MMPI-2

Assessing Personality and Psychopathology

FIFTH EDITION

John R. Graham

New York   Oxford
OXFORD UNIVERSITY PRESS

Oxford University Press, Inc., publishes works that further Oxford University's
objective of excellence in research, scholarship, and education.

Oxford   New York
Auckland   Cape Town   Dar es Salaam   Hong Kong   Karachi
Kuala Lumpur   Madrid   Melbourne   Mexico City   Nairobi
New Delhi   Shanghai   Taipei   Toronto

With offices in
Argentina   Austria   Brazil   Chile   Czech Republic   France   Greece
Guatemala   Hungary   Italy   Japan   Poland   Portugal   Singapore
South Korea   Switzerland   Thailand   Turkey   Ukraine   Vietnam

Copyright © 2012, 2006, 2000, 1994, 1991 by Oxford University Press, Inc.

For titles covered by Section 112 of the US Higher Education Opportunity Act,
please visit www.oup.com/us/he for the latest information about
pricing and alternate formats.

Published by Oxford University Press, Inc.
198 Madison Avenue, New York, New York 10016
http://www.oup.com

Oxford is a registered trademark of Oxford University Press

All rights reserved. No part of this publication may be reproduced,
stored in a retrieval system, or transmitted, in any form or by any means,
electronic, mechanical, photocopying, recording, or otherwise,
without the prior permission of Oxford University Press.

Library of Congress Cataloging-in-Publication Data
Graham, John R. (John Robert), 1940–
    MMPI-2 : assessing personality and psychopathology /
John R. Graham. — 5th ed.
        p. cm.
    Includes bibliographical references and index.
    ISBN 978-0-19-537892-4 (acid-free paper)   1. Minnesota Multiphasic Personality
Inventory. I. Title.
    RC473.M5G73 2011
    616.89′075—dc22   2010047325

Printing number: 9 8 7 6 5 4 3 2 1

Printed in the United States of America
on acid-free paper

To my best friend, Mary Ann

CONTENTS

PREFACE

The MMPI-2 is the most widely used psychological test in the United States and is commonly used in countries around the world. It is used in inpatient and outpatient mental health settings, medical centers, and correctional settings. We have seen increased applications of the MMPI-2 in the screening of applicants for jobs that involve public trust and safety. The MMPI-2 is frequently admitted as evidence in civil and criminal legal proceedings.

NEW TO THIS EDITION

- Updated research concerning all aspects of the MMPI-2
- Added chapter on MMPI-2-RF
- Reintroduced chapter on MMPI-A, based on user reviews

Approximately 700 articles, chapters, and books were published about the MMPI instruments since the last edition of this book was completed. Empirical research continues to inform our use of the tests. Some research supports long-standing practices, and other research requires changes in how we interpret the test and suggests new applications. This edition reviews much of the new research data and considers implications for MMPI-2 interpretation. This edition includes information about the development and interpretation of the latest form of the MMPI, the MMPI-2 Restructured Form (MMPI-2-RF).

Since the MMPI-A was published in 1992, considerable research has accumulated about its use. The third edition of this book included a chapter devoted to the MMMPI-A, but the fourth edition did not. Based on feedback from instructors who use this book in their graduate classes, this edition again includes a chapter concerning the development and interpretation of the MMPI-A.

Chapter 1 presents the rationale underlying the original MMPI and its development as well as information about the revision of the original test and the publication of the MMPI-2. Chapter 2 describes the MMPI-2 materials and procedures for administering and scoring the test. Chapter 3 is devoted to the Validity scales, with an expanded coverage of ways to identify overreporting and other invalidating approaches to the test. Chapter 4 describes the standard Clinical scales and suggests interpretive inferences for scores at various levels. Defining and interpreting two- and three-point code types is the focus of Chapter 5. Several approaches to the content interpretation of the MMPI-2 are discussed in Chapter 6. These include the Harris–Lingoes subscales, the Content and Content Component scales, and critical item endorsement. Chapter 7 describes the Restructured Clinical (RC) and Personality Psychopathology Five (PSY-5) scales and offers suggestions for their interpretation. Supplementary scales, including three substance abuse scales, are covered in Chapter 8. Chapter 9 examines psychometric characteristics of the MMPI-2, including reliability and validity. Chapter 10 describes the use of the MMPI-2 with special groups (e.g., older adults, ethnic minorities, medical patients, inmates) and discusses the use of the test in personnel screening. Chapter 11 presents a comprehensive strategy for interpreting MMPI-2 scores and illustrates the strategy with a sample case. Chapter 12 provides an updated discussion of computerized administration, scoring, and interpretation of the MMPI-2. This chapter presents a sample of a computerized interpretive report and compares it with a clinician-generated interpretation for the same case. Chapter 13 discusses the use of the MMPI-2 to address a variety of forensic issues, including overreporting, underreporting, competency to stand trial, and sanity. The use of the test in domestic relations and personal injury evaluations also is considered. Chapter 14 describes the development and interpretation of the newest form of the MMPI, the MMPI-2-RF. Finally, Chapter 15 is devoted to the MMPI-A and offers guidelines for interpretation of its scales. Several appendixes present technical information about the MMPI-2. One of the appendixes includes four MMPI-2 cases that can be used to practice the interpretive strategy presented in Chapter 11.

MMPI-2: Assessing Personality and Psychopathology (Fifth Edition) has two primary audiences. It should be appropriate as a text for graduate assessment courses in psychology and related disciplines. In addition, it should serve as a comprehensive guide for clinicians who interpret the MMPI instruments.

The MMPI was the most widely used personality test in the United States and around the world, and the MMPI-2 now has that same status. When the test is used appropriately by informed professionals, it contributes to accurate and useful evaluations in a variety of settings and for a variety of assessment problems. Once again, it is my hope that this book will make a contribution to more effective and appropriate use of the MMPI instruments in assessing personality and psychopathology.

Kent, OH
April, 2011

JRG

ACKNOWLEDGMENTS

I appreciate the assistance provided by others in the preparation of this revision. I am grateful to the authors and publishers who granted permission to reproduce their works. Beverly Kaemmer at the University of Minnesota Press was especially helpful in granting permissions and providing information about the MMPI instruments. Tayla Lee contributed in many ways, including reading and critiquing numerous research articles, providing helpful feedback on sections of the manuscript, organizing references, and generally being supportive. Paul Arbisi (University of Minnesota), Martin Sellbom (University of Alabama), and Yossef Ben-Porath (Kent State University) provided feedback on the MMPI-2-RF chapter. I would also like to thank those instructors whose thoughtful reviews of the previous edition of this text helped greatly in the revision process: Julia Babcock (University of Houston), Jill Holm-Denoma (University of Vermont), Peter Wilson (Trevecca Nazarene University), Clayton Shealy (University of Alabama), Nathan Weed (Central Michigan University), and Steve Akeson (Forest Inst. of Professional Psychology). Allan Harkness and John McNulty provided information about the revision of the PSY-5 scales of the MMPI-2-RF. In addition, John McNulty assisted in preparing some of the figures in Chapter 3. Meghan McElroy searched the MMPI-A literature and provided helpful summaries of studies. The following students contributed to completion of the revision in various ways: William Ajayi, William Bryant, and Lesley Hiebing. Oxford University Press provided resources for clerical support for the project. Finally, Mary Ann Stephens understands the importance of this book to me, and she provided support and encouragement throughout the preparation of this revision.

⁄⁄⁄ Development of the MMPI and MMPI-2

DEVELOPMENT OF THE ORIGINAL MMPI

Original Purpose

The Minnesota Multiphasic Personality Inventory (MMPI) was first published in 1943. The test authors, Starke Hathaway, PhD, and J. Charnley McKinley, MD, who were working in the University of Minnesota Hospitals, expected the MMPI to be useful for routine diagnostic assessments. During the 1930s and 1940s a primary function of psychologists and psychiatrists was to assign appropriate psychodiagnostic labels to individual cases. An individual interview or mental status examination and individual psychological testing usually were used with each patient. Hathaway and McKinley believed that a group-administered paper-and-pencil personality inventory would provide a more efficient and reliable way of arriving at appropriate psychodiagnostic labels.

Rationale

Hathaway and McKinley used the empirical keying approach in the construction of the various MMPI scales. This approach, which requires empirical determination of items that differentiate between groups of persons, is a common technique today, but it represented a significant innovation at the time of the MMPI's construction. Most prior personality inventories had been constructed according to a logical keying approach. With this approach, test items were selected or generated rationally according to face validity, and responses were keyed according to the subjective judgment of the test author concerning what kinds of responses were likely to be indicative of the attributes being measured. Both clinical experience and research data seriously questioned the adequacy of this logical keying approach. Increasingly, it became apparent that test takers could falsify or distort their responses to items in order to present themselves in any way they chose. Further, empirical studies indicated that the subjectively keyed responses often were not consistent with differences actually observed between groups of persons.

In the newly introduced empirical keying procedure, responses to individual test items were treated as unknowns, and empirical item analysis was utilized to identify test items that differentiated between criterion groups (e.g., depressed patients versus nonclinical individuals). Such an approach to item responses overcame many of the difficulties associated with the earlier, subjective approaches.

Clinical Scale Development

The first step in the construction of the basic MMPI scales was to collect a large pool of potential inventory items.[1] Hathaway and McKinley selected a wide variety of personality-type statements from sources such as psychological and psychiatric case histories and reports, textbooks, and earlier published scales of personal and social attitudes. From an initial pool of approximately 1000 statements, the test authors selected 504 that they judged to be reasonably independent of each other.

The next step was to select appropriate criterion groups. One criterion group, referred to as the Minnesota normals, consisted primarily of 724 relatives and visitors of medical patients in the University of Minnesota Hospitals. This group also included 265 recent high school graduates who were attending precollege conferences at the University of Minnesota, 265 Work Progress Administration workers, and 254 medical patients at the University of Minnesota Hospitals. The second major group, referred to as clinical participants, was made up of psychiatric patients at the University of Minnesota Hospitals. This second group included 221 patients representing all of the major psychiatric categories being used clinically at the time of the construction of the test. Clinical participants were divided into subgroups of discrete diagnostic samples according to their clinically determined diagnostic labels. Whenever there was any doubt about a patient's clinical diagnosis or when more than one diagnosis was given, the patient was not included in this clinical reference group. The different subgroups of clinical participants formed were hypochondriasis, depression, hysteria, psychopathic deviate, paranoia, psychasthenia, schizophrenia, and hypomania.

The next step in scale construction was to administer the original 504 test items to the Minnesota normals and to the patients in each of the clinical groups. An item analysis was conducted separately for each of the clinical groups to identify the items in the pool of 504 that differentiated significantly between the specific clinical group and a group of normal persons. Individual MMPI items that were identified by this procedure were included in the resulting MMPI scale for that clinical group. For several scales (Hypochondriasis and Depression) additional procedures were utilized to try to ensure that the scales would differentiate between patients with the diagnosed clinical condition and other persons who had some of the symptoms of the condition but were not assigned the corresponding diagnosis. For example, in constructing the Hypochondriasis scale,

---

[1] Information concerning Clinical and Validity scale development is abstracted from a series of articles by Hathaway (1956, 1965), Hathaway and McKinley (1940, 1942), McKinley and Hathaway (1940, 1944), McKinley, Hathaway, and Meehl (1948), and Meehl and Hathaway (1946).

items were added to the preliminary scale that differentiated between patients who had diagnoses of hypochondriasis and patients with somatic symptoms who did not have this diagnosis.

In an attempt to cross-validate the Clinical scales, they were administered to new groups of normal persons, patients with relevant clinical diagnoses, and sometimes also to patients with other clinical diagnoses. If significant differences were found among scores for these groups, the Clinical scales were considered to have been adequately cross-validated and thus were ready for use in the differential diagnosis of new patients whose diagnostic features were unknown.

At a somewhat later time, two additional Clinical scales were constructed. First, the Masculinity–Femininity (Mf) scale originally was intended to distinguish between homosexual and heterosexual men. Because of difficulties in identifying adequate numbers of items that differentiated between these two groups, Hathaway and McKinley subsequently broadened their approach in the construction of the Mf scale. In addition to the all too few items that discriminated between homosexual and heterosexual men, other items were identified that were differentially endorsed by men and women in the normal samples. Also, some items from the Terman and Miles Attitude–Interest Analysis Test (1936) were added to the original item pool and included in the Mf scale. Second, the Social Introversion (Si) scale was developed by Drake (1946) and came to be included as one of the basic MMPI scales. Drake selected items for the Si scale by contrasting item response frequencies for groups of college women who scored higher or lower on the introversion–extraversion scale of the Minnesota T-S-E Inventory (Benton, 1949). The Si scale was cross-validated by comparing scores of female college students who participated in many extracurricular activities with those who participated in few or no extracurricular activities. Subsequently, the scale's use was extended to men as well as women.

Validity Scale Development

Because Hathaway and McKinley were aware that test takers could falsify or distort their responses to the items in self-report inventories, they also developed four scales, hereafter referred to as the Validity scales, to detect deviant test-taking attitudes. The Cannot Say (?) score was simply the total number of items in the MMPI that the individual taking the test either omitted or responded to as both true and false. Obviously, the omission of large numbers of items, which tends to lower the scores on the Clinical scales, calls into question the interpretability of the whole resulting profile of scores.

The L scale, originally called the Lie scale of the MMPI, was designed to detect rather unsophisticated and naive attempts on the part of test takers to present themselves in an overly favorable way. The L-scale items were rationally derived and cover everyday situations in order to assess the strength of a person's unwillingness to admit even very minor weaknesses in character or personality. For example, one item involves a claim of reading every editorial in daily newspapers. Most people would be quite willing to admit that they do not read every editorial every day, but persons determined to present themselves in a favorable way might not be willing to admit to such a perceived shortcoming.

The Infrequency (F) scale of the MMPI was designed to detect individuals whose approach to the test-taking task is different from that intended by the test authors. F-scale items were selected by examining the endorsement frequency of the Minnesota normal group and identifying the items endorsed in a particular direction by fewer than 10% of the normals. Because few normal people endorse these items in that direction, a person who does endorse an item in that direction is exhibiting a deviant response. A large number of such deviant responses call into question the extent to which a person taking the test complied with the instructions. Hathaway and McKinley believed that the most common reason for elevated scores on the F scale was responding to test items without reading and considering their content.

The Correction (K) scale of the MMPI was constructed by Meehl and Hathaway (1946) to identify clinical defensiveness in test takers. It was noted that some clearly abnormal persons who took the MMPI obtained scores on the Clinical scales that were not as elevated as would be expected given their clinical status. Items in the K scale were selected empirically by comparing the responses of a group of patients who were known to be clinically deviant but who produced normal scores on the Clinical scales of the MMPI with a group of people producing normal Clinical scale scores and for whom there was no extratest indication of psychopathology. A high K-scale score was intended to indicate defensiveness and call into question the person's responses to all of the other items.

The K scale was also used later to develop a correction factor for some of the Clinical scales. Meehl and Hathaway reasoned that if the effect of a defensive test-taking attitude, as reflected by a high K score, is to lower scores on the Clinical scales, it might be possible to determine the extent to which the scores on the Clinical scales should be raised in order to reflect more accurately a person's behavior. By comparing the diagnostic efficiency of each Clinical scale with various portions of K-scale scores added as a correction factor, Meehl and Hathaway determined the appropriate weight of the K-scale score for each Clinical scale to correct for the defensiveness indicated by the K-scale score. Certain Clinical scales were not K corrected because the simple raw score on those Clinical scales seemed to result in the most accurate prediction about a person's clinical condition. Other scales have proportions of K, ranging from .2 to 1.0, added to adjust the Clinical scales appropriately.

Modified Approach to MMPI Utilization

After a decade of clinical use and additional validity studies, it became apparent that the MMPI was not adequate to successfully carry out its original purpose, namely, the valid psychodiagnosis of new patients. Although patients in any particular clinical category (e.g., depression) were likely to obtain high scores on the corresponding Clinical scale, they also often obtained high scores on other

Clinical scales. Also, many normal persons obtained high scores on one or more of the Clinical scales. Clearly, the Clinical scales were not pure measures of the symptom syndromes suggested by the scale names.

Several reasons have been suggested for the failure of the MMPI to fulfill completely its original purpose. From further research it became apparent that many of the Clinical scales of the MMPI are highly intercorrelated, making it unlikely that only a single scale would be elevated for an individual. These inter-correlations were due, to a large extent, to item overlap between scales. Also, the unreliability of the specific psychiatric diagnoses of patients used in the development of the MMPI scales contributes to their failure to differentiate among clinical groups.

Although the limited success of the MMPI scales in differentiating among clinical groups might have been bothersome in the 1940s, this limitation is not particularly critical today. Currently, practicing clinicians place less emphasis on diagnostic labels per se. Accumulating evidence suggests that psychiatric nosology is not as useful as medical diagnosis. Information in a psychiatric chart that a patient's diagnosis is schizophrenia, for example, does not tell us much about the etiology of the disorder for that individual or about recommended therapeutic procedures.

Over time, the MMPI came to be used in a way that was quite different from what was originally intended. It was assumed that the Clinical scales were indicating something other than error variance because reliable differences in scores were found among individuals known to differ in other important ways. The modified approach to the MMPI treated each of its scales as an unknown and, through clinical experience and empirical research, the correlates of each scale were identified (indeed, more than 10,000 studies were published about the MMPI). According to this approach, when a person obtained a score on a particular scale, the clinician attributed to that person the characteristics and behaviors that previous research and experience had identified for other individuals with similar scores on that scale. To lessen the likelihood that excess meaning would be attributed because of the Clinical scale names, the following scale numbers were assigned to the original scales, and today they replace the clinical labels:

PRESENT SCALE NUMBER	ORIGINAL SCALE NAME
1	Hypochondriasis (Hs)
2	Depression (D)
3	Hysteria (Hy)
4	Psychopathic Deviate (Pd)
5	Masculinity–Femininity (Mf)
6	Paranoia (Pa)
7	Psychasthenia (Pt)
8	Schizophrenia (Sc)
9	Hypomania (Ma)
0	Social Introversion (Si)

Thus, for example, among themselves, MMPI users would refer to a patient as a "four–nine" or a "one–two–three," descriptive phrases in shorthand that communicate to the listener the particular behavior descriptions associated with the "4–9" or "1–2–3" pattern.

In addition to identifying empirical correlates of high scores on each of the numbered scales, attempts were made to identify empirical correlates for low scores and for various combinations of scores on the scales (e.g., highest scale in the profile, two highest scales in the profile). Some investigators developed very complex rules for classifying individual profiles and identified behavioral correlates of profiles that meet the criteria (Gilberstadt & Duker, 1965; Marks, Seeman, & Haller, 1974). Thus, even though the MMPI was not particularly successful in terms of its original purpose (differential diagnosis of clinical groups believed in the 1930s to be discrete psychiatric types), the test can be used to generate descriptions of and inferences about individuals (normal persons and patients) on the basis of their scores. It is this behavioral description approach to the utilization of the test in everyday practice that has led to its great popularity among practicing clinicians.

DEVELOPMENT OF THE MMPI-2

Reasons for the Revision

The original MMPI was a widely used instrument. Several national surveys revealed that it was the most frequently used personality test in the United States (Harrison, Kaufman, Hickman, & Kaufman, 1988; Lubin, Larsen, & Matarazzo, 1984). It was commonly applied in inpatient (Lubin, Larsen, Matarazzo, & Seever, 1985) and outpatient (Lubin et al., 1985; Piotrowski & Keller, 1989) psychiatric and medical (Piotrowski & Lubin, 1990) settings. Counseling psychologists and community counselors used the test extensively (Bubenzer, Zimpfer, & Mahrle, 1990; Watkins, Campbell, & McGregor, 1988). Even clinicians who might seem unlikely to value the MMPI reported it to be an important assessment instrument. The use of the MMPI by members of the Society for Personality Assessment, a group typically associated with projective techniques, was second only to the Rorschach for personality assessment (Piotrowski, Shery, & Keller, 1985). Members of the American Association for Behavior Therapy indicated that it was important for professional clinicians to be skilled in the use of the MMPI (Piotrowski & Keller, 1984). Although the MMPI was developed for use with adults, it was the most widely used objective assessment measure for adolescent clients (Archer, Maruish, Imhof, & Piotrowski, 1991).

Despite its widespread use, critics expressed concern about certain aspects of the instrument. Until the publication of the MMPI-2 in 1989, the MMPI had not been revised since its publication in 1943. There were serious concerns about the adequacy of the original standardization sample, which consisted primarily of persons who were visiting friends or relatives at the University of Minnesota Hospitals. The sample was one of convenience, and little effort had been made to ensure that it was representative of the U.S. population. Standardization participants came primarily from the geographic area around Minneapolis, Minnesota. Almost all were White, and the typical person was about 35 years of age, married, residing in a small town or rural area, working in a skilled or semiskilled trade (or married to a man of this occupational level), and having about 8 years of formal education (Dahlstrom, Welsh, & Dahlstrom, 1972). Hathaway and Briggs (1957) later refined this sample by eliminating persons with incomplete records or faulty background information. The refined sample was the one typically used for converting raw scores on supplementary MMPI scales to T scores. In addition to concerns that the original standardization sample was not representative of the general population, there were concerns that the average American citizen had changed since the normative data had been collected in the late 1930s.

There also were concerns about the item content of the original MMPI. Some of the language and references in the items had become archaic or obsolete. For example, not many contemporary persons could respond meaningfully to the item involving "drop the handkerchief" because the game had not been popular among children for many years. Likewise, references to sleeping powders and streetcars were largely inappropriate for most contemporary persons.

Some of the items of the original MMPI included sexist language that was not in accord with contemporary standards concerning the use of such language in psychological tests. Certain items, such as those dealing with Christian religious beliefs, were judged inappropriate for many contemporary test takers. Many test takers felt that items dealing with sexual behavior and bowel and bladder functions were objectionable because they seemed irrelevant to personality assessment.

Because the original MMPI items had never been subjected to careful editorial review, some of them included poor grammar and inappropriate punctuation. Some of the idioms and double negatives were troublesome for many test takers with limited formal education.

Finally, there was concern that the original MMPI item pool was not broad enough to permit assessment of certain characteristics judged important by many test users. For example, few items concerned suicide attempts, use of drugs other than alcohol, and treatment-related behaviors. Although many additional scales were developed using the original MMPI item pool, the success of these scales often was limited by the inadequacy of the item pool.

MMPI researchers and users had considered the need for revision and restandardization for quite some time. In 1970 the entire MMPI Symposium was devoted to the topic of revision (Butcher, 1972). However, the enormity of the task and the unavailability of funds delayed revision plans for over a decade. In 1982 the University of Minnesota Press appointed a restandardization committee, consisting of James N. Butcher, W. Grant Dahlstrom, and John R. Graham, to consider the need for and feasibility of a revision of the MMPI.[2] Based on the

---

[2] Although not involved in the early stages of the restandardization project, Auke Tellegen later was appointed to the restandardization committee.

recommendations of the committee, a decision was made to revise the MMPI. Funds to support the revision were provided by the University of Minnesota Press. The test distributor, National Computer Systems (now Pearson Assessments), provided support in the form of test materials, forms, and scanning and scoring of data.

Goals of the Restandardization Project

From the start of the restandardization project, it was determined that every effort would be made to maintain continuity between the original MMPI and its revision. This would ensure that the considerable research base that had accumulated since the test's publication would still be relevant to the new version.

A primary goal of the project was to collect a contemporary normative sample that would be more representative of the general population than had been true of Hathaway's original sample. Additionally, efforts would be made to improve the MMPI item pool by rewriting some of the items, deleting others that had been judged to be objectionable, and generating new items that would expand the content dimensions of the item pool.

Major revisions of the existing Validity and Clinical scales were not part of the restandardization project, although it was hoped that the project would produce data that later could lead to improvements in the basic scales. Also, it was anticipated that items that were added to the item pool would be useful in generating new scales.

Preparing the Experimental Booklet

Preparing the experimental booklet (Form AX) involved several simultaneous processes. To maintain continuity between the original and revised forms of the MMPI, a decision was made to include all 550 unique items in Form AX. The second occurrences of the 16 repeated items, originally included to facilitate early machine scoring, were deleted. They no longer served any useful purpose and also disturbed many test takers who assumed incorrectly that they were included to determine if the test taker was responding consistently.

Of the 550 items, 82 were rewritten for Form AX. Some items were reworded to eliminate reference to a specific gender. In other items, idiomatic or obsolete expressions were replaced with more contemporary wordings. For example, "irritable" was substituted for "cross," "bad behavior" for "cutting up," and "often" for "commonly." References that had become dated were replaced. For example, "sleeping powders" was changed to "sleeping pills," and "bath" was changed to "bath or shower." Some changes were directed at eliminating subcultural bias. For example, "religious services" was substituted for "church."

Most of the item changes were slight, and all of them were made with the objective of preserving original meaning while using more acceptable, contemporary language. Data were collected and analyzed to ensure that changes did not significantly affect endorsement patterns (Ben-Porath & Butcher, 1989a).

A second major change in the item pool involved adding new items. The committee reviewed the content dimensions in the original MMPI item pool and sought recommendations from experts in personality measurement and clinical assessment concerning content dimensions that should be added to the pool. The committee generated 154 items that were added to the item pool, bringing the Form AX booklet length to 704 items. Items were added in content areas such as drug abuse, suicide potential, Type A behavior patterns, marital adjustment, work attitudes, and treatment amenability.

Normative Data Collection

Procedures were developed with the goal of obtaining a large normative group that was broadly representative of the U.S. population (Butcher, Dahlstrom, Graham, Tellegen, & Kaemmer, 1989). Census data from 1980 were used to guide participant solicitation. To ensure geographic representativeness, seven testing sites (Minnesota, Ohio, North Carolina, Washington, Pennsylvania, Virginia, and California) were selected. Potential participants were selected in a particular region primarily from community or telephone directories. Letters were sent to prospective participants explaining the nature of the project and asking them to participate. After an initial trial period, it was decided that individuals would be paid $15 for their participation, and couples that participated together would be paid $40. Participants were tested in groups in convenient locations in their communities. To ensure representativeness of the sample, persons from special groups were added. These included military personnel and Native Americans. In addition to completing Form AX of the MMPI, all participants completed a biographical-information form and a life-events form. Couples completed two additional forms describing the nature and length of their relationships and rating each other on 110 characteristics, using a revised form of the Katz Adjustment Scales (Katz & Lyerly, 1963).

Using these procedures, approximately 2900 participants were tested. After eliminating persons because of test invalidity or incompleteness of other forms, a final sample of 2600 community participants (1138 men and 1462 women) was constituted. Of this number, 841 couples were included in the sample. To collect test–retest data, 111 female participants and 82 male participants were retested approximately 1 week after the initial testing.

Racial composition of the sample was as follows: Caucasian, 81%; African American, 12%; Hispanic, 3%; Native American, 3%; and Asian American, 1%. Participants ranged in age from 18 to 85 years ($M = 41.04$; $SD = 15.29$) and in formal education from 3 to 20 years ($M = 14.72$; $SD = 2.60$). Most men (61.6%) and women (61.2%) in the sample were married. Approximately 32% of the men and 21% of the women had professional or managerial positions, and approximately 12% of the men and 5% of the women were laborers. The median family income was $30,000–$35,000 for men and $25,000–$30,000 for women. Approximately 3% of male participants and 6% of female participants in the normative sample indicated that they were involved in treatment for mental health problems at the time of their participation in the study.

Clearly, the normative sample for the MMPI-2 is more representative of the general population than was Hathaway's original sample. Although higher educational levels seem to be overrepresented, these reflect the types of persons who are likely to take the test. Butcher (1990a), Dahlstrom and Tellegen (1993), and Long, Graham, and Timbrook (1994) found only a negligible relationship between educational level of the MMPI-2 normative sample and scores on the MMPI-2 Validity and Clinical scales. Schinka and LaLone (1997) constituted a subsample of the MMPI-2 standardization sample that was matched to 1995 projected census data for gender, ethnic identification, age, and education. They concluded that the restandardization sample is a very close approximation of the current U.S. population and that small demographic differences (including education) between the restandardization sample and the U.S. population are not clinically meaningful.

Adolescent Data Collection

Concurrently with the adult data collection, a large normative sample of adolescent participants also was assembled. The adolescents were solicited from school rosters in most of the same cities where adult data were being collected. A separate experimental booklet (Form TX) was used, and the adolescent participants also completed biographical-information and life-events forms. Form TX included the 550 unique items in the original MMPI (some of them in rewritten form) as well as a number of the items that had been added to Form AX. In addition, new items were added to Form TX to cover content dimensions relevant to adolescents but not included in the original MMPI item pool. These data were used to develop a separate form of the test for adolescents, MMPI-A, which was published in 1992 (Butcher et al., 1992). Additional information concerning the development and use of the MMPI-A can be found in Chapter 15 of this book.

Additional Data Collection

To provide data necessary for making decisions, such as which items from the Form AX booklet would be included in the final revised booklet, data were collected from a variety of additional groups. These included psychiatric patients, alcoholics, chronic pain patients, marital counseling clients, college students, and job applicants.

Development of the Final Booklet

The final version of the revised MMPI (MMPI-2) includes 567 items from the Form AX booklet. Several criteria were employed in deciding which items were to be included in the final booklet. First, all items entering into the standard Validity and Clinical scales were provisionally included, as were items needed to score supplementary scales judged to be important. Certain items were maintained because they would be included in new scales developed from the item pool.

Table 1.1 Item Changes and Deletions for the Basic Validity and Clinical Scales

SCALE	NUMBER OF ITEMS			TYPES OF CHANGE[a]			
	DELETED	REMAINING	CHANGED	A	B	C	D
L	0	15	2	1	1	0	0
F	4	60	12	1	5	6	0
K	0	30	1	0	1	0	0
Hs	1	32	5	0	1	3	1
D	3	57	2	1	1	0	0
Hy	0	60	9	0	4	2	3
Pd	0	50	4	0	2	1	1
Mf	4	56	6	1	2	1	2
Pa	0	40	2	1	0	0	1
Pt	0	48	2	0	0	1	1
Sc	0	78	13	0	1	7	5
Ma	0	46	7	4	2	1	0
Si	1	69	6	0	3	2	1
Not on Any Scale	—	—	16	3	7	3	3

[a]A, elimination of possibly sexist wording; B, modernization of idioms and usage; C, grammatical clarification; D, simplification.

SOURCE: Excerpted (Table 1.1) from Butcher, J.N., Graham, J.R., Ben-Porath, Y.S., Tellegen, A., Dahlstrom, W.G., & Kaemmer, B. (2001). *MMPI® -2 (Minnesota Multiphasic Personality Inventory® -2): Manual for administration, scoring, and interpretation, revised edition.* Copyright © 2001 by the Regents of the University of Minnesota. Used by permission of the University of Minnesota Press. All rights reserved. "MMPI® " and "Minnesota Multiphasic Personality Inventory® " are trademarks owned by the Regents of the University of Minnesota.

From this provisional item pool, some items were deleted because they were judged on the basis of previous research (Butcher & Tellegen, 1966) to be objectionable. These items dealt with religious attitudes and practices, sexual preferences, and bowel and bladder functions. Table 1.1 indicates the number of items deleted, remaining, and changed for each Validity and Clinical scale. Not many items were changed in most scales, and even fewer were deleted from these basic scales.

In summary, the MMPI-2 is similar in most ways to the original MMPI. The MMPI-2 booklet includes the items necessary for scoring the standard Validity and Clinical scales. Although not all of the Supplementary scales that could be scored from the original MMPI can be scored from MMPI-2, many of them can. Much of the research concerning interpretation of the original MMPI still applies directly to the MMPI-2. Improvements in the MMPI-2 include a more contemporary and representative standardization sample, updated and improved items, deletion of objectionable items, and some new scales.

Current Status of MMPI-2

Although some professionals expressed understandable concerns about the comparability of the MMPI and MMPI-2 (Vincent, 1990; Ward, 1991) and the adequacy of the MMPI-2 norms (Caldwell, 1991; Duckworth, 1991b; Strassberg, 1991), subsequent research addressed these and other concerns, and the MMPI-2 has replaced the MMPI in clinical and nonclinical settings. These original concerns, as well as other psychometric issues, are discussed in detail in Chapter 9 of this book. In 1999 the test publisher, the University of Minnesota Press, discontinued publication of original MMPI materials.

Survey data indicate that the MMPI/MMPI-2 is the personality test most frequently used by clinical psychologists (86%), second in use only to the WAIS-R (94%; Camara, Nathan, & Puente, 2000). The MMPI/MMPI-2 is the personality assessment instrument most emphasized in PhD and PsyD programs (Belter & Piotrowski, 2001) and is the psychological test considered by internship directors to be most essential for practicing psychologists (Piotrowski & Belter, 1999).

An accumulating research base supports the use of the MMPI-2. Since 1989, more than 2000 articles, books, and dissertations have reported studies that included the MMPI-2. Although some of these studies used the MMPI-2 scales to evaluate other tests and constructs, most provided important information about the psychometric properties of the MMPI-2 and its use in various settings and for a wide array of purposes. Reviews of the MMPI-2 have been quite positive, with Nichols (1992) concluding that "the psychodiagnostician selecting a structured inventory for the first time will find that no competing assessment device for abnormal psychology has stronger credentials for clinical description and prediction" (p. 565).

Although the MMPI-2 has not been revised since its publication in 1989, several developments should be noted. A revised test manual (Butcher et al., 2001) presents scoring information and interpretive guidelines for some scales that were added to the MMPI-2 after its publication in 1989. Several new Validity scales, Infrequency Psychopathology (F_p; Arbisi & Ben-Porath, 1995) and Superlative Self-Presentation (S; Butcher & Han, 1995), are included, as is the Hostility (Ho; Cook & Medley, 1954) Supplementary scale. Content Component scales, developed by Ben-Porath and Sherwood (1993) to aid in interpretation of Content scale scores, are also included. A newer set of scales, the Personality Psychopathology Five (PSY-5; Harkness, McNulty, Ben-Porath, & Graham, 2002), also is included. All of these scales that have been added to the MMPI-2 will be discussed in detail in subsequent chapters of this book.

Several scales were deleted from the MMPI-2 with the publication of the revised manual. Because of substantial research indicating that the subtle–obvious subscales (Wiener, 1948) are not useful in identifying invalid responding and are unrelated to conceptually relevant extratest measures, these subscales were eliminated from the MMPI-2. In addition, Schlenger's Posttraumatic Stress Disorder scale (PS; Schlenger & Kulka, 1989) was eliminated because it was judged to be redundant with Keane's more thoroughly researched Posttraumatic Disorder scale (PK; Keane, Malloy, & Fairbank, 1984).

The revised manual includes more comprehensive recommendations than the original MMPI-2 manual for interpreting scores on all scales included in the test. A general strategy for interpreting protocols is presented and illustrated with several clinical cases.

Another development is the publication of the Restructured Clinical (RC) scales. The RC scale authors sought to improve the discriminant validity of the Clinical scales by developing a set of scales from which a common demoralization factor has been removed. The RC scales were not included in the revised manual, but they have been added to the Extended Score Report offered by Pearson Assessments, and a monograph describing the rationale, development, and interpretation of the scales has been published (Tellegen et al., 2003). The RC scales will be discussed in detail in Chapter 7 of this book.

The most recent MMPI-2 development is the introduction of an alternate form of the MMPI-2, the MMPI-2 Restructured Form (MMPI-2-RF). This form has fewer items than the MMPI-2 and includes the Restructured Clinical (RC) scales, revised versions of the MMPI-2 Validity scales, and an additional Validity scale, the Infrequency Somatic (F_s) scale. Use of the MMPI-2-RF does not permit scoring of the basic Clinical scales, the Content scales, or many of the Supplementary scales of the MMPI-2. However, the MMPI-2-RF has Higher Order scales as well as a large number of Specific Problems scales. A more detailed examination of the MMPI-2-RF is included in Chapter 14 of this book.

⧰ Administration and Scoring

QUALIFICATIONS OF TEST USERS

The MMPI-2 is easily administered and scored by hand or by computer. Although these procedures can be carried out by a properly trained and supervised clerk, secretary, or technician, the MMPI-2 is a sophisticated psychological test. Its use is restricted to qualified professionals who have adequate training in test theory, personality structure and dynamics, and psychopathology and psychodiagnosis. Before purchasing MMPI-2 materials for the first time, users must provide to the test distributor (Pearson Assessments) credentials indicating that they (1) are licensed to practice psychology independently, (2) have a graduate degree in psychology or a closely related field and have completed graduate courses in tests and measurement or a workshop or other course approved by the test distributor, or (3) have been granted the right to administer tests at this level in their jurisdiction. These criteria are consistent with standards established by the American Psychological Association and other professional organizations. Users of the MMPI-2 also should have detailed knowledge of the inventory itself. Familiarity with all material included in the MMPI-2 manual (Butcher et al., 2001) is essential. Additionally, users should be familiar with MMPI-2 interpretive procedures presented in books such as this one.

WHO CAN TAKE THE MMPI-2?

To produce meaningful MMPI-2 results, the test taker must read well enough to understand the items and respond to them appropriately. The MMPI-2 manual (Butcher et al., 2001) reports that, based on contemporary reading-proficiency levels, a sixth-grade reading level is required to comprehend the content of all the MMPI-2 items and to respond to them appropriately. If the examiner has doubt about the reading competence of a test taker, a standardized test of reading comprehension should be administered. Sometimes persons with less than a sixth-grade reading level can meaningfully complete the MMPI-2 if it is administered using a standard audio version available from the test distributor.

The MMPI-2 is intended for use with persons who are 18 years of age or older. The MMPI-A (Butcher et al., 1992) should be used with persons who are younger than 18. Because both the MMPI-A and MMPI-2 were normed on 18-year-olds, either test can be used with persons of this age. The clinician should decide for each individual case whether to use the MMPI-A or MMPI-2 with 18-year-olds. Ordinarily, the MMPI-A would be selected for 18-year-olds who are still in high school and the MMPI-2 for 18-year-olds who are in college, working, or otherwise living a more independent lifestyle. Obviously, there will be some cases where it is not clear which form should be used (e.g., an 18-year-old woman raising her young child but living in her parents' home). Shaevel and Archer (1996) demonstrated that the same test responses of 18-year-olds lead to higher Clinical scale scores when the MMPI-2 norms are used than when the MMPI-A norms are used. Osberg and Poland (2002) found that, compared with MMPI-A scores, MMPI-2 scores tended to overpathologize 18-year-old students when a self-report, symptom checklist was used as a criterion measure of psychological adjustment.

Shaevel and Archer (1996) recommended that when there is doubt about which form of the test to use with an 18-year-old, raw scores should be plotted using both sets of norms so that interpretive statements can be evaluated in the context of developmental differences and influences. As long as visual disabilities or other physical problems do not interfere, there is no upper age limit to who can take the MMPI-2.

The clinical condition of potential examinees is an important consideration in deciding who can take the MMPI-2. Completion of the test is a challenging and tedious task for many individuals. Persons who are very depressed, anxious, or agitated often find the task almost unbearable. Frequently it is possible to break the testing session into several shorter periods for such individuals. Sometimes persons who are in great distress find it easier to complete the test if the items are presented by means of the standardized audio version.

ADMINISTERING THE MMPI-2

For most persons the test can be administered either individually or in groups, using the forms of the test and answer sheets most convenient for the examiner. For persons of average or above-average intelligence, without complicating factors, such as limited reading ability or significant emotional distress, the testing time typically is between an hour and an hour and a half. For less intelligent individuals, or those with complicating factors, the testing time may exceed 2 hours. Although it might at times seem more convenient to send the MMPI-2 home to be completed, this procedure is unacceptable. The test should always be completed in a professional setting with adequate supervision. This increases the likelihood that the test will be taken seriously and that the results will be valid and useful. In forensic evaluations, examiners may be asked to verify that the responses that were scored and interpreted are indeed those of the individual under consideration. Such verification is difficult if the test was not completed under direct supervision.

Before the MMPI-2 is administered, the examiner should establish rapport with the person to be tested. The best way to ensure cooperation is to explain why the MMPI-2 is being administered, who will have access to the results, and why it is in the best interest of the test taker to cooperate with the testing. The test should be administered in a quiet, comfortable place. The examiner or a proctor should be readily available to monitor the test taking and to answer questions that may arise. Care should be taken to make sure that the test taker reads the instructions and understands them. Questions that arise during the course of testing should be handled promptly and confidentially. Most questions can be handled by referring the test taker back to the standardized test instructions.

TESTING MATERIALS

Unlike the original MMPI, the MMPI-2 exists in only one booklet form. An optional hardcover version of the booklet is available for use when a table or desk surface is not available. However, the order of the items in both the softcover and hardcover versions is identical. Items are arranged so that those required for scoring the original Validity (L, F, K) and Clinical scales appear first in the booklets. It is possible to score these standard scales by administering only the first 370 items. However, if less than the entire test is completed, some Validity scales (VRIN, TRIN, F_B, F_P FBS), the Content and Content Component scales, and many of the Supplementary scales available for MMPI-2 cannot be scored. Usually, if persons can complete 370 items, they can complete 567.

Standardized versions of the MMPI-2 are available in Spanish for North America, French for Canada, and Hmong. The MMPI-2 has been translated into more than a dozen different languages for use around the world. Persons interested in the non-English versions of the MMPI-2 should contact Pearson Assessments for more information (pearsonassessments.com).

Almost since the MMPI was first published, there have been efforts to develop short or abbreviated forms of the test. Research with the original MMPI clearly indicated that short forms were not adequate substitutes for the standard instrument (Butcher, Kendall, & Hoffman, 1980; Dahlstrom, 1980).

Several efforts have been made to develop short forms of the MMPI-2. Dahlstrom and Archer (2000) used the first 180 items of the MMPI-2 to estimate scores on the basic Validity and Clinical scales. Their data, as well as those of a subsequent study (Gass & Luis, 2001a), suggested that, although the estimated scores permit reasonable inferences about presence or absence of psychopathology, the correspondence between obtained and estimated scores was not high enough to justify clinical use of this short form. McGrath, Pogge, and Kravic (2003) used item-scale correlations as the basis for developing an MMPI-2 short form. Scores on the standard Validity and Clinical scales can be estimated from the administration of 216 items, and 297 items must be administered to permit estimation of the standard Validity and Clinical scales, several additional Validity scales, and the Content scales. McGrath et al. presented some cross-validational data suggesting that scores on their short forms estimate standard MMPI-2 scales reasonably well, although the short forms do not permit accurate estimates of code types. Additionally, the positive predictive power of some short-form scales is not adequate. Thus, except when administering the first 370 items in the booklet from which the original Validity and Clinical scales can be scored, the use of shortened forms of MMPI-2 is not acceptable.

Computer adaptive procedures permit estimates of scores on MMPI-2 scales without having to administer all of the items on the scales. Forbey and Ben-Porath (2003b) summarized previous approaches to developing computer adaptive versions of the MMPI and MMPI-2 and presented data concerning their most recent research in this area. The most common adaptive approach with the MMPI/MMPI-2 has been the countdown method. Items on a particular scale are administered until the point at which elevation on that scale is no longer possible, no matter how many additional items are endorsed in the scored direction. If exact scores are needed, in addition to the determination that the test taker will have an elevated (T > 65) score on a particular scale, the remainder of items for that scale can also be administered.

The number of items administered in a computer adaptive version of the MMPI-2 will depend on the examiner's decisions about how many and which scale scores are wanted for a particular test taker. Forbey and Ben-Porath (2003b) reported that for their nonclinical college samples, an average of approximately 16% fewer items were administered than for standard administration, resulting in an average saving of about 17 minutes in administration time. More detailed information about computer adaptive testing with the MMPI-2, including reliability and validity data for adaptive and conventional methods of administration, is presented in Chapter 12 of this book.

For persons who may have difficulty completing the standard form of the test, a standardized tape-recorded or CD version of the items is available from Pearson Assessments. Items are read and repeated in a very neutral voice, and test takers mark their answers on an answer sheet. This version is useful for semi-literate persons and for persons with disabilities that make completion of the standard form difficult or impossible. The audio version is available in English, Spanish, or Hmong.

Several early MMPI studies demonstrated that the standard booklet form and a tape-recorded form yielded very similar results (Henning, Levy, & Aderman, 1972; Reese, Webb, & Foulks, 1968; Urmer, Black, & Wendland, 1960). Differences between the two versions were no greater than for two administrations of the standard form. Wolf, Freinek, and Shaffer (1964) found that even semiliterate young adults (with reading comprehension levels below the sixth grade) produced similar results on booklet and tape-recorded forms. Simia and di Loreto (1970) found that adolescent male delinquents, who were marginally motivated to complete the MMPI and who had poor reading comprehension, were more likely to produce valid protocols with the tape-recorded than with the booklet form. Leath and Pricer (1968) reported test–retest reliability coefficients for a tape-recorded version of the MMPI that were comparable to those of the booklet form. Although all of these studies employed the original MMPI, there is no reason to believe that results would be different for the MMPI-2.

Occasionally it may seem more convenient for a clinician to read MMPI-2 items to test takers and have them record their responses or respond out loud. This is a procedure that should be avoided, because having individual clinicians read items represents a significant deviation from standardized procedures. The examiner's tone of voice, facial expressions, and other nonverbal behaviors can affect responses, and therefore scores, in unknown ways. This is especially a problem when either the test taker or the person administering the test may be motivated to produce a particular test result.

Several studies have addressed the comparability of scores resulting from standard administration of the MMPI or MMPI-2 with scores based on administration in which items were read to the test taker. Using the original MMPI, Newmark (1971) found that test takers were more defensive when responding to items presented by a live examiner. Kendrick and Hatzenbeuhler (1982), also using the original MMPI, found significant differences in scores when items were read aloud by an examiner and when the items were answered using the standard MMPI booklet.

Only one study to date has examined the effects of live oral presentation of MMPI-2 items. Edwards, Holmes, and Carvajal (1998) presented items to undergraduate students using the standard booklet and with a live examiner reading items aloud and recording responses. There were significant differences between the conditions for some Clinical scales, and generally scores were higher when the standard booklet administration was used. While the research in this area is not extensive and studies have not been particularly rigorous methodologically, results support the concern about using an administration format that deviates from standardized procedures.

Pearson Assessments, the test distributor, offers software that permits administration of the MMPI-2 by means of a personal computer. Test takers follow directions on the computer monitor, where test items are displayed, and record their responses using several identified keys on the computer keyboard. Results of research studies concerning the equivalence of computerized and conventional administrations of the original MMPI have not been completely consistent. However, a meta-analysis of the results of seven MMPI and five MMPI-2 studies (Finger & Ones, 1999) concluded that differences in results are attributable to sampling error and that the computer and booklet forms of the MMPI/MMPI-2 are psychometrically equivalent. These findings are consistent with early studies indicating that the MMPI is a very robust instrument and that administration using different forms of the original MMPI yielded comparable results (e.g., Cottle, 1950; MacDonald, 1952; Wiener, 1947). Thus, we can have considerable confidence that computerized administration of the MMPI-2 will yield results comparable to use of the standard test booklet and answer sheets. An important consideration in deciding whether to use computer administration is the computer time required. A single administration of MMPI-2 can tie up a personal computer for several hours. Other issues involved in the use of computerized versions of the MMPI-2 are considered in more detail in Chapter 12 of this book.

Several different answer sheets are available for the MMPI-2. The one to be used depends on how the examiner plans to score the test. If the test is to be hand scored, one kind of answer sheet should be used. If it is to be computer scored, a different kind of answer sheet is indicated. Before administering the test, examiners should determine how scoring will be accomplished. Reference to a Pearson Assessments catalog or the company's web site (pearsonassessmsents.com) will provide specific information about which answer sheets to use.

SCORING THE MMPI-2

Once the test taker has responded to the MMPI-2 items, scoring can be accomplished by computer or by hand. As mentioned earlier, special answer sheets must be used if computer scoring is to be done. Computer scoring can be completed in several different ways. Pearson Assessments distributes computer software that permits users to score the standard Validity and Clinical scales, as well as numerous Supplementary scales, using their own personal computers. If the test has been computer administered, test responses are stored in the computer's memory, and scoring programs can be applied directly to them. Another option, which is especially attractive for high-volume users, is to attach a scanner to a personal computer. Answer sheets are scanned quickly, and the responses are subjected to scoring programs. A final option for computer scoring is to mail the responses to Pearson Assessments in Minneapolis, where they are scored and returned to users (usually within a week). All of the computerized scoring options offered by Pearson Assessments are paid for on a per use basis. Persons interested in available computer services should contact Pearson Assessments for details.

Many persons, particularly those who are not high-volume users, may prefer to hand score the MMPI-2, using hand-scoring templates available from Pearson Assessments. Scoring keys are available for the standard Validity and Clinical scales and for numerous Supplementary scales. The scoring templates are quite easy to use. Each template is placed over an answer sheet that is designed especially for hand-scoring purposes. The number of blackened spaces is counted and represents the raw score for the scale in question. Care should be taken when scoring Scale 5 (Masculinity–Femininity) to use the scoring key appropriate for the test taker's gender. Raw scores for the standard Validity and Clinical scales are recorded in spaces provided on the answer sheet itself. For two Validity scales, VRIN and TRIN, responses to pairs of items must be transferred from the answer sheet to a separate grid to determine scores that are then recorded on the original answer sheet. For Supplementary scales, raw scores are recorded in spaces provided on separate profile sheets. Although hand scoring the MMPI-2 is a simple clerical task, it should be completed with great care, as counting and recording errors are rather common. In fact, Allard and Faust (2000) demonstrated that scoring errors are quite common for several objective personality tests and that the errors occur with both hand scoring and computer scoring that is dependent on keyboard entry of responses.

CONSTRUCTING THE PROFILE

When the MMPI-2 is scored by computer, profiles for the various sets of scales are provided in the output. When hand scoring is utilized, profile sheets are available from Pearson Assessments for the Validity, Clinical, Content, Personality Psychopathology Five, Restructured Clinical, and Supplementary scales. The standard profile sheet to be used routinely for the MMPI-2 is one that applies a K-correction (see Chapter 3) to some of the raw scores of the Clinical scales. Pearson Assessments also offers profile sheets that permit construction of non-K-corrected profiles. It is recommended that K-corrected scores be used for most clinical purposes. Almost all of the information available concerning MMPI and MMPI-2 interpretation is based on K-corrected scores. The test manual (Butcher et al., 2001) discusses circumstances in which the noncorrected scores may be preferable. Generally speaking, K-corrected scores may lead to overestimates of deviance for persons who are not clients or patients, particularly when the test taker approaches the MMPI-2 in a defensive manner. In such cases, the noncorrected scores may more accurately reflect adjustment level compared with the normative sample. Chapter 3 of this book includes a more detailed discussion of interpreting K-corrected and non-K-corrected scores.

A first step in constructing a profile following hand scoring of the standard Validity and Clinical scales is to transfer the raw scores from the answer sheet to appropriate blanks at the bottom of the profile sheet, making sure that the profile is the appropriate one for the person's gender. At this time it also is important to be certain that identifying data (name, age, date, education, etc.) are recorded on the profile sheet.

At this point the K-correction is added to the raw scores for Scales 1 (Hs), 4 (Pd), 7 (Pt), 8 (Sc), and 9 (Ma). The proportion of a person's K-scale raw score that is to be added to each of these scales is indicated on the profile form. For these scales, the total score (the original raw score plus the K-correction) is calculated and recorded in the appropriate blank on the profile sheet.

For each scale, the examiner should refer to the numbers in the column above the scale label. The number in the column corresponding to the raw score (K-corrected if appropriate) on the scale is marked by the examiner either with a small x or a small dot. Raw scores on the Cannot Say (?) scale are recorded on the profile sheet but are not plotted as part of the profile. Care should be taken when plotting the Scale 5 (Mf) scores. For men, higher raw scores yield higher T scores, whereas for women, higher raw scores yield lower T scores. After a dot or x has been entered in the column above each scale label, the MMPI-2 profile for the person examined is completed by connecting the plotted dots or xs with each other. Traditionally, the Validity scales are joined to each other but are not connected with the Clinical scale scores. Similar procedures are used to construct profiles for Content, Restructured Clinical, Personality Psychopathology Five, and Supplementary scales. However, no K-correction is used for these additional sets of scales.

Because T scores are printed at each side of the profile sheet, by plotting the scores in the manner described here, the raw scores for each scale are converted visually to T scores. A T score has a mean of 50 and a standard deviation of 10. For the Validity scales and Scales 5 and 0 the T scores used are linear, whereas for Scales 1, 2, 3, 4, 6, 7, 8, and 9 special uniform T scores are used. More information concerning characteristics of uniform T scores and differences between linear and uniform scores can be found in Chapter 9 of this book. The T-score conversions provided on the profile sheet are based on the responses of the MMPI-2 normative sample. Thus, a T score of 50 for any particular scale indicates that a person's score is equal to the average or mean score for persons of the test taker's gender in the normative sample. Scores greater than 50 indicate scores higher than the average for the normative sample, and scores below 50 indicate scores lower than the average for the normative sample. A profile of non-K-corrected scores can be constructed using the same procedures except that the K-correction is not added to raw scores before they are plotted on the profile sheet. Because separate non-K-corrected norms are used to convert raw scores to T scores, it is necessary to use a separate non-K-corrected profile sheet, which is also available from Pearson Assessments. The advantages and disadvantages of using non-K-corrected scores will be discussed in Chapter 3 of this book.

CODING THE PROFILE

Although it is possible to derive useful information by interpreting an examinee's T score on a single scale in isolation, much of the information relevant to interpretation of MMPI-2 protocols is configural in nature. Thus, in addition to interpreting individual scores, it can be helpful to consider the pattern of the scores in relation to each other. To facilitate profile interpretation, coding procedures were developed to capture most of the essential information about a profile in a concise form and for reducing the possible number of different profiles to a manageable size.

Two major coding systems were utilized with the original MMPI: Hathaway's (1947) original system and a more complete system developed by Welsh (1948). A slightly modified coding system was recommended for use when the MMPI-2 was published (Butcher & Williams, 1992). With advancements in computer technology, the usefulness of these coding systems diminished, and in the revised version of the MMPI-2 manual a coding system is no longer described or recommended. Rather, the manual recommends that one determine if the test taker's scores yield an interpretable code type.

In determining code type, each clinical scale is identified by its corresponding number (Hs—1, D—2, Hy—3, Pd—4, Mf—5, Pa—6, Pt—7, Sc—9, Ma—9, Si—0). Because most empirical research has focused on two-point and three-point code types, these are the focus of code-type interpretation. To determine a test taker's two-point code, first determine the highest and second-highest clinical scale scores (excluding 5 and 0). For example, a protocol in which the Hs (1) scale has the highest T score and the Hy (3) scale has the second-highest score would be designated provisionally as a "13" two-point code type. A protocol with the D (2) scale highest, the Pt (7) scale second highest, and the Sc (8) scale third highest would be designated provisionally as a "278" three-point code type.

As discussed in the MMPI-2 manual (Butcher et al., 2001), one should have greater confidence in inferences based on code types if the code types are defined and elevated. Definition refers to the difference in T-score points between the lowest Clinical scale score in the code type and the next highest Clinical scale score (excluding 5 and 0). Considering the measurement error of the MMPI-2 Clinical scales, a difference of at least five T-score points is needed to have confidence that a real difference exists. Thus, to have a defined two-point code, there must be a difference of at least five T-score points between the second-highest Clinical scale score and the third-highest Clinical scale score. To have a defined three-point code, there must be a difference of at least five T-score points between the third-highest Clinical scale score and the fourth-highest Clinical scale score. If a code type is not defined, it should not be the focus of the MMPI-2 interpretation, and a scale-by-scale analysis is recommended.

Code-type elevation refers to the absolute level of scales included in the code type. If T scores on all of the scales in the code type are greater than 65, the symptoms and problems associated with that code type in the interpretive literature are more likely to apply. More information about determining and interpreting MMPI-2 code types is presented in Chapter 5 of this book.

3

%% The Validity Scales

For the MMPI-2 to yield accurate and useful information, it is necessary that the person taking the test do so in the manner indicated by the standard instructions. Test takers are expected to read each item, consider its content, and give a direct and honest response to the item, using the true–false response format provided. Whenever extreme deviations from these procedures occur, the resulting protocol should be considered invalid and should not be interpreted further. Although less extreme deviations in test-taking attitudes do not necessarily invalidate test results, they should be taken into account when the resulting scores are interpreted.

Although Hathaway and McKinley expected the empirical keying procedure used in developing the MMPI to make invalid responding less likely than in earlier face-valid inventories, they recognized the importance of assessing test-taking attitudes. The four Validity indicators developed specifically to assess test-taking attitude with the original MMPI and maintained with the MMPI-2 are the Cannot Say (?), Lie (L), Infrequency (F), and Correction (K) scales. New Validity scales that have become part of the standard MMPI-2 include the Variable Response Inconsistency (VRIN), True Response Inconsistency (TRIN), Back F (F_B), Infrequency Psychopathology (F_p), Superlative Self-Presentation (S), and Symptom Validity (FBS) scales.

Research has demonstrated that, in addition to providing important information about test-taking attitudes, the Validity scales are related to some other extratest behaviors (e.g., symptoms, personality characteristics). However, this author recommends that the Validity scales be used primarily to assess test-taking attitudes and that inferences about personality and psychopathology be derived primarily from other MMPI-2 scales. The items included in each of the Validity scales, the keyed response for each item, and linear T-score transformations for raw scores are presented in appendixes of the MMPI-2 manual (Butcher et al., 2001).[1] This information for the FBS scale can be found in the FBS Test Monograph (Ben-Porath, Graham, & Tellegen, 2009).

---

[1] Although scale composition information and T-score transformations were presented in appendixes of prior editions of this book, concerns about test security led the University of Minnesota Press to adopt a policy that precludes the presentation of such information in books such as this one.

Nichols, Greene, and Schmolck (1989) stressed the importance of differentiating between invalid responding due to content-nonresponsiveness (CNR) and to content-responsive invalidity (CRF). In the former, test takers adopt an invalid approach to completing the MMPI-2 in an inconsistent way that is not related to the content of items (e.g., random responding). In the latter, test takers read and consider the content of each item and respond consistently in order to create unrealistically unfavorable or favorable impressions of themselves (i.e., overreporting or underreporting).

SCALES ASSESSING CONTENT-NONRESPONSIVENESS (CNR)

The first step in interpreting the MMPI-2 should be to determine if the test taker has responded to the items without consideration of their content. The responses may be random in nature or may follow some systematic approach (e.g., all true or all false) that is not related to item content. The Cannot Say (?), Variable Response Inconsistency (VRIN), and True Response Inconsistency (TRIN) scales are examined for this purpose. If any of these scales indicates invalid responding, the remaining scores of the MMPI-2 should not be interpreted.

Cannot Say (?) Score

The Cannot Say (?) score is simply the number of omitted items (including items answered both true and false). There are many reasons why people omit items on the MMPI-2. Occasionally, items are omitted because of carelessness or confusion. Omitted items also can reflect an attempt to avoid admitting undesirable things about oneself without directly lying. Indecisive people, who cannot decide between the two response alternatives, may leave many items unanswered. Some items are omitted because of a lack of information or experience necessary for a meaningful response.

Regardless of the reasons for omitting items, a large number of omissions can lead to lowered scores on other scales. Therefore, the validity of a protocol with many omitted items should be questioned. The MMPI-2 manual suggests that protocols with 30 or more omitted items must be considered highly suspect, if not completely invalid. This criterion seems to be too liberal. This author's own practice is to interpret with great caution protocols with more than 10 omitted items and not to interpret at all those with more than 30 omitted items. When more than a few items are omitted, it can be very helpful to determine on which scales the omitted items are scored. Obviously, even fewer than 10 omitted items can be a problem if all of the items are on a single scale. If item omissions are limited to only one or several scales, other scales may still be interpreted. Computer scoring of MMPI-2s yields an indication of the percentage of items on each scale that were answered versus omitted. Dragon and Ben-Porath (2007) found that the criterion validity of MMPI-2 substantive scales was not affected significantly when up to 10% of items were randomly omitted. Sometimes excessive item omissions are due to test takers not completing the entire MMPI-2. If excessive item omissions occur after item 370, they will not affect scores on the original Validity and Clinical scales.

As indicated in Chapter 2 of this book, the best procedure is to try to make sure that few or no items are omitted. If encouraged before beginning the MMPI-2 to answer all items, most people usually will omit only a very few. Also, if the examiner visually scans answer sheets at the time the test is completed and encourages individuals to try to answer previously omitted items, most people will complete all or almost all of the items. Programs for computer administration of the MMPI-2 typically keep track of omitted items and ask the test taker to reconsider the omitted items and answer as many of them as possible.

Variable Response Inconsistency (VRIN) Scale

The Variable Response Inconsistency (VRIN) scale was developed for the MMPI-2 as an additional validity indicator (Butcher et al., 1989, 2001). It provides an indication of a tendency to respond inconsistently to MMPI-2 items. The VRIN scale consists of 67 item response pairs with either similar or opposite content. Each time a person answers items in a pair inconsistently, one raw-score point is added to the score on the VRIN scale. For some item pairs, two true responses result in a point being scored for the scale; for other item pairs, two false responses result in a point being added; and for still other item pairs, a true response and a false response result in a point being added. This scale is very complicated to score by hand, and it is recommended that it be scored by computer (Iverson & Barton, 1999). If hand scoring is done, considerable care should be exercised to avoid errors.

A completely random response set produces a T score on the VRIN scale of 96 for men and 98 for women. In an all-true or an all-false response set the VRIN-scale T score will be near 50. Persons who deliberately overreport on the MMPI-2, as well as those who honestly admit to serious psychopathology, typically have about average T scores on the VRIN scale (Wetter, Baer, Berry, Smith, & Larsen, 1992).

The MMPI-2 manual (Butcher et al., 2001) suggests that a raw score equal to or greater than 13 (T > 80) indicates inconsistent responding that invalidates the resulting protocol. Subsequent to the publication of the MMPI-2, several empirical studies have confirmed that VRIN-scale raw scores greater than 13 are indicative of random responding (Berry, Wetter, et al., 1991; Gallen & Berry, 1996; Paolo & Ryan, 1992; Pinsoneault, 2007), although slightly lower cutoff scores may yield more accurate results in settings with unusually high base rates of random responding (Gallen & Berry, 1996).

There also are data suggesting that partial random responding produces elevated VRIN-scale scores, but the optimal cutoff scores for identifying various degrees of randomness have not been determined (Berry, Wetter, et al., 1991; Gallen & Berry, 1996; Pinsoneault, 2007). Partial random responding is most likely to occur later in the test (Berry et al., 1992; Gallen & Berry, 1996). Pinsoneault (2007) developed and evaluated subscales for the F and VRIN scales that performed somewhat better than the VRIN scale in identifying partial random responding. However, additional research with these subscales will be necessary before they are ready for clinical use.

In summary, the VRIN scale was developed to identify persons who respond to the MMPI-2 items inconsistently, typically because they did not read the content of the items and responded instead in a random or near-random way to them. The VRIN scale can be especially helpful in understanding elevated F-scale scores. A high F-scale score and a high VRIN-scale score would support the notion of random responding. However, a high F-scale score and a low or moderate VRIN-scale score would be suggestive of a protocol that did not result from random responding or confusion. Instead, the protocol probably came either from a severely disturbed person who responded validly to the items or from a person who approached the items with the intention of appearing more disturbed than really was the case. Because an all-true or all-false response set would be likely to produce a high F-scale score and an average VRIN-scale score, those sets must also be considered. The True Response Inconsistency (TRIN) scale, which is described next, is helpful in determining if a protocol is the product of a true or false response set.

True Response Inconsistency (TRIN) Scale

The True Response Inconsistency (TRIN) scale was developed for the MMPI-2 to identify persons who respond inconsistently to items by giving true responses to items indiscriminately (acquiescence) or by giving false responses to items indiscriminately (nonacquiescence) (Butcher et al., 1989, 2001). In either case, the resulting protocol is likely to be invalid and uninterpretable.

The TRIN scale consists of 20 pairs of items that are opposite in content. Because for some item pairs either two true or two false responses add a point, there are 23 response pairs in the TRIN scale. Two true responses to some item pairs or two false responses to other item pairs would indicate inconsistent responding. The TRIN raw score is obtained by subtracting the number of pairs of items to which test takers responded inconsistently with two false responses from the number of pairs of items to which they responded inconsistently with two true responses, and then adding a constant value of 9 to the difference. TRIN-scale raw scores can range from 0 to 23. Higher TRIN-scale raw scores indicate a tendency to give true responses indiscriminately, and lower TRIN-scale raw scores indicate a tendency to give false responses indiscriminately. When TRIN-scale raw scores are converted to T scores, raw scores above 9 and below 9 are converted to T scores greater than 50, with the likelihood of a true or false response set indicated by the letters "T" or "F" following the T scores. As with the VRIN scale, the TRIN scale involves complex scoring that is best done by computer (Iverson & Barton, 1999). If hand scoring is done, considerable care should be exercised.

The MMPI-2 manual (Butcher et al., 2001) suggests that TRIN-scale raw scores of 13 or greater (T > 80 in the true direction) or of 5 or less (T > 80 in the false direction) are suggestive of inconsistent responding that might invalidate the protocol. An analogue study by Wetter and Tharpe (1995) offered evidence that TRIN-scale scores are sensitive to randomly inserted true or false responses and that the TRIN scale makes a unique contribution to the detection of this response set.

SCALES ASSESSING CONTENT-RESPONSIVE INVALIDITY (CRI)

Scales for Detecting Overreporting

Sometimes persons respond to the MMPI-2 items with the intention of portraying themselves as having more problems and symptoms and as being more generally maladjusted than they really are. The motivations for this overreporting are varied. Some test takers may do so to convince mental health professionals that they are desperately in need of their help. Other test takers may be motivated to try to avoid responsibility for their actions by appearing to be very psychologically disturbed (e.g., not guilty by reason of insanity pleas) or for monetary gains (e.g., personal injury or disability claims). Regardless of motivation, it is important to detect individuals who are overreporting so that test takers will not be incorrectly described as more maladjusted than they really are. The original MMPI included scales that were helpful for detecting overreporting, and more scales designed for this purpose were developed for the MMPI-2.

Infrequency (F) Scale

The F scale of the original MMPI was developed to detect deviant or atypical ways of responding to test items, such as those that resulted when test takers did not read the items and responded randomly (Meehl & Hathaway, 1946). The 64 items in the original F scale were those answered in the scored direction by fewer than 10% of the MMPI normative sample. Several of the F-scale items were deleted from the MMPI-2 because of objectionable content, leaving the F scale with 60 items.

A factor analysis of the original F-scale items (Comrey, 1958a) identified 19 dimensions, assessing such diverse characteristics as paranoid thinking, antisocial attitudes or behavior, hostility, and poor physical health. A person can obtain a high F-scale score by endorsing items in some, but not necessarily all, of these 19 content areas. In general, and because the scales of the MMPI-2 are intercorrelated, high scores on the F scale usually are associated with elevated scores on the Clinical scales, especially on Scales 6 and 8. In the MMPI-2 normative sample, scores on the F scale are related to ethnicity, with African Americans, Native Americans, and Hispanics scoring on average three to five T-score points higher on the F scale than Caucasians (Butcher et al., 2001).

Although originally intended to identify random responding, it soon became apparent that there were explanations other than random responding for high F-scale scores. Persons who are very psychologically disturbed typically endorse a large number of F-scale items in the scored direction, as do less disturbed individuals who are attempting to appear more maladjusted than they really are. Answering items indiscriminately true or false will also lead to high F-scale scores. Determining which of these explanations was most appropriate for a specific person with an elevated F-scale score on the original MMPI was quite difficult. Fortunately, MMPI-2 scales to directly assess random responding (VRIN), indiscriminate true or false responding (TRIN), and overreporting (F_p) have made the task of understanding the reasons for high F-scale scores easier.

Empirical research has indicated that, in addition to assessing deviant and possibly invalidating approaches to completing the MMPI-2, scores on the F scale are related to some personality characteristics and behaviors. However, these same characteristics and behaviors typically can be inferred from other MMPI-2 scales for which greater research support is available. Thus, this author recommends that the F scale be used to assess test-taking approaches and not to make inferences about personality and psychopathology.

High Scores on the F Scale

It is possible to establish some ranges of T scores on the F scale and to discuss possible interpretations associated with scores in each range. The MMPI-2 manual (Butcher et al., 2001) indicates that, because of the relationship between F-scale scores and genuine psychopathology, scores on this scale may have different meanings in clinical and nonclinical settings. The manual also suggests different scores for identifying invalid responding in inpatient, outpatient, and nonclinical settings.

T > 100 (Inpatients); T > 90 (Outpatients); T > 80 (Nonclinical Settings). When T scores on the F scale are this high, the possibility of an invalidating response set should be considered. Persons who obtain scores at this level may have responded in a random way to the MMPI-2 items. The Variable Response Inconsistency (VRIN) scale, which was described earlier in this chapter, is helpful in detecting random responding. If the VRIN T-scale score is greater than 80, random responding is likely.

Some persons who obtain T scores at this level on the F scale may have had a true response bias in responding to the items. If this is the case, T scores on the True Response Inconsistency (TRIN) scale, which was described earlier in this chapter, would be expected to be greater than 80 (in the true direction). It is also possible that F-scale scores in this range have resulted from attempts to present an unrealistically negative picture when completing the MMPI-2. The Infrequency Psychopathology (F_p) scale, which will be discussed later in this chapter, is especially helpful in identifying individuals who overreported when completing the MMPI-2. Finally, among hospitalized psychiatric patients, F-scale T scores greater than 100 often are suggestive of very serious psychopathology.

T = 80–99 (Inpatients); T = 70–89 (Outpatients); T = 65–79 (Nonclinical Settings). Answering false to all or most of the MMPI-2 items can produce an F-scale score at this level. If this is the case, the TRIN-scale T score is likely to be greater than 80 (in the false direction). Persons with scores at this level may have exaggerated symptoms, perhaps as a "cry for help." However, scores at this level may also be indicative of serious psychological problems.

T = 55–79 (Inpatients); T = 55–69 (Outpatients); T = 40–64 (Nonclinical). Persons with T scores at this level on the F scale likely approached the test in a valid manner. Sometimes scores at this level indicate persons with deviant social, political, or religious convictions. Persons with scores at the upper end of this range may be accurately reporting psychological problems.

Low Scores on the F Scale [T < 54 (Inpatient and Outpatient); T < 39 (Nonclinical)]

Persons with F-scale T scores in this below-average range may be denying or minimizing psychological problems. An underreporting response set should be considered. More information about underreporting is presented later in this chapter.

Back Infrequency (F$_B$) Scale

The Back Infrequency (F$_B$) scale originally was developed for the experimental booklet used in the normative data collection for the MMPI-2 (Butcher et al., 1989). The procedures used to develop the F$_B$ scale were similar to those used in the development of the standard F scale. Since the items in the standard F scale appeared early in the experimental booklet, that scale did not assess the validity of responses to items appearing later in the 704-item booklet. The original F$_B$ scale included 64 items that appeared later in the experimental booklet to which fewer than 10% of normal individuals responded in the scored direction. The version of the F$_B$ scale included in the MMPI-2 has 40 of the original 64 items. They occur between Item No. 281 and Item No. 555 in the test booklet.

In a protocol for which the standard F-scale score is indicative of a valid approach (see the earlier description of the F scale), an elevated F$_B$-scale score could indicate that the test taker responded to items in the second half of the test booklet in an invalid manner. In this situation, the standard scales that are based on items that occur early in the booklet (L, F, and K and the Clinical scales) can be interpreted, but Supplementary scales, Content scales, and some other scales that are based on items that occur later in the booklet should not be interpreted. Of course, if the standard F-scale score is indicative of invalidity, the protocol should not be interpreted at all.

Only limited research data are available concerning optimal F$_B$-scale cutoff scores for identifying invalid records. Because of the differing number of items in the F and F$_B$ scales, raw scores on these two scales should never be compared. The MMPI-2 manual (Butcher et al., 2001) suggests that when the F$_B$ scale is significantly elevated (T > 110 in clinical settings; T > 90 in nonclinical settings) and is at least 30 T-score points higher than the F-scale T score, the test taker is likely to have changed his or her approach to the latter part of the test and that scales with items in the latter part of the test should not be interpreted.

As with the F scale, persons who respond randomly to MMPI-2 items throughout the test will have very high F_B-scale scores and high scores (T > 80) on the VRIN scale. Persons who respond true to most of the MMPI-2 items or who are overreporting psychopathology in responding to many of the items also will produce very high scores on the F_B scale. For a true response bias, the elevated F_B-scale score will be accompanied by a TRIN-scale T score greater than 80 (in the true direction). Persons who are overreporting psychopathology are likely also to have elevated scores on the F_p scale, which is described next.

Infrequency Psychopathology (F_p) Scale

Recognizing that in some clinical settings high F-scale scores are often due, at least in part, to the severe psychopathology of those who take the MMPI-2, Arbisi and Ben-Porath (1995) developed the F_p scale as a supplement to the F scale in identifying infrequent responding. The 27 items in the F_p scale are ones that were answered infrequently by both psychiatric inpatients and persons in the MMPI-2 normative sample. The resulting items are far less likely to reflect psychopathology than the F-scale items that were chosen because of infrequent responding by normal persons.

Several studies have confirmed that the F_p scale is less indicative of genuine psychopathology than the F and F_B scales are (Arbisi & Ben-Porath, 1998a; Ladd, 1998; Tolin et al., 2004). Using data collected by Graham, Watts, and Timbrook (1991), Arbisi and Ben-Porath (1995) demonstrated that the F_p scale added incrementally to the F scale in the discrimination between persons overreporting and psychiatric inpatients.

Gass and Luis (2001b) noted that four of the F_p-scale items also appear on the L scale and seem to be indicative of defensiveness rather than overreporting. They suggested that deleting these items for the F_p scale could increase its effectiveness. However, Arbisi, Ben-Porath, and McNulty (2003b) demonstrated that the original F_p scale was more effective in identifying overreporting than the revised scale suggested by Gass and Luis.

Although Arbisi and Ben-Porath (1995) did not try to establish optimal cutoff scores on the F_p scale for differentiating between overreporting and genuine psychopathology, they suggested that T scores over 100 on the F_p scale are likely to indicate overreporting. The MMPI-2 manual (Butcher et al., 2001) also suggests that an F_p scale score greater than 100 may indicate overreporting or random responding. This latter approach to the test would also result in a VRIN-scale T score greater than 80.

A study by Rogers, Sewell, and Ustad (1995) examined MMPI-2 scores of psychiatric outpatients who took the test with standard instructions and also with instructions to make their problems seem much worse than they really were. F_p-scale scores accurately identified the exaggerated protocols. The F scale was about equally effective in making this discrimination, and the F-scale and F_p-scale scores were highly correlated. Unfortunately, these investigators did not report data concerning the incremental validity of the F_p scale when used along with the F scale. However, two subsequent studies demonstrated that the F_p scale added incrementally to the F scale in the detection of prisoners who were instructed to fake bad (Gallagher, 1997) and college students who were instructed to feign schizophrenia (Bagby, Rogers, Buis, et al., 1997). Several additional studies have indicated that the F_p scale may be more accurate than the F scale in identifying psychiatric inpatients and outpatients who are instructed to exaggerate their symptoms and problems (Arbisi & Ben-Porath, 1998b; Berry et al., 1996).

Rogers, Sewell, Martin, and Vitacco (2003) conducted a meta-analysis of 65 MMPI-2 feigning studies. They concluded that, of the MMPI-2 Validity scales that are routinely scored and reported, both F and F_p are effective in identifying individuals who are feigning psychopathology. They expressed a preference for the F_p scale because optimal cutting scores were consistent across settings and there was a low probability of false positives.

High Scores on the F_p Scale

Protocols with F_p-scale scores > 100 are likely to be invalid and should not be interpreted (Butcher et al., 2001). One possible reason for such a high score is that the test taker responded inconsistently to the items, in which case the VRIN- or TRIN-scale score will be greater than 79. Another possibility is that the test taker overreported psychopathology in an attempt to appear more disturbed than he or she is in reality. F_p-scale T scores between 70 and 99 suggest some exaggeration of symptoms and problems, perhaps as a "cry for help," but the protocol could still be valid and interpretable. F_p-scale T scores < 69 suggest that the test taker accurately described current her or his mental health status.

Symptom Validity Scale (FBS)

This scale was originally called the Fake Bad Scale and was developed by Lees-Haley, English, and Glenn (1991) to detect the noncredible reporting of emotional distress among personal-injury claimants. Although not originally a part of the MMPI-2, it was subsequently added to the test, and a test monograph was published to inform users about scale development and interpretation (Ben-Porath, Graham, & Tellegen, 2009).

Items for the FBS were selected rationally based on some unpublished frequency counts of supposed malingerers' MMPI item responses and "observations of personal injury malingerers." Subsequent published research with the FBS does not support its validity for its intended purpose. In a study of overreporting in a sample of workplace accident victims, Bury and Bagby (2002) found that the FBS was ineffective in detecting feigned psychopathology and concluded that its use for this purpose is inadvisable. Butcher, Arbisi, Atlis, and McNulty (2003) analyzed data from a variety of settings and concluded that the FBS is likely to classify an unacceptably large number of individuals who are experiencing genuine psychological distress as overreporters. A meta-analysis of MMPI-2 overreporting studies (Rogers et al., 2003) revealed that the FBS has been quite ineffective in identifying persons who are giving noncredible reports of emotional distress.

Some authors have suggested that the FBS may be effective in identifying the noncredible reporting of cognitive deficits during neuropsychological examinations (Greiffenstein, Baker, Gola, Donders, & Miller, 2002; Larrabee, 2003). However, a well-conducted study by Dearth et al. (2005) found that the FBS was not as effective as the F, F_B, F_p, or Ds2 scales in identifying persons who gave noncredible responses during an analogue neuropsychological examination. None of the MMPI-2 scales studied was as effective in ruling out noncredible responding as in correctly identifying those who gave noncredible responses. Only when the base rate of noncredible responding was unrealistically high (65%) was the FBS somewhat more effective than the other scales in ruling out noncredible responding.

More recently, Nelson, Sweet, and Demakis (2006) conducted a meta-analysis of 83 studies involving the FBS's utility. Results indicated that FBS was superior to the F_B and F_p scales in differentiating between persons who gave noncredible reports of cognitive deficits compared with persons known to have such deficits. However, the FBS scale did not fare as well as the F, F_B and F_p scales in detecting noncredible reporting of emotional problems. Additional research suggested that the FBS scale is effective in identifying insufficient effort on cognitive tasks (Smart et al., 2008) and noncredible reports of pain symptoms (Bianchini, Etherton, Greve, Heinly, & Meyers, 2008). More research is needed to determine the extent to which the FBS and other MMPI-2 Validity scales can detect the overreporting of cognitive deficits during neuropsychological examination and the extent to which any of the scales adds incrementally to established motivational scales such as the Digit Memory Test (Hiscock & Hiscock, 1989), the Test of Memory Malingering (Tombaugh, 1997), or the Letter Memory Test (Inman et al., 1998).

There have been criticisms of the FBS scale claiming that the scale incorrectly classifies persons with bona fide medical problems (Butcher et al., 2003). However, Ben-Porath et al. (2009) rebutted these claims with an up-to-date literature review and original data analyses. As reported in the FBS test report (Ben-Porath et al., 2009), when appropriate cutoff scores are used few persons with genuine medical/neurological problems are incorrectly identified as noncredible responders. There also have been claims that the FBS scale is biased against women (Nichols, Greene, & Williams, 2009). However, Lee, Graham, Sellbom, & Gervais (2010) presented data suggesting that, when appropriate cutoff scores are used, the FBS scale is equally valid for men and women in differentiating between persons simulating cognitive problems and persons with bona fide cognitive problems. Dean et al. (2008) found no differences in FBS scale scores between Caucasians, Hispanics, and African Americans who were referred to a neuropsychological clinic or were patients in a vocational rehabilitation program. In summary, having reviewed existing research literature very carefully, this author has concluded that, when appropriate cutoff scores are used, the FBS scale has utility in identifying persons who give noncredible reports of cognitive deficits.

Scales for Detecting Underreporting

Lie (L) Scale[2]

As indicated in Chapter 1, the L scale originally was constructed to detect a deliberate and unsophisticated attempt to present oneself in an unrealistically favorable way (Meehl & Hathaway, 1946). All of the 15 rationally derived items in the original L scale were maintained in MMPI-2. The items deal with minor personality flaws and weaknesses to which most people are willing to admit (e.g., not reading every editorial in the newspaper every day or not liking everyone you know). However, individuals who deliberately are trying to present themselves in a very favorable way are not willing to admit even such minor shortcomings. Such people produce high L-scale scores.

Although most L-scale items are not answered in the scored direction (false) by most people, many test takers endorse several of the items in the scored direction. The average number of L items endorsed in the scored direction by persons in the MMPI-2 normative sample was approximately three. It was reported that better-educated, brighter, and more-sophisticated people from higher social classes scored lower on the L scale of the original MMPI (Graham, 1987). The relationships between T scores on the MMPI-2 L scale and these demographic characteristics are weaker than for the original test, and they probably are not very important in interpreting L-scale scores (Butcher, 1990a; Dahlstrom & Tellegen, 1993; Long, Graham, & Timbrook, 1994). However, Duris, Bjorck, and Gorsuch (2007) found that persons with strong Christian beliefs answered some L-scale items in the scored direction more often than persons in the MMPI-2 normative sample.

Persons completing the MMPI-2 in nonclinical settings (e.g., personnel screening, child custody evaluations) understandably want to present themselves in a positive way. This motivation often leads to moderately elevated scores on the L scale that do not necessarily indicate the presence of significant psychological symptoms and problems that are not being accurately reported. For example, Bathurst, Gottfried, and Gottfried (1997) reported average L-scale T scores of approximately 55 for mothers and fathers involved in child custody determinations, and Bagby, Nicholson, Buis, Radovanovic, and Fidler (1999) reported average L-scale T scores of approximately 60 for parents in a similar situation.

High Scores on the L Scale

T > 80 (Clinical and Nonclinical Settings). When the L-scale T score is equal to or greater than 80, it is likely that the test taker was not honest and frank in answering items on the inventory and may have claimed virtues and denied negative

---

[2]The reader should recognize that the descriptors listed in this and subsequent summaries are modal ones and that all descriptors will not apply necessarily to all individuals with a given score or configuration of scores. The descriptors should be viewed as hypotheses to be validated by reference to other test and nontest data.

characteristics to a greater extent than most people do. The result of such a test-taking attitude is that the person's scores on other scales may be lowered artificially in the direction of appearing better adjusted psychologically. The resulting protocol should not be interpreted. This is the level of L-scale scores typically found when test takers are instructed to appear to be very well adjusted and free of emotional problems and symptoms. When L-scale scores are at this level, profiles should be compared with the prototype for an underreporting response set that is presented later in this chapter. Scores at this level also may result from a pervasive nonacquiescence, and the TRIN-scale score (described earlier in this chapter) should be consulted to determine if this test-taking approach was utilized.

T = 65–79 (Clinical Settings); T = 70–79 (Nonclinical Settings). L-scale T scores at this level suggest the possibility that the test taker has not responded to items honestly, trying to appear as a very virtuous and well-adjusted person. Other MMPI-2 scores may not represent accurately the psychological status of the test taker, and the protocol should be interpreted very cautiously or not at all. L-scale scores at this level can also indicate a pervasive nonacquiescence response set, which can be assessed directly by referring to the TRIN scale (see the description of the TRIN scale earlier in this chapter).

T = 65–69 (Nonclinical Settings). L-scale T scores at this level are suggestive of an overly positive self-presentation. The test taker may have minimized psychological and behavioral difficulties, but the resulting protocol can be interpreted if the defensiveness is taken into account.

T = 60–64 (Clinical and Nonclinical Settings). Scores at this level may reflect an unsophisticated defensiveness in which respondents are denying negative characteristics and claiming positive ones because they judge it to be in their best interest to do so. However, the MMPI-2 protocol is likely valid and interpretable as long as this test-taking attitude and the circumstances of the evaluation are taken into account. Persons completing the MMPI-2 in nonclinical settings (e.g., personnel screening; child custody evaluations) often have L-scale scores at this level, and the scores do not necessarily indicate that significant psychological problems or symptoms are present but not being accurately reported. Persons with strong Christian or other religious beliefs may obtain scores at this level.

Average Scores on the L Scale

T = 50–59. This is an average range on the L scale, and scores at this level suggest a valid protocol.

Low Scores on the L Scale

T < 50. T scores below 50 on the L scale are considered low scores and, depending on scores on other Validity scales, may indicate overreporting of psychopathology.

(See the discussion later in this chapter concerning the identification of overreporting.) An all-true (acquiescence) response set also produces very low T scores on the L scale. The TRIN scale, which was described earlier in this chapter, can be helpful in determining if a low L-scale score is due to a true response bias.

Correction (K) Scale

When early experience with the MMPI indicated that the L scale was insensitive to several kinds of test distortion, the K scale was developed as a more subtle index of attempts by examinees to deny psychopathology and to present themselves in a favorable light or, conversely, to exaggerate psychopathology and to try to appear in a very unfavorable light (McKinley, Hathaway, & Meehl, 1948; Meehl & Hathaway, 1946). High scores on the K scale thus were thought to be associated with a defensive approach to the test, whereas low scores were thought to be indicative of unusual frankness and self-critical attitudes. The original K scale included 30 items that were empirically identified by contrasting responses of clearly disturbed psychiatric patients who produced normal scores on the MMPI with responses of a group of normal persons. The MMPI-2 version of the K scale includes all 30 of these original items. The items in the K scale cover several different content areas in which a person can deny problems (e.g., hostility, suspiciousness, family dissension, lack of self-confidence, excessive worry). The K-scale items tend to be more subtle than items in the L scale; therefore, it is less likely that defensive persons will recognize the purpose of the items and will be able to avoid detection.

Subsequent research and experience have indicated that the K scale is much more complex than was originally believed. Scores on the K scale of the original MMPI were strongly related to educational level (Graham, 1987). Better-educated persons tended to score higher on the scale. Thus, it was recommended that educational levels be taken into account in interpreting scores on the K scale. The relationship between educational level and K-scale scores of the MMPI-2 is not as strong as for the original MMPI. Although persons with less formal education score lower on the K scale than persons with more formal education, the differences are not great enough to suggest different interpretations of K-scale scores for different educational groups (Brophy, 1995; Dahlstrom & Tellegen, 1993; Long et al., 1994).

Although very high scores on the K scale typically indicate defensiveness, moderate elevations sometimes reflect greater ego strength and psychological resources (McGrath, Sweeney, O'Malley, & Carlton, 1998). There is no definite way to determine when moderately elevated K-scale scores indicate clinical defensiveness and when they indicate more positive characteristics. However, if moderately high K-scale scores are found for persons who do not seem to be disturbed psychologically and who appear to be functioning reasonably well, the possibility that the K-scale score is reflecting positive characteristics rather than defensiveness should be considered.

In addition to identifying deviations in test-taking attitudes, a statistical procedure was also developed for correcting scores on some of the Clinical scales.

(See the discussion of the K-correction in Chapter 1.) Because most of the data concerning interpretation of MMPI scores were based on K-corrected scores, the K-correction was maintained with the MMPI-2. However, several MMPI studies found that the K-correction did not lead to more accurate predictions of extratest characteristics (Clopton, Shanks, & Preng, 1987; McCrae et al., 1989; Silver & Sines, 1962; Wooten, 1984). Barthlow, Graham, Ben-Porath, Tellegen, and McNulty (2002) correlated therapist ratings of clients with K-corrected and non-K-corrected MMPI-2 scale scores and found no meaningful differences between the two sets of correlations. Of course, this study utilized two outpatient mental health samples for which little defensiveness was present. Findings in other settings where defensiveness is more likely (e.g., child custody, pre-employment screening) could be different. Sellbom, Fischler, and Ben-Porath (2007) conducted a predictive validity study using police officer applicants, a group for whom considerable defensiveness would be expected. They found that non-K-corrected scores were more closely related than corrected scores to behavioral measures of police officer misconduct.

It is difficult at this time to make a clear recommendation about using or not using the K-correction for the MMPI-2. The K-correction is still an official part of the MMPI-2, but research results tend not to support its use. It is likely that the K-correction will not be maintained in future revisions of the MMPI-2. At this time it is this author's practice to use K-corrected scores in clinical settings. Generally, corrected and noncorrected scores are quite similar in these settings, where defensiveness is not common.

However, there are some circumstances when noncorrected scores should also be examined. When assessing persons who cannot be assumed to have serious psychiatric problems (e.g., job applicants), non-K-corrected scores may give a better indication of their standing on scales in relation to the normative sample. It is especially important to use caution in nonclinical settings in interpreting moderately elevated Clinical-scale scores that result primarily, or in some cases completely, from the K-correction. To interpret K-corrected scores in these instances may lead to inaccurate inferences of maladjustment and psychopathology. The test distributor, Pearson Assessments, offers profile sheets for plotting both K-corrected and non-K-corrected scores, and many computer-generated reports include both K-corrected and non-K-corrected scores for the Clinical scales.

High Scores on the K Scale (T > 65 in Clinical Settings; T > 75 in Nonclinical Settings)

T scores at this level indicate that test takers probably approached the MMPI-2 in a very defensive manner. The higher the score, the more likely it is that the person was being clinically defensive. An underreporting response set that would invalidate the protocol should be seriously considered.

High scores on the K scale also can be indicative of a false response set. The TRIN scale can be helpful in determining if an elevated K-scale score is due to such a response set. A high K-scale score (T > 65) and a T score on the TRIN scale greater than 80 (in the false direction) strongly suggest that false responses were given to items without consideration of their content.

In nonclinical settings (e.g., personnel screening or child custody evaluations), T scores in a 65–74 range are fairly common and should not necessarily be interpreted as invalidating the test results. However, scores in this range in nonclinical settings suggest moderate defensiveness that should be taken into account as other MMPI-2 scales are interpreted.

Average Scores on the K Scale (T = 40–64)

Average scores on the K scale indicate that the test taker is likely to have presented a balanced self-view. Both positive and negative behaviors and personality characteristics are likely to have been acknowledged in responding to the MMPI-2 items.

Low Scores on the K Scale (T < 40)

Low T scores on the K scale may be indicative of a true response set or of a deliberate attempt to present oneself in an unfavorable way. (See the discussion of profile invalidity later in this chapter for details about these two response sets.) The TRIN scale can be helpful in determining if a low K-scale score indicates a true response set. A low K-scale score and a T score on the TRIN scale greater than 80 (in the true direction) strongly indicate the likelihood of a true response set. Low scores on the K scale also may indicate the exaggeration of problems as a plea for help.

Superlative Self-Presentation (S) Scale

Butcher and Han (1995) developed the S scale to assess the tendency of some persons to present themselves on the MMPI-2 as highly virtuous, responsible individuals who are free of psychological problems, have few or no moral flaws, and get along extremely well with others. This manner of self-presentation is very common in situations such as personnel screening or child custody evaluations.

The 50 items in the S scale were identified by contrasting the responses of male airline pilot applicants and men in the MMPI-2 normative sample. Butcher and Han (1995) suggested that there are five major content dimensions in the S-scale items: (1) belief in human goodness, (2) serenity, (3) contentment with life, (4) patience and denial of irritability and anger, and (5) denial of moral flaws. They also reported that S-scale scores are highly correlated with K-scale scores in the MMPI-2 normative sample: .81 for men and .92 for women. S-scale scores were less highly correlated with L-scale scores: .46 for men and .34 for women.

Higher S-scale scorers in the MMPI-2 normative study were characterized by their spouses as less dysphoric, hostile, and impulsive and as more self-confident, sociable, relaxed, cheerful, and cooperative than lower scorers on the scale. Butcher and Han (1995) concluded that higher scores on the S scale are suggestive of persons who are unrealistically reporting positive attributes and good adjustment. These investigators did not report data concerning how well this scale can detect defensiveness or underreporting response sets or the extent to which higher scores reflect these response sets rather than genuinely superior adjustment.

In a subsequent study, Baer, Wetter, Nichols, Greene, and Berry (1995) found that S-scale scores were higher when nonclinical persons took the MMPI-2 pretending to be well adjusted and psychologically and emotionally healthy in order to get a very desirable job. In addition, the S scale added to the L and K scales in discriminating between persons who took the test with standard instructions and those who pretended to be perfectly well adjusted. Baer, Wetter, and Berry (1995) also found that the S scale was effective in identifying students who tried to be very well adjusted in taking the MMPI-2. A raw score equal to or greater than 29 correctly classified 91% of the students who took the test with standard instructions and 92% of those who took it with instructions to appear very well adjusted. Bagby, Rogers, Nicholson, et al. (1997) reported that the S scale was effective in distinguishing students who completed the MMPI-2 with standard instructions and students who completed the test with instructions to try to appear very well adjusted, but that it was not as effective in distinguishing psychiatric patients who responded honestly from those who were instructed to underreport symptoms and problem. The L scale was more effective than the S scale for this latter discrimination.

Lim and Butcher (1996) found that students who were instructed to deny psychological problems or to claim excessive virtue had higher S-scale scores than when they completed the MMPI-2 with standard instructions. Optimal cutoff scores for distinguishing the two conditions varied as a function of gender and the kind of error (false positive versus false negative) that was judged to be most critical. The classification rates for the S scale were not much different from those obtained with the L scale. Unfortunately, these investigators did not determine if the S scale added incrementally to the accuracy of classification rates based on the L scale alone. Interestingly, students in the two faking conditions (denying psychological problems versus claiming excessive virtue) did not differ significantly from each other on the S scale or on the other Validity scales and indexes used in the study.

Baer and Miller (2002) conducted a meta-analysis of studies that addressed underreporting of psychopathology on the MMPI-2. They concluded that the S scale is effective in detecting underreporting, but they found no consistent support to suggest that the scale is any better than L and K in detecting underreporting. Their recommendation was that, because much more research is available for the L and K scales than for the S scale, L and K may be the more desirable approach to identifying underreporting. The results of the meta-analysis indicated that the S scale is a bit more effective than the L or K scales in detecting underreporting when test takers have been coached to avoid detection of underreporting. However, additional research is needed to verify the utility of the S scale in detecting coached underreporting and to determine optimal S-scale cutoff scores.

High Scores on the S Scale (T > 70 in Clinical Settings;
T > 75 in Nonclinical Settings)

S-scale T scores at this level suggest that the test has been completed in such a defensive manner that the results may be invalid. In clinical settings, protocols with S-scale T scores at this level probably should not be interpreted at all. In nonclinical settings, where some defensiveness is often typical, protocols with S-scale T scores above 75 should not be interpreted at all, but those with S-scale T scores between 70 and 74 may be interpreted, keeping in mind that scores on other scales may underestimate problems to a moderate degree. High scores on the S scale also can indicate a pervasive nonacquiescence response style. Scores on the TRIN scale are helpful in determining if this response set was present and accounts for the high S-scale score. If the S-scale T score is above 70 and the TRIN-scale T score is above 80 (in the false direction), it is likely that the person responded false to the MMPI-2 items without consideration of their content.

Average Scores on the S Scale (T = 40–69)

Average scores on the S scale indicate that the person was not very defensive in responding to the MMPI-2 items and that scores on the other scales are interpretable.

Low Scores on the S Scale (T < 40)

Although persons who are overreporting symptoms and problems may score well below average on the S scale, there is not sufficient research with the S scale as an indicator of overreporting to support its use for detecting this response set. Other scales, which were discussed earlier in this chapter, are more established as indicators of overreporting.

OTHER VALIDITY INDICATORS

Response Bias Scale (RBS)

Gervais, Ben-Porath, Wygant, and Green (2007) developed the 28-item Response Bias Scale (RBS) to identify persons who are overreporting cognitive symptoms and problems in forensic neuropsychological or disability assessment settings. Although this scale is not part of standard MMPI-2 scoring, it shows considerable promise in detecting noncredible reporting of cognitive deficits.

Items in the scale were identified by comparing responses of persons who failed symptom validity tests and persons who passed symptom validity tests. Somewhat less than 40% of the items in the scale are directly cognitive in nature, with the remaining items reflecting somatic symptoms, denial of antisocial behaviors, and mistrustful attitudes. The RBS was validated by comparing different groups of individuals who passed or failed symptom validity tests. Data suggested that higher scorers were more likely to fail symptom validity tests and that a raw score cutoff of 17 yielded optimal classification accuracy (PPP = .77; NP = .66). False positive classification errors (i.e., concluding that honest responders are overreporting) were minimal, although false negative errors (i.e., concluding that overresponders respond honestly) were common.

Subsequent research has supported the validity of the RBS in predicting overreporting of cognitive problems. Nelson, Sweet, and Heilbronner (2007) examined RBS scores of persons who were referred for neuropsychological evaluation in relation to cognitive complaints. The RBS was effective in differentiating between those who were presumed to have secondary gain versus those without secondary gain. Whitney, Davis, Shephard, and Herman (2008) found the RBS to be more effective than other MMPI-2 Validity scales in predicting failure on the Test of Memory Malingering. Gervais, Ben-Porath, Wygant, and Green (2008) reported that the RBS was a better predictor of memory complaint scores than other MMPI-2 Validity scales. Interestingly, there was no relationship between RBS scores and an objective measure of verbal memory. These research findings suggest that the RBS is a very promising indicator of overreporting of memory problems. Serious consideration should be given to adding the scale to standard MMPI-2 scoring.

F Minus K Index

Gough (1950) found that people who were trying to create the impression of severe psychopathology scored considerably higher on the F scale than on the K scale. He suggested that the difference between the F-scale raw score and the K-scale raw score can serve as a useful index for detecting overreporting. Gough (1950) and Meehl (1951) indicated that when such an index number was positive and greater than 9, a protocol was likely to be the product of an overreporting response set. Carson (1969) suggested that a cutoff score of 11 yielded more accurate identification of overreporting MMPI profiles. Although a single cutoff score cannot be established for all settings, whenever the F-scale raw score is greater than the K-scale raw score the possibility of overreporting should be considered, and, as the difference becomes greater, the likelihood of overreporting becomes greater. Although the F minus K index has been effective in distinguishing honest from overreported MMPI-2 protocols, most research has indicated that this index is not as effective as the F scale in making this discrimination (Graham, Watts, et al., 1991; Rogers et al., 1995, 2003).

Gough (1950) reported little success in using the F minus K index to identify persons who underreported when responding to the MMPI items. A meta-analysis of underreporting studies with the MMPI-2 revealed that while the F minus K index was somewhat effective in differentiating between underreporting and standard instruction groups, the index was less effective than the L scale and about as effective as the K scale (Baer & Miller, 2002). Thus, there is little to recommend the use of the F minus K index over these other measures.

Dissimulation (Ds) Scale

Gough (1954) developed the Ds scale to identify persons who are simulating or exaggerating psychopathology. The scale included items judged by professionals to be indicative of psychopathology but not typically endorsed by psychiatric patients. Persons who were instructed to dissimulate scored higher on this scale, but it was not as effective as the F scale in identifying overreporting (Berry, Baer, & Harris, 1991). A modified version of the Ds scale (Dsr) can be scored from the MMPI-2 items. A meta-analysis reported by Rogers et al. (2003) found that the Ds and Dsr scales were not quite as effective as the F and F_p scales in identifying overreporting. However, optimal cutoff scores for the Ds scale were quite consistent across studies. It would appear that this scale has promise in identifying overreporting on the MMPI-2 and should be included in future overreporting studies. However, the Ds and Dsr scales are not a part of standard MMPI-2 scoring output, so they are not readily available to test users.

Subtle–Obvious Index

Greene (1980, 1991) and others have suggested that the relative endorsement of subtle and obvious items of the MMPI and MMPI-2 can be helpful in identifying overreporting and underreporting response sets. As discussed in Chapter 1 of this book, there is little empirical evidence that this index is associated with overreporting on the MMPI-2. The subtle and obvious subscales no longer appear as part of the standard MMPI-2 scoring output.

Positive Malingering (Mp) Scale

The Mp scale is made up of items that were endorsed by research participants in the socially undesirable direction when responding honestly or overreporting psychopathology but in the opposite direction when underreporting (Cofer, Chance, & Judson, 1949). Persons who are underreporting when they take the MMPI-2 would be expected to score higher on the Mp scale than persons who respond honestly to the test. In a meta-analysis of studies of underreporting of psychopathology on the MMPI-2, Baer and Miller (2002) found that persons instructed to underreport on the MMPI-2 typically scored higher on the Mp scale than persons given standard instructions. However, across studies the Mp scale was no more successful in detecting underreporting than the L and K scales and even less effective than some less traditional scales such as the Superlative Self-Presentation (S) scale or Wiggins's Social Desirability (Wsd) scale. The Mp scale is not part of the standard scoring output for the MMPI-2.

Edwards Social Desirability (Esd) Scale

The items in the Esd scale (Edwards, 1957) are ones for which 10 judges unanimously agreed that endorsement in the scored direction reflected a socially desirable response. A study by Bagby, Rogers, Nicholson, et al. (1997) found that the Esd scale added significantly to the L and K scales in distinguishing psychiatric patients who took the MMPI-2 with instructions to conceal their maladjustment from patients who took the test with standard instructions. However, a meta-analysis of studies of underreporting on the MMPI-2 (Baer & Miller, 2002) indicated that the Esd scale was not as effective in identifying underreporting as many other scales and indexes included in the meta-analysis. The Esd scale is not part of the standard scoring output for the MMPI-2.

Wiggins Social Desirability (Wsd) Scale

The Wsd scale (Wiggins, 1959) is made up of 40 items answered differently by research participants who were instructed to respond to the MMPI items in a socially desirable manner and those who were instructed to answer the items honestly. Baer, Wetter, Nichols, et al. (1995) found that the Wsd scale added significantly to the L and K scales in discriminating students who were instructed to underreport in taking the MMPI-2 from students who took the test with standard instructions. In a meta-analysis of studies of underreporting on the MMPI-2, Baer and Miller (2002) reported that the Wsd scale was effective in detecting underreporting and had quite stable classification rates across studies. Although available research data are not sufficient to justify routine use of the Wsd scale for identifying underreporting on the MMPI-2, the scale seems to have enough promise that it should be included in future research studies of underreporting. The Wsd scale is not part of the standard scoring output for the MMPI-2.

Other Deception (Od) Scale

Nichols and Greene (1991) developed the Od scale by combining items in the Mp and Wsd scales and then deleting items that had the lowest item-total correlations. Bagby, Rogers, Nicholson, et al. (1997) found that the Od scale added significantly to the L and K scales in discriminating between students who were instructed to underreport when taking the MMPI-2 from those who took the test with standard instructions. However, the Od scale was not very effective in distinguishing psychiatric patients who were instructed to conceal their maladjustment from patients who took the MMPI-2 with standard instructions. A meta-analysis of studies of underreporting on the MMPI-2 (Baer & Miller, 2002) indicated that persons taking the MMPI-2 with instructions to underreport psychopathology typically scored higher on the Od scale than persons taking the test with standard instructions. Across studies included in the meta-analysis, the Od scale was even more effective than the L and K scales in detecting underreporting. This seems to be another scale for which there is not yet enough research data to support its routine use for identifying underreporting on the MMPI-2 but for which there is enough promise to indicate that it should be included in future studies of underreporting. The Od scale is not part of the standard scoring output for the MMPI-2.

Validity Scales for Specific Disorders and Specific Settings

There have been efforts to develop additional Validity scales for identifying the overreporting of symptoms associated with specific disorders. Elhai, Ruggiero, Frueh, Beckham, and Gold (2002) developed the Infrequency Posttraumatic Stress Disorder (Fptsd) scale by selecting items that were rarely endorsed by combat veterans diagnosed with PTSD. Steffan, Clopton, and Morgan (2003) developed the Malingered Depression (Md) scale by contrasting responses of students attempting to simulate depression and patients diagnosed with depression. Subsequent research with both of these scales indicated that they were no more effective than the standard Validity scales in identifying persons who were feigning the disorders. Recognizing that persons evaluated in correctional settings tended to have elevated scores on the traditional overreporting scales, Megargee (2004) developed the Infrequency Correctional (Fc) scale by identifying items endorsed by fewer than 15% of prison inmates. Using the Structured Interview of Reported Symptoms (SIRS) as a criterion, Gassen, Pietz, Spray, and Denny (2007) found that the Fc scale was superior to other MMPI-2 Validity scales in identifying inmates who were overreporting.

PROFILE INVALIDITY

Some MMPI-2 users consider any protocol invalid and uninterpretable that has more than 30 omitted items or a T score greater than 65 on one or more of the other Validity scales. Although this practice is a very conservative one that is not likely to result in considering as valid protocols that are in fact invalid, it represents an oversimplified view of protocol validity and causes many valid protocols to be discarded. For example, the MMPI-2 manual (Butcher et al., 2001) indicates that in clinical settings F-scale T scores greater than 100 can be indicative of severe psychopathology. Thus, a more sophisticated approach to profile validity is indicated.

Some persons approach the MMPI-2 with such deviant test-taking attitudes that the resulting protocols are simply not interpretable. For example, persons who respond in a random manner to the MMPI-2 items or who approach the test with a deliberate and extreme attempt to feign psychopathology will produce a protocol that should not be interpreted. Other persons may not follow the test instructions exactly, but their deviant responding is less extreme. For example, clients who are seeking psychological or psychiatric treatment for the first time may tend to exaggerate symptoms and problems to some extent as a plea for help. Parents who complete the MMPI-2 as part of child custody proceedings may do so in a moderately defensive manner. These tendencies must be taken into account when the resulting protocol is interpreted, but they do not necessarily render the protocol uninterpretable.

Deviant Response Sets and Styles

To produce a valid MMPI-2 protocol a person must read and consider the content of each item and respond to the item as true or false. Occasionally, individuals respond randomly to the items or will answer true (or false) to most items without reference to item content. Such behavior usually occurs among people who lack adequate reading skills, who are too confused to follow directions, or who have a very negative attitude toward the assessment procedure. Sometimes persons are highly motivated to appear more or less well adjusted on the MMPI-2 than is actually the case for them, and they respond to item content in terms of the impressions they want to present of themselves rather than in terms of actual self-perceptions.

In ideal circumstances the test examiner should be aware of such response tendencies. Efforts should be made to ensure that test takers follow the standard instructions for completing the MMPI-2. If cooperation cannot be elicited, the test should not be administered. However, particularly in situations in which large numbers of people are tested at once, some persons complete the MMPI-2 without following standard instructions. It is important for the MMPI-2 user to know how to detect the resulting invalid protocols. If profile invalidity is suspected, it may be helpful to consider what is known about the test taker's behavior from observation. Lack of congruence between the profile and observed behavior could be accounted for by the adoption of a response set or style.

If a particular MMPI-2 protocol is deemed invalid, the examiner may be able to discuss the situation with the test taker and re-administer the test. The examiner should indicate that the test results will not be helpful because the instruction may not have been followed and ask the individual to complete it again. Attention should be given to the standard instructions, and the test taker should be urged to follow them. Often a second testing yields a valid and interpretable protocol (Butcher, Morfitt, Rouse, & Holden, 1997; Cigrang & Staal, 2001; Gucker & McNulty, 2004). If retesting is not possible or if it does not yield a valid protocol, no interpretation should be attempted. Further, it should be understood that the only thing that an invalid protocol tells us about a person is that, because the test items were not responded to in a valid manner, the test results are not likely to present an accurate picture of what the person really is like. For example, it is tempting to conclude that a person who presents a very defensive protocol, one in which even average numbers of symptoms and problems are denied, is really a maladjusted person who is trying to conceal that maladjustment. Such a conclusion is not justified. The person could just as well be a well-adjusted person who, because of circumstances, felt the need to present himself or herself as even better adjusted than he or she really is. For example, such motivation often is present when parents complete the MMPI-2 as part of a child custody evaluation.

Random Responding

One deviant response set involves responding randomly or near randomly to the test items. A person may respond in a clearly random manner or may use an idiosyncratic response pattern, such as marking every block of eight items as true, true, false, false, true, true, false, false, or every block of six items as true, false, true, false, true, false, and repeating this pattern with each such subsequent block. There are various reasons why persons respond randomly to the test items. Sometimes they cannot read well enough to understand the items but are reluctant to inform the examiner that this is the case. Other times test takers are confused or uncooperative because they do not want to take the test but feel that they cannot directly refuse to do so. Because the responses in these various situations are made without regard to item content, the resulting protocol must be considered invalid.

The Variable Response Inconsistency (VRIN) scale, which was discussed earlier in this chapter, was developed specifically to identify random responding. According to the MMPI-2 manual (Butcher et al., 2001), VRIN-scale T scores equal to or greater than 80 indicate random responding that invalidates the protocol. Subsequent research studies have confirmed that this is the optimal VRIN-scale cutoff score for identifying random responding (Berry, Wetter, et al., 1991; Gallen & Berry, 1996; Paolo & Ryan, 1992). The profile configurations resulting from a completely random response set are shown in Figures 3.1A and 3.1B. In the random response profile, the F-, F_B-, and F_P-scale T scores are very elevated (usually greater than 100); the FBS T score is moderately elevated (low to mid 70s); the K and S scale T scores are at or near 50; and the L scale is moderately elevated (T = 60–70). The Clinical scales are characterized by generally elevated scores, usually with the highest score on Scale 8 and the second-highest score on Scale 6. T scores on Scales 5 and 0 are likely to be below 70. It should be understood that the random profiles in Figures 3.1A and 3.1B and the other invalid profiles presented in this section are modal profiles that would result if all items in the MMPI-2 were answered in the invalid manner. In practice, persons may

MMPI-2 Profile for Basic Scales

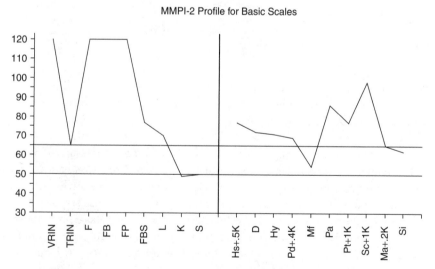

Figure 3.1A K-corrected male profile indicative of random responding.
Adapted from the *MMPI® -2 (Minnesota Multiphasic Personality Inventory® -2) Manual for Administration, Scoring, and Interpretation, Revised Edition* by James N. Butcher, John R. Graham, Yossef S. Ben-Porath, Auke Tellegen, W. Grant Dahlstrom, and Beverly Kaemmer. Copyright © 2001 by the Regents of the University of Minnesota. Used by permission of the University of Minnesota Press. All rights reserved. "MMPI® " and "Minnesota Multiphasic Personality Inventory® " are trademarks owned by the Regents of the University of Minnesota.

MMPI-2 Profile for Basic Scales

Figure 3.1B K-corrected female profile indicative of random responding.
Adapted from the *MMPI® -2 (Minnesota Multiphasic Personality Inventory® -2) Manual for Administration, Scoring, and Interpretation, Revised Edition* by James N. Butcher, John R. Graham, Yossef S. Ben-Porath, Auke Tellegen, W. Grant Dahlstrom, and Beverly Kaemmer. Copyright © 2001 by the Regents of the University of Minnesota. Used by permission of the University of Minnesota Press. All rights reserved. "MMPI® " and "Minnesota Multiphasic Personality Inventory® " are trademarks owned by the Regents of the University of Minnesota.

begin the MMPI-2 in a valid manner and then change to an invalid approach later in the test. Thus, many invalid profiles will approximate the modal ones presented here, but they will not match them exactly.

Patterns of scores on the standard Validity and Clinical scales similar to those for random responding also are obtained when individuals approach the test with an overreporting or a true or false response set. The VRIN scale is very helpful in determining when the very deviant scores should be attributed to a random response set rather than to overreporting or true or false response sets. The TRIN scale should be examined to determine if a true or false response set is likely. Obviously, a protocol resulting from random responding should not be interpreted. Characteristics of a protocol resulting from an all-true response set are described in the following section.

All-True Responding

The TRIN-scale score is very helpful in detecting a true response set. Although true responses to all items in the MMPI-2 will result in TRIN-scale T scores of 120 for men and 120 for women, any T score equal to or greater than 80 on the TRIN scale (in the true direction) indicates indiscriminate true or false responding to enough items that the resulting protocol should be considered invalid. If all of the MMPI-2 items are answered in the true direction, the resulting profiles look like the ones presented in Figures 3.2A and 3.2B. The salient features of the profile are an extremely elevated F-scale score (usually well above a T score of 100), L-, K-, and S-scale T scores well below 50, and extreme elevations on the right side of the Clinical scale profile, usually with the highest scores on Scales 6 and 8. The F_B and F_P scales will also be quite elevated, usually at about the same level as the F scale, and the FBS will be moderately elevated (T = 67 for men and T = 70 for women). Obviously, a profile resulting from all-true responding should never be interpreted.

A completely false response set will yield a TRIN-scale T score of 114 for men and 120 for women, but any T score equal to or greater than 80 on the TRIN scale (in the false direction) indicates indiscriminant false responding to enough items that the resulting protocol should be considered invalid. Persons who respond false to all of the MMPI-2 items will produce profiles like the ones shown in

Figure 3.2A K-corrected male profile indicative of all-true responding.

Adapted from the *MMPI® -2 (Minnesota Multiphasic Personality Inventory® -2) Manual for Administration, Scoring, and Interpretation, Revised Edition* by James N. Butcher, John R. Graham, Yossef S. Ben-Porath, Auke Tellegen, W. Grant Dahlstrom, and Beverly Kaemmer. Copyright © 2001 by the Regents of the University of Minnesota. Used by permission of the University of Minnesota Press. All rights reserved. "MMPI® " and "Minnesota Multiphasic Personality Inventory® " are trademarks owned by the Regents of the University of Minnesota.

MMPI-2 Profile for Basic Scales

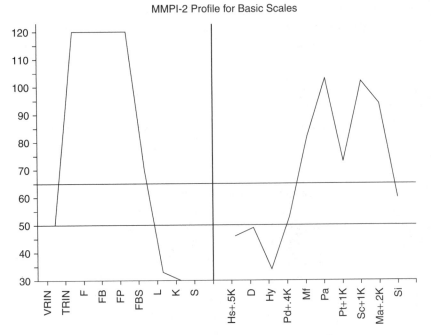

Figure 3.2B K-corrected female profile indicative of all-true responding.
Adapted from the *MMPI® -2 (Minnesota Multiphasic Personality Inventory® -2) Manual for Administration, Scoring, and Interpretation, Revised Edition* by James N. Butcher, John R. Graham, Yossef S. Ben-Porath, Auke Tellegen, W. Grant Dahlstrom, and Beverly Kaemmer. Copyright © 2001 by the Regents of the University of Minnesota. Used by permission of the University of Minnesota Press. All rights reserved. "MMPI® " and "Minnesota Multiphasic Personality Inventory® " are trademarks owned by the Regents of the University of Minnesota.

Figures 3.3A and 3.3B. Note the simultaneous elevations on the L, F, K, S, FBS, and F$_p$ scales and the more elevated scores on the left side of the Clinical scale profile. The T scores on the F$_B$ and VRIN scales will be near 50 in the all-false response set. Obviously, a protocol resulting from all-false responding should not be interpreted.

Negative Self-Presentation

Overreporting

Some persons may be motivated to present an unrealistically negative impression when completing the MMPI-2. An extreme case of negative self-presentation would be when a person deliberately responds to test items in a manner that is thought to communicate that the test taker is very psychologically disturbed when in fact that is not the case. This response set often is referred to as "faking bad" or "malingering." However, because these terms assume that there is external motivation for presenting oneself as more psychologically disturbed than is really the case, this author prefers to use the term "overreporting" to characterize this approach to the MMPI-2. To determine that overreporting can be

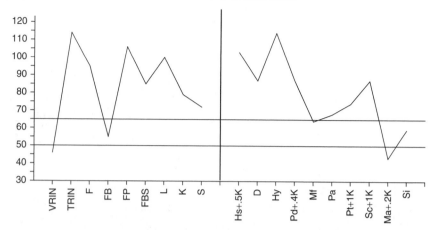

MMPI-2 Profile for Basic Scales

Figure 3.3A K-corrected male profile indicative of all-false responding.
Adapted from the *MMPI® -2 (Minnesota Multiphasic Personality Inventory® -2) Manual for Administration, Scoring, and Interpretation, Revised Edition* by James N. Butcher, John R. Graham, Yossef S. Ben-Porath, Auke Tellegen, W. Grant Dahlstrom, and Beverly Kaemmer. Copyright © 2001 by the Regents of the University of Minnesota. Used by permission of the University of Minnesota Press. All rights reserved. "MMPI® " and "Minnesota Multiphasic Personality Inventory® " are trademarks owned by the Regents of the University of Minnesota.

classified as malingering, one would need information from sources other than the MMPI-2 that the test taker had external motivation to present himself or herself as much more disturbed than is really the case.

Considerable research was conducted to ascertain the extent to which the overreporting response set could be detected by the Validity scales of the original MMPI. Schretlen (1988) reviewed 15 studies and concluded that the protocols of persons who were feigning abnormality on the MMPI could be accurately distinguished from nonpathological protocols. He added that it was more difficult to differentiate MMPI profiles that had been feigned from those produced by persons with genuine mental disorders. Berry, Baer, et al. (1991) used meta-analytic procedures to compare results of 28 studies that examined the ability of the MMPI to detect overreporting. They concluded that the MMPI Validity scales were quite successful in detecting overreporting versus honest protocols. Although discrimination between nonclinical participants answering honestly and those overreporting was easier than between nonclinical participants overreporting and psychiatric patients with bona fide psychopathology, the latter discrimination was quite respectable. The F scale seemed to produce the best discrimination, but the F minus K index also was effective. Gough's Dissimulation scale (Gough, 1950), which was described earlier in this chapter, also was an effective discriminator, but it is not routinely scored on the MMPI-2.

The Validity scales of the MMPI-2 also are quite effective in identifying persons who overreport when completing the test. As Figures 3.4A and 3.4B indicate,

MMPI-2 Profile for Basic Scales

Figure 3.3B K-corrected female profile indicative of all-false responding.
Adapted from the *MMPI® -2 (Minnesota Multiphasic Personality Inventory® -2) Manual for Administration, Scoring, and Interpretation, Revised Edition* by James N. Butcher, John R. Graham, Yossef S. Ben-Porath, Auke Tellegen, W. Grant Dahlstrom, and Beverly Kaemmer. Copyright © 2001 by the Regents of the University of Minnesota. Used by permission of the University of Minnesota Press. All rights reserved. "MMPI® " and "Minnesota Multiphasic Personality Inventory® " are trademarks owned by the Regents of the University of Minnesota.

when nonclinical persons attempt to simulate serious psychopathology on the MMPI-2, they tend to overendorse deviant items, producing scores much higher than those of seriously disturbed patients. The profiles in Figures 3.4A and 3.4B are based on data from a study by Graham, Watts, and Timbrook (1991) in which groups of male and female college students completed the MMPI-2 with standard instructions and again with instructions to present themselves as if they had serious psychological or emotional problems. The student data were compared with data from a sample of hospitalized psychiatric patients who completed the test with standard instructions. Subsequent research has found overreporting profiles very similar to those identified in this initial study (e.g., Storm & Graham, 2000; Wetter et al., 1992).

An overreporting protocol on the MMPI-2 is characterized by a very elevated F-scale T score (usually well above 100). Likewise, the F_p and F_B scales are elevated, usually at about the same level as the F scale. The FBS scale is likely to be moderately elevated (T = 80–90). Because the person who is overreporting typically is responding consistently, although not honestly, to the content of the items, both the TRIN-scale and VRIN-scale scores are not significantly elevated. Scores on the Clinical scales are very elevated, with Scales 6 and 8 typically being

FAKE–BAD, STANDARD INSTRUCTION PROFILES
COMPARED WITH MEAN PATIENT PROFILE

○ FAKE–BAD INSTR   ● PSYCHIATRIC PATIENTS   ▽ STANDARD INSTR

Figure 3.4A K-corrected profiles of male students with standard and overreporting instructions and of male psychiatric inpatients.

SOURCE: Graham, J.R., Watts, D., & Timbrook, R.E. (1991). Detecting fake-good and fake-bad MMPI-2 profiles. *Journal of Personality Assessment, 57,* 264–277. Copyright © 1991 by Lawrence Erlbaum Associates, Inc. Reproduced by permission.

FAKE–BAD, STANDARD INSTRUCTION PROFILES
COMPARED WITH MEAN PATIENT PROFILE

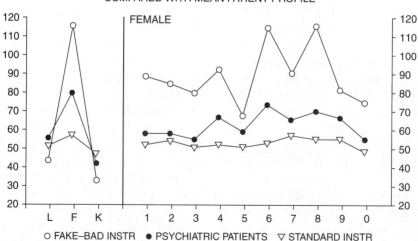

○ FAKE–BAD INSTR   ● PSYCHIATRIC PATIENTS   ▽ STANDARD INSTR

Figure 3.4B K-corrected profiles of female students with standard and overreporting instructions and of female psychiatric inpatients.

SOURCE: Graham, J.R., Watts, D., & Timbrook, R.E. (1991). Detecting fake-good and fake-bad MMPI-2 profiles. *Journal of Personality Assessment, 57,* 264–277. Copyright © 1991 by Lawrence Erlbaum Associates, Inc. Reproduced by permission.

the most elevated. Scales 5 and 0 typically are the least elevated Clinical scales in the overreporting protocol.

At first glance the overreporting profile looks similar to the profile one might expect to obtain from a person who is actually very psychologically disturbed. However, there are some important differences. Scores on the F, F_B, F_p, and FBS scales are usually higher for the overreporting protocol. The usual range of F-scale T scores for a person with severe psychopathology is 70–90, whereas in the overreporting profile the F-scale T score is well above 100. Likewise, the F_B- and F_p-scale T scores are likely to be above 100. In addition, in an overreporting protocol the Clinical scales tend to be more extremely elevated than in a valid protocol from a disturbed person.

In addition to the study of Graham, Watts, and Timbrook (1991) mentioned earlier, several other studies have confirmed the ability of MMPI-2 Validity scales to identify overreporting approaches to the test. Rogers, Sewell, and Salekin (1994) reported the results of a meta-analysis of 15 MMPI-2 overreporting studies. They concluded that the F scale has been the most effective indicator of overreporting in almost all of the studies. Utilizing receiver operating characteristic (ROC) analyses, Nicholson et al. (1997) found that the F and F_p scales and the F minus K index were most effective in identifying college students who were overreporting. Although the F minus K index has been an effective discriminator in most studies, typically this index does not add significantly to the F scale in identifying the overreporting protocols. The Obvious minus Subtle (O–S) index has shown some promise in discriminating honest responders from those who have overreported, but again it typically has not performed as well as the F scale and has not added significantly to the classification accuracy that could be achieved using the F scale alone. As noted earlier in this chapter, the MMPI-2 test publisher made a decision to discontinue inclusion of the Obvious and Subtle subscales from its scoring materials and scoring and interpretive services.

Most MMPI-2 overreporting studies have compared nonclinical individuals, typically college students, who took the test under standard instructions and/or instructions to overreport, raising some questions about how generalizable the results are to clinical settings where clients, patients, or other individuals may be motivated to feign psychopathology. Several studies have demonstrated that the F scale is effective in identifying prison inmates who took the MMPI-2 with instructions to overreport symptoms and problems (Gallagher, 1997; Iverson, Franzen, & Hammond, 1995). In the Gallagher study the F_p scale added significantly to the F scale in identifying the overreporters. In a similar study, Rogers, Sewell, and Ustad (1995) found that the F scale was the best MMPI-2 indicator of overreporting among chronic psychiatric outpatients.

Berry et al. (1996) examined scores of mental health outpatients who completed the MMPI-2 with standard instructions or with instructions to exaggerate their symptoms and problems. They found that the F, F_p, F_B, and Ds2 scales and the F minus K index were all effective in discriminating between the groups and that the Ds2 scale was the most accurate indicator. Arbisi and Ben-Porath (1998b) found that both the F and F_p scales discriminated between psychiatric inpatients who completed the MMPI-2 with standard instructions or with instructions to exaggerate their symptoms and problems. As expected, the F_p scale was a more accurate indicator than the F scale in this setting where there is a high base rate of serious psychopathology.

Although it is clear that persons who overreport when responding to the MMPI-2 produce very high F-scale scores, the optimal cutoff score for identifying overreporting is less clear. Various studies have identified optimal F-scale T-score cutoffs ranging from 75 to 120. Most studies have found that F-scale T scores greater than 100 are indicative of overreporting. However, as Graham, Watts, and Timbrook (1991) cautioned, F-scale raw scores that are beyond the T-score ceiling for the scale (120) are optimal when trying to identify overreporting among psychiatric inpatients. As mentioned earlier in this chapter, the F_p scale, which was designed specifically to identify overreporting in settings in which there is a high base rate of severe psychopathology, is a valuable addition to the F scale in inpatient settings. Although optimal cutoff scores should be determined in each setting when the MMPI-2 is used, it is clear that more confidence concerning overreporting can be had when F- and/or F_p-scale scores are more extreme.

The steps to be taken in determining if a protocol is likely to be the product of overreporting of psychological symptoms and problems were summarized by Bagby (2005), although it should be noted that the cutoff scores for the F_p scale are those recommended in the MMPI-2 manual and are somewhat different from those recommended by Bagby:

1. Check the number of omitted items.
   a. If the CNS score is equal to or greater than 30, consider the protocol invalid and do not interpret.
   b. If the CNS score is less than 30, continue to the next step.
2. Check the response inconsistency (VRIN and TRIN) scales.
   a. If the VRIN- or TRIN-scale T score is equal to or greater than 80, consider the protocol invalid and do not interpret.
   b. If both the VRIN- and TRIN-scale T scores are less than 80, continue to the next step.
3. Check the overreporting scales (F and F_B).
   a. If both the F-scale and F_B-scale T scores are less than 80, consider the protocol valid and interpretable.
   b. If either the F-scale or F_B-scale T score is equal to or greater than 80, symptom overreporting is possible; continue to next step.
4. Check the F_p-scale score.
   a. If the F_p-scale T score is equal to or greater than 100, overreporting is probable and the protocol should not be interpreted.
   b. If the F_p-scale T score is between 80 and 99, overreporting is possible; interpret the protocol with great caution; seek external information.
   c. If the F_p-scale T score is between 70 and 79, protocol validity is indeterminate; interpret the protocol cautiously; seek external information.

d. If the F_p-scale T score is less than 70, consider the protocol valid and interpretable.

Most MMPI-2 overreporting studies have instructed participants to feign serious or severe psychopathology. It is important to know whether the MMPI-2 can detect less extreme forms of overreporting. A study by Wetter et al. (1992) involved giving students instructions to feign either severe or moderate psychopathology. They found that the F scale was significantly elevated in both feigning conditions and only slightly lower for the moderate condition (T = 108) than for the severe condition (T = 119). This study suggests that the F scale can identify less extreme forms of overreporting, but different optimal cutoff scores may be needed from those that are most effective in identifying extreme overreporting.

Feigning Specific Disorders

Some studies have examined the extent to which persons can feign specific forms of psychopathology when responding to the MMPI-2 and the extent to which the MMPI-2 Validity scales can identify this test-taking approach. When non-clinical persons have been asked to feign schizophrenia, paranoid psychosis, posttraumatic stress disorder, or borderline personality disorder, they have produced scores quite similar to those of persons who are given instructions to feign general psychopathology (Bagby, Rogers, Buis, et al., 1997; Gold & Frueh, 1998; Rogers, Bagby, & Chakraborty, 1993; Sivec, Hilsenroth, & Lynn, 1995; Sivec, Lynn, & Garske, 1994; Wetter, Baer, Berry, Robison, & Sumpter, 1993; Wetter & Deitsch, 1996). Their profiles were characterized by high-ranging scores on the F scale and on Scales 6 and 8. F-scale scores were quite effective in discriminating persons who overreported symptoms of these particular disorders from persons taking the MMPI-2 with standard instructions and from patients with the actual disorders.

When nonclinical persons have been asked to feign symptoms of depression, somatoform disorder, or closed head injury, they have produced moderately high scores on the F scale and on most of the Clinical scales (Bagby, Rogers, Buis, et al., 1997; Berry et al., 1995; Sivec et al., 1994, 1995). F-scale scores have been most effective in differentiating these feigned protocols from those completed under standard conditions, but accuracy of classification has been less than for identifying the feigning of more severe forms of psychopathology.

In general, it would appear that persons who try to feign general psychopathology or specific psychopathology involving extreme and unusual symptoms produce a clearly recognizable pattern of scores on the Validity and Clinical scales. Cardinal features of the pattern are extreme elevations on the F and F_p scales and general elevation on the Clinical scales, with Scales 6 and 8 being the most elevated. When persons try to feign other specific forms of psychopathology, they produce more elevated scores than patients who actually have the disorders, and they are accurately identified by scores on the F scale. However, different optimal cutoff scores may be appropriate for identifying the feigning of some specific kinds of psychopathology, and the Validity scales may do less well for some specific kinds of feigning than others.

Effects of Coaching

As the MMPI-2 has been more widely used in forensic settings, users are concerned about the possibility that persons who want to feign psychological disturbance when they complete the MMPI-2 could do so more effectively if they have information about the symptoms of the disorder that they want to simulate and/or about how the MMPI-2 can identify overreporting. Wetter and Corrigan (1995) reported the results of a survey indicating that almost half of a sample of practicing attorneys and approximately one-third of a sample of law students indicated that they believed that clients referred for psychological testing always or usually should be given information about the validity scales of psychological tests that they will be taking.

Studies by Elhai, Gold, Frueh, and Gold (2000); Rogers et al. (1993); Wetter, Baer, Berry, and Reynolds (1994); and Wetter et al. (1993) have demonstrated that giving test takers information about the symptoms of disorders that they are asked to simulate does not permit them to avoid detection by the MMPI-2 Validity scales. Bagby, Rogers, Nicholson, et al. (1997) found that clinical psychology graduate students and psychiatric residents, who can be assumed to have considerable information about psychological testing and psychopathology, were readily detected when they attempted to feign schizophrenia on the MMPI-2.

Some research has been conducted to determine the extent to which overreporting on the MMPI-2 can be detected when test takers have been given information (coached) about how the Validity scales function and/or how to avoid detection of overreporting when completing the test. Several studies reported that it was more difficult to detect overreporting when such coaching had taken place (Rogers et al., 1993; Storm & Graham, 2000). However, even when test takers have been coached about the Validity scales, a large portion of the coached overreporters were correctly identified. Not all research in this area has yielded consistent results. Bagby, Nicholson, Bacchiochi, Ryder, and Bury (2002) found that the MMPI-2 Validity scales were equally effective in identifying coached and uncoached simulators of general psychopathology. In most studies both the F and F_p scales have been effective in identifying coached overreporters, with the F_p scale doing better in some studies.

However, Rogers et al. (1993) found that persons who were given information about how the Validity indicators of the MMPI-2 function and how to avoid detection were more effective in simulating schizophrenia without being detected by the standard Validity indicators. Two less commonly used indicators, Gough's Dissimulation (Dsr2) scale and Obvious minus Subtle (O–S) subscale scores, were relatively effective in identifying even those simulators who had been given information about the Validity scales. Viglione et al. (2001) examined the effect of giving very limited coaching and then asking test takers to overreport. They found that even giving a simple caution to avoid exaggeration of responses made detection of overreporting somewhat more difficult.

Although only limited research data are available at this time, there is reason to be concerned that some persons who are informed about how the Validity scales of the MMPI-2 function may be able to avoid detection. More research is needed to determine just how much of a problem this is and if there are more effective ways to identify the informed overreporting. Bacchiochi and Bagby (2003) reported some preliminary data suggesting that a discriminant function index to identify overreporting was less susceptible to coaching than were the MMPI-2 Validity scales.

Exaggeration

Sometimes individuals who really have psychological symptoms and problems exaggerate them in responding to the MMPI-2 items. This is a rather common occurrence among persons who are trying to communicate to others that they desperately need professional help. In these circumstances the resulting scores will depend on what actual symptoms and problems are being exaggerated. Thus, it is not possible to identify a prototype for this response set. The major clue available that such a response set might be operating is that scores on the F and F_p scales and the Clinical scales seem to be much higher than would be expected given the person's history and observations made of the person during the interview and testing.

Rogers et al. (1995) asked psychiatric outpatients to take the MMPI-2 with standard instructions and with the intention of convincing the examiner that their problems were worse than they really were and that they needed immediate hospitalization. Patients produced very similar configurations of scores in both conditions, but when they exaggerated their problems their scores were considerably higher than when they followed standard instructions. Both the F and F_p scales were quite effective in identifying the protocols produced by patients who exaggerated their symptoms and problems. Arbisi and Ben-Porath (1998b) examined scores of psychiatric inpatients who completed the MMPI-2 with standard instructions or with instructions to exaggerate their symptoms and problems. Those who exaggerated produced significantly higher scores on most scales. The F and F_p scales were both effective in identifying exaggeration, but the F_p scale was somewhat more accurate than the F scale. Exaggeration does not necessarily invalidate a protocol, but interpretations must be modified to take into account that the scores obtained represent an overreporting of symptoms and problems.

Positive Self-Presentation

Underreporting

Sometimes persons completing the MMPI-2 are motivated to deny problems and to appear better adjusted psychologically than is in fact the case. This response set is relatively common when persons complete the MMPI-2 as part of a job application process or child custody evaluation.

In the underreporting response set, the L, K, and S scales are likely to be elevated significantly, and the T scores on the F, F_B, and F_p scales are average or below average. Baer, Wetter, and Berry (1992) presented the results of a meta-analysis of data from 25 original MMPI studies in which participants completing the test with standard instructions were compared to participants instructed to appear to be extremely well adjusted emotionally. The analysis confirmed that the L and K scales were effective in discriminating between these two groups and that detection of underreporting was less accurate than detection of over-reporting. Although several less commonly used scales showed some promise in detecting underreporting of psychopathology, Baer et al. (1992) recommended that, until additional research is available about these scales, clinicians should consider the L and K scales when making judgments about underreporting of psychopathology.

In an initial MMPI-2 underreporting study, Graham et al. (1991) compared scores of male and female college students who completed the test with standard instructions and with instructions to present a very positive impression of them-selves, as if they were being evaluated for a job they really wanted. The mean profiles obtained under the two instructional sets are presented in Figures 3.5A and 3.5B. Consistent with prior research with the original MMPI, persons in the underreporting condition had somewhat lower scores on most of the Clinical scales. The Validity scale pattern previously reported for the MMPI also was present. Persons who were instructed to underreport had T scores well above 50 on the L and K scales and below 50 on the F scale. It should be noted that scores for the F_p and FBS scales were not available when the study was conducted. Graham et al. (1991) found that it was more difficult to detect underreporting than overreporting protocols.

Subsequent research with the MMPI-2 has confirmed the initial findings of Graham et al. (1991). The typical underreporting validity study has involved having students or other nonclinical participants complete the MMPI-2 with instructions to appear very well adjusted and free of psychological symptoms and problems and comparing their scores to those participants who completed the test with standard instructions.

Baer and Miller (2002) conducted a meta-analysis of 14 studies of under-reporting on the MMPI-2. They found that the MMPI-2 Validity scales were effective in discriminating between underreporters and those who completed the test with standard instructions. Although the identification of underreport-ers was not as accurate as for overreporting (e.g., Rogers et al., 1994), the overall effect size (d = 1.25) across studies was quite impressive. Persons who completed the MMPI-2 with instructions to try to appear to be very well adjusted psy-chologically tended to obtain high scores on the L, K, and S scales and aver-age or below-average scores on the F, F_B, and F_p scales. Supplemental scales and indexes also effectively identified the underreporters, although results concern-ing the incremental validity of these supplemental measures were mixed and inconclusive. Baer and Miller (2002) concluded that "relying on L and K, for

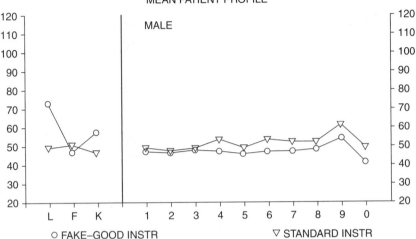

Figure 3.5A K-corrected profiles of male students with standard and underreporting instructions.

SOURCE: Graham, J.R., Watts, D., & Timbrook, R.E. (1991). Detecting fake-good and fake-bad MMPI-2 profiles. *Journal of Personality Assessment, 57,* 264–277. Copyright © 1991 by Lawrence Erlbaum Associates, Inc. Reproduced by permission.

Figure 3.5B K-corrected profiles of female students with standard and underreporting instructions.

source: Graham, J.R., Watts, D., & Timbrook, R.E. (1991). Detecting fake-good and fake-bad MMPI-2 profiles. *Journal of Personality Assessment, 57,* 264–177. Copyright © 1991 by Lawrence Erlbaum Associates, Inc. Reproduced by permission.

which much larger bodies of supporting data are available, may be the most defensible approach" (p. 24).

Although the base rates for underreporting in most studies have been approximately .50, this may not be the typical base rate in settings where underreporting is likely to be an issue. Baer and Miller (2002) estimated that the base rate for underreporting in personnel selection and child custody settings is approximately .30, and they presented positive predictive power and negative predictive power values for the Validity scales based on this estimate.

The Baer and Miller (2002) meta-analysis reached a conclusion similar to that of Graham et al. (1991) concerning optimal cutoff scores for identifying underreporting. Optimal cutoff scores are likely to vary as a function of the base rates of underreporting in particular settings, as well as on the kinds of errors (false positive versus false negative) that are judged to be most important. Obviously, setting relatively high cutoff scores will increase the likelihood that persons identified as underreporting are in fact doing so, but at the cost of mislabeling many protocols of underreporters as valid. Conversely, establishing relatively low cutoff scores will minimize the misclassification of underreported protocols as valid, but it will result in many valid protocols being labeled as underreported.

Very few studies have examined the effects of coaching on the ability of the MMPI-2 to detect underreporting. The Baer and Miller (2002) meta-analysis included only five studies where participants were coached in avoiding detection of underreporting. The Validity scales were somewhat less effective in identifying test takers who had received such coaching.

In summary, when persons complete the MMPI-2 with the intention of denying problems and symptoms and appearing much better adjusted than they really are, they tend to produce elevated scores on the L, K, and S scales and below-average scores on the F, F_B, and F_p scales. The L scale is quite effective in identifying this invalid approach to completing the MMPI-2. Although it is not possible to specify a single optimal cutoff score on the L scale for identifying underreporting protocols, raw scores greater than 5 or 6 and a Validity-scale configuration with the L-, K-, and S-scale T scores well above 50 and F-, F_B-, and F_p-scale T scores below 50 should alert examiners to the possibility that test takers may have approached the MMPI-2 in an invalid manner. Several other indicators, including the Superlative Self-Presentation (S) scale, the Positive Malingering (Mp) scale, the Wiggins Social Desirability (Wsd) scale, and the Edwards Social Desirability (Esd) scale, have shown some promise in identifying underreporting on the MMPI-2 and should be included in future research studies. Baer et al. (1995) found that the Wsd scale was especially useful in identifying persons who had been coached concerning how to underreport on the MMPI-2.

As was discussed in relation to overreporting on the MMPI-2, it is important to acknowledge what indicators of an underreporting approach to the test do and do not tell us. When we have evidence that a person has underreported in responding to the MMPI-2 items, we can conclude that the resulting scores do not give an accurate picture of the person's psychological adjustment and personality characteristics. In such a case, we do not know what the person is really like. A person who underreports in responding to the MMPI-2 could be quite well adjusted psychologically or could be quite disturbed psychologically. We cannot tell from the MMPI-2 scores which is more likely for a particular person. Other data, including interview- and history-based information, may help in making this determination.

Defensiveness

Sometimes persons are motivated to present unrealistically favorable impressions but do not do so to such an extent that their protocols should be considered invalid. For example, persons taking the MMPI-2 as part of employment screening or child custody evaluations may want to emphasize positive characteristics and minimize negative ones. The resulting scores may underestimate problems and symptoms but are not necessarily uninterpretable.

In a defensive profile the L-, K-, and S-scale scores typically are more elevated than the F-, F_B-, and F_P-scale score. T scores greater than 70 on these scales should alert the clinician that the test taker may have underreported symptoms and problems to such an extent that the protocol probably is invalid. T scores in the 60–70 range on these scales suggest underreporting that probably indicates a defensive test-taking attitude that does not necessarily invalidate the protocol.

If the Validity scales indicate defensiveness and no Clinical scale T scores are above 60, the scores are not likely to reflect accurately the psychological status of the test taker. We should not infer that the person with such a profile of scores has significant problems that are being covered up. The scores could just as well be indicative of a well-adjusted person who wanted to create an unrealistically favorable impression.

If the Validity scales indicate defensiveness and there are Clinical scale scores greater than 60, another variable should be considered. Because defensive protocols involve significant K-corrections to some of the Clinical scales, elevations on these scales may be attributed largely, or even entirely, to the K-correction. The person could have significantly elevated T scores on some Clinical scales without endorsing many (or even any) items on those scales. The K-correction itself may be enough to lead to an elevated score. In such cases, it would be inappropriate to infer significant problems and symptoms from the elevated scores. However, elevations on scales that are not K-corrected or elevations on K-corrected scales that can be attributed to endorsement of items on those scales (as opposed to the K-correction) can be interpreted in the usual manner. In such cases, the elevated scores may actually underestimate the severity of problems and symptoms.

Sometimes in a defensive profile either the L- or K-scale score is elevated but not both. This is because the two scales seem to be measuring somewhat different aspects of defensiveness. Persons who have elevated scores on the K scale are generally denying symptoms and problems. Persons who have elevated scores on the L scale are trying to present a picture of themselves as honest, moral, and conforming. Although these two aspects of defensiveness often occur simultaneously, in some circumstances they do not.

Effects of Coaching

Paralleling research reported earlier in this chapter for overreporting, several studies have examined the effects on underreporting of providing test takers with information about the Validity scales. Using a sample of nonclinical college students, Baer et al. (1995) found that the standard Validity scales were effective in detecting the students who were instructed to underreport symptoms and problems. However, when students were given information about the underreporting Validity scales, detection of underreporting was more difficult. There were two coaching conditions. One group of students was simply told that the MMPI-2 contains scales for the detection of underreporting and that they should try to appear both psychologically healthy and honest in responding to the items. Another group of students was given this same information and also tips on how to avoid being detected by the underreporting scales. The information provided was readily available from well-known MMPI and MMPI-2 textbooks. Students in both coaching conditions were more successful in underreporting without being detected, and the minimal information group was as successful as the group that received more detailed information. Baer et al. found that some less familiar scales, especially the Wiggins Social Desirability (Wsd) scale, were more effective than the traditional Validity scales in identifying coached faking. Although important as a first published study of coached underreporting, the generalization of the results of Baer et al. (1995) is limited by the use of very small groups of nonclinical students.

Baer and Sekirnjak (1997) replicated the procedures of the study of Baer et al. (1995) using outpatient mental health clients as participants. Again, clients completed the MMPI-2 with standard instructions or with instructions to underreport their symptoms. Clients in the underreporting group were either given no information about the underreporting scales or were told that the MMPI-2 contains scales for identifying underreporting, so they should try to appear psychologically healthy and honest in responding to the items. A comparison group of nonclinical adults was also available. Results were similar to those of the study of Baer et al. (1995). Clients who were instructed to underreport but were not given any information about the Validity scales were readily detected by the standard Validity scales. However, clients who were informed that the MMPI-2 contains underreporting scales were less readily detected. Several less familiar scales, including the Wiggins Social Desirability (Wsd) scale and the Superlative (S) scale, seemed to be especially promising.

In summary, it appears that persons who are informed that there are underreporting scales on the MMPI-2 and who are told to try to appear both psychologically healthy and honest are able to produce scores that resemble nonclinical persons and are difficult to detect with the traditional Validity scales. There is some preliminary indication that some less familiar scales, including Wsd and S, may be more effective than the traditional scales in detecting coached underreporting. However, more research is needed before we can conclude just how effectively coached underreporters can avoid detection and if there are ways, other than the use of the standard Validity scales, to identify the coached underreporting effectively. What is especially needed are studies with larger samples that report classification data (i.e., positive predictive power and negative predictive power) for the different test-taking conditions and the various Validity scales and indexes. In the meantime, clinicians using the MMPI-2 in settings such as employment screening or child custody evaluations, where there is strong motivation to underreport and where test takers may have been coached about the Validity scales, should be alert to the possibility that underreporting on the MMPI-2 may not be readily detected. In such instances, information in addition to the MMPI-2 scores (e.g., history, mental status, information from significant others) may be helpful in assessing the validity of self-report.

4

%% The Clinical Scales

In this chapter each MMPI-2 Clinical scale is discussed in an attempt to elucidate the dimensions of personality and psychopathology that it assesses. In addition, descriptors are presented for scores at various levels on each scale.

As previously noted, the Clinical scales of the MMPI-2 are basically the same as those found in the original MMPI. A few items were deleted from some of the scales because they had become dated or because they were judged to have objectionable content, usually having to do with religious beliefs or bowel or bladder function. Some of the items in the Clinical scales were modified slightly to modernize them, to eliminate sexist references, or to improve readability. The items included in each Clinical scale and the keyed response for each item are presented in appendixes of the MMPI-2 manual (Butcher et al., 2001). Tables for converting raw scores on the Clinical scales to T scores are also presented in the manual's appendixes.

RELIABILITY OF CLINICAL SCALES

Table 4.1 reports coefficients of internal consistency (Alphas) for the Clinical scales. Because of the empirical manner in which the Clinical scales were constructed and the absence of efforts to make the scales internally consistent, most of the scales have relatively low internal consistency coefficients. This likely reflects the varied and heterogeneous content of items in the Clinical scales. High scores on a specific Clinical scale can reflect quite different patterns of item endorsement. For example, someone with a high score on Scale 4 may have endorsed primarily items having to do with antisocial attitudes and behaviors or items suggesting negative opinions and feelings about family members or some of each kind of item.

Table 4.2 reports test–retest coefficients for subgroups of men and women in the MMPI-2 normative sample who completed the test twice with an interval of approximately one week between administrations. These data indicate that Clinical scale scores are quite stable over a relatively short period of time, with Scale 6 having the least stability and Scale 0 the most stability. Table 4.2

Table 4.1 Internal Consistency Coefficients (Alphas) for MMPI-2 Clinical Scales for Men and Women in Normative Sample

SCALE	MEN ($n = 82$)	WOMEN ($n = 111$)
1—Hs	.77	.81
2—D	.59	.64
3—Hy	.58	.56
4—Pd	.60	.62
5—Mf	.58	.37
6—Pa	.34	.39
7—Pt	.85	.87
8—Sc	.85	.86
9—Ma	.58	.61
0—Si	.82	.84

SOURCE: Excerpted (Table E-4) from Butcher, J.N., Graham, J.R., Ben-Porath, Y.S., Tellegen, A., Dahlstrom, W.G., & Kaemmer, B. (2001). *MMPI® -2 (Minnesota Multiphasic Personality Inventory® -2): Manual for administration, scoring, and interpretation, revised edition.* Copyright © 2001 by the Regents of the University of Minnesota. Reproduced by permission of the University of Minnesota Press. All rights reserved. "MMPI® " and "Minnesota Multiphasic Personality Inventory® " are trademarks owned by the Regents of the University of Minnesota.

Table 4.2 Test–Retest Coefficients for MMPI-2 Clinical Scales

SCALE	ONE-WEEK INTERVAL MMPI-2 NORMATIVE SAMPLE[a]		FIVE-YEAR INTERVAL NORMATIVE AGING SAMPLE[b]
	MEN ($n = 82$)	WOMEN ($n = 111$)	MEN ($n = 1072$)
1—Hs	.76	.75	.75
2—D	.79	.80	.71
3—Hy	.70	.74	.65
4—Pd	.79	.69	.67
5—Mf	.83	.74	.67
6—Pa	.67	.56	.55
7—Pt	.72	.68	.83
8—Sc	.72	.54	.71
9—Ma	.80	.65	.64
0—Si	.93	.92	.85

[a]SOURCE: Excerpted (Table E-1) from Butcher, J.N., Graham, J.R., Ben-Porath, Y.S., Tellegen, A., Dahlstrom, W.G., & Kaemmer, B. (2001). *MMPI® -2 (Minnesota Multiphasic Personality Inventory® -2): Manual for administration, scoring, and interpretation, Revised Edition.* Copyright © 2001 by the Regents of the University of Minnesota. Reproduced by permission of the University of Minnesota Press. All rights reserved. "MMPI® " and "Minnesota Multiphasic Personality Inventory® " are trademarks owned by the Regents of the University of Minnesota.
[b]SOURCE: Excerpted (Table 37.3) from Spiro, A., Levenson, M.R., Aldwin, C.M., & Bose, R. (2000). Change and stability in personality: A five-year study of the MMPI-2 in Older Men. In Butcher, J.N. (ed.), *Basic Sources on the MMPI-2.* Copyright © 2000 by the Regents of the University of Minnesota. Reproduced by permission of the University of Minnesota Press. All rights reserved. "MMPI® " and "Minnesota Multiphasic Personality Inventory® " are trademarks owned by the Regents of the University of Minnesota.

also reports test–retest coefficients for a group of older men who completed the MMPI-2 twice with a five-year interval between testings. As one might expect, the scores were less stable over the longer time period; however, the coefficients are comparable to those of other self-report inventories for similar time intervals.

It is noteworthy that the five-year coefficient for Scale 0 (Si) is almost as high as for the one-week interval, suggesting that characteristics associated with Scale 0 scores are likely to be quite stable.

VALIDITY OF CLINICAL SCALES

Since the MMPI's publication, hundreds of studies have examined relationships between the Clinical scales and relevant extratest characteristics such as symptoms, personality traits, diagnosis, and response to treatment. These studies were conducted in a variety of nonclinical, medical, mental health, forensic, and correctional settings. Similar studies have also been reported using the MMPI-2. Because of the continuity between the Clinical scales of the original MMPI and the MMPI-2, this research is relevant to determining the validity of the Clinical scales. The accumulated database suggests that the MMPI-2 Clinical scales are meaningfully related to conceptually relevant extratest characteristics. For example, higher scorers on Scale 1 have reported more somatic complaints than lower scorers, higher scorers on Scale 4 have been characterized as more antisocial than lower scorers, and higher scorers on Scale 8 have been more likely to show symptoms of psychotic disorders. Research findings concerning correlates of the Clinical scales in these varied settings are the primary source of the inferences that are suggested later in this chapter for higher scorers on the Clinical scales.

DEFINING HIGH AND LOW SCORES ON CLINICAL SCALES

The definition of high scores on the Clinical scales has varied considerably in the MMPI/MMPI-2 literature. Some researchers considered T scores above 70 on the original MMPI or above 65 on the MMPI-2 as high scores, others defined high scores in terms of the upper quartile in a distribution, and still others presented descriptors for several T-score levels on some scales. In this chapter, the T-score cutoffs used to indicate high scores on the Clinical scales are clearly stated, and they are not the same for all scales. For most Clinical scales, interpretive guidelines are presented for several different T-score levels.

Low scores also have been defined in different ways in the MMPI/MMPI-2 literature, sometimes as T scores below 40 and other times as scores in the lowest quartile of a distribution. This latter approach led to T scores well above 50 sometimes being considered low scores. Compared with high scores, limited information is available in the literature concerning the meaning of low scores. Some authors suggested that low scores on a particular Clinical scale indicated the absence of problems and symptoms characteristic of high scorers on that scale. Other authors suggested that low scores on some Clinical scales were associated with general maladjustment and negative characteristics. Still other authors suggested that both high and low scores on certain Clinical scales indicated similar problems and negative characteristics.

Several MMPI-2 studies have clarified the meaning of low scores on the Clinical scales. Keiller and Graham (1993) examined extratest characteristics of high-, medium-, and low-scoring persons in the MMPI-2 normative sample on eight Clinical scales. They concluded that low scores convey important information but not as much as high scores. Low scores were associated with fewer than an average number of symptoms and problems and above-average overall adjustment. In this nonclinical sample, low scores on the Clinical scales were not indicative of problems and negative characteristics.

Timbrook and Graham (1992) examined ratings of symptoms for psychiatric inpatients who had high, average, or low scores on each of the Clinical scales of the MMPI-2. As in the study of Keiller and Graham (1993), high scores of patients conveyed much more information about their clinical status than did low scores. As expected, high scorers on the Clinical scales were rated as having more severe symptoms than average scorers, and the symptoms were generally consistent with previously reported data for the MMPI Clinical scales. For several scales, ratings of symptoms differed for low and average scorers. For some scales the lower scorers were rated as having less severe symptoms than high and average scorers. For example, low-scoring women on Scale 7 were rated as less depressed than both high and average scorers on that scale. For other scales, the low scorers were rated as having more severe symptoms than average and high scorers. For example, low-scoring men on Scale 2 were rated as more uncooperative than average scorers and high scorers on that scale. Low-scoring women on Scale 9 were rated higher on unusual thought content than average scorers and high scorers on that scale. Some of the findings of the Timbrook and Graham study probably emerged because of the intercorrelations of the Clinical scales. For example, the men who had low scores on Scale 2 could have had high scores on Scale 4. This would account for the uncooperativeness associated with low scores on Scale 2. We would not necessarily expect to find that men who score low on Scale 2 but who do not score high on Scale 4 would also be rated as more uncooperative.

Graham, Ben-Porath, and McNulty (1997) studied the meaning of low scores in an outpatient mental health setting. Because relatively few low scores on the Clinical scales were found in this setting, the meaning of low scores could be ascertained only for Clinical Scales 9 and 0. Low scorers on Scale 9 did not differ significantly from average scorers in terms of symptoms and problems. However, low scorers on Scale 0 differed from average scorers and appeared to be less introverted, insecure, passive–submissive, anxious, and depressed and to have stronger achievement orientations. These characteristics were very much the opposite of high scorers on Scale 0.

Because of the inconsistent data concerning the meaning of low scores on the MMPI and the MMPI-2, this author's recommendation is to adopt a conservative approach to the interpretation of low scores on the MMPI-2 Clinical scales. In nonclinical settings (e.g., personnel selection) low scores in a valid protocol should be interpreted as indicating more positive overall adjustment than high or average scores. However, if the Validity scales indicate that the test was completed in a defensive manner, low scores in nonclinical settings should not be interpreted. In clinical settings, it is recommended that low scores on the Clinical scales not be interpreted. The exceptions are Scales 5 and 0, for which limited inferences can be made about low scorers. Any inferences that could be made about a person based on low scores could probably also be made (and with greater confidence) based on that person's high scores. Clearly, much more research is needed concerning the meaning of low scores in a variety of settings. Perhaps in the future we will have enough research data to support making specific inferences on the basis of low scores, but for now such a practice is not recommended.

INTERPRETATION OF SCORES ON CLINICAL SCALES

The approach used in this chapter will be to suggest interpretive inferences about persons who have high scores on each of the Clinical scales. In general, T scores greater than 65 are considered to be high scores, although inferences about persons with scores at several different T-score levels are presented for some scales. For Scales 5 and 0 inferences also will be suggested for below-average scores. It should be understood that the T-score levels specified have been established somewhat arbitrarily and that clinical judgment will be necessary in deciding which inferences should be applied to scores at or near the cutoff scores for the levels.

Not every inference presented in this chapter will apply to every person who has a T score at the specified level. Given the categorical nature of the original MMPI Clinical scale development (particular diagnostic group versus "normal"), greater confidence should be placed in inferences based on more extreme scores. All inferences should be treated as hypotheses to be considered in the context of other information available about the test taker. It is reasonable to infer that higher scores might also be associated with more severe symptoms and problems (e.g., depression for Scale 2). A study by Graham, Ben-Porath, Forbey, and Sellbom (2003) supported this notion. Patients with very high scores on the Clinical scales had more severe symptoms and problems than those with moderately high scores.

The descriptors that are suggested in this chapter for each Clinical scale are quite heterogeneous in nature. For example, descriptors for high scorers on Scale 8 include confused and disorganized thinking, depression, anxiety, drug abuse, and physical complaints. This wide array of potential characteristics is accounted for in part by the varied content of items in Scale 8 and in part by the general maladjustment or demoralization component that is present in each Clinical scale (Tellegen et al., 2003). In clarifying the meaning of high scores on a particular Clinical scale, it will be helpful to examine several other sources of MMPI-2 information. The Harris–Lingoes subscales and the Content and Content Component scales, which are discussed in Chapter 6 of this book, provide information about the kinds of items that were endorsed by a particular person who obtains a high score on a Clinical scale. In addition, examination of the Restructured Clinical (RC) scales, which are discussed in Chapter 7 of this book, can provide helpful information about the extent to which a high score on a Clinical scale resulted from endorsement of items having to do with the core construct for that scale (e.g., aberrant experiences for Scale 8) versus endorsement of items suggestive of general maladjustment or demoralization. Finally, consideration of other Supplementary scales can help clarify the likelihood of particular descriptors suggested for high scorers [e.g., the Addiction Admission Scale (AAS) in relation to an inference of drug abuse problems for a high scorer on Scale 8].

In summary, the descriptors listed for each Clinical scale should be considered a starting point in the interpretation, and consideration of other information will help to focus the interpretation in terms of determining which of the many descriptors are most likely for a particular person with an elevated score on a Clinical scale. The process of refining interpretations based on multiple sources of information will be discussed further and illustrated with a case in Chapter 11 of this book.

SCALE 1 (HYPOCHONDRIASIS)

Scale 1 originally was developed to identify patients who manifested a pattern of symptoms associated with a diagnosis of hypochondriasis. This syndrome was characterized in clinical terms by preoccupation with the body and concomitant fears of illness and disease. Although such fears usually are not delusional in nature, they tend to be persistent. An item deletion because of objectionable content reduced Scale 1 from 33 items in the original MMPI to 32 items in the MMPI-2.

Of all of the Clinical scales, Scale 1 seems to be the most clearly homogeneous and unidimensional. All of the items deal with somatic concerns or with general physical competence. Factor analysis (Comrey, 1957b) has indicated that much of the variance in Scale 1 is accounted for by a single factor, characterized by the denial of good health and the admission of a variety of somatic symptoms. Patients with genuine physical problems typically have somewhat elevated T scores on Scale 1 (approximately 60). Elderly persons tend to have Scale 1 scores that are slightly more elevated than those of the general adult standardization sample, probably reflecting the declining health often, but not always, associated with aging.

Interpretation of High Scores on Scale 1

For persons with extremely high scores on Scale 1 (T > 80), dramatic and sometimes bizarre somatic concerns may be present. If Scale 3 also is very elevated, the possibility of a conversion disorder should be considered. Chronic pain patients often have high scores (T = 70–80) on both Scales 1 and 3. If Scale 8 is very elevated along with Scale 1, somatic delusions may be present.

Persons with more moderate elevations on Scale 1 (T = 60–80) tend to have generally vague, nonspecific somatic complaints. When specific symptoms are elicited, they may include chronic pain, headaches, and gastrointestinal discomfort. Persons experiencing problems associated with eating often have moderately elevated scores on this scale. Chronic weakness, lack of energy, fatigue, and sleep disturbance also tend to be characteristic of high scorers. High Scale 1 scorers often are preoccupied with health problems, and they tend to develop physical symptoms in response to stress.

Medical patients with real physical problems generally obtain T scores of about 60 on this scale. When medical patients produce T scores much above 60, a strong psychological component to the illness should be suspected. Moderately high scores on Scale 1 tend to be associated with diagnoses such as somato-form disorders, somatoform pain disorders, anxiety disorders, and depressive disorders. High scorers on Scale 1 often are given prescriptions for antidepres-sant or anxiolytic medications. Acting-out behavior is rare among high Scale 1 scorers.

High Scale 1 scorers (T > 60) in both psychiatric and nonpsychiatric samples tend to be characterized by a rather distinctive set of personality attributes. They are likely to be selfish, self-centered, and narcissistic. Their outlook toward life tends to be pessimistic, defeatist, and cynical. They are generally dissatisfied and unhappy and are likely to make those around them miserable. They complain a great deal and communicate in a whiny manner. They are demanding of others and are very critical of what others do, although they are likely to express hostil-ity in rather indirect ways. High scorers on Scale 1 often are described as dull, unenthusiastic, unambitious, and lacking ease in oral expression. High scorers may not show signs of major incapacity. Rather, they appear to be functioning at a reduced level of efficiency. Problems are much more likely to be long-standing in nature than situational or transient.

Extremely high and moderately high scorers typically see themselves as phys-ically ill and are seeking medical explanations and treatment for their symptoms. They tend to lack insight concerning the causes of their somatic symptoms, and they resist psychological interpretations. These tendencies, coupled with their generally cynical outlook, suggest that they are not good candidates for traditional psychotherapy or counseling. They tend to be very critical of their therapists and may terminate therapy if they perceive the therapist as suggesting psychological reasons for their symptoms or as not giving them enough support and attention.

Summary of Descriptors for Scale 1

High scores on Scale 1 indicate persons who

1. have excessive bodily concern
2. may have conversion disorders (if T >80 and Scale 3 also is very high)
3. may have somatic delusions (if T > 80 and Scale 8 also is very high)
4. describe somatic complaints that generally are vague but if specific may include chronic pain, headaches, and gastrointestinal discomfort
5. may have problems associated with eating
6. complain of chronic weakness, lack of energy, fatigue, and sleep disturbance
7. are preoccupied with health problems and tend to develop physical symptoms in response to stress

8. if medical patients, may have a strong psychological component to their illnesses
9. frequently receive diagnoses of somatoform, pain, depressive, or anxiety disorders
10. often are given prescriptions for antidepressant or anxiolytic medications
11. are not likely to act out in antisocial ways
12. seem selfish, self-centered, and narcissistic
13. have a pessimistic, defeatist, cynical outlook toward life
14. are unhappy and dissatisfied
15. make others miserable
16. complain a great deal
17. communicate in a whiny manner
18. are demanding and critical of others
19. express hostility indirectly
20. are described as dull, unenthusiastic, and unambitious
21. lack ease in oral expression
22. may not show signs of major incapacity
23. seem to have functioned at a reduced level of efficiency for long periods of time
24. see themselves as physically ill and seek medical treatment
25. lack insight and resist psychological interpretations
26. are not very good candidates for traditional psychotherapy or counseling
27. tend to become critical of therapists
28. may terminate treatment prematurely when therapists suggest psychological reasons for symptoms or are perceived as not giving enough attention and support

SCALE 2 (DEPRESSION)

Scale 2 was developed originally to assess symptomatic depression. The primary characteristics of symptomatic depression are poor morale, lack of hope for the future, and a general dissatisfaction with one's life situation. Of the 60 items originally composing Scale 2, 57 were retained in the MMPI-2. Many of the items in the scale deal with various aspects of depression, such as denial of happiness and personal worth, psychomotor retardation and withdrawal, and lack of interest in one's surroundings. Other items in the scale cover a variety of other symptoms and behaviors, including somatic complaints, worry or tension, denial of hostile impulses, and difficulty in controlling one's own thought processes.

Scale 2 seems to be an excellent index of examinees' discomfort and dissatisfaction with their life situations. Whereas very elevated scores on this scale suggest clinical depression, more moderate scores tend to be indicative of a general attitude or lifestyle characterized by poor morale and lack of involvement. Scale 2 scores are related to age, with elderly persons scoring approximately 5–10

T-score points higher than the mean for the total MMPI-2 normative sample. Persons who recently have been hospitalized or incarcerated tend to show moderate elevations on Scale 2. These elevations may reflect dissatisfaction with current circumstances rather than clinical depression.

Interpretation of High Scores on Scale 2

High scorers on Scale 2 (particularly if the T scores exceed 70) often display depressive symptoms. They may report feeling depressed, sad, blue, unhappy, or dysphoric. They tend to feel hopeless and to be pessimistic about the future in general and more specifically about the likelihood of overcoming their problems and making a better adjustment. They may talk about committing suicide, and in clinical settings, high scorers on Scale 2 are more likely than other patients to have made suicide attempts. Self-depreciation and guilt feelings are common. Behavioral manifestations may include anhedonia, lack of energy, refusal to speak, crying, and psychomotor retardation. Patients with such high scores often are diagnosed as depressed. Other symptoms of high scorers include physical complaints, sleep disturbances, bad dreams, weakness, fatigue or loss of energy, agitation, tension, poor concentration, and fearfulness. They also are described as irritable, high-strung, and prone to worry and fretting. They often have unhealthy patterns of eating. They may have a sense of dread that something bad is about to happen to them.

High scorers also tend to feel insecure and show a marked lack of self-confidence. They report feelings of uselessness and inability to function in a variety of situations. They do not have strong achievement motivation. They act helpless and give up easily when faced with stress. They see themselves as having failed to achieve adequately in school and at their jobs.

A lifestyle characterized by withdrawal and lack of intimate involvement with other people is common. High scorers tend to be described as introverted, shy, retiring, timid, seclusive, and secretive. Also, they tend to be aloof and to maintain psychological distance from other people. They may feel that others do not care about them, and their feelings are easily hurt. They often have a severely restricted range of interests and may withdraw from activities in which they previously participated. They are extremely cautious and conventional in their activities, and they are not very creative in problem solving.

High scorers may have great difficulty in making even simple decisions, and they may feel overwhelmed when faced with major life decisions such as vocation or marriage. They tend to be very overcontrolled and to deny their own impulses. They are likely to avoid unpleasantness and will make concessions to avoid confrontations.

Because high Scale 2 scores are suggestive of great personal distress, they indicate that the examinee is likely to be motivated for treatment. Extremely high scores may indicate insufficient energy to engage actively in therapy. Patients with high scores on Scale 2 often are given antidepressant medications.

Summary of Descriptors for Scale 2

High scores on Scale 2 indicate persons who

1. display depressive symptoms (particularly if T > 70)
2. feel depressed, sad, blue, unhappy, and dysphoric
3. feel hopeless and pessimistic about the future
4. talk about committing suicide; in clinical settings may be more likely than other patients to have made suicide attempts
5. have feelings of self-depreciation and guilt
6. experience anhedonia
7. lack energy, may refuse to speak, and show psychomotor retardation
8. often are given depressive diagnoses
9. report physical complaints, sleep disturbances, bad dreams, weakness, fatigue, and loss of energy
10. are agitated, tense, and fearful
11. have poor concentration
12. are described as irritable, high-strung, and prone to worry and fretting
13. have unhealthy patterns of eating
14. may have a sense of dread that something bad is about to happen to them
15. feel insecure and lack self-confidence
16. feel useless and unable to function
17. do not have strong achievement motivation
18. act helpless and give up easily
19. feel like failures at work or in school
20. have lifestyles characterized by withdrawal and lack of involvement with other people
21. are introverted, shy, retiring, timid, seclusive, and secretive
22. are aloof and maintain psychological distance from other people
23. may feel that others do not care about them
24. have their feelings easily hurt
25. have restricted ranges of interests
26. may withdraw from activities in which they previously participated
27. are very cautious and conventional and are not creative in problem solving
28. have difficulty making decisions
29. feel overwhelmed when faced with major life decisions
30. are overcontrolled and deny own impulses
31. avoid unpleasantness and make concessions to avoid confrontations
32. because of personal distress, are likely to be motivated for psychotherapy or counseling
33. if scores are very high, may have insufficient energy to engage actively in therapy
34. often are give antidepressant medications

SCALE 3 (HYSTERIA)

Scale 3 was developed to identify patients who were having hysterical reactions to stress situations. The hysterical syndrome is characterized by involuntary psychogenic loss or disorder of function. All of the 60 items in the original version of Scale 3 were retained in the MMPI-2 version of the scale. Some of the items deal with a general denial of physical health and a variety of rather specific somatic complaints, including heart or chest pain, nausea and vomiting, fitful sleep, and headaches. Another group of items involves a general denial of psychological or emotional problems and of discomfort in social situations. Still other items have to do with having naively optimistic attitudes about other people. High raw scores are more common among women than among men in both clinical and nonclinical settings.

It is important to take into account the level of scores on Scale 3. Marked elevations (T > 80) suggest the possibility of a pathological condition characterized by classical hysterical symptomatology. It also has been noted that chronic pain patients often have Scale 3 T scores in the 70–80 range. Moderately elevated scores are associated with characteristics that are consistent with hysterical disorders but that do not include the classical hysterical symptoms. As with Scale 1, patients with genuine medical problems for whom there is no indication of psychological components to the conditions tend to obtain T scores of about 60 on this scale.

Interpretation of High Scores on Scale 3

Marked elevations on Scale 3 (T > 80) are suggestive of persons who often feel overwhelmed and who react to stress and avoid responsibility by developing physical symptoms. Their symptoms usually do not fit the pattern of any known organic disorder. They may include, in some combination, headaches, stomach discomfort, chest pains, weakness, or tachycardia. Under stress the symptoms may appear suddenly, and they are likely to disappear just as suddenly when the stress subsides.

High scorers on Scale 3 typically do not seem to be experiencing acute emotional turmoil, but they may report feeling sad, depressed, and anxious at times. They also may report lack of energy and feeling worn-out, and sleep disturbances are rather common. The most frequent diagnoses for high Scale 3 scorers in clinical settings are conversion disorder, somatoform disorder, and pain disorder. High scorers often are given prescriptions for antidepressant and anxiolytic medications.

A salient feature of the day-to-day functioning of high scorers is a marked lack of insight concerning the possible underlying causes of their symptoms. In addition, they show little insight concerning their own motives and feelings. High scorers often express rather naïve and Pollyannaish views of the world.

High scorers are often described as immature psychologically and at times even childish or infantile. They are quite self-centered, narcissistic, and egocentric, and they expect a great deal of attention and affection from others. They often use indirect and devious means to get the attention and affection they crave. When others do not respond appropriately, they may feel angry and resentful, but these feelings are likely to be denied and not expressed openly or directly.

High scorers on Scale 3 in clinical settings tend to be more interpersonally involved than many other patients. Although their needs for affection and attention drive them into social interactions, their interpersonal relationships tend to be rather superficial and immature. They seem to be interested in people primarily because of what they can get from them rather than because of a sincere interest in them.

Because of their needs for acceptance and affection, high scorers may initially be quite enthusiastic about treatment. However, they seem to view themselves as having medical problems and want to be treated medically. They are slow to gain insight into the underlying causes of their behavior and are quite resistant to psychological interpretations. If therapists insist on examining the psychological causes of symptoms, premature termination of treatment is likely. High scorers may be willing to talk about problems in their lives as long as they are not perceived as causing their symptoms, and they often respond quite well to direct advice and suggestion.

When high scorers become involved in therapy, they often discuss worry about failure in school or work, marital unhappiness, lack of acceptance by their social groups, and problems with authority figures.

Summary of Descriptors for Scale 3

High scores on Scale 3 indicate persons who

1. often feel overwhelmed
2. react to stress and avoid responsibility by developing physical symptoms (especially if T > 80)
3. may report headaches, stomach discomfort, chest pains, weakness, or tachycardia
4. have symptoms that may appear and disappear suddenly
5. typically do not seem to be experiencing acute emotional turmoil
6. may report feeling sad, depressed, and anxious at times
7. report lack of energy, feeling worn-out, and sleep disturbances
8. frequently receive diagnoses of conversion disorder, somatoform disorder, or pain disorder
9. often are given prescriptions for antidepressant and anxiolytic medications
10. lack insight concerning possible underlying causes of symptoms
11. show little insight concerning their own motives and feelings
12. often are described as psychologically immature, childish, and infantile
13. are self-centered, narcissistic, and egocentric
14. expect a great deal of attention and affection from others
15. use indirect means to get attention and affection

16. feel angry when they do not get enough attention and affection
17. do not express negative feelings openly or directly
18. may express naïve and Pollyannaish beliefs about the world
19. in clinical settings, tend to be more interpersonally involved than many patients
20. tend to have superficial and immature interpersonal relationships
21. are interested in others primarily because of what they can get from them
22. because of needs for acceptance and affection, may initially be quite enthusiastic about treatment
23. view themselves as having medical problems and want medical treatment
24. are slow to gain insight into underlying causes of their behavior
25. are quite resistant to psychological interpretations
26. may terminate treatment prematurely if therapists focus on psychological causes of symptoms
27. may be willing to talk about problems as long as they are not connected to their physical symptoms
28. often respond quite well to direct advice and suggestion
29. when involved in treatment, may discuss failure at work or school, marital unhappiness, lack of acceptance, or problems with authority figures

SCALE 4 (PSYCHOPATHIC DEVIATE)

Scale 4 was developed to identify patients diagnosed as psychopathic personality, asocial or amoral type. Whereas persons included in the original criterion group were characterized in their everyday behavior by such delinquent acts as lying, stealing, sexual promiscuity, excessive drinking, and the like, no major criminal types were included. All 50 of the items in the original scale were maintained in the MMPI-2. The items cover a wide array of topics, including absence of satisfaction in life, family problems, delinquency, sexual problems, and difficulties with authorities. Interestingly, the keyed responses include both admissions of social maladjustment and assertions of social poise and confidence.

Scores on Scale 4 tend to be related to age, with younger persons scoring slightly higher than older persons. In the MMPI-2 normative samples, Caucasians and Asian Americans scored somewhat lower on Scale 4 (5–10 T-score points) than African Americans, Native Americans, and Hispanics.

One way of conceptualizing what Scale 4 assesses is to think of it as a measure of rebelliousness. The highest scorers on the scale may rebel by acting out in antisocial and criminal ways, and moderately high scorers are likely to express their rebellion in more socially acceptable ways.

Interpretation of High Scores on Scale 4

Extremely high scores (T > 75) on Scale 4 tend to be associated with difficulty in incorporating the values and standards of society. Such high scorers are likely to engage in a variety of asocial, antisocial, and even criminal behaviors. These behaviors may include lying, cheating, stealing, sexual acting out, and excessive use of alcohol and/or other drugs.

High scorers on Scale 4 tend to be rebellious toward authority figures and often are in conflict with authorities of one kind or another. They often have stormy relationships with families, and family members tend to be blamed for their difficulties. Underachievement in school, poor work history, and marital problems are characteristic of high scorers.

High scorers are very impulsive persons who strive for immediate gratification of impulses. They often do not plan their behavior very well, and they may act without considering the consequences of their actions. They are very impatient and have a limited frustration tolerance. Their behavior may involve poor judgment and considerable risk taking. They tend not to profit from experiences and may find themselves in the same difficulties time and time again.

High scorers are described by others as immature and childish. They are narcissistic, self-centered, selfish, and egocentric. Their behavior often is ostentatious and exhibitionistic. They are insensitive to the needs and feelings of other people and are interested in others in terms of how they can be used. Although they tend to be seen as likable and generally create good first impressions, their relationships tend to be shallow and superficial. This may be in part due to rejection by the people they mistreat, but it also seems to reflect their own inability to form warm attachments with others.

In addition, high scorers typically are extroverted and outgoing. They are talkative, active, adventurous, energetic, and spontaneous. They are judged by others to be intelligent and self-confident. Although they have a wide range of interests and may become involved in many activities, they lack definite goals and their behavior lacks clear direction.

High scorers tend to be hostile and aggressive. They are resentful, rebellious, antagonistic, and refractory. Their attitudes are characterized by sarcasm, cynicism, and lack of trust. They often feel that they are mistreated by others. Both men and women with high Scale 4 scores may act in aggressive ways, but women are likely to express aggression in more passive, indirect ways. Often there does not appear to be any guilt associated with the aggressive behavior. Whereas high scorers may feign guilt and remorse when their behaviors get them into trouble, such responses typically are short-lived, disappearing when the immediate crisis passes.

Although high scorers typically are not seen as being overwhelmed by emotional turmoil, at times they may admit feeling sad, fearful, and worried about the future. They may experience absence of deep emotional response, which may produce feelings of emptiness, boredom, and depression. Among psychiatric patients, high scorers tend to receive personality disorder diagnoses, with antisocial personality disorder or passive–aggressive personality disorder occurring most frequently.

Because of their verbal facility, outgoing manner, and apparent intellectual resources, high scorers often are perceived as good candidates for psychotherapy or counseling. Unfortunately, the prognosis for change is poor. Although they may agree to treatment to avoid something more unpleasant (e.g., jail or divorce), they generally are unwilling to accept blame for their own problems, and they terminate treatment as soon as possible. In therapy they tend to intellectualize excessively and to blame others for their difficulties.

Summary of Descriptors for Scale 4

High scores on Scale 4 indicate persons who

1. have difficulty incorporating the values and standards of society
2. may engage in asocial and antisocial acts, including lying, cheating, stealing, sexual acting out, and excessive use of alcohol and/or other drugs
3. are rebellious toward authority figures
4. have stormy relationships with families
5. blame family members for difficulties
6. have histories of underachievement
7. tend to have marital problems
8. are impulsive and strive for immediate gratification of impulses
9. do not plan their behavior well
10. tend to act without considering the consequences of their actions
11. are impatient and have limited frustration tolerance
12. show poor judgment and take risks
13. tend not to profit from experiences
14. are seen by others as immature and childish
15. are narcissistic, self-centered, selfish, and egocentric
16. are ostentatious and exhibitionistic
17. are insensitive to the needs and feelings of others
18. are interested in others in terms of how they can be used
19. are likable and create good first impressions
20. have shallow, superficial relationships
21. seem unable to form warm attachments with others
22. are extroverted and outgoing
23. are talkative, active, adventurous, energetic, and spontaneous
24. are judged by others to be intelligent and self-confident
25. have wide range of interests, but behavior lacks clear direction
26. tend to be hostile, resentful, rebellious, antagonistic, and refractory
27. have sarcastic, cynical, and suspicious attitudes
28. may act in aggressive ways, although women may do so in less direct ways
29. may feign guilt and remorse when in trouble
30. are not seen as overwhelmed by emotional turmoil
31. may admit feeling sad, fearful, and worried about the future
32. experience absence of deep emotional response
33. may feel empty, bored, and depressed

34. in clinical settings are likely to receive diagnoses of antisocial or passive–aggressive personality disorder

35. may agree to treatment to avoid something more unpleasant

36. have poor prognosis for psychotherapy or counseling

37. tend to terminate treatment prematurely

38. in treatment tend to intellectualize excessively and to blame others for
difficulties

SCALE 5 (MASCULINITY–FEMININITY)

Because homosexuality was considered a mental disorder at the time that the
MMPI was being developed, Scale 5 originally was developed by Hathaway and
McKinley to identify homosexuality in men. The test authors identified only a
very small number of items that differentiated male homosexual patients from
male heterosexual patients. Thus, items also were added to the scale if they differentiated between men and women in the MMPI standardization sample. Items
from the Terman and Miles Attitude-Interest Analysis Test (1936) also were added
to the scale. Although Hathaway and McKinley considered this scale as preliminary, it has come to be used routinely in its original form.

The test authors attempted unsuccessfully to develop a corresponding scale
for identifying homosexuality in women. However, Scale 5 has been used routinely for both men and women. Fifty-two of the items are keyed in the same
direction for both sexes, whereas four items, all dealing with frankly sexual
material, are keyed in opposite directions for men and women. After obtaining
raw scores, T-score conversions are reversed for the sexes so that a high raw score
for men is transformed to a high T score, whereas a high raw score for women is
transformed to a low T score. The result is that high T scores for both men and
women are indicative of deviation from one's own sex.

In the MMPI-2, 56 of the 60 items in the original Scale 5 were maintained.
Although a few of the items in Scale 5 have frankly sexual content, most items are
not sexual in nature and cover a diversity of topics, including work and recreational
interests, worries and fears, excessive sensitivity, and family relationships.

Although the MMPI Scale 5 scores were strongly related to the amount of
formal education of examinees, the relationship is much more modest for the
MMPI-2. Butcher (1990a) reported a correlation of .35 between Scale 5 scores
and years of education for men in the MMPI-2 normative sample. For women,
the correlation was –.15. Long, Graham, and Timbrook (1994) found that men
in the MMPI-2 standardization sample with the highest educational levels (college degrees or beyond) scored more than five T-score points higher on Scale
5 than the lowest educational group (less than high school diploma). The most
educated women scored more than five T-score points lower than the least educated women. These differences probably reflect the broader interest patterns
of more educated men and women and are not large enough to necessitate different Scale 5 interpretations for persons with differing levels of education.

Scores on Scale 5 do not seem to be related to symptoms or problems for nonclinical persons (Long & Graham, 1991), psychiatric inpatients (Graham, 1988), or mental health center outpatients (Graham, Ben-Porath, & McNulty, 1999). In fact, several studies have indicated that moderate Scale 5 elevations may actually be associated with more positive functioning (Reed, Walker, Williams, McLeod, & Jones, 1996; Tanner, 1990). Although several studies have reported Scale 5 elevations for some kinds of sexual offenders (Hall, Graham, & Shepherd, 1991; Walters, 1987), relationships between Scale 5 scores and sexual aggression or other kinds of sexual problems are not established well enough to permit prediction of these problem behaviors in individual cases.

Interpretation of Scores on Scale 5

High scores for men on Scale 5 are indicative of a lack of stereotypic masculine interests. High scorers tend to have aesthetic and artistic interests, and they are likely to participate in housekeeping and child-rearing activities to a greater extent than most men.

High scores on Scale 5 are very uncommon among women. When they are encountered, they generally indicate rejection of a very traditional female role. Women having high Scale 5 scores are interested in sports, hobbies, and other activities that tend to be stereotypically more masculine than feminine, and they often are seen as assertive and competitive.

Men who score low on Scale 5 are presenting themselves as very traditionally masculine. They are likely to have stereotypically masculine preferences in work, hobbies, and other activities. Women who score low on Scale 5 are indicating that they have many stereotypically feminine interests. They are likely to derive satisfaction from their roles as spouses and mothers. However, women with low Scale 5 scores may be very traditionally feminine or may have adopted a more androgynous lifestyle. This androgynous lifestyle is more likely for women with low Scale 5 scores who also are well educated.

Summary of Descriptors for Scale 5

High Scale 5 scores for men indicate persons who

1. lack stereotypic masculine interests
2. have aesthetic and artistic interests
3. are likely to participate in housekeeping and child rearing to a greater extent than many men

High Scale 5 scores for women indicate persons who

1. may be rejecting a very traditional female role
2. are likely to be interested in sports, hobbies, and other activities that are stereotypically more masculine than feminine
3. are seen as assertive and competitive

Low Scale 5 scores for men indicate persons who

1. are presenting themselves as extremely masculine
2. tend to have stereotypically masculine preferences in work, hobbies, and other activities

Low Scale 5 scores for women indicate persons who

1. have many stereotypically feminine interests
2. are likely to derive satisfaction from their roles as spouses or mothers
3. may be traditionally feminine or more androgynous

SCALE 6 (PARANOIA)

Scale 6 originally was developed to identify patients who were judged to have paranoid symptoms such as ideas of reference, feelings of persecution, grandiose self-concepts, suspiciousness, excessive sensitivity, and rigid opinions and attitudes. Although the scale was considered as preliminary because of problems in cross-validation, a major reason for its retention was that it produced relatively few false positives. Persons who score high on the scale usually have paranoid symptoms. However, some patients with clearly paranoid symptoms are able to achieve average scores on Scale 6.

All 40 of the items in the original scale were maintained in the MMPI-2. Although some of the items in the scale deal with frankly psychotic behaviors (e.g., suspiciousness, ideas of reference, delusions of persecution, and grandiosity), other items cover such diverse topics as sensitivity, cynicism, asocial behavior, excessive moral virtue, and complaints about other people. It is possible to obtain a T score greater than 65 on this scale without endorsing any of the frankly psychotic items.

Interpretation of High Scores on Scale 6

When T scores on Scale 6 are greater than 70, and especially when Scale 6 also is the highest scale in the profile, persons may exhibit frankly psychotic behavior. Their thinking may be disturbed, and they may have delusions of persecution or grandeur. Ideas of reference also are common. They may feel mistreated and picked on, they may be angry and resentful, and they may harbor grudges. Projection is a common defense mechanism. Among psychiatric patients, diagnoses of schizophrenia or paranoid disorder are most frequent, and past hospitalizations are common.

When Scale 6 scores are within a T-score range of 60–70, frankly psychotic symptoms are not as common as for higher scores. However, persons with scores within this range are characterized by a variety of traits and behaviors that suggest a paranoid orientation. They tend to be excessively sensitive and overly responsive to the opinions of others. They feel that they are getting a raw deal out of life and tend to rationalize and to blame others for their own difficulties. Also, they are seen as suspicious and guarded and commonly exhibit hostility, resentment, and an argumentative manner. They tend to be very moralistic and rigid in their opinions and attitudes. Rationality is likely to be greatly overemphasized. Persons who score in this range may also describe depression, sadness, withdrawal, and anxiety, and they are seen by others as emotionally labile and moody. Prognosis for psychotherapy is poor because these persons do not like to talk about emotional problems and are likely to rationalize much of the time. They have great difficulty in establishing rapport with therapists. In therapy, they are likely to reveal hostility and resentment toward family members.

Summary of Descriptors for Scale 6

Extreme elevations (T > 70) on Scale 6 indicate persons who

1. may exhibit frankly psychotic behavior
2. may have disturbed thinking, delusions of persecution or grandeur, and ideas of reference
3. feel mistreated and picked on
4. feel angry and resentful
5. harbor grudges
6. utilize projection as a defense mechanism
7. in clinical settings, often receive diagnoses of schizophrenia or paranoid disorder
8. if psychiatric patients, previous hospitalizations are common

Moderate elevations (T = 60–70) on Scale 6 indicate persons who

1. have a paranoid orientation
2. tend to be excessively sensitive and overly responsive to the opinions of others
3. feel they are getting a raw deal out of life
4. tend to rationalize and blame others for difficulties
5. are suspicious and guarded
6. have hostility, resentment, and an argumentative manner
7. are moralistic and rigid in their opinions and attitudes
8. overemphasize rationality
9. may describe depression, sadness, withdrawal, and anxiety
10. are seen by others as emotionally labile and moody
11. have poor prognosis for psychotherapy
12. do not like to talk about emotional problems
13. rationalize excessively in therapy
14. have difficulty establishing rapport with a therapist
15. in therapy reveal hostility and resentment toward family members

SCALE 7 (PSYCHASTHENIA)

Scale 7 originally was developed to measure the general symptomatic pattern labeled psychasthenia. Although this diagnostic label is not used commonly today, it was popular when the scale was developed. Among currently popular diagnostic categories, the obsessive–compulsive disorder probably is closest to the original psychasthenia label. Persons given diagnoses of psychasthenia had thinking characterized by excessive doubts, compulsions, obsessions, and unreasonable fears. This symptom pattern was much more common among outpatients than among hospitalized patients, so the number of cases available for scale construction was small. All 48 items in the original scale were maintained in the MMPI-2 version of the scale. They cover a variety of symptoms and behaviors. Many of the items deal with uncontrollable or obsessive thoughts, feelings of fear and/or anxiety, and doubts about one's own ability. Unhappiness, physical complaints, and difficulties in concentration also are represented in the scale.

Interpretation of High Scores on Scale 7

Scale 7 is a reliable index of psychological turmoil and discomfort, with higher scorers experiencing greater turmoil. High scorers tend to be extremely anxious, tense, and agitated. They worry a great deal, even over small problems, and they are fearful and apprehensive. They are high-strung and jumpy and report difficulties in concentrating. High scorers often also report feeling sad and unhappy, and they tend to be pessimistic about the future. Some high scorers express physical complaints that may center on the heart, the gastrointestinal system, or the genitourinary system. Complaints of fatigue, exhaustion, insomnia, and bad dreams are common. High scorers on Scale 7 often are given anxiety disorder diagnoses.

High scorers on Scale 7 tend to be very introspective, and they sometimes report fears that they are losing their minds. Obsessive thinking, compulsive and ritualistic behavior, and ruminations, often centering on feelings of insecurity and inferiority, are common among the highest scorers. They lack self-confidence; are self-critical, self-conscious, and self-degrading; and are plagued by self-doubts. High scorers tend to be very rigid and moralistic and to have high standards of behavior and performance for themselves and others. They are likely to be perfectionist and conscientious; they may feel guilty about not living up to their own standards and depressed about falling short of goals.

In general, high scorers are neat, orderly, organized, and meticulous. They are persistent and reliable, but they lack ingenuity and originality in their approach to problems. They are seen by others as dull and formal. They have great difficulties in decision making. They do not cope well with stress, often distorting the importance of problems and overreacting to stressful situations.

High scorers tend to be shy and do not interact well socially. They are described as hard to get to know, and they worry a great deal about popularity and social acceptance. Other people often see them as sentimental, peaceable, soft-hearted, trustful, sensitive, and kind. Other adjectives used to describe them include dependent, unassertive, and immature.

Although high scorers may be motivated for treatment because they feel so uncomfortable and miserable, they are not very responsive to brief psychotherapy or counseling. Despite some insight into their problems, they tend to rationalize and intellectualize a great deal. They often are resistant to interpretations and may express hostility toward the therapist. However, they tend to remain in treatment longer than most patients, and they may show very slow but steady progress. Problems presented in treatment may include difficulties with authority figures and poor work or study habits.

Summary of Descriptors for Scale 7

High scores on Scale 7 indicate persons who

1. are experiencing psychological turmoil and discomfort
2. feel anxious, tense, and agitated
3. are worried, fearful, apprehensive, high-strung, and jumpy
4. report difficulties in concentrating
5. often report feeling sad and unhappy
6. feel pessimistic about the future
7. report physical complaints centering on the heart, genitourinary system, or gastrointestinal system
8. complain of fatigue, exhaustion, and insomnia
9. in clinical settings often are given anxiety disorder diagnoses
10. are introspective
11. may report fears that they are losing their minds
12. have obsessive thinking, compulsive and ritualistic behavior, and ruminations
13. feel insecure and inferior
14. lack self-confidence
15. are self-critical, self-conscious, and self-degrading
16. are plagued by self-doubts
17. tend to be very rigid and moralistic
18. have high standards of performance for self and others
19. are perfectionist and conscientious
20. may feel depressed and guilty about falling short of goals
21. are neat, organized, and meticulous
22. are persistent and reliable
23. lack ingenuity in their approach to problems
24. are seen by others as dull and formal
25. have difficulties in making decisions
26. do not cope well with stress
27. often distort importance of problems and overreact to stress
28. tend to be shy and do not interact well socially
29. are described as hard to get to know
30. worry about popularity and social acceptance
31. are seen by others as sentimental, peaceable, soft-hearted, sensitive, and kind
32. may be motivated for treatment because of inner turmoil

33. are not very responsive to brief therapy or counseling
34. show some insight into their problems
35. rationalize and intellectualize excessively
36. are resistant to psychological interpretations in therapy
37. may express hostility toward therapists
38. remain in treatment longer than most patients
39. make slow but steady progress in treatment
40. in treatment discuss problems that may include difficulty with authority figures and poor work or study habits.

SCALE 8 (SCHIZOPHRENIA)

Scale 8 was developed to identify patients with diagnoses of schizophrenia. This category includes a heterogeneous group of disorders characterized by disturbances of thinking, mood, and behavior. Misinterpretations of reality, delusions, and hallucinations may be present. Ambivalent or constricted emotional responsiveness is common. Behavior may be withdrawn, aggressive, or bizarre.

All 78 of the items in the original scale were maintained in the MMPI-2 version. Some of the items deal with frankly psychotic symptoms, such as bizarre mentation, peculiarities of perception, delusions of persecution, and hallucinations. Other topics covered include social alienation, poor family relationships, sexual concerns, difficulties in impulse control and concentration, and fears, worries, and dissatisfactions.

Scores on Scale 8 are related to age and ethnicity. College students often obtain T scores in a range of 50–55, perhaps reflecting the turmoil associated with that period in life. African Americans, Native Americans, and Hispanics in the MMPI-2 normative sample scored approximately five T-score points higher than Caucasians. These mildly elevated scores for ethnic minority persons do not necessarily suggest greater overt psychopathology. They may simply be indicative of the alienation and social estrangement experienced by some ethnic minority group members. Some elevations of Scale 8 are found in persons who are reporting unusual experiences, feelings, and perceptions related to the use of prescription and nonprescription drugs, especially amphetamines. Also, some persons with medical disorders such as epilepsy, stroke, or closed head injury endorse sensory and cognitive items that lead to above-average scores on Scale 8 (e.g., Dikmen, Hermann, Wilensky, & Rainwater, 1983; Dodrill, 1986; Gass, 1991, 1992; Gass & Lawhorn, 1991).

Interpretation of High Scores on Scale 8

Although one should not assign a diagnosis of schizophrenia on the basis of only the score on Scale 8, T scores greater than 75 suggest the possibility of a psychotic disorder. Confusion, disorganization, and disorientation may be present. Unusual thoughts or attitudes, perhaps even delusional in nature; hallucinations; and extremely poor judgment may be evident. High scorers often have long histories of inpatient and/or outpatient psychiatric treatment.

High scores on Scale 8 do not necessarily indicate psychotic disorders. They can be produced by an individual who is in acute psychological turmoil or by a less disturbed person who is endorsing many deviant items as a cry for help. In interpreting high scores on Scale 8, it is important to consider the possibility that they reflect the reporting of unusual symptoms associated with substance abuse problems or with medical disorders such as epilepsy, stroke, or closed head injury.

High scores on Scale 8 may suggest a schizoid lifestyle. High scorers tend to feel as if they are not a part of their social environments. They feel isolated, alienated, misunderstood, and unaccepted by their peers. They seem to believe that they are getting a raw deal from life. They are withdrawn, seclusive, secretive, and inaccessible and may avoid dealing with people and with new situations. They are described by others as shy, aloof, and uninvolved, and they often report having few or no friends.

High scorers may be experiencing a great deal of apprehension and generalized anxiety, and they often report having bad dreams and problems with concentration. They may feel sad, blue, and depressed. They may feel helpless and pessimistic about the future, and they may report suicidal ideation. They may feel very resentful, hostile, and aggressive, but they are unable to express such feelings directly. A typical response to stress is withdrawal into daydreams and fantasies, and some high scorers may have a difficult time in separating reality and fantasy.

High scorers may be plagued by self-doubts. They feel insecure, inferior, incompetent, and dissatisfied. They give up easily when confronted with problem situations and often feel like failures. Sexual preoccupation and sex-role confusion are common. Their behavior often is characterized by others as nonconforming, unusual, unconventional, and eccentric. Physical complaints may be present, and they usually are vague and long-standing in nature.

High scorers may at times be very stubborn, moody, and opinionated. At other times they are seen as generous, peaceable, and sentimental. Other adjectives used to describe high scorers include immature, impulsive, adventurous, sharp-witted, conscientious, and high-strung. Although they may have a wide range of interests and may be creative and imaginative in approaching problems, their goals generally are abstract and vague, and they seem to lack the basic information required for problem solving.

The prognosis for psychotherapy for high scorers is not good because of the long-standing nature of their problems and their inability to relate in a meaningful way to therapists. However, high scorers tend to stay in treatment longer than most patients, and eventually they may come to trust their therapists. Medical consultation to evaluate the appropriateness of psychotropic medications may be indicated. In some cases high scorers may require the structured environment of an inpatient treatment program. Focusing on specific and practical problems in therapy may be more beneficial than a more insight-oriented approach.

Summary of Descriptors for Scale 8

High scores on Scale 8 indicate persons who

1. may have a psychotic disorder (especially if T > 75)
2. may be confused, disorganized, and disoriented
3. may report unusual thoughts or attitudes and hallucinations
4. may show extremely poor judgment
5. often have histories of inpatient and/or outpatient psychiatric treatment
6. may be in acute psychological turmoil
7. may be reporting unusual symptoms associated with drug abuse or medical problems such as epilepsy, stroke, or closed head injury
8. tend to have schizoid lifestyles
9. do not feel part of their social environments
10. feel alienated, misunderstood, and unaccepted by peers
11. may feel that they are getting a raw deal from life
12. are withdrawn, seclusive, secretive, and inaccessible
13. avoid dealing with people and new situations
14. are described by others as shy, aloof, and uninvolved
15. often report having few or no friends
16. experience apprehension and generalized anxiety
17. report bad dreams and problems with concentration
18. may feel sad, blue, and depressed
19. may feel helpless and pessimistic about the future
20. may report suicidal ideation
21. feel resentful, hostile, and aggressive
22. are unable to express negative feelings directly
23. typically respond to stress by withdrawing into daydreams and fantasies
24. may have difficulty separating reality and fantasy
25. are plagued by self-doubts
26. feel insecure, inferior, incompetent, and dissatisfied
27. give up easily when confronted with problem situations
28. often feel like failures
29. may have sexual preoccupation and sex-role confusion
30. are nonconforming, unusual, unconventional, and eccentric
31. have vague and long-standing physical complaints
32. may at times be stubborn, moody, and opinionated
33. may at times be seen as generous, peaceable, and sentimental
34. are described as immature, impulsive, adventurous, sharp-witted, conscientious, and high-strung
35. have a wide range of interests
36. may be creative and imaginative in approaching problems
37. have abstract and vague goals
38. seem to lack the basic information required for problem solving

39. have a poor prognosis for psychotherapy because of the long-standing nature of their problems and inability to relate in a meaningful way to a therapist
40. tend to stay in treatment longer than most patients
41. may eventually come to trust therapists
42. may require medical referral to evaluate the appropriateness of psychotropic medications
43. in some cases may require the structured environment of an inpatient treatment program
44. may benefit most from focusing on specific and practical problems in therapy

SCALE 9 (HYPOMANIA)

Scale 9 originally was developed to identify psychiatric patients manifesting hypomanic symptoms. Hypomania is characterized by elevated mood, accelerated speech and motor activity, irritability, flight of ideas, and brief periods of depression. All 46 items in the original scale were maintained in the MMPI-2 version of the scale. Some of the items deal specifically with features of hypomanic disturbance (e.g., activity level, excitability, irritability, and grandiosity). Other items cover topics such as family relationships, moral values and attitudes, and physical or bodily concerns. No single content dimension accounts for much of the variance in scores, and most of the sources of variance represented in the scale are not duplicated in other clinical scales.

Scores on Scale 9 are related to age and ethnicity. Younger persons (e.g., college students) typically obtain scores in a T-score range of 50–60, and for elderly persons T scores below 50 are common. African Americans, Native Americans, and Hispanics in the MMPI-2 normative samples scored somewhat higher (5–10 T-score points) than Caucasians.

Scale 9 can be viewed as a measure of psychological and physical energy, with high scorers having excessive energy. When Scale 9 scores are high, characteristics suggested by other aspects of the MMPI-2 will be acted out. For example, high scores on Scale 4 suggest asocial or antisocial tendencies. If Scale 9 is elevated along with Scale 4, these tendencies are more likely to be expressed overtly in behavior.

Interpretation of High Scores on Scale 9

Extreme elevations (T > 80) on Scale 9 may be suggestive of a manic episode. Patients with such scores are likely to show excessive, purposeless activity and accelerated speech; they may have hallucinations and/or delusions of grandeur; and they are emotionally labile. Some confusion may be present, and flight of ideas is common.

Persons with more moderate elevations are not likely to exhibit severe symptoms, but there is a definite tendency toward overactivity and unrealistic self-appraisal. High scorers are energetic and talkative, and they prefer action to thought. They have a wide range of interests and are likely to have many projects going at once. However, they do not utilize energy wisely and often do not see projects through to completion. They may be creative, enterprising, and ingenious, but they have little interest in routine or details. High scorers tend to become bored and restless very easily, and their frustration tolerance is quite low. They have great difficulty in inhibiting expression of impulses, and periodic episodes of irritability, hostility, and aggressive outbursts are common. An unrealistic and unqualified optimism is also characteristic of high scorers. They seem to think that nothing is impossible, and they have grandiose aspirations. Also, they have an exaggerated appraisal of their own self-worth and self-importance and are not able to see their own limitations. High scorers have a greater-than-average likelihood of abusing alcohol and other drugs and getting into trouble with the law.

High scorers are very outgoing, sociable, and gregarious. They like to be around other people and generally create good first impressions. They impress others as being friendly, pleasant, enthusiastic, poised, and self-confident. They tend to try to dominate other people. Their relationships are usually quite superficial, and as others get to know them better they become aware of their manipulations, deceptions, and unreliability.

Despite the outward picture of confidence and poise, high scorers are likely to harbor feelings of dissatisfaction concerning what they are getting out of life. They may feel upset, tense, nervous, anxious, and agitated, and they describe themselves as prone to worry. Periodic episodes of depression may occur.

In psychotherapy, high scorers may reveal negative feelings toward domineering parents, may report difficulties in school or at work, and may admit to a variety of delinquent behaviors. High scorers are resistant to interpretations, are irregular in their attendance, and are likely to terminate therapy prematurely. They engage in a great deal of intellectualization and may repeat problems in a stereotyped manner. They do not become dependent on the therapist, who may be a target for hostility and aggression.

Summary of Descriptors for Scale 9

High scores on Scale 9 indicate persons who

1. if T > 80, may exhibit behavioral manifestations of manic episodes, including
   a. excessive, purposeless activity
   b. accelerated speech
   c. hallucinations
   d. delusions of grandeur
   e. emotional lability
   f. confusion
   g. flight of ideas
2. are overactive
3. have unrealistic self-appraisal

4. are energetic and talkative
5. prefer action to thought
6. have a wide range of interests
7. may have many projects going at once
8. do not utilize energy wisely
9. often do not see projects through to completion
10. may be creative, enterprising, and ingenious
11. have little interest in routine or detail
12. tend to become bored and restless very easily
13. have low frustration tolerance
14. have difficulty inhibiting expression of impulses
15. have periodic episodes of irritability, hostility, and aggressive outbursts
16. are characterized by unrealistic and unqualified optimism
17. have grandiose aspirations
18. have an exaggerated appraisal of self-worth
19. are unable to see their own limitations
20. have a greater-than-average likelihood of abusing alcohol and other drugs
21. may get into trouble with the law
22. are outgoing, sociable, and gregarious
23. like to be around other people
24. create good first impressions
25. impress others as friendly, pleasant, enthusiastic, poised, and self-confident
26. try to dominate other people
27. have quite superficial relationships with other people
28. eventually are seen by others as manipulative, deceptive, and unreliable
29. beneath an outward picture of confidence and poise, harbor feelings of dissatisfaction
30. may feel upset, tense, nervous, anxious, and agitated
31. may describe themselves as prone to worry
32. may experience periodic episodes of depression
33. in psychotherapy may reveal negative feelings toward domineering parents, difficulties in school or at work, and a variety of delinquent behaviors
34. have a poor prognosis for psychotherapy
35. are resistant to interpretations
36. are irregular in therapy attendance
37. are likely to terminate therapy prematurely
38. engage in a great deal of intellectualization
39. repeat problems in a stereotyped manner
40. do not become dependent on therapists
41. may make therapists targets of hostility and aggression

SCALE 0 (SOCIAL INTROVERSION)

Although Scale 0 was developed later than the other Clinical scales, it has come to be used routinely. The scale was designed to assess a person's tendency to withdraw from social contacts and responsibilities. Items were selected by contrasting high and low scorers on the Social Introversion–Extroversion scale of the Minnesota T-S-E Inventory. Only women were used to develop the scale, but its use has been extended to men as well.

All but one of the 70 items in the original scale were maintained in the MMPI-2 version. The items are of two general types. One group of items deals with social participation, whereas the other group deals with general neurotic maladjustment and self-depreciation. High scores can be obtained by endorsing either kind of item, or both. Scores on Scale 0 are quite stable over extended periods of time.

Interpretation of Scores on Scale 0

The most salient characteristic of high scorers on Scale 0 is social introversion. High scorers are very insecure and uncomfortable in social situations. They tend to be shy, reserved, timid, and retiring. They feel more comfortable when alone or with a few close friends, and they do not participate in many social activities. They may be especially uncomfortable around members of the opposite sex.

High scorers lack self-confidence, and they tend to be self-effacing. They are hard to get to know and are described by others as cold and distant. They are sensitive to what others think of them and are likely to be troubled by their lack of involvement with other people. They are overcontrolled and are not likely to display their feelings directly. They are passive, submissive, and compliant in interpersonal relationships, and they are overly accepting of authority.

High scorers also are described as serious and as having a slow personal tempo. Although they are reliable and dependable, their approach to problems tends to be cautious, conventional, and unoriginal, and they give up easily. They are somewhat rigid and inflexible in their attitudes and opinions. They also have great difficulty in making even minor decisions. They typically do not have strong needs to achieve.

High scorers tend to worry, to be irritable, and to feel anxious. They often are preoccupied with health problems. They are described by others as moody. Guilt feelings and episodes of depression may occur. High scorers seem to lack energy and do not have many interests. In treatment settings they may have difficulty forming therapeutic alliances, and they often report feeling quite uncomfortable and tense during sessions.

Low scorers on Scale 0 tend to be sociable and extroverted. They are outgoing, gregarious, friendly, and talkative. They have a strong need to be around other people, and they mix well with other people. They are seen by others as verbally fluent and expressive. They are active, energetic, and vigorous. They are interested in power, status, and recognition, and they tend to seek out competitive situations.

Summary of Descriptors for Scale 0

High scores on Scale 0 indicate persons who

1. are socially introverted
2. are very insecure and uncomfortable in social situations
3. tend to be shy, reserved, timid, and retiring
4. feel more comfortable alone or with a few close friends
5. do not participate in many social activities
6. may be especially uncomfortable around members of the opposite sex
7. lack self-confidence and tend to be self-effacing
8. are hard to get to know
9. are described by others as cold and distant
10. are sensitive to what others think of them
11. are likely to be troubled by their lack of involvement with other people
12. are quite overcontrolled and not likely to display feelings openly
13. are passive, submissive, and compliant in interpersonal relationships
14. are overly accepting of authority
15. are described as serious and as having a slow personal tempo
16. are reliable and dependable
17. tend to have a cautious, conventional, and unoriginal approach to problems
18. tend to give up easily
19. are somewhat rigid and inflexible in attitudes and opinions
20. have great difficulty making even minor decisions
21. do not have a strong need to achieve
22. tend to worry, to be irritable, and to feel anxious
23. often are preoccupied with health problems
24. are described by others as moody
25. may experience episodes of depression
26. do not have many interests
27. in treatment settings have difficulty forming therapeutic alliances
28. report feeling uncomfortable and tense during treatment sessions

Low scores on Scale 0 indicate persons who

1. are sociable and extroverted
2. are outgoing, gregarious, friendly, and talkative
3. have a strong need to be around other people
4. mix well socially
5. are seen as expressive and verbally fluent

5

⁄⁄⁄ Code Types

From the MMPI's inception, Hathaway and McKinley emphasized that configural interpretation of scores was diagnostically richer and thus more useful than interpretation that examined single scales without regard for relationships among the scales. They reasoned that persons grouped together on the basis of scores on more than one Clinical scale would be more similar to each other than those grouped together on the basis of having high scores on a single Clinical scale. Thus, it would be expected that there would be more reliable and specific behavioral correlates for configurations of scales than for single scales. Meehl (1951), Meehl and Dahlstrom (1960), Taulbee and Sisson (1957), and others also stressed configural approaches to MMPI interpretation.

Some early MMPI validity studies (e.g., Black, 1953; Guthrie, 1952; Meehl, 1951) grouped profiles according to the two highest Clinical scales in the profile and tried to identify reliable extratest behaviors that were uniquely related to each such profile type. Other investigators (e.g., Gilberstadt & Duker, 1965; Marks & Seeman, 1963) developed complex rules for classifying profiles into homogeneous groups and tried to identify extratest correlates for each group. Although clinicians initially were quite enthusiastic about this complex approach to profile classification, they became disenchanted as accumulating research and clinical evidence indicated that only a small proportion of the MMPI protocols encountered in a typical clinical setting could be classified using the code types defined by these complex classification systems (Fowler & Coyle, 1968; Huff, 1965; Meikle & Gerritse, 1970).

As interest in complex rules for classifying profiles diminished, there was a resurgence of interest in the simpler (two-scale, three-scale) approach to classification of profiles. An obvious advantage of the simpler approach is that a large proportion of the profiles encountered in most settings can be classified into categories that have been studied empirically. Marks, Seeman, and Haller (1974), in their revision and extension of the earlier work by Marks and Seeman (1963), acknowledged that no appreciable loss in accuracy of extratest descriptions resulted when they used simpler instead of their more complex rules for classifying MMPI profiles.

DETERMINING CODE TYPES

Described very simply, code types indicate which Clinical scales are the highest ones in the profile. Because Scales 5 and 0 were added after the original publication of the MMPI and do not seem to measure clinical symptoms and problems directly, these two scales typically have not been considered in determining code types. The simplest code types are high-points. A high-point code type (e.g., high-point 2) tells us that the scale, in this example Scale 2, is higher than any other Clinical scale in the profile. The high-point code type does not tell us anything about the absolute level of the highest scale or about the levels of scores on other Clinical scales. There can be only one high-point code type for any particular profile. In Chapter 4, we defined high scores on the Clinical scales in terms of absolute T-score levels and not in relation to other scales in the profile. Obviously, a person can have several or more high scores. An examination of the MMPI/MMPI-2 literature suggests that basically the same descriptors apply to high-scoring individuals, whether we are dealing with high scores or with high-point code types. Thus, no additional interpretive information will be presented in this chapter for high-point code types.

Two-point code types tell us which two Clinical scales are the highest ones in the profile. Thus, a 2–7 two-point code type tells us that Scale 2 is the highest Clinical scale in the profile and Scale 7 is the second-highest Clinical scale in the profile. For most two-point code types, the scales are interchangeable. For example, we often talk about code types such as 27/72, and we make basically the same interpretations for the 2–7 code type as we do for the 7–2 code type. Whenever order of the scales in the two-point code type makes a difference in interpretation, specific mention is made in the descriptive data for those particular code types in this chapter. As with high-point code types, two-point code types tell us nothing about the absolute level of scores for the two scales in the code type or the level of scores of other clinical scales.

Three-point code types tell us which three Clinical scales are the highest in the profile. For example, a 2–7–8 code type is one in which Scale 2 is the highest in the profile, Scale 7 is the second highest, and Scale 8 is the third highest. For most three-point code types the order of scales is interchangeable. Whenever order is important in terms of the interpretations of code types, specific mention is made when the descriptive data for those code types are presented in this chapter.

Early approaches to code type interpretation did not take into account the extent to which the code types were defined. Definition refers to the difference in scores between the scales in the code type and those not in the code type. The T-score difference between the lowest scale in the code type and the next-highest clinical scale in the profile should be considered. For example, for a two-point code type we would examine the T-score difference between the second- and third-highest scales. For a three-point code type we would examine the T-score difference between the third- and fourth-highest scales. Because the MMPI-2 Clinical scales are not perfectly reliable, small differences between scores should not be considered meaningful. Given the standard errors of measurement of the Clinical scales, T-score differences of less than five points should not be considered meaningful (Graham, Timbrook, Ben-Porath, & Butcher, 1991).

Those who argue against restricting interpretation to defined code types (e.g., Dahlstrom, 1992; Dahlstrom & Humphrey, 1996; Humphrey & Dahlstrom, 1995) seem to be ignoring measurement error. Tellegen and Ben-Porath (1996) and Ben-Porath and Tellegen (1996) offered some compelling arguments in favor of interpreting only defined code types. In addition, Berry et al. (1997) demonstrated that defined code types are stable in the face of up to 30 omitted items, whereas undefined code types often change when as few as 10 items are omitted. Graham, Smith, and Schwartz (1986) found that MMPI code types of psychiatric patients were more likely to be stable over time when they were defined. Several investigators have demonstrated that the congruence between the MMPI and MMPI-2 code types was greater when the code types were defined (Graham, Timbrook, et al., 1991; Hargrave, Hiatt, Ogard, & Karr, 1994). In a simulation study, Munley, Germain, Tovar-Murray, and Borgman (2004) found that as the degree of code-type definition increases, code-type stability also increases. They suggested that different degrees of definition may be needed for different code types.

McNulty, Ben-Porath, and Graham (1998) found that the strength and number of conceptually relevant correlates were greater for defined code types than for those that were not defined. This author's recommendation is to interpret only defined code types, ones in which the lowest Clinical scale in the code type has a score at least five T-score points higher than the next-highest Clinical scale in the profile. When such a definition is present, we can be more confident that the descriptors associated with the code type are likely to characterize the person whose profile we are interpreting. Obviously, not every MMPI-2 protocol will have a defined code type. When defined code types are not present, the code-type approach to interpretation should not be used. Rather, inferences about the examinee should be based on the levels of scores on individual scales.

Levels of scores on scales in code types have been considered in different ways. Sometimes, the levels of scores have not been taken into account. For example, the interpretation of a 27/72 code type would be similar whether the T scores on Scales 2 and 7 were above 90 or below 70. At other times, code types have been interpreted only when T scores on the scales in the code type are significantly elevated (usually > 70 with the original MMPI or > 65 with the MMPI-2).

This author believes that defined code types can be interpreted whenever the scales in the code types have T scores greater than 60. Typically, the list of descriptors for a particular code type includes both symptoms and personality characteristics. When the scores on the scales in the code types are very high, inferences concerning both symptoms and personality characteristics should be considered. When the scores on the scales in the code types are not as high, inferences about symptoms should not be made (or should be made with considerable caution), but inferences about personality characteristics would apply. It is difficult to specify a T-score level above which scores would be considered to be very high and below which they would not be considered to be very high. As a general rule, the inferences concerning symptoms probably should not be included (or included cautiously) unless T scores on the scales in the code type are greater than 65. Obviously, when T scores are considerably higher than 65 there is an even greater likelihood that inferences concerning symptoms will be appropriate.

To illustrate, let us consider a protocol in which there is a defined 27/72 code type. The list of descriptors associated with this code type (which is presented later in this chapter) includes statements about anxiety and depression as well as statements about personality characteristics, including insecurity, perfectionism, and passive–dependent relationships. If the scores on Scales 2 and 7 are high (T > 65), we would include inferences about symptoms of anxiety and depression and about the personality characteristics just listed. However, if the scores on Scales 2 and 7 are not high (T < 65), we would not make the inferences about anxiety and depression but would make inferences about insecurity, perfectionism, and passive–dependent relationships. Obviously the T-score cutoff of 65 is somewhat arbitrary, and judgment would be involved with scores that are near this level.

If the ten Clinical scales are used interchangeably and profile definition is not required, 90 two-point code types and 720 three-point code types are possible. The code types for which interpretive information is provided in this chapter are those that occur reasonably frequently in a variety of settings and for which an adequate amount of interpretive information is available in the literature.[1] Some investigators have reported correlates of infrequently occurring code types (e.g., Kelley & King, 1979c; Tanner, 1990). The results of these studies are not included in this chapter because the samples were relatively small and cross-validational studies have not been reported.

Descriptors for the various MMPI and MMPI-2 code types in this chapter are based on research studies comparing persons with a particular code type with other persons in the same setting without that code type. It should be emphasized that the descriptors for two- and three-point code types were not rationally generated by combining descriptors for the individual scales included in the code types. It also should be understood that the descriptions that follow are modal patterns and obviously do not describe unfailingly each person with a specific code type. Rather, the descriptors presented for a particular code type are more likely to apply to persons with that code type than

---

[1]The following sources were consulted in preparing the descriptors of code types: Anderson and Bauer (1985); Arbisi et al. (2003a); Archer et al. (1995); Carson (1969); Dahlstrom, Welsh, and Dahlstrom (1972); Davis and Sines (1971); Drake and Oetting (1959); Duckworth and Anderson (1986); Gilberstadt and Duker (1965); Good and Brantner (1961); Graham et al. (1999); Gynther et al. (1973); Hovey and Lewis (1967); Kelley and King (1979a,b); Lachar (1974a); Lewandowski and Graham (1972); Marks et al. (1974); Merritt, Balogh, and Kok (1998); Nelson and Marks (1985); Persons and Marks (1971); and Sellbom, Graham, and Schenk (2005).

to persons without that code type. The descriptive information is not presented separately by gender because most earlier research did not analyze data by gender and most MMPI-2 studies have found far more similarities than differences in correlates for men and women (e.g., Graham, Ben-Porath, & McNulty, 1999). For profiles that do not have defined two- or three-point code types, interpretations should be based on scores on the individual Clinical scales (see Chapter 4 of this book).

RELIABILITY OF CODE TYPES

Because MMPI/MMPI-2 interpretive strategies have emphasized configural aspects of profiles, it is important to consider the temporal stability of such configurations. Many clinicians assume that because the individual Clinical scales have reasonably good temporal stability, the configurations based on those scales also have good temporal stability. Only limited data are available concerning the stability of scale configurations for the MMPI-2. Because of the continuity between the original and revised instruments, it can be assumed that the stability of MMPI-2 configurations is very similar to the stability of configurations on the original MMPI.

Table 5.1 summarizes the results of studies that have reported stability of one-, two-, and three-point code types for the original MMPI. Although the kinds of settings and test–retest intervals have differed across studies, the results have been consistent. About one-half of persons have had the same high-point code type on two administrations, about one-fourth to one-third have had the same two-point code type, and about one-fourth have had the same three-point code type. It should be recognized that the stability indicated by these studies is lower than would be expected if the analyses had been limited to well-defined code types.

Graham, Smith, et al. (1986) concluded that no particular MMPI high- or two-point code type was significantly more stable than other code types. They also reported that configurations tended to be more stable when the scales in the code types were more elevated initially and when there was a greater difference between these scales and other scales in the profile. When code types changed from test to retest administrations, the second code type often was in the same diagnostic grouping (neurotic, psychotic, characterological) as was the first code type. From one-half to two-thirds of the code types were in the same diagnostic grouping on test and retest. When the code types were from different diagnostic groupings on test and retest, the most frequent change was from psychotic on the initial test to characterological on the retest. The implication of these data is that many of the inferences that would be made would be the same even though the patients did not have exactly the same two-point code type on the two occasions.

What about patients whose code types changed from one major diagnostic grouping on the initial test to another major grouping on the retest? Were these changes due to the unreliability of the MMPI, or did they reflect significant

Table 5.1 Percentages of High-Point, Two-Point, and Three-Point MMPI Codes Remaining the Same on Retest[a]

SOURCE	SAMPLE	N	GENDER	TEST–RETEST	HIGH POINT	TWO POINT	THREE POINT
Ben-Porath and Butcher (1989b)	College student	86	M	1–2 weeks	54	35	—
Chojnacki and Walsh (1992)	College student	86	M	1–2 weeks	64	42	43
Chojnacki and Walsh (1992)	College student	94	F	1–2 weeks	57	45	45
Graham (1977)	College student	43	M	1 week	51	35	23
Graham (1977)	College student	36	F	1 week	50	31	28
Fashingbauer (1974)	College student/psychiatric	61	M/F	1 day	63	41	23
Lichenstein and Bryan (1966)	Volunteer/ psychiatric	82	M/F	1–2 days	50	—	—
Kincannon (1968)	Psychiatric	60	M/F	1–2 days	61	—	—
Pauker (1966)	Psychiatric	107	F	13–176 days	44	25	—
Sivanich (1960)[b]	Psychiatric	202	F	2–2230 days	48	20	—
Uecker (1969)	Organic	30	M	1 week	—	23	—
Lauber and Dahlstrom (1953)	Delinquent	19	F	?	90	95	—

[a]For two-point and three-point codes, scales are used interchangeably.

[b]Used only four two-point codes (4–6, 4–2, 6–8, 2–7).

SOURCE: Graham, J.R., Smith, R.L., & Schwartz, G.F. (1986). Stability of MMPI configurations for psychiatric inpatients. *Journal of Consulting and Clinical Psychology, 54,* 375–380. Copyright © 1986 by the American Psychological Association. Adapted by permission of the publisher.

changes in the status of the patients? Graham, Smith, et al. (1986) addressed this issue to a limited extent. They studied psychiatric inpatients who produced psychotic two-point code types at the time of the initial testing and nonpsychotic code types at the time of retesting. They compared these patients with patients who had psychotic code types for both administrations or for neither administration. External psychiatric ratings of psychotic behaviors were available for patients. Patients whose code types changed from psychotic to nonpsychotic showed concomitant changes in psychiatric ratings. Patients who had nonpsychotic code types on both administrations were given relatively low psychosis ratings on both occasions. Complicating the results of the study was the finding that patients who had psychotic code types on both test and retest were given lower psychosis ratings at retest than at the time of the initial test. The psychiatrists who completed the ratings also were case managers for the patients they rated. It may be that they were reluctant to indicate that patients that they were treating, and perhaps were about ready to discharge from the hospital, had not shown decreases in psychotic behaviors.

Graham, Timbrook, et al. (1991) reported temporal stability of one-, two-, and three-point code types for the MMPI-2 normative sample The percentages of one-point, two-point, and three-point code types that remained the same for retesting a week later were 49%, 26%, and 15%, respectively. Because the subgroup of the normative sample who took the test twice was relatively small, the analysis of Graham, Timbrook, et al. could not be restricted to well-defined code types. Thus, the obtained percentages are somewhat lower than would be expected if only well-defined code types had been used in the analyses.

Ryan, Dunn, and Paolo (1995) reported code-type stability for two groups of substance abusers with test–retest intervals of 5 and 13 months. For the shorter interval, 31% of the abusers had the same one-point code type, 20% had the same two-point code type, and 14% had the same three-point code type. For the longer interval, 35% had the same one-point code type, 12% had the same two-point code type, and 6% had the same one-point code type. As with the study of Graham, Timbrook, et al. (1991), these values probably would have been higher if only defined code types had been used. In addition, some of the changes in code types for these abusers could have been reflecting actual changes that occurred during an active treatment program.

Munley et al. (2004) used a simulation design to estimate the effects on stability of varying degrees of code-type definition. As expected, they found that stability of two-point code types increased from 37% with three-point definition to 78% with ten-point definition. Consistent with these findings are those of Livingston, Jennings, Colotla, Reynolds, and Shercliffe (2006), who found that code types of injured workers were more stable over a 21-month period when the initial code types were well defined.

In summary, research findings support that code types are relatively stable over time and that well-defined code types are likely to be more stable than those that are not well defined. When code types change from one testing to another, changes typically are not dramatic, and inferences based on the two code types are likely to be very similar. Clearly, more research is needed to determine to what extent well-defined code types are stable over time and if some code types tend to be more stable than others.

VALIDITY OF CODE TYPES

The validity of code types can be demonstrated to the extent that there are relevant extratest correlates for specific code types that differentiate them from protocols that do not have the code type. Because of the similarities between the MMPI and MMPI-2, we are able to draw on research using both instruments in examining extratest correlates. Gynther, Altman, and Sletten (1973) and Lewandowski and Graham (1972) demonstrated that reliable extratest correlates could be identified for profiles that were classified according to their two highest Clinical scales. Graham, Ben Porath, et al. (1999) determined correlates of two- and three-point MMPI-2 code types for mental health center outpatients. Correlates of code types for private practice clients were identified by Sellbom, Graham, and Schenk (2005). Arbisi, Ben-Porath, and McNulty (2003a) and Archer, Griffin, and Aiduk (1995) reported correlates for commonly occurring two-point code types for psychiatric inpatients. These studies demonstrated that the MMPI-2 code-type correlates were quite stable across settings and consistent with those previously reported for the original MMPI.

INTERPRETIVE GUIDELINES FOR TWO-POINT CODE TYPES

12/21

The most prominent feature of the 12/21 code type is somatic discomfort. Individuals with this code type present themselves as physically ill, although there may be no clinical evidence of an organic basis for their symptoms. They are preoccupied with health and bodily functions, and they are likely to overreact to minor physical dysfunction. They may present multiple somatic complaints, or the symptoms may be restricted to a particular system. Although headaches and cardiac complaints may occur, the digestive system is more likely to be involved. Ulcers, particularly of the upper gastrointestinal tract, are common, and anorexia, nausea, and vomiting may be present. Individuals with the 12/21 code type also may complain of dizziness, insomnia, weakness, fatigue, and tiredness. They tend to react to stress with physical symptoms, and they resist attempts to explain their symptoms in terms of emotional or psychological factors.

Persons with the 12/21 code type may report feelings of depression, unhappiness, or dysphoria; brooding; and loss of initiative. They also may feel anxious, tense, and nervous. They are high-strung and prone to worry about many things, and they tend to be restless and irritable.

Persons with the 12/21 code type report feeling very self-conscious. They are introverted and shy in social situations, particularly with members of the opposite sex, and they tend to be somewhat withdrawn and seclusive. They harbor many doubts about their own abilities, and they are indecisive about even minor, everyday matters. They are hypersensitive concerning what other people think about them, and they may be somewhat suspicious and untrusting in interpersonal relations. They also tend to be passive–dependent in their relationships, and they may harbor anger and hostility toward people who are perceived as not offering enough attention and support.

Excessive use of alcohol may be a problem for individuals with the 12/21 code type, especially among psychiatric patients. Their histories may include blackouts, job loss, arrests, and family problems associated with alcohol abuse. Persons with the 12/21 code type most often are given diagnoses of anxiety disorders, depressive disorders, or somatoform disorders, although a small proportion of individuals with this code type have diagnoses of schizophrenia. In this latter group (schizophrenia), Scale 8 usually is elevated, along with Scales 1 and 2.

Individuals with the 12/21 code type are not seen as good risks for traditional psychotherapy. They can tolerate high levels of discomfort before becoming motivated to change. They utilize repression and somatization excessively, and they lack insight and self-understanding. In addition, their passive–dependent lifestyles make it difficult for them to accept responsibility for their own behavior. Although long-term change after psychotherapy is not likely, short-lived symptomatic changes often occur.

13/31

The 13/31 code type is more common among women and older persons than among men and younger persons. Psychiatric patients with the 13/31 code often have somatoform disorder or pain disorder diagnoses. Classical conversion symptoms may be present, particularly if Scales 1 and 3 are very elevated and Scale 2 is considerably lower than Scales 1 and 3 (i.e., the so-called conversion-V pattern). Whereas some anxiety and depression may be reported by 13/31 persons, they typically are not experiencing disabling emotional turmoil. Rather than being grossly incapacitated in functioning, the 13/31 individual is likely to continue functioning but at a reduced level of efficiency. In inpatient settings, persons with the 13/31 code sometimes report somatic delusions.

The somatic complaints presented by 13/31 persons include headaches, chest pain, back pain, and numbness or tremors of the extremities. Eating problems, including anorexia, nausea, vomiting, and obesity, are common. Other physical complaints include weakness, fatigue, dizziness, and sleep disturbance. The physical symptoms increase in times of stress, and often there is clear secondary gain associated with the symptoms.

Individuals with the 13/31 code type may present themselves as psychologically normal, responsible, and without fault. They make excessive use of denial, projection, and rationalization, and they blame others for their difficulties. They prefer medical explanations for their symptoms, and they lack insight into the psychological factors underlying their symptoms. They manifest an overly optimistic and Pollyannaish view of their situations and of the world in general, and they do not show appropriate concern about their symptoms and problems.

Persons with the 13/31 code type tend to be rather immature, egocentric, selfish, and histrionic. They are insecure and have a strong need for attention, affection, and sympathy. They are very dependent, but they are uncomfortable with the dependency and experience conflict because of it. Although they tend to be outgoing and socially extroverted, their social relationships tend to be shallow and superficial, and they lack genuine emotional involvement with other people. They tend to exploit social relationships in an attempt to fulfill their own needs. They lack skills in dealing with the opposite sex, and they may be deficient in heterosexual drive.

Individuals with the 13/31 code type harbor resentment and hostility toward other people, particularly those who are perceived as not fulfilling their needs for attention. Most of the time they are overcontrolled and likely to express their negative feelings in indirect, passive ways, but they occasionally lose their tempers and express themselves in angry, but not violent, ways. Behaving in a socially acceptable manner is important to persons with this code type. They need to convince other people that they are logical and reasonable, and they are conventional and conforming in their attitudes and values.

Because of their unwillingness to acknowledge psychological factors underlying their symptoms, persons with the 13/31 code type are difficult to motivate in traditional psychotherapy. They are reluctant to discuss psychological factors that might be related to somatic symptoms, and if therapists insist on doing so, people with this code type are likely to terminate therapy prematurely. Sometimes it is possible to get these persons to discuss problems as long as no direct link to somatic symptoms is suggested. In therapy they expect therapists to provide definite answers and solutions to their problems, and they may terminate therapy when therapists fail to respond to their demands. Because 13/31 persons tend to be suggestible, they often will try activities suggested by their therapists.

14/41

The 14/41 code type is not encountered frequently in clinical practice and is much more likely to be found for men than for women. Persons with the 14/41 code type frequently report severe somatic symptoms, particularly nonspecific headaches. They also may appear to be indecisive and anxious. Although they are socially extroverted, they lack skills with members of the opposite sex. They may feel rebellious toward home and parents, but direct expression of these feelings is not likely. Excessive use of alcohol may be a problem, and persons with the 14/41 code type may have a history of alcoholic benders, job loss, and family problems associated with their drinking behavior. In school or on the job, they lack drive and do not have well-defined goals. They are dissatisfied and pessimistic in their outlook toward life, and they are demanding, grouchy, and often referred to as "bitchy" in interpersonal relationships. Because they are likely to deny psychological problems, they tend to be resistant to traditional psychotherapy.

18/81

Persons with the 18/81 code type often harbor feelings of hostility and aggression, and they are not able to express these feelings in a modulated, adaptive manner. Either they inhibit expression almost completely, which results in feelings of being "bottled up," or they are overly belligerent and abrasive.

Individuals with the 18/81 code type feel socially inadequate, especially around members of the opposite sex. They lack trust in other people, keep them at a distance, and feel generally isolated and alienated. A nomadic lifestyle and a poor work history are common.

Psychiatric patients with the 18/81 code type often have diagnoses of schizophrenia, although diagnoses of anxiety disorders and schizoid personality disorder are sometimes given. These persons tend to be unhappy and depressed, and they may display flat affect. They often acknowledge having ideas about killing themselves. They present somatic concerns (including headaches and insomnia), which at times are so intense that they border on being delusional. Persons with this code type also may be confused in their thinking, and they are very distractible.

19/91

Persons with the 19/91 code type are likely to be experiencing a great deal of distress and turmoil. They tend to be very anxious, tense, and restless. Somatic complaints, including gastrointestinal problems, headaches, and exhaustion, are common, and they are reluctant to accept psychological explanations of their symptoms. Although on the surface persons with the 19/91 code type appear to be verbal, socially extroverted, aggressive, and belligerent, they are basically passive–dependent persons who are trying to deny this aspect of their personalities.

Individuals with the 19/91 code type often appear to have a great deal of ambition. They expect a high level of achievement from themselves, but they lack clear and definite goals. They are frustrated by their inability to achieve at a high level. The 19/91 code type is sometimes found for brain-damaged individuals who are experiencing difficulties in coping with their limitations and deficits. It should be emphasized, however, that this code type or other MMPI-2 data should not be used to diagnose brain damage.

23/32

Although persons with the 23/32 code type typically do not experience disabling anxiety, they report feeling nervous, agitated, tense, and worried, and they often experience sleep disturbances. They also report feeling sad, unhappy, and depressed, and suicidal ideations may be present. Fatigue, exhaustion, weakness, and sleep disturbances are common. They lack interest and involvement in their life situations and have difficulty getting started on projects. Decreased physical activity is likely, and somatic complaints, usually gastrointestinal in nature, may occur.

Individuals with the 23/32 code type are rather passive, docile, and dependent. They are plagued by self-doubts, and they harbor feelings of inadequacy, insecurity, and helplessness. They tend to elicit helping behaviors from other people. However, persons with the 23/32 code type are very interested in achievement, status, and power. They may appear to be competitive, industrious, and driven, but they do not really place themselves in directly competitive situations where they might experience failure. They seek increased responsibility, but they dread the stress and pressure associated with it. They often feel that they do not get adequate recognition for their accomplishments, and they are easily hurt by even mild criticism.

Persons with the 23/32 code type tend to be emotionally overcontrolled. They have difficulty expressing their feelings, and they may feel bottled up much of the time. They tend to deny unacceptable impulses, and when denial fails they feel anxious and guilty. Persons with the 23/32 code type feel socially inadequate, and they tend to avoid social involvement. They are especially uncomfortable with members of the opposite sex, and low sex drive and sexual maladjustment, including frigidity or impotence, may be reported.

The 23/32 code type is more common for women than for men. Rather than indicating incapacitating symptoms, it suggests a lowered level of efficiency for prolonged periods. Problems are long-standing, and the individuals with this code type have learned to tolerate a great deal of unhappiness. Among psychiatric patients, depressive disorder diagnoses often are assigned to persons with the 23/32 code type. Antisocial personality disorder diagnoses are rare among persons with this code type.

Response to traditional psychotherapy is likely to be poor for persons with the 23/32 code type. They are not introspective; they lack insight into their own behavior; they resist psychological formulations of their problems; and they tolerate a great deal of unhappiness before becoming motivated to change.

24/42

Persons with the 24/42 code type usually come to the attention of professionals after they have been in trouble with their families or with the law. They often appear to be angry, hostile, resentful, critical, argumentative, and untrusting. They are impulsive and unable to delay gratification of their impulses. They have little respect for social standards and often find themselves in direct conflict with societal values. Their acting-out behavior may involve excessive use of alcohol and other drugs, and their histories often include arrests, job loss, and family discord associated with substance abuse. Some patients with this code type have histories of eating disorders.

Individuals with the 24/42 code type feel frustrated by their own lack of accomplishment and are resentful of demands placed on them by other people. After periods of acting out, they may express a great deal of remorse and guilt about their misdeeds. They may report feeling depressed, anxious, and worthless, but others often question the sincerity of these expressions. Despite their resolutions to change, they are likely to act out again in the future. It has been noted in the literature that when Scales 2 and 4 are grossly elevated, suicidal ideation and attempts are quite possible. Often the suicide attempts seem to be directed at making other people feel guilty.

When they are not in trouble, 24/42 persons may seem to be energetic, sociable, and outgoing. They create favorable first impressions, but their tendencies to manipulate others produce feelings of resentment in long-term relationships. Beneath the outer facade of competent, comfortable persons, 24/42 individuals tend to be introverted, self-conscious, and passive–dependent. They harbor feelings of inadequacy and self-dissatisfaction, and they are uncomfortable in social interactions, particularly those involving the opposite sex. At times they appear to be rigid and overly intellectualized.

Personality disorder diagnoses often are given to persons with the 24/42 code type, although among persons seeking treatment, diagnoses of depression are common. Although persons with this code type may express the need for help and the desire to change, the prognosis for traditional psychotherapy is not good. They are likely to terminate therapy prematurely when the situational stress subsides or when they have extracted themselves from their current difficulties. Even when they stay in therapy, not much improvement is likely.

26/62

There is only limited research concerning the correlates of this code type. Patients with the 26/62 code type have been described as having prominent personality problems, including suspiciousness and mistrust, resentfulness, hostility, and aggressiveness. They also may be described as depressed and fatigued, and they may be preoccupied with health problems. These individuals generally do not cope well with stress, experience sleep disturbances, lack energy, and feel hopeless. Some of them have histories of suicide attempts.

27/72

Persons with the 27/72 code type tend to be anxious, tense, and high-strung. They worry excessively, and they are vulnerable to real and imagined threat. They tend to anticipate problems before they occur and to overreact to minor stress. Obsessive thoughts and compulsive behaviors often are reported. Somatic symptoms are common among persons with this code type and involve rather vague complaints of fatigue, tiredness, and exhaustion. Insomnia, anorexia, and bulimia may be reported. Persons with this code type often show symptoms of clinical depression, including feelings of sadness, weight loss, lack of energy, retarded thought processes, and suicidal ideation. They may speak slowly and hesitantly.

They feel pessimistic and hopeless about the world in general and more specifically about the likelihood of overcoming their problems, and they brood and ruminate about their problems much of the time. Individuals with the 27/72 code type are immature and have a strong need for achievement and for recognition for their accomplishments. They have high expectations for themselves, and they feel guilty when they fall short of their goals. They tend to be indecisive, and they harbor feelings of inadequacy, insecurity, and inferiority. They are intropunitive, blaming themselves for the problems in their life situations. Individuals with the 27/72 code type are rigid in their thinking and problem solving, and they are meticulous and perfectionist in their daily activities. They also may be very religious and extremely moralistic.

Persons with the 27/72 code type tend to be docile and passive–dependent in their relationships with other people. In fact, they often find it difficult to be even appropriately assertive. They have the capacity for forming deep, emotional ties, and in times of stress they become overly clinging and dependent. Not aggressive or belligerent, they tend to elicit nurturance and helping behavior from other people. Because of the intense discomfort they experience, they are motivated for psychotherapy. They tend to remain in psychotherapy longer than many patients, and slow but steady progress can be expected.

Psychiatric patients with the 27/72 code type often have diagnoses of anxiety disorder, depressive disorder, or obsessive–compulsive disorder. Diagnoses of antisocial personality disorder are rare among persons with this code type.

28/82

Persons with the 28/82 code type often report feeling anxious, agitated, tense, and jumpy. Sleep disturbance, inability to concentrate, confused thinking, and forgetfulness also characterize them. Such persons are inefficient in carrying out their responsibilities, and they tend to be unoriginal in their thinking and problem solving. They are likely to present themselves as physically ill, and somatic complaints may include dizziness, blackout spells, overeating, nausea, or vomiting. They resist psychological interpretations of their problems, and they are resistant to change. They underestimate the seriousness of their problems, and they tend to be unrealistic about their own capabilities.

Individuals with the 28/82 code type are basically dependent and ineffective, and they have problems in being assertive. They are irritable and resentful much of the time, fear loss of control, and do not express themselves directly. They attempt to deny undesirable impulses, and cognitive dissociative periods during which negative emotions are expressed may occur. Such periods are followed by guilt and depression. Persons with the 28/82 code type are sensitive to the reactions of others, and they are suspicious of the motivations of others. They may have histories of being hurt emotionally, and they fear being hurt again. They avoid close interpersonal relationships, and they keep people at a distance emotionally. This lack of meaningful involvement with other people increases their feelings of despair and worthlessness.

If both Scales 2 and 8 are very elevated, the 28/82 code type is suggestive of serious and chronic psychopathology. The most common diagnoses given to psychiatric patients with this code type are bipolar disorder and schizoaffective disorder. This is a common code type among patients who have been assigned posttraumatic stress disorder diagnoses. Individuals with this code type may be guilt-ridden and appear to be clinically depressed. Withdrawal, flat affect, soft and reduced speech, retarded stream of thought, and tearfulness also are common. Psychiatric patients with the 28/82 code type may be preoccupied with suicidal thoughts, and they may have a specific plan for doing away with themselves.

29/92

Persons with the 29/92 code type tend to be self-centered and narcissistic. They ruminate excessively about self-worth. Although they may express concern about achieving at a high level, it often appears that they set themselves up for failure. In younger persons, the 29/92 code type may be suggestive of an identity crisis characterized by lack of personal and vocational direction.

Persons with this code type report feeling tense and anxious, and somatic complaints, often centering in the upper gastrointestinal tract, are common. Although they may not appear to be clinically depressed at the time they are examined, their histories typically suggest periods of serious depression. Excessive use of alcohol may be employed as an escape from stress and pressure.

The 29/92 code type suggests individuals who are denying underlying feelings of inadequacy and worthlessness and defending against depression through excessive activity. Alternating periods of increased activity and fatigue may occur. Psychiatric patients with the 29/92 code type often have diagnoses of bipolar disorder. This code type sometimes is found for patients with brain damage who have lost emotional control or who are trying to cope with deficits through excessive activity. It should be emphasized, however, that this code type or other MMPI-2 information should not be used to diagnose brain damage.

34/43

The most salient characteristic of 34/43 persons is chronic, intense anger. They harbor hostile and aggressive impulses, but they are unable to express their negative feelings appropriately. If Scale 3 is significantly higher than Scale 4, passive, indirect expression of anger is likely. Persons with Scale 4 significantly higher than Scale 3 appear to be overcontrolled most of the time, but brief episodes of aggressive acting out may occur. Prisoners with the 4–3 code type often have histories of violent crimes. In some rare instances, individuals with the 34/43 code type successfully dissociate themselves from their aggressive acting-out behavior. Individuals with this code type lack insight into the origins and consequences of their behavior. They tend to be extrapunitive, blaming other people for their difficulties. Although others are likely to define the behavior of persons with this code type as problematic, they are not likely to view it in the same way.

Persons with the 34/43 code type are reasonably free of disabling anxiety and depression, but complaints of headaches, upper gastrointestinal discomfort, and other somatic distress may occur. Although these persons may feel upset at times, the upset does not seem to be related directly to external stress. Histories of excessive use of alcohol and other substances frequently are associated with this code type.

Many of the difficulties of persons with the 34/43 code type may stem from deep, chronic feelings of hostility toward family members. They demand attention and approval from others. They tend to be cynical and suspicious of others. They are sensitive to rejection, and they become hostile when criticized. Although outwardly they appear to be socially conforming, inwardly they are quite rebellious. They may be sexually maladjusted, and marital instability and sexual promiscuity are common. Suicidal thoughts and attempts are characteristic of individuals with the 34/43 code type; these are most likely to follow episodes of excessive drinking and acting-out behavior. Personality disorder diagnoses, especially passive–aggressive, often are associated with the 34/43 code type, and substance abuse/dependence diagnoses may also be assigned.

36/63

Individuals with the 36/63 code type may report moderate tension and anxiety and may have physical complaints, including headaches and gastrointestinal discomfort, but their problems do not seem to be acute or incapacitating. Most of their difficulties stem from deep, chronic feelings of hostility toward family members. They do not express these feelings directly, and much of the time they may not even recognize the hostile feelings. When they become aware of their anger, they try to justify it in terms of the behavior of others. In general, individuals with the 36/63 code type are defiant, uncooperative, and hard to get along with. They may express mild suspiciousness of and resentment about others, and they are very self-centered and narcissistic. They deny serious psychological problems and express a very naive, Pollyannaish attitude toward the world.

38/83

Persons with the 38/83 code type appear to be in a great deal of psychological turmoil. They report feeling anxious, tense, and nervous. Also, they are fearful and worried, and phobias may be present. Depression and feelings of hopelessness are common among 38/83 individuals, and they have difficulties in making even minor decisions. A wide variety of physical complaints (e.g., gastrointestinal and musculoskeletal discomfort, dizziness, blurred vision, chest pain, genital pain, headaches, insomnia) may be presented. They tend to be vague and evasive when talking about their complaints and difficulties.

Persons with the 38/83 code type are rather immature and dependent and have strong needs for attention and affection. They are not involved actively in their life situations, and they are apathetic and pessimistic. They approach problems in an unoriginal, stereotyped manner.

The 38/83 code type suggests the possibility of disturbed thinking, especially if both scales are quite elevated. Individuals with this code type may complain of not being able to think clearly, problems in concentration, and lapses of memory. They often express unusual, unconventional ideas, and their ideational associations may be rather loose. Obsessive ruminations, blatant delusions and/or hallucinations, and irrelevant, incoherent speech may be present. The most common diagnosis for psychiatric patients with the 38/83 code type is schizophrenia, but sometimes somatoform disorder diagnoses are assigned. Although response to insight-oriented psychotherapy is not likely to be good for persons with this code type, they often benefit from a supportive psychotherapeutic relationship.

46/64

Persons with the 46/64 code type seem to be immature, narcissistic, and self-indulgent. They are passive–dependent individuals who make excessive demands on others for attention and sympathy, but they are resentful of even the most mild demands made on them by others. Women with the 46/64 code type seem overly identified with the traditional female role and may be very dependent on men. Both men and women with this code type do not get along well with others in social situations, and they are especially uncomfortable around members of the opposite sex. They are suspicious of the motivations of others, feel that they are getting a raw deal from life, and avoid deep emotional involvement. They often have poor work histories, and marital problems are quite common. Repressed hostility and anger are characteristic of persons with the 46/64 code type. They may appear to be sarcastic, irritable, sullen, argumentative, and generally obnoxious. They seem to be especially resentful of authority and may derogate authority figures.

Individuals with the 46/64 code type tend to deny serious psychological problems. They rationalize and transfer blame to others, especially family members, accepting little or no responsibility for their own behavior. They are somewhat unrealistic and grandiose in their self-appraisals. Because they deny serious emotional problems, they generally are not receptive to traditional counseling or psychotherapy.

Among psychiatric patients, frequent diagnoses associated with the 46/64 code are passive–aggressive personality disorder and schizophrenia, paranoid type. Concerns about psychotic disorder are greater when Scales 4 and 6 are very elevated and when Scale 6 is higher than Scale 4. Psychiatric patients with this code type often have histories of substance abuse and difficulties with the law. Individuals with the 46/64 code type present vague emotional and physical complaints. They report feeling nervous and depressed, and they are indecisive and insecure. Physical symptoms may include asthma, hay fever, hypertension, headaches, blackout spells, and cardiac complaints.

47/74

Persons with the 47/74 code type may alternate between periods of gross insensitivity to the consequences of their actions and excessive concern about the effects of their behavior on others. Episodes of acting out, which may include excessive drinking and sexual promiscuity, may be followed by temporary expressions of guilt and self-condemnation. However, the remorse typically does not inhibit further episodes of acting out. Individuals with the 47/74 code type may present vague somatic complaints, including headaches and stomach pain. They also may report feeling tense, fatigued, and exhausted. They are rather dependent, insecure individuals who require almost constant reassurance of their self-worth. Passive–aggressive personality disorder diagnoses often are assigned to persons with the 47/74 code type. In psychotherapy, persons with this code type tend to respond symptomatically to support and reassurance, but long-term changes in personality are unlikely.

48/84

Individuals with the 48/84 code type do not seem to fit into their environments. They are seen by others as odd, peculiar, and queer. They are nonconforming and resentful of authority, and they may espouse radical religious or political views. Their behavior is erratic and unpredictable, and they have marked problems with impulse control. They do not seem to profit from their mistakes. They tend to be angry, irritable, and resentful, and they may act out in asocial or antisocial ways. When crimes are committed by persons with this code type, they tend to be vicious and assaultive and often appear to be senseless, poorly planned, and poorly executed. Prostitution, promiscuity, and sexual deviation are fairly common among individuals with the 48/84 code type. This is a common code type among male rapists. Excessive drinking and drug abuse (particularly involving hallucinogens) may also occur. Histories of individuals with this code type usually indicate underachievement, uneven performance, marginal adjustment, and irresponsibility.

Persons with the 48/84 code type harbor deep feelings of insecurity, and they have exaggerated needs for attention and affection. They have poor self-concepts, and it seems as if they set themselves up for rejection and failure. They may have periods during which they feel agitated and depressed and become obsessed with suicidal ideation. They are quite distrustful of other people, and they avoid close relationships. When they are involved interpersonally, they have impaired empathy and try to manipulate others into satisfying their needs. They lack basic social skills and tend to be socially withdrawn and isolated. The world is seen as a threatening and rejecting place, and their response is to withdraw or to strike out in anger as a defense against being hurt. They accept little responsibility for their own behavior, and they rationalize excessively, blaming their difficulties on other people. Persons with this code type tend to harbor serious concerns about their masculinity or femininity. Psychiatric patients with this code type are more likely than many other patients to have histories of being sexually abused. They may be obsessed with sexual thoughts, but they are afraid that they cannot perform adequately in sexual situations. They may indulge in excessive fantasy and/or antisocial sexual acts in an attempt to cope with these feelings of inadequacy.

Psychiatric patients with the 48/84 code type tend to have diagnoses of schizophrenia and/or antisocial, schizoid, or paranoid personality disorder. If both Scales 4 and 8 are very elevated, and particularly if Scale 8 is much higher than Scale 4, the likelihood of psychosis and bizarre symptomatology, including hallucinations, unusual thinking, and paranoid suspiciousness, increases.

49/94

When both scales in the 49/94 code type are very elevated a marked disregard for social standards and values is likely. Such persons frequently get in trouble with the authorities because of antisocial behavior. They have a poorly developed conscience, easy morals, and fluctuating ethical values. Alcoholism, fighting, marital problems, sexual acting out, and a wide array of delinquent acts are among the difficulties in which they may be involved. This is a common code type among persons who abuse alcohol and other substances.

Individuals with the 49/94 code type are narcissistic, selfish, and self-indulgent. They are quite impulsive and are unable to delay gratification of their impulses. They show poor judgment, often acting without considering the consequences of their acts, and they fail to learn from experience. They are not willing to accept responsibility for their own behavior, rationalizing shortcomings and failures and blaming difficulties on other people. They have a low tolerance for frustration, and they often appear to be moody, irritable, and caustic. They harbor intense feelings of anger and hostility, and these feelings are expressed in occasional emotional outbursts.

Persons with the 49/94 code type tend to be ambitious and energetic, and they are restless and overactive. They are likely to seek out emotional stimulation and excitement. In social situations they tend to be uninhibited, extroverted, and talkative, and they create a good first impression. However, because of their self-centeredness and distrust of people, their relationships are likely to be superficial and not particularly rewarding. They seem to be incapable of forming deep emotional ties, and they keep others at an emotional distance. Beneath the facade of self-confidence and security, individuals with the 49/94 code type are immature, insecure, and dependent persons who are trying to deny these aspects of themselves. A diagnosis of antisocial personality disorder is often associated with the 49/94 code type, although psychiatric patients with this code type sometimes have symptoms of paranoid or bipolar disorders.

68/86

Persons with the 68/86 code type harbor intense feelings of inferiority and insecurity. They lack self-confidence and self-esteem, and they feel guilty about perceived failures. Anxiety, depression, withdrawal from everyday activities, and emotional apathy are common. Feelings of hopelessness and pessimism and suicidal ideation may be present.

Persons with the 68/86 code type are not likely to be emotionally involved with other people, and they tend to have histories of having few or no friends. They are suspicious and distrustful of others, and they avoid deep emotional ties. They are seriously deficient in social skills, and they are most comfortable when alone. They are quite resentful of demands placed on them, and other people see them as moody, irritable, unfriendly, and negativistic. They do not make good first impressions, are seen by others as odd or strange, are not very work oriented, and do not have strong achievement orientations. In general, their lifestyles can be characterized as schizoid.

Diagnoses of paranoid or schizoid personality disorders are common among persons with this code type. Psychiatric patients with this code type often are assigned a diagnosis of schizophrenia, paranoid type, particularly if Scales 6 and 8 are both quite elevated and are considerably higher than Scale 7. Such individuals are likely to manifest clearly psychotic behavior. Thinking is described as autistic, fragmented, tangential, and circumstantial, and thought content is likely to be bizarre. Difficulties in concentrating and attending, deficits in memory, and poor judgment are common. Delusions of persecution and/ or grandeur and hallucinations may be present, and feelings of unreality may be reported.

Persons with the 68/86 code type often are preoccupied with abstract or theoretical matters to the exclusion of specific, concrete aspects of their life situations. Affect may be blunted, and speech may be rapid and at times incoherent. Effective defenses seem to be lacking, and these persons respond to stress and pressure by withdrawing into fantasy and daydreaming. Often it is difficult for persons with this code to differentiate between fantasy and reality. Medical consultation to determine appropriateness of antipsychotic medication should be considered.

69/96

Persons with the 69/96 code type are rather dependent and have strong needs for affection. They are vulnerable to real or imagined threat, and they feel anxious and tense much of the time. In addition, they may appear to be tearful and trembling. A marked overreaction to minor stress also is characteristic of persons with the 69/96 code type. A typical response to severe stress is withdrawal into fantasy. These individuals are unable to express emotions in an adaptive, modulated way, and they may alternate between overcontrol and direct, undercontrolled emotional outbursts.

Psychiatric patients with the 69/96 code type frequently have diagnoses of schizophrenia, paranoid type, and they are likely to show signs of thought disorder, especially if both scales are quite elevated. They complain of difficulties in thinking and concentrating, and their stream of thought may be retarded. They are ruminative, overideational, and obsessional. They may have delusions and hallucinations, and their speech seems to be irrelevant and incoherent. They may appear to be disoriented and perplexed, and they may show poor judgment.

78/87

Individuals with the 78/87 code type typically are in a great deal of emotional turmoil. They are not hesitant to admit to psychological problems, and they seem to lack adequate defenses to keep themselves reasonably comfortable. They report feeling depressed and pessimistic, and they may experience suicidal ideation. They also tend to be worried, tense, and anxious, and they are preoccupied with health problems. When first seen professionally, they may appear to be confused and in a state of panic. They show poor judgment and do not seem to profit from experience. They are introspective, ruminative, and overideational.

Persons with the 78/87 code type harbor chronic feelings of insecurity, inadequacy, and inferiority, and they tend to be indecisive. They lack even an average number of socialization experiences, are not socially poised or confident, and withdraw from social interactions. They are passive–dependent individuals who are unable to take a dominant role in interpersonal relationships. Mature heterosexual relationships are especially difficult for them. They often feel quite inadequate in the traditional sex role, and sexual performance may be poor. In an apparent attempt to compensate for these deficits, they may engage in rich sexual fantasies.

Diagnoses of schizophrenia, depressive disorders, obsessive–compulsive disorders, posttraumatic stress disorder, and personality disorders are all represented among individuals with the 78/87 code type. Schizoid is the most common personality disorder diagnosis assigned to persons with this code type. The relative elevations of Scales 7 and 8 are important in differentiating psychotic from nonpsychotic disorders. When Scale 8 is much higher than Scale 7, the likelihood of a psychotic disorder is greater. Even when a psychotic label is applied to persons with the 78/87 code type, blatant psychotic symptoms may not be present.

89/98

Persons with the 89/98 code type tend to be rather self-centered and infantile in their expectations of other people. They demand a great deal of attention and may become resentful and hostile when their demands are not met. Because they fear emotional involvement, they avoid close relationships and tend to be socially withdrawn and isolated. They seem especially uncomfortable in heterosexual relationships, and poor sexual adjustment is common.

Individuals with this code type are characterized as hyperactive and emotionally labile. They appear to be agitated and excited, and they may talk excessively in a loud voice. They are unrealistic in self-appraisal, and they impress others as grandiose, boastful, and fickle. They are vague, evasive, and denying in talking about their difficulties, and they may state that they do not need professional help.

Although persons with the 89/98 code type have a high need to achieve and may feel pressured to do so, their actual performance tends to be mediocre at best. Their feelings of inferiority and inadequacy and their low self-esteem limit the extent to which they involve themselves in competitive or achievement-oriented situations. They engage in excessive fantasy and daydreaming.

The 89/98 code type is suggestive of serious psychological disturbance, particularly if Scales 8 and 9 are very elevated. The modal diagnosis for persons with this code type is schizophrenia, and severe disturbance in thinking may be evident. Such individuals are likely to be confused, perplexed, and disoriented, and they may report feelings of unreality. They have difficulty concentrating and thinking, and they are unable to focus on issues. Thinking also may appear to be odd, unusual, autistic, and circumstantial. Speech may be bizarre and may involve clang associations, neologisms, and echolalia. Delusions and hallucinations may be present.

INTERPRETIVE GUIDELINES FOR THREE-POINT CODE TYPES

As stated earlier in this chapter, three-point code types tell us which three Clinical scales are the highest in the profile. Far less research has been conducted concerning three-point code types than concerning two-point code types or single-scale scores. The three-point code types included in this section are those that occur reasonably frequently in a variety of clinical settings and for which some research data are available. Because profiles classified according to three-point code types result in rather homogeneous groupings, the descriptors presented for any particular code type are likely to fit many individuals with that code type rather well. However, it must again be emphasized that the descriptions provided represent modal patterns. Not every descriptor will apply to every person with a particular three-point code type.

123/213/231

Persons with this code type usually are diagnosed as having a somatoform disorder, anxiety disorder, or depressive disorder. Somatic complaints, particularly those associated with the gastrointestinal system, are common, and often there appears to be clear secondary gain associated with the symptoms. Persons with this code type often show signs of depression, and sleep disturbance, perplexity, despondency, and feelings of hopelessness and pessimism occur. They may feel that life is a strain and may abuse alcohol and other substances as a way of coping. They seem to be in conflict about dependency and self-assertion, and they often keep other people at an emotional distance. They tend to feel fatigued, to have a low energy level, and to have low sex drive. Such persons may show relatively good work and marital adjustment, but they are not very achievement oriented and rarely take risks in their lives.

132/312

This configuration, in which Scales 1 and 3 often are significantly higher than scale 2, has been referred to as the "conversion valley." Persons with this code type may show classic conversion symptoms, and diagnoses of conversion disorder, somatoform disorder, or pain disorder are common. Physical symptoms often develop during times of increased stress. Persons with this code type use denial and repression excessively, lack insight into the causes of their symptoms, and resist psychological explanations of their problems. Although these individuals are rather sociable, they tend to be passive–dependent in relationships. It is important for them to be liked and approved of by others, and their behavior typically is conforming and conventional. They tend to seek medical treatment for their symptoms and are likely to terminate treatment prematurely if they are pressed to deal with psychological matters.

138

Persons with this code type frequently have diagnoses of schizophrenia (paranoid type) or paranoid personality disorder. They are likely to have rather bizarre somatic symptoms that may be delusional in nature. Depressive episodes, suicidal ideation, and sexual and religious preoccupation may occur. Clear evidence of thought disorder may be observed. These individuals are agitated, excitable, loud, and short-tempered. They often have histories of excessive use of alcohol and feel restless and bored much of the time. They are ambivalent about forming close relationships, and they often feel suspicious and jealous.

139

Persons with this code type often are diagnosed as having a somatoform disorder or organic brain syndrome. If they are given the latter diagnosis, they may show spells of irritation, assaultiveness, and outbursts of temper. It should be emphasized that this code type or other MMPI-2 data should not be used to arrive at organic diagnoses.

237/273/372

Persons with this code type are likely to report physical complaints and symptoms of depression and anxiety. In addition, they may find it difficult to trust other people.

247/274/472

Persons with this code type frequently have diagnoses of passive–aggressive personality disorder. This is a very common code type among patients who abuse alcohol and/or other substances. Family and marital problems are common among these individuals. They may feel depressed and pessimistic, and they may experience suicidal ideation and obsessive–compulsive thoughts and behaviors. They also may feel anxious, fearful, worried, and high-strung. They overreact to stress and undercontrol impulses. They tend to be angry, hostile, and immature, with strong unfilled needs for attention and support, and they may feel that they are getting a raw deal from life. They may be in conflict about dependency and sexuality, and they are uncomfortable around members of the opposite sex. They tend to be phobic, ruminative, and overideational, and they experience guilt associated with anger. Although they often have strong achievement needs, they are afraid to compete for fear of failing. They have difficulty enduring anxiety during treatment, and they may respond best to directive, goal-oriented treatment.

278/728

Persons with this code type are experiencing a great deal of emotional turmoil, and they tend to have rather schizoid lifestyles. They tend to feel tense, nervous, and fearful, and they have problems in concentrating and attending. They may also feel sad, depressed, despondent, pessimistic, and hopeless, and they often ruminate about suicide. Affect appears to be blunted or otherwise inappropriate. Multiple somatic complaints may be presented, and eating problems often are reported by women with this code type. Psychiatric patients with this code type are more likely than other patients to have histories of having been sexually abused. These persons lack basic social skills and are shy, withdrawn, introverted, and socially isolated. They tend to be passive in relationships. They feel inadequate and inferior. They tend to set high standards for themselves and to feel guilty when these standards are not met. They tend to show interest in obscure, esoteric subjects. They may use alcohol or other drugs as a way of coping with stress.

The diagnostic picture for the 278/728 code type is mixed. Diagnoses of depressive disorders, anxiety disorders, and psychotic disorders all occur frequently. In making a differential diagnosis it often is helpful to try to understand why Scale 8 is elevated along with Scales 2 and 7. If examination of the Harris–Lingoes subscales indicates that the Scale 8 elevation is accounted for primarily by items in the Sc3 (Lack of Ego Mastery, Cognitive) or Sc6 (Bizarre Sensory Experiences) subscales, a psychotic disorder is more likely than if items in the Sc4 (Lack of Ego Mastery, Conative) seem to account for much of the Scale 8 elevation. High scores on the Bizarre Mentation (BIZ) Content scale and/or the RC8 (Aberrant Experiences) scale also support psychotic diagnoses. Patients with the 278/728 code type often receive Axis II diagnoses of paranoid, schizoid, or schizotypal personality disorders.

468/648/684/846/864

There is not much research concerning the correlates of this code type. However, mental health center clients with this code type have been described as being in acute psychological turmoil. They were anxious, depressed, and agitated. They were more likely than other clients to have Axis I diagnoses of depression or dysthymia and Axis II diagnoses of antisocial personality disorder. They also were more likely to have histories of previous psychiatric hospitalizations, suicide attempts, and having been physically abused. Some of these clients had psychotic symptoms, including paranoid ideation. They tended to be antisocial and to have low tolerance for frustration. They were seen as critical, hostile, angry, aggressive, argumentative, and resentful. They often had family and work problems.

478/487/748/784/847/874

Although there are limited data concerning correlates of this code type, mental health center clients with the 478/748 code type have been described as having psychotic symptoms, including delusions, hallucinations, loose cognitive associations, and poor reality testing. They were characterized as eccentric and suspicious, and they tended to have histories of psychiatric hospitalizations. Depression, suicidal ideations, anxiety, and agitation also were characteristic of clients with this code type. They were seen as histrionic, insecure, and introverted persons who tended to make self-degrading comments and to engage in self-punishing behaviors.

687/867

This code type, in which Scales 6 and 8 typically are much more elevated than Scale 7, has been referred to as the "psychotic valley." It suggests very serious psychopathology, and the most common diagnosis for persons with the code type is schizophrenia, paranoid type. Hallucinations, delusions, and extreme suspiciousness are common. Affect tends to be blunted. Persons with this code type tend to be shy, introverted, and socially withdrawn, but they may become quite aggressive when drinking. They tend to have problems with memory and concentration. Although persons with this code type may not be experiencing disabling emotional turmoil, they often are unable to handle the responsibilities of everyday life and require inpatient treatment. Psychotropic medications often are prescribed.

OTHER CONFIGURAL ASPECTS

Regardless of their absolute elevations and whether or not they are the highest scales in the profile, the relative elevations of Scales 1, 2, and 3 provide important interpretive information. When Scales 1 and 3 are 10 or more T-score points higher than Scale 2, individuals probably are using denial and repression excessively. They tend to have little or no insight into their own needs, conflicts, or symptoms. They are reasonably free of depression, anxiety, and other emotional turmoil, but somatic symptoms are likely. These persons want medical explanations for their problems, resisting psychological explanations. When Scale 2 is equal to or higher than scales 1 and 3, the individuals are not likely to be so well defended, and they may report emotional turmoil and a wide variety of symptoms.

The relationship between Scales 3 and 4 gives important information about anger control. Even when these two scales are not the most elevated ones in the profile, their relative positions are meaningful. When Scale 4 is 10 or more T-score points higher than Scale 3, problems with anger control are common. Such persons tend to express anger openly without adequately considering the consequences of their actions. When Scale 3 is 10 or more T-score points higher than Scale 4, we expect persons to have adequate control and not to express anger openly. When scores on scales 3 and 4 are about equally elevated, and especially when they are both above T scores of 65, persons may be overcontrolled and not express anger openly most of the time, but periodic angry outbursts may occur.

6

///// Content Interpretation

Hathaway and McKinley utilized empirical keying procedures to construct the original MMPI Clinical scales. Items were included in a scale if they empirically differentiated between diagnostic criterion groups. Little emphasis was placed on the content of the items identified in this manner, and only for Scale 7 were attempts made to ensure internal consistency. In fact, early in the history of the MMPI some clinicians seemed to believe that examination of the content of the items endorsed by test takers would spoil the empirical approach to assessment.

More recently, clinicians and researchers have become increasingly aware that consideration of item content adds significantly to interpretation. The purpose of this chapter is to discuss some approaches to the interpretation of content dimensions of the MMPI-2. It should be emphasized that these approaches are viewed as supplementary to interpretation of the standard MMPI-2 Clinical scales and should not be used instead of them.

THE HARRIS–LINGOES SUBSCALES

Subscale Development

Because little attention was given by Hathaway and McKinley to scale homogeneity, most of the standard Clinical scales are quite heterogeneous in terms of item content. The same total raw score on a Clinical scale can be obtained by individuals endorsing very different combinations of items. Some investigators have suggested that systematic analysis of subgroups of items within the standard Clinical scales can add significantly to the interpretation of protocols (e.g., Comrey, 1957a, 1957b, 1957c, 1958b, 1958c, 1958d, 1958e; Comrey & Marggraff, 1958; Graham, Schroeder, & Lilly, 1971; Harris & Lingoes, 1955, 1968; Pepper & Strong, 1958).

The subscales developed by Harris and Lingoes (1955, 1968) represent the most comprehensive effort of this kind. Their scales have come to be widely used clinically and are routinely scored and reported by automated scoring and interpretation services. Harris and Lingoes constructed subscales for six of the ten standard Clinical scales (Scales 2, 3, 4, 6, 8, and 9). They did not develop subscales for Scales 1 or 7 because they considered them to have homogeneous content. Whereas a factor-analytic study by Comrey (1957b) suggested that Harris and Lingoes were correct about the unidimensionality of Scale 1, factor analyses of Scale 7 items have not been as conclusive. Comrey (1958d) factor analyzed Scale 7 item responses and identified several factors, but Strenger (1989) was not able to develop reliable and valid subscales for Scale 7, largely because of the homogeneity of items in the scale. Harris and Lingoes did not develop subscales for Scales 5 and 0 because these scales were not considered to be standard Clinical scales. Subsequent efforts to develop subscales for Scales 5 and 0 will be discussed later in this chapter.

Each of the Harris–Lingoes subscales was constructed rationally by examining the content of items within a standard Clinical scale and grouping together items that seemed similar in content or were judged to reflect a single attitude or trait. A label was assigned to each subscale on the basis of the investigators' clinical judgments of the content of items in the subscale. Although it was assumed that the resulting subscales would be more homogeneous than their parent scales, no statistical estimates of homogeneity were provided by Harris and Lingoes. Although 31 subscales were developed, three subscales that involve combining items from several other subscales generally are not scored or used in clinical interpretation.

Although the Harris–Lingoes subscales were constructed using the MMPI item pool, they can be scored for the MMPI-2. Several changes were made in the subscales when the MMPI-2 was developed. First, several items that were scored for some of the subscales were deleted, so the MMPI-2 has fewer items for those subscales than did the original MMPI. Although only a few items were deleted, some of the subscales were already so short that the deletions are of serious concern. Second, Harris and Lingoes included items in some of the subscales that were not in the parent scales, apparently because they were using preliminary versions of some of the Clinical scales. In the MMPI-2 the items that were in subscales but not in the parent scales were deleted from the subscales. Finally, the Harris–Lingoes subscales were renumbered to eliminate the lettered subscripts for some of the subscales.

Using psychiatric and nonclinical samples, Levitt, Browning, and Freeland (1992) compared MMPI and MMPI-2 raw scores for the Scale 4 subscales. As expected, scores were lower for the MMPI-2 subscales, which have fewer items than the corresponding MMPI subscales. However, had the investigators converted raw scores to T scores, using the appropriate norms, they would have found the differences between the MMPI and MMPI-2 scores to be quite small and probably not clinically meaningful. Chojnacki and Walsh (1994) found that the Harris–Lingoes subscale scores for a large sample of college students were quite similar for the MMPI and the MMPI-2.

The names of the 28 Harris–Lingoes subscales and the number of items in each subscale are presented in Table 6.1. The MMPI-2 booklet numbers of the

Table 6.1 Internal Consistency (Alpha) and Test–Retest Coefficients for the Harris–Lingoes Subscales

SUBSCALE		NUMBER OF ITEMS	INTERNAL CONSISTENCY[a]		TEST–RETEST RELIABILITY[b]	
			MEN (n = 1138)	WOMEN (n = 1462)	MEN (n = 82)	WOMEN (n = 111)
D1	Subjective Depression	32	.71	.74	.85	.84
D2	Psychomotor Retardation	14	.24	.28	.74	.76
D3	Physical Malfunctioning	11	.23	.29	.64	.74
D4	Mental Dullness	15	.60	.63	.76	.81
D5	Brooding	10	.63	.65	.81	.77
Hy1	Denial of Social Anxiety	6	.73	.74	.86	.85
Hy2	Need for Affection	12	.64	.62	.76	.80
Hy3	Lassitude–Malaise	15	.67	.73	.86	.88
Hy4	Somatic Complaints	17	.59	.68	.81	.77
Hy5	Inhibition of Aggression	7	.17	.11	.61	.68
Pd1	Familial Discord	9	.51	.57	.81	.73
Pd2	Authority Problems	8	.31	.23	.68	.62
Pd3	Social Imperturbability	6	.57	.55	.85	.77
Pd4	Social Alienation	13	.48	.52	.81	.75
Pd5	Self-Alienation	12	.62	.67	.78	.78
Pa1	Persecutory Ideas	17	.59	.64	.78	.69
Pa2	Poignancy	9	.39	.43	.66	.69
Pa3	Naivete	9	.56	.57	.58	.73
Sc1	Social Alienation	21	.66	.69	.78	.75
Sc2	Emotional Alienation	11	.29	.34	.69	.74
Sc3	Lack of Ego Mastery, Cognitive	10	.66	.68	.68	.64
Sc4	Lack of Ego Mastery, Conative	14	.58	.62	.76	.81
Sc5	Lack of Ego Mastery, Defective Inhibition	11	.50	.56	.72	.70
Sc6	Bizarre Sensory Experiences	20	.64	.66	.78	.67
Ma1	Amorality	6	.29	.32	.72	.78
Ma2	Psychomotor Acceleration	11	.53	.50	.81	.68
Ma3	Imperturbability	8	.43	.46	.65	.70
Ma4	Ego Inflation	9	.32	.48	.74	.58

[a]Cronbach's coefficient alpha.

[b]Average retest interval was 9 days.

SOURCE: Unpublished data from the MMPI restandardization project. John R. Graham, Department of Psychology, Kent State University, Kent, OH 44242.

Table 6.2 Intercorrelations for the Harris–Lingoes Subscales for 1138 Men and 1462 Women in the MMPI–2 Normative Sample[a]

	D	D1	D2	D3	D4	D5	
D	—	88	57	58	77	67	
D1	85	—	44	45	84	83	
D2	61	45	—	09	40	20	
D3	52	41	09	—	41	34	
D4	70	82	36	34	—	70	
D5	57	79	19	25	65	—	
	HY	HY1	HY2	HY3	HY4	HY5	
Hy	—	35	39	52	53	31	
Hy1	39	—	31	−25	−22	16	
Hy2	54	31	—	−31	−32	28	
Hy3	43	−27	−28	—	55	−16	
Hy4	45	−20	−24	53	—	−14	
Hy5	47	16	36	−09	−09	—	
	PD	PD1	PD2	PD3	PD4	PD5	
Pd	—	68	45	13	68	73	
Pd1	63	—	16	−15	46	49	
Pd2	52	19	—	32	15	15	
Pd3	13	−12	24	—	−10	−22	
Pd4	66	39	21	−07	—	71	
Pd5	67	41	21	−26	69	—	
	PA	PA1	PA2	PA3			
Pa	—	51	62	38			
Pa1	48	—	36	−39			
Pa2	57	32	—	−18			
Pa3	43	−37	−18	—			
	SC	SC1	SC2	SC3	SC4	SC5	SC6
Sc	—	83	56	76	74	73	74
Sc1	81	—	43	51	53	54	46
Sc2	52	39	—	37	70	27	31
Sc3	74	47	33	—	69	50	58
Sc4	72	50	68	69	—	40	43
Sc5	71	50	24	46	38	—	60
Sc6	68	38	26	49	32	55	—
	MA	MA1	MA2	MA3	MA4		
Ma	—	51	74	26	66		
Ma1	57	—	25	03	21		
Ma2	72	33	—	−05	41		
Ma3	28	01	−13	—	−14		
Ma4	64	21	41	−06	—		

[a]Correlations for women are above diagonal; correlations for men are below diagonal.

SOURCE: Unpublished data from the MMPI restandardization project. John R. Graham, Department of Psychology, Kent State University, Kent, OH 44242.

items in each subscale and the scored response for each item are presented in an appendix of the MMPI-2 manual (Butcher et al., 2001). Harris and Lingoes did not avoid placing an item in more than one subscale. Thus, item overlap among the subscales is considerable and may account, at least in part, for the high correlations between certain subscales. Table 6.2 summarizes these intercorrelations for men and women in the MMPI-2 normative sample.

Subscale Norms

Harris and Lingoes (1955) did not present normative data when their subscales were first described, but a later unpublished paper (Harris & Lingoes, 1968) reported means and standard deviations for a sample of psychiatric patients at the Langley Porter Clinic. Gocka and Holloway (1963) presented means and standard deviations for 68 male veteran psychiatric patients. T-score transformations for the Harris–Lingoes subscale raw scores based on data from the MMPI-2 normative sample are presented in an appendix of the MMPI-2 manual (Butcher et al., 2001).

Subscale Reliability

Harris and Lingoes (1955) reasoned intuitively that the subscales should be more homogeneous than the parent scales from which they were drawn, but they did not offer any evidence in this regard. Calvin (1974) statistically examined the homogeneity of the five Harris–Lingoes subscales for Scale 2 (Depression). He separately factor analyzed inter-item correlations for each of the five subscales and concluded that four of the subscales appeared to be unidimensional, whereas one subscale (Psychomotor Retardation) was two-dimensional (loss of interest in life activities and inhibition of hostility).

Table 6.1 reports internal consistency (alpha) coefficients for men and women in the MMPI-2 normative sample. Comparable values were reported by Kelch and Wagner (1992) for a sample of outpatient clients. Davis, Wagner, and Patty (1994) demonstrated that traditional techniques for determining internal consistency values tend to underestimate the reliabilities of some of the subscales with very few items, and they reported somewhat higher internal consistency values for some of the subscales when an alternative technique was utilized. Most of the subscales have a relatively high degree of internal consistency. However, the Hy5 subscale has unacceptably low internal consistency.

Table 6.1 also reports test–retest coefficients for men and women in the normative sample who took the MMPI-2 twice. The test–retest data suggest that the temporal stability of the subscales is less than the parent scales, but stability is adequate for most scales. As would be expected, the subscales with fewer items have lower test–retest coefficients.

Subscale Validity

Although the Harris-Lingoes subscales have been in existence for more than 50 years and have gained fairly wide usage among clinicians (largely because they are scored routinely by some automated scoring and interpretation services), only limited empirical research concerning the subscales has been published. The factor-analytic work of Comrey (1957a, 1957b, 1957c, 1958b, 1958c, 1958d, 1958e; Comrey & Marggraff, 1958) addressed the construct validity of the Harris–Lingoes subscales. Comrey reported factor analyses of the intercorrelations of items within each scale, separately for each of the Clinical scales of the MMPI (excluding Scales 5 and 0). Although there are some significant differences between the logically derived Harris–Lingoes subscales and the corresponding factor-analytically derived Comrey factors, in general the Comrey studies revealed factors within each Clinical scale that are similar to the Harris–Lingoes subscales and that supported Harris's notion that the Clinical scales are not homogeneous and unidimensional.

Lingoes (1960) factor analyzed scores on the Harris–Lingoes subscales and on the Wiener Subtle–Obvious subscales of the MMPI (Wiener, 1948) in an attempt to determine the statistical factor structure of the MMPI. He concluded that the dimensionality of the MMPI was more complex than the six standard scales from which the various subscales were derived but simpler than the 36 subscales (Harris–Lingoes and Wiener) included in his own factor analysis.

Harris and Christiansen (1946) studied pretherapy MMPI differences between neurotic patients who were judged to have been successful in psychotherapy and similar patients who were judged to have been unsuccessful. They found that the successful patients scored lower on Scales 4, 6, 8, and 9 of the MMPI, suggesting that they had more ego strength. Significant differences between successful and unsuccessful patients also were identified for eight Harris–Lingoes subscales. Successful patients scored lower on the Familial Discord, Authority Problems, and Social Alienation subscales of Scale 4; on the Persecutory Ideas subscale of Scale 6; and on the Defective Inhibition and Bizarre Sensory Experiences subscales of Scale 8. Harris and Christiansen did not address the question of whether greater accuracy of prediction of psychotherapy outcome was possible with the subscales than with only the standard Clinical scales. They felt, however, that the subscale information could lead to a better understanding of how successful therapy patients view themselves and the environments in which they live.

Gocka and Holloway (1963) correlated scores of psychiatric patients on the Harris–Lingoes subscales with other MMPI scales assessing social desirability, introversion–extroversion, and dissimulation; with some demographic variables (intelligence, occupational level, marital status); with legal competency status at the time of hospital admission; and with number of days of hospitalization. Most of the Harris–Lingoes subscales were related to the social desirability scale, and some were related to the introversion–extroversion and dissimulation scales. Few significant correlations were found between the Harris–Lingoes subscale scores and demographic variables. Two subscale scores correlated significantly with competency status, and no subscale correlated significantly with length of hospitalization.

Panton (1959) compared the Harris–Lingoes subscale scores of African American and Caucasian prison inmates. He found that Caucasian inmates scored higher on the Authority Problems subscale, suggesting that they had more authority problems and aggressive tendencies than African American inmates. African American inmates scored higher on the Persecutory Ideas, Social Alienation, and Ego Inflation subscales, suggesting more psychotic trends for African American inmates than for Caucasian inmates. Panton also compared the Harris–Lingoes subscale scores of prison inmates with the psychiatric norms presented by Harris and Lingoes (1968). He found that prison inmates scored higher than the psychiatric patients on the Social Alienation, Self-Alienation, and Amorality subscales. Prisoners scored lower than the psychiatric patients on the Subjective Depression, Psychomotor Retardation, Mental Dullness, Need for Affection, Lassitude–Malaise, Inhibition of Aggression, Lack of Ego Mastery, Cognitive, Lack of Ego Mastery, Conative, and Psychomotor Acceleration subscales.

Calvin (1975) attempted to identify extratest correlates for the Harris–Lingoes subscales for a sample of hospitalized psychiatric patients. He compared high scorers on each Harris–Lingoes subscale with other scorers on that subscale on several variables, including psychiatric diagnosis, reasons for hospitalization, nurses' ratings, and psychiatrists' ratings. Although 10 of the 28 subscales were determined to have reliable behavioral correlates, Calvin concluded that in most cases the subscales are not likely to add significantly to interpretation based on the standard Clinical scales for psychiatric patients.

Graham, Ben-Porath, and McNulty (1999) reported correlations between Harris–Lingoes subscale scores and extratest characteristics for a large sample of mental health center outpatients. Their results indicated that most of the subscales have reliable extratest correlates and that the correlates are consistent with the symptoms, behaviors, and characteristics suggested by the item content of each scale.

Several studies have demonstrated that the Harris–Lingoes subscales add important information to that provided by the Clinical scales. Prokop (1986) found that a group of chronic-pain patients obtained high scores on Scale 3 by endorsing items assessing somatic concerns rather than items indicating histrionic tendencies. Moore, McFall, Kivlahan, and Capestany (1988) compared the MMPI results of chronic-pain patients and psychotic patients and found that the chronic-pain patients obtained elevated Scale 8 scores because they endorsed items dealing with somatic symptoms and depression. By contrast, the psychotic patients obtained elevated Scale 8 scores because they endorsed items indicative of bizarre thinking, social alienation, and defective inhibition. McFall, Moore, Kivlahan, and Capestany (1988) compared groups of psychotic and nonpsychotic patients. Although both groups had similarly elevated scores on Scale 8, they had different patterns of scores on the Harris–Lingoes subscales for Scale 8. The psychotic patients scored higher on subscales indicating bizarre thinking and loss of control of impulses and emotions, whereas the nonpsychotic patients scored higher on subscales assessing depression, anxiety, and thinking difficulties.

Several studies have examined relationships between Scale 4 and the Harris–Lingoes Pd subscales and measures of psychopathy and antisocial behavior. Meloy and Gacono (1995) found that the Pd2 (Authority Problems) subscale was a better predictor than Scale 4 of scores on the Hare Psychopathy Checklist—Revised (Hare, 1991). Lilienfeld (1999) reported similar results using his Psychopathic Personality Inventory (Lilienfeld & Andrews, 1996) as a criterion measure.

Almagor and Koren (2001) examined the structural adequacy of the Harris–Lingoes subscales using large samples of Israeli and American psychiatric patients. They conducted item-level factor analyses for Scales 2, 3, 4, 6, 8, and 9 separately by country and gender. Their results generally did not support the Harris–Lingoes breakdown of most Clinical scales into specific content areas. However, their results were most consistent with the Harris–Lingoes subscales for Scales 3 and 6. The subscales that Almagor and Koren developed have superior internal consistency compared with the Harris–Lingoes subscales. Interestingly, the investigators concluded that the Clinical scales examined seemed to share a common factor assessing global distress. This factor is similar to the demoralization dimension that Tellegen et al. (2003) also identified in developing the Restructured Clinical (RC) scales (see Chapter 7 of this book for a discussion of the RC scales). Although the well-conducted study by Almagor and Koren yielded psychometrically sound subscales that could replace the Harris–Lingoes subscales, the investigators correctly concluded that determining the validity and clinical utility of their subscales will require additional research utilizing external criterion measures. It should be noted that the Almagor and Koren subscales are not part of standard MMPI-2 scoring.

Interpretive Guidelines for the Harris–Lingoes Subscales

Scores on the Harris–Lingoes subscales provide information concerning the kinds of items that were endorsed in the scored direction in obtaining a particular score on a Clinical scale. Because some of the subscales have very few items and are relatively unreliable and because there is only limited research concerning extratest correlates of the subscales, they should not be interpreted independently of their parent scales. The subscales generally should not be interpreted unless their parent scales are significantly elevated (T > 65), and interpretation should be limited to trying to understand why high scores have been obtained on the parent scales.

There are two circumstances in which the Harris–Lingoes subscales may be especially helpful. First, they sometimes can help to explain why a person receives an elevated score on a Clinical scale when that elevation was not expected from history and other information available to the clinician. For example, a patient whose primary symptom is depression could produce a profile with elevations on Scales 2, 7, and 8. The Scale 2 and Scale 7 elevations are consistent with the patient's history and with clinical observation. However, the Scale 8 elevation is somewhat troublesome. Why does this patient, for whom there is no history or clinical indication of schizophrenia or thought disorder, score relatively high on Scale 8? Reference to the Harris–Lingoes subscale scores might reveal that most of the Scale 8 elevation is coming from items in the Lack of Ego Mastery, Conative (Sc4) subscale. This subscale assesses depression and despair and whether the patient feels that life is a strain much of the time. These characteristics would be highly consistent with those based on the rest of the profile and with the patient's history.

Second, the Harris–Lingoes subscales can be very useful in interpreting Clinical scale scores that are marginally elevated (T = 65–70). It often seems that many of the interpretations suggested for a high score on a scale are not appropriate for the marginally elevated scores. For example, a person might receive a T score of 67 on Scale 4, and there would be some reluctance to attribute to that person the antisocial characteristics often suggested for high scorers on Scale 4. A high score on Pd1 (Familial Discord) of the Harris–Lingoes subscales, for example, could explain the moderately elevated score on Scale 4 without requiring inferences about more deviant asocial or antisocial behaviors. However, a high score on the Pd2 (Authority Problems) subscale would suggest a focus on the possibility of asocial or antisocial behaviors.

The Harris–Lingoes subscales can also be considered in relation to the empirical correlates for the Clinical scales. For any of the Clinical scales, a variety of behaviors and characteristics has been associated with higher scores. For example, elevated scores on Scale 4 have been associated with family problems, antisocial behavior, and absence of social anxiety. Usually, not all of the descriptors associated with elevated scores on a scale will be characteristic of any specific individual with an elevated score on that scale. Examination of the Harris–Lingoes subscales can be helpful in determining which of the many different descriptors should be emphasized. In the earlier example, if the person had an elevated score on the Familial Discord subscale and not on other Scale 4 subscales, in our interpretation we would emphasize the correlates associated with family problems. On the other hand, if the Authority Problems subscale was the only elevated Scale 4 subscale, we would emphasize the correlates having to do with acting-out behaviors.

As with many of the other scales discussed in this book, it is not possible to establish absolutely firm cutoff scores to define high scorers on the Harris–Lingoes subscales. As clinicians gain experience with the subscales, they will come to establish cutoff scores for the settings in which the MMPI-2 is used. The individual who is just beginning to use the subscales for MMPI-2 interpretation should find it useful to consider T scores greater than 65 as high scores. However, it should be noted that the brevity of several subscales, coupled with relatively high mean scores in the normative sample, makes it impossible for anyone to obtain T scores greater than 65 on several of the subscales (Krishnamurthy, Archer, & Huddleston, 1995). Thus, the Hy1 (Denial of Social Anxiety) and Pd3 (Social Imperturbability) subscales do not help in understanding why high scores were obtained on their parent scales.

The descriptions that follow for the subscales are based primarily on information provided by Harris and Lingoes (1955, 1968) and on examination of the content of the items in each subscale. The descriptions can be used to generate hypotheses concerning why persons have obtained high scores on the parent clinical scales. Because not every descriptor will be characteristic of every person who has a high score on a subscale, the hypotheses need to be evaluated in relation to other information available about the person being assessed. It should be emphasized again that the Harris–Lingoes subscales should be used to supplement the standard Validity and Clinical scales. Some of the subscales are too short and too unreliable to be used as independent scales on which to base clinical interpretation. Descriptions are not provided for low scorers on the subscales because it is difficult to know what low scores mean about the persons having them. Low scores could indicate the absence of characteristics reported by high scorers or an unwillingness to admit to having the characteristics. Therefore, it is recommended that low scores on the Harris–Lingoes subscales not be interpreted.

SUBJECTIVE DEPRESSION (D1)
High scorers on the D1 subscale report that they

1. feel unhappy, blue, or depressed much of the time
2. lack energy for coping with the problems of their everyday lives
3. are not interested in what goes on around them
4. feel nervous or tense much of the time
5. have difficulties in concentrating and attending
6. have poor appetite and trouble sleeping
7. brood and cry frequently
8. lack self-confidence
9. feel inferior and useless
10. are easily hurt by criticism
11. feel uneasy, shy, and embarrassed in social situations
12. tend to avoid interactions with other people, except for relatives and close friends.

PSYCHOMOTOR RETARDATION (D2)
High scorers on the D2 subscale report that they

1. feel immobilized and withdrawn
2. lack energy to cope with everyday activities
3. avoid other people
4. do not have hostile or aggressive impulses

PHYSICAL MALFUNCTIONING (D3)
High scorers on the D3 subscale report that they

1. are preoccupied with their own physical functioning
2. do not have good health

3. experience a wide variety of specific somatic symptoms that may include weakness, hay fever or asthma, poor appetite, nausea or vomiting, and convulsions

MENTAL DULLNESS (D4)

High scorers on the D4 subscale report that they

1. lack energy to cope with the problems of everyday life
2. feel tense
3. experience difficulties in concentrating
4. have poor memory and/or show poor judgment
5. lack self-confidence
6. feel inferior to others
7. get little enjoyment out of life
8. have concluded that life is no longer worthwhile

BROODING (D5)

High scorers on the D5 subscale report that they

1. brood, ruminate, and cry much of the time
2. lack energy to cope with problems
3. have concluded that life is no longer worthwhile
4. feel inferior, unhappy, and useless
5. are easily hurt by criticism
6. feel that they are losing control of their thought processes

DENIAL OF SOCIAL ANXIETY (Hy1)

Because it is not possible to obtain a T score greater than 65 on this subscale, it is not helpful in understanding why a high score was obtained on Scale 3.

NEED FOR AFFECTION (Hy2)

High scorers on the Hy2 subscale report that they

1. have strong needs for attention and affection from others and fear that those needs will not be met if they are more honest about their feelings and attitudes
2. have optimistic and trusting attitudes toward other people
3. see others as honest, sensitive, and reasonable
4. do not have negative feelings about other people
5. try to avoid unpleasant confrontations whenever possible

LASSITUDE–MALAISE (Hy3)

High scorers on the Hy3 subscale report that they

1. feel uncomfortable and are not in good health
2. feel weak, fatigued, or tired
3. do not have specific somatic complaints

4. have difficulties in concentrating, poor appetite, and sleep disturbance
5. feel unhappy and blue
6. see their home environments as unpleasant and uninteresting

SOMATIC COMPLAINTS (Hy4)
High scorers on the Hy4 subscale report that they

1. have many somatic complaints
2. experience pain in the heart and/or chest
3. have fainting spells, dizziness, or balance problems
4. experience nausea and vomiting, poor vision, shakiness, or feeling too hot or too cold
5. express little or no hostility toward other people

INHIBITION OF AGGRESSION (Hy5)
High scorers on the Hy5 subscale report that they

1. do not experience hostile and aggressive impulses
2. are not interested in reading about crime and violence
3. are sensitive about how others respond to them
4. are decisive

However, the internal consistency of this subscale is so low that it is not likely to be very useful in understanding why a high score was obtained on Scale 3.

FAMILIAL DISCORD (Pd1)
High scorers on the Pd1 subscale report that they

1. see their home and family situations as quite unpleasant
2. have felt like leaving their home situations
3. see their homes as lacking in love, understanding, and support
4. feel that their families are critical, quarrelsome, and refuse to permit adequate freedom and independence

AUTHORITY PROBLEMS (Pd2)
High scorers on the Pd2 subscale report that they
1. resent societal and parental standards and customs
2. have been in trouble in school or with the law
3. have definite opinions about what is right and wrong
4. stand up for what they believe
5. are not greatly influenced by the values and standards of others

SOCIAL IMPERTURBABILITY (Pd3)
Because it is not possible to obtain a T score greater than 65 on this subscale, it is not helpful in understanding why a high score was obtained on Scale 4.

SOCIAL ALIENATION (Pd4)
High scorers on the Pd4 subscale report that they

1. feel alienated, isolated, and estranged
2. feel that other people do not understand them
3. feel lonely, unhappy, and unloved
4. feel that they get a raw deal from life
5. see other people as responsible for their problems and shortcomings
6. are concerned about how other people react to them
7. experience regret, guilt, and remorse for their actions

SELF-ALIENATION (Pd5)

High scorers on the Pd5 subscale report that they

1. are uncomfortable and unhappy
2. have problems in concentrating
3. do not find daily life interesting or rewarding
4. experience regret, guilt, and remorse for past deeds but are vague about the nature of this misbehavior
5. find it hard to settle down
6. may use alcohol excessively

PERSECUTORY IDEAS (Pa1)

High scorers on the Pa1 subscale report that they

1. view the world as a threatening place
2. feel that they are getting a raw deal from life
3. feel misunderstood
4. feel that others have unfairly blamed or punished them
5. are suspicious and untrusting of other people
6. blame others for their own problems and shortcomings
7. feel that others are trying to influence or control them
8. believe that others are trying to poison or otherwise harm them

POIGNANCY (Pa2)

High scorers on the Pa2 subscale report that they

1. are more high-strung and more sensitive than other people
2. feel more intensely than others
3. feel lonely and misunderstood
4. look for risky or exciting activities to make them feel better

NAIVETE (Pa3)

High scorers on the Pa3 subscale report that they

1. have very optimistic attitudes about other people
2. see others as honest, unselfish, generous, and altruistic
3. are trusting
4. have high moral standards
5. do not experience hostility and negative impulses

SOCIAL ALIENATION (Sc1)

High scorers on the Sc1 subscale report that they

1. are getting a raw deal from life
2. believe that other people do not understand them
3. believe that other people have it in for them
4. believe that other people are trying to harm them
5. feel that their family situations are lacking in love and support
6. feel that their families treat them more as children than as adults
7. feel lonely and empty
8. have never had love relationships with anyone
9. harbor hostility and hatred toward family members
10. avoid social situations and interpersonal relationships whenever possible

EMOTIONAL ALIENATION (Sc2)

High scorers on the Sc2 subscale report that they

1. experience feelings of depression and despair and may wish that they were dead
2. are apathetic and frightened
3. have sadistic and/or masochistic needs

LACK OF EGO MASTERY, COGNITIVE (Sc3)

High scorers on the Sc3 subscale report that they

1. feel that they might be losing their minds
2. have strange thought processes and feelings of unreality
3. have problems with concentration and memory

LACK OF EGO MASTERY, CONATIVE (Sc4)

High scorers on the Sc4 subscale report that they

1. feel that life is a strain and that they experience depression and despair
2. have difficulty in coping with everyday problems and worry excessively
3. respond to stress by withdrawing into fantasy and daydreaming
4. do not find their daily activities interesting and rewarding
5. have given up hope of things getting better
6. may wish that they were dead

LACK OF EGO MASTERY, DEFECTIVE INHIBITION (Sc5)

High scorers on the Sc5 subscale report that they

1. feel that they are not in control of their emotions and impulses and are frightened by this perceived loss of control
2. tend to be restless, hyperactive, and irritable
3. have periods of laughing and crying that they cannot control

4. have experienced episodes during which they did not know what they were doing and later could not remember what they had done

BIZARRE SENSORY EXPERIENCES (Sc6)

High scorers on the Sc6 subscale report that they

1. experience feelings that their bodies are changing in strange and unusual ways
2. experience skin sensitivity, feeling hot or cold, voice changes, muscle twitching, clumsiness, problems in balance, ringing or buzzing in the ears, paralysis, and weakness
3. experience hallucinations, unusual thought content, and ideas of external influence

AMORALITY (Ma1)

High scorers on the Ma1 subscale report that they

1. perceive other people as selfish, dishonest, and opportunistic and because of these perceptions feel justified in behaving in similar ways
2. derive vicarious satisfaction from the manipulative exploits of others

PSYCHOMOTOR ACCELERATION (Ma2)

High scorers on the Ma2 subscale report that they

1. experience acceleration of speech, thought processes, and motor activity
2. feel tense and restless
3. feel excited or elated without cause
4. become bored easily and seek out risk, excitement, or danger as a way of overcoming the boredom
5. have impulses to do something harmful or shocking

IMPERTURBABILITY (Ma3)

High scorers on the Ma3 subscale report that they

1. do not experience social anxiety
2. feel comfortable around other people
3. have no problem in talking with others
4. are not concerned about the opinions, values, and attitudes of other people
5. feel impatient and irritable toward others

EGO INFLATION (Ma4)

High scorers on the Ma4 subscale report that they

1. are important persons
2. are resentful when others make demands on them, particularly if the persons making the demands are perceived as less capable
3. have been treated unfairly

SUBSCALES FOR SCALES 5 AND 0

As stated previously, Harris and Lingoes (1955, 1968) did not develop subscales for Scales 5 and 0. Their omission of these scales was consistent with other early research efforts that did not consider Scales 5 and 0 as standard Clinical scales. An early effort by Pepper and Strong (1958), who used clinical judgment in forming subgroups of items for Scale 5, received little attention among MMPI users. Graham et al. (1971) factor analyzed Scales 5 and 0 item responses of psychiatric inpatients, psychiatric outpatients, and nonclinical samples. For each of the two scales, seven factors emerged, one of which represented demographic variables included in the analyses.

Serkownek (1975) utilized the data from the factor analyses of Graham et al. (1971) to develop subscales for Scales 5 and 0. Items that loaded higher than .30 on a factor were selected for the scale to assess that factor dimension. Labels were assigned to the subscales on the basis of an examination of the content of the items included in the scale. Prior to the publication of the MMPI-2 the Serkownek subscales gained popularity among MMPI users. However, several concerns about the subscales led to a decision not to include them in the MMPI-2.

One major concern about Serkownek's Scale 5 subscales was that the factor analysis on which they were based may have had methodological problems. Graham et al. (1971) combined male and female data in their analysis, and this could have artificially produced the masculine interest and feminine interest factors. Another concern was that some of the items in the Serkownek subscales were scored in the opposite direction from the parent scales. Finally, for women the raw scores on the Scale 5 subscales were transformed to T scores in the opposite direction from the parent scale. High raw scores on Scale 5 subscales yielded high T scores, whereas for Scale 5 itself, higher raw scores yield lower T scores.

Development of the Scale 0 Subscales of the MMPI-2

Ben-Porath, Hostetler, Butcher, and Graham (1989) developed Scale 0 subscales for the MMPI-2 to replace the Serkownek subscales for that scale. These investigators also tried unsuccessfully to develop subscales for Scale 5. Factor analyses of Scale 0 item responses of male and female college students were used to construct provisional subscales. Internal consistency procedures were then used to refine the subscales. The three subscales resulting from these procedures are mutually exclusive, internally consistent, moderately independent, and representative of the major content dimensions of Scale 0. Item numbers and scored directions for each of the subscales are reported in appendixes in the MMPI-2 manual (Butcher et al., 2001). Linear T-score values for raw scores on the subscales can be found in an appendix in the MMPI-2 manual.

Reliability and Validity of the Scale 0 Subscales

Internal consistency (alpha) coefficients were computed for the subscales for college and normative samples (Ben-Porath, Hostetler, et al., 1989). These coefficients are reported in Table 6.3. Sieber and Meyers (1992) reported comparable coefficients

Table 6.3 Internal Consistency and Test–Retest Reliability Coefficients for the Scale 0 Subscales

	ALPHA COEFFICIENTS				TEST–RETEST COEFFICIENTS	
	COLLEGE		NORMATIVE		NORMATIVE	
SUBSCALE	MEN ($n = 525$)	WOMEN ($n = 797$)	MEN ($n = 1138$)	WOMEN ($n = 1462$)	MEN ($n = 82$)	WOMEN ($n = 111$)
Si1 Shyness/Self-Consciousness	.82	.82	.81	.84	.91	.90
Si2 Social Avoidance	.77	.75	.77	.75	.88	.87
Si3 Self/Other Alienation	.77	.77	.75	.78	.77	.88

SOURCE: Ben-Porath, Y.S., Hostetler, K., Butcher, J.N., & Graham, J.R. (1989). New subscales for the MMPI-2 Social Introversion (Si) Scale. *Psychological Assessment: A Journal of Consulting and Clinical Psychology, 1,* 169–174. Copyright © 1989 by the American Psychological Association. Adapted and reproduced by permission of the publisher.

for other samples of college students. The internal consistency of the subscales compares quite favorably with that of other MMPI-2 scales and subscales.

Test–retest reliability coefficients were computed for the subscales using a subsample of 82 men and 111 women from the MMPI-2 normative sample who took the test twice with approximately a 1-week interval between testings (Ben-Porath, Hostetler, et al., 1989). The test–retest coefficients are reported in Table 6.3. The temporal stability of the subscales seems to be greater than for most of the other MMPI-2 scales and subscales.

Ben-Porath, Hostetler, et al. (1989) reported some preliminary validity data for the subscales. Scores on the subscales were correlated with behavioral ratings for a sample of 822 couples from the normative sample who participated in the study together and independently rated each other. The patterns of correlations were judged to offer support for the convergent and discriminant validity of the subscales.

Sieber and Meyers (1992) examined the validity of the Scale 0 subscales by correlating them with other self-report measures of constructs that were believed to be differentially related to the three subscales. The results were very similar for men and women. These authors found that persons with elevated Si1 subscale scores were more socially anxious, were less social, and had lower self-esteem; those with elevated Si2 subscale scores were more shy and less social; and persons with elevated Si3 subscale scores possessed lower self-esteem and had a more external locus of control.

Ward and Perry (1998) confirmed the comprehensiveness, reliability, and distinctness of the Scale 0 subscales when applied to several clinical samples. Graham, Ben-Porath, and McNulty (1999) correlated scores on the Scale 0 subscales with extratest characteristics for a large sample of mental health center outpatients. Their results were consistent with previously reported characteristics and suggested that there also are reliable behavioral correlates for the subscales among mental health outpatients.

Interpretation of the Scale 0 Subscales

Examination of the Scale 0 subscales can help in clarifying the meaning of high scores on Scale 0. For example, some high scorers on Scale 0 will have high scores on both Si1 (Shyness/Self-Consciousness) and Si2 (Social Avoidance), suggesting that they are uncomfortable in social interactions and cope by avoiding most social situations. Other high scorers on Scale 0 will have high scores on Si1 but not on Si2, suggesting that, despite social discomfort, they are not likely to avoid social interactions. Because each of the Scale 0 subscales seems to be homogeneous and bipolar, both high and low scores are interpretable. Ben-Porath, Hostetler, et al. (1989) recommended that T scores of 65 or greater be considered high scores on the subscales. Although the subscale developers did not recommend any cutoff for low scores, it seems reasonable to consider T scores below 40 as low scores.

SHYNESS/SELF-CONSCIOUSNESS (Si1)
High scores on the Si1 subscale indicate persons who

1. feel shy, anxious, and uncomfortable in social situations
2. feel easily embarrassed
3. feel ill at ease in new situations
4. are not talkative or friendly
5. lack self-confidence and give up easily
6. in clinical settings, have symptoms of depression
7. in clinical settings, lack energy

Low scores on the Si1 subscale indicate persons who

1. are extroverted
2. initiate social contact with other people
3. are talkative and friendly
4. are self-confident and do not give up easily

SOCIAL AVOIDANCE (Si2)
High scores on the Si2 subscale indicate persons who

1. do not enjoy being involved with groups or crowds of people
2. actively avoid getting involved with other people
3. are shy
4. do not have high aspirations or strong achievement needs
5. in clinical settings, report depression, anxiety, somatic symptoms, and obsessive–compulsive thoughts and behaviors

Low scores on the Si2 subscale indicate persons who

1. enjoy being involved with groups or crowds of people
2. initiate social contact with other people

SELF/OTHER ALIENATION (Si3)

High scores on the Si3 subscale indicate persons who

1. have low self-esteem
2. lack interest in activities
3. feel unable to effect changes in their life situations
4. have a more external locus of control
5. are interpersonally very sensitive
6. feel insecure
7. do not have strong achievement needs
8. in clinical settings, feel depressed, sad, and hopeless
9. in clinical settings, report obsessive–compulsive thoughts and behaviors

Low scores on the Si3 subscale indicate persons who

1. have high self-esteem
2. appear to be interested in activities
3. feel able to effect changes in their life situations

THE MMPI-2 CONTENT SCALES

Whereas Harris and Lingoes formed content subscales within individual Clinical scales, Wiggins (1969) used the entire MMPI item pool to form content-based scales. Starting with 26 content categories suggested by Hathaway and McKinley (1940), Wiggins used a combination of rational and statistical procedures to develop his scales. The resulting 13 scales were psychometrically sound and seemed to represent well the content dimensions of the original MMPI. Unfortunately, when the MMPI was revised in 1989, Wiggins's scales were no longer adequate. One of the scales, Religious Fundamentalism, could no longer be scored because of item deletions. In addition, the Wiggins scales did not represent adequately the new content dimensions introduced into the MMPI-2 by the addition of new items.

Content scales based on the MMPI-2 item pool were developed by Butcher, Graham, Williams, and Ben-Porath (1990) to assess the content dimensions of the revised instrument. The Content scales were developed using a combination of rational and statistical procedures similar to that used by Wiggins (1969).

Development of the Content Scales

The first step in the development of the MMPI-2 Content scales was to define clinically relevant content areas represented by the items in Form AX of the MMPI. Twenty-two categories were rationally identified, and a definition was written for each. Three clinical psychologists served as judges and assigned items to the content categories. Judges were free to add categories, and items could be assigned to more than one category. Items assigned to a category by two or three of the judges were placed into provisional scales. Raters then met and reviewed all of the item placements. Any disagreements were discussed until there was full agreement by all three raters concerning item placement. For one of the original categories, sufficient items could not be identified, so it was dropped from further consideration.

In the next step of scale development, item responses for two samples of psychiatric patients and two samples of college students were used to identify items in the provisional scales that did not correlate highly with total scores for the scales and that detracted from internal consistency. Such items were dropped from the scales. At this stage, four additional scales were eliminated from further consideration because of unacceptably low internal consistencies. Also, the data indicated that another content category, cynicism, which had been previously identified by item factor analysis, was not represented in the Content scales. Thus, a 20-item cynicism scale was added.

Another way of ensuring appropriate item placement was to examine correlations between each item in the inventory and total scores on the provisional

Table 6.4 Reliability of the MMPI-2 Content Scales

SCALE		NUMBER OF ITEMS	INTERNAL CONSISTENCY[a]		TEST–RETEST RELIABILITY[b]	
			MEN (n = 1138)	WOMEN (n = 1462)	MEN (n = 82)	WOMEN (n = 111)
ANX	Anxiety	23	.82	.83	.90	.87
FRS	Fears	23	.72	.75	.81	.86
OBS	Obsessiveness	16	.74	.77	.83	.85
DEP	Depression	33	.85	.86	.87	.88
HEA	Health Concerns	36	.76	.80	.81	.85
BIZ	Bizarre Mentation	23	.73	.74	.78	.81
ANG	Anger	16	.76	.73	.85	.82
CYN	Cynicism	23	.86	.85	.80	.89
ASP	Antisocial Practices	22	.78	.75	.81	.87
TPA	Type A Behavior	19	.72	.68	.82	.79
LSE	Low Self-Esteem	24	.79	.83	.84	.86
SOD	Social Discomfort	24	.83	.84	.91	.90
FAM	Family Problems	25	.73	.77	.84	.83
WRK	Work Interference	33	.82	.84	.90	.91
TRT	Negative Treatment Indicators	26	.78	.80	.79	.88

[a]Cronbach's coefficient alpha.
[b]Average retest interval was 9 days.
SOURCE: Excerpted (Table E-12) from Butcher, J.N., Graham, J.R., Williams, C.L., & Ben-Porath, Y.S (1990). Development and use of the MMPI-2 Content scales. Copyright © 1990 by the Regents of the University of Minnesota. Reproduced by permission of the University of Minnesota Press. All rights reserved. "MMPI®" and "Minnesota Multiphasic Personality Inventory®" are trademarks owned by the Regents of the University of Minnesota.

Content scales. Items that correlated higher with a score from a scale other than the one on which it was placed were deleted or moved to the other scale.

A final step involved examination of the content of the items in each Content scale to determine rationally whether the items fit conceptually with the definition of the content domain. Some items that were statistically related to the total score for a scale but whose content did not seem appropriate for that scale were eliminated.

These multistage procedures yielded a set of 15 scales that were judged to be internally consistent, relatively independent, and representative of clinically relevant content dimensions in the MMPI-2 item pool. Although item overlap between scales was kept to a minimum, some overlap was permitted when the constructs assessed by the scales were conceptually related. Table 6.4 presents a listing of the 15 Content scales. Item numbers and scored directions for each of the Content scales are presented in an appendix of the MMPI-2 manual (Butcher et al., 2001).

Norms for the Content Scales

Data from men and women in the MMPI-2 normative sample (Butcher et al., 2001) were used to generate T-score conversions for the raw scores of the Content scales. The same Uniform T scores used for the Validity and Clinical scales of MMPI-2 are used with the Content scales. Raw scores for the Content scales were regressed on percentile-corresponding T scores from the uniform distribution derived for the Clinical scales. This procedure permits scores for the Content scales to be expressed on the same metric as the Clinical scales, thus ensuring comparability within the set of Content scales and between the Content scales and the Clinical scales. Uniform T-score transformations for the Content scales are reported separately for men and women in an appendix in the MMPI-2 manual.

Reliability of the Content Scales

Table 6.4 reports internal consistency (alpha) coefficients for the Content scales, based on responses of men and women in the normative sample. As would be expected, the internal consistency of the Content scales is quite high. In general, the Content scales are more internally consistent than the Clinical scales and similar in internal consistency to the Wiggins scales, which they were developed to replace.

Table 6.4 also reports test–retest reliability coefficients for the Content scales for 82 men and 111 women in the normative sample. The average retest interval was approximately nine days. These coefficients indicate that the Content scales are quite stable over this short time interval. In fact, the Content scales appear to be more stable than the basic Clinical scales.

Validity of the Content Scales

Butcher, Graham, Williams, et al. (1990) reported several kinds of preliminary validity data for the Content scales. Correlations between the Content scales and other MMPI-2 scales are reported in Table 6.5. These correlational data contribute significantly to our understanding of the construct validity of the Content scales. Some of the Content scales correlate highly with the Clinical scales, suggesting that they can be interpreted in similar ways. For example, the HEA (Health Concerns) scale and Scale 1 (Hypochondriasis) correlate .89 for men and .91 for women in the normative sample, suggesting that both are measures of health concern. Likewise, the SOD (Social Discomfort) scale and Scale 0 (Social Introversion) correlate .85 for men and .84 for women. However, other Content scales are not so highly correlated with Clinical scales with similar labels, suggesting that these scales are assessing unique characteristics as well as common ones. For example,

Table 6.5 Correlations of the MMPI-2 Content Scales with the Validity and Clinical Scales for Men and Women in the MMPI-2 Normative Samples

	?	L	F	K	Hs	D	Hy	Pd	Mf	Pa	Pt	Sc	Ma	Si
						MEN (*n* = 1138)								
ANX	−04	−27	47	−61	50	45	04	50	20	33	80	69	31	43
FRS	00	−07	24	−29	34	22	02	16	01	09	37	35	06	28
OBS	−02	−30	40	−63	40	26	−16	29	12	18	77	64	31	44
DEP	01	−17	57	−56	48	52	02	58	16	38	80	75	27	48
HEA	02	−06	47	−29	89	45	39	35	10	25	50	55	18	29
BIZ	03	−14	51	−44	38	03	−09	36	08	33	51	62	48	11
ANG	−03	−38	34	−66	33	01	−21	36	−02	15	55	53	42	19
CYN	−01	−17	39	−71	33	07	−43	26	−17	−16	51	53	42	32
ASP	−03	−34	42	−60	26	01	−36	37	−15	−12	45	50	51	18
TPA	−06	−37	29	−68	29	05	−30	22	−05	04	53	48	38	25
LSE	−01	−19	48	−52	42	42	−11	27	07	18	72	61	11	59
SOD	−01	−07	31	−31	24	39	−19	04	11	09	40	36	−20	85
FAM	02	−27	53	−55	32	21	−11	57	18	21	59	66	43	31
WRK	00	−26	53	−63	49	44	−09	41	14	21	81	73	23	59
TRT	00	−19	54	−57	46	40	−12	40	02	19	72	68	20	56
						WOMEN (*n* = 1462)								
ANX	−05	−24	47	−67	58	60	17	51	10	39	83	71	34	48
FRS	−05	02	16	−41	34	20	−01	13	00	06	39	33	11	32
OBS	−04	−26	39	−69	45	40	−06	36	08	25	79	65	36	47
DEP	00	−19	58	−63	54	63	12	61	01	44	83	77	31	55
HEA	01	−07	42	−43	91	45	48	33	00	25	55	59	29	31
BIZ	00	−07	49	−46	36	11	−03	39	−14	31	51	65	50	15
ANG	−04	−34	38	−69	39	20	−06	44	00	25	62	60	44	27
CYN	−05	−08	41	−70	41	17	−24	32	−24	−06	51	54	46	35
ASP	−05	−30	41	−57	30	09	−25	37	−28	−09	44	51	51	23
TPA	−03	−29	31	−65	32	15	−16	23	−05	13	53	49	36	28
LSE	−04	−16	44	−60	44	53	−04	31	01	23	74	61	14	65
SOD	−03	−04	28	−38	24	43	−17	06	07	19	43	35	−17	84
FAM	−01	−21	56	−57	40	32	04	61	04	33	60	72	45	33
WRK	−04	−23	50	−69	52	58	02	44	04	29	82	72	27	63
TRT	−01	−15	50	−63	45	50	−05	42	−04	26	72	69	24	61

SOURCE: Excerpted (Tables 25 & 26) from Butcher, J.N., Graham, J.R., Williams, C.L., & Ben-Porath, Y.S. (1990). *Development and use of the MMPI-2 Content scales.* Copyright © 1990 by the Regents of the University of Minnesota. Reproduced by permission of the University of Minnesota Press. All rights reserved. "MMPI® " and "Minnesota Multiphasic Personality Inventory® " are trademarks owned by the Regents of the University of Minnesota.

the correlation between the DEP (Depression) scale and Scale 2 (Depression) was .52 for men and .63 for women, suggesting that these two measures of depression are not interchangeable.

Studies reporting correlates of the Content scales have been conducted in a variety of settings. Butcher, Graham, Williams, et al. (1990) presented data concerning extratest correlates for the Content scales for 800 couples who participated in the MMPI-2 standardization project (Butcher et al., 2001). In addition to responding to the test items, these couples, most of whom were married to each other, independently rated each other on 110 items concerning personality and behavior. Ratings on these items and on factor scales derived from the items were correlated with scores on the Content scales. The resulting correlations were used to generate behavioral descriptors for high scorers on each of the Content scales. Subsequently, reliable and conceptually relevant correlates of the Content scales have been reported for psychiatric inpatients (Archer, Aiduk, Griffin, & Elkins, 1996; Dwyer, Graham, & Ott, 1992); mental health outpatients (Graham, Ben-Porath, & McNulty, 1999); college students (Ben-Porath, McCully, & Almagor, 1993); older Australian residents (Strassberg, 1991); chronic-pain patients (Strassberg & Russell, 2000); and traumatic brain injury patients (Palav, Ortega, & McCaffrey, 2001).

Some studies have examined the validity of specific Content scales. Schill and Wang (1990) reported that the Anger (ANG) Content scale correlated positively with Spielberger's anger expression measure and negatively with anger control. For men the Anger Content scale was correlated significantly with verbal expression of aggression, and for women with physical expression of aggression. O'Laughlin and Schill (1994) found that self-monitored aggression correlated positively and significantly with the Anger Content scale. Carr and Graham (1996) found that male college students who scored higher on the Anger Content scale reported experiencing anger more frequently, regardless of provocation, and that the ANG scale was not helpful in trying to predict if the anger would be expressed inwardly or outwardly. Female college students scoring higher on the ANG scale also reported experiencing anger more frequently, lacking anger control, and expressing their anger outwardly. Clark (1994) reported that in a pain management program higher Anger Content scale scores were associated with anger externalization, while higher Cynicism Content scale scores were associated with anger internalization.

Butcher, Graham, Williams, et al. (1990) reported data concerning scores of chronic-pain patients, psychiatric patients, and nonclinical persons on the Health Concerns (HEA) Content scale. As expected, chronic-pain patients scored significantly higher than the other groups on the HEA scale. A T-score cutoff of 65 on the HEA scale correctly classified most of the chronic-pain patients and incorrectly classified very few other persons. Boone (1994) reported that scores on the Depression (DEP) Content scale were highly correlated with other self-report measures of depression, hopelessness, and suicidality in a psychiatric inpatient sample.

Butcher, Graham, Williams, et al. (1990) also presented data concerning Work Interference (WRK) Content scale scores for several groups of men who would be expected to differ on this scale. The scores of pilot applicants, military personnel, alcoholics in treatment, and psychiatric inpatients were compared. The pilot applicants, who would be expected to have the most positive work attitudes, scored lowest on the WRK scale, whereas the alcoholics and psychiatric patients obtained the highest scores.

Lilienfeld (1996) reported correlations between scores on the Antisocial Practices (ASP) Content scale and extratest measures of psychopathy for several samples of college students. He concluded that the ASP scale measures some of the core personality features of psychopathy as well as generalized social deviance. Smith, Hilsenroth, Castlebury, and Durham (1999) demonstrated the utility of the ASP scale in differentiating clients with diagnoses of antisocial personality disorder from clients with other personality disorder diagnoses. Using college student participants, several studies found that scores on the Low Self-Esteem (LSE) Content scale were related to other self-report measures of negative self-value, ineptitude, and negative comparisons with others (Brems & Lloyd, 1995; Englert, Weed, & Watson, 2000; McCurdy & Kelly, 1997).

Clark (1996) examined the utility of the Negative Treatment Indicators (TRT) scale for men in a chronic-pain treatment program. Higher scorers on the TRT scale tended to show greater decreases in symptoms of depression during treatment and smaller improvements in physical capacities. Higher scorers also were more likely to terminate treatment prematurely. Clark also reported that TRT scale scores were related to several measures of anxiety, depression, and general emotional distress. Gilmore, Lash, Foster, and Blosser (2001) found that persons with higher TRT scale scores were less likely to return for treatment after a screening interview. Among persons who returned for treatment, higher TRT scale scorers were involved in treatment for fewer days and were rated as having lower motivation, poorer participation, and poorer comprehension of treatment materials. Michael et al. (2009) found that TRT scale scores were significantly related to distress and functioning at the time of intake interviews but were unrelated to changes in distress or functioning when patients received cognitive behavioral or interpersonal therapy. Craig and Olsen (2004) examined the relationship between scores on the CYN and TRT scales and several measures of success in a methadone maintenance treatment program. For their small sample of African American men neither Content scale was predictive of treatment success.

Several studies have examined the extent to which Content scale scores are related to specific clinical problems. Egeland, Erickson, Butcher, and Ben-Porath (1991) found that mothers at high risk for child abuse obtained above-average scores on all of the Content scales except Low Self-Esteem (LSE). Their highest scores were on the Antisocial Practices (ASP), Cynicism (CYN), Bizarre Mentation (BIZ), and Anger (ANG) scales. Bosquet and Egeland (2000) reported that higher ASP scores of women who completed the MMPI-2 during pregnancy were predictive of insensitivity, hostility, and harshness toward their children when they were 13–24 months old.

Hjemboe and Butcher (1991) found that the Family Problems (FAM) Content scale strongly differentiated couples in marital counseling from couples in the MMPI-2 normative sample and that FAM-scale scores were negatively and significantly related to measures of marital adjustment. Kopper, Osman, and Barrios (2001) reported significant relationships between several Content scales and self-reported suicidal ideation among college students. For women the Anger Content scale, along with several Validity and Clinical scales, contributed to the prediction of suicidal ideation, whereas for men the Type A Content scale, along with several Validity and Clinical scales, contributed to the prediction of suicidal ideation.

In a study that has implications for the use of the MMPI-2 in the area of health psychology, Kawachi et al. (1998) found that among older men scores on the Type A Content scale were significantly related to cardiovascular disease. Gass (1991) reported that some brain-injured patients obtain artificially elevated scores on some of the MMPI-2 Clinical scales because of the neurologic complaint items that those scales contain. By contrast, he concluded that the Content scales are especially useful in understanding the emotional status of brain-injured patients because these scales include relatively few neurologic complaint items.

Butcher, Graham, and Ben-Porath (1995) stressed the importance of demonstrating that new scales developed for the MMPI-2 add significantly to the prediction of relevant extratest characteristics beyond that possible using already existing scales. Several studies have demonstrated such incremental validity for the MMPI-2 Content scales. Ben-Porath, Butcher, and Graham (1991) investigated the contribution of the MMPI-2 Content scales to the differential diagnosis of schizophrenia and major depression in an inpatient psychiatric setting. They found that both the Clinical scales and the Content scales were related to the differential diagnosis of these two conditions and that the Content scales contained information relevant to this diagnostic question beyond that available from the Clinical scales. For male patients, the Depression (DEP) and Bizarre Mentation (BIZ) Content scales added to the diagnostic discrimination. For female patients, the BIZ Content scale added to the diagnostic discrimination. Wetzler, Khadivi, and Moser (1998) found that the DEP Content scale added significantly to the Clinical scales in identifying patients with depressive diagnoses, and the BIZ and DEP Content scales added significantly to the Clinical scales in identifying patients with psychotic diagnoses. Bagby et al. (2005) found that the DEP and ANX Content scales were predictive of bipolar and unipolar depression and the BIZ and LSE Content scales were predictive of schizophrenia.

Using a large sample of college students, Ben-Porath et al. (1993) found that the MMPI-2 Content scales added to the Clinical scales in the prediction of other self-report measures of relevant extratest characteristics. Archer et al. (1996) reported that for a sample of adult psychiatric inpatients, most Content scales added to the prediction of relevant self-reported and clinician-rated characteristics. Strassberg (1991) reported incremental validity for four Content scales (DEP, ANX, LSE, HEA) for a sample of older Australian residents.

Barthlow, Graham, Ben-Porath, and McNulty (1999) examined the extent to which Content scales add incrementally to the Clinical scales in predicting therapist-rated characteristics of mental health outpatients. Although the incremental validity tended to be modest, most Content scales added significantly to the variance in ratings accounted for by corresponding Clinical scales. These investigators concluded that because each set of scales (i.e., Clinical and Content) added to the other, the two sets should be used together in MMPI-2 interpretation.

In summary, there is considerable evidence to support the validity of the MMPI-2 Content scales. The scales appear to be related significantly to relevant extratest characteristics, and in most cases relationships between Content scales and extratest characteristics are stronger than between Clinical scales and those characteristics. Additionally, there have been several demonstrations that the Content scales add significantly to the Clinical scales in the prediction of relevant extratest characteristics. More research is needed to determine the extent to which these research findings can be replicated in the various settings where the MMPI-2 is used. Taken together these data indicate that the Content scales can be quite helpful in understanding persons who complete the MMPI-2 and that they add significantly to the standard Validity and Clinical scales.

However, not everyone has shared this positive view. Jackson, Fraboni, and Helmes (1997) suggested that "convergent and discriminant validity of MMPI-2 Content scales are seriously compromised by the presence of substantial, confounding, general variance" (p. 111). More specifically, they indicated that the Content scales seem to be measuring primarily social desirability and acquiescence response sets. Their arguments are similar to those previously made about scales of the original MMPI (e.g., Edwards, 1957; Jackson & Messick, 1961). Block (1965) presented data that clearly rebutted the response-set arguments (see Chapter 9). Accumulating evidence that the MMPI-2 Content scales have stable and conceptually relevant extratest correlates suggests that the scales are assessing important aspects of personality and psychopathology, which may, in part, overlap with tendencies to endorse items in stylistic ways.

Content Component Scales

Although an important goal in developing the MMPI-2 Content scales was to maximize the internal consistency of the individual scales, Ben-Porath and Sherwood (1993) suggested that for 12 of the 15 Content scales it is possible to subdivide the items to form Component scales. For example, they indicated that the items in the Antisocial Practices (ASP) Content scale could be subdivided into two clusters of items, one dealing with antisocial attitudes and the other dealing with antisocial behaviors. Ben-Porath and Sherwood reasoned that in some cases interpretation of the Content scales scores could be augmented by additional information about which kinds of items were endorsed in obtaining a particular T score on a scale.

Using data from the MMPI-2 normative sample, a college sample, and a psychiatric inpatient sample, Ben-Porath and Sherwood (1993) first factor analyzed items within each of the 15 Content scales. The results of the factor analyses were utilized to develop some preliminary Component scales. Next, several statistical

Table 6.6 MMPI-2 Content Component Scales

Fears (FRS)
  FRS1: Generalized Fearfulness
  FRS2: Multiple Fears

Depression (DEP)
  DEP1: Lack of Drive
  DEP2: Dysphoria
  DEP3: Self-Depreciation
  DEP4: Suicidal Ideation

Health Concerns (HEA)
  HEA1: Gastrointestinal Symptoms
  HEA2: Neurological Symptoms

Bizarre Mentation (BIZ)
  BIZ1: Psychotic Symptomatology
  BIZ2: Schizotypal Characteristics

Anger (ANG)
  ANG1: Explosive Behavior
  ANG2: Irritability

Cynicism (CYN)
  CYN1: Misanthropic Beliefs
  CYN2: Interpersonal Suspiciousness

Antisocial Practices (ASP)
  ASP1: Antisocial Attitudes
  ASP2: Antisocial Behavior

Type A Behavior (TPA)
  TPA1: Impatience
  TPA2: Competitive Drive

Low Self-Esteem (LSE)
  LSE1: Self-Doubt
  LSE2: Submissiveness

Social Discomfort (SOD)
  SOD1: Introversion
  SOD2: Shyness

Family Problems (FAM)
  FAM1: Family Discord
  FAM2: Familial Alienation

Negative Treatment Indicators (TRT)
  TRT1: Low Motivation
  TRT2: Inability to Disclose

SOURCE: Excerpted (Table 2) from Ben-Porath, Y.S., & Sherwood, N.E. (1993). *The MMPI-2 Content Component scales: Development, Psychometric Characteristics, and clinical application*. Copyright © 1993 by the Regents of the University of Minnesota. Reproduced by permission of the University of Minnesota Press. All rights reserved. "MMPI" " and "Minnesota Multiphasic Personality Inventory" " are trademarks owned by the Regents of the University of Minnesota.

procedures were utilized to enhance the internal consistency of the Component scales. Finally, rational analyses were employed to ensure the conceptual independence of the item clusters and to determine appropriate labels for the resulting Component scales. The resulting Content Component scales for 12 of the 15 Content scales are listed in Table 6.6. An appendix in the MMPI manual (Butcher et al., 2001) lists the items included in each Component scale (and their scored direction). Linear T-score transformations for raw scores for the Component scales, based on data from the MMPI-2 normative sample, are also presented in an appendix in the MMPI-2 manual.

Ben-Porath and Sherwood (1993) reported internal consistency coefficients for the Component scales for the normative, college, and psychiatric samples. The internal consistencies of the Component scales were quite variable and generally lower than those of their parent Content scales. The lower internal consistency of the Component scales probably can be attributed, at least in part, to the fact that they contain fewer items than the parent scales. As might be expected, for many of the Component scales, internal consistency was lower for the normative and college samples than for the psychiatric sample, perhaps reflecting the restriction of range of some of the Component scale scores in the normative sample. Ben-Porath and Sherwood (1993) pointed out that the internal consistencies of their Component scales are similar to those of the more widely used Harris–Lingoes subscales. Ben-Porath and Sherwood also reported test–retest reliability coefficients for a subsample of persons from the MMPI-2 normative sample. These coefficients also were quite variable, ranging from .47 to .90 (median = .77 for men and .79 for women). Although these coefficients are somewhat lower than those previously reported for the parent Content scales, they are comparable to those previously reported for the Harris–Lingoes subscales.

Limited data currently are available concerning the validity and utility of the Content Component scales. Ben-Porath and Sherwood (1993) reported correlations between Component scale scores and extratest ratings of persons in the MMPI-2 normative sample. Although the ratings available did not cover the full range of characteristics assessed by the Component scales and the magnitude of the resulting correlations probably was attenuated because of the restricted range of scores in the normative sample, the patterns of correlations were interpreted as offering some preliminary support for the external validity of the Component scales.

Graham, Ben-Porath, and McNulty (1999) determined extratest characteristics of the Content Component scales for a large sample of mental health outpatients. Although for many scales the correlations with extratest measures were similar for the parent Content scales and their Component scales, there were some instances where there were differential patterns of correlations. For example, having a history of being physically abusive or of committing domestic violence was more strongly related to the Explosive Behavior (ANG1) Component scale than to the Irritability (ANG2) Component scale. Clearly, more research is needed to determine the extent to which scores on the Content Component scales add significantly to the Content scales in our understanding of persons who have taken the MMPI-2.

Clark (1996) found that the Negative Treatment Indicators (TRT) Content scale and the Low Motivation (TRT1) Content Component scale were equally effective in predicting changes in depression and physical capacity for men in a chronic-pain treatment program. The Inability to Disclose (TRT2) Component scale was not very effective in predicting these changes.

Ben-Porath and Sherwood (1993) offered some guidelines for the interpretation of scores on the Content Component scales. They recommended that the Component scales be used to enhance the interpretation of the parent Content scales and not be used independently of the parent scales to generate inferences. They indicated that the Component scales should be interpreted only when T scores on a parent Content scale are equal to or greater than 60. Differential elevations on Component scales within a parent Content scale may be especially useful in specifying the symptoms and problems associated with elevations on the Content scales. This differential elevation is most likely when parent Content scale scores are moderately high (T = 60–75).

McNulty, Ben-Porath, Graham, and Stein (1997) suggested that scores on the Component scales are likely to be most helpful when the parent Content scale is elevated (T > 60) and the score on one of the Component scales is at least 10 T-score points greater than the other Component scale(s) within a parent Content scale. Their analyses of data for a sample of mental health center clients supported the notion that for some Content scales differential elevations of the Component scales added important information about which correlates of the Content scales should be emphasized or deemphasized in the interpretation.

Interpretation of the Content and Content Component Scales

The data summarized here and examination of the content of items in each Content scale can be used to generate interpretive inferences about persons who have high scores on the Content scales. As with the Harris–Lingoes subscales discussed earlier, until additional data are available users of the Content scales should consider T scores greater than 65 as high scores. Graham, Ben-Porath, et al. (1997) reported data suggesting that persons who obtain low scores (T < 40) on at least some of the Content scales are better adjusted and have fewer of the problems and symptoms associated with those scales than persons with average scores on the scales. However, until these findings are replicated in other settings, it is not recommended that low scores on the Content scales be used to generate interpretive statements. As additional validity data accumulate, it may be possible to state more precise cutoff scores when using some of the Content scales for specific purposes.

Special attention should be given to interpretation of the WRK and TRT scales. Because of the manner in which these scales were constructed, each scale seems to be saturated with general maladjustment and demoralization. Thus persons who are in a great deal of psychological turmoil and feeling demoralized are likely to obtain higher scores on these scales regardless of their specific attitudes about work or treatment. Elevated scores on these scales are most informative when there are indications that the test taker is not generally maladjusted or demoralized.

The Content Component scales should be interpreted only when the parent Content scale T score is greater than 60. In such cases, the relative T scores for Component scales for a particular Content scale should be examined. If there is a differential pattern among Component scales (i.e., one scale at least 10 T-score points higher than another scale), the item content of the Component scales may offer some additional information about which Content scale correlates should be emphasized or deemphasized in the interpretation.

It is especially important to take test-taking attitude into account when interpreting the Content scales. Because the scales contain primarily items with obvious content, scores on the scales are very susceptible to distortion related to test-taking attitude. Persons who approach the MMPI-2 in a defensive manner are likely to obtain low scores on most of the scales, and persons who exaggerate problems in taking the MMPI-2 are likely to obtain high scores on most of the scales. Clearly, the Content scales are most useful when test takers have approached the MMPI-2 in a cooperative, open manner.

Clinicians should view scores on the Content scales as direct communication between test takers and examiners. Characteristics reflected by high scores on the Content scales are those that the test takers want examiners to know about. Rapport with clients often is increased when the Content scale results are used to give feedback to clients, indicating an awareness of the things they were trying to communicate when they completed the MMPI-2.

ANXIETY (ANX)
High scores on the ANX scale are indicative of persons who

1. feel anxious, nervous, worried, and apprehensive
2. have problems with concentration
3. complain of sleep disturbance
4. are uncomfortable making decisions
5. may report obsessive–compulsive symptoms
6. may have somatic symptoms
7. may report feeling sad, blue, or depressed
8. may have suicidal ideation
9. feel that life is a strain and are pessimistic about things getting better
10. feel hopeless
11. feel insecure and lack self-confidence
12. feel overwhelmed by the responsibilities of daily life
13. in clinical settings, frequently have anxiety disorder diagnoses

ANX Content Component Scales
There are no Component scales for the ANX Content scale.

FEARS (FRS)
High scores on the FRS scale are indicative of persons who

1. feel fearful and uneasy much of the time
2. report multiple specific fears or phobias
3. are not very competitive

FRS Content Component Scales
Both the Generalized Fearfulness (FRS1) and Multiple Fears (FRS2) Component scales contain items having to do with fearfulness and anxiety. However, the FRS1 scale seems to assess a more global state of anxiety and fearfulness, whereas the FRS2 scale includes items dealing with fear associated with specific objects (e.g., lightning, animals, fire, blood).

OBSESSIVENESS (OBS)
High scores on the OBS scale are indicative of persons who

1. have great difficulty making decisions
2. are rigid and dislike change
3. fret, worry, and ruminate about trivial things
4. may feel depressed, sad, and despondent
5. lack self-confidence
6. tend to feel hopeless
7. often report sleep disturbances
8. report obsessive–compulsive symptoms
9. lack interest in things

OBS Content Component Scales
There are no Content Component scales for the OBS Content scale.

DEPRESSION (DEP)
High scores on the DEP scale are indicative of persons who

1. feel depressed, sad, blue, or despondent
2. feel fatigued and lack interest in things
3. are pessimistic and feel hopeless
4. may recently have been preoccupied with thoughts of death and suicide and may have made suicide attempts
5. cry easily
6. are indecisive and lack self-confidence
7. feel that life is a strain
8. feel guilty; feel like failures
9. are not very achievement oriented
10. have health concerns
11. often report sleep disturbances
12. feel lonely and empty much of the time
13. are emotionally withdrawn

14. have few or no friends
15. are overly sensitive interpersonally
16. have difficult interpersonal relationships
17. in clinical settings, frequently have depressive disorder diagnoses

DEP Content Component Scales

High scores on all four of the DEP Content Component scales are indicative of sadness and depression. The Lack of Drive (DEP1) Component scale has items that focus on life being empty and meaningless and on giving up hope about a better future. The Dysphoria (DEP2) Component scale focuses on mood, with high scorers indicating that they feel sad, blue, and unhappy most of the time. The Self-Depreciation (DEP3) Component scale has to do primarily with feeling inadequate and guilty about past behaviors. As the scale name indicates, the Suicidal Ideation (DEP4) Component scale has to do with the admission of recent or current thoughts of death and suicide. Four of its five items deal directly with suicidal ideation.

HEALTH CONCERNS (HEA)

High scores on the HEA scale are indicative of persons who

1. deny good physical health
2. are preoccupied with bodily functioning
3. may develop somatic symptoms in times of stress
4. feel worn out and lack energy
5. report a variety of specific somatic symptoms, including some that could be suggestive of a neurological disorder
6. do not cope well with their difficulties
7. feel anxious and overwhelmed much of the time
8. may report feeling sad, depressed, and pessimistic
9. often report sleep disturbances
10. in clinical settings, frequently have depressive disorder diagnoses

HEA Content Component Scales

The items in the Gastrointestinal Symptoms (HEA1) Component scale suggest symptoms of nausea, constipation, and stomach discomfort. The Neurological Symptoms (HEA2) Component scale has to do with sensory and motor experiences that sometimes are associated with neurological disorders (e.g., numbness in skin, convulsions, dizzy spells, balance problems). The General Health Concerns (HEA3) Component scale indicates an exaggerated general concern about illness and disease.

BIZARRE MENTATION (BIZ)

High scores on the BIZ scale are indicative of persons who

1. may have psychotic thought processes
2. may report unusual thought content

3. may report auditory, visual, or olfactory hallucinations
4. report feelings of unreality
5. may seem to be disoriented
6. feel that other people say bad things about them
7. tend to be suspicious
8. may believe that other people are trying to harm them
9. may believe that other people can read their minds or control their thinking or behavior
10. have blunted affect
11. often report having few or no friends
12. may have histories of suicide attempts
13. may have histories of substance abuse
14. may have histories of having been sexually abused
15. do not have strong achievement orientation
16. in clinical settings, frequently have psychotic diagnoses

BIZ Content Component Scales

High scores on either the Psychotic Symptomatology (BIZ1) or Schizotypal Characteristics (BIZ2) Component scales suggest the presence of psychotic symptoms. However, high BIZ1 scale scores are more likely to indicate feelings that one's thoughts and behaviors are being controlled by others.

ANGER (ANG)

High scores on the ANG scale are indicative of persons who

1. feel angry and hostile much of the time
2. are seen by others as irritable, grouchy, impatient, and stubborn
3. are aggressive, critical, and argumentative
4. may feel like swearing or smashing things
5. have temper tantrums
6. may lose control and be physically abusive
7. are impulsive and have low frustration tolerance
8. feel that they are unfairly treated
9. are very sensitive to criticism
10. often have interpersonal problems
11. may have histories of having been physically abused
12. may report feeling sad, depressed, and hopeless

ANG Content Component Scales

Persons who score significantly higher on the Explosive Behavior (ANG1) Component scale than on the Irritability (ANG2) Component scale are describing themselves as angry and resentful and sometimes losing control and striking out physically at people and things. When the reverse pattern is present (i.e., ANG2 significantly higher than ANG1), it is likely that such persons are chronically angry and resentful, but they are less likely to exhibit problems in controlling expression of these feelings.

CYNICISM (CYN)

High scores on the CYN scale are indicative of persons who

1. see other people as dishonest, selfish, and uncaring
2. are suspicious of the motives of others
3. are guarded and untrusting in relationships
4. may be hostile and overbearing
5. may be demanding themselves but resent even mild demands placed on them by others
6. are not friendly or helpful
7. have low achievement orientation
8. may have paranoid ideation
9. may have histories of having been physically abused

CYN Content Component Scales

Items in the Misanthropic Beliefs (CYN1) Component scale suggest a contemptuous and distrustful view of other people who are seen as lying to stay out of trouble, demanding more respect that they give to others, and using unfair means to gain profit or advantage. The Interpersonal Suspiciousness (CYN2) Component scale focuses on mistrust of the motives of other people and a perception that others often behave in a manner intended to get undue credit for the accomplishments of the test taker.

ANTISOCIAL PRACTICES (ASP)

High scores on the ASP scale are indicative of persons who

1. are likely to have been in trouble in school or with the law
2. believe that there is nothing wrong with getting around laws as long as they are not broken
3. may enjoy hearing about the antics of criminals
4. have generally cynical attitudes about other people, seeing them as selfish and dishonest
5. resent authority
6. blame others for their own difficulties
7. are manipulative
8. are cold-hearted
9. are self-centered
10. are viewed as dishonest, not trustworthy, and not believable
11. may have substance abuse problems
12. are aggressive, angry, and resentful
13. are impulsive
14. in clinical settings frequently have antisocial personality disorder diagnoses

ASP Content Component Scales

Higher scorers on the Antisocial Attitudes (ASP1) Component scale are expressing nonconforming attitudes (e.g., getting around a law is acceptable if you don't break it; lying to stay out of trouble is understandable), but they are not necessarily acknowledging past antisocial behaviors. The Antisocial Behaviors (ASP2) Component scale focuses on history of problems in school and with the law.

TYPE A BEHAVIOR (TPA)
High scores on the TPA scale are indicative of persons who

1. are hard-driving, fast-moving, and work-oriented
2. feel there is never enough time to get things done
3. do not like to wait or be interrupted
4. frequently are hostile, irritable, and easily annoyed
5. tend to be overbearing and critical in relationships
6. tend to hold grudges and want to get even
7. have increased risk for cardiovascular problems
8. in clinical settings, may have paranoid ideation

TPA Content Component Scales
The Impatience (TPA1) Component scale focuses on irritability toward other people and a strong dislike of having to wait or stand in line. The items in the Competitive Drive (TPA2) Component scale have to do primarily with jealousy and competitiveness in interpersonal relationships.

LOW SELF-ESTEEM (LSE)
High scores on the LSE scale are indicative of persons who

1. have very poor self-concepts
2. anticipate failure and give up easily
3. have feelings of ineptitude
4. compare themselves unfavorably with others
5. are overly sensitive to criticism and rejection
6. find it difficult to accept compliments
7. are passive in relationships
8. have difficulty making decisions
9. may have many worries and fears

LSE Content Component Scales
Persons with high scores on the Self-Doubt (LSE1) Component scale are expressing many negative attitudes about themselves. They doubt their own abilities, compare themselves unfavorably with other people, and may feel that they can never change. Persons with high scores on the Submissiveness (LSE2) Component scale are easily influenced by other people and tend to be passive and submissive in interpersonal relationships.

SOCIAL DISCOMFORT (SOD)
High scores on the SOD scale are indicative of persons who

1. are shy and socially introverted
2. are socially awkward

3. would rather be alone than around other people
4. dislike parties and other group activities
5. do not initiate conversations
6. have limited interests
7. often feel nervous
8. frequently report sleep disturbances
9. may be preoccupied with health and illness
10. may report feeling depressed and hopeless
11. are overly sensitive interpersonally
12. have low energy levels
13. may be emotionally withdrawn
14. in clinical settings, frequently have depressive disorder diagnoses

SOD Content Component Scales

While high scores on both the Introversion (SOD1) and Shyness (SOD2) Component scales suggest introversion, each scale focuses on a somewhat different aspect. The items in the SOD1 Component scale deal with a person's preference for being alone rather than around other people, particularly in groups or at parties, whereas SOD2 items focus on the uncomfortable feelings experienced when meeting new people or being the focus of attention.

FAMILY PROBLEMS (FAM)

High scores on the FAM scale are indicative of persons who

1. describe considerable discord in their current families and/or families of origin
2. describe their families as lacking in love, understanding, and support
3. resent the demands and advice of their families
4. feel angry and hostile toward their families
5. see marital relationships as involving unhappiness and lack of affection
6. often feel that they are getting a raw deal from life
7. may have histories of having been physically abused
8. may report feeling depressed and hopeless
9. in clinical settings, frequently have depressive disorder diagnoses

FAM Content Component Scales

The items in the Familial Discord (FAM1) Component scale express anger, hate, and resentment toward family members and a desire to get away from family. The Familial Alienation (FAM2) Component scale focuses on feelings that family members are not very understanding or supportive.

WORK INTERFERENCE (WRK)

High scores on the WRK scale are indicative of persons who

1. are reporting a wide variety of attitudes and behaviors that are likely to contribute to poor work performance
2. may be questioning their own career choices

3. say that their families have not approved of their career choices
4. are not ambitious and are lacking in energy
5. express negative attitudes toward co-workers
6. often feel overwhelmed and unable to cope with stress
7. feel insecure
8. often feel like failures
9. have poor self-concepts
10. are obsessive and have problems concentrating
11. have difficulty making decisions and may show poor judgment
12. feel anxious, tense, worried, and fearful
13. feel depressed, sad, and hopeless
14. may have suicidal ideation
15. have low energy level
16. do not have strong achievement orientation
17. often report somatic symptoms
18. may report sleep disturbances
19. in clinical settings, frequently have depressive disorder diagnoses

WRK Content Component Scales

There are no Component scales for the WRK Content scale.

NEGATIVE TREATMENT INDICATORS (TRT)

High scores on the TRT scale are indicative of persons who

1. have negative attitudes toward doctors and mental health treatment
2. may terminate treatment prematurely
3. feel that no one can understand them
4. believe that they have problems that they cannot share with anyone
5. give up easily when problems are encountered
6. feel unable to make significant changes in their lives
7. are experiencing intense emotional distress
8. often report sleep disturbances
9. frequently report somatic symptoms
10. feel depressed, sad, and hopeless
11. may have suicidal ideation
12. have low energy levels
13. often feel anxious and insecure
14. are poor problem solvers
15. often show poor judgment

TRT Content Component Scales

Items in the Low Motivation (TRT1) Component scale have to do with feelings of helplessness and pessimism about working out one's problems. The items in the Inability to Disclose Component scale (TRT2) indicate a person's unwillingness and/or inability to reveal personal information to others.

CRITICAL ITEMS

Critical items are those whose content has been judged to be indicative of serious psychopathology. The first set of MMPI critical items was identified by Grayson (1951) based on clinical judgment. The 38 items dealt primarily with severe psychotic symptoms and overlapped considerably with Scales F and 8. Grayson believed that responses in the scored direction to any of these items suggested potentially serious emotional problems that should be studied further. Caldwell (1969) also generated intuitively a more comprehensive set of critical items that he intended for use with computerized scoring and interpretive services. Koss, Butcher, and Hoffman (1976) investigated the validity of the Grayson and Caldwell critical items as indicators of crises, and they concluded that both sets of items performed poorly as indexes of serious malfunctioning.

Koss et al. (1976) asked clinicians to nominate MMPI items that seemed to be related to six crisis areas (acute anxiety state, depressed suicidal ideation, threatened assault, situational stress due to alcoholism, mental confusion, and persecutory ideas). The nominated items were then compared with criterion measures of the crises, resulting in a list of 73 valid critical items. Following the revision of the MMPI in 1989, the Koss–Butcher critical item set was revised to reflect changes in the item pool.

Lachar and Wrobel (1979) used a similar approach in identifying 111 critical items related to 14 problem areas frequently encountered in inpatient and outpatient samples. All but four of the original Lachar–Wrobel critical items are included in the MMPI-2. It should be noted that this set of critical items has not been revised to include new items that were added to the original MMPI item pool. To protect the integrity of the test, the content of the Koss–Butcher and Lachar–Wrobel critical items do not appear in this book. However, the categories and booklet numbers of items included in each Koss–Butcher critical item category are presented in Appendix A.

Recommendations Concerning Use of the Critical Items

Koss (1979, 1980) summarized the usefulness of critical items. She reviewed research suggesting that the Koss–Butcher and Lachar–Wrobel critical items are more valid than the Grayson or Caldwell critical items. However, Koss also pointed out some cautions in using critical items. All of the critical-item sets overlap considerably with Scales F and 8, and most critical items are keyed in the true direction. Thus, critical-item endorsements can be misleading for persons who are displaying an acquiescence response set or exaggerating their symptoms and problems.

MMPI-2 users who interpret critical-item endorsements should seriously consider Koss's (1980) cautions and recommendations. She concluded that critical items should not be used as a quick assessment of level of maladjustment. Data indicate that the critical items perform poorly in separating normal and psychiatric samples. Also, critical-item lists are not as reliable as scales because of the vulnerability to error of single-item responses. A test taker can misinterpret and/or mismark a single item, leading the test interpreter to an erroneous conclusion, whereas that same mistake in the context of a longer scale would not have much impact on the individual's total score on that scale.

The potential value of using critical items is the same as with the other content approaches discussed in this chapter. Examination of the test takers' responses can clarify the kinds of things they are telling examiners about themselves. However, critical-item responses should not be overinterpreted. In a valid MMPI-2 protocol, endorsement of critical items should lead the clinician to inquire further into the areas assessed by the items.

▨ Restructured Clinical (RC) and Personality Psychopathology Five (PSY-5) Scales

Subsequent to the publication of the MMPI-2 in 1989, some important new scales were developed using the MMPI-2 item pool. The Infrequency–Psychopathology (F_p) scale (Arbisi & Ben-Porath, 1995), which was discussed in Chapter 3 of this book, has proven very useful in identifying overreporting of symptoms, especially in settings with high base rates of serious psychopathology. Two additional substance abuse scales, the Addiction Admission Scale (AAS) and the Addiction Potential Scale (APS), were developed by Weed, Butcher, McKenna, and Ben-Porath (1992). These scales, which will be discussed in Chapter 8 of this book, add to the more familiar MacAndrew Alcoholism Scale–Revised in screening for otherwise unreported substance abuse problems. The Symptom Validity Scale (FBS) was later added to the MMPI-2 scoring and has shown promise as an indicator of overreporting of cognitive deficits. Two additional sets of scales, the Personality Psychopathology Five (PSY-5) scales (Harkness, McNulty, Ben-Porath, & Graham, 2002) and the Restructured Clinical (RC) scales (Tellegen et al., 2003), are discussed in this chapter.

RESTRUCTURED CLINICAL (RC) SCALES

As discussed in Chapter 4, the empirical methodology used in constructing the original Clinical scales of the MMPI resulted in scales that were quite heterogeneous in content and not very independent of each other. Many authors (e.g., Dahlstrom & Welsh, 1960) reported rather high intercorrelations among the MMPI Clinical scales. To some extent these relationships were due to items appearing on more than one scale. However, Welsh (1956) demonstrated that even with overlapping items removed, some of the Clinical scales were strongly intercorrelated. Early factor-analytic studies (e.g., Eichman, 1961; Welsh, 1956) revealed that a major source of variance among the Clinical scales was a factor variously labeled as anxiety, general maladjustment, or emotional distress. Factor analyses of the MMPI-2 Clinical scales have produced similar results (Butcher et al., 1989).

The empirical keying approach used in developing the MMPI Clinical scales involved contrasting separate groups of hospitalized psychiatric patients (e.g., depression, schizophrenia) and a group of nonclinical individuals. It is likely that some of the items identified for inclusion in each Clinical scale were associated with the common emotional distress and unhappiness that led to the patients seeking treatment.

While it is important to know to what extent a test taker is experiencing emotional distress, having that distress reflected in all of the Clinical scales makes it difficult to know to what extent high scores on the scales should be interpreted as indicating characteristics associated with the core constructs of the scales (e.g., depression, aberrant thinking) and to what extent they are the product of a test taker's high level of emotional distress. Clinicians often have used code types, subscales, and Content scales to help clarify the meaning of high scores on the Clinical scales.

Tellegen et al. (2003) developed the Restructured Clinical (RC) scales to overcome some of the limitations of the original Clinical scales and to help in refining interpretations of them. These authors stated that "the RC Scales were designed to preserve the important descriptive properties of the existing MMPI-2 Clinical Scales while enhancing their distinctiveness" (p. 1).

Development of the RC Scales

The description of RC scale development that follows presents the overall approach to scale construction. Some methodological details have been omitted for the sake of brevity, but they can be found in the monograph by Tellegen et al. (2003).

The first step in constructing the RC scales was to develop a general scale labeled Demoralization (RCd). It was anticipated that removal of this general factor from the Clinical scales would result in a set of restructured scales that would be less intercorrelated and have greater discriminant validity than the original Clinical scales. Based on the model of Watson and Tellegen (1985), demoralization was conceptualized as equivalent to the pleasant–unpleasant dimension of self-reported affect. Because Scale 2 and Scale 7 are known to be related to anxiety, depression, and other emotional distress, these scales were thought to contain items that would assess the demoralization dimension. Using four clinical samples, factor analyses of items in Scale 2 and Scale 7 yielded a set of items marking the demoralization factor. These items were scored in a provisional scale that was then used to identify additional demoralization markers by correlating the provisional scale with all other items in the MMPI-2. The resulting Demoralization scale was used in developing other RC scales.

The next step was designed to identify the core component of each original Clinical scale with the general demoralization factor removed. Separate factor analyses were conducted for each of the Clinical scales including items from that scale and from the provisional Demoralization (RCd) scale. Factors were extracted and rotated in a manner that yielded a clear demoralization factor, which included all of the provisional Demoralization scale items as well as items in the Clinical scales that are primarily demoralization markers, and a second factor that could be considered the substantive core for a Clinical scale (e.g., health concerns for Scale 1).

The third step in constructing the RC scales involved identifying items with high loadings on the factor representing the core of each scale to serve as a "seed" scale for each RC scale. This was accomplished by assigning to a given seed scale those items that had the highest loadings on the scale's core factor and that did not have salient loadings on the demoralization factor. An additional requirement was that an item correlated only minimally with the other core factor scales. Overlapping items were then removed, as were items that detracted from the internal consistency of a seed scale. This step was designed to make the seed scales maximally distinct in order to enhance the discriminant validity of the final RC scales.

The 12 seed scales (Demoralization plus one for each original Clinical scale except for Scale 5, which yielded two seed scales representing aesthetic/literary interests and mechanical/physical interests) were then correlated with all other MMPI-2 items in four clinical samples. Items were selected for the RC scales if they had high correlations with a particular seed scale (i.e., convergence) and low correlations with other seed scales (i.e., discrimination). Items were then deleted from a scale if they did not contribute to the scale's internal consistency or, for six scales, if they were not appropriately correlated with conceptually relevant external criterion measures. RC scales were not developed for Scales 5 and 0 because they were not judged to assess core components of psychopathology. However, Tellegen et al. (2003) indicated that restructured versions of Scale 5 and Scale 0 would be developed later.

These complex psychometric and statistical procedures resulted in restructured versions of Clinical Scales 1, 2, 3, 4, 6, 7, 8, and 9 and a Demoralization scale. The names, abbreviations, and number of items for each RC scale are reported in Table 7.1.

Table 7.1 The Restructured Clinical Scales

RCd	Demoralization (dem)	24 items
RC1	Somatic Complaints (som)	27 items
RC2	Low Positive Emotions (lpe)	17 items
RC3	Cynicism (cyn)	15 items
RC4	Antisocial Behavior (asb)	22 items
RC6	Ideas of Persecution (per)	17 items
RC7	Dysfunctional Negative Emotions (dne)	24 items
RC8	Aberrant Experiences (abx)	18 items
RC9	Hypomanic Activation (hpm)	28 items

SOURCE: Excepted from Tellegen, A., Ben-Porath, Y.S., McNulty, J.L., Arbisi, P.A., Graham, J.R., & Kaemmer, B. (2003). *MMPI® -2 (Minnesota Multiphasic Personality Inventory® -2)™ Restructured Clinical (RC) scales: Development, validation, and interpretation.* Copyright © 2003 by the Regents of the University of Minnesota. All rights reserved. Reproduced by permission of the University of Minnesota Press. "MMPI® " and "Minnesota Multiphasic Personality Inventory® " are trademarks owned by the Regents of the University of Minnesota.

Intercorrelations of RC Scales and Clinical Scales

As one would expect, given the methodology for constructing the RC scales, intercorrelations of the RC scales are lower than for the Clinical scales (Table 7.2). This greater independence for the RC scales provides the opportunity for the scales to have greater discriminant validity than the Clinical scales, an issue that will be discussed later in this chapter. Table 7.2 also reports correlations between the RC scales and the original Clinical scales for the MMPI-2 normative sample. In most comparisons, RC scales and the corresponding Clinical scales have strong positive correlations, suggesting that the scales are assessing similar but not identical constructs. The very high correlations (.89 for men and .92 for women) between RC1 and Scale 1 indicate that these two scales are essentially measuring the same construct (somatic concerns). The most interesting (and expected) exception to these patterns of correlations is for the RC3 scale and Scale 3 (−.42 for men and −.24 for women). The RC3 scale does not include the somatic items found in Scale 3; these were assigned to the RC1 scale. Items in Scale 3 indicating naive positive perceptions of other people are scored in the reverse direction for RC3, and the resulting scale is labeled Cynicism.

The data in Table 7.2 also address the extent to which the Demoralization factor was successfully removed (or at least reduced) from the RC scales compared with the original Clinical scales. Tellegen et al. (2003) concluded that the RC scales are substantially less saturated with Demoralization than are the Clinical scales. However, they also noted that several scales (especially RC2 and RC7) are not free of the Demoralization factor because of the conceptual relationships between the constructs underlying these three scales. They speculated that the somewhat higher correlations between Demoralization and the RC9 scale than between Demoralization and Scale 9 may reflect the narrower focus of the RC9 scale on hypomanic activation, an affective state similar to the negative emotionality component of Demoralization. The strong correlations between some RC scales and their Clinical scale counterparts raise the question of the extent to which the RC scales add significantly to the Clinical scales in predicting external criterion measures. This issue will be addressed later in this chapter.

Forbey, Ben-Porath, and Tellegen (2004) compared RC scales and Content scales for 1020 mental health center clients. Comparing these two sets of scales is especially interesting because the methodology used in constructing the Content scales was intended to produce more homogeneous scales than the Clinical scales, and item overlap between Content scales was minimized. Thus, one might expect the RC scales and corresponding Content scales to be more similar than the pairs of RC scales and Clinical scales. As expected, there were strong correlations between most RC scales and their corresponding Content scales (e.g., RC1 and Health Concerns; RC8 and Bizarre Mentation).

Reliability of the RC Scale

Table 7.3 reports internal consistency and test–retest reliability coefficients for the RC scales for the MMPI-2 normative sample and for the three clinical samples.

Table 7.2 Intercorrelations of MMPI-2 RC and Clinical Scales for Men (n = 1138) and Women (n = 1462) in MMPI-2 Normative Sample[a]

SCALE	RCD DEM	RC1 SOM	RC2 LPE	RC3 CYN	RC4 ASB	RC6 PER	RC7 DNE	RC8 ABX	RC9 HPM	1 HS	2 D	3 HY	4 PD	6 PA	7 PT	8 SC	9 MA
RCd	—	.40	.44	.37	.34	.36	.68	.35	.32	.45	.53	.03	.53	.36	.83	.75	.23
RC1	.47	—	.27	.25	.22	.32	.39	.40	.22	.89	.44	.37	.30	.24	.48	.56	.20
RC2	.53	.27	—	.05	.03	.08	.18	.07	.25	.37	.64	.25	.27	.20	.35	.32	.29
RC3	.42	.34	.09	—	.27	.42	.50	.37	.47	.29	.11	-.42	.22	-.19	.46	.47	.34
RC4	.36	.25	.13	.27	—	.26	.33	.38	.32	.21	.02	-.04	.63	.24	.39	.49	.43
RC6	.42	.35	.09	.45	.27	—	.40	.49	.32	.33	.16	-.06	.38	.38	.39	.49	.35
RC7	.73	.46	.31	.49	.34	.43	—	.49	.53	.43	.28	-.24	.33	.21	.82	.72	.33
RC8	.38	.39	-.01	.40	.34	.52	.46	—	.49	.37	.03	-.07	.31	.29	.50	.62	.50
RC9	.34	.28	-.16	.46	.48	.38	.49	.52	—	.21	-.21	-.25	.25	.11	.48	.51	.72
1	.52	.92	.36	.38	.24	.34	.48	.38	.27	—	.53	.41	.33	.23	.53	.56	.15
2	.66	.48	.66	.19	.09	.20	.42	.10	-.10	.56	—	.35	.34	.26	.47	.39	-.21
3	.12	.47	.21	-.24	.01	-.03	-.12	.01	-.14	.53	.35	—	.25	.32	-.05	.01	-.09
4	.57	.32	.30	.29	.64	.42	.37	.36	.31	.36	.37	.26	—	.41	.46	.55	.36
6	.42	.24	.25	-.10	.24	.41	.30	.28	.17	.24	.31	.22	.41	—	.34	.39	.15
7	.86	.55	.45	.46	.39	.45	.83	.48	.47	.59	.61	.09	.51	.43	—	.84	.33
8	.77	.59	.38	.49	.53	.58	.72	.64	.53	.60	.48	.15	.64	.47	.84	—	.46
9	.27	.27	-.22	.39	.44	.39	.34	.54	.74	.25	-.07	.01	.42	.21	.37	.51	—

[a]Correlations for men are above diagonal; correlations for women are below diagonal.

SOURCE: Excerpted (Tables 4.6 and 4.7) from Tellegen, A., Ben-Porath, Y.S., NcNulty, J.L., Arbisi, PA., and Graham, J.R., & Kaemmer, B. (2003). *MMPI®-2 (Minnesota Multiphasic Personality Inventory®-2)™ Restructured Clinical (RC) scales: Development, validation, and interpretation.* Copyright © 2003 by the Regents of the University of Minnesota. All rights reserved. Reproduced by permission of the University of Minnesota Press. "MMPI®" and "Minnesota Multiphasic Personality Inventory®" are trademarks owned by the Regents of the University of Minnesota.

Table 7.3 Internal Consistency (Alpha) Coefficients and Test–Retest Coefficients for RC Scales

| | ALPHA COEFFICIENTS | | | | | | | TEST–RETEST CORRELATIONS | |
| | NORMATIVE SAMPLE | | OUTPATIENT SAMPLE | | INPATIENT SAMPLE 1 | | INPATIENT SAMPLE 2 | NORMATIVE SAMPLE | |
SCALE	MEN (n=1138)	WOMEN (n=1462)	MEN (n=410)	WOMEN (n=610)	MEN (n=722)	WOMEN (n=501)	MEN (n=1229)	MEN (n=82)	WOMEN (n=111)
RCd (dem)	.87	.89	.93	.93	.95	.95	.93	.89	.90
RC1 (som)	.73	.78	.88	.89	.86	.88	.88	.81	.79
RC2 (lpe)	.68	.62	.83	.82	.85	.87	.84	.76	.77
RC3 (cyn)	.80	.79	.81	.80	.86	.84	.84	.76	.87
RC4 (asb)	.76	.74	.81	.77	.83	.82	.83	.90	.87
RC6 (per)	.63	.65	.80	.78	.86	.85	.85	.77	.54
RC7 (dne)	.81	.83	.87	.87	.90	.90	.89	.91	.87
RC8 (abx)	.70	.71	.81	.81	.87	.85	.84	.80	.75
RC9 (hpm)	.79	.76	.80	.78	.84	.83	.83	.88	.86

SOURCE: Excerpted (Tables 4.4 and 4.5) from Tellegen, A., Ben-Porath, Y.S., McNulty, J.L., Arbisi, PA., Graham, & Kaemmer, B. (2003). MMPI®-2 (Minnesota Multiphasic Personality Inventory®-2) ™ Restructured Clinical (RC) Scales: Development, validation, and interpretation. Copyright © 2003 by the Regents of the University of Minnesota. All rights reserved. Reproduced by permission of the University of Minnesota Press. "MMPI® " and "Minnesota Multiphasic Personality Inventory® " are trademarks owned by the Regents of the University of Minnesota.

Because internal consistency was a consideration in the development of the RC scales, it is not surprising that the RC scales have higher internal consistency values than the Clinical scales. In all samples the RC scales had quite acceptable internal consistency, with the coefficients being somewhat higher for the clinical than for the normative samples.

At this time the only test–retest reliability data available for the RC scales are for 82 men and 111 women from the MMPI-2 normative sample who completed the test twice with a retest interval of approximately one week. As the data in Table 7.3 indicate, the stability of the RC scales over this short time period is quite acceptable and in most cases greater than for the corresponding Clinical scales.

Validity of the RC Scales

The correlations between RC scales and the Clinical and Content scales, which were discussed earlier, provide some information concerning the validity of the RC scales. These correlational data indicate that most RC scales are measuring characteristics that are similar, but not identical, to their Clinical and Content scale counterparts. For several scales (e.g., RC1) the correlations are so high that it seems that the RC scales may be redundant with corresponding Clinical and/or Content scales [e.g., Scale 1 and HEA (Health Concerns)]. The RC3 scale, which was restructured more than any other scale, seems to be assessing only a part of what Scale 3 measures (naiveté/cynicism). Both the RC3 scale and the Cynicism (CYN) content scale are measuring similar characteristics. Whereas the RC3 scale seems to be a rather pure measure of misanthropic beliefs, the Cynicism scale seems to measure these beliefs along with suspiciousness.

While scale intercorrelations are of interest, the most important indicators of scale validity are relationships between scales and external criterion measures. Convergent validity is indicated when a scale correlates significantly with external criterion measures with which it is conceptually related. Discriminant validity is indicated when a scale is not related (or less related) to external criterion measures with which one would not expect strong relationships. Several studies have reported data relevant to these issues.

Tellegen et al. (2003) reported correlations between RC scales and several different kinds of external criterion measures for an outpatient mental health center sample and for two psychiatric inpatient samples. These correlations generally supported the convergent validity of the RC scales. For example, for outpatients the RC1 scale had its highest correlation with therapist ratings of somatic symptoms (.58 for men and .35 for women); the RC2 scale had its highest correlation with therapist ratings of depression (.57 for men and .34 for women); and the RC4 scale had its highest correlation with therapist ratings of antisocial behaviors (.36 for men and .35 for women).

Although the RC scales also were significantly related to some criterion measures with which they are not closely related conceptually, these correlations tended to be of lesser magnitude than correlations with conceptually relevant criterion measures. By comparison, some Clinical scales had correlations with conceptually relevant therapist ratings similar in strength to those of corresponding RC scales. The clear exception was Scale 4, for which correlations with therapist ratings of antisocial and acting-out behaviors were noticeably lower than similar correlations for the RC4 scale. The RC6 scale and Clinical Scale 6 and the RC8 scale and Clinical Scale 8 were not strongly correlated with external measures of psychotic behaviors. This likely was due to the rarity of these kinds of psychopathology in this outpatient setting.

Perhaps the most interesting thing about these data is the information provided concerning the greater discriminant validity of RC scales. Clinical scales were more likely than RC scales to be significantly correlated with therapist ratings of characteristics not conceptually related to the scales. This difference in discriminant validity was most marked for the RC4 scale versus Clinical Scale 4.

Sellbom, Ben-Porath, and Graham (2004) examined correlations between RC scales and Clinical scales and external criterion measures for 813 male and female clients at a university clinic. Their results were quite similar to those of the Tellegen et al. (2003) study of community mental health center clients. Again, most RC scales and their Clinical scale counterparts had correlations of similar strength with conceptually relevant external criterion measures. For example, the correlation between the RC1 scale and therapist ratings of somatic symptoms was .25; the corresponding correlation for Clinical Scale 1 was also .25. The RC2 scale correlated .22 with therapist ratings of depression, while Clinical Scale 2 correlated .41 with this criterion measure. Interestingly, the correlation between therapist ratings of depression and the RCd scale was .35. Correlations with therapist ratings of antisocial behavior were .35 for the RC4 scale and .25 for Clinical Scale 4. However, once again, there was evidence of greater discriminant validity for the RC scales than for the Clinical scales. More Clinical scales than RC scales were significantly correlated with general maladjustment and depression.

Forbey et al. (2004) compared the external validity of the RC scales and the Content scales using both outpatient and inpatient samples. As in the other studies cited earlier, both the RC scales and their Content scale counterparts were strongly correlated with conceptually related criterion measures. For example, the RC1 scale correlated .44 with therapist ratings of somatic symptoms, and the HEA Content scale correlated .45 with this variable. The RC4 scale and ASP Content scale correlations with therapist ratings of antisocial behaviors were .37 and .30, respectively.

However, as in the studies described earlier, the discriminant validity of the RC scales was generally greater than for the Content scales. The authors pointed out that some content scales (FRS, FAM, and ANG) assess areas not well represented by RC scales. Unfortunately, adequate criterion measures were not available in their study to examine the validity of these Content scales compared with the RC scales. They also acknowledged that the construct of social introversion is not adequately assessed by the RC scales, although development of additional restructured scales to assess this and other interpersonal constructs was anticipated.

Other studies have reached similar conclusions about the convergent and discriminant validity of the RC and Clinical scales in a variety of settings: outpatient mental health center (Sellbom, Ben-Porath & Graham, 2006; Sellbom, Graham, & Schenk, 2006; Simms, Cassilas, Clark, Watson, & Doebbeling, 2005; Wallace & Liljequist, 2005); inpatient psychiatric (Arbisi, Sellbom, & Ben-Porath, 2008; Handel & Archer, 2008); college clinics (Forbey & Ben-Porath, 2008; Osberg, Haseley, & Kamas, 2008; Sellbom & Ben-Porath, 2005); and candidates for bariatric surgery (Wygant et al., 2007). Studying clients at a university clinic, Binford and Liljequist (2008) found that the RC4 scale had better convergent and discriminant validity than Scale 4 or the ASP Content scale. However, they did not find significant differences in convergent or discriminant validity between the RCd and RC2 scales and Scale 2 or the DEP Content scale.

The utility of the RC scales in differential diagnosis has been demonstrated in several studies. Kamphuis, Arbisi, Ben-Porath, and McNulty (2008) found that the RC scales were superior to the Clinical scales in discriminating between patients with Axis I disorders (substance use or major depression) who did or did not also have Axis II disorders. Wolf et al. (2008) found that the Clinical and RC scales were equally effective in predicting PTSD diagnoses based on structured interviews, but the RC scales were superior to the Clinical scales in predicting comorbid diagnoses with PTSD.

Several investigators have factor analyzed scores on the RC scales. Tellegen et al. (2006) identified eight factors that corresponded with the eight RC scales (excluding the Demoralization scale). However, Hoelzle and Meyer (2008) concluded that a five-factor solution was optimal. An externalizing, antisocial factor was associated with elevations on RC4 and RC9. A depressive/withdrawal factor was associated with elevations on RC2 and RCd. RC1 defined a somatic factor, and RC6 and RC8 defined a psychotic factor. Finally, a cynicism factor was associated with RC3 scale elevations. It should be noted that this factor structure is similar to that reported for the RC scales in the MMPI-2-RF manual (see Chapter 14 of this book).

If all available data are considered, several conclusions about the RC scales seem appropriate. The RC scales have convergent validity that is similar to, and in some cases greater than, corresponding Clinical and Content scales. Although Demoralization is still represented to some degree in the RC scales, they are less saturated with this general factor than the Clinical or Content scales. This reduction of the Demoralization factor in the RC scales has resulted in somewhat greater discriminant validity for these scales. Some RC scales are more focused measures of important core constructs than their Clinical and Content scale counterparts. Research findings have provided important information concerning the interpretation of scores on the RC scales.

The RC scales have not been without critics. An entire issue of the *Journal of Personality Assessment* (*JPA*) (October 2006) was devoted to concerns about the RC scales and responses by the authors of the scales to these concerns. It is not possible to discuss all of the concerns and responses raised in this special issue. However, a brief summary of the major issues may be useful to readers.

In the *JPA* special issue Nichols (2006); Rogers, Sewell, Harrison, and Jordan (2006); and Butcher, Hamilton, Rouse, and Cumella (2006) expressed concerns about the manner in which the RC scales were constructed. In turn, Tellegen et al. (2006) responded to these concerns, pointing out errors of logic and presenting new data to address some of the concerns.

A major concern expressed by Nichols (2006) had to do with using demoralization as a marker of first-factor variance in MMPI-2 responses. He argued that the Demoralization (RCd) scale is too heavily weighted with depressive content and that anxiety content is diminished. Tellegen et al. (2006) reported data indicating that the RCd scale is related to both depression and anxiety to the same extent as Welsh's A scale and other first-factor markers recommended by Nichols.

Nichols (2006) also expressed concern that by adding items to RC scales that were not in corresponding Clinical scales, the RC scales "drifted" from the original constructs that the Clinical scales were constructed to measure. For example, he maintained that because the RC9 scale contains aggressive content not represented in Scale 9, the RC9 scale would not be a good measure of bipolar disorder. In response, Tellegen et al. (2006) cited research published subsequent to the publication of the RC monograph indicating that just the opposite seems to be true. In the cited research the RC9 scale was a better predictor of bipolar disorder than Scale 9. Even if the constructs measured by the RC scales are not identical to those that the Clinical scales were constructed to measure, it really does not matter as long as we have a clear understanding of what the RC scales are measuring.

In a related argument, Nichols (2006) claimed that the more homogeneous RC scales would not be good measures of more complex, heterogeneous constructs (i.e., clinical syndromes). Again Tellegen et al. (2006) cited research indicating that this is not the case. The RC scales are actually better predictors of complex criteria than are the Clinical scales.

In yet another criticism of the RC scales, Nichols (2006) maintained that the constructs measured by the RC scales can be measured by existing MMPI scales that are more widely used and empirically validated. He criticized the RC scale authors for not including data in their monograph comparing the RC scales and the Content scales. Tellegen et al. (2006) conducted additional data analyses and reported results indicating that the RC scales were superior to the Content scales in predicting most external criteria.

Caldwell (2006) expressed some of the same concerns as Nichols about paradigm shift and redundancy between the RC and Content scales. He additionally maintained that first-factor variance should not be removed from the Clinical scales because distress is part of the disorders that the Clinical scales were constructed to measure. Tellegen et al. (2006) agreed that is important to measure distress but that it should be measured only once rather than having it represented in all of the Clinical scales and therefore limiting their discriminant validity.

Butcher et al. (2006) expressed great concern that the RC3 scale is not similar at all to Scale 3. They felt that losing Scale 3 would make it difficult to identify hysterical diagnoses and to adequately understand chronic pain patients. The authors of the RC scales deliberately disassembled the components of Scale 3. The somatic component is represented in the RC1 scale. Tellegen et al. (2006) explained that when Scale 3 items were factor analyzed three factors were identified. One factor included primarily demoralization items; a second included items involving somatic symptoms; and a third involved items dealing with cynical views. A decision was made to have RC1 represent the somatic complaints and the cynical content was assigned to RC3. Tellegen et al. pointed out that the two major components of Scale 3, somatic complaints and cynical attitudes, are still represented in the MMPI-2-RF by the RC1 and RC3 scales, respectively. However, they are less confounded than in Scale 3.

Rogers et al. (2006) attempted to replicate factor analyses used by Tellegen et al. (2003) in constructing the RC scales. They were able to replicate results for five of the RC scales but not for RC4, RC8, and RC9. Tellegen et al. (2006) indicated that Rogers et al. did not use the same factor loading criteria in identifying items to be included in scales. They reported new factor analysis data using the Rogers et al. criteria and were able to replicate their results nicely.

Rogers et al. (2006) also were concerned that in a large sample of individuals whose MMPI-2 results had been submitted to Caldwell Reports, 40–45% of cases had within-normal-limits RC scale scores, perhaps suggesting that the RC scales are not adequately sensitive to psychopathology. Tellegen et al. (2006) responded by pointing out that approximately one-third of cases in the Rogers et al. sample were likely to have been quite defensive when completing the MMPI-2, having T scores equal to or greater than 65 on the L or K scales. Obviously, the defensiveness was likely to suppress scores on the RC scales.

Rogers et al. (2006) expressed concern that Tellegen et al. (2003) had not taken social desirability into account in the construction of the RC scales and that this failure would make the RC scales susceptible to noncredible responding. However, Sellbom, Ben-Porath, Graham, Arbisi, and Bagby (2005) demonstrated that the RC scales, the Clinical scales, and the Content scales were equally susceptible to overreporting and underreporting. Tellegen et al. (2006) indicated that they see social desirability as a substantive component of psychopathology that should not be removed from scales. Many years ago Block (1965) presented convincing evidence to support this view.

Interpretation of RC Scales

Clinicians who want to use the RC scales in their MMPI-2 interpretations can score and profile the scales by hand, using materials available from Pearson Assessments. Item numbers and scoring directions for the RC scales are provided in the MMPI-2 RC scales monograph (Tellegen et al., 2003). This monograph also includes uniform T-score equivalents for RC scale raw scores for the MMPI-2 normative samples. RC scale scores and profiles are available in the computerized scoring reports available from Pearson Assessments.

When interpreting any MMPI-2 scales, clinicians first need to assess the validity of test protocols. If the validity indicators suggest overreporting or underreporting that invalidates a protocol (see Chapter 3 of this book), obviously no other scales should be interpreted. However, when there is evidence of overreporting or underreporting that is not extreme enough to invalidate a protocol, the test-taking approach should be taken into account when interpreting other scales. Sellbom, Ben-Porath, Graham, et al. (2005) compared the Clinical, Content, and RC scales in terms of the extent to which scores are affected by deliberate overreporting or underreporting. Using data from several student and clinical samples, these investigators found that all three sets of scales are about equally susceptible to the effects of overreporting and underreporting. They concluded that clinicians should be cautious in the interpretation of any of these scales when there are indications that the test taker has engaged in underreporting or overreporting.

The RC scale monograph (Tellegen et al., 2003) and the research studies described here indicate that some of the RC scales can add significantly to the interpretation of MMPI-2 protocols. Not only can the scales clarify the meaning of elevated scores on the Clinical scales, they can be used to generate inferences about test takers independently of the Clinical scales.

Tellegen et al. (2003) suggested tentative interpretive guidelines for the RC scales. They recommended that, as with most MMPI-2 scales, a T score greater than 65 (approximately the 92nd percentile for the MMPI-2 normative sample) be considered a high score for most RC scales. However, for some RC scales they also discussed the meaning of even more elevated T scores. For several RC scales, interpretations of low scores (T ≤ 40) are suggested.

This author recommends the following strategy for integrating Clinical and RC scale information. First, consider that for any particular Clinical scale/RC scale pair (e.g., Scale 1 and RC1) there are four possibilities: (1) neither the Clinical nor RC scale score is high; (2) both the Clinical and RC scale scores are high; (3) the Clinical scale score is high but the corresponding RC scale score is not high; or, finally, (4) the Clinical scale score is not high but the corresponding RC scale score is high. Sellbom et al. (2004) found that in mental health center and university clinic settings, most often either both a Clinical scale and its RC scale counterpart would be elevated or neither scale would be elevated. Having only one elevated scale in the Clinical/RC pair is less common but occurs frequently enough to be important in MMPI-2 interpretation. For most Clinical/RC scale pairs, it is more common for the Clinical scale to be elevated and the corresponding RC scale not to be elevated than vice versa.

If neither the Clinical nor RC scale T score is high, no interpretations should be made of either scale. If both the Clinical and RC scale T scores are high, inferences about the core construct for the Clinical scale (e.g., health concerns for Scale 1) can be made with considerable confidence. Inferences about characteristics of the test taker in addition to those associated with the core construct may also be appropriate based on the high score on the Clinical scale. For example, a high Scale 7 score and a high RC7 scale score suggest inferences about characteristics associated with the core construct of dysfunctional negative emotions (e.g., anxiety, irritability, unhappiness). Additional inferences, based on the high Scale 7 score, would also be in order (e.g., organized, persistent, tendency to stay in treatment longer than most patients).

When the Clinical scale score is high but the RC scale score is not, one should be quite cautious about making inferences that the test taker has characteristics consistent with the core construct associated with the Clinical scale. The high Clinical scale score may very well be a product of demoralization and not indicative of characteristics associated with the core construct. In such cases, the RCd scale score also is likely to be high.

If the Clinical scale score is not high but the RC scale score is high, inferences about characteristics related to the core construct (e.g., health concerns for RC1) are appropriate. The lower Clinical scale score is likely to result from the absence of demoralization in the protocol. The person may have endorsed items consistent with the core construct for the scale but not many items having to do with demoralization, leading to a Clinical scale score that is not high. Obviously, in such cases one would not expect a high RCd scale score.

Demoralization (RCd)

The RCd scale score provides an indication of the overall emotional discomfort and turmoil that a person is experiencing. High scorers (T > 65) on this scale are likely also to have high scores on other RC, Clinical, and Content scales, especially those that have strong affective components.

Very high scores (T ≥ 80) on the RCd scale indicate persons who

1. are experiencing significant emotional turmoil
2. report feeling depressed
3. report being anxious and unable to concentrate
4. report somatic complaints that may increase in times of stress
5. feel overwhelmed by the demands of their life situations
6. feel incapable of coping with their current life circumstances
7. should be evaluated for suicide risk
8. may be motivated for treatment because of emotional distress
9. need intervention to relieve emotional distress

Moderately high scores (T = 65–79) indicate persons who

1. feel sad and unhappy
2. feel anxious much of the time
3. are dissatisfied with their life situations
4. have poor self-concepts and feel like failures
5. are pessimistic about their lives getting better

Low scores (T < 39) indicate persons who report a higher than average level of morale and life satisfaction.

Somatic Complaints (RC1)

The RC1 scale is very similar to Scale 1 and the Health Concerns (HEA) Content scale. Like these latter two scales, the cardinal feature of high scorers (T > 65) on the RC1 scale is somatic preoccupation.

High scores on the RC1 scale indicate persons who

1. report multiple somatic complaints, including gastrointestinal problems, head pain, and neurological symptoms
2. have increased somatic symptoms in times of stress
3. are quite resistant to considering psychological factors that may be related to somatic symptoms
4. if physical explanations for their somatic symptoms can be ruled out, should be further evaluated for somatoform disorders

Low scores (T < 39) indicate persons who report a sense of physical well-being.

Low Positive Emotions (RC2)

High scores (T > 65) on the RC2 scale indicate person who

1. lack positive emotional experiences in life
2. have deficits in ability to experience joy and happiness (anhedonia)
3. are unhappy and demoralized
4. are at increased risk for depression
5. lack energy to handle demands of their life situations
6. find it difficult to take charge, make decisions, and get things done
7. tend to be introverted, passive, and withdrawn in social situations
8. often feel bored and isolated
9. are pessimistic
10. have low expectations of success and are not likely to place themselves in competitive situations
11. should be evaluated for antidepressant medications
12. If T ≥ 75, may need inpatient treatment for depression
13. may have difficulty engaging in treatment because of low positive emotionality

Low scores (T < 39) on the RC2 scale indicate persons who

1. report a high level of psychological well-being
2. report a wide range of emotionally positive experiences
3. report feeling confident and energetic
4. are extraverted and socially engaged
5. are optimistic about the future

Cynicism (Rc3)

Clinical Scale 3 has two major components—somatic complaints and avowal of excessive trust of others. As mentioned earlier, the somatic complaint component was assigned to the RC1 scale. The RC3 scale assesses the second component, scored in the opposite direction from Scale 3.

High scores (T ≥ 65) indicate persons who

1. have cynical beliefs
2. see other people as untrustworthy, uncaring, and concerned only about themselves
3. are hostile and feel alienated from others
4. may have difficulty forming therapeutic relationships
5. need help in developing interpersonal trust

Low scores (T < 39) on the RC3 scale indicate persons who

1. disavow cynical beliefs
2. see others as well-intentioned and trustworthy
3. may be naive, gullible, and overly trusting of others

Antisocial Behavior (RC4)

Clinical Scale 4 is often elevated in persons with histories of antisocial attitudes and behaviors. However, because Scale 4 is quite saturated with a general Demoralization factor, high scores do not necessarily indicate antisocial proclivities. The RC4 scale is a purer measure than Scale 4 of antisocial characteristics.

High scores (T ≥ 65) on the RC4 scale indicate persons who

1. report histories of antisocial behaviors
2. find it difficult to conform to societal norms and expectations
3. are likely to have been in trouble with the law
4. are at increased risk for substance abuse
5. behave aggressively toward other people
6. are critical, argumentative, and antagonistic
7. have conflictual relationships with other people
8. may have significant family problems
9. are not likely to be motivated for treatment
10. may not be very complaint in treatment
11. need help in developing better self-control

Low scores (T < 39) on the RC4 scale indicate persons who report higher than average levels of behavioral constraint.

Ideas of Persecution (RC6)

Because the RC6 scale is less saturated with Demoralization than Scale 6, it is a purer measure of persecutory thinking.

High scores (T ≥ 65) indicate persons who

1. feel targeted, controlled, or victimized by others
2. are suspicious of the motivation of others
3. have difficulty in forming relationships
4. if T > 80, may indicate paranoid delusions and/or hallucinations
5. if T > 80, should be evaluated further for psychotic disorders
6. may have difficulty in forming therapeutic relationships

Low scores (T < 39) on this scale are not interpreted.

Dysfunctional Negative Emotions (RC7)

High scores (T ≥ 65) on the RC7 scale indicate persons who

1. report negative emotional experiences, including anxiety, fear, and irritability
2. worry excessively
3. experience intruding ideation
4. report feeling sad and unhappy
5. are insecure and excessively sensitive to perceived criticism
6. are self-critical and guilt-prone
7. ruminate and brood about perceived failures
8. may be motivated for treatment because of emotional distress
9. should be evaluated for anxiolytic medications

Low scores on the RC7 scale indicate persons who report below average levels of negative emotional experiences.

Aberrant Experiences (RC8)

Because the RC8 scale is less saturated with Demoralization than Clinical Scale 8, it has the potential to be a more focused measure of sensory, perceptual, cognitive, and motor disturbances suggestive of psychotic disorders.

High scores (T ≥ 65) on the RC8 scale indicate persons who

1. report unusual sensory, perceptual, cognitive or motor experiences
2. may experience hallucinations and/or delusions
3. may experience bizarre sensory experiences
4. have impaired reality testing
5. may report feeling anxious and/or depressed
6. have impaired occupational and interpersonal functioning
7. in mental health settings should be evaluated further for psychotic disorders
8. may require treatment in structured settings
9. should be evaluated for antipsychotic medications
10. may find it difficult to participate appropriately in treatment because of disordered thinking

Low scores (T < 39) on the RC8 scale are not interpreted.

Hypomanic Activation (RC9)

Although the RC9 scale and Clinical Scale 9 do not share many items, they seem to be very similar scales. Neither scale is heavily saturated with the Demoralization factor, and both seem to be assessing similar constructs.

High scores (T ≥ 65) on the RC9 scale indicate persons who

1. experience thought racing
2. experience high energy levels

3. have heightened mood
4. are irritable and aggressive
5. show poor impulse control
6. may engage in antisocial behaviors
7. may abuse substances
8. are sensation seekers and risk takers
9. if T > 75, may experience manic episodes
10. should be evaluated further for bipolar disorders
11. may find appropriate participation in treatment difficult because of excessive behavioral activation
12. should be evaluated for mood-stabilizing medications

Low scores (T < 39) on the RC9 scale indicate persons who have below average levels of activation and engagement with their environments.

PERSONALITY PSYCHOPATHOLOGY FIVE (PSY-5) SCALES

Widiger (1997) and others have articulated concerns about a categorical classification system of mental disorders and have suggested dimensional approaches that conceptualize personality disorders as extensions of normal range personality functioning. The Personality Psychopathology Five (PSY-5) scales were constructed to assess personality traits relevant to both normal functioning and clinical problems (Harkness, McNulty, & Ben-Porath, 1995). The conceptualization underlying the scales is similar, but not identical, to the five-factor model of personality. Although Harkness et al. subscribed to the notion of broad bandwidth personality constructs, they felt that existing scales for assessing such constructs (e.g., the NEO-PI-R, Costa & McCrae, 1992) were not adequate for assessing both normal and abnormal personality functioning.

The PSY-5 Constructs

The constructs that the PSY-5 scales were designed to measure were identified by having lay persons (hospital volunteers and college students) rate personality descriptors using the method of psychological distances. This methodology has been described in several places, but the most concise description is in a monograph published by the University of Minnesota Press (Harkness et al., 2002).

Harkness first assembled a large pool of descriptors of personality and personality disorders. One hundred and twenty descriptors of personality disorders were selected from the *Diagnostic and Statistical Manual III-R* (American Psychiatric Association, 1987) and were reworded so that they could be understood by lay persons. In addition, 16 descriptors of psychopathy (Cleckley, 1982) were similarly reworded. Finally, 94 descriptors of normal personality were generated based on personality dimensions described by Tellegen (1982). The lay raters were asked to group similar descriptors together, and these ratings were subjected to mathematical analyses to identify clusters of personality features.

The 60 clusters of personality features resulting from these procedures were then examined by other lay persons who were asked to group similar features together, and these ratings were subjected to latent root methods, yielding five broad constructs that represented both normal and abnormal personality. It is these five constructs (Aggressiveness, Psychoticism, Constraint, Negative Emotionality/Neuroticism, and Positive Emotionality/Extraversion) that were the basis for the construction of the PSY-5 scales of the MMPI-2. It should be noted that the Constraint construct later was reversed and relabeled as Disconstraint and that Positive Emotionality/Extraversion later was reversed and relabeled as Introversion/Low Positive Emotionality.

Harkness et al. (2002) provided brief descriptions of the PSY-5 constructs (appropriately reversed and relabeled). Aggressiveness (AGGR) focuses on offensive and instrumental aggression and may include enjoyment of intimidating others to accomplish one's goals. Psychoticism (PSYC) has to do with disconnection from reality, including unshared beliefs and unusual sensory and perceptual experiences, and feeling alienated and having an unrealistic expectation of harm. Disconstraint (DISC) involves risk-taking, impulsivity, and ignoring traditional moral beliefs and behaviors. Negative Emotionality/Neuroticism (NEGE) is a predisposition to experience negatively valenced emotions, to focus on problematic features of incoming information, to worry, to be self-critical, to feel guilty, and to concoct worst-case scenarios. Introversion/Low Positive Emotionality (INTR) involves limited capacity to experience joy and positive engagement and being socially introverted.

Construction of the PSY-5 Scales

Using the constructs derived from the procedures described earlier, Harkness et al. (1995) identified MMPI-2 items that were judged to be assessing each construct. First, 114 college students were trained to understand each of the PSY-5 constructs. These students then examined each MMPI-2 item and identified any that were judged to assess each construct. Items identified in this manner by a majority of raters were selected for preliminary PSY-5 scales.

Table 7.4 Personality Psychopathology-Five (PSY-5) Scales

Aggressiveness	AGGR	18 items
Psychoticism	PSYC	25 items
Disconstraint	DISC	29 items
Negative Emotionality/Neuroticism	NEGE	33 items
Introversion/Low Positive Emotionality	INTR	34 items

SOURCE: Excerpted from Harkness, A.R., McNulty, J.L., Ben-Porath, Y.S., & Graham, J.R. (2002). *MMPI®-2 Personality Psychopathology Five (PSY-5) Scales: Gaining an overview for case conceptualization and treatment planning.* Copyright © 2002 by the Regents of the University of Minnesota. All rights reserved. Reproduced by permission of the University of Minnesota Press. "MMPI® " and "Minnesota Multiphasic Personality Inventory® " are trademarks owned by the Regents of the University of Minnesota.

Experts then reviewed the preliminary scales to make sure that items in a scale could be clearly keyed to indicate the construct, were direct measures of that construct, and were relevant to only one construct. The preliminary scales were revised and then subjected to psychometric analyses based on data from four large samples. Any item that correlated more strongly with a scale other than the one on which it was keyed was deleted. An item is not scored on more than one PSY-5 scale. Uniform T scores were generated for each raw score based on data from the MMPI-2 normative sample. Table 7.4 lists the PSY-5 scales and the number of items in each scale. Item numbers and scored directions for each of the PSY-5 scales can be found in the MMPI-2 manual (Butcher et al., 2001). Tables for converting raw scores on the PSY-5 scales to Uniform T scores can also be found in the MMPI-2 manual.

Reliability of the PSY-5 Scales

Harkness et al. (1995) reported internal consistency coefficients for the MMPI-2 normative sample and for three clinical samples (Table 7.5), and Trull, Useda, Costa, and McCrae (1995) published similar data for two samples of psychiatric patients. Subsequently, internal consistency data were reported for college students (Sharpe & Desai, 2001) and Dutch psychiatric patients (Egger, De Mey, Derksen, & van der Staak, 2003). In all of these nonclinical and clinical samples, the PSY-5 scales had acceptable internal consistency (> .60). In general, the scales were a bit more internally consistent for clinical than for nonclinical samples.

Because the PSY-5 scales are thought to measure rather enduring personality characteristics, scores on these scales should be relatively stable over time. Harkness et al. (1995) reported test–retest reliability coefficients for the MMPI-2 normative sample (one-week interval) and for the Boston VA Normative Aging sample (five-year interval). Trull et al. (1995) reported test–retest coefficients for

Table 7.5 Internal Consistency (Alpha) Coefficients for PSY-5 Scales

	ALPHA COEFFICIENTS				
SCALE	NORMATIVE ($n = 2567$)	COLLEGE ($n = 2928$)	PSYCH. A[a] ($n = 328$)	PSYCH. B[b] ($n = 156$)	CDC ($n = 1196$)
AGGR	.68	.71	.70	.73	.72
PSYC	.70	.74	.84	.78	.74
DISC	.71	.69	.73	.68	.75
NEGE	.84	.84	.88	.88	.86
INTR	.71	.74	.86	.85	.81

NOTE: AGGR = Aggressiveness, PSYC = Psychoticism, DISC = Disconstraint, NEGE = Negative Emotionality/Neuroticism, INTR = Introversion/Low Positive Emotionality; a = state hospital psychiatric patients, b = private hospital psychiatric patients, c = chemical dependency.
SOURCE: Excerpted (Tables 1 and 2) from MMPI® -2 Personality Psychopathology Five (PSY-5) Scales. Gaining an overview for case conceptualization and treatment planning by Allan R. Harkness, John L. McNulty, Yossef S. Ben-Porath, and John R. Graham. Copyright © 2002 by the Regents of the University of Minnesota. All rights reserved. Reproduced by permission of the University of Minnesota Press. "MMPI® " and "Minnesota Multiphasic Personality Inventory® " are trademarks owned by the Regents of the University of Minnesota.

Table 7.6 Test–Retest Reliability Coefficients for PSY-5 Scales

SCALE	1-WEEK[a]	3-MONTH[b]	6-MONTH[b]	5-YEAR[c]
AGGR	.82	.65	.62	.74
PSYC	.78	.83	.67	.69
DISC	.88	.84	.86	.74
NEGE	.88	.78	.84	.82
INTR	.84	.76	.70	.79

NOTE: AGGR = Aggressiveness, PSYC = Psychoticism, DISC = Disconstraint, NEGE = Negative Emotionality/ Neuroticism, INTR = Introversion/Low Positive Emotionality; [a] 5 = 111 men and women in MMPI-2 normative sample, [b] = 44 psychiatric outpatients, [c] = approximately 959–998 men in Boston VA Normative Aging Sample. SOURCE FOR 1-WEEK DATA: Excerpted (Table 3) from Harkness, A.R., McNulty, J.L., Ben-Porath, Y.S., & Graham, J.R. (2002). *MMPI® -2 Personality Psychopathology Five (PSY-5) Scales: Gaining an overview for case conceptualization and treatment planning.* Copyright © 2002 by the Regents of the University of Minnesota. All rights reserved. Reproduced by permission of the University of Minnesota Press. "MMPI® " and "Minnesota Multiphasic Personality Inventory® " are trademarks owned by the Regents of the University of Minnesota. SOURCE FOR 3-MONTH AND 6-MONTH DATA: Trull, T.J., Useda, J.D., Costa, P.T., & McCrae, R.R. (1995). Comparison of the MMPI-2 Personality Psychopathology Five (PSY-5), the NEO-PI, and the NEO-PI-R. *Psychological Assessment, 7,* 508–516. Copyright © 1995 by the American Psychological Association. Reproduced by permission. SOURCE FOR 5-YEAR DATA: Harkness, A.R., Spiro, A., Butcher, J.N., & Ben-Porath, Y.S. (1995, August). *Personality Psychopathology Five (PSY-5) in the Boston VA Normative Aging Study.* Paper presented at the 103rd Annual Convention of the American Psychological Association, New York. Reproduced by permission from the authors.

the PSY-5 scales for psychiatric patients for whom repeat MMPI-2s were available after 3 and 6 months. The reliability coefficients for these various samples are reported in Table 7.6. These coefficients suggest that the PSY-5 scales are temporally stable even for patients who are undergoing psychiatric treatment and for nonpatients over relatively long periods of time.

Validity of the PSY-5 Scales

Bagby, Ryder, Ben-Dat, Bacchiochi, and Parker (2002) reported data that support the construct validity of the PSY-5 scales. These investigators conducted confirmatory factor analyses of items in the PSY-5 scales for college student and psychiatric patient samples. They reported a good fit between the hypothesized model underlying the PSY-5 scales and their factor-analytic results.

Some validity studies have examined relationships between PSY-5 scales and scales from other self-report inventories. Harkness et al. (1995) correlated PSY-5 scales with scales from Tellegen's Multidimensional Personality Questionnaire (MPQ; Tellegen, 1982). Given that MPQ constructs were the basis, at least in part, for the determination of the PSY-5 constructs, it is not surprising that expected relationships between the two sets of scales were obtained. For example, the PSY-5 Aggressiveness scale's highest correlation was with the MPQ Aggression scale, and the PSY-5 Disconstraint scale correlated most highly (and negatively) with the MPQ Constraint super factor scale. Harkness et al. also correlated PSY-5 scales with scales from the 16PF. Again, correlations between the sets of scales were consistent with definitions of the PSY-5 constructs. For example, the PSY-5 Disconstraint scale had its highest positive correlation with the 16PF Happy-Go-Lucky versus Sober scale and its highest negative correlations with the Conscientious versus Expedient and Assertive versus Humble scales of the 16PF.

PSY-5 scales have also been correlated with scores on the NEO and NEO-PI-R for older nonclinical men (Trull et al., 1995) and psychiatric patients (Bagby, Sellbom, Costa, & Widiger, 2008; Egger et al., 2003). Data from these studies demonstrated expected patterns of relationships that generally supported the construct validity of the PSY-5 scales.

Sharpe and Desai (2001) examined relationships between PSY-5 scale scores and scales from the Buss and Perry Aggression Questionnaire (AQ; Buss & Perry, 1992). Aggressiveness (AGGR) scale scores were significantly correlated with the total score and all subscale scores of the AQ. However, the AGGR scale was especially important in predicting scores on the Verbal Aggression subscale of the AQ, a measure that seems to be assessing an assertiveness or instrumental component of aggression. Harkness et al. (2002) reported correlations between PSY-5 scales and scales from the SCL-90-R. Most of the PSY-5 scales were significantly correlated with many SCL-90-R scales. This apparent lack of discriminant validity may be explained, at least to a large extent, by the high intercorrelations between the SCL-90-R scales.

PSY-5 scales also have been correlated with history variables for male and female mental health center clients (Harkness et al., 2002) and for men and women referred to a court clinic for forensic evaluations (Petroskey, Ben-Porath, & Stafford, 2003). PSY-5 scales were correlated with expected history variables (e.g., Aggressiveness with history of being physically abusive; Introversion/Low Positive Emotionality with history of previous suicide attempts). Harkness et al. (2002) also reported relationships between PSY-5 scales and therapist ratings of their clients. Again, expected relationships were observed. The highest correlation for the AGGR scale was with therapist ratings of aggressive behavior, and the highest correlation for the DISC scale was with therapist ratings of antisocial behavior. Although the NEGE and INTR scales were correlated significantly with many therapist ratings, it is interesting to note that the ratings having to do with anger and antisocial behaviors were noticeably lacking among the correlates for these two scales.

Using a sample of private practice clients, Wygant, Sellbom, Graham, and Schenk (2006) found that the PSY-5 scales added incrementally to the Clinical and Content scales in predicting personality disorder criteria. The AGGR scale was most related to criteria for narcissistic, antisocial, and paranoid disorders; PSYC was most related to borderline, paranoid, and schizotypal disorders; DISC was most strongly related to antisocial disorders; and INTR was most strongly related to avoidant disorders. NEGE was significantly related to all of the personality disorders, but it was most strongly related to borderline and schizotypal disorders.

A study by Miller, Kaloupek, Dillon, and Keane (2004) demonstrated that the PSY-5 scales can be helpful in understanding the diversity of symptoms reported by patients with diagnoses of posttraumatic stress disorder (PTSD). Three groups of PTSD patients were identified on the basis of cluster analysis of

PSY-5 scale scores: (1) low pathology, (2) externalizing, and (3) internalizing. The low pathology group had PSY-5 scale scores within a normal range, the externalizing group was characterized by high negative emotionality and low constraint, and the internalizing group was characterized by high negative emotionality and low positive emotionality. The groups differed in terms of comorbid disorders, with the externalizers showing higher rates of alcohol-related and antisocial personality disorders and the internalizers showing higher rates of panic and major depressive disorder. The findings suggested that premorbid personality characteristics may influence the expression of posttraumatic symptomatology.

Caillouet, Boccaccini, Varela, Davis, and Rostow (2010) examined relationships between PSY-5 scale scores and several measures of negative job performance of law enforcement officers. The PSY-5 scales were only mildly related to supervisor ratings of job misconduct. However, stronger relationships were found between PSY-5 scale scores and involuntary employment termination. The relationships were stronger among officers who did not have elevated L and K scale scores, with elevated scores on the AGGR and DISC scales having the strongest relationships.

Taken together, these various studies suggest strong support for the construct validity of the PSY-5 scales. The PSY-5 scales seem to be related to important personality characteristics and behaviors that are consistent with the constructs underlying the scales. Although some extratest characteristics are related to more than one PSY-5 scale, there are some data suggesting that the scales have discriminant validity. For example, Petroskey et al. (2003) found that the AGGR scale was positively correlated with antisocial personality disorder diagnoses and histories of violence among criminal offenders but negatively correlated with or unrelated to diagnoses of depression and anxiety disorders. The Psychoticism (PSYC) scale was positively related to diagnoses of schizophrenia but unrelated to antisocial personality disorder diagnoses. A.R. Harkness (personal communication, December 8, 2004) found that correlations between PSY-5 scales and Demoralization (RCd) were modest compared with other MMPI-2 scales.

In summary, research involving the PSY-5 scales indicates that they are a useful source of information about the underlying personality characteristics of clinical and nonclinical test takers. Harkness and Lilienfeld (1997) and Harkness and McNulty (2006) have made some interesting suggestions concerning the use of information about personality traits, such as that provided by the PSY-5 scales, in treatment planning. Vendrig, Derksen, and de Mey (2000) found that pain patients with higher scores on the Introversion/Low Positive Emotionality (INTR) scale showed greater improvements in treatment satisfaction and self-rated emotional change. However, the PSY-5 scales were not related to measures of physical change (e.g., pain intensity, fear of movement).

PSY-5 Facet Scales

Based on research indicating that lower-level facets of other Five Factor Model instruments led to better predictive accuracy in the area of personality psychopathology, Arnau, Handel, and Archer (2005) used Principal Components Analysis to derive subscales for the MMPI-2 PSY-5 scales. Using large derivational and replication samples drawn from a variety of mental health and correctional settings, facet scales were developed for each of the PSY-5 scales. Arnau et al. opined that the facet scales have potential clinical utility in helping to identify content areas contributing to PSY-5 scale elevations.

Arnau, Handel, Archer, Bisconer, and Gross (2004) examined correlates of the PSY-5 scales and their facet scales for a sample of patients admitted to a state psychiatric hospital. Criterion measures were extracted from patients' clinical records. Correlates of the PSY-5 scales were consistent with those previously reported by Harkness et al. (2002) and others. There also was some support for differential correlates for the PSY-5 facet scales.

Quilty and Bagby (2007) conducted psychometric and structural analyses of the PSY-5 facet scales using a sample of more than 1000 psychiatric patients. They concluded that the reliability and discriminant validity of the Arnau et al. (2005) facet scales were mostly inadequate. They further concluded that the facet scales do not represent stable, independent, lower order facet markers and that the use of the scales in clinical settings is premature. A similar conclusion was reached by Wang, Zhang, Shi, Zhou, and Li (2010), who examined internal consistency reliability and convergent and discriminant validity of the PSY-5 scales in the MMPI-2 normative sample. Although Quilty and Bagby were able to identify facets in their own data, they concluded that their facets also were not sufficiently reliable and valid to justify their clinical use.

Given the limited reliability and discriminant validity of the facet scales and the failure to replicate them in other settings, their clinical use at this time is not recommended. It should be noted that the PSY-5 facet scales are not included in MMPI-2 scoring or interpretive reports.

Interpretation of the PSY-5 Scales

Harkness et al. (2002) provided some preliminary guidelines for interpreting scores on the PSY-5 scales. Based on item response theory, it was determined that high scores (T > 65) on all five scales are interpretable. Only for the Disconstraint (DISC) and Introversion/Low Positive Emotionality (INTR) scales was interpretation of low scores (T ≤ 40) recommended. However, subsequent research has indicated that low scores on the Aggressiveness (AGGR) scale also can be interpreted and that low scorers on this scale had characteristics that were basically opposite those of high scorers (Weisenburger, Harkness, McNulty, Graham, & Ben-Porath, 2008). Harkness et al. acknowledged that their interpretive guidelines are likely to be modified, refined, and expanded as more research is conducted with the PSY-5 scales. The interpretive inferences that follow are based on the Harkness et al. recommendations and this author's examination of research concerning the PSY-5 scales.

Aggressiveness (AGGR)

Both high and low scores on this scale are interpreted. High scores (T > 65) on the AGGR scale indicate persons who

1. are both verbally and physically aggressive
2. may use aggression to dominate and control others
3. may enjoy intimidating other people
4. may react aggressively when provoked
5. have histories of behavioral problems in school
6. have histories of arrests
7. if male, often have histories of committing domestic violence
8. in clinical or forensic settings, tend to have diagnoses of antisocial personality disorder
9. in treatment may attempt to control and dominate therapists
10. in treatment may benefit from discussion of the costs and benefits of their aggressiveness

Low scores (T ≤ 40) indicate persons who are passive, submissive, and not very aggressive in interactions with other people.

Psychoticism (PSYC)
Low scores are not interpreted for this scale. High scores (T > 65) on the PSYC scale indicate persons who

1. are experiencing a disconnection from reality
2. may experience unshared beliefs and/or unusual sensory or perceptual experiences
3. may report delusions of reference
4. may have bizarre, disoriented, or circumstantial thinking
5. have an unrealistic expectation of harm
6. feel alienated
7. have few or no friends
8. have poor work histories
9. are not very achievement oriented
10. in therapy may benefit from frequent opportunities to engage in reality checking

Disconstraint (DISC)
Both high and low scores are interpreted for this scale. High scores (T > 65) on the DISC scale indicate persons who

1. are impulsive and lack self-control
2. take physical risks
3. are easily bored by routine and seek out excitement
4. are less bound by traditional moral constraints
5. often have histories of substance abuse
6. often have histories of school problems and arrests
7. in forensic settings tend to have histories of violence and antisocial personality disorder diagnoses
8. in treatment may benefit from exploring more constructive ways to satisfy needs for novelty, excitement, and risk-taking

Low scores (T ≤ 40) on the DISC scale indicate persons who

1. are self-controlled and not impulsive
2. do not take many physical risks
3. have high tolerance for boredom
4. tend to follow rules and laws
5. may respond better to structured treatment approaches

Negative Emotionality/Neuroticism (NEGE)

Low scores on this scale are not interpreted. High scores (T > 65) on the NEGE scale indicate persons who

1. have a predisposition to experience negative affect
2. focus on problematic features of incoming information
3. concoct worst-case scenarios
4. may have few or no friends
5. are self-critical
6. worry excessively
7. feel guilty
8. may report feeling sad or blue
9. are pessimistic
10. are not very achievement oriented
11. in clinical settings may have histories of suicide attempts
12. in clinical settings often receive diagnoses of depression or dysthymia
13. are very anxious
14. may report somatic symptoms
15. may benefit from therapy designed to identify and deal with their tendencies to process information in anxiety-producing ways

Introversion/Low Positive Emotionality (INTR)

Both high and low scores on this scale are interpreted. High scores (T > 65) on the INTR scale indicate persons who

1. seem to have little capacity to experience joy and pleasure
2. are socially introverted
3. have low need to achieve
4. report feeling sad, blue, or depressed
5. report somatic symptoms
6. often feel anxious
7. are pessimistic about the future
8. in clinical settings tend to have diagnoses of depression
9. in clinical settings may have histories of suicide attempts
10. tend to show little emotional response in therapy

Low scores on the INTR scale(T ≤ 40) indicate persons who

1. have the capacity to experience joy and pleasure
2. are quite sociable
3. have lots of energy
4. if scores are very low, may exhibit symptoms of hypomania
5. are likely to be quite emotionally responsive in therapy

▨ Supplementary Scales

In addition to its utilization in the construction of the Validity and Clinical scales, the original MMPI item pool was used to develop numerous other scales by variously recombining the 567 items using item-analytic, factor-analytic, and intuitive procedures. Dahlstrom, Welsh, and Dahlstrom (1972, 1975) identified more than 450 Supplementary scales. The scales had quite diverse labels, ranging from more traditional ones, such as "Dominance" and "Suspiciousness," to more unusual ones, such as "Success in Baseball." The scales varied considerably in terms of what they were supposed to measure, the manner in which they were constructed, their reliabilities, the extent to which they were cross-validated, the availability of normative data, and the amount of additional validity data that were generated. The scales also varied in terms of how frequently they were used in clinical and research settings. Some scales were used only by their constructors, whereas others were employed extensively in research studies and used routinely in clinical interpretation of the MMPI. Caldwell (1988) offered interpretive information for many of the Supplementary scales of the original MMPI.

Not all Supplementary scales were maintained in the MMPI-2 (Butcher et al., 1989, 2001) because that would have increased the length of the booklet beyond a point judged acceptable for routine clinical use. For the most part, the extent to which existing research data supported a scale's reliability and validity determined which scales were retained. However, some scales were maintained on the basis of less scientific criteria. For example, the Harris–Lingoes subscales were judged to be a very helpful supplementary source of information in interpreting the Clinical scales. The Wiener Subtle–Obvious subscales were maintained because some persons believe that they are useful in detecting certain response sets that invalidate profiles. As will be discussed later in this chapter, the Subtle–Obvious subscales subsequently were deleted from MMPI-2 scoring and interpretive materials because accumulating research did not support their use.

Levitt (1990) determined how many MMPI-2 items are available for scoring some commonly used Supplementary scales. He concluded that certain Supplementary scales not included in the MMPI-2 manual can still be scored.

However, no MMPI-2 norms are readily available for use with these additional scales.

In addition to maintaining some of the existing Supplementary scales, new scales were developed for the MMPI-2. Several new Validity scales (described in Chapter 3 of this book) and Content scales (described in Chapter 6 of this book) were developed. Other scales also were developed as part of the restandardization project and will be described in this chapter. Subsequent to the publication of the MMPI-2, several additional scales for assessing substance abuse and marital distress were published. They too will be described in this chapter.

The same format will be used for discussing each Supplementary scale. Scale development information will be presented, and reliability and validity data will be reported. Interpretive suggestions for each scale also will be given. As with the Clinical and Validity scales, no absolute cutoff scores can be specified for the Supplementary scales. In general, T scores greater than 65 should be considered as high scores. Whenever information about specific cutoff scores for a scale is available, the information will be presented. The higher the scores are, the more likely it is that the interpretive information presented will apply. As with other scales discussed earlier in this book, low scores should not be interpreted for most of the Supplementary scales. There is not enough research information available to have confidence in interpretive statements based on low scores. For several scales for which data concerning the meaning of low scores are available, the interpretation of low scores is discussed in this chapter.

Although an attempt was made to rely on research studies for interpretive information, in some cases examining item content was necessary in generating descriptors. For Supplementary scales that were developed from the original MMPI and maintained in the MMPI-2, research data from the original MMPI also were used to generate interpretive suggestions. Because these scales are essentially the same in the two versions of the test, this approach seems appropriate. It should be emphasized that the Supplementary scales are not intended to replace the standard Validity and Clinical scales. Rather, they are to be used in addition to them.

Archer, Elkins, Aiduk, and Griffin (1997) concluded that the Supplementary scales did not add much to the Clinical scales in predicting self-reported and psychologist-rated symptoms of psychiatric inpatients. However, it should be noted that their study did not include conceptually relevant extratest measures for most of the Supplementary scales. Graham, Ben-Porath, and McNulty (1999) were able to identify meaningful correlates for many Supplementary scales in their study of community mental health center clients.

The composition and scoring of each Supplementary scale are presented in an appendix of the MMPI-2 manual (Butcher et al., 2001). It should be noted that most of the Supplementary scales can be scored only if the entire 567-item MMPI-2 is administered. The test distributor (Pearson Assessments) provides scoring keys for the Supplementary scales discussed in this chapter. An appendix in the MMPI-2 manual presents T-score conversions for the Supplementary scales, and the test distributor provides profile sheets for plotting scores on most of the

Supplementary scales. The norms used to transform raw scores to T scores are the same ones used for the standard Validity and Clinical scales. Linear T-score transformations are used for all of the Supplementary scales discussed in this chapter. All of the Supplementary scales described in this chapter are included in the Extended Score Report available from Pearson Assessments, and scores for most of the Supplementary scales are also included in other computer-generated reports available from Pearson Assessments.

ANXIETY (A) AND REPRESSION (R) SCALES

Scale Development

Whenever the basic Validity and Clinical scales of the MMPI or MMPI-2 have been factor analyzed to reduce them to their most common denominators, two basic dimensions have emerged consistently (e.g., Block, 1965; Butcher et al., 1989; Eichman, 1961, 1962; Welsh, 1956). Welsh (1956) developed the Anxiety (A) and Repression (R) scales to assess these two basic dimensions.

By factor analyzing MMPI scores for male Veterans Administration patients, Welsh identified a factor that he originally labeled "general maladjustment" and later called "anxiety." This factor was defined by high positive loadings from Scales 7 and 8 and a high negative loading from the K Scale. The A scale was developed to assess this factor by identifying items that were most highly associated with it. After being administered to new groups of psychiatric patients, the scale was refined by using internal consistency procedures. The original Anxiety (A) scale included 39 items, all of which are included in the MMPI-2 version of the scale. Welsh suggested from an examination of the items that the content of the A-scale items falls into four categories: thinking and thought processes, negative emotional tone and dysphoria, pessimism and lack of energy, and malignant mentation. The items are keyed in such a way that high scores on the A scale are associated with greater psychopathology.

The Repression (R) scale was constructed by Welsh (1956) to measure the second major dimension emerging from factor analyses of the basic Validity and Clinical scales of the MMPI. This factor was defined by positive loadings from Scales 1, 2, and 3 and a negative loading from Scale 9. A procedure similar to that used in developing the A scale also was employed with the R scale. It resulted in a final scale containing 40 items, 37 of which are included in the MMPI-2 version of the scale. Welsh suggested the following clusters based on the content of the R-scale items: health and physical symptoms; emotionality, violence, and activity; reactions to other people in social situations; social dominance, feelings of personal adequacy, and personal appearance; and personal and vocational interests.

Reliability and Validity

Welsh (1965) reported reliability data for the A and R scales based on unpublished research by Kooser and Stevens. For 108 college undergraduates, the split-half reliability coefficients for the A and R scales were .88 and .48, respectively. Gocka (1965) reported Kuder–Richardson 21 (internal-consistency) values of .94 and .72 for the A and R scales, respectively, for 220 male Veterans Administration psychiatric patients. For the MMPI-2 normative sample, internal-consistency coefficients for the A scale were .89 for men and .90 for women. Corresponding internal-consistency coefficients for the R scale were .67 and .57 (Butcher et al., 1989, 2001). Thus, it appears that the A scale is quite internally consistent, whereas the R scale is less so.

Temporal stability data have been reported for both the MMPI and MMPI-2 versions of the A and R scales. When 60 college sophomores were given the scales on two occasions, separated by 4 months, test–retest reliability coefficients for the A and R scales were .70 and .74, respectively (Welsh, 1956). Test–retest coefficients for the A scale for college students, with a 6-week interval, were .90 for men and .87 for women. Corresponding values for the R scale were .85 and .84, respectively (Moreland, 1985b). For the MMPI-2 normative sample, test–retest reliabilities (with an average interval of one week) for the A scale were .91 for men and .91 for women. Test–retest reliabilities for the R scale were .79 for men and .77 for women (Butcher et al., 1989, 2001). Thus, the stability of scores on the A and R scales over these relatively short periods of time seems to be quite acceptable.

It has been suggested by some researchers that the major sources of variance in MMPI responses are associated with response sets. A response set exists when persons taking a test answer the items from a particular perspective or attitude about how they would like the items to show themselves to be. Edwards (1964) argued that the first factor of the MMPI, the one assessed by the A scale, simply assesses examinees' willingness, while describing themselves on the test, to endorse socially undesirable items. Messick and Jackson (1961) suggested that R scale scores simply indicate the extent to which examinees are unwilling to admit (acquiesce) on the test to many kinds of emotional difficulties. This interpretation appears to be supported by the fact that all of the items in the R scale are keyed in the false direction. Block (1965) refuted the response set or bias arguments by demonstrating that the same two major factor dimensions emerge even when the MMPI scales were altered to control for social desirability and acquiescence effects with the use of techniques developed by Edwards (1964) and others. Block also was able to identify through his research reliable meaningful extratest correlates for his two factor dimensions.

Welsh (1956) reported some unpublished data supplied by Gough for a group of normal persons. Gough found that A-scale scores correlated negatively with the L and K Scales and with Scale 1 of the MMPI and correlated positively with the F Scale and with Scales 9 and 0. Gough also reported that high A-scale scorers showed slowness of personal tempo, pessimism, vacillation, hesitancy, and inhibitedness. Sherriffs and Boomer (1954) found that high A-scale scorers showed more self-doubts in examination situations. Welsh (1956) reported an unpublished study by Welsh and Roseman indicating that patients who showed the most positive change during insulin shock therapy also showed marked decreases in A-scale scores after such therapy. There also is evidence that A-scale scores tend to decrease during psychiatric hospitalization (Lewinsohn, 1965). Duckworth and Duckworth (1975) suggested that a high A-scale score indicates that a person is experiencing enough discomfort to be motivated to change in psychotherapy. Block and Bailey (1955) identified reliable extratest correlates for scores on the A scale in a military setting. Graham et al. (1999) reported that mental health center clients with higher scores on the A scale had a wide variety of symptoms, including anxiety, depression, and somatic complaints, and they were more likely than lower scorers to have histories of inpatient mental health treatment and suicidal ideation. The correlates from these various studies are included in the discussion of the interpretation of A-scale scores that appears later in this section.

Welsh (1956) reported that in the study by Welsh and Roseman patients who were judged as most improved during their course of insulin shock therapy showed decreases in R-scale scores in addition to the decreases in A-scale scores. Lewinsohn (1965) found only small changes in R-scale scores during psychiatric hospitalization. Welsh (1956) reported data provided by Gough indicating that in a sample of normal persons, R-scale scores were positively correlated with the L and K scales and with Scales 1 and 2 of the MMPI and negatively correlated with Scale 9. Duckworth and Duckworth (1975) described high R-scale scorers as denying, rationalizing, and lacking self-insight. Block and Bailey (1955) identified extratest correlates of R-scale scores in a military setting. Archer et al. (1997) found that R-scale scores were positively related to ratings of psychomotor retardation for women in an inpatient psychiatric setting. Graham et al. (1999) identified relatively few correlates of the R scale among mental health center clients. However, higher scoring male and female clients were seen as preoccupied with health and presenting somatic complaints. Male clients with higher scores were seen as nervous and depressed, lacking energy, and having restricted affect. They also were more concrete in their thinking and felt pessimistic. Higher scoring female clients also were seen as anxious, introverted, and shy. These women often felt overwhelmed and that life is a strain. They expressed many fears and were lacking in energy. The correlates from these various studies are included later in connection with the interpretation of scores on the R scale.

Interpretation of High A-Scale Scores

High scores on the A scale indicate persons who

1. are generally maladjusted
2. are anxious and uncomfortable
3. are depressed
4. have somatic complaints
5. have a slow personal tempo
6. may admit having suicidal ideation
7. are pessimistic
8. are apathetic, unemotional, and unexcitable
9. are shy and retiring

10. lack confidence in their own abilities
11. are hesitant and vacillating
12. are inhibited and overcontrolled
13. are influenced by diffuse personal feelings
14. are defensive
15. rationalize and blame others for difficulties
16. lack poise in social situations
17. are conforming and overly accepting of authority
18. are submissive, compliant, and suggestible
19. are cautious
20. are fussy
21. if men, have behavior that tends to be seen as effeminate
22. are seen as cool, distant, and uninvolved
23. become confused, disorganized, and maladaptive under stress
24. are likely to have histories of inpatient mental health treatment
25. are uncomfortable enough to be motivated to change in psychotherapy

In summary, persons scoring high on the A scale, if from a normal population, are rather miserable and unhappy. High A-scale scorers in a psychiatric setting are described as neurotic, maladjusted, submissive, and overcontrolled and are likely to have histories of previous mental health treatment. Because of their discomfort, high A-scale scorers usually are highly motivated for counseling or psychotherapy.

Interpretation of High R-Scale Scores

High scores on the R scale indicate persons who

1. are passive/submissive
2. are unexcitable
3. are conventional and formal
4. are slow and painstaking
5. may show psychomotor retardation
6. are introverted
7. have somatic complaints

In summary, high R-scale scorers are introverted, internalizing individuals who have adopted careful and cautious lifestyles.

EGO STRENGTH (Es) SCALE

Scale Development

The Ego Strength (Es) scale was developed by Barron (1953) specifically to predict the response of neurotic patients to individual psychotherapy. The original Es scale had 68 items, of which the MMPI-2 version of the scale includes 52. To identify items for the original Es scale, item responses of 17 patients who were judged as clearly improved after six months of psychotherapy were compared with item responses of 16 patients who were judged as unimproved after six months of psychotherapy. Items are scored in the direction most often chosen by the improved patients. The Es-scale items deal with physical functioning, seclusiveness, moral posture, personal adequacy, ability to cope, phobias, and anxieties.

Reliability and Validity

Barron (1953) reported that the odd–even reliability of the Es scale for a sample of 126 patients was .76. Gocka (1965) reported a Kuder–Richardson 21 (internal-consistency) value of .78 for the Es scale for 220 male Veterans Administration psychiatric patients. For men and women in the MMPI-2 normative sample, internal-consistency values for the Es scale were .60 and .65, respectively. Schuldberg (1992) reported that for a sample of college students the internal consistency of the MMPI-2 Es scale was slightly higher than that of the original MMPI Es scale.

Barron (1953) reported a test–retest reliability coefficient of .72 for a group of 30 patients, using a test–retest interval of 3 months. Moreland (1985b) reported test–retest coefficients for male and female college students (with a 6-week interval) of .80 and .82, respectively. Test–retest coefficients for subsamples of men and women in the MMPI-2 normative sample were .78 and .83, respectively (Butcher et al., 1989, 2001).

The Es scale was cross-validated by Barron (1953) using three different samples of neurotic patients for whom ratings of improvement during brief, psychoanalytically oriented psychotherapy were available. Because pretherapy Es-scale scores were positively related to assessed improvement for all three samples, Barron concluded that the Es scale is useful in predicting responsiveness to psychotherapy. Unfortunately, subsequent attempts by others to cross-validate the Es scale as a predictor of response to psychotherapy or other treatment approaches have yielded inconsistent findings. Some data indicate that psychiatric patients who change most during treatment have higher pretreatment Es-scale scores than patients who show less change (e.g., Wirt, 1955, 1956), whereas other data suggest that change in treatment is unrelated to pretreatment Es-scale scores (Ends & Page, 1957; Fowler, Teel, & Coyle, 1967; Getter & Sundland, 1962; Sullivan, Miller, & Smelser, 1958).

Distler, May, and Tuma (1964) found that pretreatment Es-scale scores were positively related to hospitalization outcome for male psychiatric patients and negatively related to hospitalization outcome for female psychiatric patients. Sinnett (1962) reported that Veterans Administration psychiatric patients with higher pretreatment Es-scale scores showed more personality growth during treatment, which included psychotherapy, than did patients with lower scores, but pretreatment Es-scale scores were unrelated to assessed symptomatic change for these same patients. Shepherd (1997) reported that mental health center clients with higher pretreatment Es-scale scores were rated as more improved at the termination of treatment than clients with lower Es-scale scores. Consistent with the earlier findings of Sinnett (1962), Shepherd found that pretreatment scores of clients were not significantly related to changes in severity of symptoms during the course of treatment.

Dahlstrom et al. (1975) tried to explain the inconsistent findings concerning the relationship between Es-scale scores and treatment outcome. They suggested that when high Es-scale scores occur for persons who obviously are having difficulties but who are denying them, the high Es-scale scores may not be predictive of a favorable treatment outcome. However, high Es-scale scores for persons who admit to emotional problems may suggest a favorable response to treatment. Clayton and Graham (1979) were not able to validate the hypothesis of Dahlstrom et al. with a sample of hospitalized psychiatric patients. It is clear from the existing literature that the relationship between Es-scale scores and treatment outcome is not a simple one and that factors such as kind of patients, type of treatment, and nature of the outcome measure must be taken into account. In general, however, high Es-scale scores are predictive of positive personality change for neurotic patients who receive traditional, individual psychotherapy.

It is necessary to be very cautious in interpreting Es-scale scores in protocols that are suggestive of defensiveness. In such circumstances, Es-scale scores tend to be artificially high and are not predictive of positive response to therapy. Likewise, caution should be exercised in interpreting Es-scale scores in protocols suggestive of exaggeration of symptoms. In such circumstances, Es-scale scores tend to be artificially low and are not predictive of a negative response to therapy.

There also are research data indicating that the Es scale can be viewed as an indication of overall psychological adjustment. Higher scores on the Es scale are associated with more favorable adjustment levels as assessed by other MMPI-2 indexes and extratest criteria. Schuldberg (1992) found that MMPI-2 Es-scale scores of college students were positively related to other self-report measures of psychological health. Graham et al. (1999) reported that mental health center clients with higher Es-scale scores were rated as having fewer symptoms, feeling less that life is a strain, and coping better with stress than clients with lower Es-scale scores. In addition, clients with higher Es-scale scores were seen as having more energy, being more competitive, and having more interests. Archer et al. (1997) reported that Es-scale scores were negatively related to ratings of psychomotor retardation and unusual thought content in an inpatient psychiatric setting.

Es-scale scores tend to be lower for psychiatric patients than for nonpatients and for people receiving psychiatric or psychological treatment than for persons not involved in such treatment (Gottesman, 1959; Himelstein, 1964; Kleinmuntz, 1960; Quay, 1955; Spiegel, 1969; Taft, 1957). It has been reported that the Es scale fails to differentiate between delinquent and nondelinquent adolescents (Gottesman, 1959). However, Weaver and Wootton (1992) found that adolescent juvenile delinquents who committed more serious crimes had lower Es-scale scores than delinquents who committed less serious crimes.

Whereas Es-scale scores tend to be higher for neurotic patients than for psychotic patients, the scale fails to discriminate among more specific diagnostic categories (Hawkinson, 1961; Rosen, 1963; Tamkin, 1957; Tamkin & Klett, 1957).

Windle (1994) found that male alcoholics who had made suicide attempts had lower Es-scale scores than other male alcoholics. Rosch, Crowther, and Graham (1991) reported that female college students being treated for bulimia had lower Es-scale scores than female students being treated for other problems and female students who were not in treatment.

There are some data indicating that Es-scale scores tend to increase during the course of psychotherapy or other treatment procedures. Lewinsohn (1965) reported that psychiatric patients showed an increase in level of Es-scale scores from hospital admission to discharge. However, Barron and Leary (1955) found that Es-scale scores did not change more for patients who received individual or group psychotherapy than for patients who remained on a waiting list for a similar period of time. It also was reported that psychotherapy patients who were self-referred scored higher on the Es scale than those who were referred by someone else (Himelstein, 1964), suggesting that high Es-scale scorers are more aware of internal conflicts than are low Es-scale scorers.

Scores on the Es scale are related positively to intelligence (Tamkin & Klett, 1957; Wirt, 1955) and to formal education (Tamkin & Klett, 1957). The relationship between Es-scale scores and age is less clear. Tamkin and Klett (1957) found no relationship between Es-scale scores and age, but Getter and Sundland (1962) reported that older persons tended to score lower on the Es scale. Consistent gender differences in Es-scale scores have been reported, with men obtaining higher raw scores than women (Butcher et al., 1989; Distler et al., 1964; Getter & Sundland, 1962; Taft, 1957). This gender difference originally was interpreted as reflecting the greater willingness of women to admit to problems and complaints (Getter & Sundland, 1962). However, a reasonable alternative explanation of the gender difference on the Es scale is that men score higher than women because the scale contains a number of items dealing with masculine role identification (Holmes, 1967).

Interpretation of High Es–Scale Scores

From the previous discussion, it may be concluded that high scorers on the Es scale generally tend to show more positive change during treatment than do low scorers. However, the relationship between Es-scale scores and treatment prognosis is not a simple one, and patient and treatment variables must be taken into account. High Es-scale scorers tend to be better adjusted psychologically, and they are more able to cope with problems and stresses in their life situations. In addition, high scores on the Es scale indicate persons who

1. have fewer and less severe symptoms
2. lack chronic psychopathology
3. are stable, reliable, and responsible
4. are tolerant and lack prejudice
5. are alert, energetic, and adventuresome
6. may be sensation seekers
7. are determined and persistent

8. are self-confident, outspoken, and sociable
9. are intelligent, resourceful, and independent
10. have a secure sense of reality
11. deal effectively with others
12. create favorable first impressions
13. gain acceptance of others
14. are opportunistic and manipulative
15. are energetic and have many interests
16. if men, have an appropriately masculine style of behavior
17. are hostile and rebellious toward authority
18. are competitive/work oriented
19. may be sarcastic and cynical
20. seek help because of situational problems
21. can tolerate confrontations in psychotherapy

In summary, people with high Es-scale scores appear to be fairly well adjusted emotionally. In nonpsychiatric settings, such people are not likely to have serious emotional problems. Among persons with emotional problems, high Es-scale scores suggest that problems are likely to be situational rather than chronic, that the individuals have psychological resources that can be drawn on in helping them to solve the problems, and that the prognosis for positive change in counseling or psychotherapy is good.

Interpretation of Low Es–Scale Scores

In many ways persons with low scores on the Es scale are the opposite of those with high scores. Lower scorers are likely to have more severe problems that are less likely to be situational in nature. They do not seem to have many psychological resources for coping with stress, and the prognosis for change in treatment for these persons is not very positive.

DOMINANCE (Do) SCALE

Scale Development

The Dominance (Do) scale was developed by Gough, McClosky, and Meehl (1951) as part of a larger project concerned with political participation. Because the 60-item scale included 28 MMPI items, it was possible to score an abbreviated version of the scale from standard administration of the MMPI. The MMPI-2 version of the Do scale has 25 of the 28 items.

To develop the Do scale, high school and college students were given a definition of dominance (strength in face-to-face personal situations; ability to influence others; not readily intimidated or defeated; feeling safe, secure, and confident in face-to-face situations) and were asked to nominate peers who were most and least dominant. High- and low-dominance criterion groups were defined on the basis of these peer nominations, and both groups were given a 150-item questionnaire, which included some MMPI items. Analyses of the responses identified items that differentiated between high- and low-dominance criterion groups. The items are keyed in such a way that a high score on the Do scale is suggestive of high dominance. The Do-scale items deal with a number of different content areas, including concentration, obsessive–compulsive behaviors, self-confidence, discomfort in social situations, concern about physical appearance, perseverance, and political opinions.

Reliability and Validity

Gough et al. (1951) reported an internal-consistency coefficient (Kuder–Richardson 21) of .79 for the 60-item Do scale, and Gocka (1965) reported a Kuder–Richardson 21 value of .60 for the 28-item Do scale for 220 male Veterans Administration psychiatric patients. Internal-consistency (alpha) coefficients for men and women in the MMPI-2 normative sample were .74 and .79, respectively (Butcher et al., 2001).

A test–retest coefficient of .86 for Marine Corps officers was reported by Knapp (1960). Moreland (1985b) reported test–retest coefficients (6-week interval) for male and female college students of .82 and .83, respectively. Test–retest coefficients (1-week interval) for subsamples of men and women in the MMPI-2 normative sample were .84 and .86, respectively (Butcher et al., 2001).

Gough et al. (1951) found that a raw-score cutoff of 36 on the 60-item scale identified 94% of their high- and low-dominance high school students, whereas a raw-score cutoff of 39 on the 60-item scale identified 92% of high- and low-dominance college students. Correlations between Do-scale scores based on the 28 MMPI items and peer ratings and self-ratings of dominance were .52 and .65, respectively, for college students and .60 and .41, respectively, for high school students.

Knapp (1960) found that Marine Corps officer pilots scored significantly higher on the 28-item Do scale than did enlisted men. The mean scores for the officers and enlisted men were quite similar to mean scores reported for high- and low-dominance high school and college students. Knapp interpreted his data as supporting the use of the Do scale as a screening device in selecting officers. However, Olmstead and Monachesi (1956) reported that the MMPI Do scale was not able to differentiate between firefighters and fire captains. Eschenback and Dupree (1959) found that Do-scale scores did not change as a result of situational stress (a realistic survival test). It would be interesting to know whether Do-scale scores change as individuals change their dominance roles (e.g., when an enlisted person becomes an officer). Unfortunately, no data of this kind are currently available.

Hedayat and Kelly (1991) reported a correlation of .86 between Do-scale scores of female psychiatric day-treatment clients and ratings of dominance completed by staff members. Archer et al. (1997) found that Do-scale scores of psychiatric inpatients were positively related to a measure of grandiosity that was provided by staff members. Graham et al. (1999) reported correlates of the Do scale for clients at a community mental health center. Clients with higher

Do-scale scores tended to have fewer symptoms, including anxiety, depression, and somatic complaints; they were less passive and socially awkward; and they were more achievement oriented.

Interpretation of High Do-Scale Scores

High scorers on the Do scale see themselves and are seen by others as stronger in face-to-face personal situations, as not readily intimidated, and as feeling safe, secure, and self-confident. Although there is some evidence to suggest that high scores on the Do scale are more common among persons holding positions of greater responsibility and leadership, no data are available concerning the adequacy of performance in such positions as a function of Do-scale scores. Also, high Do-scale scores may indicate persons who

1. appear poised and self-assured
2. are secure and self-confident
3. appear to feel free to behave in a straightforward manner
4. are optimistic
5. are resourceful and efficient
6. are realistic and achievement oriented
7. feel adequate to handle problems
8. are persevering
9. have a dutiful sense of morality
10. have a strong need to face reality
11. are comfortable in social situations
12. if psychiatric patients, are likely to have fewer symptoms, including anxiety, depression, and somatic complaints, and may be rather grandiose

In summary, high scorers on the Do scale are people who are confident of their abilities to cope with problems and stresses in their life situations. Psychiatric patients with higher scores on the Do scale are likely to have fewer symptoms, including anxiety, depression, and somatic complaints.

SOCIAL RESPONSIBILITY (Re) SCALE

Scale Development

The Social Responsibility (Re) scale was developed by Gough, McClosky, and Meehl (1952) as part of a larger project concerning political participation. The original scale contained 56 items, with 32 items coming from the MMPI item pool. A score based on the 32 MMPI items could be obtained, and normative data were available for the 32-item Re scale. In the MMPI-2, 30 of the original 32 MMPI items were retained.

The samples used in constructing the Re scale consisted of 50 college fraternity men, 50 college sorority women, 123 social science students from a high school, and 221 ninth-grade students. In each sample, the most and least responsible individuals were identified. Responsibility was defined as willingness to accept the consequences of one's own behavior, dependability, trustworthiness, integrity, and sense of obligation to the group. For the high school and college samples, peer nominations were used to identify persons high and low in responsibility. Teachers provided ratings of responsibility for the ninth-grade sample. MMPI item responses of the most and least responsible persons in each sample were examined. Items that revealed the best discrimination between most and least responsible persons in all samples were included in the Re scale. The content of the MMPI-2 version of the Re scale deals with concern for social and moral issues; disapproval of privilege and favor; emphasis on duties and self-discipline; conventionality versus rebelliousness; trust and confidence in the world in general; and poise, assurance, and personal security (Gough et al., 1952).

Reliability and Validity

Gough et al. (1952) reported an uncorrected split-half reliability coefficient of .73 for the 56-item scale for a sample of ninth-grade students. Gocka (1965) reported a Kuder–Richardson 21 (internal-consistency) value of .63 for the 32-item Re scale for 220 male Veterans Administration psychiatric patients. Internal-consistency (alpha) coefficients for men and women in the MMPI-2 normative sample were .67 and .61, respectively (Butcher et al., 2001).

Moreland (1985b) reported test–retest coefficients (6-week interval) for male and female college students of .85 and .76, respectively. Test–retest coefficients (with 1-week interval) for subsamples of men and women in the MMPI-2 normative sample were .85 and .73, respectively (Butcher et al., 2001). Gough and his colleagues reported correlations of .84 and .88 between Re-scale scores based on all 56 items and scores based on the 32 MMPI items in the Re scale for their college and high school samples.

Correlations between MMPI Re-scale scores and criterion ratings of responsibility in the derivation samples were .47 for college students and .53 for high school students. For college students, the correlation between MMPI Re-scale scores and self-ratings of responsibility was .20, and the correlation between these two variables for high school students was .23. Optimal cutoff scores for the MMPI Re scale yielded correct classification of 78% and 87%, respectively, of the most and least responsible individuals in the various derivation samples. Gough et al. (1952) reported some limited cross-validational data for the total (56-item) Re scale. They obtained a correlation of .22 between scores and ratings of responsibility for a sample of medical students. A correlation of .33 between Re-scale scores and ratings of positive character integration was reported for a sample of fourth-year graduate students.

In two studies, persons with higher Re-scale scores tended to have positions of leadership and responsibility. Knapp (1960) found that Marine Corps officers scored significantly higher on the MMPI Re scale than did enlisted men. Olmstead and Monachesi (1956) reported that fire captains scored higher on the MMPI Re scale than firefighters, but the difference was not statistically significant.

Duckworth and Duckworth (1975) suggested that the Re scale measures acceptance (high score) or rejection (low score) of a previously held value system, usually that of one's parents. For persons above the age of 25, high Re-scale scorers tend to accept their present value system and intend to continue using it, and low scorers may be questioning their current value system or rejecting their most recently held value system. For younger persons, high Re-scale scores indicate that they accept the value system of their parents, whereas low Re-scale scores indicate questioning or rejection of parental value systems. Duckworth and Duckworth also suggested that high Re-scale scorers, regardless of age, are more rigid in acceptance of existing values and are less willing to explore others' values. They also indicated that older persons tend to score higher than younger persons on the Re scale and that college students who are questioning parental values often receive quite low Re-scale scores.

Graham et al. (1999) determined correlates of the Re scale for mental health center clients. Clients with higher Re-scale scores had fewer symptoms, including anxiety, depression, and somatic complaints. They were seen as more secure and less socially awkward than other clients.

Interpretation of High Re-Scale Scores

High Re-scale scorers tend to see themselves and are seen by others as willing to accept the consequences of their own behavior, as dependable and trustworthy, and as having integrity and a sense of responsibility to the group. They also are more likely than low Re-scale scorers to be in positions of leadership and responsibility. High Re-scale scorers are rigid in acceptance of existing values and are unwilling to explore others' values. Younger persons with high Re-scale scores tend to accept the values of their parents. Also, high scores may indicate persons who

1. have deep concern over ethical and moral problems
2. have a strong sense of justice
3. set high standards for themselves
4. reject privilege and favor
5. place excessive emphasis on carrying their own share of burdens and duties
6. are secure and self-confident
7. are comfortable in social situations
8. have trust and confidence in the world in general
9. if psychiatric patients, tend to have fewer symptoms, including anxiety, depression, and somatic complaints, than other clients

In summary, high Re-scale scorers have incorporated societal and cultural values and are committed to behaving in a manner consistent with those values. They place high value on honesty and justice. They are confident, secure persons. Among psychiatric patients, higher scorers on the Re scale suggest fewer symptoms, including anxiety, depression, and somatic complaints.

COLLEGE MALADJUSTMENT (Mt) SCALE

Scale Development

The College Maladjustment (Mt) scale was constructed to discriminate between emotionally adjusted and maladjusted college students (Kleinmuntz, 1961). Mt-scale items were selected from the MMPI item pool by comparing responses of 40 adjusted male and female students and 40 maladjusted male and female students. The adjusted students had contacted a university clinic to arrange for a routine mental health screening examination as part of teacher certification procedures, and none of them admitted to a history of psychiatric treatment. The maladjusted students had contacted the same clinic for help with emotional problems and had remained in psychotherapy for three or more sessions. Item-analytic procedures identified 43 items that discriminated between the adjusted and maladjusted students. The MMPI-2 Mt scale has 41 of the original 43 items, with items scored such that higher scores on the scale are more indicative of greater maladjustment. Kleinmuntz (1961) found that scores on the 43-item scale administered separately corresponded quite well to Mt-scale scores derived from a standard MMPI administration.

Barthlow, Graham, Ben-Porath, and McNulty (2004) factor analyzed items in the Mt scale and identified three interpretable factors. A factor labeled "Low Self-Esteem" was represented by items having to do with lack of self-confidence and negative comparisons of self with others. A second factor, labeled "Lack of Energy," was represented by items having to do with feeling tired and having difficulty in starting to do things. A third factor, labeled "Cynicism/Restlessness," had somewhat more heterogeneous content than the other factors and was represented by items having to do with negative impressions of other people, restlessness, and having ideas that are too bad to talk about.

Reliability and Validity

Internal-consistency (alpha) coefficients for men and women in the MMPI-2 normative sample were .84 and .86, respectively (Butcher et al., 2001). Lauterbach, Garcia, and Gloster (2002) reported an alpha coefficient of .85 for a large sample of male and female college students. The test–retest coefficients (one-week interval) for both men and women in the MMPI-2 normative sample were .90 (Butcher et al., 2001). When Kleinmuntz (1961) administered the Mt scale to college students twice with an interval of 3 days, a test–retest reliability coefficient of .88 was obtained. Moreland (1985b) reported test–retest coefficients (6-week interval) for male and female college students of .89 and .86, respectively.

Kleinmuntz (1961) reported that college students who completed the Mt scale when they entered college and later sought "emotional" counseling scored higher on the scale than did a similar group of students who sought out "vocational-academic" counseling. Using a Mt-scale cutoff of 15, Parker (1961) was able to classify correctly 74% of maladjusted students who completed the Mt scale at the time they sought counseling, but only 46% when the Mt scale was completed as part of a battery administered at the time of college admission. Parker's data and Kleinmuntz's own data led Kleinmuntz (1961) to conclude that the Mt scale is more accurate when it is used for identifying existing emotional problems than when it is used for predicting future emotional problems. Higher Mt-scale scores for maladjusted than for adjusted students were reported subsequently in several different settings (Kleinmuntz, 1963).

Several studies have found that higher Mt-scale scores are associated with the presence of symptoms of psychopathology, including depression, anxiety, and posttraumatic stress disorders (Lauterbach, Garcia, & Gloster, 2002; Svanum & Ehrmann, 1993; Wilderman, 1984). However, scores on the Mt scale were not related to symptoms of substance abuse disorders. Female students tend to obtain higher Mt-scale raw scores than male students, and students with poorer academic performance score higher than those with better academic performance (Lauterbach et al., 2002). Among clients at a university-based clinic, higher Mt scores were related to level of emotional turmoil and distress (e.g., depression, anxiety, insecurity) but did not seem to be strongly related to acting-out behaviors (Barthlow et al., 2004). Correlations between Mt-scale scores and maladjustment were similar to those of other MMPI-2 scales and indexes associated with maladjustment, and the Mt scale added little to the other MMPI-2 measures of maladjustment (e.g., Welsh's A, the Es scale, mean score on the eight Clinical scales).

Interpretation of High Mt-Scale Scores

Because of variations in Mt-scale scores among college settings, it is not possible to identify a cutoff score above which students should be considered to be maladjusted. However, among college students within a given setting, higher Mt-scale scores are more suggestive of psychological maladjustment. The scale seems to be most sensitive to emotional turmoil and less related to acting-out behaviors. Because the Mt scale has not been studied systematically in settings other than colleges and universities, its use is not recommended with persons who are not college students. In addition to suggesting general maladjustment, high Mt-scale scores for college students may indicate persons who

1. are ineffectual
2. are pessimistic
3. procrastinate
4. are anxious and worried
5. develop somatic symptoms during times of increased stress
6. feel that life is a strain much of the time

POSTTRAUMATIC STRESS DISORDER (PK) SCALE

Scale Development

The Posttraumatic Stress Disorder (PK) scale was developed by Keane, Malloy, and Fairbank (1984) by contrasting the MMPI item responses of 60 male Vietnam combat veterans who had diagnoses of PTSD based on structured interviews and a psychophysiological assessment procedure and 60 male veterans who had diagnoses other than PTSD. They identified 49 items that these two groups answered significantly differently. A raw cutoff score of 30 correctly classified 82% of veterans used in developing the scale and also 82% of cross-validation groups of PTSD and non-PTSD veterans. In the MMPI-2 version of the PK scale, three items that appeared twice in the original PK scale were eliminated and one item was slightly reworded.

The content of the PK-scale items is suggestive of great emotional turmoil. Some items deal with anxiety, worry, and sleep disturbance. Others are suggestive of guilt and depression. In their responses to certain items test takers are reporting the presence of unwanted and disturbing thoughts, and in others they are describing lack of emotional control. Feeling misunderstood and mistreated is also represented in item content. Although PK-scale scores typically are determined from the administration of the entire MMPI-2, Lyons and Scotti (1994) demonstrated that scores based on a separate administration of the PK scale were quite congruent with scores based on administration of the entire MMPI-2. However, a major disadvantage of the stand-alone administration is that important information concerning test-taking attitudes is lost when the Validity scales cannot be scored. Lyons and Scotti (1994) and Trent, Rushlau, Munley, Bloem, and Driesenga (2000) found no significant differences in PK-scale scores between African American and Caucasian male veterans who had been referred to a trauma recovery program.

Reliability and Validity

Internal-consistency coefficients for the PK scale for men and women in the MMPI-2 normative sample were .85 and .87, respectively. A test–retest reliability coefficient of .87 was reported for subsamples of men and women in the MMPI-2 normative sample.

Subsequent to the development of the PK scale by Keane et al. (1984), other investigations of its utility in diagnosing veteran PTSD patients have been published (Butler, Foy, Snodgrass, Hurwicz, & Goldfarb, 1988; Cannon, Bell, Andrews, & Finkelstein, 1987; Gayton, Burchstead, & Matthews, 1986; Hyer, Fallon, Harrison, & Boudewyns, 1987; Hyer, Woods, Summers, Boudewyns, & Harrison, 1990; Munley, Bains, Bloem, & Busby, 1995; Orr et al., 1990; Query, Megran, & McDonald, 1986; Vanderploeg, Sisson, & Hickling, 1987; Watson, Kucala, & Manifold, 1986). In virtually all of these studies, patients with PTSD diagnoses obtained significantly higher PK-scale scores than comparison groups (nonpatients, substance abusers, and general psychiatric patients). However, classification rates using the PK scale have varied from study to study and generally have been somewhat lower than in the original study of Keane et al. (1984). Classification rates have been higher when more reliable diagnoses have been utilized. The raw cutoff score of 30, which was identified in the study of Keane et al., was not optimal in some other studies. Optimal cutoff scores have ranged from 8.5 to 30. Generally, the scale has been more effective in discriminating between

PTSD patients and nonpatients than between PTSD patients and patients with other diagnoses. Lyons and Wheeler-Cox (1999) reviewed MMPI-2 PK-scale research studies and concluded that a raw score cutoff of > 28 was optimal for discriminating veterans with posttraumatic stress disorder from those with other disorders.

Several studies have reported positive correlations between PK-scale scores and symptoms of PTSD as determined by structured interviews or other methods (Adkins, Weathers, McDevitt-Murphy, & Daniels, 2008; McFall, Smith, Roszell, Tarver, & Malas, 1990; Neal et al., 1994; Neal, Hill, Hughes, Middleton, & Busuttil, 1995; Sloan, Arsenault, Hilsenroth, & Harvill, 1996; Watson, Juba, Anderson, & Manifold, 1990; Watson et al., 1994). Berk et al. (1989) found that veterans who experienced greater noncombat traumas scored significantly higher on the PK scale. Patients with symptoms of posttraumatic stress disorder who did not meet criteria for a PTSD diagnosis scored higher than other patients on the PK scale but not as high as patients with PTSD diagnoses. Watson, Kucala, Manifold, Vassar, and Juba (1988) did not find significant differences in PK-scale scores for veterans with delayed-onset PTSD and those with undelayed-onset PTSD. Kenderdine, Phillips, and Scurfield (1992) found that veterans with PTSD diagnoses and substance abuse problems scored significantly higher on the PK scale than veterans with PTSD diagnoses who did not also have substance abuse problems.

Most of the PK-scale research to date has focused on combat-related PTSD. However, several studies have suggested that scores on the PK scale may also be related to civilian trauma. Koretzky and Peck (1990) reported that several small groups of civilian PTSD patients who had experienced life-threatening events (violent criminal victimization, industrial accidents, car or train accidents) obtained higher scores on the PK scale than a group of general psychiatric patients. The PK scale correctly classified 87% of persons in one comparison and 88% in another. However, the civilian PTSD groups had lower mean PK-scale scores than those reported previously for combat-related PTSD groups. In addition, the optimal cutoff score for classifying these civilian groups was different from that typically reported for combat groups. Sloan (1988) studied 30 male survivors of the crash landing of an airplane immediately after the crash and several later times. He found that the mean PK-scale scores of these men were relatively high immediately after the crash and that they decreased markedly during a 12-month period after the crash. McCaffrey, Hickling, and Marrazo (1989) compared two small groups of civilians who had experienced traumatic events (typically motor vehicle accidents). The group that had been diagnosed with PTSD had higher PK-scale scores than the group with other diagnoses. Sinnett, Holen, and Albott (1995) reported that female clients in two private practice settings who were abuse victims scored higher on the PK scale than other female clients in these settings who were not abuse victims. Noblitt (1995) similarly reported that a small group of mostly female psychiatric patients who reported having experienced ritual abuse scored higher on the PK scale than patients who did not report such abuse. Bowler, Hartney, and Ngo (1998) found that approximately half of a sample of persons who had been assigned PTSD diagnoses following a chemical spill had T scores greater than 65 on the PK scale.

Haisch and Meyers (2004) found that PK-scale scores of police officers were significantly related to job stress, job pressure, and perceived lack of support on the job. Duckworth and Iezzi (2005) studied individuals reporting chronic pain following motor vehicle accidents. Those with higher PK scores had more physical impairment and greater psychological distress and used more maladaptive pain coping strategies.

There is accumulating evidence that scores on the PK scale are related to general distress (Lyons & Wheeler-Cox, 1999). For example, depressed patients without posttraumatic stress disorders had higher PK-scale scores than nonpatients, and more than 20% of women with somatization disorder diagnoses had PK-scale raw scores of 28 or higher. It may be that very high PK-scale scores are indicative of posttraumatic stress disorder but more moderate elevations on the scale reflect general distress and not specifically posttraumatic stress.

Fairbank, McCaffrey, and Keane (1985) indicated that caution should be used with the PK scale because it may be susceptible to distortion by veterans who are motivated to appear to have PTSD in order to gain monetary compensation. The authors suggested that exaggeration be considered when the F-scale T score is greater than 88. However, Hyer et al. (1987) found that many PTSD patients had very high F-scale scores and that their MMPIs would have been considered invalid according to the criterion of Fairbank et al. (1985).

Litz et al. (1991) demonstrated that the MMPI and MMPI-2 versions of the PK scale work equally in identifying PTSD. However, because the MMPI-2 version includes three fewer items than the MMPI version, scores on the two versions should not be compared directly. Lyons and Keane (1992) recommended using different cutoff scores for the MMPI and MMPI-2 PK scales. They suggested that adding two raw-score points to the MMPI-2 PK-scale scores would make them comparable to MMPI PK-scale scores. In other words, a raw-score cutoff of 28 on the MMPI-2 PK scale would be equivalent to a raw-score cutoff of 30 on the MMPI PK scale. Wetzel and Yutzy (1994) offered empirical support for this suggested adjustment of cutoff scores.

In summary, there appears to be considerable evidence that scores on the PK scale are related to PTSD diagnoses among veterans. Studies, such as that by Keane et al. (1984), which have used well-defined criteria to establish the diagnosis of PTSD, report higher classification rates than other studies that have used less reliable diagnostic procedures. Using the PK scale to classify veterans as PTSD or non-PTSD will produce more false-positive than false-negative errors. It is not clear to what extent scores on the PK scale are susceptible to faking by persons who are motivated to appear to have PTSD but who really do not have the disorder. Because higher PK-scale scores of mental health clients tend to be associated with more symptoms of psychological maladjustment (Graham et al., 1999), the use of the scale to arrive at differential diagnoses between PTSD versus other disorders may be limited. The utility of the PK scale in identifying PTSD associated with noncombat stress needs to be researched more fully. As with other MMPI-2 scales, it is not responsible clinical practice to use a single scale to assign diagnostic labels.

Interpretation of High PK-Scale Scores

High scorers on the PK scale are likely to be manifesting many of the symptoms and behaviors typically associated with PTSD. When high PK-scale scores are encountered in persons who have experienced combat-related stress, the possibility of PTSD should be explored carefully. It is far less clear to what extent high PK-scale scores in other circumstances indicate the appropriateness of a PTSD diagnosis.

In addition to being associated with diagnoses of posttraumatic stress disorder, high scores on the PK scale indicate persons who

1. are reporting intense emotional distress
2. report symptoms of anxiety and sleep disturbance
3. feel guilty and depressed
4. may be having unwanted and disturbing thoughts
5. fear loss of emotional and cognitive control
6. feel misunderstood and mistreated

MARITAL DISTRESS SCALE (MDS)

Scale Development

The Marital Distress Scale (MDS) of the MMPI-2 was developed by Hjemboe, Almagor, and Butcher (1992) to assess distress in marital relationships. Tentative items were selected by correlating MMPI-2 item responses with scores on the Dyadic Adjustment Scale (DAS; Spanier, 1976) for 150 couples involved in marital counseling and 392 couples from the MMPI-2 normative sample. The DAS is a 31-item inventory assessing relationship consensus, cohesion, affection, and satisfaction. Additional items were added to the tentative MDS on the basis of correlations between other MMPI-2 items and scores on the tentative scale. Items were later eliminated if their content was judged not to be specifically related to marital distress or if their removal led to improved discriminant validity. The final scale consists of 14 items. The content of certain items seems to be related obviously to marital distress (e.g., having quarrels with family members; believing one's home life is unpleasant). Several items in the scale have less obvious relationships to marital distress (e.g., not being able to make up one's mind; feeling that one's life goals are not within reach). The items are scored in the direction most often chosen by persons experiencing less positive marital adjustment. Although Hjemboe et al. (1992) reported uniform T-score equivalents for raw scores on the MDS, the T scores presented in the MMPI-2 manual are linear T scores.

Reliability and Validity

Hjemboe et al. (1992) reported an internal-consistency (alpha) coefficient of .65 for the developmental sample. Alpha coefficients for men and women in the MMPI-2 normative sample were .61 and .68, respectively. Test–retest reliability coefficients for men and women in the MMPI-2 normative sample were .78 and .81, respectively.

The MDS was validated by correlating it with DAS scores for the combined marital counseling and normative groups. The correlation between the two measures was –.55. The ability of the MDS to discriminate between persons with high and low levels of marital distress was compared with that of several other relevant MMPI-2 scales: Pd (Psychopathic Deviate), Harris–Lingoes Pd1 subscale (Familial Discord), and the FAM (Family Problems) Content scale. Regression analysis indicated that the MDS accounted for more of the variance in DAS scores than did any of the other measures. When marital adjustment groups were formed on the basis of extremely high or low scores on the DAS, a T-score cutoff of 60 on the MDS correctly classified slightly more persons overall (88%) than did the Pd1 subscale (85%), the Pd scale (83%), or the FAM scale (84%). However, the MDS correctly classified a higher percentage of the high-marital-distress persons (63%) than did the other scales. The results of the study of Hjemboe et al. (1992) are somewhat difficult to evaluate because most of the persons used in the validity analyses were also used for scale development purposes.

Graham et al. (1999) identified correlates of MDS scores for mental health center clients. For male clients higher MDS scores were associated with higher therapist ratings of family problems, but this relationship was not observed for female clients. Interestingly, MDS scores of male clients were even more strongly related to a wide variety of symptoms and negative characteristics, including depression, anger, and suicidal ideation.

O'Reilly, Graham, Hjemboe, and Butcher (2003) found that MDS scores were related to the number of marital problems reported by couples involved in marital counseling and added significantly to other MMPI-2 scales in predicting number of marital problems. However, the MDS also seemed to be assessing general maladjustment in a manner similar to other MMPI-2 measures such as Welsh's Anxiety (A) scale, the Ego Strength (Es) scale, and the mean T score for the eight Clinical scales.

Interpretation of MDS Scores

Because limited data are available concerning the validity of the MDS, the scale should be interpreted cautiously. High scores (T > 60) may be indicative of significant marital distress, and additional assessment in this area is recommended. Obviously, the scale may not be of much help when assessing persons who are admitting to marital problems and seeking help for them. However, when the MMPI-2 is used as part of a more general assessment, high MDS scores should alert clinicians that marital problems may be underlying other symptoms such as anxiety or depression.

In addition to suggesting distress in marriages or other intimate relationships, high scores on the MDS indicate persons who

1. are generally maladjusted
2. may be experiencing depression
3. may feel like failures much of the time
4. feel that life is a strain
5. are angry
6. have few or no friends and may feel rejected by other people

HOSTILITY (Ho) SCALE

Scale Development

The Hostility (Ho) scale was one of several developed by Cook and Medley (1954) to predict the rapport of teachers with pupils in a classroom. Teachers who scored very high or very low on the Minnesota Teacher Attitude Inventory (MTAI), an instrument known to predict teacher–pupil interactions, were identified and their MMPI responses compared. Of the 250 items that these groups endorsed significantly differently, 77 whose content most clearly reflected hostility were included in a preliminary version of the Ho scale. The preliminary scale was refined by having five clinical psychologists independently select the items most clearly related to hostility, resulting in a final 50-item scale. All but one of the items in the MMPI version of the Ho scale are included in the MMPI-2. Brophy (1997) reported that Ho-scale raw scores are somewhat lower (approximately three points) for the MMPI-2 normative sample than for the original MMPI normative sample.

Cook and Medley (1954) indicated that those who score high on the Ho scale are hostile persons who have little confidence in other people; see people as dishonest, unsocial, immoral, ugly, and mean; and believe that others should be made to suffer for their sins. Although developed specifically in relation to teacher–pupil interactions, Cook and Medley (1954) suggested that because the Ho-scale items do not directly relate to school settings, the scale could prove to be useful in the selection of salespeople, military personnel, and others who must be able to establish rapport with other people and maintain group morale.

Costa, Zonderman, McCrae, and Williams (1986) factor analyzed Ho-scale item responses of medical patients referred for coronary arteriography. They found two interpretable factors, which they labeled as "cynicism" and "paranoid alienation." However, they concluded that because of the strong correlation between the factors and the similarity of item content, the factors should be considered different aspects of a single trait measured by the Ho scale. These investigators concluded that "cynical mistrust" might be a better label than "hostility" for this trait. Barefoot, Dodge, Peterson, Dahlstrom, and Williams (1989) developed six rational subsets of Ho-scale items: cynicism, hostile affect, aggressive responding, hostile attribution, social avoidance, and other. They reported data suggesting that the first three of these subsets were most strongly related to health problems in lawyers. Based on data from Finnish college students,

Greenglass and Julkunen (1991) concluded that the Ho scale assesses a single underlying dimension, which they labeled "cynical distrust." Houston, Smith, and Cates (1989) used a small sample of undergraduate students and identified two clusters of items that they labeled "overt cynical mistrust" and "covert cynical mistrust." Students identified according to their endorsements of these two clusters of items exhibited different physiological responsivity during periods of stress. Han, Weed, Calhoun, and Butcher (1995) factor analyzed Ho-scale item responses for a mixed sample of persons in the MMPI-2 normative sample, couples in marital counseling, substance abusers, and general psychiatric patients. They identified four clusters of items, which overlapped considerably with those of Barefoot et al. (1989): cynicism, hypersensitivity, aggressive responding, and social avoidance. In summary, although there has not been clear agreement concerning the factor structure of the Ho scale, all analyses have identified cynicism as a primary component. Aggressive responding and social avoidance have also been identified as components of the Ho scale in more than one study.

Reliability and Validity

Cook and Medley (1954) reported an internal consistency coefficient of .86 for the Ho scale for 200 graduate students in education. Internal consistency coefficients for the Ho scale for men and women in the MMPI-2 normative sample are .87 and .85, respectively. The test–retest coefficients for subsamples of men and women in the MMPI-2 normative sample were .85 and .88, respectively. Barefoot, Dahlstrom, and Williams (1983) reported a 1-year test–retest reliability coefficient of .86 for medical students, and Shekelle, Gale, Ostfeld, and Paul (1983) reported a 4-year test–retest reliability coefficient of .84 for 1877 middle-aged male employees.

Preliminary validity data were obtained by Cook and Medley (1954) by correlating Ho-scale scores of male and female graduate students with their scores on a measure of teacher–pupil interactions. The correlations were −.44 for men, −.45 for women, and −.44 for men and women combined. Subsequent studies of college students (Brown & Zeichner, 1989; Hardy & Smith, 1988; Hart, 1966; Houston & Vavak, 1991; Pope, Smith, & Rhodewalt, 1990; Smith & Frohm, 1985; Swan, Carmelli, & Rosenman, 1991), employed women (Houston & Kelly, 1989), married couples (Smith, Saunders, & Alexander, 1990), adults in the MMPI-2 normative sample (Han et al., 1995), healthy men (Carmody, Crossen, & Wiens, 1989), and medical patients (Blumenthal, Barefoot, Burg, & Williams, 1987) have added to the construct validity of the Ho scale. In these studies, high scorers tended to experience more anger and were more likely to display overtly hostile behavior than lower Ho-scale scorers. They were more irritable, antagonistic, and resentful. High scorers on the Ho scale also were more cynical, suspicious, and untrusting. They were not very friendly, attributed hostility to others, and blamed others for their problems. These high scorers perceived and sought less social support. Previous research has indicated that there is a strong neuroticism component to the Ho scale, with higher scorers having higher levels of anxiety, depression, and somatic complaints and lower self-esteem (Blumenthal et al., 1987).

Graham et al. (1999) determined correlates of the Ho scale in an outpatient mental health center. They found that the primary characteristic being measured by the Ho scale was cynicism. In addition, Ho-scale scores were highly correlated with measures of psychological distress and general maladjustment. Although Ho-scale scores were strongly correlated with scores on the Anger Content scale for both men and women, correlations with extratest measures of hostility/aggression were very modest for men and not significant for women. They concluded that clinicians who use the Ho scale in outpatient clinical settings should be cautious not to infer that high scorers will be more hostile or aggressive than those with lower scores. High scores may also indicate a cynical mistrust of others, emotional distress, and general maladjustment.

Interest in the Ho scale increased dramatically following research indicating that the anger component of the Type A personality construct was related significantly to health problems, especially coronary heart disease (e.g., Williams et al., 1980). Following evidence that patients undergoing coronary angiography were more likely to have severe coronary artery disease if they had high Ho-scale scores, three prospective studies offered support for the link between hostility, as measured by the Ho scale, and significant health problems. Barefoot et al. (1983) conducted a 25-year follow-up of physicians who had completed the MMPI during medical school and found that Ho-scale scores were positively related to subsequent coronary heart disease incidence and to mortality from all causes. Shekelle et al. (1983) reported that Ho-scale scores predicted myocardial infarction and cardiac deaths at 10-year follow-up and coronary heart disease deaths and death from all causes at 20-year follow-up. Barefoot et al. (1989) found that Ho-scale scores were related to early mortality for lawyers who had taken the MMPI in law school approximately 25 years earlier. A meta-analysis of 83 studies identified consistent but modest relationships between hostility (often but not always measured with the Ho scale) and coronary heart disease (Booth-Kewley & Friedman, 1987).

Not all studies have supported the relationship between Ho-scale scores and serious health problems. Colligan and Offord (1988) found that unusually large proportions of normal people and general medical patients obtained Ho-scale scores higher than cutoffs proposed by previous researchers, suggesting a more conservative interpretation of Ho scores as predictors of coronary heart disease. Maruta et al. (1993) reported that in a 20-year follow-up study of 620 general medical patients the Ho score was a significant predictor of the development of coronary heart disease. However, when age and sex were controlled, the Ho score was no longer a significant predictor.

There has been much speculation concerning the mechanisms that link hostility and heart disease and other health problems. Smith (1992) described several models that have been offered to explain these mechanisms. The psychophysiological reactivity model suggests that hostile people show larger increases in blood pressure, heart rate, and stress-related hormones in response to potential stressors and that these increases lead to significant health problems. Smith concluded that the evidence for this model is mixed and that relationships between hostility and physiological reactivity are likely to be quite complex.

The psychosocial vulnerability model posits that hostile people experience a more taxing interpersonal environment, encountering higher levels of interpersonal conflict and lower levels of social support. These experiences make hostile people more vulnerable to disease because of increased physiological reactivity and absence of social support to buffer the effects of stress.

The transactional model holds that hostile people actually create, through their own actions, more frequent, severe, and enduring contacts with stressors. These experiences could lead to greater physiological reactivity and more serious health problems.

The health behaviors model suggests that hostile people may be at greater risk of disease, at least in part because of poor health habits. It may be that their cynicism causes them to discount information linking certain behaviors and health problems. Support for this model comes from studies that have found that persons with higher Ho-scale scores are more likely to smoke, to use alcohol, and to be overweight and less likely to engage in positive health behaviors such as regular exercise (e.g., Bunde & Suls, 2006).

The constitutional vulnerability model suggests that the apparent association between hostility and health problems may reflect an underlying constitutional weakness that accounts for personality characteristics, including hostility, and health problems. Evidence that hostility may be determined, at least in part, by genetic factors lends some support to this model.

Smith (1992) concluded that regardless of the model to which one subscribes, the relationship between personality factors and serious health problems is an important avenue for future research. Given previous findings concerning the relationship between Ho-scale scores and heart disease and other serious health problems, it is likely that this scale will continue to receive considerable attention among health psychologists.

Interpretation of Ho-Scale Scores

Higher scores on the Ho scale tend to be associated with cynicism, higher levels of experienced anger and overtly hostile behavior, and greater risk for serious health problems such as coronary heart disease. In mental health settings higher Ho-scale scores are related to cynicism, emotional distress, and general maladjustment. The Ho scale is not a very good predictor of overt hostility and aggression among mental health clients. In summary, higher Ho-scale scores indicate persons who

1. are very cynical, suspicious, and mistrusting
2. experience higher levels of anger, especially in interpersonal situations
3. are seen as unfriendly
4. attribute hostility to others
5. blame others for their problems
6. perceive and seek less social support
7. have higher levels of anxiety, depression, and somatic complaints

8. have poor self-concepts
9. are at increased risk for serious health problems
10. are not well adjusted psychologically

OVERCONTROLLED–HOSTILITY (O–H) SCALE

Scale Development

Megargee, Cook, and Mendelsohn (1967) suggested that there are two major types of persons who commit acts of extreme physical aggression. Habitually aggressive (undercontrolled) persons have not developed appropriate controls against the expression of aggression, so when they are provoked they respond with aggression of an intensity proportional to the degree of provocation. Chronically overcontrolled persons have very rigid inhibitions against the expression of any form of aggression. Most of the time the overcontrolled individuals do not respond even with aggression appropriate to provocation, but occasionally, when the provocation is great enough, they may act out in an extremely aggressive manner. Megargee and his associates believed that the most aggressive acts typically are committed by overcontrolled rather than undercontrolled persons.

The original Overcontrolled–Hostility (O–H) scale was constructed by identifying items that were answered differently by extremely assaultive prisoners, moderately assaultive prisoners, prisoners convicted of nonviolent crimes, and men who had not been convicted of any crime. Items were scored so that higher scores on the O–H scale were indicative of more assaultive (overcontrolled) persons. The original O–H scale had 31 items, and the MMPI-2 version of the scale includes 28 of the items.

Reliability and Validity

Megargee et al. (1967) reported a coefficient of internal consistency (Kuder–Richardson 21) of .56 for the O–H scale for a combined group of criminals and college students. Internal-consistency (alpha) coefficients for men and women in the MMPI-2 normative sample were .34 and .24, respectively (Butcher et al., 2001). Clearly, the O–H scale is not very internally consistent. Moreland (1985b) reported test–retest coefficients for male and female college students of .72 and .56, respectively. Test–retest coefficients for men and women from the MMPI-2 normative sample were .68 and .69, respectively (Butcher et al., 2001).

Results of research comparing O–H-scale scores of violent and nonviolent offenders have been mixed. Some studies (e.g., Deiker, 1974; Fredericksen, 1976; Megargee et al., 1967) found that more violent criminals scored higher on the O–H scale than less violent offenders. Other studies (e.g., Fisher, 1970; Hutton, Miner, Blades, & Langfeldt, 1992) failed to find O–H-scale differences between assaultive and nonassaultive prisoners. Verona and Carbonell (2000) reported that one-time violent female offenders had higher O–H-scale scores than nonviolent offenders. Consistent with Megargee's conceptualization of overcontrolled persons, repeat violent offenders did not score differently on the O–H scale from nonviolent offenders. Although samples utilized were too small to have adequate statistical power to achieve significance, Salekin, Ogloff, Ley, and Salekin (2002) found that adolescent murderers scored higher on the O–H scale than other violent offenders, nonviolent offenders, and nonoffenders.

Lane (1976) suggested that some of the negative findings concerning the relationship between the O–H scale and violent offending could be due to the manner in which the O–H scale was administered and to a confounding of race and the assaultiveness. Although no data were presented to support the contention, Lane stated that the O–H scale must be administered in the context of the entire MMPI. Hutton et al. (1992) found that African American forensic psychiatric patients scored somewhat higher (M = 65.57) than Caucasian patients (M = 59.86) on the O–H scale, but the relationship between O–H-scale scores and relevant extratest measures did not differ for these two groups.

Archer et al. (1997) reported that O–H-scale scores of psychiatric inpatients were positively related to extratest measures of grandiosity and negatively related to measures of uncooperativeness. Graham et al. (1999) found that therapists rated male mental health center clients with high O–H-scale scores as less depressed than other male clients, and these high-scoring men were less likely to have been arrested. Female clients with high O–H-scale scores were rated as more optimistic than other female clients. High-scoring male and female clients presented themselves as less depressed, hostile, and obsessive–compulsive. There is little evidence to suggest that high scores on the O–H scale in groups other than prisoners are associated with violent acts.

Caldwell (2005) suggested that the O–H scale can provide information about parenting characteristics in child custody evaluations, stating that high-scoring parents may bottle up anger and express it in undercontrolled ways. However, Bow, Flens, Gould, and Greenhut (2005) cited survey data indicating that clinicians who used the MMPI-2 in child custody evaluations did not find the O–H scale to be very useful. This author could find no data published in peer-review journals concerning behaviors associated with O–H scale scores in settings where custody evaluations are conducted.

Interpretation of High Scores on the O–H Scale

In correctional settings, high scores on the O–H scale tend to be associated with aggressive and violent acts. However, the validity of the O–H scale is such that individual predictions of violence from scores are not likely to be very accurate. In addition, cutoff scores for predicting violence would have to be established separately in each setting where the scale is used. The O–H scale has potential use in other settings because it tells clinicians something about how persons typically respond to provocation. Higher scorers on the O–H scale tend not to respond to provocation appropriately most of the time, but occasional exaggerated aggressive responses may occur. High scores also may be indicative of persons who

1. typically do not express angry feelings
2. are more socialized and responsible
3. have strong needs to excel

4. are dependent on others
5. are trustful
6. describe nurturing and supportive family backgrounds
7. if psychiatric inpatients, tend to be rather grandiose but cooperative
8. if mental health center clients, present themselves as having fewer symptoms and negative characteristics than other clients

Interpretation of Low Scores on the O–H Scale

Relatively few data exist concerning the interpretation of low scores on the O–H scale. In fact, Megargee (2000) indicated that T scores below 65 are meaningless. Low scorers are not expected to display the overcontrolled–hostility syndrome described for high scorers. However, low scorers may be either chronically aggressive persons or persons who are quite appropriate in the expression of their aggression.

MACANDREW ALCOHOLISM SCALE–REVISED (MAC-R)

Scale Development

The MacAndrew Alcoholism (MAC) scale (MacAndrew, 1965) was developed to differentiate alcoholic from nonalcoholic psychiatric patients. The scale was constructed by contrasting the MMPI responses of 200 male alcoholics seeking treatment at an outpatient clinic with responses of 200 male nonalcoholic psychiatric outpatients from the same facility. These analyses identified 51 items that differentiated the two groups. Because MacAndrew was interested in developing a subtle scale, two of the 51 items that deal directly with excessive drinking behavior were eliminated from the scale. The items are keyed in the direction selected most often by the alcoholic patients. Schwartz and Graham (1979) reported that the major content dimensions of the MAC scale are cognitive impairment, school maladjustment, interpersonal competence, risk taking, extroversion and exhibitionism, and moral indignation. Weed, Butcher, and Ben-Porath (1995) factor analyzed the MAC-R items for a mixed sample of alcoholics and psychiatric patients. They found four of the same factors reported by Schwartz and Graham (i.e., cognitive impairment, school maladjustment, interpersonal competence, and risk taking). In addition, they identified clusters of items that they labeled as harmful habits and masculine interests.

Four of the original MAC-scale items were among those eliminated from the MMPI-2 because of objectionable content. Because the MAC scale typically is interpreted in terms of raw scores, a decision was made to maintain a scale of 49 items in the MMPI-2. Thus, the four objectionable items were replaced with four new items that were selected because they differentiated alcoholic and nonalcoholic men (Butcher et al., 1989).

Reliability and Validity

Internal consistency data were not reported for the original MAC scale. The MAC-R scale does not seem to have particularly good internal consistency.

Internal consistency (alpha) coefficients for the MMPI-2 normative sample were .56 for men and .45 for women (Butcher et al., 2001). Butcher, Graham, and Ben-Porath (1995) reported alpha coefficients of .51 and .61, respectively, for a composite sample of male and female substance abusers, psychiatric patients, and nonpatients. Miller, Shields, Campfield, Wallace, and Weiss (2007) reviewed 210 studies in which MAC/MAC-R data were reported and found that reliability data were reported for only 9% of the studies. The median internal consistency value for these studies was .48. Factor analyses of the MAC/MAC-R items reported by Schwartz and Graham (1979) and Butcher et al. (1995) indicated that neither version of the scale is unidimensional.

Moreland (1985b) reported test–retest reliability coefficients (6-week interval) for the MAC scale with samples of normal college men and women. The coefficients were .82 and .75, respectively. For subsamples of men and women in the MMPI-2 normative sample, test–retest reliability coefficients (1-week interval) for the MAC-R scale were .62 and .78, respectively. These relatively modest test–retest reliability coefficients for normal samples can be explained, at least in part, by limited variability of scores in these groups.

Several studies reported that MAC-scale scores did not change significantly during addiction treatment programs ranging in length from 28 to 90 days or during a 1-year follow-up period after treatment (Chang, Caldwell, & Moss, 1973; Gallucci, Kay, & Thornby, 1989; Huber & Danahy, 1975; Rohan, 1972; Rohan, Tatro, & Rotman, 1969). Hoffman, Loper, and Kammeier (1974) compared the MMPI scores of male alcoholics at the time of treatment to MMPIs completed 13 years earlier when they had entered college and found no significant changes in MAC-scale scores over this extended period of time. Apfeldorf and Hunley (1975) reported high MAC-scale scores for male veterans with histories of alcohol abuse who were no longer abusing alcohol when they completed the MMPI. Average MAC-R-scale scores of recovering male and female alcoholics were below cutoff scores suggestive of substance abuse problems (Rouhbakhsh, Lewis, & Allen-Byrd, 2004). However, MAC-R data were not available for these individuals before they were considered to be recovering, so it is difficult to determine if these scores represent a decrease from earlier scores that were significantly higher.

MacAndrew (1965) reported cross-validation data for his scale. A raw-score cutoff of 24 correctly classified approximately 82% of the alcoholic and nonalcoholic persons. Subsequent research confirmed that persons who abuse alcohol and/or other substances scored higher on the MAC scale than nonabusers (Apfeldorf & Hunley, 1975; Rhodes, 1969; Rich & Davis, 1969; Rohan, 1972; Rosenberg, 1972; Schwartz & Graham, 1979; Uecker, 1970; Williams, McCourt, & Schneider, 1971).

Research concerning the MAC-R also has indicated that substance-abusing individuals score higher than nonabusers (e.g., Cavaiola, Strohmetz, Wolf, & Lavender, 2002; Clements & Heintz, 2002; Rouse, Butcher, & Miller, 1999; Stein, Graham, Ben-Porath, & McNulty, 1999; Wasyliw, Haywood, Grossman, & Cavanaugh, 1993; Weed et al., 1995). Cooper-Hakim and Viswesvaran (2002) reported results of a meta-analysis of 161 studies involving the MAC and MAC-R scales. They concluded that with a raw score cutoff of 27, 72% correct classification of abusers and nonabusers was achieved. The more traditional cutoff score of 24 also yielded 72% correct classification. Craig (2005) reviewed 71 MAC-R studies published between 1988 and 2001 and concluded that the scale "significantly correlates with measures of alcohol and substance abuse in both male and female adolescents and adults across a diverse spectrum of the use-abuse continuum" (p. 444).

There also are data suggesting that drug addicts score higher than other psychiatric patients but not differently from alcoholics on the MAC scale (Fowler, 1975; Kranitz, 1972). Graham (1978) reported that pathological gamblers scored similarly to alcoholics and heroin addicts on the MAC scale. Brown and Fayek (1993) reported that patients who abused alcohol and cocaine had higher MAC-R-scale scores than those who abused only alcohol. First-time and repeat DWI offenders scored significantly higher than nonoffenders on the MAC-R scale (Cavaiola et al., 2002).

Hoffman et al. (1974) located MMPIs of male alcoholics in treatment; these MMPIs had been completed approximately 13 years previously when the men entered college. The MAC-scale scores of these men were higher than scores of their classmates who had not received treatment for alcoholism. There also are data suggesting that persons who drink excessively but who are not alcoholics score higher on the MAC scale than persons who do not drink excessively (Apfeldorf & Hunley, 1975; Williams et al., 1971). Several studies have reported that the MAC scale also seems to be effective in identifying adolescents who have significant problems with alcohol and/or drug abuse (Gantner, Graham, & Archer, 1992; Wisniewski, Glenwick, & Graham, 1985; Wolfson & Erbaugh, 1984). However, Colligan and Offord (1990) found that the MAC scale did not discriminate well between male adolescent substance abusers and nonabusers.

Several studies have suggested caution in using the MAC scale with African Americans (Graham & Mayo, 1985; Walters, Greene, & Jeffrey, 1984; Walters, Greene, Jeffrey, Kruzich, & Haskin, 1983). Although African American alcoholics tend to obtain scores suggestive of substance abuse problems, classification rates in these studies have not been very good because nonalcoholic African Americans also tend to score rather high on the MAC scale. It should be noted that the African American samples have involved military personnel or veterans. The extent to which these findings are generalizable remains to be determined. Likewise, additional research is needed to determine to what extent the MAC-R scale is effective with other minority groups. Greene, Robin, Albaugh, Caldwell, and Goldman (2003) reported that MAC-R scores were not related to several different measures of substance abuse among members of two American Indian tribes. Although the MAC scale was developed using data from male substance abusers and psychiatric outpatients, it has come to be used with both men and women. However, data suggest that the scale does not work as well with women as with men (Gottesman & Prescott, 1989; Schwartz & Graham, 1979).

Not all MAC-scale validity studies have reported positive results (Miller & Streiner, 1990; Snyder, Kline, & Podany, 1985; Svanum, McGrew, & Ehrmann, 1994; Zager & Megargee, 1981). After reviewing 74 empirical studies, Gottesman and Prescott (1989) questioned the routine use of the MAC scale in clinical and employment settings. They concluded that the evidence for the use of the MAC scale to identify substance abusers is not as compelling as many users assume. Further, accuracy of classification using the MAC scale is considerably lower when the scale is used in settings where the base rate for substance abuse is markedly different from that of the setting in which the scale was developed. The observations made by Gottesman and Prescott are appropriate, but their recommendation that the MAC scale not be used outside of research settings does not seem justified. Although most of the studies they reviewed used a cutoff score of 24 in discriminating abusers from nonabusers, a somewhat higher cutoff score (T = 27) is probably more appropriate. Further, their recommendation seems to imply that whether a person is or is not a substance abuser would be decided on the basis of MMPI (or MMPI-2) data only. Of course, no decisions about substance abuse should be made on the basis of MAC- (or MAC-R-) scale scores alone. High scores on the scale should alert clinicians to obtain corroborating information concerning the possibility of substance abuse.

At times the MAC scale has been described as assessing an addiction-prone personality. It has been suggested that higher MAC scorers are at greater risk for developing substance abuse problems even if they are not currently abusing substances. The existing literature simply does not support such interpretations. The relationships between MAC-scale scores and current substance abuse do not speak to the issue of predicting such abuse in persons who currently are not abusers.

It has been suggested that the MAC scale measures general antisocial tendencies and not specifically substance abuse. Data concerning this possibility are mixed. Schwartz and Graham (1979) concluded that the MAC scale was not measuring general antisocial behavior in a large sample of hospitalized psychiatric patients. However, Levenson, Aldwin, Butcher, DeLabry, Workman-Daniels, and Bosse (1990) reported that older men with arrest histories but without drinking problems scored as high on the MAC scale as older men with drinking problems but without arrest histories. Zager and Megargee (1981) reported that young male prisoners scored relatively high on the MAC scale regardless of the extent to which they reported having drinking problems.

As Ward and Jackson (1990) suggested, there is evidence that MAC-scale scores may be a function of both psychiatric diagnosis and substance use/abuse. Substance-abusing patients who have other psychiatric diagnoses (i.e., MacAndrew's secondary alcoholics) tend to obtain relatively low scores on the MAC scale (e.g., Ward & Jackson, 1990) and are not easily discriminated from psychiatric patients who do not abuse substances. Patients with diagnoses of antisocial personality disorder often obtain relatively higher scores on the MAC scale whether or not they abuse substances (e.g., Wolf, Schubert, Patterson, Grande, & Pendleton, 1990). Thus, nonabusing patients with diagnoses of antisocial personality disorder are often misidentified as having substance abuse problems.

Interpretation of Scores on the MAC–R Scale

Except for four objectionable items that have been replaced, the MAC-R scale is essentially the same as the original scale. Thus, the interpretation of the scale can be similar to the interpretation of the original MAC scale. High scores on the MAC-R scale suggest the possibility of alcohol or other substance abuse problems. Obviously, it would not be responsible clinical practice to reach conclusions about substance abuse without obtaining corroborating information from other sources.

The following guidelines are based on this author's review of empirical research literature on the MAC and MAC-R. In general, raw scores of 28 and above on the MAC-R scale are suggestive of substance abuse problems. In such cases, additional information about alcohol and drug use should be obtained. Scores between 24 and 27 are suggestive of substance abuse, but at this level there will be many false positives (i.e., nonabusers who are identified as abusers because of their scores). Scores below 24 suggest that substance abuse problems are not very likely. Incorrect classification of nonabusers as abusers is especially likely to occur for individuals who have many of the characteristics often associated with the diagnosis of antisocial personality disorder. Substance-abusing patients who also have other psychiatric diagnoses, such as schizophrenia or major affective disorders, are likely to have relatively low scores on the MAC-R scale and may not be identified as having substance abuse problems on the basis of this scale. African Americans who abuse substances are likely to obtain elevated MAC-R-scale scores, but the tendency for nonabusing African Americans to have elevated scores on the scale will lead to more false positives than with Caucasian subjects.

Although most items on the MAC-R scale are not obviously related to substance use/abuse, some data suggest that alcoholics who take the MMPI/MMPI-2 with intentions of hiding problems or shortcomings may produce lower scores on the MAC-R scale than when they take the test more honestly (Otto, Lang, Megargee, & Rosenblatt, 1988; Wasyliw et al., 1993). Using a MAC-scale cutoff score of 24, 84% of alcoholics who took the test with standard instructions were identified correctly, whereas only 65% of alcoholics who took the test with instructions to hide problems and shortcomings were correctly identified. However, almost all of the persons who were trying to hide problems and shortcomings were identified by the MMPI Validity scales and indexes. These data suggest caution in interpreting MAC-R-scale scores when the Validity scales of the MMPI-2 indicate that the test taker has approached the MMPI-2 in a defensive manner.

In addition to the possibility of substance abuse, high scores on the MAC-R scale may indicate persons who

1. are socially extroverted
2. are exhibitionistic
3. are self-confident and assertive
4. may experience blackouts

5. enjoy competition and risk taking
6. have difficulties in concentrating
7. have histories of behavior problems in school or with the law
8. are aggressive
9. if mental health patients, may be more likely than other patients to have made suicide attempts

ADDICTION ADMISSION SCALE (AAS)

Scale Development

Weed, Butcher, McKenna, and Ben-Porath (1992) developed the Addiction Admission Scale (AAS), emphasizing items in the MMPI-2 that have obvious content related to substance abuse (e.g., having a drug or alcohol problem; expressing true feelings only when drinking). A tentative scale composed of 14 items was refined using internal-consistency procedures, resulting in the elimination of three items that did not contribute to scale homogeneity. Scores on the 11-item version of the scale were correlated with each of the other MMPI-2 items. Two additional items were identified for inclusion in the scale. Thus, the final AAS has 13 items. Raw scores on the AAS are transformed to linear T scores using the MMPI-2 normative data.

Reliability and Validity

Weed et al. (1992) reported an internal-consistency coefficient (alpha) of .74 for a combined sample of substance abusers, psychiatric patients, and persons in the MMPI-2 normative sample. In a comprehensive literature review, Miller et al. (2007) found only two studies that reported internal consistency data for the AAS. The median value was .58. Weed et al. reported test–retest reliability coefficients of .89 and .84, respectively, for men and women in the MMPI-2 normative sample. Factor analysis of the AAS items yielded one very strong factor associated with admission of problem drinking, and two weaker factors, one reflecting the use of drugs other than alcohol and the other having to do with social problems associated with alcohol or drug use (Weed et al., 1995).

The utility of the AAS was examined by Weed et al. (1992) using samples of substance abusers (832 men, 380 women), psychiatric inpatients (232 men, 191 women), and the MMPI-2 normative sample (1138 men and 1462 women). For both men and women, the substance abusers had the highest mean AAS scores and persons in the normative sample had the lowest mean scores. The mean scores of the psychiatric patients were between the means of the other two groups. Other research has supported the relationship between AAS scores and various indicators of substance abuse. In the MMPI-2 normative sample (Butcher et al., 1989) higher AAS scorers were more likely to be described by their partners as drinking excessively and using nonprescription drugs. In several studies, mental health patients with higher AAS scores were more likely to have indicators of substance abuse (Stein et al., 1999; Wong & Besett, 1999), and similar relationships were observed in a forensic setting (Ben-Porath & Stafford, 1993) and for college student samples (Clements & Heintz, 2002; Svanum et al., 1994). Rouse et al. (1999) reported that psychotherapy patients with substance abuse problems scored significantly higher on the AAS than those without substance abuse problems.

Although Weed et al. (1992) did not recommend cutoff scores for the AAS, examination of their data suggests that a T score of 60 yielded optimal classification. When men with AAS T scores greater than 60 were considered to be substance abusers and those with T scores equal to or below 60 nonabusers, 72% of the substance abusers, 51% of the psychiatric patients, and 87% of persons in the normative sample were correctly classified. A T-score cutoff of 60 for women yielded correct classification of 58% of substance abusers, 66% of psychiatric patients, and 95% of persons in the normative sample. Greene, Weed, Butcher, Arredondo, and Davis (1992) reported similar classification rates for the AAS with substance abuse and general psychiatric samples. Although classification rates in other studies have varied (e.g., Clements & Heintz, 2002; Stein et al., 1999), in general the data have suggested that T scores greater than 60 on the AAS are suggestive of substance abuse problems that should be evaluated carefully with other corroborating data.

It appears that the AAS has promise in discriminating between substance abusers and nonabusers. However, the AAS may be less useful in discriminating between substance abusers and general psychiatric patients. Using the AAS for this purpose may lead to many psychiatric patients being misclassified as substance abusers. However, this may reflect the nature of the psychiatric samples used in previous studies. The study of Weed et al. (1992) did not eliminate from the psychiatric samples patients who also had alcohol and/or drug problems. In fact, Greene et al. (1992) reported that between 10 and 20% of psychiatric patients in the study's setting typically received a diagnosis of alcohol or drug dependence.

Interpretation of AAS Scores

Although future research may clarify the usefulness of the AAS in various settings, it is clear that persons who obtain high scores (T > 60) on the AAS are openly acknowledging substance abuse problems, and additional assessment in this area is indicated. The meaning of low scores on the AAS is less clear. Because the content of the items in the AAS is obviously related to substance abuse, persons not wanting to reveal substance abuse problems can easily obtain lower scores. Therefore, it is difficult to determine if low scores indicate the absence of substance abuse problems or simply reveal denial of such problems in persons who actually abuse substances. Examination of the Validity scales of the MMPI-2 could be helpful in this regard. One should not interpret low AAS scores in a defensive profile. Validity patterns suggesting exaggeration are of less concern because persons are not often motivated to appear to have alcohol or drug problems when they really do not have them. However, in certain forensic cases this motive should be considered (e.g., a case in which a defendant could receive a more favorable outcome if judged to be drug dependent).

In addition to the possibility of substance abuse problems, high scores on the AAS may indicate persons who

1. in mental health or forensic settings, may have diagnoses of substance abuse or dependence
2. have histories of acting-out behavior
3. are impulsive
4. are risk takers
5. have poor judgment
6. are angry and aggressive
7. are critical and argumentative
8. have family problems
9. are agitated/moody

ADDICTION POTENTIAL SCALE (APS)

Scale Development

The Addiction Potential Scale (APS) was developed by Weed et al. (1992) using the MMPI-2 item pool. The 39 items in the scale are those that 434 men and 164 women in an inpatient chemical-dependency program answered differently from 120 male and 90 female psychiatric inpatients and 584 men and 706 women in the MMPI-2 normative sample. The substance abusers included persons who abused alcohol only, other drugs only, or both alcohol and other drugs. Several tentative items were eliminated from the scale because their content obviously related to substance abuse. The items are keyed in the direction most often chosen by the substance abusers. Raw scores on the APS are transformed to linear T scores using the MMPI-2 normative data.

The content of the items in the APS is quite heterogeneous, and many of the items do not seem to have obvious relevance to substance use or abuse. Some items seem to be related to extroversion, excitement seeking, and risk taking. Other seem to assess self-doubts, self-alienation, and cynical attitudes about other people. Sawrie et al. (1996) factor analyzed the items in the APS and identified five major clusters of items: (1) satisfaction/dissatisfaction with self, (2) powerlessness/lack of self-efficacy, (3) antisocial acting out, (4) surgency, and (5) risk taking/recklessness. A somewhat different factor structure for the APS was reported by Weed et al. (1995), who considered a six-factor solution to be most interpretable: (1) harmful habits, (2) positive treatment attitudes, (3) forthcoming, (4) hypomania, (5) risk taking, and (6) passivity.

Reliability and Validity

Although items included in the APS were based, in part, on their contribution to internal consistency, no internal-consistency coefficients were reported by the scale's developers. Weed et al. (1995) later reported alpha coefficients of .70 and .73, respectively, for men and women in a combined sample of substance abusers, psychiatric patients, and nonpatients. Alpha coefficients for men and women in the MMPI-2 normative sample were .48 and .43, respectively. In a comprehensive literature review, Miller et al. (2007) found only two studies that reported internal consistency data for the APS. The median value was .58. The test–retest reliability coefficients for men and women in the MMPI-2 normative sample (one-week interval) were .89 and .84, respectively (Butcher et al., 2001).

In cross-validating the APS, Weed et al. (1992) drew different participants from the same settings used in scale development. They reported data suggesting that the APS discriminated quite well between substance abusers and persons in the normative sample and between substance abusers and psychiatric patients. Although the scale developers did not recommend cutoff scores for the APS, examination of their data reveals that the optimal T-score cutoff for both male and female participants seemed to be 60. When men with T scores greater than 60 were considered to be substance abusers, and those with T scores equal to or less than 60 nonabusers, 71% of the substance abusers, 86% of persons in the normative sample, and 82% of the psychiatric patients were correctly classified. A T-score cutoff of 60 for women correctly classified 70% of the substance abusers, 87% of the normative sample, and 81% of the psychiatric patients. By lowering the cutoff score, greater proportions of substance abusers could be correctly classified, but more persons in the normative sample and more psychiatric patients were incorrectly classified as substance abusers. Classification rates in subsequent studies have generally been lower than those reported by Weed et al., and the APS generally did a poorer job of identifying substance abusers than either the MAC-R scale or the AAS (e.g., Greene et al., 1992; Rouse et al., 1999; Stein et al., 1999). Although the APS has been related to various indicators of substance abuse, it also seems to indicate a general need to admit serious personal problems and to profess a desire for change (Weed et al., 1995).

Interpretation of APS Scores

The limited data available concerning the APS suggest that it has some promise for discriminating between persons who abuse substances and those who do not. However, the APS does not seem to be as effective as either the MAC-R scale or the AAS in identifying substance abuse problems in a variety of settings. The label of "Addiction Potential" suggests that the scale assesses a potential for or vulnerability to substance abuse, whether or not that abuse is currently taking place. At this time there are no data concerning this very important issue. Available data address the ability of the scale to identify persons who currently are abusing substances or have done so in the past. The extent to which the scale can predict future abuse and can identify current abuse by persons who are denying abuse remains to be investigated.

Despite the limited data available concerning the APS, it should be considered as one indicator of possible substance abuse problems. Of course, it is not appropriate to reach conclusions about substance abuse on the basis of MMPI-2 scores alone. High APS scores (T > 60) should alert clinicians that additional information concerning possible substance abuse should be obtained. However, when MAC-R scale or AAS scores are suggestive of substance abuse and the APS score is not, greater weight should be given to the MAC-R and AAS scores.

MASCULINE GENDER ROLE (GM) AND FEMININE GENDER ROLE (GF) SCALES

Scale Development

Peterson and Dahlstrom (1992) developed the Masculine Gender Role (GM) and Feminine Gender Role (GF) scales for the MMPI-2 as separate measures of the masculine and feminine components in the bipolar Masculinity–Femininity (Mf) scale of the MMPI. Items in the GM scale were those endorsed in the scored direction by a majority of men in the MMPI-2 normative sample and endorsed in that same direction by at least 10% fewer women in the MMPI-2 normative sample. Correspondingly, items in the GF scale were those endorsed in the scored direction by a majority of women in the MMPI-2 normative sample and endorsed in that same direction by at least 10% fewer men in the MMPI-2 normative sample. Only 9 of 47 items in the GM scale and 16 of the 46 items in the GF scale also appear on the Mf scale.

Examination of the content of the items in the GM scale suggests that they deal primarily with the denial of fears, anxieties, and somatic symptoms. Some GM-scale items have to do with interest in stereotypically masculine activities, such as reading adventure stories, and with denial of interests in stereotypically feminine occupations, such as nursing and library work. Other groups of GM-scale items have to do with denial of excessive emotionality and presentation of self as independent, decisive, and self-confident.

The largest group of items in the GF scale has to do with the denial of asocial or antisocial acts, such as getting into trouble with the law or at school and excessive use of alcohol or other drugs. Many GF-scale items also have to do with liking stereotypically feminine activities, such as cooking and growing houseplants, and with disliking stereotypically masculine activities, such as reading mechanics magazines and auto racing. A number of GF-scale items involve admissions of excessive sensitivity. There are also several items expressing early identification with a female figure and satisfaction with being female.

Reliability and Validity

Internal-consistency (alpha) coefficients for the GM scale for men and women in the MMPI-2 normative sample were .67 and .75, respectively (Butcher et al., 2001). Johnson, Jones, and Brems (1996) reported an internal consistency coefficient of .79 for the GM scale for a sample of male college students. Test–retest reliability coefficients (one-week interval) for the GM scale for subsamples of men and women in the MMPI-2 normative sample were .82 and .89, respectively (Butcher et al., 2001).

The internal-consistency (alpha) coefficient for the GF scale was .57 for both men and women in the MMPI-2 normative sample (Butcher et al., 2001). Johnson et al. (1996) reported an internal-consistency coefficient of .82 for a sample of female college students. Test–retest reliability coefficients (one-week interval) for the GF scale were .85 and .78, respectively, for men and women in the MMPI-2 normative sample (Butcher et al., 2001).

Peterson and Dahlstrom (1992) suggested that the conjoint interpretation of the GM and GF scales can yield a gender-role typology similar to that used with other instruments. Used in this manner, a high score on the GM scale and a low score on the GF scale would indicate stereotypic masculinity; a high score on the GF scale and a low score on the GM scale would indicate stereotypic femininity; high scores on both the GM and GF scales would indicate androgyny; and low scores on both the GM and GF scales would indicate an undifferentiated orientation. However, subsequent research by Johnson et al. (1996) did not support this use of the GM and GF scales. These researchers found that the GM and GF scales had only modest correlations with other sex-role measures (e.g., Bem Sex-Role Inventory, Sex-Role Behavior Scale) and that classifying students as masculine, feminine, androgynous, or undifferentiated using the GM and GF scales was not very accurate.

Peterson and Dahlstrom (1992) reported some preliminary data concerning behavioral correlates of the GM and GF scales for men and women in the MMPI-2 normative sample. GM-scale scores for both men and women were positively related to high self-confidence, persistence, and lack of feelings of self-reference and other positive characteristics. GF-scale scores were related to negative characteristics, including hypercritical behavior and poor temper control for men and misuse of alcohol and nonprescription drugs for men and women. Research by Castlebury and Durham (1997), which involved college student participants, supported the notion that for both men and women higher GM scale scores are associated with greater self-confidence and general well-being. Similar results were reported by Woo and Oei (2006, 2008) for mental health patients.

Interpretation of GM- and GF-Scale Scores

The limited research that has been published about the GM and GF scales does not support their use as measures of sex roles. High scorers (both men and women) on the GM scale are likely to be better adjusted than those who score lower on this scale. However, better MMPI-2 measures of psychological adjustment are available, so the routine use of the GM and GF scales is not recommended. They should be considered experimental scales to be used for research purposes only.

SUBTLE–OBVIOUS SUBSCALES

Wiener (1948) differentiated between MMPI items that were easy to detect as indicating emotional disturbance and items that were relatively difficult to detect as indicating emotional disturbance. The former were labeled as obvious items and the latter as subtle items. Wiener rationally developed Obvious and Subtle subscales for Scales 2, 3, 4, 6, 8, and 9 of the original MMPI, hypothesizing that test takers who were trying to fake bad on the MMPI would endorse many of the obvious and few of the subtle items in the Clinical scales. Correspondingly, test takers who were trying to fake good on the MMPI would endorse many of the subtle items and few of the obvious items in the Clinical scales. It seems likely that the subtle items came to be identified only by chance in the original item analyses. Had Hathaway and McKinley cross-validated their item analyses, these items probably would not have been included in the Clinical scales.

Considerable research evidence indicates that nontest behaviors are most accurately predicted by the obvious rather than by the subtle items (Burkhart, Gynther, & Fromuth, 1980; Duff, 1965; Gynther, Burkhart, & Hovanitz, 1979; Mihura, Schlottmann, & Scott, 2000; Osberg & Harrigan, 1999; Snyter & Graham, 1984; Weed, Ben-Porath, & Butcher, 1990). In fact, including subtle items in the Clinical scales may actually detract from the prediction of criterion variables.

The data concerning the utility of the Subtle–Obvious subscales in detecting deviant test-taking attitudes are somewhat more complex. Persons who were known to be exaggerating psychopathology when responding to MMPI items tended to endorse many more obvious than subtle items. However, because all of the Clinical scales except Scale 9 have many more obvious than subtle items, persons who actually have considerable psychopathology also endorse more obvious than subtle items (Schretlen, 1988). Thus, the differential endorsement of the subtle and obvious items is not particularly useful in differentiating between exaggerated profiles and valid profiles indicating severe psychopathology. Several studies have demonstrated that the standard Validity scales are better able than the Subtle–Obvious subscales to detect malingering (Anthony, 1971; Berry, Baer, & Harris, 1991; Dubinsky, Gamble, & Rogers, 1985; Grossman, Haywood, Ostrov, Wasyliw, & Cavanaugh, 1990; Schretlen, 1988; Timbrook, Graham, Keiller, & Watts, 1993).

When test takers are instructed to fake good on the MMPI or MMPI-2, they endorse fewer obvious items than under standard instructions. Interestingly, with the fake-good instructions persons tend to endorse more of the subtle items than with standard instructions. This may be because the subtle items are seen by test takers as representing socially desirable attitudes or actions (Burkhart, Christian, & Gynther, 1978). It is also possible that more subtle items are endorsed with fake-good instructions because most subtle items are keyed in the false direction, and persons who are faking good may have a naysaying response bias (Timbrook et al., 1993). Studies that have examined the utility of the Subtle–Obvious subscales in identifying fake-good response sets have not found them to be very useful (Dubinsky et al., 1985; Schretlen, 1988; Timbrook et al., 1993).

Several conclusions can be reached concerning the Subtle–Obvious subscales. First, the subtle items probably were included in the Clinical scales because the item analyses were not cross-validated. Second, it is the obvious and not the subtle items that are most related to extratest behaviors. Third, although persons who approach the MMPI-2 with motivation to minimize or to exaggerate psychopathology may endorse the subtle and obvious items differentially, the

Subtle–Obvious subscales do not permit very accurate differentiation of faked and valid profiles. Fourth, the standard Validity scales of the MMPI-2 work as well as or better than the Subtle–Obvious subscales in identifying these deviant response sets. In apparent response to these research findings, the MMPI-2's publisher no longer includes the Subtle–Obvious subscales in MMPI-2 test materials, scoring services, or interpretive reports.

🕭 Psychometric Considerations

It is very important for test users to understand the strengths and weaknesses of the MMPI-2 so they can evaluate the appropriateness of its use in various settings and for various purposes. This chapter provides a summary of information concerning the psychometric properties of the MMPI-2. Information about specific scales is included in chapters in this book in which the scales are examined in detail. Because of the continuity between the original MMPI and the MMPI-2, some information about both versions is included.

The MMPI was the most widely used psychological test in the United States (Harrison, Kaufman, Hickman, & Kaufman, 1988; Keller & Piotrowski, 1989; Lubin, Larsen, & Matarazzo, 1984; Piotrowski & Lubin, 1990). Far more research articles have been published about the MMPI than about any other psychological test (Graham & Lilly, 1984; Kramer & Conoley, 1992). Reviewers of the MMPI were generally positive about its utility. Alker (1978) concluded that the MMPI could provide reliable indications of psychological treatments that will or will not work for specific patients. King (1978) concluded his review of the MMPI by stating: "The MMPI remains matchless as the objective instrument for the assessment of psychopathology ... and still holds the place as the sine qua non in the psychologist's armamentarium of psychometric aids" (p. 938).

Although there were some criticisms of the MMPI-2 (e.g., Adler, 1990; Duckworth, 1991b; Helmes & Reddon, 1993; Strassberg, 1991), reviews of the MMPI-2 in the *Eleventh Mental Measurements Yearbook* were quite positive. Archer (1992a) described the MMPI-2 as "a reasonable compromise of the old and the new; an appropriate balance between that which required change (norms) and that which required preservation (standard scales). It should prove to be a worthy successor to the MMPI" (p. 561). Nichols (1992) agreed with Archer, commenting that "what was broke was fixed, what was not broke was left alone" (p. 567), and adding that "the psychodiagnostician selecting a structured inventory for the first time will find that no competing assessment device for abnormal psychology has stronger credentials for clinical description and prediction"(p. 567).

STANDARDIZATION

Unlike many of the projective techniques, the MMPI was well standardized in terms of materials, administration, and scoring. Essentially the same items, scales, and profile sheets were used from its inception in the 1930s until the publication of the MMPI-2 in 1989. Although there were variations in the ways in which scores were interpreted, most users based interpretations on the sizable MMPI research literature. This standardization of materials and procedures ensured that data collected in diverse settings were comparable and led to the accumulation of a significant database for interpreting results.

Although some changes were made in the MMPI-2, considerable effort was made to maintain continuity between the original test and the revised version. Although some items were updated, a few deleted, and new ones added, the basic item pool is quite similar to that of the original MMPI. The MMPI-2 maintains the true–false response format of the original test. The basic Validity and Clinical scales remain essentially unchanged. Scores are arrayed on a profile sheet that bears strong resemblance to the original. Although uniform T scores are used for eight of the Clinical scales, the resulting scores are very similar to the linear T scores of the original MMPI (Graham, Timbrook, Ben-Porath, & Butcher, 1991; Tellegen & Ben-Porath, 1992). Clearly, the continuity that exists between the two versions of the test makes much of what we have learned about the MMPI relevant to the MMPI-2.

SCALE CONSTRUCTION

As was discussed briefly in Chapter 1, the Clinical scales of the MMPI were constructed according to empirical keying procedures. Items were selected for inclusion in a scale if patients diagnosed as having a particular clinical syndrome (e.g., hypochondriasis, depression) responded to the items differently from nonclinical persons. For some scales comparisons also were made between patients with a particular clinical diagnosis and patients with other diagnoses. The reader interested in details concerning original scale construction should consult a series of articles by Hathaway and his associates in *Basic Readings on the MMPI* (Dahlstrom & Dahlstrom, 1980). To ensure continuity between the original and revised instruments, the MMPI-2 maintains the basic Clinical scales with only minor deletions and changes (see Table 1.1 in Chapter 1 of this book). Scale 5 had the most items deleted (four), and these dealt primarily with objectionable sexual content. Ben-Porath and Butcher (1989a) studied the 82 rewritten items in the MMPI-2 and concluded that they are psychometrically equivalent to the original items. Correlations between raw scores on the original Clinical scales and the Clinical scales of the MMPI-2 are all above .98 (Graham, 1988).

Although the empirical keying approach used to construct the original MMPI scales was an improvement over the face-valid approach used in earlier personality inventories, the scale construction procedures were rather unsophisticated by current psychometric standards. The clinical samples were often very small. For example, only 20 criterion cases were used to select items for Scale 7. Although the test authors stressed that they tried to identify criterion groups composed of patients with only one kind of psychopathology, no data were presented concerning the reliability of the criterion placements. For most scales, cross-validation procedures were employed. The statistical analyses were not very sophisticated, and often only descriptive statistics were presented.

Because no attempt was made to ensure that items would appear on only one scale, there is considerable overlap between some of the scales. For example, 13 of the 39 items in Scale 6 of the MMPI-2 also appear in Scale 8. This item overlap contributes to high intercorrelations among the scales and limits the extent to which scores on a single scale contribute uniquely to prediction of appropriate criterion measures. The intercorrelations of the basic MMPI-2 scales for the normative sample are presented in Appendix B at the end of this book. It should be noted that Hathaway did not view item overlap and lack of homogeneity as problems, maintaining that external validity was the most relevant characteristic. However, most contemporary psychometricians view item overlap as problematic because it limits the discriminant validity of scales. This issue will be addressed later in this chapter.

The empirical keying approach used with the MMPI did not emphasize item content and scale homogeneity. Hathaway and McKinley (1940) noted that the MMPI item content was heterogeneous, but they did not give attention to homogeneity of the individual scales. As a result, the internal consistency of the scales is not very high. Information about the internal consistency of MMPI-2 scales was presented in earlier chapters of this book.

Various strategies have been used in developing Supplementary scales for the MMPI and the MMPI-2. Certain scales (e.g., Ego Strength scale, MacAndrew Alcoholism scale) used empirical keying procedures similar to those employed in developing the Clinical scales. Other scales (e.g., the Harris–Lingoes subscales) were constructed rationally with no attention given to external validity. Still other scales (e.g., the Content scales) were constructed using a combined rational and statistical procedure that ensured greater item homogeneity. Additional Supplementary scales have been developed for the MMPI-2 utilizing combinations of these various methods.

NORMS

Test norms provide a summary of results obtained when the test is given to a representative sample of individuals. The sample is referred to as the normative or standardization sample. A person's score on a test typically has meaning only when it is compared with a normative sample.

Original MMPI Norms

The primary nonclinical participants used in constructing the original scales of the MMPI included 724 individuals who were visiting friends or relatives at the University of Minnesota Hospitals. Only persons who reported that they were under the care of a physician were excluded from the sample. Other nonclinical participants used in various phases of scale development were 265 high school graduates who came to the University of Minnesota Testing Bureau for precollege guidance, 265 skilled workers involved with local Works Progress Administration projects, and 243 medical patients who did not report psychiatric problems.

Only the 724 hospital visitors were included in the sample that was used to determine T-score values for the original MMPI. Almost all of the persons in the standardization sample were Caucasians, and the typical person was about 35 years old, married, residing in a small town or rural area, working in a skilled or semiskilled trade (or married to a man of this occupational level), and having about 8 years of formal education (Dahlstrom, Welsh, & Dahlstrom, 1972). Hathaway and Briggs (1957) later refined this sample by eliminating persons with incomplete records or faulty background information. The refined sample was the one typically used for converting raw scores on MMPI supplementary scales to T scores.

Although some data collected from nonclinical samples in a variety of research projects suggested that the original MMPI norms were still appropriate, concern was expressed that the MMPI norms had become outdated. Colligan, Osborne, and Offord (1980) collected contemporary data from nonclinical persons in the same geographic area where the original MMPI norms had been collected. These investigators found that on some MMPI scales contemporary samples endorsed more items in the scored direction than did the original MMPI normative sample. The data of Colligan et al. were of limited utility because their sample was limited geographically and demographically. In addition, their data were presented as normalized T scores. Although Colligan et al. argued that normalized scores were appropriate, Hsu (1984) offered convincing arguments to the contrary, and Graham and Lilly (1986) demonstrated that the use of normalized T scores led to underdiagnosis of psychopathology in psychiatric patients.

MMPI-2 Norms

The MMPI-2 normative sample is larger and more representative than that of the original MMPI (Butcher et al., 2001). The 1138 men and 1462 women in the MMPI-2 normative sample were selected from diverse geographic areas of the United States, and their demographic characteristics closely paralleled 1980 census data. They were community residents who were solicited randomly for participation in the restandardization study. Approximately 3% of the men and 6% of the women indicated that they were in treatment for mental health problems at the time of their participation in the study. The revised MMPI-2 manual (Butcher et al., 2001) includes data indicating that the norms are even more representative of 1990 census data.

The normative sample includes representatives of minority groups. For men, 82% were Caucasians, 11% were African Americans, 3% were Hispanics, 3% were Native Americans, and less than 1% were Asian Americans. For women, 81% were Caucasians, 13% were African Americans, 3% were Hispanics, 3% were Native Americans, and 1% were Asian Americans. Although the MMPI-2 normative sample does not match census data exactly, it is far more ethnically diverse than the original MMPI standardization sample.

Although the educational level of persons in the MMPI-2 normative sample (approximately 15 years) is somewhat higher than that of the general population in the 1980 census data, it probably is representative of persons to whom the MMPI-2 is likely to be administered. Persons with little or no formal education are represented in the census data but are not likely to take the MMPI-2. Butcher (1990b) reported that persons of different educational levels obtain different mean scores on some MMPI-2 scales, but the differences are small and probably not clinically important. Long, Graham, and Timbrook (1994) compared MMPI-2 scores of men and women of differing educational and family income levels. They concluded that the effects of educational level and family income are minimal and probably not clinically meaningful. Only for Scale 5 for men were Clinical scale differences greater than five T-score points across educational levels, and there were no differences of this magnitude or greater for the family income levels.

Schinka, LaLone, and Greene (1998) concluded that demographic characteristics (e.g., gender, age) contributed little to most MMPI-2 scales in discriminating between a sample of psychiatric inpatients and a subsample of the MMPI-2 normative sample. The exception among the Validity and Clinical scales was Scale 5, where, as would be expected, gender was an important variable. For the Content scales, gender added significantly to the discrimination only for the Fears and Antisocial Practices scales. For several Supplementary scales, including MAC-R, GM, GF, R, and Re, demographic characteristics added incrementally to the discrimination between patients and the normative sample.

In response to critiques of the MMPI-2 normative sample as inappropriate because its educational level is higher than that of the U.S. population, Schinka and LaLone (1997) compared MMPI-2 scores for the entire normative sample and a census-matched subsample. They found a meaningful T-score difference (approximately three points) only for Scale 1 (Hypochondriasis). They concluded that the MMPI-2 normative sample is not a robust source of bias in the interpretation of MMPI-2 profiles and that the use of the standard MMPI-2 norms is indicated. Consistent with earlier suggestions by Timbrook and Graham (1994), they stressed the importance of determining if MMPI-2 interpretations are differentially accurate for persons with differing demographic characteristics.

Long et al. (1994) analyzed how well the MMPI-2 scales predicted conceptually relevant extratest characteristics of persons of different educational and family income levels in the MMPI-2 normative sample. For both education and income, some Clinical scales underpredicted symptoms for lower levels and overpredicted symptoms for higher levels, although the errors in prediction were not very large. Because lower socioeconomic participants had obtained higher MMPI scores, some earlier writers assumed that the MMPI scales would overpathologize them. Interestingly, the results of the study of Long et al. were in the opposite direction, with scores underpredicting problem behaviors of lower socioeconomic persons to a modest extent rather than overpredicting them.

Persons in the MMPI-2 normative sample ranged in age from 18 to 85 years. In a separate project, normative data were collected from large, diverse samples of adolescents. Based on those data, a decision was made to develop a separate version of the test (MMPI-A) for adolescents (Butcher, Williams, et al., 1992). Analyses of MMPI-2 scores were conducted for various subgroupings of the normative sample. These analyses indicated that separate norms were not needed for persons of differing ages, geographic areas, or ethnic minority status.

Gendered versus Non-gendered Norms

As with the original MMPI, there were important differences in raw scores between the men and women, so separate norms were developed for these two groups. Use of gendered norms is based on the assumption that the differences in raw scores between men and women reflect differing degrees of willingness to admit to symptoms and problems rather than actual differences in those characteristics.

The use of separate norms for men and women is problematic when the MMPI-2 is used in employment screening. The Civil Rights Act of 1991 explicitly prohibits consideration of race, color, religion, national origin, or sex in employment practices. The use of gendered norms is seen as violating this prohibition. Thus, non-gendered norms were developed and are included in the Extended Score Report and in two Minnesota Reports (Personnel and Forensic), which are available from Pearson Assessments. Non-gendered T scores are based on 1138 men and 1138 women in the MMPI-2 normative sample (Ben-Porath & Forbey, 2003). The use of non-gendered norms is appropriate in employment screening applications of the MMPI-2 or whenever the use of gendered norms is prohibited.

Ben-Porath and Forbey (2003) compared gendered and non-gendered scores for all MMPI-2 scales at varying levels of scores. Although they found significant differences for some scales, they concluded that different interpretations would not be reached about individuals based on gendered versus non-gendered scores. However, those who use non-gendered norms need to be aware of how scores are likely to differ from those that would be obtained with gendered norms. Such information can be found in the Ben-Porath and Forbey monograph.

In summary, whereas the normative sample for the original MMPI was small and not very representative of the general population of the United States, the normative sample for MMPI-2 is large and representative of the population on major demographic variables. This represents an important improvement in the instrument. Research conducted to date in response to criticisms that the MMPI-2 normative sample is not representative of the U.S. population, especially in terms of educational level, has suggested that the differences between the MMPI-2 normative sample and the U.S. population are rather small and not a source of bias or error in the interpretation of the MMPI-2. However, additional research is needed to determine to what extent, if any, MMPI-2 scale scores are differentially accurate in predicting conceptually relevant behaviors of persons with differing demographic characteristics. This issue will be discussed in detail in Chapter 10 of this book.

K-Corrected versus Non-K-Corrected Norms

As discussed in Chapters 1 and 3 of this book, The K (Correction) scale was developed to identify persons who completed the MMPI in a defensive manner by denying symptoms, problems, and negative characteristics to a greater extent than the average person. In addition, Hathaway and McKinley introduced a correction factor for some of the Clinical scales to adjust scores to take into account under-reporting of symptoms and problems (above-average K-scale scores) or over-reporting of symptoms and problems (below-average K-scale scores). Optimal weights for the K-correction, as it came to be called, were determined by comparing the classification accuracy that resulted when corrected and uncorrected Clinical scale scores were used to classify individuals as nonclinical or as patients having a diagnosis corresponding to the scale being studied. The effects on classification accuracy of adding various proportions of test takers' K-scale scores (i.e., none, .1K, .2K, etc.) were examined. The resulting K-correction weights became a standard part of the original MMPI and were used routinely in research studies and in clinical practice. Although subsequent research (e.g., Clopton, Shanks, & Preng, 1987; McCrae et al., 1989; Silver & Sines, 1962; Wooten, 1984) generally did not indicate increased extratest validity for K-corrected scales, and in fact sometimes indicated decreased validity for the corrected scores, the decision was made to maintain the K-correction for the MMPI-2. The argument for doing so was that decades of MMPI validity research was based on K-corrected scores, and to change to uncorrected scores could render that large research base inappropriate for guiding MMPI-2 interpretations.

Research conducted since the MMPI-2 was published also has not supported the routine use of K-corrected Clinical scale scores. Weed and Han (1992) concluded that the standard K-correction failed to produce higher correlations between Clinical scale scores and ratings of symptoms and personality characteristics for couples in the MMPI-2 normative sample or for couples involved in marriage counseling. Instead, they found that for four of the five traditionally corrected Clinical scales higher correlations were found with spousal ratings for uncorrected than for K-corrected scores. Archer, Fontaine, and McCrae (1998) examined the K-correction with psychiatric inpatients and found few meaningful differences between corrected and uncorrected Clinical scale scores and clinicians' ratings of the patients. Barthlow, Graham, Ben-Porath, Tellegen, and McNulty (2002) reported similar results for samples of community mental health center and university clinic clients. There were few differences between K-corrected Clinical scale scores and uncorrected scores in terms of correlations with conceptually relevant therapist ratings of client characteristics. When K-corrected scores yielded slightly higher correlations than uncorrected scores, optimal K-scale weights were not the ones that are routinely used.

Studies conducted in clinical settings where defensiveness is not common may not adequately test the value of the K-correction with very defensive test takers. However, data from studies that used more defensive samples have yielded similar results. Detrick, Chibnall, and Rosso (2001) correlated K-corrected and uncorrected MMPI-2 Clinical scale scores with scores from the Inwald Personality Inventory (IPI) for a large sample of police officer applicants. The IPI assesses a variety of problems, including alcohol/drug use, legal difficulties, and job difficulties, and is a well-respected instrument in the area of safety officer screening. In almost all comparisons, K-corrected Clinical scale scores had lower correlations with conceptually relevant IPI scales than did uncorrected scores.

Ben-Porath and Forbey (2004) presented data for a variety of clinical and nonclinical samples, including several that were described earlier. They found that correlations between uncorrected Clinical scale scores and conceptually relevant criterion measures (self-report and therapist ratings) were consistently stronger than correlations between K-corrected scores and the criterion measures. Interestingly, Ben-Porath and Forbey also examined correlates of two-point code types based on uncorrected and K-corrected scores. As one would expect, there was not much congruence between code types determined in these two ways. However, the correlates of code types were remarkably similar for those based on uncorrected and K-corrected scores. In many instances, stronger correlates were identified for code types based on the uncorrected scores. In summary, research data do not support the routine use of K-corrected Clinical scale scores. Although current practice is to use K-corrected scores routinely, this practice probably needs to be reexamined.

One has to be especially careful in using K-corrected scores in settings where defensiveness is common (e.g., employment screening, child custody evaluations). In these settings, K-corrected scores may overpathologize test takers. Very high K-scale scores, which may be for persons without significant problems, can yield high T scores that may be incorrectly interpreted as indicative of symptoms and problems. Fortunately, uncorrected norms are available for the MMPI-2 Clinical scales. The test distributor (Pearson Assessments) offers non-K-corrected profile sheets for plotting uncorrected scores, and non-K-corrected scores are available in the Extend Score Report available from Pearson Assessments. In cases where K-scale scores are not much above or below average, corrected and uncorrected scores will yield similar results. However, when the K scale is much above or below average, the corrected scores may give a distorted picture of the individual's psychological adjustment. Until some official position about uncorrected scores is taken by the test publisher, it is this author's recommendation that in nonclinical applications of the MMPI-2 both K-corrected and uncorrected scores be generated and that emphasis be placed on the uncorrected scores when K-scale scores are significantly above or below average.

T-SCORE TRANSFORMATIONS

As indicated in Chapter 2 of this book, raw scores on the various MMPI-2 scales are converted to T scores to facilitate interpretation. With the original MMPI, raw scores were converted to linear T scores having a mean of 50 and a standard deviation of 10. Because raw scores for the MMPI and MMPI-2 scales are not normally distributed, linear T scores, which maintain the same distributions as the raw scores on which they are based, do not have exactly the same meaning for every scale. For example, a T score of 70 on any particular Clinical scale of the original MMPI did not necessarily have the same percentile value as a T score of 70 on another MMPI Clinical scale. Although the percentiles were not greatly different from one scale to another, the differences sometimes led to problems in profile interpretation.

For the eight basic Clinical scales (excluding Scales 5 and 0), the MMPI-2 utilizes a different kind of T-score transformation from that used with the original MMPI. This transformation, called a Uniform T score, ensures that a T score of a given level (e.g., 65) has the same percentile value for all Clinical scales (Butcher et al., 2001). A composite (or average) distribution of raw scores of the MMPI-2 normative sample on the eight basic Clinical scales was derived. The distribution of each of the eight Clinical scales was adjusted so that it would match this composite distribution. This procedure resulted in Uniform T scores that are percentile equivalent and whose distributions are closely matched in terms of skewness and kurtosis (Tellegen & Ben-Porath, 1992). The change in the distribution of any particular scale is not great, so the profile retains most of its familiar characteristics. Percentile equivalents for various Uniform T scores are reported in Appendix C at the end of this book.

Although it has been suggested by some that the use of Uniform T scores significantly affects scale elevations and configurations, this is not the case. The MMPI-2 manual (Butcher et al., 1989) presented data concerning profile elevation and linear versus Uniform T scores. Raw scores of psychiatric patients were transformed to both linear and Uniform T scores using the MMPI-2 normative data, and the numbers of patients with elevated scores were calculated. There were only negligible differences between the numbers based on linear and Uniform T scores. Graham, Timbrook, et al. (1991) compared congruence of MMPI and MMPI-2 code types using both linear and Uniform T-score transformations. Again, the effect of using Uniform T scores on code-type congruence was negligible.

Uniform T scores were not derived for Scales 5 and 0 or for the Validity scales because the distributions of scores for these scales differ from those of the eight Clinical scales. For these scales, linear T-score transformations, comparable to those used with the original MMPI, were derived. Uniform T scores also are used for the Content scales, the Personality Psychopathology Five (PSY-5) scales, and the Restructured Clinical (RC) scales. Linear T scores are used for other MMPI-2 Supplementary scales.

COMPARABILITY OF THE MMPI AND THE MMPI-2

Because of the desire to use research based on the original MMPI to inform interpretation of MMPI-2 scores, it was necessary to demonstrate the comparability of scales from the two instruments. Several studies reported data suggesting that raw scores on the standard Validity and Clinical scales of the MMPI-2 and of the original MMPI are remarkably similar for samples of college students (Ben-Porath & Butcher, 1989b; Chojnacki & Walsh, 1992) and for nonclinical and clinical samples of adults (Graham, 1988). Given that most scales have the same, or nearly the same, items in both versions of the test, this comparability is expected.

It also was important to know to what extent T scores for MMPI-2 scales are comparable to T scores for the original MMPI. For most scales the contemporary normative sample endorsed more items in the scored direction than did the original MMPI normative sample. The difference in mean raw scores for the MMPI and MMPI-2 normative samples typically was between one and two points. However, men and women in the MMPI-2 normative sample scored somewhat lower than their counterparts in the MMPI normative sample on the L scale. Men in the MMPI-2 normative sample scored slightly lower than men in the MMPI normative sample on Scale 1, and women in the MMPI-2 normative sample scored slightly lower than women in the MMPI normative sample on Scale 7.

The somewhat higher raw scores for the MMPI-2 normative sample could indicate that the sample is more pathological than the original sample, but this seems unlikely given that the differences were consistent across most Clinical scales. A more likely explanation has to do with the instructions given to test takers. Persons in the original MMPI normative sample were permitted, and even encouraged, to omit items if they felt unable to answer them. By contrast, persons in the MMPI-2 normative sample were given the instructions that have been in use since the original MMPI was published. These instructions encourage test takers to try to respond to every statement in the test. Thus, persons in the MMPI-2 normative sample omitted many fewer items than persons in the MMPI normative sample. In the process of answering more items, persons in the MMPI-2 normative sample endorsed more items in the scored direction.

Because of the differences in raw scores between the MMPI and MMPI-2 normative samples, a particular raw score does not yield the same T score for both tests. Because raw scores tend to be higher for the MMPI-2 normative sample than for the MMPI normative sample, a specific raw score for most scales will yield a lower T score for the MMPI-2 than for the original MMPI. Although the differences in T scores between the two instruments vary a bit by scale and by level of scores on a scale, the average difference is about five T-score points, i.e., MMPI-2 T scores tend to be about five T-score points lower than would be the case if the same person had obtained the same raw scores on the original MMPI. These findings led to a recommendation in the MMPI-2 manual (Butcher et al., 1989) that MMPI-2 T scores between 65 and 69 be considered potentially significant in interpreting MMPI-2 results.

If all of the MMPI-2 scales differed from their corresponding MMPI scales in the same direction and by the same amount, MMPI and MMPI-2 code types and other configurations would be the same for both versions of the test. That differences are not equal for all scales leads to some lack of congruence in configural aspects of the MMPI and MMPI-2 profiles. The MMPI-2 manual

(Butcher et al., 1989) reported data concerning the congruence of MMPI and MMPI-2 code types for a sample of 232 male and 191 female psychiatric patients. Approximately two-thirds of the patients had the same two-point code type for both versions of the test.

Graham, Timbrook, et al. (1991) refined the analyses of the psychiatric patient data by including only well-defined code types (i.e., those in which the lowest scale in the code type was at least five T-score points higher than the next-highest Clinical scale in the profile). They found that congruence of two-point code types increased markedly. Similar increases in congruence rates were also noted for one- and three-point code types. Graham, Timbrook, et al. reported corresponding analyses for the MMPI-2 normative sample and noted even higher congruence rates for well-defined code types.

Dahlstrom (1992) reported data concerning comparability of specific MMPI and MMPI-2 two-point code types for the MMPI-2 normative sample and concluded that some code types are quite comparable and others are not. However, Dahlstrom's findings are difficult to interpret because he chose not to take code-type definition into account in his analyses. Ben-Porath and Tellegen (1996) and Tellegen and Ben-Porath (1996) offered some compelling arguments in favor of interpreting only well-defined code types.

Lachar, Hays, and Buckle (1991), using a sample of 100 psychiatric inpatients, found that 60% had the same MMPI and MMPI-2 two-point code types. Harrell, Honaker, and Parnell (1992) determined concordance rates for MMPI and MMPI-2 high-point and two-point code types for their sample of psychiatric outpatients and inpatients. For both defined and undefined code types, concordance was not significantly different from concordance of code types based on two administrations of either the MMPI or the MMPI-2. Data concerning congruence of MMPI and MMPI-2 code types also have been reported for brain-injured patients (Miller & Paniak, 1995), psychiatric outpatients (Edwards, Morrison, & Weissman, 1993), hospitalized substance abusers (Legan & Craig, 1996), veterans with diagnoses of posttraumatic stress disorder (Litz et al., 1991), and peace officers (Hargrave et al., 1994).

Clavelle (1992) asked clinicians to indicate how similar MMPI and MMPI-2 profile pairs were to each other and how similar or different their interpretations would be for each pair of profiles. Clinicians indicated that 92–96% of their diagnoses and 89–93% of their interpretations would be essentially the same or only slightly different from one version of the test to the other. Poorly defined MMPI-2 code types were more likely to be viewed as somewhat different or quite different from the MMPI. However, Clavelle asked clinicians to indicate how they would interpret the profiles, but actual interpretations were not made and compared. Timbrook (1998) compared interpretations that clinicians made of MMPI and MMPI-2 profiles for the sample patients and found that the interpretations were quite similar.

In summary, existing data indicate that MMPI and MMPI-2 code types are quite congruent for normative, college student, and a variety of psychiatric inpatient and outpatient samples. Congruence rates are higher for well-defined code types than for code types that are not well defined. Several studies have indicated that the congruence of MMPI and MMPI-2 code types, while not very high on an absolute level, is not significantly lower than congruence of code types based on two administrations of either the MMPI or the MMPI-2.

Some differences between scores on the MMPI and the MMPI-2 are expected, and, as pointed out by Ben-Porath and Graham (1991), such differences are necessary if the MMPI-2 is to be an improvement over the MMPI. If both versions yielded exactly the same scores, there would be little to justify or recommend the revised instrument. Critics of the MMPI-2 (e.g., Caldwell, 1991; Duckworth, 1991a, 1991b) seemed to conclude that in cases where the MMPI and MMPI-2 results are not comparable, something is wrong with the MMPI-2. This assumption may not be justified. Graham, Timbrook, et al. (1991) identified persons from the MMPI-2 normative sample for whom well-defined MMPI and MMPI-2 two-point code types were not congruent. They compared descriptions based on each code type for each person and determined their accuracy by comparing the descriptions with information provided by persons who knew these persons very well. Results indicated that the descriptions based on the MMPI-2 were at least as accurate as the MMPI-based descriptions, and perhaps even more accurate. Timbrook (1998) compared the accuracy of clinicians' descriptions of patients based on MMPI or MMPI-2 profiles and found them to be equally accurate, as determined by comparing the descriptions with extratest information about the patients. Morrison, Edwards, and Weissman (1994) found that MMPI and MMPI-2 scores were equally effective in predicting diagnoses of 200 mental health outpatients.

Another important consideration is the extent to which specific MMPI-2 code types have extratest correlates similar to corresponding code types on the MMPI. For example, are the correlates of an MMPI-2 4–8 two-point code type similar to the correlates of an MMPI 4–8 two-point code type? Several studies have identified empirical correlates for MMPI-2 code types for samples of psychiatric inpatients (Arbisi, Ben-Porath, & McNulty, 2003a; Archer, Griffin, & Aiduk, 1995; Moreland & Walsh, 1991), mental health center outpatients (Graham, Ben-Porath, & McNulty, 1999), and private practice clients (Sellbom, Graham, & Schenk, 2005). The correlates identified in these studies are quite consistent with those previously reported for MMPI code types. These findings support the notion that MMPI-2 code types can be interpreted similarly to their MMPI counterparts.

RELIABILITY

Internal Consistency

Because of the empirical keying procedures used in constructing the basic Validity and Clinical scales of the original MMPI, little attention was given by the test authors to internal consistency of most of these scales. Dahlstrom, Welsh, and Dahlstrom (1975) summarized MMPI internal-consistency data for a variety of samples. A meta-analysis of MMPI studies conducted by Parker, Hanson, and Hunsley (1988) determined an average internal-consistency coefficient of .87 across scales and across a number of samples.

The MMPI-2 manual (Butcher et al., 2001) reports internal-consistency values for the Clinical, Content, and Supplementary scales of the MMPI-2. These values are included in Chapters 4, 6, and 8 of this book. The manual does not include internal consistency coefficients for the Personality Psychopathology Five (PSY-5) scales or the Restructured Clinical (RC) scales. However, these coefficients have been reported elsewhere and are summarized in Chapter 7 of this book. As expected, the Clinical scales, which were constructed without concern about internal consistency, are less internally consistent than the Content, PSY-5, and RC scales, which were constructed with the goal of having internally consistent scales.

Factor analyses of items within each standard scale of the MMPI have indicated that most of the scales are not unidimensional (Ben-Porath, Hostetler, et al., 1989; Comrey, 1957a, 1957b, 1957c, 1958a, 1958b, 1958c, 1958d, 1958e; Comrey & Marggraff, 1958; Graham, Schroeder, & Lilly, 1971). The one exception seems to be Scale 1, where most of the variance is associated with a single dimension—concern about health and bodily functioning. Because little attention was given to internal consistency when the original MMPI scales were constructed, it is not surprising that the scales are not as internally consistent as other scales that were developed according to internal consistency procedures.

Factor analyses of the Clinical scales of the MMPI-2, which were conducted as part of the development of the RC scales, support earlier findings that these scales are not very homogeneous or internally consistent (Tellegen et al., 2003). In their development of subscales for Scale 0, Ben-Porath, Hostetler, et al. (1989) conducted item-level factor analyses and identified three rather distinct factors: Shyness/Self-Consciousness, Social Avoidance, and Self/Other Alienation.

Although the Content scales were intended to be quite homogeneous and internally consistent, subsequent analyses have suggested that at least some of them are not unidimensional. Ward (1997) conducted confirmatory factor analyses of the Depression (DEP) and Anxiety (ANX) content scales of the MMPI-2 and identified three factors for each scale. Brems and Lloyd (1995) factor analyzed items in the Low Self-Esteem (LSE) Content scale and identified three dimensions that they labeled as Ineptitude, Negative Self-Value, and Negative Comparison with Others. Ben-Porath and Sherwood (1993) used factor-analytic procedures in the development of Content Component scales. Their results, which are described in Chapter 6 of this book, suggested that most of the Content scales are not unidimensional.

The major advantage of having scales that are unidimensional and internally consistent is that scores on such scales are likely to have stronger associations with conceptually relevant extratest characteristics (convergent validity) and weaker relationships with extratest measures that are not conceptually relevant (discriminant validity). Thus, for example, we would expect a Clinical scale (e.g., Scale 4) and its Restructured Clinical scale counterpart (RC4) to have strong positive correlations with extratest measures of antisocial behavior (e.g., arrests), with the RC scale perhaps having a somewhat stronger correlation. However, because of its greater internal consistency we would expect that the RC4 scale would be less correlated than Clinical Scale 4 with other less conceptually related criterion measures (e.g., depression, anxiety). Data reported by Tellegen et al. (2003) are consistent with these expectations. For male clients at a mental health center, correlations with therapist ratings of antisocial behavior were .13 for Clinical scale 4 and .36 for RC4; correlations with therapist ratings of depression were .45 for Clinical scale 4 and .23 for RC4.

Temporal Stability

That scores on tests of ability, interest, and aptitude should have high temporal stability is quite accepted by most psychologists. What should be expected from tests of personality and psychopathology in this regard is not as clear. Although personality test scores should not be influenced by sources of error variance, such as room temperature or lack of sleep, it must be recognized that many personality attributes and symptoms change over relatively short periods of time. Dahlstrom (1972) pointed out that some of the inferences made from personality test data involve current emotional status, whereas others deal with personality structure. Scales assessing personality structure should have relatively high temporal stability, but those designed to measure current emotional status should be sensitive to rather short-term fluctuations. This is particularly true in clinical settings in which individuals are experiencing heightened levels of distress that might be expected to decrease over time and with treatment.

From the MMPI's inception there has been an awareness of the importance of scale stability. Schwartz (1977) summarized temporal stability data for the individual Validity and Clinical scales of the MMPI (see Table 4.2 in this book) and concluded that the temporal stability of the original MMPI scales was not related systematically to gender or MMPI form used. Further, no MMPI scale appeared to be consistently more stable than other scales. A meta-analysis conducted by Parker et al. (1988) reported an average stability coefficient for MMPI scales across a variety of samples to be .74. This value was only slightly lower than the value of .82 that was reported for the Wechsler Adult Intelligence Scale. In summary, short-term temporal stability of the original MMPI scales compared favorably with that of scores from other psychological tests.

The MMPI-2 manual (Butcher et al., 2001) reports test–retest reliability coefficients for the MMPI-2 Clinical, Content, and Supplementary scales for 82 men and 111 women in the normative sample. The retest interval was approximately one week. These reliability data were reported previously in this book when the development of these various scales was discussed.

Spiro, Butcher, Levenson, Aldwin, and Bose (2000) compared MMPI-2 scores for more than 1000 men who were participants in the Boston VA Normative Aging Study who took the test twice with an interval between testings of approximately 5 years (see Table 4.2 in this book). Test–retest correlations for the Clinical, Content, and Supplementary scales were only slightly lower than those reported in the MMPI-2 manual (Butcher et al., 2001) for a much shorter (1 week) interval. It should be noted that the participants were not mental health clients or patients and that their MMPI-2 scores were about average for both testings. One would expect scores of clients or patients to be somewhat less stable over this longer period of time, particularly for scales that assess primarily emotional turmoil and other psychiatric symptoms.

Examination of the test–retest reliability coefficients for the various sets of MMPI-2 scales suggests that all of the scales are quite stable over shorter periods of time, with typical stability coefficients ranging from .75 to .85. The more internally consistent scales (e.g., Content scales, RC scales, PSY-5 scales) seem to be a bit more stable than the Clinical scales. Data from a nonclinical sample of men suggest that the MMPI-2 scales also are generally stable over much longer periods of time. Because MMPI/MMPI-2 interpretive strategies have emphasized configural aspects of profiles, it is important to consider the temporal stability of such configurations.

Many clinicians assume that because the individual Clinical scales have reasonably good temporal stability, the configurations based on those scales also have good temporal stability. Table 5.1 in this book summarizes stability data for MMPI code types. Because of the continuity between the original and revised instruments, it can be assumed that the stability of MMPI-2 code types is very similar to the stability of code types on the original MMPI. Chapter 5 of this book should be consulted for a more detailed discussion of the stability of code types.

FACTOR STRUCTURE

Scale-Level Factor Structure

Two dimensions emerged consistently when scores on the basic MMPI Validity and Clinical scales were factor analyzed (Block, 1965; Eichman, 1961, 1962; Welsh, 1956). Scales 7 and 8 had high positive loadings on Factor I, and the K scale had a high negative loading on this factor. Welsh and Eichman both labeled this factor "Anxiety," whereas Block scored it in the opposite direction and called it "Ego Resiliency." Welsh developed the Anxiety (A) scale to assess this dimension. This scale seems to assess a general maladjustment dimension.

Scales 1, 2, and 3 had high positive loadings on Factor II, and Scale 9 had a moderately high negative loading on this factor. Welsh and Eichman labeled this dimension "Repression," and Block called it "Ego Control." Welsh developed the Repression (R) scale to assess this dimension. This scale seems to assess denial, rationalization, lack of insight, and overcontrol of needs and impulses.

The MMPI-2 manual (Butcher et al., 1989) reports results of factor analyses of the MMPI-2 scales for persons in the normative sample. The results of these analyses are quite consistent with previous studies reported in the literature for the original MMPI. One major factor seems to be related to general maladjustment and psychotic mentation, whereas another major factor seems to be more related to neurotic characteristics. Weaker factors seem to be related to gender-role identification and social introversion. The factor structure was somewhat different for men and women, suggesting that certain MMPI-2 patterns may have somewhat different interpretive meanings for each gender. Quereshi and Kleman (1996) factor analyzed MMPI-2 scores of college students and reported results very congruent with those for the MMPI-2 normative sample.

Item-Level Factor Structure

Some investigators factor analyzed or cluster analyzed responses to the entire original MMPI item pool (Barker, Fowler, & Peterson, 1971; Chu, 1966; Johnson, Null, Butcher, & Johnson, 1984; Lushene, 1967; Stein, 1968; Tryon, 1966; Tryon & Bailey, 1965). Most of these early studies were limited by small sample sizes or analyses based on subsets of the total MMPI item pool. Only the study of Johnson et al. (1984) utilized a very large sample (more than 11,000 persons) and analyzed the entire item pool in a single computational pass.

Using replication procedures, Johnson et al. (1984) identified the following 21 factors in the MMPI item pool: Neuroticism—General Anxiety and Worry, Psychoticism—Peculiar Thinking, Cynicism—Normal Paranoia, Denial of Somatic Problems, Social Extroversion, Stereotypic Femininity, Aggressive Hostility, Psychotic Paranoia, Depression, Delinquency, Inner Directedness, Assertiveness, Stereotypic Masculinity, Neurasthenic Somatization, Phobias, Family Attachment, Well-Being—Health, Intellectual Interests, Rebellious Fundamentalism, Sexual Adjustment, and Dreaming. The authors noted the similarity of these factors to the content dimensions represented in the Wiggins content scales and in the original content categories presented by Hathaway and McKinley. They also commented that the item pool seemed to be measuring more aspects of personality than merely emotional stability. Waller's (1999) factor analysis of the MMPI item responses of a very large sample of psychiatric and medical patients yielded 16 factors that were very similar to those identified in the Johnson et al. study.

Leonelli, Chang, Bock, and Schilling (2000) conducted an exploratory item-level full-information factor analysis on the MMPI-2 normative sample. This method of factor analysis, which is based on item response theory, avoids some of the problems inherent in using phi coefficients or tetrachoric coefficients as input to factor analysis. Their analysis yielded 10 interpretable factors that they labeled Distrust, Self-Doubt, Fitness, Serenity, Rebelliousness, Instrumentality, Irritability, Artistry, Sociability, and Self-Reliance. They concluded that differences between their results and those of Johnson et al. with the MMPI were most likely a function of the different procedures used for the factor analyses.

RESPONSE SETS AND STYLES

Over the years some critics (e.g., Edwards, 1957, 1964; Edwards & Clark, 1987; Edwards & Edwards, 1992; Messick & Jackson, 1961) argued that the MMPI scales were of limited utility because most of the variance in their scores could be attributed to response sets or styles. Similar claims also have been made about the MMPI-2 scales (Helmes & Reddon, 1993; Jackson, Fraboni, & Helmes, 1997).

Messick and Jackson (1961) argued that persons who obtained high scores on the MMPI scales did so primarily because of an acquiescence response style (i.e., a tendency to agree passively with inventory statements). In support of their argument, Messick and Jackson pointed out that the standard MMPI scales were not balanced for proportion of items keyed as true or false. Further, it was shown that scores on Welsh's Anxiety scale (a measure of one major source of variance in MMPI responses) correlated positively with an acquiescence measure.

Edwards (1957, 1964) maintained that scores on the standard scales of the MMPI were grossly confounded with a social desirability response set. Persons who obtained higher scores on the Clinical scales were hypothesized to be more willing to admit to socially undesirable behaviors, whether or not these behaviors really were characteristic of them. Major support for this position came from data indicating that scores on the standard MMPI scales and on Welsh's Anxiety scale had high negative correlations with a social desirability scale.

Although many persons argued against the acquiescence and social desirability interpretations of the MMPI scales, Block (1965) most thoroughly reviewed the arguments in support of acquiescence and social desirability and pointed out some statistical and methodological problems. He also presented new evidence that clearly rebutted the arguments. Block modified the standard MMPI scales, balancing the number of true and false items within each scale. Contrary to the prediction of Messick and Jackson, the factor structure of the MMPI with these modified scales was essentially the same as with the standard scales. Block also developed a measure of Welsh's Anxiety scale that was free of social desirability influences. Correlations between this modified Anxiety scale and standard MMPI scales were essentially the same as for Welsh's original scale. Finally, Block demonstrated that the MMPI scales had empirical correlates with important extratest behaviors even when the effects of social desirability and acquiescence were removed.

Although such definitive data have not been presented for the MMPI-2, the continuity between the MMPI and MMPI-2 suggests that similar demonstrations could be made for the revised instrument. In addition, many studies have demonstrated that the MMPI-2 Clinical, Content, and Supplementary scales have conceptually relevant correlates across several settings (e.g., Archer, Aiduk, Griffin, & Elkins, 1996; Butcher, Graham, Williams, & Ben-Porath, 1990; Graham et al., 1999). Such findings indicate that the MMPI-2 scales are measuring more than general response sets.

In summary, the criticism directed at the MMPI by critics such as Messick, Jackson, and Edwards was severe. However, the MMPI withstood their challenges. Because of the continuity between the original MMPI and the MMPI-2, the data presented by Block concerning response sets probably can be generalized to the MMPI-2 as well. In addition, empirical validity data suggest that the MMPI-2 scales are clinically useful in a variety of settings.

VALIDITY

Issues in Determining Validity

Generalizability of Correlates

The MMPI/MMPI-2 literature includes results of several large-scale research studies that established the extratest correlates of MMPI scales. It is important to know if scales have the same meaning in the various settings in which they are used. The MMPI was intended for use in an inpatient psychiatric setting, but it and its successor, the MMPI-2, have come to be used in varied settings, including outpatient, forensic, correctional, and employment screening. Are we to interpret MMPI-2 scores the same regardless of the settings in which the test was completed? As detailed throughout this book, there is consistent support for the notion that the MMPI/MMPI-2 scales assess clinical status (e.g., degree of maladjustment, symptom presentation) similarly in various settings. However, when the scales are used for purposes other than those for which they were developed, it is necessary to demonstrate their validity in relation to these other characteristics. For example, if the MMPI-2 is to be used to predict success in a particular kind of treatment program (e.g., inpatient substance abuse), we must have empirical evidence that the scales are indeed predictive of patients' outcomes.

Test Bias

Questions have often been raised about the appropriateness of using the MMPI/MMPI-2 with persons who are members of ethnic minority or other subcultural groups. These questions are appropriate because the MMPI scales were developed and normed on almost exclusively Caucasian samples. How well do the research findings based on the majority culture apply to persons in these minority groups? Chapter 10 of this book includes a review of research concerning the use of the MMPI-2 with special groups, including ethnic minorities. Most of the research to date has compared African American and Caucasian groups, mainly because African Americans have composed the largest minority group. As the composition of the U.S. population changes, it becomes more important to study other minority groups as well. The basic conclusion that is expressed in Chapter 10 is that the MMPI-2 scales seem to have the same meaning in majority and minority groups that have been studied so far.

Early studies of the MMPI with ethnic minorities relied on comparisons of mean scores of minority and majority groups, with the assumption that higher scores for minority groups reflected a bias in the test that made its use with such persons questionable. However, as Pritchard and Rosenblatt (1980) and Timbrook and Graham (1994) pointed out, the more appropriate way to assess potential bias is to compare the extent to which scores of majority and minority groups are related to conceptually relevant extratest measures. Arbisi, Ben-Porath, and McNulty (2002) illustrated a methodology for assessing bias on the MMPI-2. With samples of African American and Caucasian psychiatric patients, they used a step-down hierarchical multiple regression procedure that yielded tests of ethnic bias involving slope and intercept. Readers wanting more detailed information about this rather complicated procedure should consult the article by Arbisi et al. (2002). Although there was evidence of bias for some MMPI-2 scales, with minor underprediction of psychopathology for African Americans, differences in predictive accuracy were small and not clinically meaningful.

Specific Norms

There have often been suggestions in the MMPI/MMPI-2 literature that separate norms are appropriate for groups of persons who differ from the normative samples. Should we be comparing African American test takers with other African Americans, older test takers with other older persons, or public safety applicants with other public safety applicants? At times there can be value in understanding how an individual compares with others with similar demographic characteristics or in similar circumstances. However, the use of specific norms limits the inferences that we can make about persons based on test scores. For example, we are not likely to know if an MMPI-2 score at a particular T-score level has the same meaning when the T score is based on a general normative group as when it is based on a normative group similar to the individual taking the test. If specific norms are to be used, separate validity studies should be conducted to determine the relationship of T scores based on the specific norms to relevant extratest measures. Because such research has not been reported in the literature, it generally is not appropriate to use specific norms (as opposed to the general MMPI-2 norms) in interpreting test results.

Convergent and Discriminant Validity

Empirical validity refers to the extent to which test scores are related to extratest characteristics of test takers. Convergent validity is demonstrated when scores on a scale are significantly related to conceptually relevant extratest measures. For example, results indicating that scores on Scale 4 (Psychopathic Deviate) of the MMPI-2 are significantly and positively related to histories of arrests and other antisocial behaviors would be seen as evidence of the convergent validity of Scale 4. Discriminant validity is demonstrated to the extent that scores on a scale are not related to extratest measures that are not conceptually relevant to what the scale is intended to measure. For example, finding that Scale 4 scores are not significantly related to extratest measures of depression, anxiety, or thought disorder would be evidence of discriminant validity of Scale 4. If Scale 4 scores are significantly related to conceptually relevant extratest measures and to conceptually irrelevant extratest measures, the scale would be characterized as having good convergent validity but poor discriminant validity. In this latter situation it would be very difficult to know if high Scale 4 scores should be interpreted as indicating antisocial behaviors or the other characteristics that are related to high scores on the scale.

As Helmes and Reddon (1993) and Tellegen et al. (2003) have pointed out, there is considerable evidence for the convergent validity of many MMPI-2 scales, but evidence of discriminant validity is generally lacking. This is due, at least in part, to the heterogeneity of item content of many MMPI-2 scales. For example, in addition to items dealing with antisocial attitudes and behaviors, Scale 4 includes items having to do with depression and dysphoria. In addition, Welsh (1956) and others have demonstrated that many MMPI/MMPI-2 scales are saturated with a general factor that has been variously labeled as general maladjustment, neuroticism, or demoralization. This factor is a major reason that many MMPI-2 scales relate to a variety of extratest characteristics in addition to the core constructs that the scales were designed to measure. Tellegen et al. developed the Restructured Clinical (RC) scales as measures of core constructs with the general demoralization factor removed or reduced. As discussed in Chapter 7 of this book, the RC scales generally have better discriminant validity than corresponding Clinical and Content scales.

Incremental Validity

Incremental validity refers to the extent to which a scale or other assessment measure adds to other already existing or more easily obtained assessment information in the understanding or prediction of conceptually relevant characteristics. To justify the use of the MMPI-2, we need evidence that inferences or predictions based on MMPI-2 scores are more accurate than those based on other information that is more easily obtained (e.g., demographics, history, interview). Data reviewed later in this chapter indicate that the MMPI/MMPI-2 adds to demographic information, impressions based on interview, and other psychological test measures. Butcher, Graham, and Ben-Porath (1995) argued that any new MMPI-2 scales should have incremental validity in comparison with already existing scales. For example, the Depression Content scale should add incrementally to Scale 2 in predicting extratest measures of depression (e.g., therapist ratings). Early MMPI studies rarely addressed the issue of incremental validity, but more recent studies have done so.

Classification Accuracy

MMPI/MMPI-2 validity studies typically have reported results as differences in scores between groups (e.g., alcoholic versus nonalcoholic, schizophrenia versus major affective disorder, treatment completers versus premature terminators) or relationships between scores and extratest measures (e.g., Depression Content scale scores and therapist ratings of depression, Ego Strength scale scores and ratings of improvement in psychotherapy). Although such data are informative, it is difficult for clinicians who use the MMPI-2 to translate them into decisions about clients. For example, how do significant Addiction Admission Scale (AAS) score differences between clients for whom there is or is not clear evidence of substance abuse problems translate into inferences about the likelihood that a client with a particular score on the AAS has a substance abuse problem? Butcher et al. (1995) maintained that the most informative validity information is classification accuracy. For example, what is the probability that a client with an AAS T score greater than 60 will have a substance abuse problem?

Positive predictive power and negative predictive power provide specific information about the likelihood that a target behavior (e.g., substance abuse) will or will not be present for persons with a particular score on a scale (e.g., AAS). Positive predictive power indicates the probability that a person with a score above a specified cutoff (e.g., AAS T score greater than 60) indeed has a particular problem (e.g., substance abuse). Negative predictive power indicates the probability that a person with a score at or below a specified cutoff does not have a particular problem. Specific information on how to calculate positive and negative predictive powers is presented by Butcher et al. (1995). Unfortunately, most MMPI/MMPI-2 research has not provided these important classification statistics. Sometimes they can be calculated from data presented in research reports, but most often they cannot. Complicating the matter of classification accuracy is that predictive powers vary as a function of cutoff score used and base rates of target behaviors in a particular setting.

Validity of the Original MMPI

Because of the continuity between the MMPI and the MMPI-2, validity studies of both versions are relevant to an evaluation of the validity of the MMPI-2. In Volume II of *An MMPI Handbook*, Dahlstrom et al. (1975) cited over 6000 studies involving the MMPI. In trying to reach conclusions about the validity of the original MMPI, it is helpful to group research studies into three general categories. First, some studies compared the MMPI profiles of relevant criterion groups. Most of these studies identified significant differences on one or more of the MMPI scales among groups formed on the basis of diagnosis, severity of disturbance, treatment outcomes, and numerous other criteria. Lanyon (1968) published average or typical profiles for many of these criterion groups. Efforts to develop classification rules to discriminate among diagnostic groups also added to our understanding of the validity of the MMPI (Goldberg, 1965; Henrichs, 1964; Meehl & Dahlstrom, 1960; Peterson, 1954; Taulbee & Sisson, 1957).

A meta-analysis of 403 control and psychiatric samples indicated that the MMPI was effective in discriminating between psychiatric and control groups, neurotic and psychotic groups, and depression and anxiety disorder groups (Zalewski & Gottesman, 1991). In a different meta-analysis, Parker et al. (1988) found that the average validity coefficient for MMPI studies conducted between 1970 and 1981 was .46. Although this average coefficient was somewhat lower than for the Wechsler Adult Intelligence Scale (.62), Parker et al. concluded that the MMPI had acceptable validity. Atkinson (1986) applied meta-analytic procedures to a sample of MMPI studies conducted between 1960 and 1980. The results indicated that MMPI scores accounted for approximately 12% of the variance in criterion measures across many samples. It was noted that the MMPI was more valid when studies were conceptually based rather than undirected and when more reliable criterion measures were employed.

A second category of studies included efforts to identify empirical correlates of MMPI scales and configurations. Extratest correlates of high or low scores on individual Clinical scales have been identified for adolescents (Archer, Gordon, Giannetti, & Singles, 1988; Hathaway & Monachesi, 1963), normal college students (Black, 1953; Graham & McCord, 1985), student nurses (Hovey, 1953), normal Air Force officers (Block & Bailey, 1955; Gough, McKee, & Yandell, 1955), medical patients (Guthrie, 1949), and psychiatric patients (Boerger, Graham, & Lilly, 1974; Hedlund, 1977). Correlates for configurations of two or more MMPI scales were reported for normal adults (Hathaway & Meehl, 1952), normal college students (Black, 1953), medical patients (Guthrie, 1949), and psychiatric patients (Boerger et al., 1974; Gilberstadt & Duker, 1965; Gynther, Altman, & Sletten, 1973; Lewandowski & Graham, 1972; Marks, Seeman, & Haller, 1974; Meehl, 1951). The results of the numerous empirical correlate studies are summarized in Chapters 4 and 5 of this book. Clinicians drew heavily on the results of these studies in making inferences about MMPI scores and configurations. These data suggested that there are reliable extratest correlates for MMPI scores and configurations, but they also indicated that exactly the same correlates may not always be found for persons of differing demographic backgrounds.

A third category of studies considered the MMPI scores and the person interpreting them as an integral unit and examined the accuracy of clinical inferences based on the MMPI. In an early study of this type, Little and Shneidman (1959) asked expert test interpreters to provide diagnoses, ratings, and descriptions based on data from the MMPI, Rorschach, Thematic Apperception Test (TAT), and Make a Picture Story (MAPS) Test. The accuracy of these judgments was determined by comparing them with judgments based on extensive case history data. The average correlations between judges' descriptions based on the MMPI, Rorschach, TAT, and MAPS were .28, .16, .17, and .11, respectively. Kostlan (1954) reported data suggesting that the MMPI leads to the most accurate inferences when it is used in conjunction with social case history data. Sines (1959) reported a mean correlation of .38 between judgments based on MMPI and interview data and criterion ratings provided by patients' therapists. In a study limited to MMPI data, Graham (1967) reported correlations between MMPI-based descriptions and criterion descriptions of .31, .37, and .29 for judges of high, medium, and low experience, respectively. Other studies (Graham, 1971a, 1971b; Henrichs, 1990) have indicated that judges can learn to make more accurate inferences from MMPI data if they are given feedback concerning their performance.

Reviewing clinical judgment research, of which the previously cited studies are a part, Goldberg (1968) concluded that, in general, clinical judgments tend to be rather unreliable, only minimally related to the confidence and the amount of experience of test judges, relatively unaffected by the amount of information available to judges, and rather low in validity on an absolute basis. Based on a meta-analysis, Grove, Zald, Lebow, Snitz, and Nelson (2000) concluded that mechanical (statistical) prediction techniques were approximately 10% more accurate than clinical predictions.

In his reviews of the clinical judgment literature, Garb (1984, 1989) was more optimistic, concluding that adding MMPI data to demographic information led to significant increases in validity of inferences. Graham and Lilly (1984) pointed out that compared with Rorschach and other projective techniques, personality descriptions based on the MMPI have been relatively more accurate. Also, descriptions based on MMPI data have been more accurate than descriptions based on judges' stereotypes of typical patients. When MMPI data have been used in conjunction with social history and/or interview data, the resulting descriptions have been more valid than when the MMPI data have been used alone.

Validity of the MMPI-2

Although the congruence between scores on the original MMPI and the MMPI-2 make it possible to draw on decades of MMPI research in interpreting at least some MMPI-2 scales, it is important that the validity of the MMPI-2 also be established by comparing its scores with relevant extratest measures. Of course, evidence concerning external validity is especially important for scales (e.g., RC and PSY-5) that were not part of the original MMPI. Since the MMPI-2 was published in 1989, information about the test has been published in more than 3000 articles, chapters, and books. Many, but certainly not all, of these publications have dealt with the validity of the MMPI-2. It is beyond the scope of this chapter to review large numbers of these individual studies. Many of these studies were reviewed in earlier chapters in which the various sets of scales (Validity, Clinical, Content, Supplementary, RC, PSY-5) were discussed. In the sections that follow summaries of research findings and conclusions about validity will be presented for each set of MMPI-2 scales. It is not appropriate to make judgments about the validity of an assessment technique in a very general way. Rather, it is important to determine the validity of specific scales and configurations of scales in relation to specific symptoms, problems, and behaviors.

Validity Scales

One of the very positive features of the MMPI-2 is the inclusion of scales designed specifically to determine if test takers approached the test in the manner intended or if they adopted a deviant test-taking attitude (e.g., random responding, overreporting, underreporting) that makes it less likely that the resulting MMPI-2 scores will accurately portray their symptoms, problems, and other characteristics. Research concerning the extent to which the Validity scales fulfill this important function was reviewed in Chapter 3 of this book.

There is good evidence that the Variable Response Inconsistency (VRIN) scale is effective in identifying persons who respond to the MMPI-2 items without consideration for their content (i.e., random responding). Extreme elevations on the True Response Inconsistency (TRIN) scale are indicative of an all-true or all-false response set. Moderately elevated TRIN-scale scores are found relatively frequently in protocols of test takers in clinical settings, and their meaning has not been established.

A great deal of research has focused on detection of overreporting, and there is consistent support for the Infrequency (F) and Infrequency Psychopathology (F_p) scales as very good indicators of this response set. In most clinical settings, either of these scales is a good measure of overreporting. However, in settings where serious psychopathology is common, the F_p scale, which is less influenced than the F scale by genuine psychopathology, seems to be a bit more accurate in identifying overreporting. Likewise, F_p seems to work a bit better in identifying overreporting in situations where test takers have received some coaching about how to overreport on the MMPI-2 without being detected as doing so. Research has indicated clearly that it is more difficult to detect overreporting when test takers have been coached concerning how to avoid being detected as overreporters, but the F and F_p scales still do a reasonable job of identifying coached overreporters.

Far less research has addressed the identification of underreporting on the MMPI-2. However, there seems to be consistent evidence that the Lie (L) scale is the best indicator of underreporting. The Correction (K) and Superlative (S) scales also detect underreporting, but they typically have not added much to the L scale in this regard. Some other measures, which are not currently part of MMPI-2 scoring, have shown promise as indicators of underreporting, and they probably should be included in future studies of underreporting. These measures include the Positive Malingering (Mp), Wiggins Social Desirability (Wsd), and Edwards Social Desirability (Esd) scales.

Research concerning the effectiveness of K-corrected scores generally has not supported the routine use of the K-correction. In fact, most research studies have reported greater extratest validity for scores that have not been corrected. When K-corrected scores have had greater extratest validity than uncorrected scores, the optimal K weights have not been those that are routinely used. It is especially important to consider uncorrected scores in nonclinical situations (e.g., employment screening, child custody evaluations) where underreporting is common and where elevated Clinical scale scores may be an artifact of the K-correction and do not accurately reflect the status of test takers.

Clinical Scales

Because the Clinical scales of the MMPI-2 are essentially the same as those of the original MMPI, we would expect that extratest correlates would be very similar for corresponding scales in the two instruments. This indeed has been demonstrated empirically. Correlates of individual MMPI-2 Clinical scales have been reported for couples in the MMPI-2 normative sample, psychiatric inpatients, mental health center outpatients, and private practice clients. The data offer consistent support for the convergent validity of the MMPI-2 Clinical scales. Scores on the Clinical scales correlate significantly with extratest measures with which they are conceptually related. For example, presentation of somatic symptoms is a cardinal feature of Scale 1, and higher scores on Scale 4 are associated with various kinds of externalizing behaviors. As one would expect, correlates of MMPI-2 Clinical scales are very consistent with those reported for the Clinical scales of the original MMPI.

Consistent with the Helmes and Reddon (1993) critique of Clinical scales being too heterogeneous, having overlapping items, and being intercorrelated, the Clinical scales of the MMPI-2 do not seem to have very good discriminant validity. Although scores on the Clinical scales are correlated with conceptually related extratest measures, they have been found to be related to extratest measures that are not conceptually related to the scales. For example, as stated earlier, higher Scale 4 scores are associated with antisocial behaviors in clinical settings, but they also are significantly related to various extratest measures of depression. Tellegen et al. (2003) recognized the problem of poor discriminant validity and attributed it to the Clinical scales being saturated with a general demoralization component. The Restructured Clinical (RC) scales, which were discussed in Chapter 7 of this book, were developed by reducing the Demoralization factor in each Clinical scale and retaining items that assess the core component of the scale (e.g., antisocial characteristics for Scale 4). Initial data indicate that the RC scales have convergent validity as good as, or in some cases better than, the original Clinical scales and that most have better discriminant validity. Thus, the RC scales are likely to provide purer measures of the core constructs associated with the scales and thus clarify the meaning of high scores on the Clinical scales.

One cannot assume that the correlates of scales identified in one setting (e.g., psychiatric inpatient) will apply to the scales when used in a different setting (e.g., prisoners). When the Clinical scales are used for their intended purpose, the assessment of mental health symptoms and problems, they should (and do) have very similar correlates across settings. A high Scale 1 score, for example, indicates above-average somatic symptoms regardless of setting. However, when attempts are made to use the Clinical scales to assess characteristics for which they were never intended (e.g., effective parenting), the validity of the scales for these different purposes needs to be established. Existing research with both the MMPI and MMPI-2 does not support the use of the Clinical scales to assess characteristics such as type of criminal offending or parenting styles.

Code Types

As discussed in Chapter 5 of this book, MMPI and MMPI-2 Clinical scale interpretation has emphasized the consideration of configurations of scores (i.e., code types). Because persons who are classified on the basis of more than one Clinical scale are more similar to each other than those classified on the basis of high scores on a single scale, more specific and reliable correlates can be established for code types than for individual Clinical scales.

Several large-scale research studies have identified extratest correlates of commonly occurring code types for psychiatric inpatients (Arbisi et al., 2003a; Archer et al., 1995), mental health center outpatients (Graham et al., 1999), and private practice clients (Sellbom et al., 2005). Correlates for most code types were very similar across these three studies and consistent with previously reported code-type correlates for the original MMPI (Gynther et al., 1973; Lewandowski & Graham, 1972). Because of limitations in sample sizes, these research studies typically investigated only a limited number of code types. Thus, there are many possible code types for which we have little or no data to guide interpretations. As recommended elsewhere in this book, in such cases clinicians should interpret scores on individual Clinical scales.

As discussed in Chapter 5 of this book, early approaches to code-type interpretation identified code types solely on the basis of the highest two or three Clinical scales in the profile. No consideration was given to the relative elevation of these highest scales in comparison with other Clinical scales. Graham,

Timbrook, et al. (1991) stated that interpretable code types exist only when the lowest scale in a two- or three-point code type is at least five T-score points higher than the next highest Clinical scale score (i.e., code-type definition). Code types tend to be more stable when they are more defined (Munley, Germain, Tovar-Murray, & Borgman, 2004). McNulty, Ben-Porath, and Graham (1998) found that the strength and specificity of correlates was greater for defined code types than for those that were not defined.

When one examines the array of correlates for specific two- or three-point code types, it is evident that some have to do with psychiatric symptoms (e.g., depression, paranoid delusions), whereas others have to do with personality characteristics (e.g., introversion, interpersonal sensitivity). In Chapter 5 of this book I recommended that when scales in a defined code type are elevated (T > 65) both symptom and personality descriptors should be considered but when the scales in a defined code type are not elevated only the personality descriptors are likely to apply. This recommendation is based on data concerning the meaning of moderately high versus very high scores on individual Clinical scales. However, no research findings have yet been published concerning differential inferences for code types with differing levels of scale elevation.

Other MMPI-2 Scales

Content and Content Component Scales

Since their publication in 1992, the Content scales of the MMPI-2 have been researched frequently. Some studies have examined extratest correlates for the entire set of 15 Content scales using samples of psychiatric inpatients (Archer et al., 1996), mental health center outpatients (Graham et al., 1999), private practice clients (Sellbom et al., 2005), college students (Ben-Porath, McCully, & Almagor, 1993), and couples in the MMPI-2 normative sample (Butcher et al., 1992). Correlates of individual Content scales have been remarkably similar for these various samples. Generally, correlations between Content scale scores and conceptually relevant extratest characteristics have been stronger than those between corresponding Clinical scales and the extratest measures. In addition, discriminant validity (i.e., correlations between Content scale scores and extratest measures that are not conceptually related to them) has been better than for the Clinical scales.

Other research has examined the extent to which Content scale scores add to scores on corresponding Clinical scales in predicting conceptually relevant extratest characteristics. In most cases incremental validity has been demonstrated for the Content scales (Archer et al., 1996; Barthlow, Graham, Ben-Porath, & McNulty, 1999; Ben-Porath et al., 1993). However, it should be noted that Clinical scales also added incrementally to the Content scales in predicting conceptually relevant extratest characteristics, suggesting that both sets of scales should be utilized in MMPI-2 interpretation. Simonds, Handel, and Archer (2008) found that some Content scales added to the SCL-90-R in predicting conceptually relevant criterion measures. Studies examining the validity of specific Content scales were summarized in Chapter 6 of this book.

Although the Content scales were intended to be very homogeneous in terms of item content, Ben-Porath and Sherwood (1993) demonstrated that most Content scales could be partitioned into components, and they developed scales to assess these components. To date little research has been conducted concerning the Content Component scales. Ben-Porath and Sherwood reported extratest correlates of the Content component scales for couples in the MMPI-2 normative sample, and Graham et al. (1999) reported correlates of the scales for mental health center outpatients. McNulty, Ben-Porath, Graham, and Stein (1997) demonstrated that, when a Content scale is elevated (T > 60), differential elevation of its component scales helps in determining which correlates are to be emphasized and deemphasized.

Restructured Clinical (RC) Scales

As discussed in Chapter 7 of this book, the Restructured Clinical (RC) scales were developed to provide purer measures of the core constructs associated with the Clinical scales while reducing the extent to which the scales are influenced by general maladjustment or demoralization. One would expect that the RC scales would have strong correlations with conceptually relevant extratest measures (convergent validity) and would be less correlated than their corresponding Clinical scales with nonrelevant criterion measures (discriminant validity). To date the published data concerning the validity of the RC scales have suggested that most scales have convergent validity equal to or greater than the corresponding Clinical scales and better discriminant validity than the Clinical scales.

The Personality Psychopathology Five (PSY-5) Scales

The PSY-5 scales were constructed to assess personality traits relevant to both normal functioning and clinical problems and are related to the Five-Factor Model (FFM) of personality. Several studies have reported relationships between PSY-5 scales and scales from other instruments based on the FFM. Correlates of the PSY-5 scales also have been reported for mental health center clients (Harkness, McNulty, Ben-Porath, & Graham, 2002) and individuals undergoing evaluations at a court-sponsored clinic (Petroskey, Ben-Porath, & Stafford, 2003). Relationships between the PSY-5 scales and extratest measures were consistent with the constructs underlying the PSY-5 scales. For example, the Aggressiveness (AGGR) scale was positively related to histories of being physically abusive, and high scores on the Introversion/Low Positive Emotionality (INTR) scale were positively related to depression and previous suicide attempts. The PSY-5 scales are conceptually related to personality disorder characteristics, and empirical relationships have been reported between PSY-5 scales and other self-reported characteristics of personality disorders in private practice clients (Wygant, Sellbom, Graham, & Schenk, 2004).

Supplementary Scales

The MMPI and MMPI-2 item pools have been used by researchers to develop scales to assess many psychological constructs (e.g., ego strength, hostility). The

Supplementary scales that are included in the MMPI-2 manual (Butcher et al., 2001) and for which hand-scoring materials and computerized scoring are available were discussed in some detail in Chapter 8. These scales were developed using factor analysis, empirical keying, and rational/statistical procedures. The amount of validity research available varies considerably for the supplementary scales. Some scales, such as the MacAndrew Alcoholism (MAC) scale and its slightly revised version (MAC-R) and the Keane Posttraumatic Stress Disorder (PK) scale, have been the subjects of dozens of methodologically sound studies. Other scales, such as the Masculine Gender Role (GM) and Feminine Gender Role (GF) scales, have had very little research conducted concerning their validity.

Graham et al. (1999) reported empirical correlates for the Supplementary scales in an outpatient mental health setting. Archer, Elkins, Aiduk, and Griffin (1997) examined the incremental validity of MMPI-2 Supplementary scales for psychiatric inpatients. Sellbom et al. (2005) determined empirical correlates for the Supplementary scales for private practice clients. These studies identified meaningful correlates for some scales that were consistent across settings. There also have been studies of the validity of individual Supplementary scales. Research concerning the Supplementary scales was reviewed in detail in Chapter 8 of this book, and readers interested in a particular supplementary scale are referred to that chapter.

10

▨ Use with Special Groups

The original MMPI was developed for use with adult psychiatric patients. Its norms were based primarily on adult Caucasians living in the cities and towns surrounding the University of Minnesota. Understandably, questions were raised concerning the use of the instrument with persons whose demographic characteristics were different from those of the normative sample or in other than traditional psychiatric settings. This chapter reviews information concerning the use of the MMPI-2 with persons who differ from those used in the development of the original test and the norming of both the MMPI and MMPI-2. Because of the continuity between the two versions of the test, both MMPI and MMPI-2 research is considered.

ADOLESCENTS

Although the original MMPI was intended for use with adults, it quickly became popular as an instrument for assessing adolescents (e.g., Hathaway & Monachesi, 1963). However, many concerns were expressed about its use with adolescents (e.g., Archer, 1987; Williams, 1986). It was suggested that many of the MMPI items were inappropriate for younger persons. Moreover, research studies demonstrated that the use of the adult MMPI norms overpathologized adolescent test takers (Archer, 1984, 1987; Klinge, Lachar, Grisell, & Berman, 1978). Unofficial norms were developed for use with younger persons (Marks, Seeman, and Haller, 1974). Some studies indicated that the use of these adolescent norms seemed to underpathologize disturbed adolescents assessed in clinical settings (Archer, Stolberg, Gordon, & Goldman, 1986; Klinge & Strauss, 1976), whereas other research supported the notion that scores based on these adolescent norms more accurately portrayed the clinical status of adolescents in a variety of clinical settings (e.g., Wimbish, 1984).

In 1992 a version of the MMPI developed specifically for use with adolescents was published (Butcher, Williams, Graham, Archer, Tellegen, Ben-Porath, & Kaemmer). The MMPI-A is appropriate for persons between the ages of 14 and 18.

Because both the MMPI-2 and the MMPI-A can be used with 18-year-olds, clinicians must decide which version is most appropriate for each 18-year-old. Generally, it is advisable to use the MMPI-2 for mature 18-year-olds who are in college or otherwise living independently from parents and the MMPI-A for less mature 18-year-olds who have not adopted independent lifestyles. The MMPI-A is discussed in detail in Chapter 15 of this book. For readers who are interested in even more information about the MMPI-A, several excellent reference books are available (Archer, 2005; Archer & Krishnamurthy, 2002; Butcher & Williams, 2000).

OLDER ADULTS

Original MMPI

The apparent relationship between age and MMPI scores was noted quite early (e.g., Brozek, 1955). Although research results have not been totally consistent, most MMPI studies found that older persons obtained somewhat higher scores on Scales 1, 2, 3, and 0 and lower scores on Scales 4 and 9 (e.g., Butcher et al., 1991; Gynther, 1979; Leon, Gillum, Gillum, & Gouze, 1979; Lezak, 1987). These differences between scores of older and younger persons should not be interpreted as indicating that the older persons are necessarily more psychologically disturbed. Rather, they may reflect realistic increases in concern about health and decreases in activity and energy levels that often, but not always, accompany the aging process (Segal, Hersen, VanHasselt, Silberman, & Roth, 1996). In an interesting exception to typical findings, Fow, Sittig, Dorris, Breisinger, and Anthony (1994) found that older adults being evaluated for admission to a chronic-pain treatment program scored lower on most MMPI scales than younger persons undergoing the same evaluations.

Taylor, Strassberg, and Turner (1989) studied groups of elderly community residents and elderly psychiatric patients. They found that MMPI T scores based on the standard norms were significantly higher than average for both groups. However, the scores significantly discriminated between the community and psychiatric groups. In addition, scores of the elderly psychiatric patients were related in expected ways to information obtained from a structured psychiatric interview. They concluded that the MMPI, as generally applied, is valid for use with older adults.

Swenson (1961) suggested that the use of the standard MMPI norms resulted in inaccurate inferences about older adults. Using data from 31 men and 64 women, Swenson constructed T-score norms and recommended their use with older adults. Colligan, Osborne, Swenson, and Offord (1983) reported age-specific data for larger groups of persons. The data of Colligan et al. were later reanalyzed by Colligan and Offord (1992) to provide estimates of what differences should be expected between general norms and persons in specific age groups. Consistent with other studies, older adults (60–99 years of age) scored slightly higher (1–4 T-score points) on Scales 1, 2, and 0 and slightly lower (1–6 T-score points) on

Scales 4 and 9. It should be noted that these data were cross-sectional in nature, making it difficult to determine if scores changed with increasing age or if the observed differences were due to cohort effects.

In deciding whether to use age-specific norms it is necessary to consider the purposes for which the assessment is being conducted. If the purpose is to compare a specific older adult with other persons of similar age, age-specific norms may be appropriate. However, the use of age-specific norms can mask important differences between older and younger persons. For example, it could be important to know that a specific older adult has greater somatic concern than the average adult (regardless of age). The use of norms that compare older adults only with other older adults would not reveal this somatic concern. We do not know from existing research findings if inferences about older adults that are based on age-specific norms would be as accurate as those based on general norms. Most studies of the relationship between MMPI scores and age have used cross-sectional designs. Large samples of persons were subdivided into age groups and their MMPI scores were compared. Such designs did not take into consideration that differences could be attributable to cohort effects. It may be that MMPI scores did not change as persons aged. Rather, differences in age groups may reflect the different times at which individuals were growing up. However, a longitudinal study by Leon et al. (1979) found differences between older and younger persons similar to those resulting from cross-sectional studies. Koeppl, Bolla-Wilson, and Bleecker (1989) failed to replicate age-related differences reported in earlier studies and suggested that the earlier results could have been due to geographic, societal, and population factors.

Several conclusions can be reached about the relationship between age and scores on the original MMPI. Older persons tended to obtain slightly higher scores on Scales 1, 2, 3, and 0 and slightly lower scores on Scales 4 and 9. It is not clear to what extent these differences can be attributed to the cross-sectional designs used in most studies and to what extent they indicate that scores change as individuals age. The differences in MMPI scores between older adults and adults in general probably do not reflect greater psychopathology in the elderly. Rather, they may indicate realistic changes in health concerns, energy levels, and other attitudes that often, but not always, occur as persons age.

MMPI-2

The MMPI-2 normative sample included persons ranging in age from 18 to 84 years (mean = 41.71; Butcher et al., 2001). However, older adults (70 years of age or older) were somewhat underrepresented (4.6% of men; 5.3% of women). Although the MMPI-2 manual does not report scores separately by age groups, the committee that developed the MMPI-2 conducted appropriate analyses and concluded that age-specific norms were not needed (Butcher et al., 1989).

Butcher et al. (1991) compared scores of men in the MMPI-2 normative sample with those of a group of healthy elderly men from the Normative Aging Study (NAS). Ages of men in the NAS ranged from 40 to 90 years (mean = 61.27). Scores of the two groups of men were very similar. Of the 567 MMPI-2 items, only 14 differed by more than 20% in endorsement percentages between the two groups. Interestingly, the item with the greatest difference in endorsement had to do with enjoying the use of marijuana, supporting earlier speculation that differences between older and younger persons may reflect cohort effects. The content of the remaining items that were endorsed differently by the groups suggests that the older men were indicating less stress and turmoil in their lives and greater satisfaction and contentment.

Within each of their samples, Butcher et al. (1991) compared scores of men of different ages. The differences between age groups in each sample were consistent with previously reported data for the original MMPI. However, the differences were small and probably not clinically important. Butcher et al. concluded that the differences may represent the single or combined effects of cohort factors and age-related changes in physical health status rather than age-related changes in psychopathology per se. They also concluded that special, age-related norms for the MMPI-2 are not needed for older men. Spiro, Butcher, Levenson, Aldwin, and Bose (2000) compared MMPI-2 scores of men in the Boston Normative Aging Study who took the test twice with a five-year interval. Consistent with findings for the original MMPI, they found significant but small changes on several scales, including Scales 1, 2, and 3.

Priest and Meunier (1993) studied a small group of elderly women (60+ years of age) who were attending an elder hostel program and found that the scores of these women were quite similar to those of women in the MMPI-2 normative sample. Strassberg, Clutton, and Karboot (1991) reported that older adult men and women in Australia who were not in clinical settings had MMPI-2 scores very similar to those of older adults in the United States. They had modest elevations on Clinical Scales 1 and 2 and the Low Self-Esteem Content scale and somewhat below-average scores on Scales 4, 6, and 9. Interestingly, Strassberg et al. also reported that the Clinical and Content scale scores of the Australian older adults were related significantly to conceptually relevant extratest characteristics. Aaronson, Dent, Webb, and Kline (1996) reported that older male VA domiciliary residents endorsed fewer MMPI-2 critical items than younger residents. These results are difficult to interpret because the older residents also were more defensive, suggesting that they could have underreported actual symptoms and problems.

Considering both MMPI and MMPI-2 data, it seems appropriate to conclude that there may be some differences between scores of older adults and adults in general. However, the differences tend to be small (less than five T-score points) and not clinically important. They may reflect changes in concerns, attitudes, and behaviors that often, but not always, are associated with aging. The use of age-specific norms for older adults does not seem appropriate. Because differences associated with normal aging are small, clinically elevated scores (T > 65) on MMPI-2 scales of older adults are likely to indicate the same kinds of symptoms and problems that have been associated with such elevated scores for younger adults. Future research should utilize longitudinal designs and determine the accuracy of scores based on standard and age-specific norms.

ETHNIC MINORITIES

Almost all of the psychiatric patients and nonpatients used in the development of the original MMPI were Caucasians, and the MMPI norms were based primarily on the responses of Caucasian adult community residents in Minnesota. Therefore, there was understandable concern that the MMPI might not be appropriate for assessing members of ethnic minority groups.

As Timbrook and Graham (1994) indicated, there have been two general approaches to studying possible bias against minority group members on the MMPI/MMPI-2. Most studies have examined mean score differences between minority and majority groups, assuming that higher scores for minority group members indicate that the test is biased against them. A second approach, which unfortunately has been far less common than the first, has been to determine if MMPI/MMPI-2 scores are equally valid for majority and minority group members (i.e., do the scales relate to conceptually relevant extratest measures equally well?). As early as 1980, Pritchard and Rosenblatt recognized that the presence or absence of mean scale differences between minority and majority groups does not address directly the issue of test bias. They emphasized the importance of determining the relative empirical validity of scales for minority and majority group members.

Dahlstrom, Lachar, and Dahlstrom (1986) and Greene (1987) presented detailed reviews of the literature concerning the use of the original MMPI with members of ethnic minority groups. More recently Hall, Bansal, and Lopez (1999) completed a meta-analytic review of more than 30 years of research concerning the use of the MMPI/MMPI-2 with members of ethnic minority groups.

Several issues are very important in conducting research concerning the appropriateness of using the MMPI-2 with members of ethnic minority groups. First, past research has often failed to acknowledge the heterogeneity of cultural backgrounds represented in groups such as Hispanics or American Indians and have either not identified subgroup identity or included persons from varied backgrounds under a single ethnicity rubric. Allen (1998) pointed out that there are 510 federally recognized native entities in the United States. Persons with Mexican, Puerto Rican, Cuban, and Spanish backgrounds often are simply described as "Hispanic." Second, the importance of acculturation as a moderating variable has rarely been considered in any systematic way.

In the sections that follow, an attempt will be made to summarize what is known about the appropriateness of using the MMPI-2 with members of ethnic minority groups. As will become obvious to the reader, research concerning this issue has been limited, with most of it having been conducted with the original MMPI and concentrating on comparisons between African American and Caucasian groups.

African Americans

Original MMPI

A basic concern has been that, because African Americans were not included in the scale development or the normative sample, the MMPI might be biased against such persons. Early studies reporting that African Americans obtained higher scores than Caucasians on some of the MMPI Clinical scales reinforced concerns about possible test bias (e.g., Ball, 1960; Butcher, Ball, & Ray, 1964). A general finding was that African Americans tended to score higher (approximately five T-score points) than Caucasians on Scales F, 8, and 9. Later studies found that differences between African Americans and Caucasians were small and not clinically meaningful or did not exist when groups were matched for age, education, and other demographic characteristics (Dahlstrom et al., 1986; Penk, Robinowitz, Roberts, Dolan, & Atkins, 1981).

Several other factors also were found to be related to MMPI differences between African Americans and Caucasians. When invalid profiles were excluded from the analyses, differences lessened dramatically (Costello, Tiffany, & Gier, 1972). Several studies also indicated that persons who were more identified with the African American culture differed more from Caucasians on the MMPI (Costello, 1977; Harrison & Kass, 1968).

Finding significant test score differences between majority and minority group members does not necessarily mean that a test is biased. As Pritchard and Rosenblatt (1980) pointed out, for a test to be biased the accuracy of inferences or predictions based on test scores must be different for majority and minority group members. Several kinds of MMPI studies bear on this issue.

If scores of minority and majority group members accurately reflect levels of symptoms and maladjustment, one would not expect significant differences between Caucasians and African Americans who have been assigned the same psychiatric diagnoses. Cowan, Watkins, and Davis (1975) and Davis (1975) found that matched groups of African Americans and Caucasians with diagnoses of schizophrenia did not have significantly different MMPI scores. Similarly, Johnson and Brems (1990) compared the MMPI scores of 22 African American and 22 Caucasian psychiatric inpatients who had been matched for age, gender, and psychiatric diagnoses. They found no significant differences in scores between the African American and Caucasian patients. Nelson, Novy, Averill, and Berry (1996) compared small groups of Caucasians and African Americans who were being treated at a chronic-pain center. Female African American patients scored significantly higher than Caucasian female patients on Scales F, 5, and 0, and male African American patients scored significantly higher than male Caucasian patients on Scales F, 8, and 9. Because no external measures of psychopathology were available for these patients, it is not known if the significant differences were associated with differences in actual severity of psychopathology.

Other studies have compared extratest correlates of MMPI scales and code types for African Americans and Caucasians. The results of these studies have been mixed. Gynther et al. (1973) were able to demonstrate reliable correlates of very high F-scale scores for Caucasian patients but not for African American patients. However, Smith and Graham (1981) found no significant differences in F-scale correlates for African American and Caucasian psychiatric patients. Elion and Megargee (1975) concluded that Scale 4 is sensitive to antisocial behavior patterns for African Americans and Caucasians. Clark and Miller (1971) reported that the cardinal features of the 8–6 code type were similar for African Americans and Caucasians. Several other studies found differences in code-type correlates for African Americans and Caucasians (Gynther et al., 1973; Strauss, Gynther, & Wallhermfechtel, 1974).

Another approach to studying potential test bias has been to determine if MMPI differences between African Americans and Caucasians are associated with important extratest differences. Butcher, Braswell, and Raney (1983) found that MMPI differences between African American and Caucasian psychiatric inpatients were meaningfully associated with actual symptomatic differences. Dahlstrom et al. (1986) reported analyses suggesting that MMPI scores were not differentially related to psychopathology for African American and Caucasian psychiatric patients. Dahlstrom et al. suggested that the higher MMPI scores of African Americans, especially young men, could reflect the various coping and defense mechanisms to which some minority group members resort in their efforts to deal with the special circumstances they too often encounter in the United States today. These investigators made reasonable recommendations concerning the interpretation of the MMPIs of African Americans. They felt that the best procedure was to accept the pattern of MMPI scores that results from the use of the standard norms and, when profiles of African Americans are markedly deviant, make special effort to explore in detail their life circumstances to understand as fully as possible the nature and degree of their problems and demands and the adequacy of their efforts to deal with them.

MMPI-2

As was discussed earlier, the normative sample for the MMPI-2 includes African Americans in approximately the same proportion as in the 1980 census. This is certainly an improvement over the original MMPI and may increase the likelihood that the MMPI-2 will be useful in assessing African Americans. However, inclusion of African Americans in the normative sample does not necessarily mean that the test is not biased. We must still determine if significant MMPI-2 differences exist between African Americans and Caucasians. We should determine if African Americans and Caucasians with the same MMPI-2 scores or code types should be described in similar ways.

Appendix H of the original MMPI-2 manual (Butcher et al., 1989) reported MMPI-2 summary data separately for the various ethnic groups included in the normative sample. African Americans scored slightly higher than Caucasians on most scales. However, T-score differences of more than five points occurred only for Scale 4 for women (six T-score points). It is important to recognize that the African American and Caucasian groups were not matched for age, socioeconomic status, or other demographic variables. As stated earlier, MMPI differences between African Americans and Caucasians were much smaller when such variables were taken into account. The MMPI-2 restandardization committee interpreted these summary data as indicating that separate norms were not needed for minority groups. No data were presented concerning whether these small differences between African Americans and Caucasians in the normative samples were associated with extratest differences.

Timbrook and Graham (1994) compared the scores of African Americans and Caucasians in the MMPI-2 normative sample who were matched for age, education, and family income. They found that the African American men scored significantly higher than the Caucasian men only on Scale 8. The African American women scored significantly higher than the Caucasian women on Scales 4, 5, and 9. In all instances, the differences were less than five T-score points. Timbrook and Graham also determined the accuracy with which MMPI-2 scores predicted ratings of conceptually relevant characteristics of the African Americans and Caucasians. Accuracy of prediction did not differ for any scale for African American and Caucasian men. For women, the only significant difference in predictive accuracy was that Scale 7 slightly underpredicted anxiety ratings of African Americans. The authors concluded that for persons in the MMPI-2 normative sample, there was no evidence of bias against African Americans.

McNulty, Graham, Ben-Porath, and Stein (1997) compared MMPI-2 scores of African American and Caucasian clients of a community mental health center. Male African American clients scored significantly higher than male Caucasian clients only for the L scale and the Fears (FRS) Content scale. Female African American clients scored significantly higher than female Caucasian clients only for Scale 9 and the Low Self-Esteem (LSE) Content scale. No significant differences between African Americans and Caucasians were found in relationships between MMPI-2 scores and therapist ratings of conceptually relevant client characteristics. These authors concluded that the MMPI-2 was not biased against African Americans in this outpatient mental health setting. Castro, Gordon, Brown, Anestis, and Joiner (2008) conducted a similar study in a different outpatient mental health center setting. They found that African American clients scored significantly higher than Caucasian clients on Scales 1, RC1, RC3, RC6, and RC8. However, using information from a client application form, they found no support for the conclusion that the MMPI-2 scales predicted differentially for the African American and Caucasian clients.

Arbisi, Ben-Porath, and McNulty (2002) found that African American inpatients scored meaningfully higher than Caucasian inpatients on Scales 4, 6, and 9; on the BIZ and FAM Content scales; and on the MAC-R scale. However, regression analyses indicated that differences in predictive accuracy between African American and Caucasian patients were small and not clinically significant.

Shondrick, Ben-Porath, and Stafford (1992) reported MMPI-2 data for 106 Caucasian and 37 African American men who were undergoing forensic evaluations. Scores of the two groups on the Validity and Clinical scales were remarkably similar. The groups differed significantly only on Scale 9, with African Americans scoring approximately seven T-score points higher than Caucasians. Because no data were presented concerning extratest characteristics of Caucasians and African Americans, we do not know if the Scale 9 differences are indicative of actual behavioral differences.

Frueh, Smith, and Libet (1996) reported that male African American patients with diagnoses of posttraumatic stress disorder scored higher than Caucasian patients with this diagnosis on Scales 6 and 8 and the F–K index. Because no external measures of severity of psychopathology were compared, it is not clear if African Americans actually had more severe psychopathology than Caucasians. The authors speculated that the difference on the F–K index could suggest that the African American patients could have been overreporting their symptoms in order to get attention and treatment in a facility with predominantly Caucasian staff. In a follow-up study, Frueh, Gold, de Arellano, and Brady (1997) found that African American and Caucasian patients with diagnoses of posttraumatic stress disorder did not differ on any MMPI-2 scales or indexes or on external ratings of psychopathology or diagnoses.

Monnot, Quirk, Hoerger, and Brewer (2009) examined the accuracy of MMPI-2 scales in predicting SCID-based psychiatric diagnoses in a large sample of African American and Caucasian patients. Because of the large sample size, many significant differences in MMPI-2 scores were found between the two groups of patients. However, for only one Clinical scale (Scale 9) and two RC scales (RC2 and RC6) were differences clinically meaningful, with African American patients scoring higher than Caucasian patients. Regression analyses revealed that there were slope and prediction biases for many of the scales studied. In general, MMPI-2 scales modestly overpredicted the presence of conceptually relevant diagnoses for African American patients. The results of this study are difficult to interpret because of the use of only patients involved in chemical dependency treatment, most of whom had substance abuse diagnoses.

A meta-analytic study by Hall et al. (1999) examined the results of 25 studies of African American and Caucasian men and 12 studies of African American and Caucasian women. These authors concluded that, although African American men scored higher than Caucasian men on seven MMPI/MMPI-2 scales and African American women scored higher than Caucasian women on eight scales, the effect sizes associated with ethnicity were small and not clinically meaningful. For no scale did the average difference between African American and Caucasian groups exceed five T-score points.

Very little is known about differences between African Americans and Caucasians on the Supplementary scales of the MMPI or MMPI-2. Greene (1991) summarized several MMPI studies and concluded that fewer differences between African Americans and Caucasians have been found for the Supplementary than for the standard Validity and Clinical scales. Hutton, Miner, Blades, and Langfeldt (1992) reported that African American forensic inpatients scored significantly higher than Caucasian forensic inpatients on the Overcontrolled Hostility (O–H) scale. However, this difference is difficult to interpret because for neither group were O–H-scale scores significantly related to external variables that the scale was designed to assess. Shondrick et al. (1992) found that African American and Caucasian men undergoing forensic evaluations differed significantly on only two of the MMPI-2 Content scales. African Americans scored significantly higher on the Cynicism (CYN) and Antisocial Practices (ASP) scales. Again, no data were presented concerning the extent to which the African Americans and Caucasians differed on relevant extratest characteristics.

As indicated in Chapter 8 of this book, several studies have suggested caution in using the MacAndrew Alcoholism (MAC) scale with African Americans (Graham & Mayo, 1985; Walters, Greene, & Jeffrey, 1984; Walters, Greene, Jeffrey, Kruzich, & Haskin 1983). These studies indicated that African American alcoholics tend to obtain relatively high scores on the MAC, but classification rates for African Americans are not very good because nonalcoholic African American psychiatric patients also tend to obtain rather high MAC scores. All of these studies used military personnel or veterans, so the extent to which the findings can be generalized to other African Americans is unclear. However, until additional information is available, caution should be exercised when the MAC-R is used with African Americans.

Although more research is needed concerning MMPI-2 differences between African Americans and Caucasians, some tentative conclusions may be reached. Differences between African Americans and Caucasians are small when groups are matched on variables such as age and socioeconomic status. When differences are found, they tend to be associated with relevant extratest characteristics and probably should not be attributed to test bias. Only small MMPI-2 differences have been reported between African Americans and Caucasians in the normative sample, in a forensic setting, in an outpatient mental health setting, and in an inpatient mental health setting. Thus, these studies suggest that the MMPI-2 is not biased against African Americans and that its scales predict conceptually relevant characteristics of African Americans and Caucasians equally well.

Hispanics

Original MMPI

Velasquez, Ayala, and Mendoza (1998) summarized more than 170 studies involving Hispanics, but Greene (1987) identified only 10 published empirical studies comparing Hispanic and Caucasian groups on the MMPI. Although there were some significant differences between Hispanics and Caucasians in these studies, Greene concluded that there was no pattern to them. The data did not support Greene's earlier contention (Greene, 1980) that Hispanics frequently score higher on the L scale and lower on Scale 5. It also appeared that there were fewer differences between Hispanics and Caucasians on the MMPI than between African Americans and Caucasians.

Campos (1989) conducted a meta-analysis of 16 studies that compared Hispanics and Caucasians and concluded that the only consistent finding was that Hispanics scored higher (approximately four T-score points) than Caucasians on the L scale. Campos also concluded that the limited data available suggested that the MMPI predicts job performance of peace officers equally well for Hispanic and Caucasian groups.

Several studies have reported that there are marked similarities between MMPI characteristics of Hispanic and Caucasian psychiatric patients who have the same diagnoses. Velasquez, Callahan, and Carrillo (1991) found that the patterns of MMPI scores for Mexican American psychiatric inpatients were very similar to previously reported data for Caucasian patients. Velasquez, Callahan, and Carrillo (1989) studied a small group of Hispanic sex offenders and concluded that their MMPI profile patterns were similar to those previously reported for Caucasian sex offenders. Velaquez and Callahan (1990a) reported that Hispanic alcoholics scored significantly lower than Caucasian alcoholics on Scales 4, 5, and 0 of the MMPI but that the profile patterns of the two groups of alcoholics were similar. Venn (1988) found that a small sample of Mexican American alcoholics scored significantly higher than a matched sample of Caucasian alcoholics only on the L scale. Velasquez and Callahan (1990b) found that, although there were some significant differences between Hispanic and Caucasian patients with diagnoses of schizophrenia, the most frequent code type for both groups was 28/82.

Velasquez, Callahan, and Young (1993) compared small groups of male Hispanic and Caucasian patients with diagnoses of schizophrenia, major depression, or antisocial personality disorder. After correcting for multiple statistical tests, there were few differences associated with ethnicity. The Hispanic patients with diagnoses of schizophrenia scored higher than the Caucasian patients with diagnoses of schizophrenia only for Scale 1; the Hispanic patients with diagnoses of major depression scored differently (lower) from Caucasian patients with this diagnosis only for Scale 5; and no significant differences were found between the scores of Hispanic and Caucasian patients with diagnoses of antisocial personality disorder.

Nelson et al. (1996) compared small samples of Hispanic and Caucasian pain patients and found that for both men and women the Hispanic patients scored significantly higher than the Caucasian patients only on Scale 1. In addition, the Hispanic women scored significantly higher than the Caucasian women on Scale 5.

Several studies have examined MMPI scores of Hispanic worker compensation claimants. Clark, Velasquez, and Callahan (1992) concluded that a Spanish-language version of the MMPI-2 was useful with Hispanic claimants, but no comparisons were made with Caucasian claimants. DuAlba and Scott (1993) reported that Hispanic worker compensation claimants were more likely than Caucasian claimants to have elevated scores on Scales 1, 2, and 3.

Little information is available concerning Hispanic–Caucasian differences on the Supplementary scales of the MMPI. McCreary and Padilla (1977) found no meaningful differences between Hispanic and Caucasian prisoners on most Supplementary scales. However, Hispanic prisoners scored higher than Caucasian prisoners on the Overcontrolled–Hostility (O–H) scale. Page and Bozlee (1982) found no differences between Hispanic and Caucasian substance abusers on the MacAndrew Alcoholism (MAC) scale. Although Lapham et al. (1995) reported that a higher percentage of Hispanic driving while intoxicated (DWI) offenders scored above a previously published cutoff score on the MAC scale, no extratest data were available to examine the possibility of actual differences between the groups of offenders in alcohol use/abuse. Dolan, Roberts, Penk, Robinowitz, and Atkins (1983) found no meaningful differences between Hispanic and Caucasian heroin addicts on the Wiggins content scales. Although Montgomery, Arnold, and Orozco (1990) found that Mexican American college students scored slightly higher than Caucasian college students on most MMPI scales, these differences diminished when scale validity, age, and level of acculturation were controlled.

In summary, it would appear that there have been more similarities than differences reported between MMPI scores of Hispanics and Caucasians. The differences reported between these two groups have not been consistent across studies. The differences are difficult to interpret for several reasons. First, there have not been many studies concerning MMPI characteristics of Hispanics, and the samples utilized typically have been quite small. Second, there is considerable heterogeneity among persons designated as Hispanic. Typically studies have not indicated whether the Hispanics were Mexican American, Cuban, or Puerto Rican. Finally, most studies have not controlled for differences between Hispanic and Caucasian groups on variables such as socioeconomic status or level of acculturation. However, when variables such as socioeconomic status have been controlled, differences have been smaller.

MMPI-2

An official Spanish-language version of the MMPI-2 is available from Pearson Assessments. Not much research has yet been published concerning scores of Hispanics on the MMPI-2. Appendix H of the original MMPI-2 manual (Butcher et al., 1989) reported scores separately for Caucasians and Hispanics in the normative sample. Although ethnic backgrounds of the Hispanics were not described, the geographical areas in which the normative data were collected suggest that most were Mexican Americans. Careful examination of these data reveals that Hispanic men ($n = 35$) in the normative sample scored slightly higher than Caucasian men on most scales. However, none of the differences between Hispanic and Caucasian men was greater than five T-score points. Hispanic women ($n = 38$) in the normative sample scored higher than Caucasian women on all scales except L, K, and 0. On the L and K scales the Hispanic women scored lower than the Caucasians, and on Scales 5 and 0 there were no differences between the two groups. For Scales F, 1, 4, 7, 8, and 9, the differences were greater than five T-score points.

It appears that the differences between Hispanic and Caucasian men in the normative sample are small and not clinically meaningful. The larger differences between Hispanic and Caucasian women in the normative sample are of more concern. However, it should be noted that the ethnic groups in the normative sample were not matched for variables such as age or education. Additional analyses controlling for these variables are indicated.

Whitworth and McBlaine (1993) reported that Hispanic college students scored higher on the L scale and lower on Scales K, 3, and 4 than the Caucasian students, but the mean differences were less than five T-score points and not likely to be meaningful. They also observed that the differences between Hispanics and Caucasians were smaller than differences previously reported between Caucasians and African Americans. Whitworth and Unterbrink (1994) found that Hispanic college students scored higher than Caucasian students on the L and F scales and lower on the K scale, but all of these differences were less than five T-score points. After correcting for multiple statistical tests, the Hispanic students scored higher than the Caucasian students on Scales 8 and 9, but again the differences were not very large and probably not meaningful. Whitworth and Unterbrink also found that the Hispanic students scored higher than the Caucasian students on 13 MMPI-2 Content scales, but only for the Family Problems (FAM) and Cynicism (CYN) scales were the differences larger than five T-score points.

A meta-analytic study by Hall et al. (1999) examined the results of 13 studies that compared MMPI/MMPI-2 scores of male Caucasians and male Hispanics and found that the Hispanic men scored higher than the Caucasian men on the L, F, and K scales and lower on all of the Clinical scales. They concluded that the differences between these groups have been small and probably not clinically meaningful. The largest effect of ethnicity was for the L scale, where Hispanic men scored higher than Caucasian men, and Scale 5, where Hispanic men scored significantly lower than Caucasian men. However, even these differences were less than five T-score points.

Adequate data do not exist to permit conclusions concerning how Hispanic–Caucasian differences should be interpreted. We need to know if, when such differences occur, they are associated with important extratest differences between the groups. For example, are Hispanic women who score higher than Caucasian women on Scale 4 more likely to have the antisocial characteristics typically associated with higher scores on this scale? Based on the data that have been published concerning the meaning of MMPI differences between African Americans and Caucasians, we can speculate that Hispanic–Caucasian differences will be associated with important extratest differences and not attributable to test bias.

Some relevant information about the validity of the MMPI-2 with Hispanic patients comes from a study by Fantoni-Salvador and Rogers (1997). Spanish versions of the MMPI-2 and the Diagnostic Interview Schedule were administered to mental health patients for whom Spanish was the sole or preferred language. MMPI-2 code types were significantly related to diagnoses of depression and schizophrenia but not to diagnoses of anxiety or alcohol dependence disorders. The Addiction Admission Scale was a good predictor of substance dependence. Classification data indicated that for Hispanic patients the MMPI-2 scales are more effective at ruling out than ruling in disorders for individual patients.

Velasquez et al. (1998) summarized more than 170 studies involving Hispanic participants. Unfortunately, most of the studies have not been published, so their results and conclusions are difficult to evaluate. Most of the studies involved comparisons between Hispanic and other ethnic groups. Many found higher scores for Hispanic groups on some MMPI/MMPI-2 scales, but none reported the extratest data that would permit conclusions concerning the meaning of the scale differences. Some of the studies reported data suggesting that Hispanics with differing psychological symptoms and diagnoses differed significantly from each other on the MMPI/MMPI-2 scales.

Several authors (Butcher, Cabiya, Lucio, & Garrido, 2007; Velasquez, 1995; Velasquez et al., 1997, 1998) have made recommendations for using the MMPI-2 with Hispanic individuals. Some of these recommendations apply to the general use of the test (e.g., administer the entire test; explain to test takers how completing the MMPI-2 will be helpful to them). It has also been recommended that test users should always consider the impact of acculturation on MMPI-2 performance. However, data concerning the relationships between measures of acculturation and MMPI-2 scores of Hispanics have been mixed. For example, whereas Canul and Cross (1994) found higher L scores for less acculturated Mexican Americans, Lessenger (1997) found no significant relationships between acculturation scores and MMPI-2 scores of 100 male Hispanic substance abusers.

Several conclusions can be reached concerning the use of the MMPI-2 with Hispanics. First, a determination must be made concerning whether the Spanish or English version of the test should be used. Obviously, one should use the form corresponding to the language with which the test taker is most facile. Second, moderately elevated scores (T = 50–60) may very well be the product of low acculturation, so that variable needs to be determined and taken into consideration. Given the rather consistent finding that Hispanics obtain somewhat elevated L-scale scores, care should be taken not to infer defensiveness from L-scale T scores that are below 60. Finally, very high scores (T > 65) on the Clinical and Content scales are likely to reflect the same symptoms and problems that have been reported for Caucasians on these scales.

American Indians

Original MMPI

Greene's review (1987) identified only seven studies that compared MMPI scores of American Indians and Caucasians. Although the American Indians tended to score higher than Caucasians on some Clinical scales, there was no clear pattern to these differences across the studies. In an early study, Arthur (1944) compared MMPI scores of a small group of adolescent and young adult American Indians with scores of Caucasian college students. She concluded that there were more similarities than differences between the groups and that the MMPI scores realistically assessed the circumstances of the American Indians and Caucasians. Herreid and Herreid (1966) studied groups of native and nonnative Alaskan college students. They found that the natives obtained somewhat higher MMPI scores than the nonnatives, although only one difference (Scale 5 for women) was as large as five T-score points. Data were not available to examine relationships between differences in MMPI scores and actual differences in extratest characteristics.

Several studies have compared MMPI scores of American Indian alcoholics with scores of other groups of alcoholics. Kline, Rozynko, Flint, and Roberts (1973) examined a small group of male American Indian alcoholics. They reported that, compared with groups of Caucasian alcoholics reported previously in the literature, the American Indians had more deviant MMPI scores. However, there was no attempt to determine if these more deviant scores were associated with more deviant extratest characteristics. Uecker, Boutilier, and Richardson (1980) compared American Indian and Caucasian alcoholics and concluded that the groups were very similar in terms of MMPI scores. However, the Caucasians scored significantly higher than the American Indians on Scales 4 and 5. Page and Bozlee (1982) compared very small groups of American Indian and Caucasian male alcoholics and concluded that the groups were more similar than different. Venn (1988) compared a small sample (*n* =16) of male American Indian alcoholic inpatients with a sample of male Caucasian alcoholic inpatients matched for age and marital status. Although the sample of American Indians was too small to permit generalization to other American Indians, this study also found no significant differences between the groups on MMPI Validity or Clinical scales.

It is interesting to note that no significant differences between American Indian and Caucasian alcoholics were reported for the MacAndrew Alcoholism scale in the two studies that considered that scale (Page & Bozlee, 1982; Uecker et al., 1980). In a somewhat later study, Lapham et al. (1995) compared alcohol scale scores of Caucasians and American Indians who were first-time DWI offenders and found a higher percentage (22%) of American Indians scored above a previously published cutoff score on the MAC scale than did Caucasian offenders (15%). However, no extratest data were available concerning the extent to which there might have been actual differences in alcohol use/abuse between the Caucasian and American Indian offenders.

Borzecki, Wormith, and Black (1988) compared MMPI scores of male native and nonnative psychiatric offenders in Canada. When the groups were not matched for intelligence and educational level, the native offenders scored significantly higher than the nonnative offenders on Scales L, F, and 1 and significantly lower on Scale 5. However, none of these differences was more than five T-score points. When the native and nonnative offender groups were matched for intelligence and educational level, differences in MMPI scores were much smaller. Borzeki et al. concluded that the MMPI is appropriate for use with native offenders in Canada.

Only two MMPI studies involving American Indian psychiatric patients were reported. Pollack and Shore (1980) compared several different diagnostic groups of patients from Pacific Northwest tribes and concluded that the MMPI scores were very similar across diagnostic groups. However, they saw their data as demonstrating a significant cultural influence on the MMPI results of these groups of American Indians. Butcher et al. (1983) included a small group of American Indians in their study of psychiatric inpatients. They found that the MMPI scores of the American Indian patients were less deviant than those of Caucasian or African American patients.

Taken together, the results of these MMPI studies of American Indians suggest that there were few important differences between American Indians and Caucasians on the MMPI. What was lacking in all of the studies described here was the inclusion of extratest data that could be used to determine if MMPI differences are associated with other relevant characteristics.

MMPI-2

There are 38 American Indian men and 39 American Indian women in the MMPI-2 normative sample. Appendix H of the original MMPI-2 manual (Butcher et al., 1989) summarized scores for these two groups. American Indians scored higher than Caucasians on most scales. The American Indian men scored more than five T-score points higher than the Caucasian men on Scales F and 4. The American Indian women scored more than five T-score points higher than the Caucasian women on Scales F, 1, 4, 5, 7, and 8. Although the American Indian groups were small and not necessarily similar to the Caucasian groups in terms of age, socio-economic status, or other demographic characteristics, the differences between American Indian and Caucasian groups are potentially important. However, no data were included that would indicate if the MMPI-2 differences are associated with important extratest characteristics.

Robin, Greene, Albaugh, Caldwell, and Goldman (2003) compared MMPI-2 Validity, Clinical, Content, and Supplementary scale scores of 535 Southwestern and 297 Plains American Indian tribal members with scores of persons from the MMPI-2 normative sample. Although differences between the two American Indian tribes were expected, no meaningful differences were found for any MMPI-2 scales. However, meaningful differences between the combined tribal groups and the normative sample were found. The American Indians had mean-ingfully higher scores for Validity scales L and F; for Clinical scales 4, 8, and 9; for the HEA, BIZ, CYN, ASP, and TRT Content scales; and for the AAS and MAC-R scale. Although differences between groups for these scales were smaller when they were matched for age, gender, and education, they were still large enough to be clinically meaningful.

In a companion study to that of Robin et al. (2003), Greene, Robin, Albaugh, Caldwell, and Goldman (2003) used the same two tribal groups and calcu-lated correlations between MMPI-2 scores and measures of clinical symptoms and behaviors generated from a modified version of the Schedule for Affective Disorders and Schizophrenia (SADS; Endicott & Spitzer, 1978). Meaningful cor-relations ($\geq .30$) were obtained between most MMPI-2 scales and conceptually relevant measures from the SADS. For example, breaking rules was correlated with Scale 4 and the Antisocial Practices Content scale, suicide attempts with the Depression Content scale, and alcohol and drug use with the AAS. The MAC-R scale was not correlated meaningfully with any of the measures of alcohol or drug problems, supporting earlier concerns about the appropriateness of this scale with American Indians. This finding is especially troubling because the Robin et al. study reported that American Indians scored meaningfully higher on the MAC-R scale than the persons in the MMPI-2 normative sample. It should be noted that the SADS provided conceptually relevant measures for only some MMPI-2 scales. Correlates of other scales remain to be demonstrated in future studies.

Pace et al. (2006) examined MMPI-2 scores of two American Indian tribes, Eastern Woodland Oklahoma and Southwest Plains Oklahoma, and compared their scores with data for the MMPI-2 normative sample. Both tribal groups scored significantly and meaningfully higher than the normative sample for most of the MMPI-2 Validity and Clinical scales. Acculturation level was not a significant factor in MMPI-2 scale differences. The authors concluded that the MMPI-2 should be used with great caution with American Indians and that scores should be interpreted in the context of clients' unique beliefs and predicaments. This caution is consistent with this author's position that MMPI-2 results should always be interpreted taking into account such factors for all who complete the test. Absent from the Pace et al. study was criterion information that would have informed interpretation of elevated scores for members of these two tribes.

What conclusions can be reached about using the MMPI-2 with American Indians? First, one should expect American Indians to obtain moderately high scores on many MMPI-2 scales. These scores may likely be reflecting cultural factors rather than psychopathology. However, when T scores on Clinical and Content scales are above 65, the scores probably reflect the same symptoms and problems for American Indians as they do for Caucasians. Special caution should be used in inferring substance abuse problems from the MacAndrew Alcoholism scale–Revised (MAC-R). However, high scores on the Addiction Admission Scale (AAS) are likely to reflect substance abuse problems, as the items in that scale have obvious substance use and abuse content. Additional research is needed to establish more clearly relationships between MMPI-2 scores and conceptually relevant extratest characteristics of American Indians. Future research should more carefully consider the heterogeneity of American Indian tribes and the extent to which findings for one tribe will apply equally well to other tribes.

Asian Americans

An official Hmong version of the MMPI-2 is available from Pearson Assessments. Although the MMPI-2 has been translated into other Asian languages, these other versions are not readily available. Readers interested in them should consult an edited book titled *International Adaptations of the MMPI-2* (Butcher, 1996). Research studies often have utilized heterogeneous groups of Asian Americans, so it is difficult to know to which particular Asian American groups the findings are most applicable.

Original MMPI

Few research studies are available concerning MMPI scores of Asian Americans. Dahlstrom et al. (1986), Greene (1987), and Kwan (1999) summarized published and unpublished studies involving comparisons of Asian American and Caucasian samples. The studies typically utilized very small samples and heterogeneous groups of Asian Americans. In most studies Asian Americans obtained higher scores than Caucasians on many MMPI scales, although the differences typically were small and probably not very meaningful. The most consistent finding was that Asian Americas scored significantly higher than Caucasians on Scale 0, suggesting greater social introversion. Because extratest measures were not available, it was not possible to determine if differences in MMPI scores were associated with actual differences in psychopathology. Marsella, Sanborn, Kameoka, Shizuru, and Brennan (1975) reported that Asian American (Chinese, Japanese) college students residing in Hawaii had higher scores on Scale 2 of the MMPI than Caucasian college students. Interestingly, the Asian American students also had higher scores on the Beck Depression Inventory, suggesting that the higher scores on Scale 2 could be reflecting differences in symptoms of depression.

Several studies reported similarities between Asian American and Caucasian psychiatric patients with diagnoses of somatization disorders (Tsushima & Onorato, 1982) or chronic pain (Tsushima & Stoddard, 1990). Two MMPI studies conducted with Chinese participants in Hong Kong suggested that a Chinese translation of the MMPI could be clinically useful. Lee, Cheung, Man, and Hsu (1992) found significant differences between chronic low back pain patients and community residents. Consistent with U.S. data, the low back pain patients were significantly elevated on Scales 1, 2, and 3. However, unlike U.S. patients, the Chinese low back pain patients also had elevated scores on Scales 7 and 8. Cheung and Song (1989), using a Chinese translation of the MMPI, found that a nonclinical sample of Chinese residents had higher scores than the U.S. norms on Scales F, 2, and 8. However, the patterns of scores for major mental disorders were quite similar for Chinese and U.S. patients.

MMPI-2

Because very few Asian Americans were included in the MMPI-2 normative sample (6 men, 13 women), it is not appropriate to reach conclusions about differences between Asian Americans and Caucasians on the MMPI-2. However, the data in Appendix H of the original MMPI-2 manual (Butcher et al., 1989) suggest that there were few differences between the Asian Americans and Caucasians included in the normative sample and that the Asian Americans did not score consistently higher than the Caucasians.

Stevens, Kwan, and Graybill (1993) compared a small sample of foreign-born Chinese college students with a matched sample of Caucasian college students. The Chinese men scored significantly higher than the Caucasian men on Scale 0, suggesting that they were more introverted than the Caucasians. The Chinese women scored higher than the Caucasian women on the L scale, suggesting that they presented themselves as somewhat more virtuous. Similar results were reported by Robers (1992) for Chinese American students.

Tran (1996) and Dong and Church (2003) reported that Vietnamese Americans had MMPI-2 scores within a normal range, but their scores were slightly higher than the normative sample, especially for Scales F and 8. Dong and Church assessed the degree of trauma that the Vietnamese refugees had experienced and found a significant correlation between severity of trauma and mean elevation of MMPI-2 Clinical scales, suggesting that their somewhat elevated scores were assessing psychological symptoms related to the traumatic experiences. Dong and Church also assessed acculturation levels of their participants and reported that less acculturated refugees had higher MMPI-2 scores.

Tsai and Pike (2000) compared Asian American college students (mostly Chinese, Vietnamese, and Korean) with varying degrees of acculturation with a group of Caucasian college students. They found that the low acculturated students had higher scores than the Caucasian students on most MMPI-2 scales, with the greatest differences on the F scale and Scale 8. The highly acculturated students did not differ meaningfully from the Caucasian students. However, as Kwon (2002) pointed out, the design did not control for socioeconomic differences between groups, making it difficult to have confidence that differences were due only to differing levels of acculturation.

Additional research is needed concerning MMPI-2 differences between Asian Americans and Caucasians. It will be especially important to determine if MMPI-2 differences between these groups are associated with differences in important extratest characteristics. Based on studies involving the original MMPI, it seems likely that such an association will be found. Okazaki and Sue (1995) stressed the importance of considering the acculturation levels of Asian Americans when conducting psychological assessments. They recommended that assessors "be more conservative and cautious in interpreting the results of less acculturated individuals whose scores deviated from the American norms" (p. 117).

Several conclusions can be reached about the use of the MMPI-2 with Asian Americans. First, scores of nonclinical Asian Americans are likely to be within normal limits, although some moderately high scores (T scores between 50 and 60) may be expected. These moderately elevated scores are likely to be the product of experienced stress and/or level of acculturation and probably do not reflect significant psychopathology. However, MMPI-2 T scores that are very high (T > 65) are likely to reflect symptoms and problems consistent with the findings that have been reported for Caucasian test takers.

MEDICAL PATIENTS

The original MMPI was used frequently by psychologists in medical settings (Piotrowski & Lubin, 1990). Patients were accepting of completing MMPIs requested by their physicians, and physicians found the MMPI useful with their patients (Swenson, Rome, Pearson, & Brannick, 1965). The MMPI-2 also is widely used in medical settings. A survey revealed that almost 90% of health psychologists use the MMPI-2 (Piotrowski & Lubin, 1990), and it is the psychological test most frequently used by neuropsychologists (Camara, Nathan, & Puente, 2000).

Osborne (1979) and Henrichs (1981) presented overviews of the use of the MMPI in medical settings, and Arbisi and Butcher (2004) summarized uses of the MMPI-2 in such settings. It will not be possible in this chapter to review even briefly the voluminous research literature concerning the relationship between MMPI/MMPI-2 data and characteristics of medical patients. Rather, suggestions will be made about ways in which the MMPI-2 can be helpful in working with patients with medical problems.

Screening for Psychopathology

One important use of the MMPI with medical patients has been to screen for serious psychopathology that has not been reported or that has been minimized by patients. The indicators of serious psychopathology discussed elsewhere in this book (e.g., overall scale elevation) should be considered when examining the profiles of medical patients.

Many clinicians assume that medical problems are necessarily very emotionally distressing to patients and that this distress will be reflected in highly deviant scores on the MMPI-2. It is important to develop some expectations concerning typical MMPI-2 scores and profiles produced by medical patients. Swenson, Pearson, and Osborne (1973) reported summary MMPI data for approximately 25,000 male and 25,000 female patients at the Mayo Clinic. The mean Clinical scale scores for both male and female patients fell within normal limits. The Validity scales suggested a slightly defensive test-taking attitude. T scores on Scales 1, 2, and 3 were near 60. Apparently, the medical problems of these patients were not psychologically distressing enough to lead to grossly elevated scores on the MMPI scales. Colligan et al. (2008) reported MMPI-2 scores for 590 female and 653 male family medicine outpatients. The patients' average scores were quite similar to previous reports of MMPI scores of medical patients. Scores on the L, K, and S scales were slightly above average. All Clinical scale scores were within normal limits, with scores on Scales 1, 2, and 3 being approximately five T-score points above the mean for the MMPI-2 normative sample. Clinical scale T scores greater than 65 indicate that the possibility of significant psychological problems be explored thoroughly. Graham, Barthlow, Stein, Ben-Porath, and McNulty (2002) examined various MMPI-2 measures and concluded that the mean T score for eight Clinical scales (1, 2, 3, 4, 6, 7, 8, and 9) was most related to extratest measures of maladjustment. Obviously, higher mean scores for this index indicate greater psychological maladjustment.

Screening for Substance Abuse Problems

Substance abuse problems are quite common among persons being treated primarily for medical conditions. The MMPI-2 can be useful in alerting clinicians to the possibility of substance abuse. Some patients develop physical symptoms because of chronic substance abuse, some develop substance abuse problems because of their medical problems, and some have substance abuse problems that are not directly related to their physical symptoms. Regardless of the reasons for the relationship between substance abuse problems and medical problems, early awareness of these problems facilitates treatment planning.

Research with the original MMPI did not reveal a single pattern of MMPI scales associated with substance abuse problems (e.g., Graham & Strenger, 1988). However, there is convincing evidence that Scale 4 is likely to be elevated among groups of persons who abuse substances. Because Scale 4 typically is not significantly elevated among groups of medical patients, significant Scale 4 elevation (T > 65) suggests that the possibility of abuse of substances should be considered.

Fordyce (1979) suggested that chronic-pain patients can easily become addicted to narcotics, barbiturates, or muscle relaxants. He reported that such persons often obtain elevations on Scales 2 and 9. When both of these scales are elevated above 65, the possibility of addiction to prescription medications should be explored.

The 24/42 two-point code type often is found among male alcoholics in treatment, and this same code type and the 46/64 code type often are found for female alcoholics in treatment. Neither of these code types is common among medical patients who do not abuse alcohol. Thus, when these code types are encountered in medical patients (particularly if the T scores are greater than 65), the possibility of alcohol abuse should be explored carefully.

The MacAndrew Alcoholism Scale–Revised (MAC-R) was described in Chapter 8 of this book. Although the original MAC scale was developed by comparing the item responses of male alcoholic outpatients and male psychiatric outpatients, subsequent research indicated that the scale was useful for identifying substance abuse problems of various kinds for men and women in a variety of settings (Graham & Strenger, 1988). If significant elevation is found on the MAC-R scale scores for patients in a medical setting, careful consideration should be given to the possibility that these persons are abusing substances. As discussed in Chapter 8 of this book, MAC-R scale raw scores of 28 or above suggest that the possibility of substance abuse problems should be explored. Scores between 24 and 27 are somewhat suggestive of such abuse. Scores below 24 suggest that substance abuse problems are not very likely. It should be emphasized that research concerning the MAC and the MAC-R scales has emphasized abuse of alcohol and other nonprescribed drugs. Little is known about the extent to which the MAC-R is sensitive to the abuse of prescribed drugs, such as those used by chronic-pain patients.

Medical patients with T scores greater than 60 on the Addiction Admission Scale (AAS) (Weed et al., 1992) are openly reporting substance abuse problems, and additional assessment in this area is indicated. Because most of the items in the AAS have content obviously related to substance abuse, the absence of elevated scores on this scale should not be interpreted as indicating the absence of substance abuse problems. Such scores could indicate either actual absence of or conscious denial of significant substance abuse problems.

T scores greater than 60 on the Addiction Potential Scale (APS) (Weed et al., 1992) also should alert clinicians that additional information concerning possible substance abuse should be obtained. However, as discussed in Chapter 8 of this book, research findings concerning the validity of the APS have been mixed, suggesting that scores on this scale should be given less consideration than scores for the MAC-R and especially for the AAS.

Organic versus Functional Etiology

Although the original MMPI sometimes was used to try to determine if the somatic symptoms presented by patients were organic or functional in origin, it is never appropriate to use the MMPI-2 alone to diagnose an organic condition or to rule out such a condition. The most that the MMPI-2 can do is to give some information concerning the underlying personality characteristics of the patient. This information can be used, along with other available information, to make inferences concerning the compatibility of the personality characteristics and a functional explanation of symptoms.

Osborne (1979) and Keller and Butcher (1991) summarized studies with the original MMPI that tried to determine if patients' symptoms were functional or organic in nature. The symptoms studied have included low back pain, sexual impotence, neurologic complaints, and others. In general, the research indicated that patients with symptoms that were exclusively or primarily psychological in origin tended to score higher on Scales 1, 2, and 3 than patients with similar symptoms that were clearly organic in origin. Particularly common among groups of patients with symptoms of psychological origin was the 13/31 two-point code type. When this code type was found, and Scales 1 and 3 were elevated above T > 65 and were considerably higher than Scale 2, the likelihood of functional origin increased. However, Osborne (1979) and Keller and Butcher (1991) pointed out that the differences between the functional and organic groups have not been large enough to permit predictions in individual cases.

Several MMPI supplementary scales were developed specifically to try to determine if physical symptoms are of functional or organic origin. Two of the most commonly used were the Low Back Pain Scale (Lb; Hanvik, 1949, 1951) and the Caudality Scale (Ca; Williams, 1952). Because of inadequate research data to support the usefulness of these scales, they were not included in the MMPI-2.

Establishing Homogeneous Subtypes

Some investigators have used the MMPI to establish homogeneous subtypes within a particular medical disorder. Most of this research has been in relation to chronic pain. The goals underlying the subtyping approach have been to identify etiological factors that are unique to particular subtypes and to determine specific treatment interventions that are appropriate for the subtypes.

Sometimes the subtyping has been based on MMPI code types or other configural aspects of test performance. Keller and Butcher (1991) reviewed this literature and concluded that MMPI researchers consistently had identified two subtypes of pain patients. One subtype was characterized by the "conversion-V" pattern (Scales 1 and 3 as highest scales and both considerably higher than Scale 2, which is third highest in the profile). The second subtype was characterized by elevated scores on Scales 1, 2, and 3, but without significant differences among these three scales. Slesinger, Archer, and Duane (2002) reported that MMPI-2 code types involving Scales 1, 2, and 3 were very common among patients in an inpatient chronic-pain program. There were some suggestions in the MMPI literature that there are differential treatment outcomes associated with these various code types. However, Keller and Butcher concluded that using this approach to predict treatment outcome was not very effective.

Other investigators have used more sophisticated procedures (e.g., cluster analysis) to identify homogeneous MMPI subgroups among pain patients (e.g., Costello, Hulsey, Schoenfeld, & Ramamurthy, 1987; Costello, Schoenfeld, Ramamurthy, & Hobbs-Hardee, 1989; Kinder, Curtiss, & Kalichman, 1992). Four cluster types have emerged consistently (the conversion-V pattern, the neurotic triad pattern, the normal-limits profile, and the general elevation profile). Interestingly, Strassberg, Tilley, Bristone, and Oei (1992) cluster analyzed MMPI scores of Australian chronic-pain patients and found three clusters that were very similar to clusters previously reported for pain patients in the United States.

Keller and Butcher (1991) studied 590 chronic-pain patients, identifying three MMPI-2 clusters that were similar to those previously reported for the original MMPI. The clusters differed from each other primarily in terms of scale elevation rather than scale configuration. Few differences between clusters were identified in patient characteristics as determined from clinical records. They concluded that the MMPI-2 is useful with chronic-pain patients primarily as a way to assess general level of distress and disability and that Scale 2 was especially useful in this regard.

Using hierarchical cluster analysis, Riley and Robinson (1998) identified four MMPI-2 cluster types among pain patients that were very similar to those previously reported for the MMPI. Riley and Robinson demonstrated that relationships between psychological variables (e.g., cognitive coping and activity level) were different for the cluster types, suggesting that differential approaches to treating chronic pain might be indicated for patients with differing code types. Gatchel, Mayer, and Eddington (2006) found that chronic pain patients with more than four elevated Clinical scale scores were more likely to have Axis I diagnoses than patients with normal limits profiles and that patients with normal limits profiles were more likely than those with other types of profiles to be employed one year after pain treatment. Haggard, Stowell, Bernstein, and Gatchell (2008) reported that chronic pain patients with more than four elevated Clinical scale scores had more physical diagnoses and reported poorer physical and mental health than patients with normal limits profiles.

The cluster-analytic methodology has also been applied to MMPI data for other kinds of medical patients. For example, Robinson, Greene, and Geisser (1993) analyzed data for two groups of pain patients and a group of patients awaiting heart transplants. The clusters for the pain groups were very similar to those previously reported for pain patients, but the clusters for cardiac patients were somewhat different from those of the pain patients. Basically, the cardiac patient data yielded four clusters that differed primarily in terms of the severity of psychopathology indicated by the profiles. Bombardier, Divine, Jordan, Brooks, and Neelon (1993) cluster analyzed MMPI scores for a group of patients with heterogeneous medical conditions, including neurological, gastrointestinal, musculoskeletal, and cardiovascular disorders. Their results were very similar to those for the cardiac patients in the study of Robinson et al. (1993). Four clusters were identified that differed primarily in terms of the severity of psychopathology suggested by the profiles.

Regardless of how subtypes are determined, the clinical utility of this approach depends on demonstrating empirically that there are important extratest differences associated with the cluster types. As Keller and Butcher (1991) pointed out, most studies have generated interpretive schemata based on the supposed significance of various scale configurations, but data to support these schemata are very limited. Kinder et al. (1992) reported that MMPI cluster groups of headache patients differed in terms of level of affective distress assessed by non-MMPI measures. Bombardier et al. (1993) found that the clusters identified for patients with heterogeneous medical conditions differed on measures of symptom severity external to the MMPI and changes in functional impairment and depression 6 months after treatment.

Clearly, if the subtyping approach is to be useful with the MMPI-2, future research must concentrate on establishing empirically that persons in the various subtypes differ in important ways (e.g., in their responsiveness to treatment interventions of various kinds). Existing data seem to indicate that medical patients can be categorized according to the severity of psychopathology suggested by their MMPI-2 scores and that patients in the most severe groups tend to be more distressed and in some ways may respond less well to medical treatment than patients whose MMPI-2s suggest less severe psychopathology.

Psychological Effects of Medical Conditions

The MMPI-2 can be used to understand how persons with medical problems are affected psychologically by them. When it is used for this purpose, the clinician should consider indicators of emotional disturbance that have been discussed previously in this book. For example, high scores on Scale 2, the Depression (DEP) Content scale, the Low Positive Emotions (RC2) scale, or Demoralization (RCd) scale suggest that medical patients are experiencing dysphoria/depression, and elevated scores on Scale 7, Welsh's Anxiety scale, the Anxiety (ANX) Content scale, or the Dysfunctional Negative Emotions (RC7) scale indicate that medical patients are anxious, worried, and tense.

Patients with such varied disorders as head injury (Diamond, Barth, & Zillmer, 1988; Nockleby & Deaton, 1987), stroke (Gass & Lawhorn, 1991), chronic pain (Keller & Butcher, 1991; Slesinger et al., 2002), eating disorders (Cumella, Wall, & Kerr-Almeida, 2000), fibromyalgia (Gerson & Fox, 2003), and cancer (Chang, Nesbit, Youngren, & Robison, 1988) may have MMPI-2 scores suggestive of significant psychological distress and maladjustment. Sometimes the distress is in the form of exaggerated somatic concerns, which will be reflected in high scores on Scales 1 and 3, the Somatic Complaints (RC1) scale, and the Health Concerns (HEA) Content scale, but often it is expressed in symptoms of depression, which will be reflected in high scores on Scale 2, the Depression (DEP) Content scale, the Demoralization (RCd) scale, and the Low Positive Affect (RC2) scale, or anxiety, which will be reflected in high scores on Scale 7, the Anxiety (ANX) Content scale, Welsh's Anxiety (A) scale, and the Dysfunctional Negative Emotions (RC7) scale.

Interpreting high MMPI-2 scores for medical patients can be challenging because some items in the MMPI-2 scales may reflect symptoms and behaviors that are the products of particular medical disorders. For example, patients could endorse items suggesting problems with concentration and attention related to anxiety, but the items could also reflect deficits directly related to traumatic brain injury.

Gass (1991) and Alfano, Paniak, Christopher, and Finlayson (1993) identified MMPI-2 items that are associated with traumatic brain injury and developed procedures for correcting scores on some scales to remove the effects of these items. Gass (1992) developed a similar correction factor for use with stroke patients. When the correction factors were applied to scores of brain-injured and stroke patients, corrected scores tended to be significantly lower than uncorrected scores. It was opined that the corrected scores portrayed the emotional status of patients more accurately. Similarly, Nelson, Elder, Groot, Tehrani, and Grant (2004) identified MMPI-2 items that persons with epilepsy could answer in the scored direction because of symptoms related to their epilepsy. When MMPI-2 scales were corrected to remove these items, lower scores were obtained for most scales. However, no data were presented to address whether the corrected scores more accurately reflected the psychological status of patients than the uncorrected scores.

Arbisi and Ben-Porath (1999) reviewed the use of correction factors with brain-injured patients and expressed concerns about their routine use. An important danger in using the correction factors is that the items, although related to the medical disorders (e.g., traumatic brain injury), could also be indicative of important psychological disorders (e.g., depression). Thus, the corrected scores could underestimate the severity of the psychological disorders. According to Arbisi and Ben-Porath, there is inadequate evidence to support the notion that corrected scores more accurately portray the psychological status of patients than do uncorrected scores. Empirical research is needed to determine the relative validity of corrected and uncorrected scores. Arbisi and Ben-Porath also expressed some methodological concerns about the manner in which the correction factors have been applied to scores. Their article should be consulted for details of those concerns.

Response to Medical Treatment

The MMPI-2 also can provide important information concerning how medical patients are likely to respond psychologically to medical interventions. Several examples can be given to illustrate this potential use. Henrichs and Waters (1972) investigated the extent to which MMPIs administered preoperatively to cardiac patients could predict emotional or behavioral reactions to surgery. Based on prior literature concerning cardiac patients, five types were conceptualized, and rules for classifying MMPI profiles into these types were developed. The rules were able to classify 97% of MMPIs given to patients preoperatively. Postoperative course was recorded for all patients to determine if they had behavioral or emotional problems. The occurrence of such postoperative problems was significantly different for the different MMPI types. Only 6% of patients who were in the well-adjusted MMPI type preoperatively had postoperative emotional or behavioral problems. By contrast, 44% of persons having preoperative MMPIs indicating serious disturbance had postoperative behavioral or emotional problems. Henrichs and Waters pointed out that different types of preoperative interventions could be developed to address anticipated postoperative problems.

Sobel and Worden (1979) demonstrated that the MMPI was useful in predicting psychosocial adjustment of patients who had been diagnosed as having cancer. The MMPI typically was administered following the diagnosis of cancer, and patients were studied for 6 months following this testing. Patients were classified as having high distress or low distress at follow-up on the basis of multiple measures of emotional turmoil, physical symptoms, and effectiveness of coping with the demands of daily living. Using discriminant analyses of MMPI scores, 75% of patients were correctly classified as having high distress or low distress. The authors pointed out that interventions could be developed to assist cancer patients who are considered to be at high risk for psychosocial problems.

Barrash, Rodriguez, Scott, Mason, and Sines (1987) identified 10 MMPI subtypes among patients who were going to have gastric bypass surgery. These subtypes were differentially related to post-surgery weight loss over a 10–14 month follow-up period. Tsushima, Bridenstine, and Balfour (2004) conducted a similar study with the MMPI-2 with a one-year follow-up. Less successful patients had higher pre-surgery scores on Scales, F, 3, 5, 6, and 7 and the Health Concerns (HEA) Content scale. Higher scores on Scale 5 and HEA were the best predictors of poor post-surgery weight loss.

Several studies have used the MMPI to predict response to chronic-pain treatment programs. Akerlind, Hornquist, and Bjurulf (1992) found that overall elevation on the Clinical scales, especially on Scales 1 and 3, was predictive of poorer development of work capacity during a follow-up period of 6 to 12 years. Gatchel, Polatin, and Kinney (1995) compared chronic-pain patients who had or had not returned to work following treatment and found that Scale 3 was the only MMPI scale that predicted work status, with those who had not returned to work having higher Scale 3 scores. Vendrig, Derksen, and de Mey (1999) used selected MMPI-2 scales to predict improvement in Dutch pain patients following a four-week outpatient intervention program. Scales indicative of emotional distress were negatively related to improvement in self-reported pain intensity and disability, but no MMPI-2 scales were predictive of changes in physical abilities following the intervention. Also studying Dutch patient responses to an intervention program, Vendrig (1999) found that only the Harris–Lingoes Lassitude–Malaise (Hy3) subscale was predictive of return to work following the intervention, with higher scores associated with failure to return to work.

Dancyger, Sunday, Eckert, and Halmi (1997) used MMPI scores to predict outcome of inpatient treatment of bulimia 10 years after treatment. Admission MMPI scores were not related to outcome, but higher discharge scores on Scales 1 and 6 and lower scores on Scale 4 were predictive of worse outcome. These three scales together accounted for approximately 25% of the variance in outcome 10 years later. Edwin, Andersen, and Rosell (1988) reported that MMPI scores did not predict response to treatment for anorexia nervosa patients. However, there were some modest relationships between MMPI scales and outcome for some subtypes. For bulimic subtypes higher Scale 9 scores were associated with more negative outcomes, and for restricting subtypes higher Scale 3 scores were associated with more positive outcomes.

In summary, a general finding in the literature has been that persons who are well adjusted emotionally before they develop serious medical problems and/or before they are treated for such problems seem to handle the illness-related stress better than persons who are emotionally less well adjusted. Additionally, better-adjusted persons seem to have better posttreatment courses than do less well-adjusted persons. However, not all studies have found positive relationships between MMPI results and response to medical interventions (e.g., Guck, Meilman, & Skultety, 1987). Although the MMPI-2 seems to have a great deal of potential in predicting response to medical interventions, there is a need for additional research to establish more clearly the extent to which the MMPI-2 can and should be used for this purpose.

Psychological Effects of Medical Treatment

Several investigators have used the MMPI to examine psychological status following medical interventions. For example, Clark and Klonoff (1988) identified five clusters of MMPI profiles of patients awaiting coronary bypass surgery. The different clusters were associated with different degrees of anxiety and depression before surgery, and these differences were also present at the same levels after surgery. Kirkcaldy and Kobylinska (1988) compared breast cancer patients after they had undergone treatment (mastectomy or chemotherapy). They found that both groups of patients had more deviant MMPI scores than a control group of healthy nurses. Unfortunately, no pretreatment MMPI data were reported, so it is not possible to determine if the distress suggested by the MMPI scores of the patients resulted from the treatment or was present prior to the interventions.

Predisposing Factors

Numerous research projects have sought to identify factors that place persons at risk for serious medical problems such as coronary heart disease or cancer. The MMPI has been utilized in some of these projects. In a number of early studies the MMPI was administered to persons who already had a serious medical disorder, and the results were compared with those of healthy persons. These studies were of little value because it was not possible to determine if the psychological characteristics assessed by the MMPI had predisposed the persons to the disorders or had resulted from the disorders.

More sophisticated prospective studies have also been reported. In these studies large groups of persons have been assessed using a variety of procedures, including the MMPI, and followed for many years to determine which of them developed serious medical disorders. Although the MMPI Clinical scales were analyzed in some of these prospective studies (e.g., Persky, Kempthorne-Rawson, & Shekelle, 1987), most have focused on the Hostility (Ho) scale (Cook & Medley, 1954) of the MMPI. This scale, which was discussed in more detail in Chapter 8 of this book, originally was developed to predict performance of classroom teachers. Subsequently, it became obvious that the scale assessed hostility and lack of confidence in other people.

Several studies have reported that persons with lower Ho-scale scores are less likely than persons with higher scores to develop coronary heart disease (CHD). Williams et al. (1980) studied men and women who had diagnoses of CHD. Angiography indicated that those with higher Ho-scale scores were more likely to have significant occlusion of at least one artery. Although these results are very interesting, they are of limited utility because the study was cross-sectional in nature.

Barefoot, Dahlstrom, and Williams (1983) conducted a 25-year follow-up study of 255 physicians who had completed the MMPI while in medical school. They found that higher Ho-scale scorers were more likely to have been diagnosed as having CHD and that mortality from all causes was greater for persons with higher Ho-scale scores. Shekelle et al. (1983) evaluated 1877 male employees of the Western Electric Company 10 and 20 years after an initial assessment that included the MMPI. They found that even after other risk factors such as blood pressure and cholesterol levels were factored out, persons with higher Ho-scale scores were more likely to receive CHD diagnoses during the follow-up period.

Colligan and Offord (1988) cautioned that higher Ho-scale scores are not necessarily associated with a greater risk for CHD. They studied groups of contemporary normal persons, general medical patients, persons undergoing treatment for alcoholism, and persons hospitalized for psychiatric treatment and found that many persons in these groups had Ho-scale scores that would suggest that they were at risk for CHD. Of course, this was not a prospective study, so we do not know how many of the persons with higher Ho-scale scores, in fact, developed CHD.

Several prospective studies have failed to replicate the earlier relationship between Ho-scale scores and CHD. Hearn, Murray, and Luepker (1989) conducted a 33-year follow-up study of men who had taken the MMPI when they entered the University of Minnesota. Higher Ho-scale scores did not predict CHD mortality, CHD morbidity, or total mortality either before or after adjustment for baseline risk factors. Leon, Finn, Murray, and Bailey (1988) studied 280 men who had been healthy when they completed the MMPI in 1947. In a 30-year follow-up there was not a significant relationship between Ho-scale scores and CHD. Similarly, McCranie, Watkins, Brandsma, and Sisson (1986) completed a follow-up study of persons who had taken the MMPI when in medical school. Ho-scale scores were not significant predictors of CHD incidence or total mortality in this sample.

The Type A Content scale has been linked to CHD. Among a group of older (mean age = 61 years) men free of CHD, higher scorers on the Type A scale were significantly more likely to experience CHD death or nonfatal myocardial infarction during a follow-up period of approximately seven years (Kawachi et al., 1998).

In summary, there are data suggesting that the MMPI-2, especially the Ho scale, may be helpful in identifying psychological risk factors in CHD. However, research results have not been completely consistent. Studies have differed in terms of participant age, geographic location, follow-up period, and methods used to assess CHD. Additional research is needed to clarify the extent to which the Ho scale or other scales of the MMPI-2 can be used clinically to assess psychological risk for CHD and other serious medical disorders. Future research in this area should take into account other MMPI-2 scales, such as the Anger, Cynicism, and Type A Content scales.

The MMPI has also been used to predict future pain symptoms. Fordyce et al. (1992) conducted a prospective study of more than 1600 industrial employees who completed the MMPI and were followed for an average of three years. The Harris-Lingoes Lassitude-Malaise (Hy3) subscale was significantly related to whether or not the workers filed a back injury report during the follow-up period. Applegate et al. (2005) conducted a study involving more than 2300 individuals who completed the MMPI at the time of entry into college between 1964 and 1966. They were surveyed in 1997 to determine the presence of various chronic pain symptoms. Although scores on Scales 1, 3, and 5 for men and Scales 1, 3, and 6 for women were significantly related to number of pain symptoms in later life, the relationships were very modest and probably not clinically meaningful.

PERSONNEL SCREENING

The MMPI was developed in a psychiatric hospital setting, and most of the research done with the instrument has been conducted in clinical settings. However, the use of the MMPI in nonclinical settings increased dramatically in the years before its revision (Graham & McCord, 1985). The MMPI and MMPI-2 have been used frequently in selecting employees for sensitive occupations (e.g., safety officers, airline pilots) and students for training programs (Butcher, 1979, 1985).

Using the MMPI-2 to screen for psychopathology among applicants is most justified when individuals are being considered for employment in occupations involving susceptibility to occupational stress, personal risk, and personal responsibility (Butcher, 1991). Such sensitive occupations include those of air traffic controller, airline pilot, police officer, firefighter, and nuclear power plant operator. Routine use of the MMPI-2 for personnel selection is not recommended. For many jobs the primary requirements are appropriate ability and training, and personality factors may be relatively unimportant or irrelevant. Consistent with the Americans with Disabilities Act, the psychological screening process, which typically includes administration of the MMPI-2, is undertaken only after conditional offers of employment have been extended to applicants. Results of psychological evaluations can lead to withdrawal of conditional offers.

Research data suggest that the MMPI and MMPI-2 can be used effectively to screen for psychopathology in nonclinical groups. Lachar (1974b) demonstrated that the MMPI could predict serious psychopathology leading to dropouts among Air Force cadets. More recently, Carbone, Cigrang, Todd, and Fiedler (1999) reported that MMPI-2 scores added to biographical information in predicting who did and did not complete basic military training. Strupp and Bloxom (1975) found that men with certain MMPI code types were likely to have difficulty with personal adjustment, graduating from college, finding a job, and deciding on a career. Richard, Wakefield, and Lewak (1990) reported that congruence of responses to MMPI items was a reliable predictor of marital satisfaction.

There also are data suggesting that the MMPI could be used to predict effective hotline workers (Evans, 1977), competent clergy (Jansen & Garvey, 1973), and successful businesspeople (Harrell & Harrell, 1973). The success of police applicant selection is well documented (e.g., Bernstein, 1980; Beutler, Storm, Kirkish, Scogin, & Gaines, 1985; Costello, Schoenfeld, & Kobos, 1982; Hartman, 1987; Inwald, 1988). The MMPI also has been used successfully in selecting physicians' assistants (Crovitz, Huse, & Lewis, 1973), medical assistants (Stone, Bassett, Brousseau, Demers, & Stiening, 1972), psychiatric residents (Garetz & Anderson, 1973), clinical psychology graduate students (Butcher, 1979), nurses (Kelly, 1974), firefighters (Avery, Mussio, & Payne, 1972), probation officers (Solway, Hays, & Zieben, 1976), and nuclear power plant personnel (Dunnette, Bownas, & Bosshardt, 1981). In virtually all of these studies the most effective way to use the MMPI has been to exclude persons with very elevated scores on one or more of the Clinical scales. Liao, Arvey, Butler, and Nutting (2000) reported small but significant relationships between some MMPI-2 scales and frequency and duration of injuries among firefighters. Higher scores on Scales 3 and 0 were associated with more frequent injuries, and higher scores on Scale 4 were associated with longer periods of time from injury to return to work. A puzzling finding was that higher scores on Scale 8 were associated with shorter periods of time from injury to return to work.

Detrick, Chibnall, and Rosso (2001) summarized studies of relationships between pre-employment MMPI-2 scores and subsequent job performance. Generally, higher scores on MMPI-2 scales were associated with poorer job performance (e.g., Hargrave & Hiatt, 1987; Hiatt & Hargrave, 1988; Pallone, 1992). Higher scores on Scales 4 and 9 were especially predictive of poor job performance (e.g., Bartol, 1991; Costello, Schneider, & Schoenfeld, 1996). Interestingly, Neal (1986) found that moderately high scores on the K scale were associated with more positive supervisory ratings.

Hargrave et al. (1994) compared MMPI and MMPI-2 scores of peace officers and concluded that the two versions of the test yielded comparable profiles. Flynn, Sipes, Grosenbach, and Ellsworth (1994) conducted a field project demonstrating the viability of using a computerized administration of the MMPI-2 to assess personality characteristics of military aviators that could be related to job success.

Kornfeld (1995) reported descriptive MMPI-2 data for Caucasian and ethnic minority applicants for police officer positions in small and medium towns. As had been reported previously for the MMPI, most applicants were quite defensive. Interestingly, the mean scores of Caucasian and ethnic minority applicants were quite similar. However, it should be noted that the minority sample included only five Hispanics, four African Americans, and two Asian Americans. Similarly defensive MMPI-2 results were also reported by Detrick et al. (2001) for police officer applicants in small to midsized suburban cities. Scores on the L and K scales were in the 60–65 T-score range. Differences between gendered and ungendered scores were trivial.

Detrick et al. (2001) compared MMPI-2 scores of their police officer applicants with scores on the Inwald Personality Inventory (IPI), a well-established instrument for predicting law enforcement job performance. Modest but significant correlations were obtained between MMPI-2 and IPI scores. Interestingly, relationships between the two instruments were stronger when non-K-corrected MMPI-2 scores were used. The issue of K-corrected versus non-K-corrected scores was discussed in detail in Chapters 3 and 9 of this book.

Sellbom, Fischler, et al. (2007) examined relationships between police officer integrity and misconduct and MMPI-2 scores. The MMPI-2s were administered to police officer candidates after a conditional offer of employment was rendered. For those who were eventually hired various measures of employment problems were noted (e.g., breaking rules and regulations, citizen complaints, supervisor ratings, and involuntary dismissal). Although high scores on Scales 8 and 9 and low scores on Scale 3 were related to problem behaviors, the RC3, RC4, RC6, and RC8 scale scores were even more predictive of problems. Consistent with other research reviewed in this book, non-K-corrected scores on the Clinical scales were more strongly related to problem behaviors than K-corrected scores.

Butcher (1994) reported data for 437 pilot applicants for a major airline. Consistent with earlier studies with the original MMPI, the applicants were generally quite defensive. Butcher speculated that because the L and K scales were developed in clinical settings, their utility in personnel selection may be limited and that new measures of defensiveness may be needed. The Superlative (S; Lim & Butcher, 1996) scale, which was described in Chapter 3 of this book, may prove to be useful in this regard. Because elevated scores on the MMPI-2 Clinical scales were quite rare in the pilot applicant sample, Butcher recommended that T scores greater than 60 should be considered extreme in these kinds of settings.

The Negative Work Attitudes (WRK) Content scale was developed to measure personality characteristics that might be associated with poor job performance. Butcher, Graham, Williams, and Ben-Porath (1990) reported some preliminary data concerning WRK scale scores of men who could be assumed to have differing levels of work performance. Airline pilots, who were assumed to have highly successful work skills, scored well below the mean for the MMPI-2 normative sample, and active-duty military personnel, who volunteered to participate and were as a group not experiencing occupational problems, scored at about the mean for the MMPI-2 normative sample. Alcoholics and hospitalized psychiatric patients, who typically have very poor work histories, scored well above the mean for the normative sample. Although these group data are encouraging, research is needed in which scores on the WRK scale are compared with measures of actual job performance. It also should be recognized that the WRK scale appears to be saturated with general maladjustment/demoralization and that test takers who are demoralized or depressed are likely to have elevated WRK scale scores that may have little to do with negative work attitudes.

Because most test takers in personnel selection situations have scores suggestive of defensive responding, this issue deserves careful consideration. Some clinicians re-administer the MMPI-2 when an initial testing results in scores indicating a degree of defensiveness that invalidates the results. Other clinicians deal with anticipated defensiveness by instructing test takers to avoid trying to present themselves in an unrealistically favorable way when responding to MMPI-2 items. Several research studies have addressed the effects of these practices on test scores.

Butcher et al. (1997) examined MMPI-2 scores of airline pilot applicants. They found that 73% of the applicants produced valid results on an initial testing. The applicants who produced invalid results were asked to complete the MMPI-2 again after having received altered instructions that explained how the MMPI-2 scales were constructed and being told that because of defensiveness their results would not help the psychologists understand them. On retest 79% of the applicants who initially produced invalid results produced valid results. Their Validity scale scores were less defensive and resembled scores of applicants who had produced valid results on the first administration of the MMPI-2. Similar results were obtained by Cigrang and Staal (2001) in their study of applicants for military training instructor positions. They found that 83% of applicants who produced invalid MMPI-2 results on a first testing produced valid results when retested with altered instructions that stressed that they should be more open when responding to the MMPI-2 items.

Butcher, Atlis, and Fang (2000) reasoned that, because giving altered instructions designed to reduce defensiveness deviates from standardized test administration procedures, it is important to know to what extent such altered instructions affect scores of people more generally. Do persons who complete the MMPI-2 initially with such altered instructions obtain different scores from persons who complete the test with standard instructions? A sample of 218 college students completed the MMPI-2 with altered instructions very similar to those used in the Butcher, Morfitt, Rouse, and Holden (1997) study, and their scores were compared with 150 college students who completed the test with standard instructions. The scores of male students in the two conditions did not differ significantly for any scales. For women, students who received the altered instructions had lower scores on the L, K, and S scales. However, the differences were judged to be trivial.

In summary, persons completing the MMPI-2 in personnel selection situations often produce moderately defensive scores, and some applicants respond so defensively that their results are considered invalid. When asked to retake the MMPI-2 with instructions to be more open and honest in responding to items, most applicants produce valid results. Because the use of altered instructions intended to avoid anticipated defensiveness during initial assessment does not seem to affect scores significantly, the standard MMPI-2 norms can be utilized in such circumstances. Given that research concerning this issue is rather preliminary, it is this author's recommendation that standard instructions for completing the MMPI-2 be used in initial administration with applicants. However, for those applicants who produce invalid results, re-administration of the MMPI-2 with emphasis on following the standard instructions may produce valid protocols.

Pearson Assessments markets a computerized MMPI-2 interpretive report intended for use in personnel selection situations (Butcher, 2001). This report provides profiles of scores on the standard Validity and Clinical scales and several Supplementary scales and lists of scores on many other Supplementary scales. In keeping with Americans with Disabilities Act guidelines, both gendered and nongendered T scores are provided for the Clinical and Content scales. A narrative interpretation of scores and an Adjustment Rating Report also are available. Based on a set of MMPI-2 decision rules, examinees are rated on several important adjustment variables: Openness to Evaluation, Social Facility, Addiction Potential, Stress Tolerance, and Overall Adjustment.

Although no studies have yet been published concerning the validity of the evaluations provided in the *Revised Personnel System*, Butcher (1989b) summarized several studies utilizing the MMPI version of the report. Butcher (1988) compared ratings of overall level of adjustment of airline pilot applicants based on the decision rules used in the *Revised Personnel System* with corresponding ratings by experienced clinicians. There was striking agreement between the computer rules and the experienced clinicians. Muller and Bruno (1988) compared evaluations of police applicants based on the *Revised Personnel System* decision rules with evaluations based on other data (interview, background check, polygraph). The MMPI decision rules were quite effective in identifying persons who subsequently were rejected on the basis of other data as psychologically unsuited for the job of police officer. Although these data concerning the validity of evaluations based on the *Revised Personnel System* are encouraging, research is needed in which evaluations based on the *Revised Personnel System* are compared with reliable measures of actual job performance.

CORRECTIONAL SETTINGS

The MMPI was used in prison settings as early as 1945. Dahlstrom et al. (1975) reviewed the major ways in which the MMPI has been used in correctional settings and presented lists of references concerning such use. Megargee (2006) provided a comprehensive account of how the MMPI-2 can be used in criminal justice and correctional settings. Megargee and Carbonell (1995) described the various ways in which the MMPI and MMPI-2 have been used to classify prisoners and to predict their behavior while incarcerated and after their release from prison. The most sophisticated use of the MMPI-2 in correctional settings involves a configural system developed by Megargee, Bohn, Meyer, and Sink (1979) for the original MMPI. Megargee (1994, 1997) revised the classification system for the MMPI-2. Megargee's system and other ways in which the MMPI has been used in correctional settings are described in Chapter 13 of this book.

11

⟁ An Interpretive Strategy

In 1956 Paul Meehl made a strong plea for a "good cookbook" for psychological test interpretation. Meehl's proposed cookbook was to include detailed rules for categorizing test responses and empirically determined extratest correlates for each category of test responses. The rules could be applied automatically by a nonprofessional worker (or by a computer) with the interpretive statements selected for a particular type of protocol from a larger library of statements. Although efforts have been made to construct such cookbooks (e.g., Gilberstadt & Duker, 1965; Marks & Seeman, 1963; Marks, Seeman, and Haller, 1974), the current status of psychological test interpretation is far from the automatic process Meehl envisioned. All tests, including the MMPI-2, provide opportunities for standardized observation of the current behavior of examinees. On the basis of these test behaviors, inferences are made about other extratest behaviors. The clinician serves as both information processor and clinical judge in the assessment process. The major purpose of this chapter is to suggest one approach (but by no means the only one) to using MMPI-2 data to make meaningful inferences about examinees.

The MMPI-2 should be used to generate hypotheses or inferences about an examinee, for the interpretive data presented earlier will not apply completely and unfailingly to each person with specified MMPI-2 scores. In interpreting MMPI-2 scores, one is dealing with probabilities. A particular extratest characteristic is more likely than another to apply to a person with a higher score on a scale than a person with a lower scale on that scale, but there can never be complete certainty that it will. The inferences generated from an individual's MMPI-2 scores should thus be validated against other test and nontest information available about that individual.

The MMPI-2 is most valuable as an assessment tool when it is used in conjunction with other psychological tests, interview and observational data, and appropriate background information. Although blind interpretation of the MMPI-2 certainly is possible and in fact is the procedure involved in computerized interpretations, such interpretations should be used only to generate hypotheses, inasmuch as more accurate person-specific inferences are likely to occur when the MMPI-2 is viewed in the context of all information available about an individual. This position is consistent with research findings by investigators such as Kostlan (1954) and Sines (1959).

Two kinds of interpretive inferences can be made on the basis of MMPI-2 data. First, some characteristics of an examinee with particular MMPI-2 scores are those that differentiate that examinee from other persons in a particular setting (e.g., hospital or clinic). For example, it is possible to infer from a hospitalized patient's MMPI-2 scores that he or she is likely to abuse alcohol or other substances. Because most patients do not abuse substances, this inference clearly differentiates this particular patient from most other patients. A second kind of inference is one that involves a characteristic common to many individuals in a particular setting. For example, the inference that a hospitalized psychiatric patient does not know how to handle stress in an effective manner is one that probably is true for most patients in that setting. Although the differential, patient-specific inferences tend to be more useful than the general ones, the latter are important in understanding an individual case, particularly for clinicians and others involved in the treatment process who might not have a clear understanding of what behaviors are shared by most persons in a particular setting.

Whereas Meehl envisioned the assessment process as dealing exclusively with nontest behaviors that are directly and empirically tied to specific aspects of test performance, the current status of the assessment field is such that only limited relationships of this kind have been identified. Often it is possible and necessary to make higher-order inferences about examinees based on a conceptualization of their personalities. For example, currently no clear data indicate that a particular kind of MMPI-2 profile is predictive of a future suicide attempt. However, if we have inferred from an individual's MMPI-2 scores that he or she is extremely depressed, agitated, and emotionally uncomfortable; is impulsive; and shows poor judgment much of the time, the higher-order inference that such a person has a higher risk of suicide than patients in general is a logical one. Although it is legitimate to rely on such higher-order inferences in interpreting the MMPI-2, one should have greater confidence in the inferences that are more directly related to MMPI-2 scores and configurations.

A GENERAL STRATEGY

In his own clinical work this author utilizes an approach to MMPI-2 interpretation that involves trying to answer the following questions about each MMPI-2 protocol:

1. What was the test-taking attitude of the examinee, and how should this attitude be taken into account in interpreting the protocol?
2. What is the general level of adjustment (or maladjustment) of the examinee?
3. What other characteristics (e.g., symptoms, attitudes, defenses) can be inferred about or expected from the examinee?

4. What diagnostic labels are consistent with the MMPI-2 scores produced by the examinee?
5. What are the implications for treatment of the examinee?

Test-Taking Attitude

The ideal examinee is one who approaches the task of completing the MMPI-2 in a serious and cooperative manner. This individual reads each MMPI-2 item and responds to the item in an honest, direct manner. When such an ideal situation is realized, the examiner can be confident that the test responses are a representative sample of the examinee's behavior and can proceed with the interpretation of the protocol. However, as suggested in Chapter 3 of this book, for various reasons examinees may approach the MMPI-2 with an attitude that deviates from the ideal situation described here. Specification of test-taking attitude for each individual examinee is important because such differential attitudes must be taken into account in generating inferences from the MMPI-2 scores. In addition, such attitudes may be predictive of similar approaches to other nontest aspects of the examinee's life situation.

Qualitative aspects of an examinee's test behavior often serve to augment inferences based on the more quantitative scores and indexes. One such factor is the amount of time required to complete the MMPI-2. As stated in Chapter 2 of this book, the typical examinee takes between 60 and 90 minutes to complete the test. Excessively long testing times may be indicative of indecisiveness, psychomotor retardation, confusion, or passive resistance to the testing procedures. Extremely short times suggest that examinees were quite impulsive in responding to the test items or did not read and consider their content.

Examinees occasionally become very tense, agitated, or otherwise upset in the MMPI-2 test-taking situation. Such behavior may be predictive of similar responses to other stressful situations. Some examinees, who are obsessive or indecisive, write qualifications to their true–false responses in the margins of the answer sheet.

Although the qualitative features of test performance just discussed can offer important information about an examinee, the Validity scales are the primary objective sources of inferences about test-taking attitude. The Cannot Say (?) score indicates the number of items omitted by the examinee. A large number of omitted items may indicate indecisiveness, ambivalence, or an attempt to avoid admitting negative things about oneself without deliberately lying. Examinees who answer all or most of the items are not availing themselves of this simplistic way of attempting to present a positive picture of themselves.

The Variable Response Inconsistency (VRIN) and True Response Inconsistency (TRIN) scales offer additional information concerning the possibility of response sets that can invalidate the protocol (see Chapter 3 of this book). High scores on the VRIN scale indicate that the examinee probably responded to the items without reading and considering their content. When the TRIN-scale T score is high (in either the true or false direction), the possibility of a yea-saying or nay-saying response set must be considered.

Scores on the F scale reflect the extent to which an examinee's responses to a finite pool of items compare to those of the normative sample, with higher F-scale scores reflecting greater deviance. Scores that are considerably higher than average suggest that examinees are admitting to many clearly deviant behaviors and attitudes. There are several reasons for such admissions (see Chapter 3 of this book). Examinees might have responded to the test items randomly or with a deliberate intention of appearing very emotionally disturbed. Another possibility is that the examinees are emotionally disabled and are using the MMPI-2 as a vehicle to express a cry for help. F-scale scores that are considerably below average indicate that the examinees are admitting fewer than an average number of deviant attitudes and behaviors. They may be overly defensive and trying to create unrealistically positive pictures of themselves. F-scale scores in the average range indicate that the examinees have been neither hypercritical of themselves nor overly denying in responding to the test items.

Whereas F-scale scores provide information about examinees' attitudes in responding to the first 361 items of the test, the Back-Page Infrequency (F_B) scale provides similar information for items that occur later in the test booklet. F_B-scale scores should be interpreted very similarly to those of the standard F scale. The F_p scale was developed to detect overreporting in settings where there is a high base rate of serious psychopathology (see Chapter 3 of this book). Compared with the F scale, high scores (T > 100) on the F_p scale are less likely to indicate genuine psychopathology and more likely to indicate overreporting. Very high scores on the Symptom Validity Scale (FBS) suggest that the examinee reported a large number of responses that are unusual even for someone with serious medical problems (see Chapter 3 of this book).

Above-average scores on the L scale indicate that examinees may have presented themselves as more virtuous than they really are. When L-scale scores are moderately high, the protocol can be interpreted but adjustments should be made to take into account the examinee's defensiveness (see Chapter 3 of this book). Extremely high scores on the L scale indicate that the protocol is invalid and should not be interpreted (see Chapter 3 of this book).

The K scale can serve as another index of defensiveness. Above-average K-scale scores indicate that examinees have been overly defensive, whereas below-average scores indicate lack of defensiveness and a highly self-critical attitude (see Chapter 3 of this book). Average-range scores on the K scale suggest that examinees have been neither overly defensive nor overly self-critical in endorsing the MMPI-2 items. As discussed in Chapter 3 of this book, high scores on the S scale also indicate an attempt to present oneself as highly virtuous, responsible, free of psychological problems, having few or no flaws, and getting along well with others.

The configuration of the Validity scales also is important for understanding examinees' test-taking attitudes. In general, persons who are approaching the test with the intention of presenting themselves in an overly favorable way have L-, K-, and S-scale scores greater than scores on the F, F_B, F_p and FBS scales. On the other hand, persons who are using the test to be overly self-critical and/or to exaggerate their problems produce L-, K-, and S-scale scores that are significantly lower than the F-, F_B-, F_P-, and FBS-scale scores.

In summary, a first step in interpreting the MMPI-2 is to make some judgments concerning the test-taking attitude of the examinee. If the decision is made that the test was approached in a manner that invalidates the protocol (e.g., inconsistent responding, underreporting, overreporting), no additional interpretation of the scores is in order. Invalid protocols do not tell us anything meaningful about test takers other than how they likely approached the MMPI-2. Scores other than those on the Validity scales should not be viewed as providing an accurate assessment of the test taker. If there are less extreme response sets operating (e.g., defensiveness or exaggeration), it may be possible to make some tentative interpretations of the profile, but adjustments in interpretations must be made to take into account these response sets.

Adjustment Level

There are several important components to psychological adjustment level. First, how emotionally comfortable or uncomfortable are examinees? Second, how well do they carry out the responsibilities of their life situations regardless of how conflicted and uncomfortable they might be? For most people these two components are very much related. Persons who are psychologically comfortable tend to function well and vice versa. However, for certain individuals (e.g., those with anxiety disorder diagnoses) a great deal of discomfort and turmoil can be present, but adequate functioning continues. For other persons (e.g., some individuals with diagnoses of chronic schizophrenia or antisocial personality disorder), serious impairment in coping with responsibilities can be found without great emotional discomfort. The MMPI-2 permits inferences about both of these aspects of adjustment level.

Several MMPI-2 scales are excellent indicators of experienced distress. Elevated scores on Clinical Scale 2, the Depression (DEP) Content scale, and the RCd and RC2 scales suggest that the examinee is feeling depressed and demoralized. Elevated scores on Clinical Scale 7, the Anxiety (ANX) Content scale, and the RC7 scale indicate that the examinee is likely to be experiencing considerable anxiety.

Overall elevation on the Clinical scales is a simple but meaningful index of the extent to which an examinee is not coping well with the demands of his or her life situation. In general, as more of the Clinical scales are elevated (and as the degree of elevation increases), the probability is greater that serious psychopathology and impaired functioning are present. An index of scale elevation can be obtained by calculating the average T scores for eight Clinical scales (excluding Scales 5 and 0), with higher average scores indicating poorer coping. Graham, Barthlow, Stein, Ben-Porath, and McNulty (2002) demonstrated that this simple index was strongly related to maladjustment in mental health center clients as assessed by intake workers and therapists. Scores on several other MMPI-2 scales also are related to coping. Welsh's Anxiety (A) scale, Barron's Ego Strength (Es) scale, and the RCd scale are related to coping. High scorers on the A and RCd scales and low scorers on the Es scale are not likely to be coping very well. The RC2 (Low Positive Emotions) scale indicates someone who lacks positive emotional engagement with the world. Scale 7 (Psychasthenia) and the RC7 (Dysfunctional Negative Emotions) scale are good measures of anxiety, irritability, and other forms of aversive reactivity. It may also be helpful to check responses to the critical items. These items deal with some blatantly psychotic behaviors and attitudes, sexual deviation, excessive use of alcohol, homicidal and/or suicidal impulses, and other manifestations of serious maladjustment. As was discussed in Chapter 6 of this book, care should be taken not to overinterpret these individual item responses. Because of concerns about test security, individual items cannot be reproduced in this book. However, the item numbers for the various critical item categories are presented in Appendix A of this book.

Characteristic Traits and Behaviors

A next step in the interpretive process is to describe the test taker's symptoms, traits, behaviors, attitudes, defenses, and so forth in enough detail to allow an overall understanding of the person. Although not every protocol permits inferences about all of the following points, in general I try to make statements or inferences about each of these:

1. symptoms
2. major needs (e.g., dependency, achievement, autonomy)
3. perceptions of the environment, particularly of significant other people in the examinee's life situation
4. reactions to stress (e.g., coping strategies, defenses)
5. self-concept
6. sexual identification
7. emotional control
8. interpersonal relationships
9. psychological resources

Inferences about these various aspects of behavior and personality are based on analysis of defined code types and scores on individual Clinical, Content, RC, PSY-5, and Supplementary scales. Code types and scores on the various scales should be considered, the appropriate sections of this book should be consulted, and appropriate hypotheses or inferences for each source should be recorded for additional processing.

Because inferences based on well-defined code types are more likely to apply to a particular examinee with that code type than inferences based on a single MMPI-2 scale, we generally begin by determining if a protocol has a defined code type (see Chapter 5 of this book for details concerning defined code types). If no three- or two-point defined code type is identified, no inferences are generated on the basis of configurations of the Clinical scales, and you should consider each Clinical scale individually. However, if you determine that there is a defined code type, you should consult Chapter 5 of this book and generate inferences associated with that code type. If the scales in the defined code type are elevated (T > 65), you should include inferences having to do with symptoms as well as those having to do with personality characteristics. However, if the scales in the defined code type have T scores between 60 and 65, you should emphasize inferences about personality characteristics and not those associated with symptoms.

Next you should examine each MMPI-2 score and determine if any inferences are appropriate for a score at its level. If a defined code type was identified, you should not consider individually the Clinical scales that make up the code type. However, other Clinical scales should be examined to determine if inferences are appropriate for scores at their levels. Then you would move on to consider all other MMPI-2 scores, generating additional inferences about scales when their scores indicate that this is appropriate.

High scores on the Clinical scales typically suggest many inferences with varying content. Obviously, not all of the inferences for a scale will apply to everyone with a high score on that scale. For example, high scores on Scale 4 lead to inferences that include family problems, antisocial behaviors, and negative emotionality (e.g., depression and worry). Examination of some other MMPI-2 scales can sometimes clarify the meaning of a high score on a Clinical scale for a particular person. The Harris–Lingoes subscales (see Chapter 6 of this book) may indicate greater focus on some inferences over others. For example, if a high Scale 4 score is accompanied by a high score on the Pd2 subscale (Authority Problems), you should focus on the antisocial aspects. However, if the high Scale 4 score is accompanied by a high score on the Pd1 subscale (Family Problems) but not on the Pd2 subscale, you should focus on the inferences having to do with family problems. Obviously, if scores on the Harris–Lingoes subscales are very similar to each other, these scales will not be helpful in clarifying the meaning of a high Clinical scale score.

The Content scales can also be used to clarify the interpretation of high scores on Clinical scales. Again, let's consider the example of a high score on Scale 4, suggesting possible antisocial behaviors, family problems, and negative affect. If you find that the Antisocial Practices (ASP) Content scale also is high, you should focus on the antisocial inferences for Scale 4. However, if the ASP scale is not very high but the Family Problems (FAM) Content scale is high, you should focus on the inferences having to do with family problems and not on those having to do with antisocial behaviors.

Examination of the Restructured Clinical (RC) scales can also help focus interpretations of the Clinical scales. If there is a high score for a Clinical scale (e.g., Scale 4) and the corresponding RC scale (e.g., RC4) is also high, the focus should be on the core construct of the Clinical scale (e.g., antisocial behavior). However, if a Clinical scale score is high but the corresponding RC scale score is not high, it is likely that the Clinical scale is high because the test taker endorsed many items having to do with demoralization and not because of characteristics associated with the core construct. In this case, you would expect the Demoralization (RCd) scale also to be high. Occasionally, an RC scale score will be high and its corresponding Clinical scale score will not be high. In such cases, the high RC scale score suggests a focus on the core constructs that the scale assesses. The absence of a high score on the corresponding Clinical scale is likely due to the absence of great personal distress, and you would not expect the RCd scale to be high.

The Content Component scales can potentially be of assistance in determining the focus of inferences associated with a high Content scale score. Much like the Harris–Lingoes subscales for the Clinical scales, the Content Component scales can clarify the kinds of symptoms and behaviors associated with a high score on a particular Content scale. For example, if there is a high score on the Anger (ANG) Content scale that is accompanied by a higher score on the Explosive Behavior (ANG1) scale than on the Irritability (ANG2) Content Component scale, you should emphasize the inferences based on the ANG scale that have to do with problems with anger control. However, if there is a high Anger (ANG) Content scale score with the ANG2 scale score higher than the ANG1 scale score, inferences about problems with anger control are less critical. Ben-Porath and Sherwood (1993) emphasized that the Content Component scales for a particular Content scale should be interpreted only when the T score on the Content scale is greater than 60 and when there is a difference of at least 10 T-score points between Content Component scale scores.

This part of the interpretive process typically will yield a large number of inferences. Because some of the MMPI-2 scales are not independent of each other, there may be considerable overlap in the inferences that have been generated. It is a simple matter to eliminate obviously redundant ones. Initially there may appear to be inconsistencies among the various inferences that have been generated. You should first consider the possibility that the apparent inconsistencies are accurately reflecting different facets of the examinee's personality and behavior. Consider, for example, a profile with high scores (T > 65) on both Scales 2 and 4. The Scale 2 score suggests sensitivity to the needs and feelings of others, whereas the Scale 4 score suggests insensitivity to the needs and feelings of others. It is possible that the same individual may show both characteristics at different times. In fact, research with the 24/42 code type indicates that persons with this code type tend to alternate between periods of great sensitivity to others and periods of gross insensitivity to others.

Sometimes inconsistencies in inferences cannot be reconciled as easily as in this example. In these instances you must decide in which inferences to have the most confidence. In general, inferences based on defined code types will be more accurate than those based on a single scale. Greater confidence should be placed in inferences that occur for several scales than in those that occur for only a single scale. Inferences based on scales with very high scores should receive greater emphasis than those based on moderately high scores. Finally, greater emphasis should be placed on inferences based on scales that are more valid for the particular characteristic in question. While beginning MMPI-2 users may have limited information about relative validity of scales, as users become more informed about the test, more information will be available to inform this issue.

As mentioned earlier in this chapter, some inferences about an examinee do not result directly from scores on a scale or from configurations of scales. Rather, they are higher-order inferences generated from a basic understanding of the examinee. For example, there are no data indicating that scores on particular MMPI-2 scales are predictive of suicide attempts. However, it would be reasonable to be concerned about such attempts in a person whose MMPI-2 scores led to inferences of serious depression, agitation, impulsivity, and poor judgment.

Diagnostic Impressions

Although the usefulness of psychiatric diagnoses has been questioned by many clinicians, referral sources often request information about diagnosis. In addition, it often is necessary to assign diagnostic labels for purposes such as insurance claims, disability status, or competency status. Many of the interpretive sections in earlier chapters of this book presented diagnostic inferences for two- and three-point code types and for individual scales. Inferences relevant to diagnoses would have been recorded earlier as you considered code types and scores on the individual scales. You should keep in mind that one cannot assign diagnoses based solely on MMPI-2 data. The criteria for most diagnoses include information not available from test data (e.g., age at onset of symptoms; previous occurrences of the problem behavior). You should determine the diagnoses that are most consistent with the MMPI-2 data and then consider these possible diagnoses in the context of everything else that is known about a particular person.

In using the MMPI-2 for diagnostic purposes, you should consider that most research studies concerning diagnostic inferences were based on the original MMPI. However, because of the continuity between the original MMPI and the MMPI-2, data based on the original instrument are applicable to the MMPI-2. It also is important to know that most of the studies of the relationship between MMPI data and diagnoses were conducted prior to the publication of the DSM-IV. In presenting diagnostic inferences for particular scores and configurations of scores in this book, the earlier diagnostic labels were translated into more contemporary ones.

Treatment Implications

A primary goal of many assessments is to make meaningful recommendations about treatment. Sometimes, when demand for treatment exceeds the resources available, the decision is whether or not to accept a particular person for treatment. Such a decision may involve clinical judgment about how much the person needs treatment as well as how likely the person is to continue in treatment and respond favorably. When differential treatment procedures are available, the assessment may be useful in deciding which procedures are likely to be most effective. When the decision has been made before the assessment that a person will receive a particular treatment procedure, the assessment still can be helpful in providing information about problem areas to be considered in treatment and alerting the therapist (or others involved in treatment) to assets and liabilities that could facilitate or hinder progress in therapy. The MMPI-2 can provide information relevant to all of these aspects of treatment. Butcher (1990b) and Finn (1996, 2007) have provided interesting descriptions of how the MMPI-2 can be useful in relation to treatment. Results of a meta-analysis reported by Poston and Hanson (2010) indicated that psychological assessment as a treatment intervention produces positive outcomes and enhances the treatment process.

Many of the inferences generated from well-defined code types and scores on individual scales have direct relevance to treatment considerations. Of special importance is the pattern of scores on the Validity scales. A defensive pattern (L-, K-, and S-scale scores considerably higher than scores on the F-family of scales) suggests that the examinee is not willing to talk about problems or symptoms and is not likely to be very receptive to therapeutic intervention. By contrast, an examinee whose scores on the F-family of scales are considerably higher than the L-, K-, and S-scale scores is admitting to problems, symptoms, and emotional distress. This person is likely to be motivated to begin treatment and talk about problems.

MMPI-2 indicators of personal distress and emotional turmoil are relevant to treatment planning. Generally, persons in more distress are more receptive to therapeutic intervention and may be willing to tolerate the effort and discomfort of therapy in order to feel better. As discussed in earlier chapters, primary indicators of distress include the Demoralization (RCd) scale, Welsh's Anxiety (A) scale, Clinical Scales 2 and 7, the RC2 and RC7 scales, and Content scales such as Depression, Fears, and Anxiety.

Well-defined code types and high scores on individual scales can provide additional information relevant to treatment, and those inferences would have been recorded earlier in the interpretive process as each of these sources was considered. At this point in the process, you can simply go back through the recorded inferences and extract those that have direct relevance to treatment. For example, high Scale 4 scorers typically are not accepting responsibility for any of their difficulties, may agree to treatment only to avoid more unpleasant circumstances, and tend to terminate treatment prematurely. On the other hand, persons with the 27/72 code type are agreeable to treatment because of their emotional distress, tend to remain in treatment longer than most patients, and can be expected to show slow but steady progress in treatment. These are just a few of the treatment-related inferences stemming from examination of code types and individual scales.

Several of the MMPI-2 scales were developed specifically to provide information about treatment. The Ego Strength (Es) scale, which was discussed in Chapter 8 of this book, was designed to predict response to psychotherapy. In dealing with individuals who are admitting problems and voluntarily seeking treatment, higher Es-scale scores indicate a more favorable response to individual psychotherapy. With other kinds of persons and/or treatment procedures the relationship between Es-scale scores and treatment outcome is less clear, but in general, higher Es-scale scores can be interpreted as suggestive of greater psychological resources that can be used in treatment. However, it should be noted that persons who approach the MMPI-2 in a defensive manner tend to have relatively high Es-scale scores that are not indicative of a positive prognosis for treatment. Also, persons who are exaggerating problems and symptoms tend to have very low Es-scale scores, which do not necessarily indicate a negative prognosis.

The Negative Treatment Indicators (TRT) Content scale was designed to assess attitudes that would indicate a negative response to treatment. Higher scorers on the TRT scale may be unwilling or unable to change their life situations, pessimistic about the possibility of positive change, uncomfortable discussing problems with others, and rigid and noncompliant in therapy. A limitation of the TRT scale is that its scores are strongly related to maladjustment in general and depression and demoralization in particular. Therefore, persons who are depressed, demoralized, or generally maladjusted may have elevated TRT-scale scores that do not necessarily reflect negative attitudes about treatment.

As was discussed earlier in relation to characteristic traits and behaviors, many of the inferences about treatment will not come directly from scores on specific MMPI-2 scales or configurations of scales. Rather, they are higher-order inferences based on other inferences that already have been made about the examinee. For example, if it has been inferred from the MMPI-2 that an examinee is in a great deal of emotional turmoil, it can further be inferred that this person is likely to be motivated enough to change in psychotherapy. On the other hand, if it has been inferred that a person is very reluctant to accept responsibility for her or his own behavior and blames others for problems and shortcomings, the prognosis for traditional psychotherapy is very poor. A person who has been described on the basis of MMPI-2 scores as very suggestible is apt to respond more favorably to direct advice than to insight-oriented therapy. A person described as antisocial (based on elevations on Scales 4 and 9), who enters therapy rather than going to jail, is likely to terminate therapy prematurely. Obviously, there are many other examples of higher-order inferences related to treatment.

As was discussed earlier in this chapter in relation to characteristic traits and behaviors, inferences based on a particular set of MMPI-2 scores may include some inconsistencies. These should be addressed in the same manner described earlier, giving greater weight to the inferences based on code types and those based on higher scores on individual scales.

Specific Referral Questions

The interpretive strategy that has just been discussed is intended to help the clinician generate as many meaningful inferences as possible about test takers' MMPI-2s. It should be recognized that the MMPI-2 sometimes is administered as part of an evaluation intended to address specific questions or issues. For example, a court-ordered evaluation may ask about competency to stand trial, a police department may want recommendations about which applicants to hire, or another psychologist may want an opinion about the suicide potential of a client. Unless these specific questions or issues are dealt with directly, it is unlikely that the MMPI-2 interpretation will be regarded as useful. Sometimes the MMPI-2 data are directly relevant to the issue of concern. For example, scores on the substance abuse scales

(MAC-R, AAS) permit inferences about alcohol or other drug problems. At other times, conclusions about issues of concern are dependent on clinical integration of many different kinds of MMPI-2 data and higher-order inferences.

AN ILLUSTRATIVE CASE

To illustrate the strategy just discussed, an actual case (Jeff) will now be considered, and a step-by-step analysis of the MMPI-2 protocol will be presented. As a practice exercise, readers can interpret Jeff's scores and then compare their interpretations with the ones presented in this section. All of Jeff's scores can be found in the Extended Score Report that is appended to this chapter.

Background Information

Jeff is a 24-year-old Caucasian man. He has never been married and lives with his older sister and her family. He graduated from high school with somewhat below-average grades. He did not get into trouble in school. He did not participate in sports or other school activities, and he did not have any close friends. He has never had a serious romantic relationship. Since completing high school he has had several jobs in fast-food restaurants and service stations, and he currently is unemployed.

The MMPI-2 was administered to Jeff when he requested services at a local community mental health center. He was cooperative and completed the MMPI-2 in about 90 minutes. Jeff had not previously been involved with mental health services. He was referred to the mental health center by emergency room staff at a local hospital. Apparently, during a period of excessive drinking he took a large number of aspirin. He was treated at the emergency room and released. Jeff admitted that he had been feeling increasingly upset and depressed lately. His sister had encouraged him to seek professional help, and she came with him for his intake appointment.

Test-Taking Attitude

Jeff completed the MMPI-2 in about an average amount of time for a mental health outpatient, indicating that he was neither excessively indecisive nor impulsive in responding to the items. He omitted no items, suggesting that he was cooperative and did not use this rather simple way of avoiding unfavorable self-statements. The VRIN-scale T score of 46 does not suggest random responding. The TRIN scale raw score of 9 (T = 50) is not suggestive of all-true or all-false responding. Jeff's T score of 55 on the F scale suggests that he was admitting somewhat more than an average number of deviant attitudes and behaviors. The F-scale score is not high enough to suggest random responding, an overreporting response set, or any other approach to the test that would invalidate the protocol. His T score of 71 on the Back-Page Infrequency (F_B) scale suggests that he endorsed more items appearing later in the test booklet than in the first part; however, the score is not high enough to suggest invalidity. The Infrequency–Psychopathology (F_P) scale T score of 41 is below average and does not suggest overreporting, and his Symptom Validity Scale (FBS) T score of 59 suggests somewhat more than an average number of somatic complaints but not enough to suggest noncredible responding.

His T score of 48 on the L scale is slightly below average, so we may infer that he was not claiming virtues and other positive characteristics that he does not really have. His S-scale T score of 41 also is somewhat below average, indicating that he did not try to present himself as highly virtuous, responsible, and free of psychological problems. Jeff's T score of 41 on the K scale indicates that he was not defensive. In fact, he was somewhat self-critical in responding to the items, an approach that is common among persons seeking mental health services. In summary, Jeff seems to have approached the MMPI-2 in an honest and open manner, admitting to some symptoms and problem behaviors. There are no indications that he approached the MMPI-2 in an invalid manner. Therefore, interpretation of the Clinical, Content, Restructured Clinical, Personality Psychopathology Five, and Supplementary scales can be undertaken.

Adjustment Level

Several MMPI-2 scales are excellent indicators of experienced distress. Elevated scores on Clinical Scale 2 (T = 81), the Depression (DEP) Content scale (T = 77), and RCd (T = 79) suggest that Jeff is feeling depressed and demoralized. Elevated scores on Clinical Scale 7 (T = 77), the Anxiety (ANX) Content scale (T = 80), and RC7 (T = 77) indicate that he also may be experiencing considerable anxiety and may report difficulties in concentrating and attending.

Overall elevation on the Clinical scales is a simple but meaningful index of the extent to which Jeff is not coping well with the demands of his life situation. In general, as more of the Clinical scales are elevated (and as the degree of elevation increases), the probability is greater that serious psychopathology and impaired functioning are present. An index of scale elevation can be obtained by calculating the average T score for eight Clinical scales (excluding Scales 5 and 0), with higher average scores indicating poorer coping. Jeff's mean score of 63.9 (indicated as Profile Elevation on the Extended Score Report) suggests that he is coping less well than the average person and is likely to experience impairment in important aspects of functioning. Scores on several other MMPI-2 scales also are related to coping. Jeff's high scores on Welsh's Anxiety scale (T = 81) and the RCd scale (T = 79) indicate that he is not coping very well. His very low score on the Ego Strength (Es) scale (T = 30) suggests that Jeff has limited psychological resources for coping with the demands of his life situation. In summary, Jeff appears to be experiencing considerable emotional distress and is not coping very effectively.

Characteristic Traits and Behaviors

At this point in the interpretation we want to generate as many inferences about Jeff as we possibly can from his MMPI-2 scores. A first step in trying to generate inferences is to determine if Jeff has a well-defined code type and, if he does, to consult Chapter 5 of this book to generate inferences based on the code type. It is best to start with the most complex code type for which interpretive information is available. When scales 5 and 0 are excluded, Jeff's three highest scores are on Clinical Scales 2, 7, and 6 (in that order). Because there is not a five T-score point difference between scores on Scale 6 (his third-highest Clinical scale) and Scale 3 (his fourth-highest Clinical scale), a defined three-point code type does not exist. Thus, no inferences are made on the basis of the configuration of these three highest scales. However, there is a nine T-score point difference between his scores on Scale 7 (his second-highest Clinical scale) and Scale 6 (his third highest Clinical scale). Thus, Jeff has a defined two-point code type.

27/72 Code Type

This is a commonly occurring code type among mental health outpatients, and considerable information is available concerning its correlates. The two scales in the code type are quite elevated and the code type is well defined. Therefore, we are confident that inferences based on the code type are likely to fit him well. Because the scales in the code type are quite elevated, we can make inferences both about symptoms and personality characteristics commonly associated with the code type.

Reference to Chapter 5 of this book indicates that numerous inferences about Jeff can be made on the basis of the 27/72 code type. He is reporting symptoms of clinical depression that may include weight loss, slow personal tempo, and slowed thought processes. He seems to be extremely pessimistic about the world in general and more specifically about the likelihood of overcoming his problems, and he tends to brood about his problems much of the time.

Jeff also is reporting symptoms of anxiety. He is likely to feel anxious, nervous, tense, high-strung, and jumpy. He worries excessively and is vulnerable to real and imagined threat. He tends to anticipate problems before they occur and to overreact to minor stress. Vague somatic symptoms and complaints of fatigue, tiredness, and exhaustion may be reported.

Jeff seems to have a strong need for achievement and for recognition of his accomplishments. He has high expectations for himself, and he feels guilty when he falls short of his goals. He tends to be indecisive and to harbor feelings of inadequacy, insecurity, and inferiority. He is intropunitive, blaming himself for the problems in his life. He tends to be rigid in his thinking and problem solving, and he is meticulous and perfectionistic in his daily activities. He may be very religious and moralistic.

Jeff tends to be rather docile and passive–dependent in his relationships with other people. In fact, he often finds it difficult to be even appropriately assertive. He has the capacity for forming deep emotional ties, and in times of stress he may become overly dependent and clinging. He is not aggressive or belligerent, and he tends to elicit nurturance and helping behavior from other people.

Clinical Scales

Next, the Clinical scale scores should be examined to determine what, if any, inferences are appropriate for each of them. The Clinical scales that are included in the defined code type (Scales 2 and 7 in this sample case) are not used individually to generate inferences because such inferences would be largely redundant with and less focused than those based on the code type.

Scale 1 (T = 57)
This is an average score, so no inferences would be made on the basis of this scale. Scores on the RC1 (Somatic Complaints) and HEA (Health Concerns) Content scales are consistent with the average score on Scale 1.

Scale 2 (T = 81)
Because this scale is part of a defined code type, additional inferences would not be generated.

Scale 3 (T = 64)
This is an average score, so no inferences would be made on the basis of this scale.

Scale 4 (T = 62)
This is an average score, so no inferences would be made on the basis of this scale.

Scale 5 (T = 48)
This is an average score. It suggests that Jeff's interests and attitudes are similar to those of most men.

Scale 6 (T = 68)
Although this score represents a significant elevation, the score is not high enough to lead to inferences concerning psychotic symptoms and behavior. Rather, we would expect Jeff to be excessively sensitive and overly responsive to the opinions of others. He feels that he is getting a raw deal from life. He is suspicious and guarded in relationships. He tends to rationalize and blame others for difficulties and may be hostile, resentful, and argumentative in relationships. He may appear to overemphasize rationality and to be moralistic and rigid in opinions and attitudes. Examination of the Harris–Lingoes subscales for Scale 6 is not helpful because all T scores are between 50 and 60. T scores of 39 on the Bizarre Mentation Content scale, 52 on the RC8 (Aberrant Experiences) scale, and 41 on the RC6 (Ideas of Persecution) scale reinforce the inference that Jeff is not likely to be experiencing psychotic symptoms. These average or below-average scores, along with the very high RCd scale score (T = 79), suggest that the high score on Scale 6 is to a large extent the product of Jeff's endorsement of many items in the scale having to do with personal distress.

Scale 7 (T = 77)
Because this scale is part of a defined code type, additional inferences would not be made.

Scale 8 (T = 56)
This is an average score, so no inferences would be made based on this scale.

Scale 9 (T = 45)
This is an average score, so no inferences would be made based on this score.

Scale 0 (T = 74)
This high score suggests that Jeff is socially introverted, shy, timid, reserved, and retiring. He is not likely to participate in many social activities and when he does he probably feels very insecure and uncomfortable. He is especially likely to feel uncomfortable around members of the opposite sex. He may feel more comfortable alone or with a few close friends. Jeff lacks self-confidence and is likely to be described by others as cold, distant, and hard to get to know. He is quite troubled by lack of involvement with other people. He tends to be overcontrolled and is not likely to display feelings openly. He is submissive and compliant in interpersonal relationships and is overly accepting of authority. He is described as having a slow personal tempo. He also is described as cautious, conventional, and unoriginal in his approach to problems, and he gives up easily when things are not going well. He is somewhat rigid and inflexible in attitudes and opinions, and he may have great difficulty making even minor decisions. He enjoys work and gets pleasure from productive personal achievement. He tends to worry, to be irritable, and to feel anxious. Others describe him as moody, and he may experience episodes of depression characterized by lack of energy and lack of interest in the activities of daily living.

Examination of the Scale 0 (Social Introversion) subscales sometimes helps clarify the primary reasons for an elevation on Scale 0. Jeff's scores on two of the Scale 0 subscales are high. The T score of 74 on the Si1 (Shyness/Self-Consciousness) subscale indicates that he feels quite shy, embarrassed, and ill at ease around other people. The T score of 68 on the Si3 (Self/Other Alienation) subscale suggests that he has low self-esteem and feels unable to effect changes in his life. The absence of a high score (T = 58) on the Si2 (Social Avoidance) scale may mean that despite his social discomfort, Jeff is not totally avoiding social activities.

Restructured Clinical (RC) Scales

Demoralization—RCd (T = 79)
This high score suggests that Jeff is reporting a great deal of overall emotional discomfort. He feels discouraged, generally demoralized, insecure, and pessimistic. He has a poor self-concept, expecting to fail in various aspects of his life. He feels helpless, overwhelmed, and incapable of coping with his current circumstances.

Somatic Complaints—RC1 (T = 48)
Because this is an average score, no inferences would be made on the basis of this scale.

Low Positive Emotions—RC2 (T = 60)

Because this is an average score, no inferences would be made on the basis of this scale.

Cynicism—RC3 (T = 41)

Because this is an average score, no inferences would be made on the basis of this scale.

Antisocial Behavior—RC4 (T = 68)

The moderately high score on this scale suggests that Jeff may find it difficult to conform to societal norms and expectations and may engage in some antisocial acts. He may be viewed by others as being antagonistic, angry, and argumentative. A history of conflictual family relationships and poor achievements is likely, and substance misuse should be considered.

Ideas of Persecution—RC6 (T = 41)

Because this is an average score, no inferences would be made on the basis of this scale.

Dysfunctional Negative Emotions—RC7 (T = 77)

The high score on this scale suggests that Jeff has a tendency to have negative emotional experiences, including anxiety, irritability, and other forms of aversive reactivity. He tends to ruminate and worry excessively, is sensitive to criticism, and feels guilty and insecure. He tends to be preoccupied about self-perceived failures. He may experience intrusive, unwanted ideation.

Aberrant Experiences—RC8 (T = 52)

Because this is an average score, no inferences would be made on the basis of this scale.

Hypomanic Activation—RC9 (T = 47)

Because this is an average score, no inferences would be made on the basis of this scale.

Content Scales

As stated in Chapter 6 of this book, the Content scales of the MMPI-2 are much more homogeneous than the Clinical scales and can be helpful in understanding Jeff's symptoms, problems, and behaviors. Jeff has eight Content scale scores equal to or greater than 65. We would next generate inferences based on each of these high Content scale scores.

Anxiety—ANX (T = 80)

The very high score on this scale suggests that Jeff is feeling anxious, nervous, worried, and apprehensive. He may have problems concentrating, his sleep may be disturbed, and he may be uncomfortable making decisions. He also may report feeling that life is a strain and that he is pessimistic about things getting better. He lacks self-confidence and feels overwhelmed by the responsibilities of daily life.

Fears—FRS (T = 57)

Because this is an average score, no inferences would be made based on this scale.

Obsessiveness—OBS (T = 77)

The high score on this scale suggests that Jeff frets, worries, and ruminates about trivial things. He may engage in compulsive behaviors such as counting or hoarding. He has difficulty making decisions. He is rigid and dislikes change. He lacks self-confidence, lacks interest in things, and may feel dysphoric and despondent.

Depression—DEP (T = 77)

The high score on this scale indicates that Jeff is experiencing symptoms of depression. He feels sad, blue, and despondent, and he may cry easily. He feels fatigued and lacks interest in things. He feels pessimistic and hopeless. He may recently have been preoccupied with thoughts of death and suicide. He lacks self-confidence and often feels guilty. He feels lonely and empty much of the time. He may be expressing health concerns. Jeff had T scores greater than 65 for four of the five Depression Content Component scales. However, because differences between these four scales are not at least 10 T-score points, they are of little help in helping to focus our interpretation of the Depression scale score. It should be noted that Jeff endorsed only one item in the Suicidal Ideation (DEP4) content component scale, and that item did not have to do directly with suicide.

Health Concerns—HEA (T = 51)

Because this is an average score, no inferences would be made based on this scale.

Bizarre Mentation—BIZ (T = 39)

Because this is a below average score, we would not expect Jeff to be experiencing psychotic symptoms.

Anger—ANG (T = 70)

The high score on this scale suggests that Jeff feels angry and hostile much of the time. He may feel like swearing or smashing things and may at times have temper tantrums during which he is quite verbally aggressive. Others see him as irritable, grouchy, impatient, and stubborn. Although there is not a difference of 10 T-score points between the two ANG Content Component scales, we would note that the Explosive Behavior (ANG1) scale was eight points lower than the Irritability (ANG2) scale, suggesting that Jeff is not likely to act out angry feelings very readily.

Cynicism—CYN (T = 41)

Because this is an average score, no inferences would be made based on this scale.

Antisocial Practices—ASP (T = 47)

Because this is an average score, no inferences would be made based on this scale.

Type A Personality—TPA (T = 53)

Because this is an average score, no inferences would be made based on this scale.

Low Self-Esteem—LSE (T = 72)

Based on the high score on this scale, we would expect Jeff to have a very poor self-concept. He anticipates failure and gives up easily. He is overly sensitive to criticism and rejection. He is likely to be passive in relationships, and it may be difficult for him to accept compliments from others. He worries and frets a great deal, and he has difficulty making decisions. Because the Submissiveness (LSE2) Content Component scale is significantly more elevated than the Self-Doubt (LSE1) scale, greater emphasis would be placed on inferences having to do with passivity and submissiveness.

Social Discomfort—SOD (T = 68)

The high score on this scale suggests that Jeff is shy and socially introverted. He would rather be alone than around other people. It is difficult for him to initiate conversations, and he dislikes parties and other group activities. Because the two Social Discomfort Content Component scale scores are not at least 10 points different from each other, these scores are not helpful in focusing the interpretation of the SOD scale.

Family Problems—FAM (T = 44)

Because this is an average score, no inferences would be made based on this scale.

Work Interference—WRK (T = 81)

Jeff may be reporting some negative attitudes and characteristics that are likely to lead to poor work performance. He may have rather negative perceptions of co-workers. He may not be very confident about his career or vocational choices and feels that his family does not approve of his choices. Because Jeff appears to be depressed and demoralized, we would be quite tentative in making such inferences.

Negative Treatment Indicators—TRT (T = 66)

The marginally elevated score of 66 on the Negative Treatment Indicators scale suggests that Jeff may have some characteristics that are likely to interfere with psychological treatment. Because the Low Motivation (TRT1) Content Component scale is 11 T-score points higher than the Inability to Disclose (TRT2) Content Component scale, the interpretation would focus more on the lack of motivation to change in treatment than on inability to disclose personal information in treatment. However, because other scores indicate that he is likely to be depressed and demoralized, inferences about treatment based on the TRT scale would be rather tentative.

Supplementary Scales

Jeff's scores on some of the Supplementary scales discussed in Chapter 8 of this book can be used to generate additional inferences about him.

Anxiety—A (T = 81)

The very high score on this scale suggests that Jeff is likely to be experiencing considerable emotional turmoil, including anxiety and depression. In addition, he is not likely to be coping very well with the demands of his life situation.

Repression—R (T = 65)

Because this score is only moderately high, not much emphasis should be placed on it in the interpretation of Jeff's MMPI-2. However, a score at this level indicates that Jeff tends to be passive in relationships. He may be described by others as slow, painstaking, unexcitable, and clear-thinking. He tends to be conventional and formal in his attitudes.

Ego Strength—Es (T = 30)

Low scores on this scale tend to be associated with poor adjustment and limited psychological resources. In addition, Jeff is presenting himself as overwhelmed by and unable to respond to the demands of his life situation.

Dominance—Do (T = 30)

The very low score on this scale suggests that Jeff is not very strong in face-to-face situations and is lacking in self-confidence.

Responsibility—Re (T = 39)

This relatively low score likely reflects Jeff's lack of self-confidence and social discomfort.

College Maladjustment—Mt (T = 81)

Because Jeff is not a college student, this scale would not be interpreted.

Posttraumatic Stress Disorder Scale—PK (T = 75)

The PK scale is useful only when we know that we are dealing with persons who have been exposed to extraordinary stressors (such as combat experiences). Because we have no information suggesting that Jeff has been exposed to such stressors, we would make no inferences about him based on this scale. His high score likely is reflecting the personal distress that has been inferred from other scales.

Marital Distress—MDS (T = 51)
Because Jeff is not married, this scale would not be interpreted.

Hostility—Ho (T = 48)
Because this is an average score, no inferences would be made based on this scale.

Overcontrolled–Hostility—O–H (T = 35)
Because low scores on this scale are not interpreted, no inferences would be made.

MacAndrew Alcoholism Scale–Revised—MAC-R (Raw Score = 23)
This is a borderline score on the MAC-R screening measure of alcohol and drug problems. The score is not high enough to permit us to have confidence in inferences about Jeff's use or abuse of substances.

Addiction Admission Scale—AAS (T = 70)
The high score on this scale indicates that in responding to the MMPI-2 items, Jeff acknowledged substance abuse problems and behaviors associated with the abuse. Additional information should be obtained about his patterns of substance use and abuse.

Addiction Potential Scale—APS (T = 76)
Because of the conflicting research concerning the relationship between this scale and substance-related problems, no inferences would be made based on this scale.

Masculine Gender Role—GM (T = 32) and Feminine
Gender Role—GF (T = 50)
As discussed in Chapter 8 of this book, there is not enough research to support making inferences based on these scales.

Personality Psychopathology Five (Psy-5) Scales

Aggressiveness—AGGR (T = 33)
The low score on this scale suggests that Jeff is passive, submissive, and not very aggressive in interactions with other people.

Psychoticism—PSYC (T = 49)
Because this is an average score, no inferences would be made on the basis of this scale.

Disconstraint—DISC (T = 54)
Because this is an average score, no inferences would be made on the basis of this scale.

Negative Emotionality/Neuroticism—NEGE (T = 78)

The very high score on this scale suggests that Jeff has a predisposition to experience negatively valenced affects and emotions, to focus on problematic features of incoming information, to worry, to be self-critical, to feel guilty, and to concoct worst-case scenarios. He is likely to experience anxiety, depression, and sad mood. Diagnoses of depression or dysthymia should be considered.

Introversion/Low Positive Emotionality—INTR (T = 68)

The moderately high score on this scale suggests that Jeff has limited capacity to experience joy and positive engagement. He tends to be socially introverted and has a low need to achieve. His symptoms are likely to include depression, anxiety, and somatic complaints.

Resolving Inconsistent Inferences

A review of the inferences that were generated concerning Jeff's characteristic traits and behaviors indicates a striking consistency among them. However, several of the inferences appear to be somewhat inconsistent. It may be helpful to discuss how these apparent inconsistencies would be handled.

One of the inferences based on the 27/72 code type was that Jeff may express vague somatic concerns. However, average scores on other more specific indicators of somatic symptoms (Scales 1, RC1, HEA) suggest that somatic symptoms would not be a primary part of Jeff's presenting complaints.

Jeff's T score of 70 on the Anger (ANG) Content scale led to inferences that he is angry and hostile much of the time, that he may have temper tantrums during which he is verbally aggressive, and that others may describe him as irritable and grouchy. Examination of the Anger Content Component scales is not particularly helpful because the two scales do not differ from each other by at least 10 T-score points. However, we would note that the Explosive Behavior (ANG1) scale was eight points lower than the Irritability (ANG2) scale. This difference is in the direction that would lead us to infer that Jeff is not very likely to express anger openly and directly. Review of Jeff's critical-item endorsements indicates that he admitted to feeling like smashing things and having a strong urge to do something harmful or shocking. He is often said to be hotheaded and easily angered. Based on all of this information, we would probably conclude that Jeff harbors a great deal of anger and resentment that does not usually get expressed openly. However, he may occasionally vent the angry feelings in verbal outbursts.

On the basis of the 27/72 code type and the high score on Scale 0, it was inferred that Jeff has a strong need for achievement and is likely to enjoy work and get pleasure from productive personal achievement. A high score on the Work Interference (WRK) Content scale led to the inference that Jeff lacks ambition and energy and may have attitudes and behaviors that would interfere with job performance. Because inferences based on code types are likely to be more accurate than those based on individual scales and because there has been much more empirical research concerning the 27/72 code type and Scale 0 than concerning the Work Interference Content scale, we would have greater confidence in the inferences that Jeff has a strong need to achieve and is likely to enjoy work. We would also consider that the WRK scale often is high for persons like Jeff who are experiencing a great deal of personal distress, regardless of their work performance. Background information about Jeff suggests that he has had a number of low-level jobs and that at least some were lost because of problems with supervisors. Thus, although we cannot resolve these somewhat inconsistent inferences, it appears that this would be an important area to explore during therapy.

The 27/72 code type suggests that Jeff tends to be self-blaming, but the high score on Scale 6 led to an inference that he tends to blame others. Again, because we tend to have more confidence in inferences based on code types than those based on individual scales, we would probably describe Jeff as self-blaming. That the Scale 6 score was only moderately high (T = 68) also suggests that we should have more confidence in the inference that he is self-blaming. In addition, we know from Jeff's Demoralization (RCd) scale score that his elevated Scale 6 score is likely to be due, in large part, to great personal distress.

The T score of 68 on the Antisocial Behavior (RC4) scale led to inferences of antisocial characteristics that can include difficulty conforming to societal norms, legal difficulties, and behaving aggressively toward others. However, Jeff's T scores of 62 on Scale 4 and 47 on the Antisocial Practice (ASP) Content scale are not consistent with these antisocial characteristics. There is no simple way to resolve these apparent inconsistencies. However, we would expect that if Jeff has some problems with social conformity and acceptance of authority, he is not likely to act out in illegal ways.

Finally, Jeff's high scores on Scale 2, the Demoralization (RCd) scale, and the Depression (DEP) Content scale would lead to concerns about suicidal ideation and perhaps intent. Because this obviously is a very serious issue, it should be mentioned in the interpretation. However, we would also want to note that examination of Jeff's critical-item endorsement indicates that he did not endorse any of the items dealing directly with suicidal ideation or attempts.

Integration of Inferences

Having dealt with apparent inconsistencies in inferences about Jeff, the next step would be to examine all of the inferences concerning characteristic traits and behaviors and to organize them into meaningful categories. Earlier in this chapter a list of possible categories was suggested.

Symptoms

There is clear agreement from many aspects of the MMPI-2 protocol that Jeff is experiencing a great deal of emotional turmoil. He is likely to be clinically depressed, he seems to feel sad and unhappy, and he may be showing signs of psychomotor retardation. He lacks energy and has lost interest in things going on around him. He may cry easily. Life seems to be a strain for him, and he is pessimistic about things ever getting better for him. At times he may feel that life is not worthwhile, but in responding to the MMPI-2 items, he did not endorse the items dealing directly with suicidal ideation or attempts.

Jeff also appears to feel anxious, tense, and nervous. He is high-strung, jumpy, agitated, and apprehensive. He worries excessively and is vulnerable to real and imagined threat. He may have a sense of dread that something bad is going to happen to him. He is likely to be experiencing difficulties in concentrating and attending. His thinking may be obsessive and his behavior compulsive. He is likely to be quite indecisive, even about very trivial matters. Perceived lack of control over thoughts and emotions may cause him to fear that he is losing his mind. Jeff may report vague somatic concerns, but these are not likely to be central to his presenting complaints.

Jeff's high score on the Addiction Admission Scale (AAS) indicates that he is openly admitting to misuse of alcohol or other drugs and the problems associated with the misuse. Clearly, additional information about substance use is needed.

Major Needs

Many of the inferences generated from Jeff's MMPI-2 scores suggest that he has very strong unfulfilled dependency needs. He is likely to be passive–dependent in relationships, and he worries about not being popular and socially accepted. Jeff seems to harbor above-average levels of anger and resentment. Most of the time he does not express these negative feelings directly. However, occasional temper tantrums and verbal outbursts of anger may occur. Jeff seems to have rather strong abasement needs. He often evaluates himself negatively and compares himself unfavorably with others. Jeff seems to have strong needs to achieve and to receive recognition for his accomplishments, but insecurity and fear of failure keep him from placing himself in many directly competitive situations.

Perceptions of the Environment

Jeff sees the world as a demanding place and feels incapable of responding to the demands of his daily life. He has a sense of dread that bad things are going to happen to him. He seems to feel that his needs are not met by others and that he is getting a raw deal from life. He may be cynical, skeptical, and suspicious about the motives of other people.

Reactions to Stress

Jeff's MMPI-2 scores suggest that he feels poorly equipped to deal with stress. He is vulnerable to real and imagined threat, tends to anticipate problems before they occur, and often overreacts to minor stress. During times of increased stress he may develop somatic symptoms and become increasingly clinging and dependent. Although he prefers to use denial and repression as defenses, these mechanisms do not seem to be working well for him now. As a result, he is overwhelmed with emotional turmoil. At times Jeff may respond to stress by withdrawing into fantasy and daydreaming, and at other times he may seek escape from stress through the use of alcohol and/or other drugs.

Jeff appears to be a responsible, conscientious person. He is likely to be neat, organized, and persistent in his approach to problems. However, he is also likely to be quite cautious, conventional, and rigid. He is rather indecisive about most things in his life. He is a rather poor problem solver and often may show poor judgment. He tends to give up easily when faced with increasing stress.

Self-Concept

Jeff's MMPI-2 scores indicate that he has an extremely negative self-concept. He is plagued by feelings of inadequacy, insecurity, and inferiority. He is quite self-critical and often compares himself unfavorably with other people. He has high expectations for himself and feels guilty when he falls short of his goals. He blames himself for the problems in his life and feels hopeless and unable to effect life changes.

Sexual Identification

Not many inferences were generated about Jeff's sexual identification. His average Scale 5 score would suggest that his interests and attitudes are likely to be similar to those of most men. His high Scale 0 score indicates that he may be especially uncomfortable around women. He did not endorse the critical items that would suggest that he is dissatisfied with his sex life, that he has engaged in unusual sex practices, or that he has been in trouble because of his sexual behavior.

Emotional Control

Jeff is likely to be emotionally overcontrolled much of the time. He tends to deny his impulses and is not likely to display feelings openly. He tends to emphasize rational rather than emotional aspects of situations. Although he is not likely to express anger and resentment openly most of the time, during occasional tantrums these feelings may get expressed verbally. He is so emotionally uncomfortable at this time that he may cry easily.

Interpersonal Relationships

Jeff is a shy, socially introverted person. Although he has the capacity to form deep emotional ties and very much wants to be involved with others, his poor self-concept causes him to feel quite uncomfortable in social situations. He is likely to avoid large gatherings and may feel most comfortable when with a few close friends. He is troubled by his limited interactions with other people, and he feels lonely much of the time. In relationships Jeff is likely to be passive, submissive, and compliant. He is very unassertive and likely to make concessions to avoid confrontations.

Other people's perceptions of Jeff are quite variable. Sometimes he is seen as sentimental, peaceable, and soft-hearted, and he elicits nurturance and helping behavior from others. At other times he is seen as moody, irritable, dull, and moralistic. His shyness may be misinterpreted by others as indicating that he is aloof, cold, and distant.

Jeff has ambivalent feelings about other people. He is drawn to them because they represent sources of gratification for his strong dependency needs. However, he also has negative perceptions of other people. He seems to view them as not being very understanding and supportive. He is quite sensitive to criticism, and his feelings are easily hurt. At times he can be rather blunt and harsh in social interactions. Jeff may have some negative attitudes about co-workers that are likely to interfere with productive work.

Psychological Resources

Because the MMPI-2 scales tend to emphasize psychopathology and negative characteristics and because Jeff has many high scores on the scales, most of the inferences generated tend to be negative. However, a review of the inferences previously generated reveals a few that could be viewed as psychological resources. Although he often feels like a failure, Jeff has strong needs to receive recognition for his accomplishments. He is neat, meticulous, persistent, and reliable. He has the capacity for forming deep emotional ties. Others sometimes see him in positive ways (e.g., sensitive, kind, soft-hearted, and peaceable) and react to him in nurturant and helping ways.

Diagnostic Impressions

As was discussed earlier in this chapter, it is not possible to assign psychiatric diagnoses solely on the basis of psychological test data. The criteria for most diagnoses include information that cannot be obtained from psychological test data. However, we can make statements concerning the diagnoses that are most consistent with Jeff's MMPI-2 results.

The MMPI-2 data consistently suggest that Axis I diagnoses of depressive disorder (major depression or dysthymia) and generalized anxiety disorder should be considered. The 27/72 code type and high scores on Clinical scales 2 and 7; the RCd, RC2, and RC7 scales; and the Depression (DEP) and Anxiety (ANX) Content scales support these diagnoses. The 27/72 code type and a high score on the Obsessiveness (OBS) Content scale indicate that an Axis I diagnosis of obsessive–compulsive disorder should be considered. The very high score on the Addiction Admission Scale (AAS) is consistent with substance use disorders, and more information about substance use should be obtained. There are no direct empirical data that would lead to inferences about Axis II diagnoses. However, the descriptions of symptoms and personality characteristics that were generated about Jeff are consistent with Axis II diagnoses of dependent and obsessive–compulsive personality disorders.

Implications for Treatment

Many indicators in Jeff's MMPI-2 data suggest that he is in a great deal of emotional turmoil and is not likely to be meeting the responsibilities of daily life in an effective manner. Because of his intense distress, he is likely to be motivated for psychotherapy. The 27/72 code type indicates that Jeff is likely to remain in treatment longer than most patients and can be expected to show slow positive change during treatment. However, there are indications of characteristics that are likely to interfere with effective therapy. He may not have the energy to participate effectively in traditional psychotherapy. A referral to assess the appropriateness of antidepressant medication should be considered. His very low score on the Ego Strength (Es) scale suggests that he has limited psychological resources that can be utilized in treatment. Based on the high score on Scale 7, we would expect that he will rationalize and intellectualize a great deal in therapy. He probably would be resistant to psychological interpretations and could come to express significant hostility toward a therapist. The high score on the Negative Treatment Indicators (TRT) content scale indicates that he might have negative attitudes toward doctors and mental health treatment. He may feel that other people cannot really understand his problems, and he seems to believe that he is helpless to change major aspects of his life. His rigidity and tendency to give up easily in stressful situations could be liabilities in treatment.

As stated earlier, Jeff's scores on the substance abuse scales of the MMPI-2 indicate that he may have problems with alcohol and/or other drugs. If corroborating information supports the inferences concerning substance abuse, a treatment plan should include a substance abuse component.

Summary

The preceding analysis of this single case is lengthy in its presentation because it is meant as a teaching–learning tool for the beginning MMPI-2 user. The experienced user would write a much briefer interpretation of the protocol. Specifically, the following is what the author might write about Jeff in a clinic chart, to the referring source, or for his own psychotherapy notes.

The MMPI-2 protocol produced by Jeff appears to be valid. He was not overly defensive in responding to the MMPI-2 items. He admitted to some deviant attitudes and behaviors, but this admission is seen as an accurate reporting of problems.

Jeff appears to be having some significant psychological problems. He is experiencing a great deal of emotional distress. He feels overwhelmed and unable to respond to the demands of daily life. He seems to be clinically depressed and anxious. He is pessimistic about the future and at times may feel that life is not worthwhile. However, he is not reporting suicidal plans or intent at this time. He may report vague somatic symptoms and difficulties in concentrating and attending. His thinking may be obsessive and his behavior compulsive.

Jeff sees the world as a demanding place and feels that his needs are not being met by other people. Although he typically engages in denial and repression, these defenses do not seem to be working very well for him at this time.

Jeff has an extremely negative self-concept. He is plagued by feelings of inadequacy, insecurity, and inferiority. At times he may blame himself for the problems in his life, but at other times he tends to rationalize and blame others.

Although Jeff may be harboring feelings of anger and resentment, he typically does not express feelings openly. However, brief verbal outbursts of anger may occur during temper tantrums.

Jeff is shy, timid, and socially introverted. Although he seems to want to be involved with other people and has the capacity to form deep emotional ties, he tends to withdraw from many social interactions in order to protect himself from the criticism and rejection that he has come to expect. In relationships he is likely to be passive, submissive, and unassertive. He can be expected to make concessions in order to avoid unpleasant confrontations. He seems to have negative perceptions of other people, seeing them as neither understanding nor supportive of him.

Jeff's MMPI-2 data are consistent with DSM-IV Axis I diagnoses of depressive disorder (major depression or dysthymia), generalized anxiety disorder, and obsessive–compulsive disorder. Substance use disorders should be ruled out. His symptoms and personality characteristics are consistent with Axis II diagnoses of dependent and obsessive–compulsive personality disorders.

Jeff is not coping very well with the demands of his life situation and needs psychological treatment. Because of his intense psychological discomfort, he is likely to be receptive to psychotherapy. If his distress is so severe that it interferes with his ability to participate meaningfully in psychotherapy, a medical referral to evaluate the appropriateness of antidepressant and antianxiety medications should be considered. Although he is not likely to respond well to brief psychotherapy, he probably will stay in treatment longer than many patients and may show slow but steady progress. If corroborating information indicates that he is abusing alcohol and/or other drugs, a substance abuse component should be included in his treatment plan.

ADDITIONAL PRACTICE CASES

MMPI-2 data are presented for four additional cases in Appendix D at the end of this book. These cases can be used to practice the various aspects of MMPI-2 interpretation and feedback that are described in this chapter.

GIVING FEEDBACK TO CLIENTS

Although most persons who take the MMPI-2 are interested in their test performance and many expect to receive feedback about their test results, often such feedback is not given or is not given in a comprehensive and systematic way. In addition to client expectations, there are other important reasons for routinely giving feedback about MMPI-2 results (Butcher, 1990b; Finn, 1996; Pope, 1992). In many circumstances clients have legal rights to information about their test results. Also, according to the Ethical Principles of Psychologists (American Psychological Association, 2002), psychologists have the professional responsibility to provide clients with information about test results in a manner that can be easily understood.

In addition, giving feedback about MMPI-2 results to clients can be clinically beneficial. If handled well by clinicians, feedback can be a vehicle for establishing good rapport with clients. Feedback also can be helpful to clients in understanding why treatment is being recommended, suggesting possible problem areas to be explored in treatment, and identifying resources that can be utilized in treatment. In fact, some preliminary data suggest that receiving assessment feedback is associated with a significant decline in symptomatic distress and a significant increase in self-esteem (Finn & Tonsager, 1992; Newman & Greenway, 1997; Poston & Hanson, 2010). Finn (1996) developed detailed procedures for using MMPI-2 results as a therapeutic intervention. When the MMPI-2 is repeated during treatment, discussion of changes in results can help the client and therapist assess treatment progress and define additional treatment goals.

As discussed in Chapter 2 of this book, valid and interpretable test results are more likely to be obtained if, prior to test administration, the examiner explains why the MMPI-2 is being administered, who will have access to the test results, and why it is in the client's best interest to cooperate with the testing. At this time the examiner can also explain that the client will be given feedback about test results and will have an opportunity to ask general questions about the test and specific questions about test results. Clients often ask for a written report of test results and interpretations. In most cases, it is not a good idea to provide such a report because the clinician cannot be sure that the client will understand everything in the report. Instead, indicate that you will be willing to meet with the client after the testing has been completed, discuss the results, and give the client an opportunity to ask questions and make comments.

General Guidelines

1. Communicate in a manner that is easily understood by the client. Some clients will be able to understand rather complex and technical explanations, whereas others will require greatly simplified explanations.
2. Use vocabulary that the client can understand. Avoid psychological jargon. If you use psychological terms, take the time to explain exactly what they mean.
3. Present both positive and negative aspects of the client's personality and functioning. Finding positive things to say may be rather difficult in the case of certain clients, but it is usually possible to do so. Clients are much more likely to accept interpretations if you maintain a balance between positive and negative characteristics.
4. Avoid terms such as "abnormal," "deviant," or "pathological." It is helpful to explain that most symptoms and negative characteristics are shared by most people but perhaps are not possessed by individuals to the same extent as by a particular client.
5. Do not overwhelm the client with a long list of adjectives. Instead, limit your interpretations to a few of the most important things you want the client to hear and understand, and explain each as fully as possible to ensure that the client understands what you are trying to communicate.
6. Encourage clients to make comments and ask questions about what you have said. This often provides additional information about clients and makes them feel that they are a part of the process.

7. Do not argue with clients or otherwise try to convince them that your interpretations are correct. This will increase their defensiveness and can jeopardize your future role as therapist or counselor.

8. When the discussion of the test results has been completed, ask the client to summarize the major points that have been covered. This will increase the likelihood that the client will remember what has been discussed and will give you an opportunity to clarify any misunderstandings that clients might have about what was discussed.

General Explanation of the MMPI-2

To increase the likelihood that the client will have confidence in your interpretations and take the feedback seriously, you should indicate that the MMPI has been used by psychologists for more than 50 years, that there have been thousands of research studies concerning what MMPI scores mean, and that the test was revised and updated in 1989. You could also point out that the test is the most widely used psychological test in the world.

Before giving specific feedback about a client's MMPI-2 results, you should spend some time explaining in general how the test was developed and how it is interpreted. You may want to illustrate your explanation by referring to an MMPI-2 profile. It is a good idea not to use the client's own profile at this time. Clients may be so anxious about their own scores that it will be difficult for them to attend to what you are saying.

Scale Development

Typically, it is not very difficult to explain to clients how the MMPI-2 scales were developed. For most people the empirical construction of the basic scales is easy to understand and makes sense. Having an understanding of these procedures increases the client's confidence in the test and in your interpretations.

You should explain that the MMPI-2 is made up of a large number of statements to which true or false responses are given. The basic MMPI-2 scales were developed by comparing the item responses of a group of patients having specific kinds of problems (e.g., anxiety and depression) with the responses of persons who were not having any serious psychological problems. You should avoid mentioning that the groups were defined according to psychiatric diagnoses. If a client persists in asking what the scale abbreviations (e.g., Sc) stand for, you should give honest answers but emphasize that these labels are not important in the way that the MMPI-2 is used today. You should then point out that the client's responses were scored for each of these scales. It is helpful to show the client a profile sheet (not his or her own yet) and point out that each number at the top and bottom of the sheet corresponds to one of these original scales.

As was mentioned in Chapter 6 of this book, the Content scales of the MMPI-2 represent direct communication between the client and the clinician. High scores on any of these scales indicate that the client wants you to know about certain symptoms, problems, and characteristics. Because you may want to present scores on some of the Content scales to support inferences about a client, you should mention how these scales were developed. It probably will be sufficient to indicate that each of these scales is made up of items in the test with similar content. For example, the items in the Anxiety Content scale all have to do with various aspects of anxiety.

Norms

You should then indicate that the client's score on each of these scales is compared with scores of a large group of persons living in communities throughout the United States. Avoid referring to "normals" or "norms," because clients who have scores different from this group may label themselves as "abnormal." You can again refer to a profile sheet, indicating that most people obtain scores near the lower heavy black line on the profile sheet. If clients ask about the meaning of the numbers along the left or right sides of the profile (T scores) you should explain in very simple terms what they mean. Otherwise, it probably is best not to deal directly with the T scores. You can also point out that because scores above the upper heavy black line (T > 65) are rare, we tend to emphasize them in our interpretations. These high scores indicate the likelihood of problems similar to those of persons involved in the original development of the scales (e.g., anxiety and depression). Because the meaning of low scores is not very clear at this time, you can simply indicate that scores below the lower heavy black line (T = 50) indicate that the client is not likely to have problems similar to those of people involved in the development of these scales.

Validity Scales

You should emphasize that we can gain useful information about clients from their MMPI-2 results only if they have followed the test instructions (i.e., read each item and responded honestly as the item applies to them). Indicate that there are special MMPI-2 scales to help us determine if the instructions have been followed. Mention that these scales tell us if a person left too many items unanswered (?), responded to the items without really reading them (VRIN), was defensive and denying (L, K, and S scales), or exaggerated problems and symptoms (F, F_B, F_p, FBS). You should spend more time explaining the Validity scales if the client's scores suggest that the results may be invalid or of questionable validity.

Sources Of Interpretive Statements

After you are confident that the client understands how the scales were developed and what is meant by high scores, you should explain how interpretive inferences are made on the basis of these scores. Emphasize that the inferences are based on extensive study of persons who have obtained high scores on the various scales. For example, when we have studied persons who have had high scores on Scale 2, we have found that they reported feeling more depressed than persons scoring lower on Scale 2. You can also mention that such studies have been done concerning persons who obtain high scores on several of the scales at the same time (e.g., 2 and 7). In interpreting a specific client's scores, we infer that the client will have problems and characteristics similar to persons we have studied who have had similar scores. Clients often ask about the meaning of specific MMPI-2 items. You should acknowledge that their responses to such items are important because they represent something that the clients want us to know but that we tend to emphasize scale scores rather than individual item responses in our interpretations.

Organizing the Feedback

Once you are confident that the client has a basic understanding of how the MMPI-2 was developed and how it is interpreted, you are ready to present feedback about his or her specific results. There is no correct or incorrect way of organizing your feedback. However, you may find it helpful to organize it by using some of the categories described earlier in this chapter: (1) test-taking attitudes, (2) overall adjustment level, (3) characteristic traits and behaviors (e.g., symptoms, needs, self-concept, interpersonal relationships, psychological resources), and (4) treatment implications.

Illustration

Assuming that a general explanation of the MMPI-2 has been given, we can illustrate the specific feedback that we might give to Jeff, the person whose MMPI-2 was interpreted previously. You will remember that Jeff is a 24-year-old man who took the MMPI-2 at a mental health center where he had been referred after emergency treatment following ingestion of a large number of aspirin.

After explaining how the MMPI-2 was developed and how it is interpreted generally, you could begin by pointing out to Jeff that he was very cooperative in completing the MMPI-2. He omitted no items, and his average scores on the L, F, and K scales, and on several additional validity scales, suggest that he carefully read each item and responded to it honestly and thoughtfully as it applied to him. Therefore, you have confidence that his scores on the other scales will give an accurate picture of what he is like.

Next, you should indicate that he seems to be in a great deal of emotional turmoil. His high scores on several scales (Scale 2, RCd, DEP) indicate that he is likely to be depressed and dissatisfied with his current life situation, and his high scores on Scales 7, RC7, and ANX indicate that he is likely to feel anxious, tense, and nervous much of the time. You could add that he seems to be lacking in self-confidence (high scores on Scales 2 and 7 and on the Low Self-Esteem Content scale). High scores on Scale 0 and on the Social Discomfort Content scale suggest that he is shy, introverted, and uncomfortable around people that he does not know well. The high score on the Work Interference Content scale suggests that his psychological problems may interfere with work performance.

You could point out that several scores suggest that he feels that he cannot cope with the demands of his everyday life situation. The most important source of this inference is the very low score on the Ego Strength (Es) scale. You could explain that this means he feels he just does not know how to cope with every-thing that is happening in his life at this time.

You probably then would want to point out that in his responses to items on the AAS scale he clearly admitted to substance-related problems. You could speculate that he might be using alcohol and/or other drugs as a way of trying to handle some of the discomfort that he is feeling.

You could indicate that the high score on Scale 6 could mean that he sees the world as a rather demanding place and feels that he gets a raw deal from life. He may be somewhat suspicious and skeptical of the motives of other people. His high score on the Anger Content scale suggests that he is resentful of this perceived mistreatment.

Based on the inferences that have been made about psychological turmoil and feeling overwhelmed by the demands of everyday life, you might indicate that he probably is feeling the need for some professional psychological help. You could emphasize that when people are in so much turmoil, they generally are willing to get involved in treatment and often show positive changes as a result of treatment. However, you would probably want to add that the moderately high score on the Negative Treatment Indicators content scale suggests that he may have reservations about sharing his feelings with other people because he does not think that they will understand them and that he may feel unable to bring about changes in his own life.

The concerns about substance abuse suggest that additional assessment of this possibility is indicated. If he readily admits to such problems, you would want to encourage him to consider involvement with Alcoholics Anonymous or some other program designed to help individuals deal with substance abuse problems.

At this point, having described many of Jeff's problem areas and negative characteristics, you should balance the feedback by mentioning some positive aspects of his MMPI-2 results. You could point out that his high scores on Scales 2 and 7 indicate that he is likely to be a persistent, conscientious, and reliable person. These high scores, coupled with his high score on Scale 0, indicate that he has a strong need to achieve, probably enjoys work, and gets pleasure from productive personal achievement.

The reader will note that many of the inferences made about Jeff earlier in this chapter have not been addressed in the feedback session. In keeping with the recommendation made earlier in this section, feedback should be limited to a few of the most important things that you want to communicate to Jeff. Although you should have encouraged Jeff's questions and reactions through-out the feedback session, near the end of the session you should ask very directly if he has any questions or comments about the feedback or any aspect of his MMPI-2 results. You would end the feedback session by having Jeff summarize what had been discussed, which would give you the opportunity to determine if he had misunderstood or misinterpreted some aspects of the feedback. If he had, you should carefully restate your interpretations and again ask Jeff to repeat what he heard.

If you were going to be Jeff's therapist or counselor, you might want to mention that you and he probably will discuss the MMPI-2 results again at various times during treatment. If you plan to re-administer the MMPI-2 during treatment, you should mention this possibility to him and indicate that it will give you and him an opportunity to examine possible changes as treatment progresses.

CHAPTER APPENDIX

Minnesota Multiphasic
Personality Inventory®-2

MMPI®-2
Minnesota Multiphasic Personality Inventory®-2
Extended Score Report

ID Number:	000182672
Age:	24
Gender:	Male
Date Assessed:	09/02/1998

PEARSON   🕮 *PsychCorp*

Copyright © 1989, 1994, 2000, 2003, 2006 by the Regents of the University of Minnesota. All rights reserved.
Portions reproduced from the MMPI-2 test booklet. Copyright © 1942, 1943 (renewed 1970), 1989 by the Regents of the
University of Minnesota. All rights reserved. Portions excerpted from the *MMPI-2 Manual for Administration, Scoring, and
Interpretation, Revised Edition.* Copyright © 2001 by the Regents of the University of Minnesota. All rights reserved.
Distributed exclusively under license from the University of Minnesota by NCS Pearson, Inc.

Minnesota Multiphasic Personality Inventory and **MMPI** are registered trademarks of the University of Minnesota.
Pearson, the **PSI logo,** and **PsychCorp** are trademarks in the U.S. and/or other countries of Pearson Education, Inc., or its
affiliate(s).

TRADE SECRET INFORMATION
Not for release under HIPAA or other data disclosure laws that exempt trade secrets from disclosure.

[5.1 / 153 / 2.3.17]

Reproduced by permission of the University of Minnesota Press. All rights reserved. "MMPI® " and
"Minnesota Multiphasic Personality Inventory® " are trademarks owned by the University of Minnesota.

MMPI-2 VALIDITY AND CLINICAL SCALES PROFILE

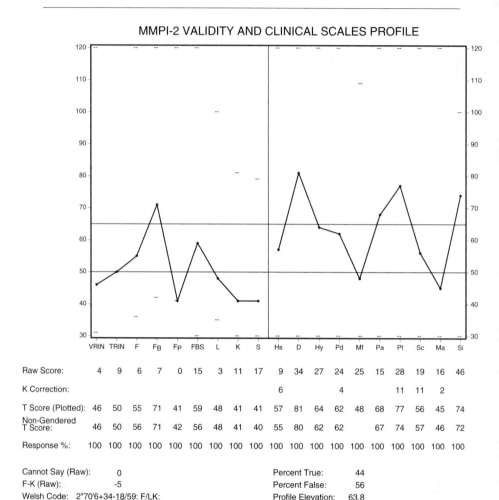

	VRIN	TRIN	F	FB	Fp	FBS	L	K	S	Hs	D	Hy	Pd	Mf	Pa	Pt	Sc	Ma	Si
Raw Score:	4	9	6	7	0	15	3	11	17	9	34	27	24	25	15	28	19	16	46
K Correction:										6			4		11	11	2		
T Score (Plotted):	46	50	55	71	41	59	48	41	41	57	81	64	62	48	68	77	56	45	74
Non-Gendered T Score:	46	50	56	71	42	56	48	41	40	55	80	62	62		67	74	57	46	72
Response %:	100	100	100	100	100	100	100	100	100	100	100	100	100	100	100	100	100	100	100

Cannot Say (Raw):   0
F-K (Raw):   -5
Welsh Code: 2"70'6+34-18/59: F/LK:

Percent True: 44
Percent False: 56
Profile Elevation: 63.8

The highest and lowest T scores possible on each scale are indicated by a "--".

For information on FBS, see Ben-Porath, Y. S., & Tellegen, A. (2006). The FBS: Current Status, a report on the Pearson web site (www.pearsonassessments.com/tests/mmpi_2.htm).

MMPI-2 **NON-K-CORRECTED** VALIDITY/CLINICAL SCALES PROFILE

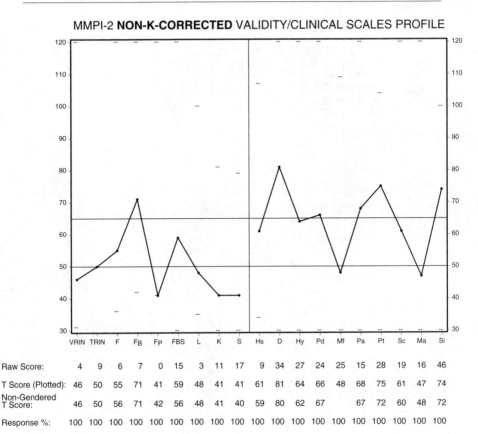

	VRIN	TRIN	F	F$_B$	Fp	FBS	L	K	S	Hs	D	Hy	Pd	Mf	Pa	Pt	Sc	Ma	Si
Raw Score:	4	9	6	7	0	15	3	11	17	9	34	27	24	25	15	28	19	16	46
T Score (Plotted):	46	50	55	71	41	59	48	41	41	61	81	64	66	48	68	75	61	47	74
Non-Gendered T Score:	46	50	56	71	42	56	48	41	40	59	80	62	67		67	72	60	48	72
Response %:	100	100	100	100	100	100	100	100	100	100	100	100	100	100	100	100	100	100	100

Cannot Say (Raw):	0	Percent True:	44
Profile Elevation:	65.4	Percent False:	56

The highest and lowest T scores possible on each scale are indicated by a "--".

Non-K-corrected T scores allow interpreters to examine the relative contributions of the Clinical Scale raw score and the K correction to K-corrected Clinical Scale T scores. Because all other MMPI-2 scores that aid in the interpretation of the Clinical Scales (the Harris-Lingoes subscales, Restructured Clinical Scales, Content and Content Component Scales, PSY-5 Scales, and Supplementary Scales) are not K-corrected, they can be compared most directly with non-K-corrected T scores.

For information on FBS, see Ben-Porath, Y. S., & Tellegen, A. (2006). The FBS: Current Status, a report on the Pearson web site (www.pearsonassessments.com/tests/mmpi_2.htm).

MMPI-2 RESTRUCTURED CLINICAL SCALES PROFILE

	RCd dem	RC1 som	RC2 lpe	RC3 cyn	RC4 asb	RC6 per	RC7 dne	RC8 abx	RC9 hpm
Raw Score:	19	2	7	2	12	0	17	2	11
T Score (plotted):	79	48	60	41	68	41	77	52	47
Non-Gendered T Score:	77	47	61	41	71	43	75	52	48
Response %:	100	100	100	100	100	100	100	100	100

The highest and lowest T scores possible on each scale are indicated by a "--".

LEGEND

dem= Demoralization   **cyn** = Cynicism   **dne** = Dysfunctional Negative Emotions
som= Somatic Complaints   **asb** = Antisocial Behavior   **abx** = Aberrant Experiences
lpe = Low Positive Emotions   **per** = Ideas of Persecution   **hpm**= Hypomanic Activation

---

For information on the RC scales, see Tellegen, A., Ben-Porath, Y.S., McNulty, J.L., Arbisi, P.A., Graham, J.R., & Kaemmer, B. 2003. The MMPI-2 Restructured Clinical (RC) Scales: Development, Validation, and Interpretation. Minneapolis: University of Minnesota Press.

320

MMPI-2 CONTENT SCALES PROFILE

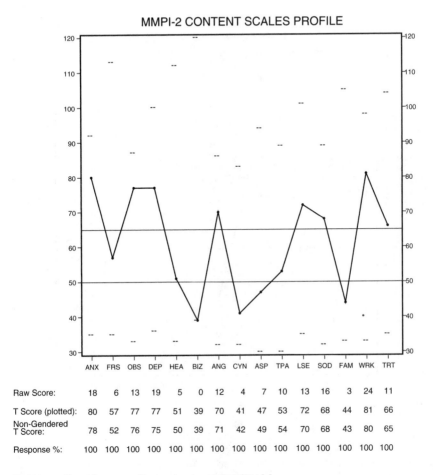

	ANX	FRS	OBS	DEP	HEA	BIZ	ANG	CYN	ASP	TPA	LSE	SOD	FAM	WRK	TRT
Raw Score:	18	6	13	19	5	0	12	4	7	10	13	16	3	24	11
T Score (plotted):	80	57	77	77	51	39	70	41	47	53	72	68	44	81	66
Non-Gendered T Score:	78	52	76	75	50	39	71	42	49	54	70	68	43	80	65
Response %:	100	100	100	100	100	100	100	100	100	100	100	100	100	100	100

The highest and lowest T scores possible on each scale are indicated by a "--".

321

MMPI-2 SUPPLEMENTARY SCALES PROFILE

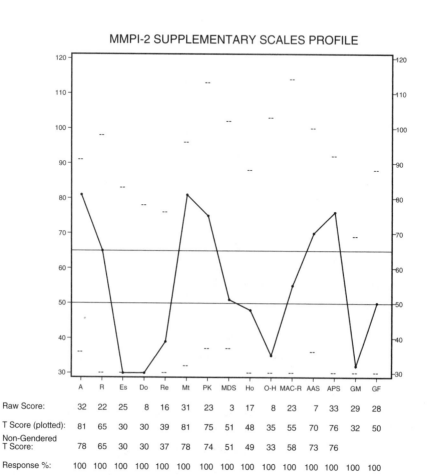

	A	R	Es	Do	Re	Mt	PK	MDS	Ho	O-H	MAC-R	AAS	APS	GM	GF
Raw Score:	32	22	25	8	16	31	23	3	17	8	23	7	33	29	28
T Score (plotted):	81	65	30	30	39	81	75	51	48	35	55	70	76	32	50
Non-Gendered T Score:	78	65	30	30	37	78	74	51	49	33	58	73	76		
Response %:	100	100	100	100	100	100	100	100	100	100	100	100	100	100	100

The highest and lowest T scores possible on each scale are indicated by a "--".

MMPI-2 PSY-5 SCALES PROFILE

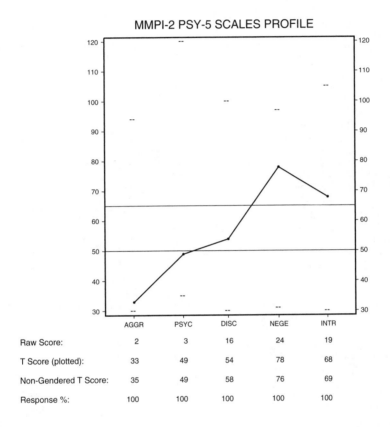

	AGGR	PSYC	DISC	NEGE	INTR
Raw Score:	2	3	16	24	19
T Score (plotted):	33	49	54	78	68
Non-Gendered T Score:	35	49	58	76	69
Response %:	100	100	100	100	100

The highest and lowest T scores possible on each scale are indicated by a "--".

ADDITIONAL SCALES
(to be used as an aid in interpreting the parent scales)

	Raw Score	T Score	Non-Gendered T Score	Resp %
Harris-Lingoes Subscales				
Depression Subscales				
Subjective Depression (D_1)	20	85	82	100
Psychomotor Retardation (D_2)	8	65	64	100
Physical Malfunctioning (D_3)	6	75	73	100
Mental Dullness (D_4)	8	77	76	100
Brooding (D_5)	5	68	65	100
Hysteria Subscales				
Denial of Social Anxiety (Hy_1)	0	30	30	100
Need for Affection (Hy_2)	8	55	55	100
Lassitude-Malaise (Hy_3)	13	97	94	100
Somatic Complaints (Hy_4)	2	48	46	100
Inhibition of Aggression (Hy_5)	2	40	39	100
Psychopathic Deviate Subscales				
Familial Discord (Pd_1)	2	51	51	100
Authority Problems (Pd_2)	5	60	64	100
Social Imperturbability (Pd_3)	0	30	30	100
Social Alienation (Pd_4)	5	56	55	100
Self-Alienation (Pd_5)	10	82	82	100
Paranoia Subscales				
Persecutory Ideas (Pa_1)	3	58	58	100
Poignancy (Pa_2)	3	55	54	100
Naivete (Pa_3)	6	56	55	100
Schizophrenia Subscales				
Social Alienation (Sc_1)	4	55	54	100
Emotional Alienation (Sc_2)	4	78	78	100
Lack of Ego Mastery, Cognitive (Sc_3)	3	60	61	100
Lack of Ego Mastery, Conative (Sc_4)	10	92	92	100
Lack of Ego Mastery, Defective Inhibition (Sc_5)	3	61	60	100
Bizarre Sensory Experiences (Sc_6)	2	51	50	100
Hypomania Subscales				
Amorality (Ma_1)	1	42	44	100
Psychomotor Acceleration (Ma_2)	8	63	64	100
Imperturbability (Ma_3)	0	30	30	100
Ego Inflation (Ma_4)	3	50	50	100
Social Introversion Subscales				
Shyness/Self-Consciousness (Si_1)	13	74	72	100
Social Avoidance (Si_2)	5	58	59	100
Alienation--Self and Others (Si_3)	11	68	67	100

	Raw Score	T Score	Non-Gendered T Score	Resp %
Content Component Scales				
Fears Subscales				
Generalized Fearfulness (FRS$_1$)	2	62	58	100
Multiple Fears (FRS$_2$)	4	54	50	100
Depression Subscales				
Lack of Drive (DEP$_1$)	7	79	77	100
Dysphoria (DEP$_2$)	4	74	69	100
Self-Depreciation (DEP$_3$)	6	83	84	100
Suicidal Ideation (DEP$_4$)	1	62	62	100
Health Concerns Subscales				
Gastrointestinal Symptoms (HEA$_1$)	0	44	44	100
Neurological Symptoms (HEA$_2$)	0	40	40	100
General Health Concerns (HEA$_3$)	4	72	72	100
Bizarre Mentation Subscales				
Psychotic Symptomatology (BIZ$_1$)	0	44	44	100
Schizotypal Characteristics (BIZ$_2$)	0	41	41	100
Anger Subscales				
Explosive Behavior (ANG$_1$)	4	64	67	100
Irritability (ANG$_2$)	7	72	71	100
Cynicism Subscales				
Misanthropic Beliefs (CYN$_1$)	1	36	37	100
Interpersonal Suspiciousness (CYN$_2$)	3	48	49	100
Antisocial Practices Subscales				
Antisocial Attitudes (ASP$_1$)	4	43	45	100
Antisocial Behavior (ASP$_2$)	3	59	64	100
Type A Subscales				
Impatience (TPA$_1$)	6	68	70	100
Competitive Drive (TPA$_2$)	3	50	51	100
Low Self-Esteem Subscales				
Self-Doubt (LSE$_1$)	5	64	64	100
Submissiveness (LSE$_2$)	6	83	79	100
Social Discomfort Subscales				
Introversion (SOD$_1$)	10	65	67	100
Shyness (SOD$_2$)	6	68	67	100
Family Problems Subscales				
Family Discord (FAM$_1$)	2	45	44	100
Familial Alienation (FAM$_2$)	1	49	50	100

	Raw Score	T Score	Non-Gendered T Score	Resp %
Negative Treatment Indicators Subscales				
Low Motivation (TRT$_1$)	5	71	69	100
Inability to Disclose (TRT$_2$)	3	60	61	100

Uniform T scores are used for Hs, D, Hy, Pd, Pa, Pt, Sc, Ma, the content scales, the content component scales, and the PSY-5 scales. The remaining scales and subscales use linear T scores.

OMITTED ITEMS

Those items for which there is no response or for which both true and false responses have been entered are considered "omitted." The potential for lowering the elevation of individual scales or the overall profile and rendering the administration invalid increases with the number of omitted items. Defensiveness, confusion, carelessness, and indecision are among the common reasons for omitting items. Examination of the content of the items that were omitted by the respondent may reveal specific problem areas or suggest reasons for their not responding appropriately to all items. Following are the items that were omitted:

None omitted.

CRITICAL ITEMS

The MMPI-2 contains a number of items whose content may indicate the presence of psychological problems when endorsed in the deviant direction. These "critical items," developed for use in clinical settings, may provide an additional source of hypotheses about the respondent. However, caution should be used in interpreting critical items since responses to single items are very unreliable and should not be treated as scores on full-length scales -- for example, an individual could easily mismark or misunderstand a single item and not intend the answer given. The content of the items and the possibility of misinterpretation make it important to keep the test results strictly confidential. Special caution should be exercised when interpreting these items in nonclinical settings.

Acute Anxiety State (Koss-Butcher Critical Items)
 3.
 10.
 15.
 39.
140.
172.
218.
223.
469.

Depressed Suicidal Ideation (Koss-Butcher Critical Items)
 9.
 38.

 65.
 71.
 95.
130.
233.
273.
388.

411.
454.
485.
518.

Threatened Assault (Koss-Butcher Critical Items)
37.
85.
213.
389.

Situational Stress Due to Alcoholism (Koss-Butcher Critical Items)
264.
487.
489.
518.

Mental Confusion (Koss-Butcher Critical Items)
31.
299.
325.

Persecutory Ideas (Koss-Butcher Critical Items)
124.

251.

Antisocial Attitude (Lachar-Wrobel Critical Items)
27.

35.
105.
266.

Family Conflict (Lachar-Wrobel Critical Items)
21.

Somatic Symptoms (Lachar-Wrobel Critical Items)
175.
229.

464.

Anxiety and Tension (Lachar-Wrobel Critical Items)
15.
172.
218.

223.
261.
299.
405.

Sleep Disturbance (Lachar-Wrobel Critical Items)
  39.
140.
328.
471.

Deviant Thinking and Experience (Lachar-Wrobel Critical Items)
122.

Depression and Worry (Lachar-Wrobel Critical Items)
  3.
 10.
 65.
 73.
130.
273.
339.

411.
415.
454.

Substance Abuse (Lachar-Wrobel Critical Items)
168.

264.
429.

Problematic Anger (Lachar-Wrobel Critical Items)
 85. At times I have a strong urge to do something harmful or shocking. (True)
213. I get mad easily and then get over it soon. (True)
389. I am often said to be hotheaded. (True)

End of Report

NOTE: This and previous pages of this report contain trade secrets and are not to be released in response to requests under HIPAA (or any other data disclosure law that exempts trade secret information from release). Further, release in response to litigation discovery demands should be made only in accordance with your profession's ethical guidelines and under an appropriate protective order.

ITEM RESPONSES

```
  1: 2     2: 1     3: 2     4: 2     5: 2     6: 1     7: 1     8: 1     9: 2    10: 2
 11: 2    12: 1    13: 2    14: 1    15: 1    16: 2    17: 2    18: 2    19: 1    20: 1
 21: 1    22: 2    23: 2    24: 2    25: 2    26: 1    27: 1    28: 2    29: 1    30: 2
 31: 1    32: 2    33: 1    34: 1    35: 1    36: 2    37: 1    38: 1    39: 1    40: 2
 41: 1    42: 2    43: 2    44: 2    45: 2    46: 1    47: 1    48: 1    49: 2    50: 2
 51: 1    52: 1    53: 2    54: 2    55: 1    56: 1    57: 1    58: 2    59: 2    60: 2
 61: 1    62: 2    63: 2    64: 2    65: 1    66: 2    67: 1    68: 1    69: 1    70: 1
 71: 1    72: 2    73: 1    74: 2    75: 1    76: 2    77: 1    78: 1    79: 2    80: 2
 81: 2    82: 1    83: 1    84: 2    85: 1    86: 1    87: 1    88: 1    89: 1    90: 1
 91: 1    92: 2    93: 1    94: 2    95: 2    96: 2    97: 2    98: 1    99: 2   100: 2
101: 2   102: 1   103: 2   104: 2   105: 1   106: 1   107: 1   108: 1   109: 1   110: 2
111: 2   112: 1   113: 1   114: 2   115: 2   116: 1   117: 1   118: 2   119: 2   120: 1
121: 1   122: 2   123: 1   124: 1   125: 1   126: 1   127: 1   128: 1   129: 1   130: 1
131: 2   132: 1   133: 2   134: 2   135: 1   136: 1   137: 2   138: 2   139: 1   140: 2
141: 2   142: 1   143: 2   144: 2   145: 2   146: 2   147: 2   148: 2   149: 2   150: 2
151: 2   152: 2   153: 2   154: 1   155: 2   156: 2   157: 2   158: 1   159: 1   160: 2
161: 1   162: 2   163: 1   164: 1   165: 1   166: 2   167: 1   168: 1   169: 2   170: 2
171: 1   172: 2   173: 2   174: 2   175: 1   176: 1   177: 1   178: 2   179: 1   180: 2
181: 2   182: 2   183: 1   184: 1   185: 1   186: 2   187: 2   188: 1   189: 1   190: 2
191: 2   192: 1   193: 2   194: 1   195: 2   196: 1   197: 2   198: 2   199: 2   200: 2
201: 2   202: 1   203: 1   204: 1   205: 2   206: 1   207: 2   208: 1   209: 2   210: 1
211: 2   212: 2   213: 1   214: 1   215: 2   216: 2   217: 1   218: 1   219: 2   220: 2
221: 2   222: 1   223: 2   224: 1   225: 1   226: 1   227: 2   228: 2   229: 1   230: 1
231: 2   232: 2   233: 1   234: 1   235: 2   236: 2   237: 1   238: 2   239: 2   240: 2
241: 2   242: 2   243: 1   244: 1   245: 2   246: 2   247: 2   248: 2   249: 1   250: 2
251: 1   252: 2   253: 2   254: 2   255: 1   256: 2   257: 2   258: 2   259: 2   260: 1
261: 2   262: 2   263: 2   264: 1   265: 1   266: 2   267: 2   268: 2   269: 2   270: 2
271: 1   272: 1   273: 1   274: 2   275: 1   276: 1   277: 2   278: 1   279: 2   280: 2
281: 1   282: 2   283: 2   284: 1   285: 1   286: 2   287: 2   288: 2   289: 1   290: 1
291: 2   292: 2   293: 2   294: 2   295: 1   296: 2   297: 2   298: 2   299: 1   300: 2
301: 2   302: 1   303: 2   304: 2   305: 1   306: 2   307: 2   308: 2   309: 1   310: 1
311: 2   312: 2   313: 2   314: 1   315: 2   316: 2   317: 2   318: 1   319: 2   320: 1
321: 2   322: 2   323: 2   324: 2   325: 1   326: 1   327: 2   328: 1   329: 2   330: 1
331: 1   332: 2   333: 2   334: 2   335: 1   336: 2   337: 1   338: 2   339: 1   340: 2
341: 1   342: 2   343: 1   344: 1   345: 2   346: 2   347: 1   348: 2   349: 2   350: 2
351: 2   352: 2   353: 2   354: 2   355: 1   356: 2   357: 1   358: 2   359: 2   360: 1
361: 2   362: 1   363: 1   364: 1   365: 2   366: 2   367: 1   368: 1   369: 1   370: 1
371: 2   372: 2   373: 1   374: 2   375: 1   376: 2   377: 2   378: 1   379: 2   380: 2
381: 2   382: 2   383: 1   384: 1   385: 2   386: 1   387: 2   388: 2   389: 1   390: 1
391: 1   392: 2   393: 2   394: 1   395: 2   396: 1   397: 2   398: 2   399: 2   400: 1
401: 2   402: 2   403: 1   404: 1   405: 2   406: 1   407: 2   408: 1   409: 1   410: 2
411: 1   412: 2   413: 2   414: 2   415: 1   416: 2   417: 1   418: 2   419: 1   420: 1
421: 1   422: 1   423: 2   424: 1   425: 2   426: 2   427: 1   428: 1   429: 2   430: 1
431: 2   432: 2   433: 1   434: 1   435: 2   436: 1   437: 2   438: 2   439: 2   440: 1
```

441: 2 442: 1 443: 2 444: 2 445: 2 446: 1 447: 2 448: 2 449: 2 450: 2
451: 2 452: 2 453: 1 454: 1 455: 1 456: 2 457: 1 458: 2 459: 1 460: 2
461: 1 462: 1 463: 2 464: 1 465: 2 466: 2 467: 2 468: 2 469: 1 470: 2
471: 1 472: 2 473: 1 474: 1 475: 1 476: 2 477: 1 478: 2 479: 2 480: 2
481: 2 482: 1 483: 2 484: 2 485: 1 486: 1 487: 1 488: 2 489: 1 490: 2
491: 1 492: 2 493: 1 494: 1 495: 2 496: 2 497: 2 498: 2 499: 1 500: 2
501: 1 502: 2 503: 1 504: 2 505: 2 506: 2 507: 1 508: 2 509: 1 510: 2
511: 2 512: 2 513: 1 514: 1 515: 2 516: 2 517: 1 518: 1 519: 1 520: 2
521: 2 522: 2 523: 1 524: 2 525: 2 526: 1 527: 2 528: 2 529: 2 530: 2
531: 2 532: 2 533: 2 534: 2 535: 1 536: 2 537: 2 538: 2 539: 1 540: 1
541: 2 542: 1 543: 2 544: 2 545: 1 546: 2 547: 1 548: 2 549: 1 550: 1
551: 2 552: 1 553: 1 554: 1 555: 2 556: 1 557: 2 558: 2 559: 2 560: 2
561: 1 562: 2 563: 2 564: 2 565: 2 566: 1 567: 2

▧ Computerized Administration, Scoring, and Interpretation

In an era of almost unbelievable advances in computer technology, it is not at all surprising that there have been increasing efforts to automate the assessment process. Automation in psychological assessment occurs whenever computers perform functions previously carried out by clinicians. Computers can be used to administer, score, and interpret tests. Although automation has been applied to a variety of psychological tests, objective personality inventories, such as the MMPI-2, lend themselves most readily to automation. Butcher (1987) pointed out that increasing applications of computers in psychology are altering the ways psychologists function. Inconsistent data have been reported concerning the frequency of use of computerized testing procedures. Ball, Archer, and Imhof (1994) surveyed clinical psychology practitioners and found that two-thirds used computers in psychological evaluations, most often for scoring and interpretation. Camara, Nathan, and Puente (2000) surveyed clinical psychologists and neuropsychologists and found that only approximately 10% of psychological tests were scored by computer and even smaller percentages were administered (approximately 3%) or interpreted (approximately 4%) by computer. Reasons for these apparently inconsistent findings are not clear. Additional data are needed to help us better understand current practices concerning the use of computers in psychological assessment. Also, we need data concerning the use of computers specifically with the MMPI-2.

Computers have some definite advantages over human clinicians in the assessment enterprise. First, they are very efficient. Operations that would take a person minutes, or even hours, to complete can be performed by computers in seconds. Second, computers are accurate and reliable. Assuming that accurate information has been programmed into a computer, there is almost perfect reliability in the functions that are performed. Third, the computer has far greater storage capacity than the human clinician. A virtually infinite number of bits of information can be stored by the computer, to be called on as needed in the assessment process. Fourth, the flexibility provided by computer technology offers the possibility of developing tests or sets of test items tailored to the individual examinee. Programs can be written to interact with the examinee so that the answer to any specific item determines the next item to be presented, skipping irrelevant data and/or exploring some areas in more depth. Although such computer-tailored assessment procedures have been employed in ability testing and diagnostic interviewing, this potential has not been widely exploited in personality assessment (Butcher, Keller, & Bacon, 1985). However, there have been several demonstrations that adaptive testing procedures can be applied to the MMPI and the MMPI-2 (Ben-Porath, Slutske, & Butcher, 1989; Butcher et al., 1985; Handel, Ben-Porath, & Watt, 1999; Roper, Ben-Porath, & Butcher, 1991, 1995).

COMPUTERIZED ADMINISTRATION

Instead of using the traditional test booklets and answer sheets, the MMPI-2 can be completed on a computer terminal or personal computer. The typical procedure is for test takers to sit at the computer while the test items are individually displayed on a monitor. A response is made to each item by pressing designated keys on the keyboard. Each response is recorded automatically and saved in the computer's memory for later processing. Programs can permit changes in responses after they are made, and omitted items can be presented again at the end of the test. More information about computerized administration is available from the test distributor, Pearson Assessments.

Automated administration has several advantages. Many persons find it more interesting than the traditional procedure and are more motivated to complete the task (Carr, Ghosh, & Ancill, 1983; Evan & Miller, 1969; Greist & Klein, 1980; Honaker, Harrell, & Buffaloe, 1988; Lucas, Mullin, Luna, & McInroy, 1977; Pinsoneault, 1996; Rozensky, Honor, Rasinski, Tovian, & Herz, 1986). Because response data are entered directly into the computer, no professional or clerical time is used for this purpose. However, a major disadvantage is that each administration consumes an hour or more of computer time. Also, some persons, particularly upset and confused clients or patients, may be overwhelmed by the task.

The MMPI-2 is a very robust instrument. Various forms of the original MMPI (e.g., booklet, audio tape recording) yielded essentially equivalent results. However, the equivalence of the computer-administered and more traditional versions of the test must be demonstrated (American Psychological Association, 1986).

Moreland (1985a); Honaker (1988); and Watson, Thomas, and Anderson (1992) reviewed studies that compared scores obtained from computerized administration of the MMPI with scores obtained from a standard booklet administration. They concluded that, although there were some differences in scores for the two forms of administration, differences were small and probably not clinically meaningful. Finger and Ones (1999) reported results of a meta-analysis of seven MMPI and five MMPI-2 studies that compared computerized and standard test administrations. They concluded that the two forms are psychometrically equivalent and that small differences reported in some studies likely were due to sampling error.

In summary, it would appear that differences between computerized and standard administrations of the MMPI-2 are small and not clinically important. This is especially true when the procedures used for computerized administrations offer test takers response options similar to those available in the standard administration. Clinicians opting to use computer administration of the MMPI-2 should use only the software provided by the test distributor. The use of nonstandardized software for test administration increases the likelihood that resulting scores will not be comparable to those that would have been obtained if the test had been administered using standard procedures.

COMPUTER-ADAPTIVE ADMINISTRATION

A significant advantage of computerized administration of the MMPI-2 is the potential to adapt the administration to the specific purposes for which the test is being used and specific characteristics of test takers. Most applications of computer-adaptive testing have been in the areas of ability and achievement testing, where items can be adaptively administered according to preliminary determinations of appropriate difficulty level. Adaptive testing is more difficult to accomplish with scales that are not homogeneous psychometrically.

Butcher et al. (1985) proposed the countdown method for adaptive administration of the MMPI. Items in a scale are administered only until it becomes impossible for a person to achieve a score at a predetermined level (e.g., T > 65). If it is determined that the cutoff cannot be reached, no additional items from the scale have to be administered. Of course, if one wants to know a person's exact T score, rather than just knowing that it is greater than 65, the remaining items in the scale can be administered. Butcher et al. demonstrated that this technique led to a 21–31% reduction in number of administered items. Similar savings have been demonstrated for the countdown method for the MMPI-2 (Forbey & Ben-Porath, 2004; Forbey, Ben-Porath, Graham, & Black, 2004; Handel et al., 1999; Roper et al., 1991).

Handel et al. (1999) and Forbey and Ben-Porath (2004) demonstrated that scores based on a computer-adaptive version of the MMPI-2 were as reliable as those based on two conventional computer administrations. Their studies also found that the validity of MMPI-2 scores based on computer-adaptive administration were as valid as scores based on conventional computer administration, using college student samples and other self-report measures as criteria. Only the Handel et al. study utilized participants in a clinical setting.

Forbey and Ben-Porath (2004, 2007) reported the development of computer-adaptive versions of the MMPI-2. They studied two types of adaptive administration. In one type they administered only the number of items needed to determine if an examinee would exceed a T score of 60 on a scale. In another type they administered items needed to determine the exact score on a scale if the T score was above 65. Their data suggested that there were significant time savings

when either adaptive type was compared with a standard computer administration. They found that correlations between scores from their three administration procedures (conventional adaptive, classification adaptive, full score
adaptive) and other self-report measures of conceptually relevant characteristics
were comparable. Forbey and Ben-Porath (2007) also developed adaptive mod-
ules that permit administration of only selected scales for screening and other
uses in various clinical, correctional, and employee assistance settings.

COMPUTERIZED SCORING

Programming a computer to score the MMPI-2 is not a very difficult task. The
computer's memory stores information that determines which items and which
responses are scored for each scale. Dozens, and even hundreds, of scales can
be scored in a matter of seconds. Because test norms also can be stored in the
computer's memory, raw scores on the various scales can be converted easily to
T scores, and profiles based on these T scores can be plotted. This entire process can be accomplished in a fraction of the time that it would take to score and
plot even the basic Validity and Clinical scales by hand. The use of MMPI-2 scoring information and norms is covered by copyright standards, so permission to
develop scoring programs must be obtained from the test publisher, the University
of Minnesota Press.

Several different procedures for computer scoring of the MMPI-2 are offered
by Pearson Assessments. Software is available for scoring using personal computers. If the test is computer administered, the individual responses are saved in
the computer's memory and are ready for immediate scoring. If a test booklet and
answer sheet are used, an examiner or clerk can use the computer keyboard to
enter the responses. With a little practice, the 567 items can be entered in a very
short time (10 to 15 minutes). For high-volume users, special answer sheets can
be processed by scanners that can be attached to personal computers. Another
option is for special answer sheets to be used and mailed to Minneapolis for scoring. Ordinarily the resulting scores are sent by return mail within 24 hours of
receipt. Persons who anticipate using computerized scoring should consult with
the test distributor to determine the most convenient and economical method
for their particular circumstances and to make sure that appropriate materials
are used.

COMPUTERIZED INTERPRETATION

Automated interpretation of the MMPI-2 is not as simple and straightforward as
administration and scoring. Interpretive statements are written for various scores
and patterns of scores, and these statements are stored in the computer's memory.
When a test is administered and scored, the computer searches its memory to find
interpretive statements that previously were judged to be appropriate for these
particular scores and patterns of scores. These statements are then selected and
printed.

It is important to distinguish between automated and actuarial interpretation (Graham & Lilly, 1984). Automation refers to the use of computers to store interpretive statements and to select and assign particular statements to particular scores and patterns of scores. Decisions about which statements are to be assigned to which scores may be based on research, actuarial tables, or clinical experience. Regardless of how the decisions are made initially, they are made automatically by the computer after the test is administered and scored. Actuarial interpretations are ones in which the assignment of interpretive statements to scores and patterns of scores is based entirely on previously established empirical relationships between test scores and the behaviors included in the interpretive statements. Experience and intuition play no part in actuarial interpretation. This is the procedure that Meehl seemed to have in mind when he made his plea for a "good cookbook" for test interpretation (Meehl, 1956).

The MMPI-2 interpretive services currently available are not actuarial in nature. They are what Wiggins (1973) called automated clinical prediction. On the basis of published research, clinical hypotheses, and clinical experience, clinicians generate interpretive statements judged to be appropriate for particular sets of test scores. The statements are stored in the computer and called on as needed. The accuracy (validity) of these kinds of interpretations depends on the knowledge and skill of the clinicians who generated the interpretive statements. The validity of these interpretations should not be assumed and needs to be demonstrated as much as the validity of a test (Moreland, 1985a).

Unlike scoring programs, interpretive programs are not controlled by copyright procedures. As long as scoring and generation of T scores are not included, there are no restrictions on the development of programs for interpreting MMPI-2 scores. Some programs are written by persons with considerable knowledge of the MMPI-2 research literature and adequate experience with the original and revised instruments. Others are written by persons knowing very little about the test. Because most interpretive services do not make available the algorithms underlying their programs, it is difficult to evaluate their accuracy. Ben-Porath and Butcher (1986) suggested that potential users of computerized interpretation services should ask the following questions before deciding which service, if any, will be used:

1. To what extent has the validity of the reports been studied?
2. To what extent do the reports rely on empirical findings in generating interpretations?
3. To what extent do the reports incorporate all of the currently available validated descriptive information?
4. Do the reports take demographic variables into account?
5. Are different versions of the reports available for various referral questions (e.g., employment screening versus clinical diagnosis)?
6. Do the reports include practical suggestions?
7. Are the reports periodically revised to reflect newly acquired information?

These seem to be reasonable questions for potential users to ask of the services they are considering. Additionally, they should find out who actually wrote the interpretive programs and determine the professional qualifications of the writers. Services that cannot or will not provide answers to these questions should not be considered seriously.

Williams and Weed (2004b) identified and reviewed eight commercially available MMPI-2 computerized interpretation services—Automated Assessment Associates; Behaviordata, Inc.; Caldwell Reports; Pearson Assessments; Psychological Assessment Resources; Psychometric Software, Inc.; PsychScreen, Inc.; and Western Psychological Services. Three of the services offered MMPI-2 scoring in addition to interpretations. While most services permitted scoring and interpretation on clinicians' personal computers, two offered only a mail-in option. Weed et al. evaluated each of the services, excluding the two that offered only a mail-in option, in terms of ease of installation, ease of data input, ability to edit report output, readability of reports, and adequacy of software and report documentation. Although most services were judged to have both strengths and weaknesses, Pearson Assessments and Psychological Assessment Resources were evaluated most positively on most dimensions.

According to guidelines established by the American Psychological Association (1986), the validity of computer-based interpretations of MMPI-2 scores should not be assumed, but rather needs to be demonstrated. Yet Williams and Weed (2004b) concluded that computerized interpretation services do not provide users with much direct evidence in support of the use of their programs.

Several methodologies have been utilized in evaluating computerized interpretations. Some studies have assessed consumer satisfaction with computer-generated interpretations. Drawing on users' knowledge of clients whose MMPI-2 results have been submitted for computer-based interpretations, users have been asked to rate individual reports in terms of clarity, accuracy, and usefulness. Early studies (e.g., Adams & Shore, 1976; Eyde, Kowal, & Fishburne, 1991; Green, 1982; Webb, Miller, & Fowler, 1969, 1970) found that users were generally satisfied with the computerized interpretations. However, a methodological limitation of these studies is that they did not control for what Meehl (1956) called the Barnum effect, that is, descriptive statements being considered as highly accurate despite their lack of discrimination among individuals. In addition, the studies did not assess the external validity of inferences included in the reports.

A more recent study by Williams and Weed (2004a) controlled for the Barnum effect in its research design. MMPI-2 answer sheets for clients from four settings (inpatient, outpatient, college counseling, and prison) were randomly assigned to one of eight commercially available services, the same ones mentioned earlier in relation to another of their studies (Williams & Weed, 2004b). The services generated reports based on each client's MMPI-2 responses and a modal report for each of the four settings based on mean scores for the setting. Therapists who submitted the MMPI-2 answer sheets were sent a report for each client. Although reports were sometimes based on a client's actual MMPI-2 responses and sometimes on the mean scores for a particular setting, the therapists were not told that some reports were not actually based on their clients' responses. Therapists rated each report on the following 10 dimensions, using a seven-point scale: conciseness, confirmation of therapist's impressions of client, usefulness for diagnosis and/or treatment, accuracy, provision of new information, presence of contradictory information, omission of important information, organization and clarity, presence of useless information, and appropriateness of diagnostic considerations. Reports from each service were evaluated by comparing therapist ratings of the reports based on individual MMPI-2 responses with reports based on mean scores for the setting in which each client was evaluated. Most reports based on average scores for settings were not evaluated positively on most of the 10 dimensions. Thus, there did not seem to be much of a Barnum effect. Ratings of reports based on patients' actual MMPI-2 scores were generally evaluated much more positively by therapists. Williams and Weed summarized average therapist evaluations of reports for the 10 dimensions listed here. Except for reports provided by one service, the computer-based interpretations were generally judged rather positively. Each service seemed to have strengths and weaknesses. Readers who are interested in how each service's reports were evaluated on each dimension should consult the Williams and Weed article.

Some studies (e.g., Bringmann, Balance, & Giesbrecht, 1972) evaluated computer-generated reports by comparing them with reports generated by clinicians examining test scores. Generally, computer-generated and clinician-generated reports were judged to be comparable. However, such studies are of limited value because the validity of the clinician-generated reports was unknown.

An interesting study by Epstein and Rotunda (2000) examined the extent to which computer-generated and clinician-generated reports added to basic MMPI-2 scores and demographic information. Licensed psychologists who received a computer-generated report in addition to an MMPI-2 profile and demographic information provided less accurate symptom ratings than those who received a clinician-generated report in addition to an MMPI-2 profile and demographic information. A complicating factor in this study was that the computer-generated report was based only on MMPI-2 scores, whereas the clinician-generated report was based on a complete psychological evaluation that could have included information from interviews and other psychological tests.

The most definitive evaluation of computer-generated MMPI-2 interpretations is to determine the external validity of statements and inferences included in the computer-generated reports. Several early studies examined the external validity of computer-generated MMPI reports by comparing statements in the reports with ratings of test-takers based on therapist ratings or clinical records (Anderson, 1969; Chase, 1974; Crumpton, 1975; Hedlund, Morgan, & Master, 1972). Although the results of these studies generally supported the validity of computer-generated inferences, methodological issues, including small sample sizes and questionable reliability of criterion ratings, limited confidence in their findings. Using a Q-sort procedure, McNeal (1997) compared the validity of computer-based MMPI-2 interpretations and clinician-based blind interpretations of MMPI-2 profiles. Accuracy of each kind of inferences was assessed by comparing them with descriptions generated by patients' therapists. Both kinds of interpretations were found to be significantly related to criterion ratings provided by therapists, but the computer-based and clinician-based interpretations did not differ from each other in validity.

In summary, research results support the usefulness of computer-based MMPI-2 interpretations. Such interpretations generally are evaluated by clinicians as useful and accurate. Each of the commercially available services has both strengths and weaknesses. It would be premature at this time to recommend any particular service for general clinical use. What clearly is needed is more research concerning the external validity of computer-based MMPI-2 inferences.

ISSUES CONCERNING THE USE OF COMPUTERIZED INTERPRETATIONS

There are important issues involved in the use of computerized MMPI-2 interpretations. One has to do with the extent to which adequately trained clinicians integrate the automated reports with other information available about test takers. Although most of the services advise users that inferences in the test reports need to be verified by other data sources, in practice some clinicians use the automated reports instead of a comprehensive assessment. This is not responsible clinical practice. Tanner (2007) developed free MMPI-2 interpretive software that is available only to users who promise to rewrite the computer-generated statements to take into account additional information about patients.

Another concern is that because they are computer generated, the automated reports are seen as valid and questions rarely are asked about research demonstrating their validity. In fact, Ziskin (1981) recommended the use of automated reports in forensic cases because the computer-generated profiles and reports are viewed by judges and jurors as more scientific. Despite these perceptions, the validity of automated interpretations must be demonstrated empirically.

The qualifications of users of automated services are very important. Although services purport to assess the qualifications of potential users to make sure that they use the interpretive reports appropriately, many users of the services may not be qualified professionally to use them. Some psychologists who are trained and licensed to practice psychology do not know enough about the MMPI-2 to evaluate the appropriateness of the automated interpretations. The services also are available to physicians, social workers, and others who are licensed to offer mental health services. Often, the members of these other professions are not adequately trained to evaluate the appropriateness of the automated interpretations.

Some services list scores for large numbers of supplementary scales, some of which are experimental in nature. Although information about the development, reliability, and validity of these scales sometimes is provided in materials supplied to users, the typical reader of computerized reports does not have readily accessible information permitting informed decisions about the relative importance to attach to the various scores provided. It would be very helpful if reports would indicate which scales are considered to be experimental so users could exercise appropriate caution in interpreting them.

Most services also provide numerous indexes, such as the Goldberg index and the Henrichs modification of the Meehl–Dahlstrom rules. The guidelines of the American Psychological Association indicate that when such indexes are presented in computerized interpretations, information concerning hit rates and other validity data should be available to users. Such information typically has not been provided by computer services.

Automated services for the MMPI-2 typically list critical items that test takers have endorsed in the scored direction. Although critical-item endorsements represent an important additional source of inferences concerning test takers, many users of the services overinterpret such endorsements. Each critical item is, in fact, a single-item scale whose reliability is very questionable. Thus, extreme caution must be exercised in interpreting the critical items.

As Butcher (1978) noted, automated interpretive systems often become fixed at a rather naive level. Although the potential exists for modifying the systems as new interpretive data become available, there has been a tendency not to change systems that have been operating smoothly and producing a profit for companies. Butcher discussed several instances in which, in response to critics, only minor cosmetic changes or no changes were made in existing interpretive programs.

PROFESSIONAL GUIDELINES FOR COMPUTERIZED ASSESSMENT

In an effort to try to address some of the potential problems involved in the use of automated assessment services, in 1966 the American Psychological Association developed some interim standards for such services (Fowler, 1969). The standards made it clear that organizations offering the services have primary responsibility for ensuring that the services are used by qualified persons and for demonstrating the reliability and validity of the interpretations included in the reports. In 1986 the Committee on Professional Standards and the Committee on Psychological Tests and Assessment of the American Psychological Association published updated guidelines for computer-based tests and interpretations (American Psychological Association, 1986). These updated guidelines state that it is the responsibility of test developers of computer-based test services to demonstrate the equivalence of computerized and conventional versions of a test. Developers offering interpretations of test scores should describe how the interpretive statements are derived from the original scores and should make clear the extent to which interpretive statements are based on quantitative research versus clinical opinion. When statements in an interpretive report are based on expert clinical opinion, users should be given information that will allow them to weigh the credibility of the opinion.

Developers are expected to provide whatever information is needed to qualified professionals engaged in scholarly review of their interpretive services.

The updated guidelines make it very clear that professionals are responsible for any use they make of computer-administered tests or computer-generated interpretations. Users should be aware of the method employed in generating the scores and interpretations and be sufficiently familiar with the test to be able to evaluate its applicability to the purpose for which it will be used. The user should judge, for each test taker, the validity of the computerized test report based on the user's professional knowledge of the total context of testing and the test taker's performance and characteristics.

Clearly, the developers of computerized testing services and the clinicians who use them share responsibility for ensuring that the results are valid and are used appropriately. In the past, it has seemed that each of these parties has assumed that the other has major responsibility.

SAMPLE OF COMPUTERIZED INTERPRETIVE REPORT

To illustrate computerized interpretation of the MMPI-2, the answer sheet of the person discussed in detail in Chapter 11 (Jeff) was scored and interpreted using a service provided by Pearson Assessments, and the resulting computer report is presented in its entirety in an appendix to this chapter.

The Minnesota Report: Adult Clinical System—Revised (4th Edition) (Butcher, 2005) was authored almost entirely by one expert, Dr. James N. Butcher, incorporating both his knowledge of research data and his clinical experience. The program is built hierarchically around code-type interpretations (Butcher, 1989a; Butcher et al., 1985). If a profile fits an established code type, a standard report for that configural pattern is printed. Additions and modifications are based on scores on other scales. If the profile does not fit an established code type, the report is based on a scale-by-scale analysis.

The Minnesota Report relies heavily on research findings on the original MMPI and the MMPI-2 and the report author's clinical experience with the original and revised versions of the test (Butcher, 1993). According to the user's guide for the Minnesota Report (Butcher, 1993), several demographic and situational variables are taken into consideration in generating interpretive statements about scores. Gender, age, educational level, marital status, and type of setting in which the test was completed are all considered.

Several different options are available for persons who want to use the MMPI-2 computerized services provided by Pearson Assessments. The Extended Score Report includes scores for the standard Validity and Clinical scales and a large number of other scales and indexes. In addition to the Minnesota Adult Clinical Report, which is the one illustrated in this chapter, there are interpretive reports available for use in personnel selection and in forensic and criminal justice and correctional settings. Readers wanting more information about these services should consult a recent Pearson Assessments catalog or contact Pearson Assessments.

As the reader can see in the sample report, the Minnesota *Adult Clinical Report* includes scores for the Validity and Clinical scales and for a large number of Supplementary scales. Some of these scores are profiled (Validity scales, Clinical scales, Content scales, some Supplementary scales), and others are listed along with corresponding T-score values. The report also presents raw scores and T scores for five subscales of the Superlative Self-Presentation (S) scale. For each scale for which scores are reported, there is an indication of the percentage of items in the scale that were completed (as opposed to omitted).

The Welsh Code, which is printed beneath the Clinical and Supplementary scales profile, indicates the ordering of the Clinical scales (from highest to lowest), with symbols inserted to indicate T-score levels of scores. Other indexes, such as the mean profile elevation (an average T score for eight Clinical scales) and percentage of true and false responses, are calculated and reported.

The narrative portion of the report contains several sections. The first section deals with the validity of the profile. If the profile is judged to be invalid, scores are reported, but no further interpretive statements are made. The second section provides a description of the most salient symptoms suggested by the test results. The third section presents data concerning the frequency with which the particular pattern of scores occurs in the MMPI-2 normative sample and in several clinical samples. The fourth section gives statements concerning the likelihood that the symptoms and other characteristics described in other sections are likely to remain stable or change over time. The fifth section describes the most likely manner in which the test taker interacts with other people. This section states whether or not the scores suggest code-type definition. The sixth section comments on symptoms and characteristics that should be considered in relation to diagnoses. The seventh and final section of the narrative addresses treatment considerations. The report also lists critical items that were endorsed in the scored direction along with the frequencies with which each item was endorsed by the MMPI-2 normative sample and a large sample of mental health outpatients. The content of the test items is included in the actual reports. To protect the integrity of the test, item content does not appear here because books are available to the general public. The last information presented in the report is a listing of individual item responses to the 567 items in the MMPI-2.

It is important to note that the Minnesota Report includes cautionary statements indicating that the descriptions, inferences, and recommendations contained in the report need to be verified by other sources of clinical information and that the information in the report should be most appropriately used by a trained, qualified test interpreter.

COMPARISON OF COMPUTERIZED AND CLINICIAN-GENERATED INTERPRETATIONS

A comparison of the computerized and the clinician-generated interpretations for the case that was presented in Chapter 11 (Jeff) reveals considerable agreement between the interpretations. However, the clinician-generated report seems to be more comprehensive in its description of Jeff, and its inferences are a bit more integrated than is the case for the computerized interpretation.

Both interpretations conclude that the MMPI-2 results are valid and interpretable. Both interpretations indicate that the configuration of Clinical scale scores is well defined and is likely to be stable over time.

The two interpretations are remarkably similar in describing Jeff as experiencing emotional turmoil and feeling overwhelmed by the responsibilities of daily life. Both interpretations describe depression, anxiety, and somatic symptoms. The possibility of suicidal ideation is raised in both interpretations. The computerized interpretation indicates that there is a strong possibility that he has seriously contemplated suicide, whereas the clinician-generated interpretation states that Jeff did not endorse items dealing directly with suicide attempts or plans. Both interpretations mention lack of energy, problems with concentration, obsessiveness, guilt, and indecision, and they state that at times Jeff may feel out of control of his thought processes.

The two interpretations are quite similar concerning diagnoses that should be considered. For Axis I these include depressive, anxiety, and alcohol and drug use disorders. Both interpretations indicate that Jeff's symptoms and behaviors are consistent with Axis II diagnoses of dependent and obsessive–compulsive personality disorders.

Descriptions of Jeff's personality characteristics and behaviors are remarkably similar in the two interpretations. Jeff is described as a shy, insecure, passive–dependent person who is not appropriately assertive in relationships. Although he is capable of forming intimate relationships, his insecurity often interferes with them. Both interpretations note that Jeff is likely to be experiencing anger and resentment. The clinician-generated interpretation infers that the anger and resentment may result from perceptions of other people as not very understanding, supportive, or trustworthy. The clinician-generated interpretation also indicates that Jeff is not likely to express negative feelings openly most of the time but may do so in occasional emotional outbursts. Both interpretations describe Jeff as shy and socially uncomfortable. The clinician-generated interpretation raises the possibility that other people may misinterpret Jeff's shyness as aloofness and emotional distancing.

Positive statements about Jeff are noticeably lacking in the computerized interpretation. The clinician-generated interpretation describes some positive characteristics, including persistence, reliability, strong need to achieve, and capacity to form deep emotional ties.

Both interpretations indicate that Jeff is in need of mental health services. Because of his intense discomfort, he is likely to be receptive to treatment, but he has a low capacity for self-change. Both interpretations suggest the possibility of medication to alleviate symptoms of depression. The computerized interpretation suggests several specific therapeutic approaches, such as cognitive-behavioral therapy and assertiveness training, and suggests that negative work attitudes should be addressed in treatment. Both interpretations indicate that a substance abuse component to treatment be considered.

The clinician-generated interpretation indicates that Jeff is likely to stay in treatment longer than many patients, will not respond well to brief therapy, and will show slow but steady progress over time. The clinician-generated interpretation also mentions several characteristics that may interfere with effective treatment. Jeff is described as having limited psychological resources that could be utilized in therapy. He also can be expected to rationalize and intellectualize excessively and to resist psychological interpretations. He tends to be rigid and to give up easily when things are not going well. He may come to express considerable hostility toward the therapist.

The clinician-generated interpretation includes inferences about Jeff's personality and behavior not directly addressed by the computerized interpretation. Jeff is described as trying to handle stress through the use of denial, repression, and withdrawal into fantasy and daydreaming. He is described as cynical and suspicious of the motives of other people. He has a strong need for recognition for his accomplishments. Although the Work Interference (WRK) Content scale suggests characteristics that could interfere with work performance, Jeff seems to derive satisfaction from productive work.

In summary, the overall agreement between the computerized and clinician-generated interpretations is remarkable. Although there are some specific differences in emphasis, the descriptions that emerge from the two interpretations are very similar. The agreement is not really unexpected. The clinician who developed the interpretive program for the Minnesota Report and the clinician who did the interpretation in Chapter 11 were basing their interpretations on basically the same research data. For this sample case, the clinician-generated interpretation is more detailed than the computerized interpretation.

The comparison of the two interpretations for this sample case should not be considered as general support for the validity of computerized interpretations of the MMPI-2. However, it should be noted that the clinician-generated interpretation was completed before the author had access to the computerized interpretation. Consideration must be given to the fact that the case used for this comparison is not a very difficult or complicated one. There is a clearly defined two-point code type that has been researched extensively. Few internal inconsistencies are present. There very well might be less agreement between computerized and clinician-generated interpretations of less clear-cut MMPI-2 protocols.

CONCLUSIONS AND RECOMMENDATIONS

The use of computers for the administration of the MMPI-2 is not likely to become a widespread practice. The computer time required to complete the test using a personal computer is so great that in most settings this form of administration is not practical. However, it appears that the scores resulting from computer-administered versions of the MMPI-2 are comparable to those of paper-and-pencil versions. The use of computerized scoring of the MMPI-2 permits the clinician to obtain scores on numerous MMPI-2 scales in a very efficient manner. Only scoring programs that are officially sanctioned by the test publisher are legal. Computerized interpretation of MMPI-2 scores is not covered by copyright standards. Persons are free to develop computer programs for interpreting scores. As a result, many different interpretive services are available to clinicians. The accuracy (validity) of these interpretations needs to be demonstrated empirically and cannot be assumed, and it is the responsibility of the developers of the computerized interpretations to do so. It is the responsibility of the users of the services to obtain information needed to make intelligent decisions concerning the use of the interpretations.

This author is in agreement with Matarazzo (1986) and Fowler and Butcher (1986) that computerized interpretations should not serve as the equivalent of or substitute for a comprehensive psychological assessment conducted by a properly trained clinician. The automated reports are intended as professional-to-professional consultations, and the hypotheses generated are to be considered in the context of other information available about examinees. It is the responsibility of the users of these reports to determine to what extent the interpretations apply to particular test takers. When used in this manner by qualified professionals, the automated interpretive reports have considerable potential. When used instead of a comprehensive psychological assessment conducted by a qualified clinician, their use is irresponsible and not recommended.

MMPI®-2
Minnesota Multiphasic
Personality Inventory®-2

Outpatient Mental Health Interpretive Report

MMPI®-2

The Minnesota Report™: Adult Clinical System-Revised, 4th Edition

James N. Butcher, PhD

ID Number:	182672
Age:	24
Gender:	Male
Marital Status:	Never Married
Years of Education:	12
Date Assessed:	09/02/1998

Setting was not specified. This report was processed for an "Outpatient Mental Health" setting.

PEARSON

🔵 *PsychCorp*

Copyright © 1989, 1993, 2001, 2005 by the Regents of the University of Minnesota. All rights reserved.
Portions reproduced from the MMPI-2 test booklet. Copyright © 1942, 1943 (renewed 1970), 1989 by the Regents of the
University of Minnesota. All rights reserved. Portions excerpted from the *MMPI-2 Manual for Administration, Scoring, and
Interpretation, Revised Edition.* Copyright © 2001 by the Regents of the University of Minnesota. All rights reserved.
Distributed exclusively under license from the University of Minnesota by NCS Pearson, Inc.

Minnesota Multiphasic Personality Inventory and **MMPI** are registered trademarks and **The Minnesota Report** is a
trademark of the University of Minnesota. **Pearson,** the **PSI logo,** and **PsychCorp** are trademarks in the U.S. and/or other
countries of Pearson Education, Inc., or its affiliate(s).

TRADE SECRET INFORMATION
Not for release under HIPAA or other data disclosure laws that exempt trade secrets from disclosure.

[9.4 / 153 / 2.3.17]

Reproduced by permission of the University of Minnesota Press. All rights reserved. "MMPI® ,"
"Minnesota Multiphasic Personality Inventory® ," and "The Minnesota Report™" are trademarks owned by the University of Minnesota.

MMPI-2 VALIDITY PATTERN

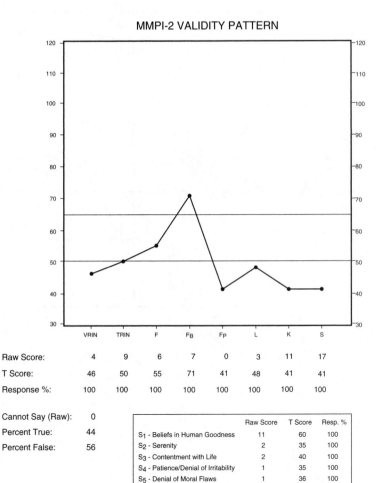

	VRIN	TRIN	F	FB	Fp	L	K	S
Raw Score:	4	9	6	7	0	3	11	17
T Score:	46	50	55	71	41	48	41	41
Response %:	100	100	100	100	100	100	100	100

Cannot Say (Raw): 0

Percent True: 44

Percent False: 56

	Raw Score	T Score	Resp. %
S1 - Beliefs in Human Goodness	11	60	100
S2 - Serenity	2	35	100
S3 - Contentment with Life	2	40	100
S4 - Patience/Denial of Irritability	1	35	100
S5 - Denial of Moral Flaws	1	36	100

MMPI-2 CLINICAL AND SUPPLEMENTARY SCALES PROFILE

	Hs	D	Hy	Pd	Mf	Pa	Pt	Sc	Ma	Si		MAC-R	APS	AAS	PK	Ho	MDS
Raw Score:	9	34	27	24	25	15	28	19	16	46		23	33	7	23	17	*
K Correction:	6			4			11	11	2								
T Score:	57	81	64	62	48	68	77	56	45	74		55	76	70	75	48	*
Response %:	100	100	100	100	100	100	100	100	100	100		100	100	100	100	100	*

Welsh Code: 2"70'6+34-18/59: F/LK:

Profile Elevation: 63.8

*MDS scores are reported only for clients who indicate that they are married or separated.

MMPI-2 CONTENT SCALES PROFILE

	ANX	FRS	OBS	DEP	HEA	BIZ	ANG	CYN	ASP	TPA	LSE	SOD	FAM	WRK	TRT
Raw Score:	18	6	13	19	5	0	12	4	7	10	13	16	3	24	11
T Score:	80	57	77	77	51	39	70	41	47	53	72	68	44	81	66
Response %:	100	100	100	100	100	100	100	100	100	100	100	100	100	100	100

PROFILE VALIDITY

This is a valid MMPI-2 clinical profile. The client was cooperative with the evaluation and appears to be willing to disclose personal information.

The clinical setting in which this MMPI-2 was taken has not been indicated. The report has been processed as though "Outpatient Mental Health Program" was indicated. The report may not be as specific as it would have been if the actual assessment setting had been designated.

SYMPTOMATIC PATTERNS

The personality and behavioral descriptions provided by this MMPI-2 profile code incorporated correlates of D and Pt. These descriptions are likely to be a good match with the empirical literature because of the client's well-defined profile type. The client's MMPI-2 clinical profile reflects much psychological distress at this time. He has major problems with anxiety and depression. He tends to be high-strung and insecure, and he may also be having somatic problems. He is probably experiencing loss of sleep and appetite and a slowness in personal tempo.

Individuals with this profile often have high standards and a strong need to achieve, but they feel that they fall short of their expectations and then blame themselves harshly. This client feels quite insecure and pessimistic about the future. He also feels quite inferior, has little self-confidence, and does not feel capable of solving his problems.

In addition, the following description is suggested by the client's scores on the content scales. He endorsed a number of items suggesting that he is experiencing low morale and a depressed mood. He reports a preoccupation with feeling guilty and unworthy. He feels that he deserves to be punished for wrongs he has committed. He feels regretful and unhappy about life, and he seems plagued by anxiety and worry about the future. He feels hopeless at times and feels that he is a condemned person. He has difficulty managing routine affairs, and the items he endorsed suggest a poor memory, concentration problems, and an inability to make decisions. He appears to be immobilized and withdrawn and has no energy for life. He views his physical health as failing and reports numerous somatic concerns. He feels that life is no longer worthwhile and that he is losing control of his thought processes.

According to his response content, there is a strong possibility that he has seriously contemplated suicide. The client's recent thinking is likely to be characterized by obsessiveness and indecision. He endorses statements that show some inability to control his anger. He may physically or verbally attack others when he is angry.

Long-term personality factors identified by his PSY-5 scale elevations may help provide a clinical context for the symptoms he is presently experiencing. He tends to view the world in a highly negative manner and usually develops a worst-case scenario to explain events affecting him. He tends to worry to excess and interprets even neutral events as problematic. His self-critical nature prevents him from viewing relationships in a positive manner. He also shows a meager capacity to experience pleasure in life. Persons with high scores on INTR (Introversion/Low Positive Emotionality) tend to be pessimistic.

PROFILE FREQUENCY

Profile interpretation can be greatly facilitated by examining the relative frequency of clinical scale patterns in various settings. The client's high-point clinical scale score (D) occurred in 7.2% of the MMPI-2 normative sample of men. However, only 2.4% of the sample had D as the peak score at or above a T score of 65, and only 1.1% had well-defined D spikes. This elevated MMPI-2 profile configuration (2-7/7-2) is very rare in samples of normals, occurring in less than 1% of the MMPI-2 normative sample of men.

This high-point MMPI-2 score on the D scale is relatively frequent in various outpatient settings. In the Pearson outpatient sample, the high-point clinical scale score on D occurred in 12.7% of the men. Moreover, 9.0% of the male outpatients had the D scale spike at or above a T score of 65, and 3.8% had well-defined D scale scores. His elevated MMPI-2 profile configuration (2-7/7-2) is relatively common in outpatient men. It occurred in 4.8% of the men in the Pearson outpatient sample. The 2-7 profile code was the second most frequent two-point code in outpatient men when both scales were at or above a T score of 65.

He scored relatively high on APS and AAS, suggesting the possibility of a drug- or alcohol-abuse problem. The base rate data on his profile type among residents in alcohol and drug programs should also be evaluated. His MMPI-2 profile code, including D and Pt, is the second most frequent two-point code among men in alcohol- and drug-abusing populations. Over 13.8% of the men in substance-abuse treatment programs had this pattern (McKenna & Butcher, 1987).

PROFILE STABILITY

The relative elevation of the highest scales in his clinical profile reflects high profile definition. If he is retested at a later date, his peak scores on D and Pt are likely to retain their relative salience in his retest profile.

INTERPERSONAL RELATIONS

He appears to be quite passive and dependent in interpersonal relationships and does not speak up for himself even when others take advantage of him. He avoids confrontation and seeks nurturance from others, often at the price of his own independence. He forms deep emotional attachments and tends to be quite vulnerable to being hurt. He also tends to blame himself for interpersonal problems. Individuals with this profile are often experiencing psychological distress in response to stressful events. The intense feelings may diminish over time or with treatment.

He appears to be rather shy and inhibited in social situations, and he may avoid others for fear of being hurt. He has very few friends, and others think he is hard to get to know. He is quiet, submissive, and conventional, and he lacks self-confidence in dealing with other people. Individuals with this passive and withdrawing lifestyle are often unable to assert themselves appropriately and are frequently taken advantage of by others. Personality characteristics related to social introversion tend to be stable over time. His generally reclusive behavior, introverted lifestyle, and tendency toward interpersonal avoidance may be prominent in any future test results.

The client's scores on the content scales suggest the following additional information concerning his interpersonal relations. He feels intensely angry, hostile, and resentful of others, and he would like to get back at them. He is competitive and uncooperative, tending to be very critical of others.

DIAGNOSTIC CONSIDERATIONS

Individuals with this profile tend to be considered neurotic and receive diagnoses such as Dysthymic Disorder or Anxiety Disorder. They may also receive an Axis II diagnosis of Dependent or Compulsive Personality Disorder.

His extremely high scores on the addiction proneness indicators suggest the possible development of an addictive disorder. In his responses to the MMPI-2, he acknowledged some problems with excessive use or abuse of addictive substances. Further evaluation of substance use or abuse problems is strongly recommended.

TREATMENT CONSIDERATIONS

Individuals with this MMPI-2 pattern are usually feeling a great deal of discomfort and tend to want help for their psychological problems. The client's self-esteem is low and he tends to blame himself too much for his difficulties. Although he worries a great deal about his problems, he seems to have little energy left over for action to resolve them.

Symptomatic relief for his depression may be provided by antidepressant medication. Psychotherapy, particularly cognitive behavioral treatment, may also be beneficial.

The passive, unassertive personality style that seems to underlie this disorder might be a focus of behavior change. Individuals with these problems may learn to deal with others more effectively through assertiveness training.

The client's scores on the content scales indicate attitudes and feelings that suggest a low capacity for change. His potentially high resistance to change might need to be discussed with him early in treatment in order to promote a more positive attitude.

In any intervention or psychological evaluation program involving occupational adjustment, his negative work attitudes could become an important problem to overcome. He has a number of attitudes and feelings that could interfere with work adjustment.

His acknowledged problems with alcohol or drug use should be addressed in therapy.

ADDITIONAL SCALES

	Raw Score	T Score	Resp %
Personality Psychopathology Five (PSY-5) Scales			
Aggressiveness (AGGR)	2	33	100
Psychoticism (PSYC)	3	49	100
Disconstraint (DISC)	16	54	100
Negative Emotionality/Neuroticism (NEGE)	24	78	100
Introversion/Low Positive Emotionality (INTR)	19	68	100
Supplementary Scales			
Anxiety (A)	32	81	100
Repression (R)	22	65	100
Ego Strength (Es)	25	30	100
Dominance (Do)	8	30	100
Social Responsibility (Re)	16	39	100
Harris-Lingoes Subscales			
Depression Subscales			
Subjective Depression (D_1)	20	85	100
Psychomotor Retardation (D_2)	8	65	100
Physical Malfunctioning (D_3)	6	75	100
Mental Dullness (D_4)	8	77	100
Brooding (D_5)	5	68	100
Hysteria Subscales			
Denial of Social Anxiety (Hy_1)	0	30	100
Need for Affection (Hy_2)	8	55	100
Lassitude-Malaise (Hy_3)	13	97	100
Somatic Complaints (Hy_4)	2	48	100
Inhibition of Aggression (Hy_5)	2	40	100
Psychopathic Deviate Subscales			
Familial Discord (Pd_1)	2	51	100
Authority Problems (Pd_2)	5	60	100
Social Imperturbability (Pd_3)	0	30	100
Social Alienation (Pd_4)	5	56	100
Self-Alienation (Pd_5)	10	82	100
Paranoia Subscales			
Persecutory Ideas (Pa_1)	3	58	100
Poignancy (Pa_2)	3	55	100
Naivete (Pa_3)	6	56	100

	Raw Score	T Score	Resp %
Schizophrenia Subscales			
Social Alienation (Sc_1)	4	55	100
Emotional Alienation (Sc_2)	4	78	100
Lack of Ego Mastery, Cognitive (Sc_3)	3	60	100
Lack of Ego Mastery, Conative (Sc_4)	10	92	100
Lack of Ego Mastery, Defective Inhibition (Sc_5)	3	61	100
Bizarre Sensory Experiences (Sc_6)	2	51	100
Hypomania Subscales			
Amorality (Ma_1)	1	42	100
Psychomotor Acceleration (Ma_2)	8	63	100
Imperturbability (Ma_3)	0	30	100
Ego Inflation (Ma_4)	3	50	100

Social Introversion Subscales (Ben-Porath, Hostetler, Butcher, & Graham)

	Raw Score	T Score	Resp %
Shyness/Self-Consciousness (Si_1)	13	74	100
Social Avoidance (Si_2)	5	58	100
Alienation--Self and Others (Si_3)	11	68	100

Content Component Scales (Ben-Porath & Sherwood)

	Raw Score	T Score	Resp %
Fears Subscales			
Generalized Fearfulness (FRS_1)	2	62	100
Multiple Fears (FRS_2)	4	54	100
Depression Subscales			
Lack of Drive (DEP_1)	7	79	100
Dysphoria (DEP_2)	4	74	100
Self-Depreciation (DEP_3)	6	83	100
Suicidal Ideation (DEP_4)	1	62	100
Health Concerns Subscales			
Gastrointestinal Symptoms (HEA_1)	0	44	100
Neurological Symptoms (HEA_2)	0	40	100
General Health Concerns (HEA_3)	4	72	100
Bizarre Mentation Subscales			
Psychotic Symptomatology (BIZ_1)	0	44	100
Schizotypal Characteristics (BIZ_2)	0	41	100
Anger Subscales			
Explosive Behavior (ANG_1)	4	64	100
Irritability (ANG_2)	7	72	100
Cynicism Subscales			
Misanthropic Beliefs (CYN_1)	1	36	100
Interpersonal Suspiciousness (CYN_2)	3	48	100

	Raw Score	T Score	Resp %
Antisocial Practices Subscales			
Antisocial Attitudes (ASP$_1$)	4	43	100
Antisocial Behavior (ASP$_2$)	3	59	100
Type A Subscales			
Impatience (TPA$_1$)	6	68	100
Competitive Drive (TPA$_2$)	3	50	100
Low Self-Esteem Subscales			
Self-Doubt (LSE$_1$)	5	64	100
Submissiveness (LSE$_2$)	6	83	100
Social Discomfort Subscales			
Introversion (SOD$_1$)	10	65	100
Shyness (SOD$_2$)	6	68	100
Family Problems Subscales			
Family Discord (FAM$_1$)	2	45	100
Familial Alienation (FAM$_2$)	1	49	100
Negative Treatment Indicators Subscales			
Low Motivation (TRT$_1$)	5	71	100
Inability to Disclose (TRT$_2$)	3	60	100

Uniform T scores are used for Hs, D, Hy, Pd, Pa, Pt, Sc, Ma, the content scales, the content component scales, and the PSY-5 scales. The remaining scales and subscales use linear T scores.

CRITICAL ITEMS

The following critical items have been found to have possible significance in analyzing a client's problem situation. Although these items may serve as a source of hypotheses for further investigation, caution should be used in interpreting individual items because they may have been checked inadvertently.

The percentages of endorsement for each critical item by various reference groups are presented in brackets following the listing of the item. The endorsement percentage labeled "N" is the percentage of the MMPI-2 normative sample of 1,138 men who endorsed the item in the scored direction. Endorsement percentages for the normative sample are reported for all critical items. When available, endorsement percentages for the setting are also reported. The designation "Op" refers to a sample of 10,510 male outpatients (Pearson, 1993).

Acute Anxiety State (Koss-Butcher Critical Items)

Of the 17 possible items in this section, 9 were endorsed in the scored direction:

3.

10.

15.

39.

140.

172.

218.

223.

469.

Depressed Suicidal Ideation (Koss-Butcher Critical Items)

Of the 22 possible items in this section, 13 were endorsed in the scored direction:

9.

38.

65.

71.

95.

130.

233.

273.

388.

411.

454.

485.

518.

Threatened Assault (Koss-Butcher Critical Items)

Of the 5 possible items in this section, 4 were endorsed in the scored direction:

37.

85.

213.

389.

Situational Stress Due to Alcoholism (Koss-Butcher Critical Items)

Of the 7 possible items in this section, 4 were endorsed in the scored direction:

264.

487.

489.

518.

Mental Confusion (Koss-Butcher Critical Items)

Of the 11 possible items in this section, 3 were endorsed in the scored direction:

31.

299.

325.

Persecutory Ideas (Koss-Butcher Critical Items)

Of the 16 possible items in this section, 2 were endorsed in the scored direction:

124.

251.

Antisocial Attitude (Lachar-Wrobel Critical Items)

Of the 9 possible items in this section, 4 were endorsed in the scored direction:

27.

35.

105.

266.

Family Conflict (Lachar-Wrobel Critical Items)

Of the 4 possible items in this section, 1 was endorsed in the scored direction:

21.

Somatic Symptoms (Lachar-Wrobel Critical Items)

Of the 23 possible items in this section, 3 were endorsed in the scored direction:

175.

229.

464.

Anxiety and Tension (Lachar-Wrobel Critical Items)

Of the 11 possible items in this section, 7 were endorsed in the scored direction:

15.

172.

218.

223.

261.

299.

405.

Sleep Disturbance (Lachar-Wrobel Critical Items)

Of the 6 possible items in this section, 4 were endorsed in the scored direction:

39.

140.

328.

471.

Deviant Thinking and Experience (Lachar-Wrobel Critical Items)

Of the 10 possible items in this section, 1 was endorsed in the scored direction:

122.

Depression and Worry (Lachar-Wrobel Critical Items)

Of the 16 possible items in this section, 10 were endorsed in the scored direction:

3.

10.

65.

73.

130.

273.

339.

411.

415.

454.

Substance Abuse (Lachar-Wrobel Critical Items)

Of the 3 possible items in this section, 3 were endorsed in the scored direction:

168.

264.

429.

Problematic Anger (Lachar-Wrobel Critical Items)

Of the 4 possible items in this section, 3 were endorsed in the scored direction:

85.

213.

389.

End of Report

NOTE: This MMPI-2 interpretation can serve as a useful source of hypotheses about clients. This report is based on objectively derived scale indices and scale interpretations that have been developed in diverse groups of patients. The personality descriptions, inferences, and recommendations contained herein need to be verified by other sources of clinical information because individual clients may not fully match the prototype. The information in this report should only be used by a trained and qualified test interpreter. The report was not designed or intended to be provided directly to clients. The information contained in the report is technical and was developed to aid professional interpretation.

This and previous pages of this report contain trade secrets and are not to be released in response to requests under HIPAA (or any other data disclosure law that exempts trade secret information from release). Further, release in response to litigation discovery demands should be made only in accordance with your profession's ethical guidelines and under an appropriate protective order.

ITEM RESPONSES

1: 2	2: 1	3: 2	4: 2	5: 2	6: 1	7: 1	8: 1	9: 2	10: 2
11: 2	12: 1	13: 2	14: 1	15: 1	16: 2	17: 2	18: 2	19: 1	20: 1
21: 1	22: 2	23: 2	24: 2	25: 2	26: 1	27: 1	28: 2	29: 1	30: 2
31: 1	32: 2	33: 1	34: 1	35: 1	36: 2	37: 1	38: 1	39: 1	40: 2
41: 1	42: 2	43: 2	44: 2	45: 2	46: 1	47: 1	48: 1	49: 2	50: 2
51: 1	52: 1	53: 2	54: 2	55: 1	56: 1	57: 1	58: 2	59: 2	60: 2
61: 1	62: 2	63: 2	64: 2	65: 1	66: 2	67: 1	68: 2	69: 1	70: 1
71: 1	72: 2	73: 1	74: 2	75: 1	76: 2	77: 1	78: 1	79: 2	80: 2
81: 2	82: 1	83: 1	84: 2	85: 1	86: 1	87: 1	88: 1	89: 1	90: 1
91: 1	92: 2	93: 1	94: 2	95: 2	96: 2	97: 2	98: 1	99: 2	100: 2
101: 2	102: 1	103: 2	104: 2	105: 1	106: 1	107: 1	108: 1	109: 1	110: 2
111: 2	112: 2	113: 1	114: 2	115: 2	116: 1	117: 1	118: 2	119: 2	120: 1
121: 1	122: 1	123: 1	124: 1	125: 1	126: 1	127: 1	128: 1	129: 1	130: 1
131: 2	132: 1	133: 2	134: 2	135: 1	136: 1	137: 2	138: 2	139: 1	140: 1
141: 2	142: 1	143: 2	144: 2	145: 2	146: 2	147: 2	148: 2	149: 2	150: 2
151: 2	152: 2	153: 2	154: 1	155: 2	156: 2	157: 2	158: 1	159: 1	160: 2
161: 1	162: 2	163: 1	164: 1	165: 1	166: 2	167: 1	168: 1	169: 2	170: 2
171: 1	172: 1	173: 2	174: 2	175: 1	176: 1	177: 1	178: 2	179: 1	180: 2
181: 2	182: 2	183: 1	184: 2	185: 1	186: 2	187: 2	188: 1	189: 1	190: 2
191: 2	192: 1	193: 2	194: 1	195: 2	196: 1	197: 2	198: 2	199: 2	200: 2
201: 2	202: 1	203: 1	204: 1	205: 2	206: 1	207: 2	208: 1	209: 2	210: 1
211: 2	212: 2	213: 1	214: 1	215: 2	216: 2	217: 1	218: 1	219: 2	220: 2
221: 2	222: 1	223: 2	224: 1	225: 1	226: 1	227: 2	228: 2	229: 1	230: 1
231: 2	232: 2	233: 1	234: 1	235: 2	236: 2	237: 1	238: 2	239: 2	240: 2
241: 2	242: 2	243: 1	244: 1	245: 2	246: 2	247: 2	248: 2	249: 1	250: 2
251: 1	252: 2	253: 2	254: 2	255: 1	256: 2	257: 2	258: 2	259: 2	260: 1
261: 2	262: 2	263: 2	264: 1	265: 1	266: 2	267: 2	268: 2	269: 2	270: 2
271: 1	272: 1	273: 1	274: 2	275: 1	276: 1	277: 2	278: 1	279: 2	280: 2
281: 1	282: 2	283: 2	284: 1	285: 1	286: 2	287: 2	288: 2	289: 1	290: 1
291: 2	292: 2	293: 2	294: 2	295: 1	296: 2	297: 2	298: 2	299: 1	300: 2
301: 2	302: 1	303: 2	304: 2	305: 1	306: 2	307: 2	308: 2	309: 1	310: 1
311: 2	312: 2	313: 2	314: 1	315: 2	316: 2	317: 2	318: 1	319: 2	320: 2
321: 2	322: 2	323: 2	324: 2	325: 1	326: 1	327: 2	328: 1	329: 2	330: 1
331: 1	332: 2	333: 2	334: 2	335: 1	336: 2	337: 1	338: 2	339: 1	340: 2
341: 1	342: 2	343: 1	344: 1	345: 2	346: 2	347: 1	348: 2	349: 2	350: 2
351: 2	352: 2	353: 2	354: 1	355: 2	356: 1	357: 1	358: 2	359: 2	360: 1
361: 2	362: 1	363: 1	364: 1	365: 2	366: 2	367: 2	368: 1	369: 1	370: 1
371: 2	372: 2	373: 1	374: 2	375: 1	376: 2	377: 1	378: 1	379: 2	380: 2
381: 2	382: 2	383: 1	384: 1	385: 2	386: 1	387: 2	388: 2	389: 1	390: 1
391: 1	392: 2	393: 2	394: 1	395: 2	396: 1	397: 2	398: 2	399: 2	400: 1
401: 2	402: 2	403: 1	404: 1	405: 2	406: 1	407: 2	408: 1	409: 1	410: 2
411: 1	412: 2	413: 2	414: 2	415: 1	416: 2	417: 1	418: 2	419: 1	420: 1
421: 1	422: 1	423: 2	424: 1	425: 2	426: 2	427: 1	428: 1	429: 2	430: 1
431: 2	432: 2	433: 1	434: 1	435: 2	436: 1	437: 2	438: 2	439: 2	440: 1

441: 2 442: 1 443: 2 444: 2 445: 2 446: 1 447: 2 448: 2 449: 2 450: 2
451: 2 452: 2 453: 1 454: 1 455: 1 456: 2 457: 1 458: 2 459: 1 460: 2
461: 1 462: 1 463: 2 464: 1 465: 2 466: 2 467: 2 468: 2 469: 1 470: 2
471: 1 472: 2 473: 1 474: 1 475: 1 476: 2 477: 1 478: 2 479: 2 480: 2
481: 2 482: 1 483: 2 484: 2 485: 1 486: 1 487: 1 488: 2 489: 1 490: 2
491: 1 492: 2 493: 1 494: 1 495: 2 496: 2 497: 2 498: 2 499: 1 500: 2
501: 1 502: 2 503: 1 504: 2 505: 2 506: 2 507: 1 508: 2 509: 1 510: 2
511: 2 512: 2 513: 1 514: 1 515: 2 516: 2 517: 1 518: 1 519: 1 520: 2
521: 2 522: 2 523: 1 524: 2 525: 2 526: 1 527: 2 528: 2 529: 2 530: 2
531: 2 532: 2 533: 2 534: 2 535: 1 536: 2 537: 2 538: 2 539: 1 540: 1
541: 2 542: 1 543: 2 544: 2 545: 1 546: 2 547: 1 548: 2 549: 1 550: 1
551: 2 552: 1 553: 1 554: 1 555: 2 556: 1 557: 2 558: 2 559: 2 560: 2
561: 1 562: 2 563: 2 564: 2 565: 2 566: 1 567: 2

13

░░ Forensic Applications of the MMPI-2

Psychologists are being asked more and more frequently to offer expert opinions about a variety of legal issues. Their opinions often are based, at least in part, on psychological assessment data (Borum & Grisso, 1995), and the MMPI-2 frequently is the source of these data. Lees-Haley (1992) surveyed forensic psychologists and found that they used the MMPI or MMPI-2 more frequently than any other assessment instrument. Lally (2003) surveyed 64 diplomates in forensic psychology and found that the MMPI-2 was recommended or judged as acceptable for use in a variety of forensic evaluations, including malingering, mental state at time of offense, risk of physical or sexual violence, competency to stand trial, and competency to waive Miranda rights.

Another survey of 100 experts in neuropsychology revealed that the MMPI/ MMPI-2 ranked second to the Wechsler Intelligence Scales in frequency of use in forensic evaluations (Lees-Haley, Smith, Williams, & Dunn, 1996). A survey of mental health professionals who conducted child custody evaluations found that the MMPI/MMPI-2 was used in 84% of the evaluations that they conducted (Hagen & Castagna, 2001). Australian psychologists who do forensic evaluations also use the MMPI-2 frequently (Martin, Allan, & Allan, 2001). Thus, it seems clear that the MMPI-2 is a very popular instrument among psychologists who conduct forensic evaluations.

Several factors make the MMPI-2 an attractive instrument among forensic psychologists (Pope, Butcher, & Seelen, 2000). Unlike many other assessment procedures, the MMPI-2 uses a standard set of items and is administered and scored in a standardized manner. Its scales are reliable, and interpretation of its scores is based on a vast body of empirical research. Of special appeal to forensic psychologists is that the MMPI-2 includes validity scales designed to detect deviant test-taking attitudes (e.g., underreporting, overreporting). Because many persons evaluated in forensic settings have motivation to present themselves in unrealistically positive or negative ways, the Validity scales are particularly useful. In addition, psychologists offering expert testimony based on MMPI-2 results find that it is easy to communicate the basis of their opinions to nonpsychologists.

Ogloff (1995) searched a computerized legal database and found that the MMPI and the MMPI-2 have been employed frequently in both state and federal cases. The legal issues addressed have included workers' compensation/ employment disability, criminal responsibility, competency to stand trial, child custody/parenting, murder/death penalty issues, and employment screening/ discrimination.

ADMISSIBILITY OF MMPI-2 EVIDENCE

Ogloff (1995) pointed out that it is the responsibility of a judge to determine whether expert testimony meets the legal criteria for admissibility. If expert testimony is based on test results, the judge must also make a determination of the admissibility of the test results. In most jurisdictions the criteria for admissibility of expert testimony currently are based on the Federal Rules of Evidence (FRE) and a United States Supreme Court decision concerning the admissibility of scientific evidence (*Daubert v. Merrell Dow Pharmaceuticals, Inc.*, 1993).

Prior to the adoption of the FRE in 1976, most jurisdictions used an early court decision (*Frye v. United States*, 1923) which stated that to be admissible, scientific evidence must be generally accepted by the field in which it is offered, that it is used in the relevant areas of the field, and that the techniques used in producing the evidence comport with the state of the art in the field (Ogloff, 1995). The FRE adopted a more liberal view of expert testimony, maintaining that general acceptance is not a requirement for admissibility of evidence and that all evidence that is relevant to the issue at hand is admissible.

In its *Daubert* decision, the U.S. Supreme Court ruled that the FRE displaced the earlier *Frye* test of general acceptance as a standard for determining admissibility of scientific evidence and expert testimony based on that evidence (*Daubert v. Merrell Dow Pharmaceuticals, Inc.*, 1993). The *Daubert* decision also stated some specific issues to be considered in determining admissibility of evidence. Trial judges are to determine whether expert witnesses are proposing to testify to scientific knowledge that will assist the trier of fact to understand and determine a fact in issue. A technique is considered to be scientific to the extent that (1) it leads to hypotheses or statements that can be (or have been) tested empirically, (2) information is available concerning error rates associated with the technique, and (3) it has been subjected to peer review and publication. Although general acceptance of a technique within a scientific community is not a requirement for admissibility of evidence based on that technique, such acceptance can be offered in support of its admissibility. Although most jurisdictions follow a standard based on *Daubert*, some states still use the *Frye*-based standard of general acceptance within a field.

The MMPI-2 fares quite well on all of these criteria. Its development and validation have been firmly based in empirical research. Error rates (e.g., positive predictive power, negative predictive power) have been established for many uses of the test. There is a very large body of MMPI and MMPI-2 research that has been published in peer-reviewed scientific journals. That the MMPI-2 is widely used by psychologists and that it has received very positive evaluations by reviewers (see Archer, 1992a; Nichols, 1992) indicate acceptance by the scientific community of psychologists.

Ogloff (1995) reviewed cases in which courts have commented on admissibility of MMPI-based testimony and concluded that when the MMPI has been used for purposes for which it has been validated (e.g., determining a person's current mental state), its results have been readily admitted as evidence. When the MMPI has been used to address issues less directly related to a person's current mental state (e.g., sanity at a time somewhat removed temporally from the time of the evaluation), the reactions of courts concerning admissibility have been mixed. More recently, Bow, Gould, Flens, and Greenhut (2006) surveyed forensic psychologists and found that 95% of respondents indicated that the MMPI-2 meets Daubert criteria. Ogloff and Douglas (2003) cautioned psychologists to limit expert testimony based on MMPI-2 results to issues in which there is clear scientific evidence that its scores are related to the behaviors in question.

SOME IMPORTANT ISSUES IN USING THE MMPI-2 IN FORENSIC SETTINGS

Norms

Several issues are especially important in deciding to what extent the MMPI-2 will be useful in forensic settings. Should the standard MMPI-2 norms be used, or are special forensic norms needed? This issue becomes especially important in relation to forensic questions in which those being assessed typically differ in a systematic way from the standard norms. For example, parents completing the MMPI-2 in relation to child custody issues typically produce a defensive pattern on the MMPI-2 Validity scales (Bathurst, Gottfried, & Gottfried, 1997). However, it is appropriate to use the standard MMPI-2 norms for all applications of the test. These are the norms that have been utilized in determining the meaning of scores on the MMPI-2 scales, and to use other norms would render this important research base useless. Norms for specific forensic purposes (e.g., child custody, personal injury) may one day be developed, but their use will require research evidence concerning the meaning of scores based on these specific norms.

Correlates of Scales and Code Types

Most of the research concerning the correlates of MMPI/MMPI-2 scores and code types has been based on participants in various mental health settings (e.g., hospitals, clinics). An important question is the extent to which the scales and configurations of scales have similar correlates in forensic settings. For example, does significant elevation on Scale 2 indicate greater likelihood of clinical depression in both clinical and forensic settings? If not, then the MMPI-2 cannot be interpreted similarly in the two settings.

In relation to psychopathology and personality characteristics, we would expect the MMPI-2 scales to have similar correlates in clinical and forensic settings. Decades of research have established that the scales have very similar symptom and personality correlates across settings that have included psychiatric inpatients, mental health outpatients, college counselees, medical patients, and nonclinical student and community groups. Several studies have confirmed that the MMPI-2 scales have similar correlates in forensic settings. In a study conducted at a criminal court forensic diagnostic center, Ben-Porath and Stafford (1993) identified correlates for MMPI-2 scales that were quite congruent with previously reported correlates in other settings. For example, Scale 2 scores were related positively to sad mood, Scale 4 scores were related positively to alcohol abuse, and Scale 8 scores were related positively to number of previous psychiatric hospitalizations. Also, scores on the Anger Content scale were related positively to histories of violent behavior, scores on the Antisocial Practices Content scale were related positively to a variety of criminal activities, scores on the Family Problems Content scale were related positively to marital problems, and scores on three substance abuse scales (MacAndrew Alcoholism Scale–Revised, Addiction Admission Scale) were related positively to abuse of alcohol and other substances. Unfortunately, this sample did not include a large proportion of severely emotionally disturbed persons, and thus many previously reported correlates could not be studied.

Ricketts (2003) reported that the MMPI-2 Content scales and Content Component scales were related to symptoms and problems of forensic cases evaluated at a court-sponsored clinic in ways that were very similar to those reported previously for psychiatric patients. For example, the Depression (DEP) Content scale was significantly related to diagnoses of depression, and the Family Problems (FAM) Content scale to histories of poor family relationships. Petroskey, Ben-Porath, and Stafford (2003) found that correlates of the MMPI-2 Personality Psychopathology 5 scales were very similar for forensic and mental health samples. In summary, there currently are data demonstrating directly that the MMPI-2 scales are related to psychopathology and personality characteristics in similar ways in forensic and clinical settings.

When the MMPI-2 scales are used to infer behaviors or characteristics different from those that have been previously studied, it is important to demonstrate that the scales are actually related to these behaviors and characteristics. For example, we should not assume that MMPI-2 scales will be related to variables such as criminal history, adjustment to incarceration, or offenses against persons versus property offenses. These relationships must be established through empirical research.

Osberg and Poland (2001) examined relationships between MMPI-2 scales and number of previous criminal offenses. They found that higher scorers on Scale 9 and on several Harris–Lingoes subscales reported more offenses. Megargee and Carbonell (1995) reviewed studies in which the MMPI was used to predict behavior and adjustment of incarcerated offenders. They concluded that the standard MMPI scales have been helpful in understanding and predicting behavior in correctional settings. Sellbom, Ben-Porath, and Stafford (2009) found that four MMPI-2 scales (Scale 4, RC4, ASP, and DISC) were significantly related to extratest measures of psychopathy and antisocial behaviors, with RC4 having the strongest relationship with the extratest variables.

Megargee and his colleagues (Megargee, Bohn, Meyer, & Sink, 1979) developed an MMPI classification system for use in correctional settings and demonstrated that the system permitted accurate prediction of many relevant institutional behaviors of inmates. The classification system, which will be described in greater detail later in this chapter, has been modified for use with the MMPI-2 (Megargee, 1994, 1997). The work of Megargee and his colleagues supports the notion that the MMPI-2 scales and classification systems based on the scales have relevant extratest correlates among persons who have been convicted of criminal behaviors. Later in this chapter we will consider how the MMPI-2 relates to constructs that are largely legal (as opposed to clinical) in nature (e.g., criminal responsibility, competency).

Use with Ethnic Minorities

There has long been concern that because the MMPI was developed and normed primarily on Caucasians it (and its successor, the MMPI-2) may not be appropriate for use with members of ethnic minority groups (see Chapter 10 of this book). Although many early MMPI studies reported scale score differences between African Americans and Caucasians, a review by Greene (1987) and a meta-analysis by Hall, Bansal, and Lopez (1999) concluded that there has been no consistent pattern of differences and that there have been more studies that have found no differences than have found differences. Some investigators (e.g., Elion & Megargee, 1975; McNulty, Graham, Ben-Porath, & Stein, 1997; Pope, Butcher, & Seelen, 2000; Pritchard & Rosenblatt, 1980; Timbrook & Graham, 1994) have argued that the best way to determine if the MMPI/MMPI-2 can be used appropriately with members of ethnic minority groups is to determine if its scales predict extratest characteristics and behaviors equally well for minority and majority groups. Timbrook and Graham (1994) found that the MMPI-2 scales predicted equally well for Caucasians and African Americans in the MMPI-2 normative sample, and McNulty, Graham, et al. (1997) reported similar findings for Caucasian and African American community mental health center clients.

Several studies have addressed directly the possibility of MMPI/MMPI-2 differences between African Americans and Caucasians in forensic settings. Holcomb and Adams (1982) compared MMPI scores of African American and Caucasian murderers and found that the two groups were more similar than different. The African American murderers scored slightly higher on Scale 9 and slightly lower on Scale 0 than the Caucasian murderers. Elion and Megargee (1975) demonstrated that Scale 4 scores validly differentiated levels of social deviance among young African American men.

Ben-Porath, Shondrick, and Stafford (1995) examined the association between race and MMPI-2 scores in Caucasian and African American men who were undergoing court-ordered forensic psychological evaluations. They concluded that overall the Caucasians and African Americans produced highly comparable MMPI-2 scores. The two groups did not differ significantly for any of the Validity or Clinical scales. However, the African Americans scored higher than the Caucasians on the Cynicism and Antisocial Practices Content scales. In a follow-up study, Gironda (1999) found that the MMPI-2 scales predicted extratest characteristics equally well for Caucasian and African American men undergoing these court-ordered evaluations.

Although only limited data are available concerning the comparable accuracy of predicting extratest characteristics of members of majority and minority groups in forensic settings, data from other settings would suggest that the MMPI-2 scales will be equally accurate for Caucasians and African Americans. It will be important for additional studies to determine the accuracy of prediction for other minority groups (e.g., Hispanics, American Indians, Asian Americans) in forensic settings.

Profiling

Psychologists who are involved in forensic evaluations often are asked to determine if the MMPI-2 scores of a particular person indicate that the person did or did not commit a specific crime (e.g., murder, sexual aggression), will or will not behave in particular ways in the future (e.g., function as a good or bad parent, become violent), or has or has not experienced some particular damages (e.g., emotional distress associated with a traumatic incident). This process has been referred to as "profiling" and involves specifying the typical MMPI-2 scores of a particular group (e.g., murderers, sexual aggressors, good or bad parents) and then determining the probability that a person does or does not match the prototype.

There has been very little empirical support for the notion that there are typical MMPI/MMPI-2 profiles associated with particular crimes or other forensic-related behaviors and that important decisions about persons in forensic settings can be made by comparing their test results to these typical profiles. For example, Marshall and Hall (1995) concluded that the MMPI was not very useful to the courts in determining the guilt or innocence of committing a sexual offense, largely because research has failed to identify a typical set of MMPI scores associated with sexual offending. Although Ridenour, Miller, Joy, and Dean (1997) reported that the MMPI-2 could accurately identify child molesters, the generalizability of their findings is questionable because they used a normal comparison group, rather than a group of offenders who were not child molesters, and they did not cross-validate their findings.

Butcher (1995) indicated that no single pattern of MMPI or MMPI-2 scores exists among persons who are claiming psychological damages in personal injury litigation. Otto and Collins (1995) reached a similar conclusion concerning the use of the MMPI-2 in child custody evaluations. Their review of the literature failed to identify studies of the relationship between MMPI or MMPI-2 patterns and good or bad parenting.

In summary, it seems clear that there is not sufficient empirical research to support the profiling approach to the use of the MMPI-2 in forensic settings. Persons known to have committed particular offenses (e.g., sexual offending) or to have particular characteristics (e.g., good parenting skills) are not likely to produce a specific set of MMPI-2 scores. Thus, the MMPI-2 is of limited utility in assisting courts to determine if an accused person has or has not committed particular crimes or if persons involved in civil litigation have or do not have particular characteristics (e.g., good or bad parenting skills, psychological damages). This does not mean that the MMPI-2 cannot be of any help in these determinations. Some of the inferences that can be made accurately from MMPI-2 scores can be highly relevant to issues that courts are addressing. For example, MMPI-2 results strongly suggesting that a parent in a child custody evaluation is likely to have severe substance abuse problems would be very helpful to the court in deciding what arrangements are in the best interests of the children in this family.

Administering the MMPI-2

It is always appropriate to administer the MMPI-2 in circumstances in which monitoring is available from persons specifically trained to do so. This is especially important in forensic evaluations because it will ensure that the clinician will later be able to testify that she or he is sure that the person in question completed the test under standard conditions and without help from others and without opportunities to consults books or other sources that could influence the results.

Sometimes it is desirable to administer the MMPI-2 to a person whose first language is not English. Pearson Assessments offers a standardized Spanish version of the test. Questions concerning administering the MMPI-2 in languages other than English or Spanish should be directed to Pearson Assessments. Butcher (1996) presented important information about using the MMPI-2 with persons whose first language is not English or who are from cultures different from that of the United States.

The usual way to administer the MMPI-2 is using the standard test booklets and answer sheets on which examinees mark responses to the test items. The reading level required to complete the test validly in this manner is approximately the sixth grade. However, some persons with limited formal education can understand the items better if they are presented using a standard tape-recorded version of the test available from Pearson Assessments. Software also is available for computerized administration of the MMPI-2 items. As indicated in Chapter 2 of this book, these various ways of administering the MMPI-2 are likely to yield comparable results. However, the MMPI-2 items should not be read to test takers because factors such as the examiner's tone of voice, facial expressions, and other nonverbal behaviors can affect responses. Several studies demonstrated that scores obtained when items were read to test takers were not comparable to those obtained from standard administration of the test (Edwards, Holmes, & Carvajal, 1998; Kendrick & Hatzenbuehler, 1982; Newmark, 1971).

Standardized administration of the MMPI-2 involves having examinees complete all 567 items. Various "short forms" have been developed for the MMPI and the MMPI-2. Because research clearly suggested that the short forms do not yield results comparable to the standard form (Butcher, Kendall, & Hoffman, 1980; Dahlstrom, 1980; Gass & Luis, 2001a), such forms of the MMPI-2 are to be avoided. The one exception is that administration of the first 370 items of the MMPI-2 permits scoring of the standard Validity and Clinical scales and their subscales. However, administering less than the entire test leads to the loss of potentially important information because many other scales include items that appear later than item 370 in the booklet.

Sometimes clinicians decide to administer MMPI-2 scales out of the context of the entire test. For example, they might extract the items in the MacAndrew Alcoholism Scale–Revised, print them in a separate form, and administer only these items to examinees. Research results concerning the comparability of scales administered out of the context of the entire test have been mixed. Therefore, it is best not to use this practice.

Scoring the MMPI-2

Once administration of the MMPI-2 has been completed, several scoring options are available (see Chapter 2 of this book). Hand scoring is quite time consuming but more practical when the volume of MMPI-2 use is low. Care should be taken to ensure the accuracy of hand scoring, as it is quite easy to make errors that can be embarrassing, although usually not critical. Computerized scoring is fast and economical if large numbers of tests are administered. The accuracy of computerized scoring is high, although errors can be made during the data entry stage if responses are entered using a computer keyboard. In forensic cases it is important to recheck data entry to ensure that errors have not been made.

An important advantage of computerized scoring is that scores on many scales, subscales, and indexes typically are generated. Having this array of scores can be quite advantageous, but it also can be problematic. During expert testimony clinicians may be asked questions about scores and indexes that they did not use in their interpretation and about which they are not well informed. Clinicians who use computerized scoring should familiarize themselves with all of the scores and indexes that are contained in the scoring reports that they utilize.

Interpreting the MMPI-2

As stated earlier in this chapter, one of the advantages of using the MMPI-2 in forensic evaluations is that interpretation typically is done in a rather standardized manner by relying on the extensive empirical research literature concerning the meaning of scores. Clinicians are advised to limit their interpretations to issues for which the MMPI-2 has been adequately validated and to avoid making interpretations that cannot be supported by reference to empirical research. When questioned about the validity of MMPI-2 inferences made in forensic evaluations, it usually will be sufficient to cite secondary sources such as this book. However, clinicians using the MMPI-2 in forensic settings should be prepared to identify and cite specific research studies to support their inferences. My practice is to make only statements in forensic reports and during expert testimony that can be supported by reference to specific empirical research literature. Although this often means making many fewer statements than might be made in clinical settings, it certainly makes defending my interpretations much easier.

SOME FORENSIC USES OF THE MMPI-2

Detecting Invalid Responding

Random Responding
Persons taking the MMPI-2 in forensic settings sometimes respond to the items randomly rather than on the basis of their content. There are various reasons for this random responding, including inability to read well enough to understand the items, uncooperativeness, and confusion. Obviously, it is important to identify persons who respond in this manner so that their scores will not be interpreted as accurate indicators of their mental status. As discussed in Chapter 3 of this book, the Variable Response Inconsistency (VRIN) scale is the most effective way to identify random responding. Raw scores of 13 or greater on the VRIN scale indicate that the examinee was likely to have responded randomly and that other MMPI-2 scores should not be interpreted.

All-true or All-false Responding
Sometimes persons taking the MMPI-2 will decide to respond true or false to almost all of the items in the test without consideration of their content. The scores resulting from this approach to the test should not be interpreted as accurate indicators of what the examinees are really like. As discussed in Chapter 3 of this book, the True Response Inconsistency (TRIN) scale is the best way to identify this invalid response set. Raw scores of 13 or greater on the TRIN scale suggest an all-true response set that invalidates the protocol, while raw scores of 5 or less on the TRIN scale suggest an all-false response set that invalidates the protocol.

Overreporting
As discussed earlier in this chapter, persons taking the MMPI-2 in forensic settings often are strongly motivated to present themselves as much more psychologically disturbed and maladjusted than they really are. Examples of situations in which this tendency might be present include evaluations of persons in relation to pleas of not guilty by reason of insanity or incompetency to stand trial or evaluations of persons who are claiming psychological damages because of some traumatic event such as an automobile accident or medical malpractice. Grossman and Wasyliw (1988) estimated that up to 41% of insanity defendants clearly malingered during psychological evaluations. Similarly, Gallagher, Ben-Porath, and Briggs (1997) reported that 16% of male inmates admitted to deliberately distorting their responses on the MMPI-2.

As discussed in detail in Chapter 3 of this book, the Infrequency (F) scale is an effective indicator of overreporting on the MMPI-2. Optimal F-scale cutoff scores for identifying overreporting have differed from study to study and setting to setting. However, whenever T scores on the F scale are greater than 100 the possibility of overreporting should be considered seriously. The higher the F-scale scores are, the more likely it is that examinees approached the MMPI-2 with the intention of appearing more maladjusted than they really are. The Infrequency Psychopathology (F_p) scale (see Chapter 3 of this book) also is a very good indicator of overreporting. Because the F_p scale is less affected by actual psychopathology than is the F scale, it is especially useful in settings where the base rate of psychopathology is high. As with the F scale, optimal F_p-scale cutoff scores for identifying overreporting have varied. However, whenever a test taker has a T score greater than 100 on the F_p scale, overreporting should be suspected.

Unfortunately, most research concerning overreporting has not been conducted in forensic settings. However, there is no reason to believe that the indicators of overreporting that have worked well in other settings would not also work well in forensic settings. In fact, several studies conducted in forensic settings have supported the utility of the MMPI-2 Validity scales in identifying overreporting. Hawk and Cornell (1989) found that criminal defendants who were judged by clinicians to be overreporting scored significantly higher on the MMPI F scale and on the F-K index than age-matched psychotic and nonpsychotic criminal defendants who were judged not to be overreporting. Similar results were reported by Roman, Tuley, Villanueva, and Mitchell (1990) for cases evaluated in a forensic state hospital. Bagby, Rogers, and Buis (1994) and Bagby, Buis, and Nicholson (1995) demonstrated that the F scale was quite effective in differentiating between students who were instructed to malinger on the MMPI-2 and both general psychiatric patients and forensic inpatients. Iverson, Franzen, and Hammond (1995) found that the F scale was quite effective in identifying minimum security inmates who were given instructions to malinger psychopathology in completing the MMPI-2. Gallagher (1997) also found that the F scale effectively identified male malingerers at a correctional reception center. In his study, the F_p added significantly to the discrimination between prisoners who were instructed to malinger and correctional psychiatric patients who were assumed to have taken the MMPI-2 honestly.

Several studies have addressed the utility of the MMPI-2 Validity scales in identifying feigned symptoms of posttraumatic stress disorder. Bury and Bagby (2002) found that, while the F and F_B scales were effective in this regard, the F_p scale had the highest predictive powers. Gough's Dissimulation Scale (Ds2), which is not part of the standard MMPI-2 scoring, was also quite effective. Elhai et al. (2004) found that persons who were asked to feign symptoms of posttraumatic stress disorder resulting from child sexual abuse obtained much higher scores on the F and F_p scales than actual victims of child sexual abuse. However, this study did not report predictive powers for the scales. As discussed in Chapter 3 of this book, Lees-Haley, English, and Glenn (1991) developed the Fake-Bad Scale (FBS) to detect malingering of emotional distress among personal injury claimants. However, subsequent research has not supported the validity of the FBS for that purpose (Ben-Porath, Graham, & Tellegen, 2009; Bury & Bagby, 2002; Butcher, Arbisi, Atlis, & McNulty, 2003; Rogers, Sewell, Martin, & Vitacco, 2003).

Berry et al. (1995) found that persons who were instructed to feign symptoms of closed-head injury obtained higher scores than patients with closed-head injuries on the F, F_B, F_p, and Ds2 scales of the MMPI-2. However, this study did not report predictive powers for these scales in relation to discriminating between the malingering and patient groups. Ben-Porath, Graham, et al. (2009) reviewed research concerning the FBS and concluded that, if appropriate cutoff scores are used, the scale has promise in identifying persons who are overreporting cognitive and somatic symptoms.

Underreporting

There are some circumstances in forensic settings in which examinees have strong motivation to underreport symptoms and try to appear better adjusted psychologically than they really are. Obvious examples include parents who are evaluated in relation to child custody issues or persons who are seeking release from psychiatric or correctional facilities.

As discussed in Chapter 3 of this book, it is much more difficult to identify underreporting than overreporting on the MMPI-2. However, there are data indicating that persons who try to appear better adjusted than they really are when completing the MMPI-2 are likely to produce above-average scores on the L and K scales. It is not possible to specify exact cutoff scores on these scales that will be effective across various settings, but whenever T scores on these scales are greater than 60, the likelihood of underreporting should be considered seriously. Obviously, the higher the L- and K-scale scores are, the more likely it is that defensiveness or underreporting has occurred. Several other scales, including the Positive Malingering (Mp) scale, the Edwards Social Desirability (Esd) scale, the Wiggins Social Desirability (Wsd) scale, the Other Deception (Od) scale, and the Superlative Self-Presentation (S) scale, have shown some promise in identifying underreporting. However, none of these other scales has had enough research support to justify its routine use for identifying underreporting. In a recent study Bagby et al. (1995) concluded that the L scale and the Mp scale were equally effective in identifying persons instructed to fake good when completing the MMPI-2 in comparison with forensic patients who completed the test with standard instructions. More detailed information about the identification of underreporting on the MMPI-2 was reported in Chapter 3 of this book.

Coaching

Psychologists who use the MMPI-2 in forensic settings are understandably concerned about the possibility that examinees can prepare themselves to underreport or overreport without being detected by the Validity scales. A survey by Wetter and Corrigan (1995) revealed that almost half of a sample of practicing attorneys and approximately one-third of a sample of law students reported that they felt obligated to give their clients information about the Validity scales of psychological tests that they would be taking.

Data concerning effects of coaching on MMPI-2 Validity scales and indexes were presented in detail in Chapter 3 of this book. In summary, giving examinees specific information concerning the symptoms of disorders that they are trying to simulate when completing the MMPI-2 did not affect the accuracy with which the Validity scales and indexes could identify the overreporters. However, giving examinees specific information about the nature of the Validity scales and how they work decreased the likelihood that overreporting would be correctly identified by the Validity scales and indexes. Although the traditional Validity scales were especially affected by this kind of coaching, several research studies have suggested that some less commonly used indicators, including Gough's Dissimulation (Dsr2) scale and Obvious minus Subtle (O–S) subscale scores, were relatively effective in identifying even those overreporters who were given specific information about the Validity scales. It is not known if this finding resulted because the overreporters were not coached concerning these less commonly used indicators or if these indicators will be effective even when examinees have been given specific information about them. At any rate, clinicians using the MMPI-2 in forensic settings should be aware that persons who have been given specific information about the MMPI-2 Validity scales may be able to underreport or overreport without being detected. It may be time for the development of a new generation of validity indicators that will not be affected by coaching. In this regard, Bacchiochi and Bagby (2003) developed a discriminant function index for the MMPI-2 to detect overreporting. The index, which was based on 39 MMPI-2 scales, was more effective than individual Validity scales in detecting coached overreporting (See Chapter 3 of this book).

Assessing Clinical Condition

The primary purpose for which the original MMPI scales were developed and for which both the MMPI and MMPI-2 scales have been most comprehensively validated is the assessment of the clinical condition of test takers. Initially, the emphasis was on the assignment of diagnostic labels, but through the years there has been less emphasis placed on labels and more emphasis placed on identifying a wide array of symptoms, behaviors, and characteristics that are related to how well test takers are functioning in their life situations. Therefore, it is appropriate to use the MMPI-2 to generate inferences concerning the clinical condition or status of persons assessed in forensic settings.

The MMPI-2 scales were constructed in such a way that higher scores on most scales indicate more symptoms and problems and greater maladjustment. Thus, the most direct indicator of maladjustment is the extent to which scales are elevated. Generally, T scores greater than 65 are considered to be clinically significant. Graham, Barthlow, Stein, Ben-Porath, and McNulty (2002) studied seven different measures of general maladjustment on the MMPI-2, using both self-reported symptom severity and clinicians' rating of symptom severity as criteria. They concluded that the mean T score for eight Clinical scales (1, 2, 3, 4, 6, 7, 8, 9) was the best indicator of general maladjustment in an outpatient mental health setting. Although their results have not been replicated in a forensic setting, there is reason to believe that this measure would be effective there as well. The MMPI-2 Content scales were also constructed such that higher scores indicate more problems and poorer adjustment. The more Content scale T scores that are above 65, the more maladjusted the person is likely to be.

Some MMPI-2 Supplementary scales have been related to overall level of maladjustment. Welsh's Anxiety (A) scale is related to general maladjustment, with higher scores indicating greater maladjustment. The Ego Strength (Es) scale also is related to general maladjustment because it assesses the psychological resources that are available for coping with the demands of one's life situation. Unlike most other MMPI-2 scales, higher Es-scale scores indicate greater adjustment, and lower Es-scale scores indicate greater maladjustment. However, as indicated in Chapters 6 and 7 of this book, scores on the Content scales and on the Es scale are directly affected by deviant test-taking attitudes. Persons who approach the test defensively tend to obtain artificially high scores, whereas those who exaggerate problems and symptoms when taking the MMPI-2 tend to obtain artificially low scores.

As indicated in Chapter 3 of this book, there is some research indicating that higher scores on the F scale are likely to indicate greater maladjustment. However, F-scale scores also are related to test-taking attitudes, with test takers who overreport obtaining very high scores and defensive persons obtaining low scores. Because motivation to distort (positively as well as negatively) is so great in many forensic situations, the F scale is not a particularly good indicator of level of maladjustment in these settings.

Screening for Substance Abuse

Often it is important to determine if persons undergoing forensic evaluations have significant substance abuse problems. For example, this possibility may be raised as a mitigating circumstance in relation to criminal charges, it can be important in making decisions about child custody decisions, or it can be related to disposition of criminal cases. Although it is not possible or appropriate to conclude that a person is or is not a substance abuser solely on the basis of test data, the MMPI-2 has three scales that were designed specifically to identify substance abuse problems. Elevated scores on these scales serve as indicators of the possibility of substance abuse problems that should be investigated further, using other sources of information such as reports of significant others and/or physical test results. Although the three substance abuse scales, MacAndrew Alcoholism Scale–Revised (MAC-R), Addiction Admission Scale (AAS), and Addiction Potential Scale (APS), were described in detail in Chapter 8 of this book, their use will be summarized briefly here.

MacAndrew Alcoholism Scale–Revised (MAC-R)

Designed for the original MMPI, this empirically derived scale was maintained in the MMPI-2. Its 49 items are ones that outpatient male alcoholics answered differently from other outpatient male psychiatric patients. Dozens of research studies have demonstrated that scores on this scale are related to excessive use of alcohol and other drugs for both men and women and both adolescents and adults (see Graham & Strenger, 1988, for a review). Although most MAC/MAC-R studies have not been conducted in forensic settings, a study by Ben-Porath and Stafford (1993) indicated that scores on the MAC-R scale are related to a wide variety of problems with alcohol and drugs in a sample of persons evaluated at a forensic diagnostic center.

In Chapter 8 of this book some guidelines were presented for interpreting scores on the MAC-R scale. Raw scores below 24 are contraindicative of substance abuse problems. Raw scores between 24 and 27 are considered to be borderline scores; possible substance abuse problems should be explored from other data sources. Raw scores of 28 or higher are strongly suggestive of substance abuse problems. However, other collateral information should be sought before reaching conclusions about substance abuse.

Several investigators have cautioned against using the MAC-R scale with African Americans and members of other ethnic minority groups. Some early studies suggested that nonabusing African Americans tend to obtain high scores on the MAC scale (e.g., Walters, Greene, & Jeffrey, 1984; Walters, Greene, Jeffrey, Kruzich, & Haskin, 1983). However, several other studies have not found significant MAC-R scale differences between African Americans and Caucasians (McClinton, Graham, & Ben-Porath, 1995; Ben-Porath et al., 1995). The study of Ben-Porath et al. is especially important because it was conducted at a criminal court diagnostic clinic. The study of McClinton et al. also concluded that the MAC-R, AAS, and APS worked equally well in identifying substance abuse problems for African American and Caucasian mental health center clients.

Addiction Admission Scale (AAS)
This scale contains MMPI-2 items that have obvious content related to substance abuse. When persons obtain high scores on this scale, they are openly admitting to the misuse of alcohol and/or other drugs. The scale's developers recommended that T scores greater than 60 be considered significant, and several subsequent research studies have supported this cutoff score for identifying substance abuse problems (see Chapter 8 of this book). Thus, T scores greater than 60 on the AAS should be interpreted as an open admission of excessive use of alcohol and/or other drugs. Because the content of the AAS items is so obviously related to substance abuse, persons who want to hide substance abuse problems can easily avoid detection on this scale. Thus, T scores below 60 on this scale are basically uninterruptible. They could indicate the absence of substance abuse problems or the denial of substance abuse problems by persons who really have such problems.

Addiction Potential Scale (APS)
This scale was empirically developed in a manner similar to the MAC. However, items in the APS are ones that persons with alcohol problems answered differently from other psychiatric patients and persons in the MMPI-2 normative sample. Because the content of items in the APS is not obviously related to substance abuse, it is not as easily faked as the AAS. However, research concerning the validity of the APS has yielded mixed results, with some studies indicating that its scores are related to substance abuse and others indicating that they are not (see Chapter 8

for more details). What seems clear, however, is that the APS does not seem to add much to the MAC-R or the AAS in identifying substance abuse problems.

Some General Concerns

Although the MMPI-2 substance abuse scales can provide important information about the possibility of substance abuse problems, there are several issues that should be kept in mind when using them in forensic settings. First, most of the research concerning these scales has not been conducted in forensic settings. However, a study by Ben-Porath and Stafford (1993) has suggested that the scales also are related to substance abuse problems in forensic settings. Second, current research does not address how persons score on the substance abuse scales when they previously abused substances but no longer do. Clinical and anecdotal evidence suggests that scores on the MAC-R scale are likely to remain high even after persons have stopped abusing substances. Third, research to date has addressed only abuse of nonprescription drugs, so little is known about the substance abuse scales in relation to abuse of prescription drugs. Finally, it is important to keep in mind that no conclusions should be reached about substance abuse based only on the MMPI-2 scales. High scores on these scales should be seen as one indicator that substance abuse problems may exist and that corroborating information should be collected.

Predicting Dangerousness

Predicting future violent or dangerous behavior is relevant to many of the purposes for which forensic assessments are conducted (e.g., civil commitment, release from prison or hospital, child custody). Heilbrun and Heilbrun (1995) discussed the importance of these predictions and the role that the MMPI-2 can and cannot play in them. Their conclusion, with which this author agrees, was that there is no direct and accurate way to predict from MMPI-2 scores which individuals will or will not act dangerously or violently in the future. In fact, there is little evidence to support the notion that data from any psychological tests are able to predict dangerous or violent behavior directly (e.g., Monahan, 1981).

As Heilbrun and Heilbrun (1995) pointed out, predicting dangerousness involves the consideration of many different kinds of information. Historical data (e.g., having acted dangerously in the past), demographic characteristics (e.g., being young, male, and of lower socioeconomic status), mental status (e.g., having psychotic symptoms), and dynamic factors (e.g., substance abuse, marital problems) all are related in complex ways to acting in dangerous ways. In addition, it is important to understand base rates for aggression for persons belonging to different groups. For example, it has been reported that approximately 12% of persons with mental disorders, including schizophrenia, mania or bipolar disorder, major depression, substance abuse or dependence, obsessive–compulsive disorder, panic disorder, or phobia, admitted to having acted violently in the past year. Approximately 2% of persons without these mental disorders reported having acted violently in the past year (Swanson, Holzer, Ganju, & Jono, 1990).

Sellbom, Ben-Porath, Lilienfeld, Patrick, and Graham (2005) studied the prediction of violent recidivism among offenders undergoing treatment in a batterers' intervention program. The RC4 and RC9 scales predicted recidivism even when historical and demographic variables were taken into account.

Obviously, much of the information that is relevant to predicting dangerousness is available from sources other than the MMPI-2. However, Heilbrun and Heilbrun (1995) suggested several ways that the MMPI-2 can add information relevant to predicting dangerousness. There are data suggesting that psychopathy (as measured by Scale 4 of the MMPI-2) is related to acting dangerously, particularly when coupled with below-average intelligence (Heilbrun, 1979). However, Sellbom and Ben-Porath (2006) cautioned that Scale 4 is too heterogeneous in content to be used in this manner and suggested that the RC4 scale would be a more appropriate scale for such predictions.

Several other MMPI-2 scales and code types have been related to acting in physically aggressive ways. Persons in correctional settings who score higher on the Overcontrolled–Hostility (O–H) scale are more likely to display extreme physical aggression than those who score lower on this scale (see Chapter 8 of this book). Scores on the Anger (ANG) Content scale suggest problems with the control of anger (see Chapter 6 of this book). The 4–3 code type also has been associated with problems with anger control (see Chapter 5 of this book), but Fraboni, Cooper, Reed, and Saltstone (1990) found that neither the 4–3 nor the 48/84 code types successfully discriminated between violent and nonviolent offenders. No differences in Clinical or Content scale scores were found between groups of female offenders who had murdered their child, a partner, or a nonfamily adult (McKee, Shea, Mogy, & Holden, 2001).

Unfortunately, the relationships between these MMPI-2 measures and the likelihood of acting dangerously are so modest that using them to make individual predictions about dangerousness is not appropriate (e.g., Nussbaum, Choudhry, & Martin-Doto, 1996). Nonetheless, these measures serve as sources of information, to be considered along with other data, relevant to dangerousness. Weiss (2000) discussed the integration of MMPI-2 scores and other information in trying to predict dangerousness among felons incarcerated in Israel.

Megargee and his colleagues (1979) developed a configural system for classifying the MMPI scores of inmates, and the system has been modified for use with the MMPI-2 (Megargee, 1994). Evidence was presented that membership in certain categories in their system was strongly related to aggressive behavior while in prison. Hutton, Miner, and Langfeldt (1993) demonstrated that the Megargee typology also can reliably and usefully describe different categories of patients in a forensic psychiatric setting. It should be noted that at least one study has questioned the utility of the Megargee typology with African American forensic patients (Hutton & Miner, 1995).

In summary, there is not adequate research evidence to support the notion that there are MMPI-2 scales or profiles that directly predict dangerous or violent behavior. Historical, demographic, and contextual variables are very important in making such predictions. However, there are MMPI-2 scales and configurations of scales that provide some information relevant to the prediction of dangerousness. This information should be considered along with other kinds of information, rather than being used directly to make predictions about dangerousness.

Assessing Sanity

Rogers and McKee (1995) defined insanity as "a legal term used to describe the acquittal...of a criminal defendant because of a severe mental disorder on the basis of specified legal criteria" (p. 104). Although the specific criteria differ from one jurisdiction to another, all sets of criteria require the presence of some mental disorder or mental retardation. Criteria usually also include cognitive incapacity (i.e., lack of awareness of the wrongfulness of the act) and volitional incapacity (i.e., inability to refrain from the criminal behavior in question). Many jurisdictions exclude abnormalities that result from repetitive antisocial behavior.

Because determinations of legal insanity typically involve reaching conclusions about a person's mental status at a time distant from that of the evaluation and because insanity is defined in very narrow legal terms, psychological tests, including the MMPI-2, tend not to be very useful in determining legal sanity. Existing research does not support the notion that there are specific aspects of MMPI-2 results that are related directly to legal insanity. Rogers and McKee (1995) reviewed the limited database concerning MMPI results of defendants judged to be legally sane or insane and concluded that there were few meaningful differences between these two classes of defendants. They also presented some of their own MMPI-2 data on legally sane and insane persons and reached a similar conclusion, although they found that defendants judged to be insane were likely to have lower scores on Scale 4 and on the Antisocial Practices (ASP) Content scale than defendants judged to be sane.

Given the legal definition of insanity, it is not surprising that there is no typical profile or set of scores on the MMPI-2 that indicates insanity. However, Rogers and McKee (1995) suggested several ways in which the MMPI-2 can contribute relevant information to an insanity evaluation. First, because defendants who make not guilty by reason of insanity (NGRI) pleas may be strongly motivated to exaggerate their emotional problems, it is important to assess their test-taking attitudes. As discussed in a previous section of this chapter, the MMPI-2 Validity scales and indexes are quite effective in identifying persons who are overreporting when they complete the test. Second, the vast research literature concerning the correlates of scales and code types permits accurate inferences about symptoms and personality characteristics that can add to the data on which determinations of sanity versus insanity are based. Third, several MMPI-2 scales, especially Scale 4, the RC4 scale, and the Antisocial Practices (ASP) Content scale, offer information about antisociality that can address, at least in part, the criterion that excludes abnormalities that are related only to repetitive antisocial behavior.

In summary, existing research does not support the notion that there are specific MMPI-2 scales, code types, or patterns of scores that directly indicate that someone was legally sane or insane at the time that an act was committed. This determination should result from consideration of a comprehensive database including information from a variety of sources. However, the MMPI-2 can add useful information concerning the possibility of overreporting, current symptoms and behaviors indicative of severe mental disorder, and the likelihood of repetitive antisocial behavior.

Assessing Competency to Stand Trial

Psychologists often are asked to offer opinions about a defendant's competency to stand trial on criminal charges. Competency in this context has to do with whether the defendant has the ability to consult meaningfully with his or her attorney with a reasonable degree of understanding and has a rational as well as factual understanding of the proceedings against her or him (*Dusky v. United States*, 1960). Ogloff (1995) concluded that, because the competency criteria are functional and do not focus on the defendant's mental state or character, the MMPI-2 has limited utility for such evaluations. Offering a somewhat different perspective, Lawrence (1985) concluded that "psychological test results in competency evaluations are not only useful as an adjunct to other collected data, but are often indispensable" (p. 86).

Clearly, a determination concerning competency to stand trial requires information that cannot be obtained from tests like the MMPI-2. Using either clinical interview and/or standardized competency instruments, assessors should collect relevant information from defendants, attorneys, and others who might be aware of such information. However, there are several important ways in which the MMPI-2 can add to the database. Defendants who are claiming to be incompetent to stand trial sometimes overreport severe psychopathology as a reason for their claimed incompetency. As discussed in an earlier section of this chapter, the Validity scales of the MMPI-2 can be very useful in detecting such over-reporting. Previous research has documented that having a psychotic diagnosis is associated with being judged incompetent to stand trial (e.g., Daniel, Beck, Herath, Schmitz, & Menninger, 1985; Rogers, Gillis, McMain, & Dickens, 1988). Thus, the presence of indicators of severe psychopathology in an MMPI-2 protocol that is judged to be valid and interpretable suggests the possibility that emotional problems could be interfering with a defendant's ability to communicate effectively with his or her attorney and/or to have a rational understanding of the proceedings against her or him. Obviously, information from the MMPI-2 should be considered along with many other kinds of information in making determinations about competency.

Not much empirical research has been conducted concerning MMPI/ MMPI-2 differences between defendants judged to be competent versus incompetent to stand trial. Several studies found that incompetent defendants tend to have more elevated scores on the F scale and several Clinical scales, especially Scale 6 (e.g., Cook, 1969; Maxon & Neuringer, 1970). Other research has failed to find significant and meaningful MMPI differences between competent and incompetent defendants (e.g., Rogers et al., 1988). It may very well be that most defendants who are really incompetent to stand trial are not able to complete tests like the MMPI-2 in a valid manner and therefore have been excluded from previous research studies (Cook, Pogany, & Johnston, 1974; Rogers et al., 1988). Miller (2004) studied criminal defendants who were found incompetent to stand trial because of mental illness. MMPI-2 scores were correlated with scores from the Structured Interview of Reported Symptoms (SIRS; Rogers, 1992), an established instrument for identifying over-reporting of psychopathology. The F, F_B, and F_p scales of the MMPI-2 were highly correlated with most SIRS scores, suggesting that they are good indicators of overreporting of symptoms.

Domestic Relations Evaluations

With approximately half of all new marriages in the Unites States ending in divorce (Otto & Collins, 1995) and many of the divorcing couples having minor children, domestic relations courts are quite busy making decisions about custody and visitation arrangements. Although it has been estimated that mental health professionals offer expert opinions in a relatively small proportion (10–25%) of child custody cases (Melton, Petrila, Poythress, & Slobogin, 1987; Melton, Weithorn, & Slobogin, 1985), the absolute number of cases involving mental health professionals is quite large.

Domestic relations courts have great latitude in making decisions about child custody and visitation arrangements. Although specific standards may differ between jurisdictions, most criteria are modeled after the Uniform Marriage and Divorce Act (UMDA) of 1979 or Michigan's Child Custody Act (MCCA) of 1970, as modified in 1992 (Otto & Collins, 1995). These acts direct courts to make decisions that are "in the best interests of the child." Specific guidelines are stated, and several of them deal with matters about which psychologists are trained to offer expert opinions. Among other criteria, the UMDA indicates that courts should consider the interaction and interrelationship of children with their parents and other persons who may significantly affect their best interests; children's adjustment to home, school, and community; and the mental and physical health of all individuals involved. The MCCA directs courts to consider the love, affection, and emotional ties existing between children and significant adults; the capacity of the parties involved to give children love, affection, and guidance; and the physical and mental health of the parties involved. Clearly, the training and experience of psychologists qualify them to offer opinions about such matters. Otto, Buffington-Vollum, and Edens (2003) have provided a comprehensive discussion of psychological assessment in child custody cases.

It is important to consider the sources of information that psychologists utilize in developing opinions about what is best for a particular child. Interviews with parents and children and observations of parent–child interactions seem to be the most frequent sources of information (Bow & Quinnell, 2001). Hagan and Castagna (2001) surveyed psychologists who conducted child custody evaluations and found that the MMPI-2 was the most frequently used test, being employed in 84% of the evaluations of adults.

It is clear that much of the information on which expert opinions about child custody and visitation arrangements are based should come from sources other than psychological test data (American Psychological Association, 1994). Review of school, legal, and treatment records; interviews with children and significant adults; and observations of children interacting with significant adults provide much of the information that is needed. However, additional relevant information can be obtained from MMPI-2 results. Domestic relations courts typically have been quite receptive to expert opinion based (in full or in part) on MMPI and MMPI-2 data (Otto & Collins, 1995).

In virtually every jurisdiction, the mental health of parents and other significant adults (e.g., stepparents, grandparents, other caregivers) is an important consideration in deciding what is in the best interests of children. Because the MMPI was developed to assess clinical condition and both the MMPI and MMPI-2 have been validated for this purpose, MMPI-2 data are directly relevant to this important consideration.

Before assessing clinical condition from MMPI-2 results, it is very important to consider the test-taking attitudes of the persons being evaluated. Most parents who are assessed as part of child custody proceedings approach psychological testing in a defensive manner. They understandably want to present a very favorable impression, and in trying to do so they tend to minimize symptoms and problems and to endorse items that they believe will make them appear to be honest, conscientious, virtuous, and well-adjusted persons. Several studies have reported MMPI-2 scores of parents who completed the test as part of child custody evaluations. Mean scores have suggested moderate levels of defensive responding and absence of significant elevations on the Clinical scales (Bagby, Nicholson, Buis, Radovanovic, & Fidler, 1999; Bathurst et al., 1997; Siegel, 1996; Strong, Greene, Hoppe, Johnson, & Olesen, 1999). The typical pattern on the Validity scales is one with above-average scores on the L and K scales and below-average scores on the F scale.

Thus, we have come to expect some moderate defensiveness in the MMPI-2 results of parents evaluated as part of child custody or visitation proceedings. It is important to consider what such results do and do not indicate about these individuals. When the T scores on the L and/or K scales are between 50 and 65, the results are very typical for the circumstances and probably do not indicate an attempt to deny or hide significant psychological problems. However, if the T scores on the L and/or K scales are greater than 65, the results should be considered invalid and uninterruptible. In this circumstance, it is not possible to know if the extreme defensiveness does or does not indicate serious emotional problems that the test taker is trying to deny or hide. All that is clear is that the absence of elevations on other scales, which is likely to accompany the very defensive pattern on the Validity scales, does not necessarily indicate good adjustment. In this circumstance, other sources of information will be helpful in trying to make a determination about psychological adjustment.

Occasionally, adults assessed as part of child custody or visitation proceedings will produce a pattern on the Validity scales suggesting the open admission, and perhaps even exaggeration, of problems and symptoms. Typically, F-scale scores will be well above average, and L- and K-scale scores are typically at average or below-average levels. Several possible interpretations of this pattern of scores should be considered. First, the person may have such serious psychological problems that revealing them cannot be avoided even in a situation in which the demand characteristics are clearly to try to do so. Second, the pattern may reflect a person who is overreporting problems and symptoms because he or she really does not want custody. This may occur when a grandparent or some other person has pressured the parent to seek custody that the parent really does not want. Again, information from other sources will be helpful in trying to decide which interpretation is more appropriate.

Assuming that the Validity scale scores are not suggestive of extreme defensiveness or exaggeration, MMPI-2 scores and code types can be interpreted very much as they can in other settings. Previous chapters in this book have provided detailed interpretive information. However, it may be helpful to summarize briefly the most important sources of MMPI-2 information concerning clinical condition. The level of scores on the Clinical, Content, and Supplementary scales is the best index of maladjustment. With very few exceptions, MMPI-2 scales were constructed such that higher scores indicate greater maladjustment. The more scales that are significantly elevated (i.e., $T > 65$), the more maladjusted persons are likely to be. Graham, Barthlow, Stein, Ben-Porath, and McNulty (2002) found that the mean T score for eight Clinical scales (1, 2, 3, 4, 6, 7, 8, and 9) was the most effective way to assess general maladjustment as measured by self-reported severity of symptoms and clinicians' rating of symptom severity.

Several MMPI-2 Supplementary scales have been demonstrated to be good indexes of general maladjustment. Although Welsh (1956) chose the label of "anxiety" for his scale that was developed to assess a major factor dimension of the MMPI, subsequent research indicated that scores on the Anxiety (A) scale are related to a wide variety of measures of general maladjustment. Thus, higher A-scale scores indicate greater maladjustment. The Ego Strength (Es; Barron, 1953) scale was developed to predict response to individual psychotherapy, but subsequent research has indicated that higher Es-scale scores are related to more positive adjustment, and lower Es-scale scores are related to greater maladjustment. As discussed in Chapter 8 of this book, scores on the Es scale are related to test-taking attitudes. Persons who approach the MMPI-2 in a defensive manner tend to have artificially high Es-scale scores that do not necessarily indicate more positive adjustment. Conversely, persons who exaggerate when completing the MMPI-2 have artificially low Es-scale scores that do not necessarily indicate greater maladjustment.

Inferences about specific kinds of problems and symptoms can be made on the basis of elevations on individual Clinical, Content, and Supplementary scales (see Chapters 4, 6, and 8 of this book) and well-defined code types (see Chapter 5 of this book). For example, higher scores on Scale 2 and on the Depression (DEP) Content scale tend to be associated with symptoms of clinical depression, and higher scores on Scale 4 and on the Antisocial Practices (ASP) Content scale tend to be associated with a variety of acting-out behaviors.

Substance abuse problems of parents can have quite negative effects on their children, and it is unlikely that parents involved in custody or visitation proceedings will readily admit to having such problems. It is possible to use the MMPI-2 as a source of information about the likelihood of substance abuse problems. The MacAndrew Alcoholism Scale–Revised (MAC-R), the Addiction Potential Scale (APS), and the Addiction Admission Scale (AAS) provide information about possible substance abuse problems. An earlier section of this chapter offered specific guidelines for interpreting scores on these three substance abuse scales. Several things should be kept in mind when interpreting scores on these scales. First, never conclude on the basis of MMPI-2 data alone that someone is or is not a substance abuser. Scores on the substance abuse scales should be used to generate hypotheses or inferences that are then validated using data from other available sources. Second, persons who previously abused substances but no longer do so may continue to score at higher levels on the substance abuse scales. Third, the possibility of substance abuse problems does not necessarily disqualify a person as custodial parent. It is one important piece of information to be considered in the context of the overall custody evaluation.

The MMPI/MMPI-2 literature does not include many empirical studies that examined relationships between test scores and effective parenting. There is no single scale or pattern of scales that is related directly to effective or ineffective parenting (Otto & Collins, 1995). In a study of parents of children with asthma, Mrazek, Klinnert, Mrazek, and Macey (1991) found that mothers who were judged to have parental difficulties tended to have lower scores on the K and Es scales and higher scores on Scales F, 2, and 4. Heinicke, Diskin, Ramsey-Klee, and Oates (1986) found that maternal warmth, as measured by the MMPI during pregnancy, was related to responsiveness to infant needs and aggression modulation when their children were two years of age.

Several studies demonstrated that parents of emotionally disturbed children tended to have more deviant MMPI scores, particularly those associated with antisocial tendencies (Otto & Collins, 1995). However, it is not possible from these studies to conclude that the problems suggested by the more elevated MMPI scores of parents of disturbed children caused the children's problems. Perhaps parents develop their own problems in response to the stress of coping with their disturbed children. Another area of MMPI/MMPI-2 research that has relevance to child custody evaluations is that of parental abuse of children. Unfortunately, research in this area has not revealed a clear profile that identifies parents as abusers or is associated with abuse (Otto & Collins, 1995).

Ezzo, Pinsoneault, and Evans (2007) compared MMPI-2 scores of parents involved in custody litigation whose parental rights had been suspended because of suspected child maltreatment with scores of parents involved in custody litigation where child maltreatment was not suspected. The former group scored significantly higher than the latter on 7 of 10 Clinical scales. However, for no Clinical scale was the mean T score for the suspected maltreatment group greater than 65. The authors concluded that MMPI-2 scores could not be used to determine if child maltreatment had or had not occurred.

Although MMPI-2 scores do not permit direct inferences concerning how effective persons are likely to be as parents, many of the inferences that are made in the course of a comprehensive MMPI-2 interpretation can provide potentially relevant information. For example, if a person has been described, based on his or her MMPI-2 scores, as impulsive, unstable, unpredictable, and aggressive and as having very poor judgment, this would certainly be relevant to how this person might be expected to function in the parental role. However, it is important to make clear that inferences about parenting often are not directly related to MMPI-2 scores. Rather, they are higher order inferences based on demonstrated relationships between MMPI-2 scores and behaviors and characteristics that might reasonably be expected to be related to effectiveness of parenting. It should also be kept in mind that parental characteristics that might be in the best interests of one child may not necessarily be in the best interests of another child who has different needs.

Guidelines for child custody evaluations (American Psychological Association, 1994) caution psychologists to avoid overinterpreting assessment data, especially drawing conclusions not adequately supported by research data. The MMPI-2 can play an important role in such evaluations, but users should keep in mind that there are limitations to its contributions and should use the test as one of several sources of assessment information.

Personal Injury Evaluations

Psychologists often are called on to evaluate the mental status of individuals who allege that they have suffered psychological damages as a result of some traumatic event in which they were involuntary participants or witnesses. The events that allegedly have caused such damages include vehicle accidents, violent assaults, medical malpractice, sexual harassment, and many other negative experiences. Persons claiming psychological damages because of events of these kinds vary in terms of gender, age, ethnicity, and socioeconomic status. Ogloff (1995) summarized legal cases in which MMPI evidence or MMPI-based testimony has been accepted by courts in relation to personal injury claims. It would appear that expert testimony based, at least in part, on MMPI results has been admitted readily in these kinds of cases.

Psychologists typically are asked to address several issues in personal injury evaluations (Pope et al., 2000). First, does the person claiming to have been psychologically damaged really have significant psychological or emotional problems? Because there often is strong motivation in these kinds of cases for the claimants to exaggerate problems and symptoms, it becomes very important to assess the credibility of the reported symptoms and problems. Second, are the current psychological or emotional problems directly attributable, at least in part, to the traumatic event that is being claimed as the cause of the problems? In this regard, it becomes very important to determine if there was a preexisting condition that could account, at least in part, for the damages that are being blamed on a particular traumatic incident. Likewise, it is important to determine if there have been other events subsequent to the one that is being blamed that could account, at least in part, for current psychological problems. Finally, psychologists often are asked to make some statements about the likely course of recovery from current psychological problems.

The MMPI-2 is well suited to address some of these issues and not as well suited to address others. The Validity scales of the MMPI-2 can be very useful in assessing the extent to which claimants are presenting accurate reports of their symptoms and problems and the extent to which they are exaggerating such problems. Because its Clinical scales were developed to assess mental status (i.e., clinical condition) and have been well validated in this regard, the MMPI-2 can address directly problems and symptoms currently being experienced by claimants. Although not totally useless in regard to preexisting conditions, other traumatic events that could account for current problems and symptoms, or likely course of recovery from current problems, the MMPI-2 is of limited utility in relation to these issues.

As discussed in some detail in Chapter 3 of this book and in earlier sections of this chapter, one very important feature of the MMPI-2 in relation to forensic evaluations is that it includes Validity scales that are very helpful in determining if persons completing the test did so candidly or if they were overreporting or underreporting problems and symptoms. In personal injury evaluations, where the motivation to present an unrealistically negative picture of one's psychological status often is strong, it is especially important to be able to address the issue of credibility.

Binder and Rohling (1996) conducted a meta-analysis and concluded that litigation was associated with symptom severity. Consistent with this general finding, Youngjohn, Davis, and Wolf (1997) found that persons with diagnoses of head injury who were involved in litigation concerning their injuries tended to have more deviant MMPI-2 scores than nonlitigants, even when severity of injury was equated. In a similar study, Dush, Simons, Platt, Nation, and Ayres (1994) found that chronic-pain patients who were involved in litigation concerning their injuries had more deviant MMPI scores than nonlitigant pain patients. However, we do not know to what extent the higher scores of litigating patients reflected an exaggeration of symptoms and the extent to which patients with more severe symptoms are more likely to litigate than those with less severe symptoms.

As discussed previously, the F scale is an effective measure of overreporting on the MMPI-2, with higher scores indicating greater likelihood of overreporting. Because scores on the F scale also are related to genuine psychopathology, the F_p scale, which was designed to minimize the effect of psychopathology, adds to the detection of malingering. When persons respond to the MMPI-2 items claiming symptoms and problems that they do not really have, they tend to produce higher F-scale and F_p-scale scores than most persons with genuine psychopathology who respond honestly to the items. Although it is not possible to specify exact cutoff scores above which overreporting is likely, when

F-scale and F_p-scale T scores are above 100, the possibility of overreporting should be explored carefully. In these cases it can be very helpful to compare the entire set of scores to the overreporting prototype presented in Chapter 3 of this book.

Some efforts have been made to develop measures specifically to identify overreporting in persons who are claiming emotional disturbance stemming from physical injuries. As discussed in Chapter 3 of this book, Lees-Haley et al. (1991) developed the Fake-Bad Scale (FBS), now labeled the Symptom Validity Scale, to detect malingering of emotional distress among personal injury claimants. However, subsequent research did not support the validity of the FBS for its intended purpose and suggested that the scale may be a measure of general maladjustment rather than of overreporting. More recently, Larrabee (2003) suggested that the FBS may be effective in identifying the overreporting of cognitive deficits during neuropsychological examinations. Dearth et al. (2005) found that the FBS was not as effective as other MMPI-2 Validity scales (e.g., F scale, F_p scale) in identifying persons who feigned cognitive problems during an analogue neuropsychological examination. Several studies have demonstrated that persons who overreport symptoms of brain injury are accurately detected by the MMPI-2 Validity scales (e.g., Berry et al., 1995). However, it is not at all clear that any of the MMPI-2 Validity scales adds incrementally to established motivational scales (e.g., Test of Memory Malingering; Tombaugh, 1997) in detecting the overreporting of cognitive deficits.

Sometimes persons involved in forensic evaluations have a tendency to exaggerate symptoms and problems that they really have. For example, someone who has developed genuine anxiety following an automobile accident may overstate the symptoms of anxiety when completing the MMPI-2. As discussed in Chapter 3 of this book, this exaggeration of genuine psychopathology is rather difficult to identify with the MMPI-2 Validity scales. If in a forensic setting F-scale T scores are quite high (> 100), scores on the Clinical scales are likely to be higher than would be expected given other information available about the test taker, and the overall pattern of MMPI-2 scores does not fit the prototype for overreporting (see Chapter 3 of this book), the possibility of exaggeration of symptoms and problems should be explored carefully. Unfortunately, no data are available concerning optimal cutoff scores for identifying persons with genuine psychopathology who are exaggerating.

In Chapter 3 of this book and in an earlier section of this chapter the effects of coaching on the ability of MMPI-2 scales to detect underreporting and overreporting were discussed. Existing research suggests that giving test takers information about the disorders that they are trying to feign has little effect on the accuracy with which the Validity scales can identify the feigning. However, when test takers are given specific information about the MMPI-2 Validity scales and how they work, they often produce test results that do not accurately reflect their clinical condition and that do not suggest the strong possibility of overreporting.

Because the MMPI-2 scales were designed to assess clinical condition, once the likelihood of overreporting has been ruled out, scores on the Clinical, Content, and Supplementary scales can address directly the presence or absence of current psychopathology. The indicators of serious psychopathology have been discussed previously in this chapter and in earlier chapters of this book. Basically, higher scores on most MMPI-2 scales indicate more serious psychopathology. Graham et al. (2002) concluded that the mean T score for eight Clinical scales (1, 2, 3, 4, 6, 7, 8, and 9) was the most effective way to assess general maladjustment with the MMPI-2.

In many personal injury cases claimants maintain that they have suffered posttraumatic stress disorder (PTSD) as a result of some traumatic event. There is extensive research literature concerning the identification of persons with PTSD from their MMPI/MMPI-2 scores. Although persons with PTSD tend to produce very high scores on the F scale and on many of the Clinical scales, especially Scales 2, 4, 7, and 8, their scores on these scales do not seem to differ systematically from persons with other kinds of serious psychopathology (e.g., Keane, Malloy, & Fairbank, 1984). Platt and Husband (1987) concluded that there does not appear to be a typical MMPI profile that characterizes PTSD accident victims who are involved in litigation. A much more fruitful approach has been the development of supplementary scales to assess PTSD. The most widely used and researched of these is the Posttraumatic Stress Disorder (PK) scale (Keane et al., 1984).

As discussed in Chapter 8 of this book, there is strong evidence that scores on the PK scale are related to diagnoses of PTSD. However, most of the research on the PK scale has utilized combat veterans. Several studies have found that civilian PTSD patients who had experienced life-threatening events (e.g., criminal victimization, industrial or vehicle accidents) scored higher on the PK scale than general psychiatric patients, but the civilians with PTSD scored lower than veterans with PTSD, suggesting that different cutoff scores are needed for civilian use. Despite these several promising studies, the utility of the PK scale in identifying PTSD associated with noncombat stress remains to be demonstrated.

PRESENTING EXPERT OPINIONS BASED ON THE MMPI-2

A detailed discussion of how to write forensic reports and how to prepare and present expert testimony in court is beyond the scope of this chapter. Others have presented very helpful suggestions about these issues (e.g., Brodsky, 1991; Pope et al., 2000; Weiner, 1987, 1995). Only in extraordinarily rare cases will the MMPI-2 be the only source of support for expert opinions. Typically, historical information, clinical interviews, and other assessment data will also be available and will be integrated with MMPI-2 data in support of expert opinions. This section will offer some guidelines concerning the presentation of expert testimony that is based on MMPI-2 results. However, many of the guidelines also will apply to testimony based on other assessment data.

1. Be familiar with the MMPI-2. Although psychologists have an ethical and professional responsibility to be familiar with all techniques that they employ, it is especially important for them to be well informed about instruments used in conducting forensic evaluations, where every statement is likely to be scrutinized, questioned, or challenged. Clinicians should understand how the original MMPI scales were developed and how the MMPI-2 scales are related to those of the original instrument. It is especially important to have a full understanding of the Validity scales and how they can be used to identify deviant test-taking attitudes. Knowledge about the normative sample with which test takers are being compared is essential. An understanding of the research literature relevant to the MMPI-2 interpretations that are being made in a particular case is critical. This literature may never have to be discussed, but one should always be prepared to do so.

2. Be sure that the MMPI-2 is appropriate for the particular forensic issues that are in question. One of the most common mistakes that is made by psychologists who use the MMPI-2 in forensic evaluations is trying to use the instrument for purposes for which it is not suited and for which it has not been adequately validated. In previous sections of this chapter information was given about issues that can be addressed appropriately with MMPI-2 data. The MMPI-2 is very well suited for identifying deviant test-taking attitudes and for assessing current clinical condition. As Weiner (1995) pointed out, test data, including the MMPI-2, are not well suited for concluding what someone is likely to have done in the past or is likely to do in the future. Such postdictions and predictions should be made cautiously.

3. Be sure that the MMPI-2 was administered appropriately and scored correctly. As was discussed in Chapter 2 of this book, the MMPI-2 should be administered in a standardized way, in a professional setting, and with appropriate supervision. Psychologists should be in a position to verify that these procedures were followed and that the test results that are being discussed are, in fact, those of the person who is the focus of the evaluation. Care should be taken to ensure the accuracy of hand scoring of item response. Computer scoring of test responses is quite reliable, but if keyboard entry is utilized, it is important to ensure that the data were entered correctly.

4. Be familiar with all aspects of any computerized scoring and interpretation services that are utilized. Butcher (1995) discussed the advantages of utilizing computerized interpretations in forensic evaluations. They tend to be more thorough and better documented than more traditional interpretations. They reduce the likelihood that information will be selectively emphasized or ignored by clinicians. They are rapid, efficient, and reliable, and there are data suggesting a high level of external validity. However, interpretations typically contain many scores and indexes, some of which are not very familiar to most clinicians. Even if some of these scores and indexes are not emphasized in a particular interpretation, it can be very embarrassing for

clinicians not to be able to respond meaningfully to questions about them. It also is important that users of computerized interpretations understand how the interpretive statements are generated and that they have made determinations about which of the statements in the reports apply to a particular person. The descriptions included in the interpretive reports are based on a particular MMPI-2 prototype, and not every descriptor will apply to every person for whom a computerized interpretation is generated.

5. Limit inferences based on MMPI-2 data to those that can be supported by empirical research. It is this author's practice to make only statements in forensic reports or in expert testimony for which supporting empirical research can be cited. This means that far fewer statements are made than in other kinds of assessment situations, but it makes it much easier to defend what is said if the statements and inferences are challenged. Typically, experts can respond to challenges using secondary sources such as this book, but they should be prepared to cite original research reports if pressed to do so.

6. Present information about the MMPI-2 in a manner that will be understandable to the recipients of the information. This is an obligation that psychologists have in all assessment situations, but it is especially critical in forensic evaluations where the recipients of the interpretations are lay persons (e.g., attorneys, judges, juries). Chapter 11 of this book included guidelines for presenting feedback about MMPI-2 results to persons who have taken the test. These same guidelines are applicable to the presentation of MMPI-2 results and interpretations to lay persons in forensic settings.

Psychologists should not assume that the persons to whom information is being communicated have any background concerning the MMPI-2. Prior to presenting information about any particular person who has taken the MMPI-2, psychologists should educate their audiences by describing the development of the MMPI-2 scales, the norms utilized in interpreting scores, the ways in which the Validity scales can detect deviant responding, and the empirical nature of interpretations. Visual aids, such as sample profile sheets, often are useful in this regard.

Information should be presented using language that will be understood readily by the audience, and technical jargon should be avoided. It is preferable to make statements about the likelihood of certain characteristics and behaviors among persons who produce MMPI-2 results similar to those of the person being evaluated than to make definitive statements that the person who was evaluated does or does not have such characteristics and behaviors. For example, it would be better to state that persons with a 48/84 two-point code type often show very poor judgment than to state that a particular person who produced a 48/84 code type shows very poor judgment.

It is important to keep in mind that inferences made on the basis of MMPI-2 data really are probability statements. A person with a particular code type is more likely to have certain characteristics than someone without that code type, or a person with a very high score on a scale is more likely to have certain characteristics than a person with a lower score on that scale. Because no psychological test, including the MMPI-2, is perfectly valid for any purpose, we can never be absolutely confident that every characteristic that has been associated with a particular score or configuration of scores will fit every person who has that score or configuration. Attorneys often will try to get psychologists to assign probability values to particular inferences, for example, what proportion of persons with the 48/84 code type actually show poor judgment. Although there is a strong research base underlying inferences such as these from MMPI-2 data, it generally does not permit these kinds of specific probability statements to be made.

In summary, the MMPI-2 can be very useful in addressing some issues that are being considered in forensic settings. It is especially useful in assessing deviant test-taking attitudes (e.g., overreporting or underreporting) and determining current clinical condition. However, psychologists are cautioned to limit their MMPI-2 interpretations to areas for which the test was developed and for which adequate validity data are available.

CORRECTIONAL SETTINGS

The earliest studies of the MMPI in relation to criminal activities were conducted by Hathaway and Monachesi (1953, 1957) and Capwell (1945). These investigators found significant relationships between MMPI scale scores (especially Scale 4) and juvenile delinquency for both boys and girls. Through the years since the publication of the original MMPI, numerous studies have examined the utility of the MMPI (and now MMPI-2) in correctional settings. Although it is often assumed that inmates will be uncooperative and likely to produce invalid protocols if required to complete the MMPI-2, this does not seem to be the case. McNulty et al. (2003) reported that approximately 79% of inmates who were administered the MMPI-2 at their time of entry into the correctional system produced valid protocols. This rate of profile validity is very similar to that encountered in many clinical settings.

Megargee and Carbonell (1995) presented an excellent review of the research literature concerning the use of the MMPI-2 in correctional settings, and their review provides the structure for this section. Megargee's 2006 book, *Using the MMPI-2 in Criminal Justice and Correctional Settings*, includes comprehensive guidelines for interpreting MMPI-2 data in correctional settings. These authors described the vital role that classification procedures play in correctional settings. Efficient and valid systems for classifying offenders contribute significantly to effective utilization of the limited resources available in virtually all correctional settings. Various ways of using the MMPI and MMPI-2 to classify prisoners and to predict their behavior while incarcerated and after release have been developed and examined empirically.

According to Megargee and Carbonell (1995), previous research typically has identified significant relationships between standard MMPI scales (especially Scales F and 4) and criminal behavior. Likewise, Scales F and 4 (and sometimes Scales 8 and 9) have been related to disciplinary infractions in prison and to repeat offenses after release. Unfortunately, the magnitude of these relationships has been so modest that accurate prediction in individual cases is not likely. Supplementary scales have been developed specifically to predict institutional and post-release behaviors (e.g., Panton, 1958). Megargee and Carbonell concluded that these supplementary scales have tended to be related only modestly to criterion behaviors and typically have not added much to prediction that could be achieved using standard scales such as F and 4. Linear combinations of standard and Supplementary scales have not yielded predictive accuracy much greater than for individual scales.

Megargee Classification System

Megargee and his associates (Megargee et al., 1979) developed a configural system for classifying the MMPI results of prisoners and determined empirically the criterion variables (e.g., institutional adjustment) that were related to membership in the various categories that they identified. These investigators used hierarchical profile analysis to identify clusters among the MMPIs of offenders. Classification rules were developed for placing offenders into the groups defined by the cluster analyses. Following some use of the system with other samples of offenders, the original classification rules were refined and expanded.

The resulting classification system involved 10 types of offender MMPIs and explicit rules for classifying offenders into the type to which they were most similar. Megargee (1979) reported that in a variety of correctional settings, mechanical application of the rules classified about two-thirds of offender profiles. Most of the remaining one-third of the profiles could be classified by clinicians using published guidelines and additional data. Overall, 85 to 95% of offender profiles could be classified using the 10 profile types. Although the derivational work for the Megargee system took place in a federal facility and involved primarily youthful male offenders, subsequent data indicated that the classification system also worked well in other settings (e.g., state prisons; Nichols, 1980; forensic psychiatric units; Bohn, Carbonell, & Megargee, 1995; Wrobel, Wrobel, & McIntosh, 1988) and with other kinds of offenders (e.g., women; Schaffer, Pettigrew, Blouin, & Edwards, 1983).

Subsequent research found significant differences between the Megargee types on demographic characteristics, criminal behavior patterns, rated personality characteristics, measures of institutional adjustment (including frequency of disciplinary infractions, incidence of reports to sick call, interpersonal relations, and work performance), and recidivism rates. (See Megargee, Carbonell, Bohn, & Sliger, 2001, for a review of these research findings.)

With the revision of the MMPI it became necessary to revise the classification system. Megargee (1994) developed a new set of rules for classifying male offenders on the basis of MMPI-2 scores and found that 91% of the cases could be classified. Megargee (1997) extended the MMPI-2-based classification system to female offenders. Some modifications were made in the rules that had been developed for men, resulting in the classification of more than 98% of the female offenders. Sliger (1997) used Megargee's revised rules to classify MMPI-2s of female federal inmates and examined extratest characteristics of women in each category of the typology. Megargee et al. (2001) described the development of both the MMPI and MMPI-2 classification rules for male and female inmates. They also summarized research findings concerning differences among the Megargee types concerning social, educational, work, and health histories; psychological adjustment; prison adjustment; and recidivism. Implications for management and treatment of offenders in the basic Megargee types also were discussed. Readers contemplating the use of the Megargee classification system should consult books authored by Megargee et al. (2001) and Megargee (2006) for more detailed information about the system.

Criminal Justice and Correctional Report

Pearson Assessments offers a *Criminal Justice and Correctional Report* (Megargee, 2000). The report provides MMPI-2 Validity, Clinical, Content, and Supplementary scale scores that have proved most useful in criminal justice settings over the years. The user's guide for the report provides useful information about the interpretation of these various scales in correctional settings. Offender type (Able, Baker, etc.), based on Megargee's classification system, is indicated, along with the frequency with which the type occurs.

Based on MMPI-2 data on other criminal offenders, nine behavioral dimensions are rated on a three-point scale (below average, average, above average): (1) Need for Mental Health Assessment/Programming, (2) Socially Deviant Behavior/Attitudes, (3) Extraversion, (4) Leadership Ability/Dominance, (5) Hostile Peer Relations, (6) Conflict with Authorities, (7) Positive Response to Supervision, (8) Positive Response to Academic Programming, and (9) Positive Response to Vocational Programming. It should be noted that each of these dimensions is evaluated relative to other criminal offenders.

Next, possible problem areas are addressed. Only areas where the MMPI-2 data indicate that there may be difficulties are addressed in this section. Possible problem areas include (1) difficulties with alcohol or substance abuse, (2) thought disorder, (3) depressive affect or mood disorder, (4) extensive use of sick call, (5) overcontrolled hostility, (6) manipulation or exploitation of other inmates, (7) anger control, (8) awkward or difficult interpersonal relationships, and (9) family problems. Again, statements in this section compare each inmate with other criminal offenders. Finally, the report lists critical items endorsed having to do with self-injury or suicide.

The Criminal Justice and Correctional Report is an excellent and economical way to extract important information about offenders from their MMPI-2 data. The user's guide provides very useful information about the meaning of MMPI-2 scales in correctional settings. The ratings of behavioral dimensions and possible problem areas are based on a synthesis of many years of MMPI/MMPI-2 research. However, it will be important to demonstrate the validity of the specific ratings and inferences in the report in relation to extratest measures.

◩ MMPI-2 Restructured Form (MMPI-2-RF)

The MMPI-2-RF is the most recent development in the long history of the MMPI. As described in Chapter 7 of this book, Tellegen, Ben-Porath, et al. (2003) developed the Restructured Clinical (RC) scales to remove a common demoralization element from the original Clinical scales and to construct scales that would assess the core clinical construct of each Clinical scale. The RC scales have concurrent validity as good as or better than corresponding Clinical scales and better discriminant validity than the corresponding Clinical scales. However, Ben-Porath and Tellegen (2008b) recognized that the RC scales did not measure all the important characteristics that could be assessed by MMPI-2 item pool.

The test's authors (Ben-Porath & Tellegen, 2008b), state that the MMPI-2 RF "is a revised, 338-item version of the MMPI-2 designed to provide an exhaustive and efficient assessment of clinically relevant variables measurable with the instrument's item pool" (p. 1). The MMPI-2-RF has 50 scales. The 9 RC scales of the MMPI-2 represent the core of the revised version and are augmented by 7 revised Validity scales, 1 new Validity scale, 3 new Higher-Order scales, 23 new Specific Problems scales, 2 new Interest scales, and revised versions of the Personality Psychopathology Five (PSY-5) scales. Table 14.1 lists all 50 of the MMPI-2-RF scales. According to the website (pearsonassessments.com) of the test's distributor, "the MMPI-2-RF provides a valuable alternative to the MMPI-2 test, not a replacement. The MMPI-2 test continues to be published and fully supported by the University of Minnesota Press and distributed exclusively by Pearson."

DEVELOPMENT OF THE MMPI-2-RF SCALES

Validity Scales

The MMPI-2-RF has eight Validity scales. Seven of these scales are revised versions of MMPI-2 Validity scales, and one, Infrequent Somatic Responses (F_s), is a new scale. Raw scores for all these validity scales are converted to linear T scores

Table 14.1 MMPI-2-RF Scales

Validity Scales	
VRIN-r	Variable Response Inconsistency
TRIN-r	True Response Inconsistency
F-r	Infrequent Responses
F_p-r	Infrequent Psychopathology Responses
F_s	Infrequent Somatic Responses
FBS-r	Symptom Validity
L-r	Uncommon Virtues
K-r	Adjustment Validity
Higher-Order (H-O) Scales	
EID	Emotional/Internalizing Dysfunction
THD	Thought Dysfunction
BXD	Behavioral/Externalizing Dysfunction
Restructured Clinical (RC) Scales	
RCd	Demoralization
RC1	Somatic Complaints
RC2	Low Positive Emotions
RC3	Cynicism
RC4	Antisocial Behavior
RC6	Ideas of Persecution
RC7	Dysfunctional Negative Emotions
RC8	Aberrant Experiences
RC9	Hypomanic Activation
Specific Problems Scales	
Somatic Scales	
MLS	Malaise
GIC	Gastrointestinal Complaints
HPC	Head Pain Complaints
NUC	Neurological Complaints
COG	Cognitive Complaints
Internalizing Scales	
SUI	Suicidal/Death Ideation
HLP	Helplessness/Hopelessness
SFD	Self-Doubt
NFC	Inefficacy
STW	Stress/Worry
AXY	Anxiety
ANP	Anger Proneness
BRF	Behavior-Restricting Fears
MSF	Multiple Specific Fears
Externalizing Scales	
JCP	Juvenile Conduct Problems
SUB	Substance Abuse
AGG	Aggression
ACT	Activation
Interpersonal Scales	
FML	Family Problems
IPP	Interpersonal Passivity
SAV	Social Avoidance
SHY	Shyness
DSF	Disaffiliativeness
Interest Scales	
AES	Aesthetic–Literary Interests
MEC	Mechanical–Physical Interests

Table 14.1 *Continued*

Personality Psychopathology Five (PSY-5) Scales	
AGGR-r	Aggressiveness—Revised
PSYC-r	Psychoticism—Revised
DISC-r	Disconstraint—Revised
NEGE-r	Negative Emotionality/Neuroticism—Revised
INTR-r	Introversion/Low Positive Emotionality— Revised

SOURCE: Excerpted (Table 1.1) from Ben-Porath, Y.S., & Tellegen, A. (2008). *MMPI-2-RF manual for administration, scoring, and interpretation.* Copyright © 2008 by the Regents of the University of Minnesota. Reproduced by permission of the University of Minnesota Press. All rights reserved. "Minnesota Multiphasic Personality Inventory-2-RF® " and "MMPI-2-RF® " are trademarks owned by the Regents of the University of Minnesota.

($M = 50$; $SD = 10$) based on responses of the MMPI-2-RF normative sample. As with the MMPI-2, the Cannot Say (CNS) scale is simply the count of unanswered items and items answered both true and false.

Variable Response Inconsistency–Revised (VRIN-r) and True Response Inconsistency–Revised (TRIN-r) Scales

These scales were constructed using procedures very similar to those used in constructing the VRIN and TRIN scales of the MMPI-2 (see Chapter 3). However, some additional criteria were added to achieve greater independence of the two inconsistency measures.

The VRIN-r scale consists of 53 item–response pairs. When scoring this scale, a point is assigned whenever a test taker responds to two items within a pair in an inconsistent manner. For example, if someone says that he or she wakes up fresh and rested most mornings and also says that sleep is fitful and disturbed, a point would be assigned on the VRIN-r scale. The VRIN-r raw score is simply the number of inconsistencies identified in responses to the pairs of items. Raw scores are converted to linear T scores. Higher scores indicate a greater degree of inconsistent responding. Interpretive guidelines for the VRIN-r scale are presented later in this chapter.

The TRIN-r scale consists of 26 pairs of negatively correlated items for which either two true or two false answers to a pair of items indicate inconsistent responding. The TRIN-r raw score is the number of true–true responses to the item pairs minus the number of false–false answers to the item pairs. A higher difference score indicates a tendency to respond in an acquiescent content-nonresponsive manner (yea-saying), whereas a lower difference score indicates a tendency to respond in a counteracquiescent content-nonresponsive manner (nay-saying). Difference scores are converted to linear T scores, and T scores lower than 50 are reflected. For example, a T score of 40 is reflected as a T score of 60. Thus, TRIN-r T scores cannot be lower than 50. Higher T scores indicate noncontent responsiveness of either an acquiescent or counteracquiescent type, with the former being designated with the letter *T* and the latter with the letter *F* in scoring reports. Interpretive guidelines for the TRIN-r scale are presented later in this chapter.

Infrequent Responses-Revised (F-r) Scale

The F-r scale consists of 32 items that were endorsed in the keyed direction by 10% or fewer of both men and women in the MMPI-2 normative sample. Some items that met this criterion were not included in the F-r scale because they also appeared on other infrequency scales or on the L-r or K-r scales. Raw scores are converted to linear T scores, with higher scores indicating greater endorsement of items rarely endorsed by persons in the normative sample. Interpretive guidelines for the F-r scale are presented later in this chapter.

Infrequent Psychopathology Responses-Revised (F_p-r) Scale

Recognizing that persons with serious psychopathology tended to get higher scores on the Infrequency (F) scale of the MMPI-2, Arbisi and Ben-Porath (1995) developed the F_p scale to identify invalid responding in settings where the base rate of serious psychopathology is high. They chose items for the F_p scale that were endorsed infrequently by persons in both the MMPI-2 normative sample and an inpatient psychiatric sample. They demonstrated that the F_p scale was less sensitive than the F scale to genuine psychopathology. Subsequent research indicated that the F_p scale was quite effective in identifying persons who overreported when responding to the MMPI-2 items (e.g., Rogers, Sewell, Martin, & Vitacco, 2003).

The F_p-r scale retained 18 of the 27 items from the F_p scale of the MMPI-2 and added three items. Four items that are also in the L scale were deleted, as were three items that are included in the F_s scale. Two additional F_p items were dropped because analyses indicated that they did not function as effectively as other items in the scale, and three items not in the original F_p scale were added because they improved the effectiveness of the scale. Raw scores are converted to linear T scores. Higher scores on the resulting 21-item F_p-r scale suggest overreporting of psychopathology. Interpretive recommendations for this scale are presented later in this chapter.

Infrequent Somatic Responses (F_s) Scale

This scale was developed by Wygant, Ben-Porath, and Arbisi (2004) to identify the reporting of uncommon somatic symptoms. The 16 items in the F_s scale were endorsed by 25% or less of men and women in several large samples of medical patients. Raw scores are converted to linear T scores. Higher scores on the F_s scale indicate greater likelihood of noncredible reporting of somatic symptoms and complaints. Interpretive guidelines for this scale are presented later in this chapter.

Symptom Validity Scale-Revised (FBS-r)

This scale is an abbreviated version of the FBS scale of the MMPI-2. Thirty of the 43 items in the original FBS scale were included because they are in the 338-item MMPI-2-RF item pool. Raw scores are converted to linear T scores. Higher scores on this scale indicate the likelihood of noncredible reporting of cognitive deficits. Interpretive recommendations for the FBS-r scale are presented later in this chapter.

The Uncommon Virtues (L-r) and Adjustment Validity (K-r) Scales

These scales were developed to identify underreporting on the MMPI-2-RF. To create the underreporting scales, items in the Lie (L), Correction (K), Superlative Self-Presentation (S), and Wiggins Social Desirability (Wsd) scales of the MMPI-2 were factor analyzed. Two distinct factors emerged, and two separate scales were developed by selecting items that loaded substantially on one factor but not on the other factor. The scale reflecting the first factor was labeled Uncommon Virtues (L-r) and consists of 14 items, 11 from the L scale and 3 from the Wsd scale of the MMPI-2. The scale reflecting the second factor was labeled Adjustment Validity (K-r), and all of its 14 items are from the K scale of the MMPI-2. Raw scores on the L-r and K-r scales are converted to linear T scores. Higher scores on these two scales suggest greater likelihood of underreporting of symptoms and problems and/or the claiming of more virtuous behavior than the average person. Interpretive guidelines for the L-r and K-r scales are presented later in this chapter.

Higher-Order (H-O) Scales

Tellegen and Ben-Porath (2008) developed a set of Higher-Order scales that would capture the major dimensions represented by the MMPI-2-RF scales and provide an organizational structure for the interpretation of its substantive scales. Factor analyses of the RC scales in three clinical samples yielded three consistent factors: Emotional/Internalizing Dysfunction (EID), Thought Dysfunction (THD), and Behavioral/Externalizing Dysfunction (BXD). Scales were constructed to measure these three dimensions by correlating the three factor scores with the 567 items in the MMPI-2 item pool. Most of the items in the EID scale come from the RCd, RC2, and RC7 scales, most of the items in the THD scale come from the RC6 and RC8 scales, and most of the items in the BXD scale come from the RC4 and RC9 scales. Thus, the Higher-Order scales represent, in dimensional form, three commonly occurring MMPI-2 code types (27/72, 68/86, and 49/94). Interpretive guidelines for the Higher-Order scales are presented later in this chapter.

Restructured Clinical (RC) Scales

The nine RC scales of the MMPI-2-RF are identical to the RC scales of the MMPI-2. The construction of these scales was discussed in Chapter 7 of this book. Interpretive guidelines for the RC scales were presented in Chapter 7, and they are summarized again later in this chapter.

Specific Problems (SP) Scales

Recognizing that the RC scales do not assess all the important clinical constructs represented in the MMPI-2 item pool, Ben-Porath and Tellegen (2008b) developed 23 SP scales. The SP scales were constructed to measure distinctive Clinical scale components not represented by the RC scales, RC scale facets warranting separate assessment, and clinically significant attributes not assessed by RC scales.

The exact procedures used to construct each of the SP scales are not reported in Tellegen and Ben-Porath (2008). However, the authors provide an overview of how the scales were constructed. It seems that initially the authors relied on their own ideas about what additional constructs should be measured. Numerous item factor analyses were conducted to identify constructs and items to assess them. In the construction of each scale, efforts were made to minimize the contribution of demoralization to the scales (see Chapter 7). After a preliminary set of constructs had been identified, experts were asked to suggest additional constructs (beyond the RC scales, the PSY-5 scales, and the preliminary list of SP scales). Based on these suggestions and additional data analyses, a final set of 23 SP scales was established. A list of these scales can be found in Table 14.1. Interpretive guidelines for each of these scales are presented later in this chapter.

Interest Scales

The two Interest scales of the MMPI-2-RF were based on factor analyses of items in the Masculinity–Femininity scale of the MMPI-2. These analyses identified two relatively independent dimensions for which scales were developed. The first scale is labeled Aesthetic–Literary Interests (AES) and has seven items having to do with interest in writing, music, and theater. The second scale is labeled Mechanical–Physical Interests (MEC) and has nine items having to do with interest in fixing or building things, outdoor activities, and sports. Guidelines for the interpretation of the Interest scales are presented later in this chapter.

Personality Psychopathology Five (PSY-5) Scales

The PSY-5 scales of the MMPI-2-RF are revised versions of the MMPI-2 PSY-5 scales that were described in detail in Chapter 7. These scales provide a conceptual link between the MMPI instruments and modern models of personality and psychopathology. Starting with the 96 PSY-5 items that are retained in the MMPI-2-RF item pool, Harkness and McNulty (2007) used internal consistency and external criterion information to revise each of the PSY-5 scales. They discarded 22 of the 96 PSY-5 items that did not contribute to scale reliability and validity. They added 30 other items from the MMPI-2-RF item pool that improved scale reliability and validity. Some of these items were selected based on previous research in which lay persons selected MMPI-2 items that were judged to be associated with each PSY-5 scale, while other items were added to scales based on correlations between existing scales and other items in the MMPI-2-RF item pool. These procedures resulted in 104 items assessing the PSY-5 constructs. The MMPI-2-RF PSY-5 scales are listed in Table 14.1, and interpretive guidelines are presented later in this chapter.

ADMINISTRATION AND SCORING

User Qualifications

As with the MMPI-2, the MMPI-2-RF is to be used only by persons with appropriate education and training in the use of clinical assessment instruments. The test distributor, Pearson Assessments, has established minimum qualifications for users of tests of this kind. Their website (pearsonassessments.com) provides details concerning these qualifications. Basically, users are to be adequately trained in the administration and interpretation of clinical assessment instruments. This training can be obtained through completion of degree programs and/or continuing education workshops.

Administration

As with the MMPI-2, the MMPI-2-RF should be administered in a professional way. The test taker's ability to read and comprehend the items should be determined. A fifth grade reading level is required. The test is usually administered by means of either a printed booklet or computer software. When the booklet is used, responses are recorded on a separate answer sheet. When computer administration is used, responses are recorded by pressing designated keys on the keyboard. The Pearson Assessments catalog or website (pearsonassessments.com) should be consulted to determine what test materials and software are available. For persons with borderline reading levels or with visual disabilities, a standardized audio version of the test is available. Reading items aloud to test takers is discouraged because the practice deviates from the standardized procedures for test administration. Subtle changes in tone of voice or body language can affect responses. Tests should always be administered under supervised conditions. Either a qualified user or someone trained by a qualified user in test administration procedures should administer the test. The test should never be given to someone to take outside a supervised setting. Ben-Porath and Tellegen (2008b) indicate that booklet and answer sheet administration typically takes 35–50 minutes, and computer administration typically takes 25–35 minutes.

Scoring

If the MMPI-2-RF was administered using the printed booklet and separate answer sheet, several scoring methods are available. Answer sheets can be mailed to Pearson Assessments, and scoring and/or interpretive reports will be mailed back within 24–48 hours. Hand scoring can be accomplished using scoring templates and profile sheets available from the test distributor. Responses can also be entered by hand using a keyboard and computer software available from the test distributor. High-volume users can score the test efficiently by means of a scanner attached to a personal computer. If the test was administered by means of personal computer, responses are saved and scoring is accomplished efficiently by appropriate software. Pearson Assessments offers a *Score Report* that provides scores and profiles for all 50 MMPI-2-RF scales and has the option of providing mean data for various comparison groups (e.g., mental health outpatients, psychiatric inpatients, prisoners, medical conditions, substance abuse). A narrative computerized *Interpretive Report* is also available. It provides scores and profiles for all 50 scales and has the option of reporting mean data for various comparison groups. Users also have the option of identifying the sources of inferences included in the report. A sample *Interpretive Report* is appended to this chapter. The case (Jeff) was also interpreted in Chapter 11 of this book when the MMPI-2 interpretive strategy was discussed.

PSYCHOMETRIC CHARACTERISTICS

Normative Sample

The normative sample for the MMPI-2-RF is essentially the same as for the MMPI-2. Details concerning the MMPI-2 sample were reported in Chapter 9 of this book. Only nongendered norms are available for the MMPI-2-RF. Having nongendered norms conforms to the provision in the Civil Rights Act of 1991 that prohibits consideration of sex in employment practices. Ben-Porath and Forbey (2003) found that nongendered norms for the MMPI-2 yielded T scores that generally were not meaningfully different from those generated using gendered norms.

The nongendered sample was created by combining data for all 1138 men in the MMPI-2 sample and data from 1138 women selected randomly from the 1462 women in the MMPI-2 sample. Because at the time that the MMPI-2-RF was developed the MMPI-2 norms were almost 20 years old, Tellegen and Ben-Porath (2008) compared MMPI-2-RF scores derived from a 1990 college student sample with scores of a similar college student sample tested with the MMPI-2-RF approximately 20 years later. They found that MMPI-2-RF scores generated from the two cohorts were essentially interchangeable, suggesting that it is appropriate to use the 1989 norms for the MMPI-2-RF. Detailed information about the MMPI-2-RF normative sample can be found in Ben-Porath and Tellegen (2008b).

Standard Scores

For most MMPI-2 scales raw scores are converted to Uniform T scores (see Chapter 9). A primary advantage of Uniform T scores is that scores at a particular level have the same percentile meaning across scales. Thus, comparisons between scores on scales are easily made. Similarly, raw scores on most MMPI-2-RF scales are converted to Uniform T scores by means of the same procedures used with the MMPI-2. Linear T scores are used for the Validity scales and the two Interest scales, however, because distributions of raw scores for these scales are not similar to those of the other MMPI-2-RF scales.

Reliability

Tables 3.2–3.6 in Tellegen and Ben-Porath (2008) report test–retest coefficients, internal consistency coefficients (Cronbach's alpha), and estimates of standard error of measurement (SEM) for all the MMPI-2-RF scales for normative, mental health inpatient, and mental health outpatient samples. Internal consistency and test–retest estimates for the Validity scales vary across scales and samples, but they generally are much lower than those demonstrated for the substantive scales. This is to be expected because of the limited variability of these scales in samples where test takers are likely to be cooperative and to give credible responses. However, the standard error of measurement for each of the Validity scales is small enough to justify the kinds of interpretation discussed later in this chapter.

Test–retest reliability data were based on a combined gender subset (82 men and 111 women) of individuals from the MMPI-2 normative sample who completed the test twice with a median test–retest interval of seven days. Test–retest reliability coefficients for the Higher-Order scales tended to be in the .80 to .90 range. The lowest value was for the Thought Dysfunction (THD) scale in the normative sample, where the base rate for this kind of serious psychopathology was very low.

Consistent with data reported in Chapter 7, temporal stability of the RC scales was generally good, ranging from .89 for RC4 to .64 for RC6. Again, the lower value for RC6 is likely due to the low base rate of this kind of serious psychopathology in the normative sample. Test–retest coefficients for the SP and Interest scales ranged from .54 to .93, with most values falling between .70 and .80 in the normative sample. Scales with more items tended to be more stable than scales with fewer items. It should be noted that some of the SP scales have as few as four or five items. Test–retest reliability coefficients for the revised PSY-5 scales were acceptable and ranged from .80 for PSYC-r to .93 for DISC-r.

Internal consistency coefficients (Cronbach's alpha) for the Higher-Order scales were quite high in the clinical samples, with typical values falling in the .80s and .90s. As expected, values were lower in the normative sample, likely due to restriction of range. As reported previously, the RC scales had good internal consistency, with values for the clinical samples generally in the .80s and .90s and for the normative sample in the .70s and .80s. As would be expected, the internal consistencies of the SP scales, which have fewer items than the Higher order or RC scales, were lower than for the longer scales. Alpha coefficients for the SP scales varied from a low of .34 to a high of .86, with most values falling in the .60s and .70s in the normative sample. SEMs for the SP scales were only slightly higher than the SEMs for the Higher-Order and RC scales. Internal consistency coefficients (alpha) for the PSY-5 scales in the normative sample ranged from .69 for PSYC-r to .77 for NEGE-r. Corresponding values in clinical samples were slightly higher.

In summary, the internal consistency and temporal stability of the H-O, RC, and PSY-5 scales are good and comparable to those of other self-report scales. The somewhat lower reliabilities of the SP and Interest scales suggest that test users should have more confidence in interpreting scores on these scales that are more elevated, as opposed to those that are only marginally elevated.

Validity

Since the MMPI-2-RF is a relatively new form of the test, only limited additional research is available to guide interpretation of its scales. No validity data are presented in Ben-Porath and Tellegen (2008b). However, Tables A.1–A.136 in Tellegen and Ben-Porath (2008) include more than 50,000 correlations between MMPI-2-RF scale scores and external criteria for a variety of samples, including college students, community mental health center clients, psychiatric patients, substance abusers, criminal defendants, and disability claimants. Criterion measures consisted of therapist ratings, intake information, record reviews, and other self-report instruments. The test authors seem to base many of their interpretative recommendations on these correlational data. The sections that follow summarize validity data reported in Tellegen and Ben-Porath (2008), as well as research published in professional journals or presented at professional conferences.

Validity Scales

Cannot Say (CNS) Scale

Ben-Porath and Tellegen (2008b) indicate that excessive item omissions are associated with lowered scores on some scales and that when 15 or more total items are omitted, scores on some substantive scales may not accurately reflect characteristics of the test taker. The manual also indicates that scales can be interpreted when at least 90% of items from an individual scale are answered. This recommendation coincides with past research that demonstrated that little interpretive validity is lost when up to 10% of items in scales are omitted (Dragon & Ben-Porath, 2007).

Inconsistent Responding Scales (VRIN-r and TRIN-r)

Ben-Porath and Tellegen (2008b) indicate that when VRIN-r T scores are between 70 and 79, substantive scales should be interpreted cautiously; when VRIN-r T scores are ≥ 80, the test taker likely responded to items so inconsistently that scores on other scales should not be interpreted. For the MMPI-2, several studies demonstrated that a T score of 80 on the VRIN scale was optimal for identifying random responding (Gallen & Berry, 1996; Paolo & Ryan, 1992). Given the similarity between the VRIN and VRIN-r scales, one would expect that the recommended T-score cutoff of 80 is also appropriate for the VRIN-r scale.

In a simulation study in which varying percentages of random responses were inserted into MMPI-2-RF protocols, Handel, Ben-Porath, Tellegen, and Archer (2010) demonstrated that the MMPI-2 VRIN scale and the MMPI-2-RF VRIN-r scale were similarly affected by the insertion of random responses. The external validity of RC scales was partially compromised when the VRIN and VRIN-r T scores were between 70 and 79; when the T scores were ≥ 80, validity was compromised to an extent that the RC scales should not be interpreted. Thus, the results of this simulation study support the interpretive guidelines for the VRIN-r scale that are reported in Ben-Porath and Tellegen (2008b).

Ben-Porath and Tellegen (2008b) recommends that a TRIN-r scale T score ≥ 80 be interpreted as indicating fixed (true or false) responding that invalidates the protocol. Research with the MMPI-2 indicated that the TRIN scale was sensitive to the insertion of randomly inserted true or false responses (Wetter & Tharpe, 1995). Given the similarity between the TRIN and TRIN-r scales, one would expect that the TRIN-r scale also is sensitive to fixed responding. Handel et al. (2010) reported results of a simulation study in which varying percentages of true or false responses were inserted into MMPI-2-RF protocols. They found that TRIN-r scores became greater as the percentage of inserted true or false items increased. They also reported that the insertion of up to 10% true or false responses into the protocol did not affect the external validity of the RC scales. However, as percentages of inserted responses increased, the correlations between RC scales and external criteria were lower. Thus, their results support the interpretive guidelines given for the TRIN-r scale in Ben-Porath and Tellegen (2008b).

Overreporting Scales (F-r, F_p-r, F_s, FBS-r)

The F-r, F_p-r and FBS-r scales appear to be very similar to their MMPI-2 counterparts. Tellegen and Ben-Porath (2008) report correlations between the MMPI-2 and MMPI-2-RF Validity scales in several different settings. Correlations differed across settings, but in settings that showed sufficient variability in scores, the MMPI-2-RF and corresponding MMPI-2 scales were highly correlated.

Given the similarities between the MMPI-2-RF scales and the corresponding MMPI-2 scales, similar interpretations can probably be made for MMPI-2-RF overreporting scales. Research discussed in Chapter 3 has consistently demonstrated that the F, F_p, and FBS scales of the MMPI-2 tend to be higher for persons who are overreporting symptoms and problems than for persons who give credible responses (Rogers et al., 2003). The research further indicates that the F_p scale is more sensitive to overreporting than the F scale in settings with a high base rate of severe psychopathology. The FBS scale seems to be most sensitive to exaggeration of cognitive and somatic symptoms (Ben-Porath, Graham, & Tellegen, 2009).

Ben-Porath and Tellegen (2008b) recommend cutoff scores and interpretive guidelines for each of the overreporting scales. The recommendations, which are similar but not identical to those for the MMPI-2 (Butcher et al., 2001), are summarized later in this chapter.

Limited research has addressed the use of the MMPI-2-RF scales in identifying overreporting. In a series of three studies, Wygant et al. (2009) examined the overreporting scales in several different civil forensic settings. In the first study, persons with head injuries were asked to complete the MMPI-2 in a manner that would suggest that they could not return to work and should receive disability compensation, and their F-r-, F_p-r-, FBS-, and F_s-scale scores were compared to scores of head-injured patients who completed the test with standard instructions. In the second study, veterans being treated for medical but not psychiatric problems were asked first to complete the MMPI-2 with standard instructions. Half of the veterans then completed the test a second time with standard instructions, and half completed the test again with instructions to exaggerate their medical problems.

The third study involved individuals who completed the MMPI-2 and cognitive symptom validity tests (SVTs). Two groups were formed according to whether the participants passed or failed the SVTs. With only one exception, across the studies persons in the overreporting simulation conditions scored significantly higher on the MMPI-2-RF overreporting scales than the comparison groups. Interestingly, the exception was that the head injury simulation group did not score significantly higher than the head injury comparison group on the FBS-r scale. In the personal injury study, persons who failed the SVTs scored significantly higher on all the MMPI-2-RF overreporting scales than those who passed the SVTs.

Wygant et al. (2009) also examined classification accuracies for the MMPI-2-RF overreporting scales. The FBS-r, F-r, and F_s scales yielded the most accurate classification of head-injured individuals versus persons simulating head injury. Classification was less accurate for the F_p-r scale, probably because this scale is most sensitive to feigned symptoms of severe psychopathology, which are not likely in individuals who overreport in this medicolegal context.

Sellbom, Toomey, Wygant, Kucharski, and Duncan (2010) used a known-groups design to examine the extent to which the MMPI-2-RF Validity scales could detect overreporting in a criminal forensic setting. Participants were men for whom psychological evaluations were conducted in a federal court setting. Scores on the Structured Interview for Reported Symptoms (SIRS; Rogers, Bagby, & Dickens, 1992) were used to identify participants who were overreporting (n = 27) or not over reporting (n = 98). MMPI-2-RF scale scores were derived from MMPI-2 protocols. The four overreporting scales of the MMPI-2-RF (F-r, F_p-r, F_s, FBS-r) were compared for the overreporting and non-overreporting groups. Overreporters scored significantly higher than non-over-reporters on all four scales, but effect sizes were greatest for the F-r and F_p-r scales. Each of these two scales accounted for unique variance in differentiating between over-reporters and non-over-reporters. Classification accuracy data supported the cutoff scores recommended for the F-r and F_p-r scales in Ben-Porath and Tellegen (2008b).

In summary, the overreporting scales of the MMPI-2-RF seem to function similarly to their MMPI-2 counterparts. All the overreporting scales are sensitive to overreporting of various kinds. Optimal cutoff scores differ from scale to scale and according to the base rates of invalid responding. Until additional research is available concerning optimal cutoff scores in a variety of settings, the interpretive guidelines (Ben-Porath and Tellegen (2008b) and included later in this chapter should be followed.

Underreporting Scales (L-r, K-r)

As reviewed in Chapter 3, the MMPI-2 literature contains many studies indicating that the L scale is sensitive to underreporting. A meta-analysis by Baer and Miller (2002) that compared findings across 14 studies determined that the L scale is very sensitive to underreporting. Baer and Miller concluded that optimal cutoff scores for determining underreporting that invalidates protocols are likely to vary from setting to setting, with somewhat higher scores needed in nonclinical settings, where the base rate of underreporting is greater than in most clinical settings.

Ben-Porath and Tellegen (2008b) indicate that T scores between 70 and 79 on the L-r scale indicate an overly virtuous self-presentation and that scores on the substantive scales should be interpreted with caution because they may underestimate the problems assessed by the scales. The manual further recommends that when L-r scale T scores are $\geq$ 80 absence of elevation on substantive scales is not interpretable. However, elevated scores on substantive scales are interpretable, but it should be recognized that the scores may underestimate the magnitude of the problems that they assess. The manual is silent concerning differential cutoff scores for clinical and nonclinical settings.

Sellbom and Bagby (2008) reported the results of two MMPI-2-RF under-reporting studies. In one study college students and patients with diagnoses of schizophrenia completed the MMPI-2 with instructions to under-report symptoms and problems, and their L-r scale scores were compared with students who completed the test with standard instructions. As expected, both underreporting groups had higher L-r scale scores than the students who completed the MMPI-2-RF with standard instructions. In a second study, Sellbom and Bagby compared L-r scale scores of students who completed the test with standard instructions, students who completed the test with instructions to under-report problems, and parents who completed the test as part of child custody proceedings. As in the first study, both underreporting groups had higher L-r scale scores than the students who completed the test with standard instructions.

In summary, the L-r scale of the MMPI-2-RF is very similar to the L scale of the MMPI-2. Eleven of the 14 items in the L-r scale are also in the L scale. Research with both the L scale and L-r scale support the sensitivity of the L-r scale to underreporting. For now it seems appropriate to use the cutoff scores reported in Ben-Porath and Tellegen (2008b). Future research should address optimal cutoff scores and determine whether different cutoff scores are needed in clinical and nonclinical settings.

Chapter 3 reviews research concerning the use of the MMPI-2 K scale in identifying underreporting of symptoms and problems. Baer and Miller (2002) conducted a meta-analysis of 14 MMPI-2 underreporting studies and concluded that the K scale is effective in identifying persons who under-report symptoms and problems. They also concluded that optimal cutoff scores for identifying underreporting may differ from setting to setting. Recognizing that persons who complete the MMPI-2 in nonclinical settings (e.g., employment screening) generally have higher K-scale scores, the MMPI-2 manual (Butcher et al., 2001) recommends different cutoff scores for clinical and nonclinical settings.

Ben-Porath and Tellegen (2008b) indicate that K-r scale T scores between 60 and 69 can indicate either very good psychological adjustment or underreporting of symptoms and problems. For individuals who are not especially well adjusted, scores in this range likely indicate underreporting, and scores on substantive scales should be interpreted with caution. The manual further indicates that K-r T scores $\geq$ 70 suggest underreporting to an extent indicating the need for great caution in interpreting scores on substantive scales, since those scores are likely to reflect underestimation of the test takers' actual symptoms and problems. As with the L-r scale, the manual is silent concerning the need for different cutoff scores for clinical and nonclinical settings.

In the same two studies reported for the L-r scale, Sellbom and Bagby (2008) compared scores of students who completed the MMPI-2 with standard instructions, students who completed the MMPI-2 with instructions to appear to be free of psychological problems, patients with diagnoses of schizophrenia who were instructed to avoid revealing their symptoms, and parents who completed the test as part of child custody proceedings. As with the L-r scale, all three underreporting groups had higher K-r scale scores than the standard instruction group. The authors did not address the issue of K-r scale cutoff scores for identifying underreporting. Sellbom and Bagby demonstrated that, although the L-r and K-r scales are correlated, each identified unique variance in underreporting.

In summary, the MMPI-2 K scale and the MMPI-2-RF K-r scale are very similar. In fact, all 14 items in the K-r scale are also in the K scale. Lacking specific evidence concerning optimal K-r scale cutoff scores, it is appropriate to use those presented in Ben-Porath and Tellegen (2008b) and included later in this chapter. The recommended cutoff scores are very similar to those recommended for the MMPI-2 K scale, except that a T score as low as 60 on the K-r scale may indicate underreporting. Future research should examine optimal K-r scale cutoff scores for determining underreporting in different settings and determine whether different cutoff scores are indicated in clinical and nonclinical settings.

Higher-Order Scales

In general, the correlations reported in Tellegen and Ben-Porath (2008) support both the convergent and discriminant validity of the Higher-Order scales. Higher scores on the EID scale are associated with many aspects of emotional distress, including feeling overwhelmed, vulnerable, and helpless. Depression and, to some extent, anxiety are prominent for high EID scale scorers. Higher scores on the EID scale are unrelated, or in some settings negatively related, to measures of externalizing behaviors such as getting in trouble with the law or abusing substances. In inpatient psychiatric settings, EID scale scores are also meaningfully related to symptoms of psychotic disorders (e.g., delusions, hallucinations).

Higher scores on the THD scale are associated with indicators of psychotic disorder. High scorers often receive psychotic diagnoses, and they may report auditory or visual hallucinations and delusions of persecution or grandeur. Higher scores are not strongly related to severe emotional distress or to externalizing behaviors such as getting into trouble with the law or abusing substances.

Higher scores on the BXD scale are associated with a wide variety of externalizing behaviors. Higher scores have been associated with trouble at home, at work, and with the law and with histories of substance abuse. Low tolerance for frustration and stormy interpersonal relationships are associated with higher scores. Higher BXD scores are not related to many indicators of emotional distress, but some high scorers may report anxiety and depression. Higher scores are not strongly related to symptoms of psychotic disorder.

Thus, it would seem that examination of scores on the three Higher-Order scales can provide important information about the general nature of problems that a test taker may be experiencing. However, more precise inferences about test takers are based on more specific substantive scales (i.e., RC, Specific Problems, and PSY-5 scales).

Restructured Clinical (RC) Scales

Because the RC scales of the MMPI-2-RF are identical to the RC scales of the MMPI-2, the validity data presented in Chapter 7 apply to the MMPI-2-RF scales. Since the publication of the RC scales (Tellegen, Ben-Porath, et al., 2003), a sizable body of research literature has accumulated concerning their utility in a variety of settings and for a variety of purposes. That research indicates that the RC scale authors were largely successful in developing a set of scales that captured the core constructs of the original Clinical scales while reducing, but not totally eliminating, the effect of the demoralization that was present in the Clinical scales. External correlate data suggest that the RC scales have convergent validity that is equal to or in some cases greater than the original Clinical scales and considerably greater discriminant validity. Ben-Porath and Tellegen (2008a) and Tellegen, Ben-Porath, and Sellbom (2009) summarized the results of studies concerning the validity of the RC scales.

Specific Problems Scales: Somatic/Cognitive Scales

The five Somatic/Cognitive SP scales were developed to assess general preoccupation with poor health as well as presentation of more specific somatic symptoms and cognitive deficits. The Malaise (MLS) scale indicates the extent to which the test taker is presenting himself or herself as being in poor health and debilitated by physical problems, whereas the content of the other four scales focuses on circumscribed symptoms and problems. Because of the brevity of the scales and the homogeneity of their item content, persons who obtain high scores on a scale are likely to have endorsed items consistent with the label of the scale. However, the pattern of correlations of each Somatic/Cognitive scale with external criterion measures (Tellegen & Ben-Porath, 2008) indicates that anyone who scores high on any cognitive/somatic scale in a clinical setting also is likely to have the characteristics described for the MLS scale (e.g., feeling overwhelmed and unable to cope).

Gironda and Clark (2009) examined MMPI-2-RF Somatic/Cognitive scales in two samples of patients in chronic pain programs. Using several validated pain-specific measures as criteria, the authors concluded that the MMPI-2-RF scales possess good convergent and discriminant validity in relatively impaired chronic pain samples.

Using a large sample ($n = 1741$) of disability claimants evaluated in a private-practice setting, Gervais, Ben-Porath, and Wygant (2009) explored relationships between scores on the Cognitive Complaints (COG) scale, objective measures of cognitive deficits, and self-reported cognitive deficits. COG scale scores were not significantly correlated with age and only weakly correlated with education ($r = .17$). Scores on the COG scale were not significantly related to objective cognitive and memory measures. However, COG scale scores were related to subjective reports of cognitive and memory problems. This relationship was present even when insufficient cognitive effort and symptom exaggeration were partialed out.

Specific Problems (SP) Scales: Internalizing Scales

The nine Internalizing SP scales address particular aspects of internalizing dysfunction inherent in elevations on the Emotional/Internalizing Dysfunction (EID) scale and the RCd (Demoralization), RC2 (Low Positive Emotions), and RC7 (Dysfunctional Negative Emotions) scales. The scales are relatively short (4–9 items), and the content of items in each scale is quite homogeneous. Thus, persons who have elevated scores on a scale likely have endorsed items consistent with the label of the scale. As reported in Tellegen and Ben-Porath (2008) the intercorrelations of the nine scales are relatively high. External correlate data indicate that the scales have relatively good convergent validity (i.e., they relate to criterion measures that are consistent with the purposes of the scales), but evidence of discriminant validity is limited. Most of the scales are also related to depression, anxiety, and other indicators of general emotional distress.

Specific Problems Scales: Externalizing Scales

The four SP Externalizing scales deal with acting-out behavior, and each of the scales addresses specific manifestations of this behavior. Items in the Juvenile Conduct Problems (JCP) scale have to do with getting in trouble at school and with the law, items in the Substance Abuse (SUB) scale deal with the use and misuse of alcohol and/or other drugs, items in the Aggression (AGG) scale deal with anger and acting out in aggressive ways, and items in the Activation (ACT) scale describe periods of excessive energy and excitement. While some of the external correlates presented in Tellegen and Ben-Porath (2008) are quite consistent with specific item content, all four Externalizing scales are meaningfully related to a wide variety of acting-out behaviors. In other words, each scale seems to have good convergent validity, but discriminant validity within the realm of externalizing behaviors is not very good. For example, scores on the SP AGG scale are significantly correlated with therapist ratings of angry resentment, but scores on the JCP and SUB scales also are related to angry resentment.

Specific Problems Scales: Interpersonal Scales

The five SP Interpersonal scales address test takers' relationships with other people. Interestingly, the scales are not highly correlated with each other. In fact, the Family Problems (FML) scale is negatively correlated with the Interpersonal Passivity scale. As reported in Tellegen and Ben-Porath (2008), while all of the Interpersonal scales are correlated with external measures of introversion, each scale seems to be associated with a particular aspect of introversion. The Interpersonal Passivity (IPP) scale is related to low assertiveness, the Shyness (SHY) scale is related to social anxiety, the Social Avoidance scale is related to low gregariousness, and the Disaffiliativeness (DSF) scale is related to low warmth and low social closeness. Scores on all these scales also are positively related to indicators of emotional distress (e.g., anxiety, depression).

Interest Scales

As stated earlier in this chapter, all of the items in the two MMPI-2-RF Interest scales are from the Masculinity–Femininity scale of the MMPI-2. Persons scoring higher on Aesthetic–Literary Interests (AES) are reporting interest in occupations and activities that are aesthetic or literary in nature, whereas high scorers on the Mechanical–Physical Interests (MEC) scale are reporting interest in occupations and activities that are mechanical or physical in nature. The two Interest scales are not correlated with each other for men and have only a modest intercorrelation (.11) for women. Examination of external correlates reported in Tellegen and Ben-Porath (2008) for the two scales indicates that neither scale is meaningfully related to serious psychopathology. Men who score higher on the AES scale are described by others as not having stereotypically masculine interests and as rejecting a traditional gender role. Men and women who score higher on the AES scale are also seen as conscientious, optimistic, and open to experience. Both men and women who score high on the MEC scale are described by others as having stereotypically masculine interests. Men scoring higher on the MEC scale are described as not rejecting a traditional gender role, whereas higher scoring women are described as rejecting a traditional gender role.

Personality Psychopathology-Five Scales-Revised (PSY-5)

Examination of correlations between the original MMPI-2 PSY-5 scales and the MMPI-2-RF PSY-5 scales and external criterion measures reported in Tellegen and Ben-Porath (2008) suggests that the original and revised scales are associated with essentially the same test taker characteristics. However, the DISC-r scale seems to be more strongly related to antisocial characteristics than the original scale, especially for men. Although higher scorers on the NEGE-r scale tend to have multiple indicators of emotional distress, the revised scale seems to focus more on depression and suicidal ideation than on other indicators of emotional distress. Interpretive guidelines for the PSY-5-r scales are presented later in this chapter.

MMPI-2 VERSUS MMPI-2-RF

The MMPI-2-RF is not intended as a replacement for the MMPI-2. Rather it should be viewed as another form of the test that has advantages and disadvantages compared with the MMPI-2. Test users should make a decision about which form of the test best meets their needs for particular assessments.

Before examining some of the advantages and disadvantages of each form, it is important to consider ways in which the forms are similar. Both the MMPI-2 and the MMPI-2-RF utilize a self-report approach to assessment. In this approach test takers are asked to describe themselves (in the case of the MMPI-2 and MMPI-2-RF by agreeing or disagreeing with statements about themselves). Interested readers may wish to consult Ben-Porath (2003) for a discussion of the advantages and disadvantages of the self-report methodology.

A major concern about self-report approaches to assessment is the credibility of test takers' responses. Sometimes they respond in ways that compromise the integrity of resulting scores. One of the features of the MMPI that contributed to its extraordinary popularity over many decades was the inclusion of validity scales specifically designed to assess response credibility. Both the MMPI-2 and MMPI-2-RF include validity scales that seem to function similarly for the two forms.

Recurring criticisms of the original MMPI included the heterogeneity of the Clinical scales, their saturation with a common demoralization component, and item overlap between the scales. Tellegen et al. (2003) developed the RC scales to address these issues. Identical versions of the RC scales are available in both the MMPI-2 and the MMPI-2-RF.

When the MMPI-2 was developed, the linear T-score transformations of raw scores were replaced with Uniform T-score transformations. The Uniform T scores assure comparability across scales (see Chapter 9 for more information about Uniform T scores). Both the MMPI-2 and MMPI-2-RF utilize Uniform T scores for most scales.

An important feature of any psychological test is the normative sample used to add meaning to scores of individual test takers. Test norms were updated when the MMPI-2 was published (Butcher et al., 2001), and the MMPI-2-RF uses a slightly smaller subsample of the MMPI-2 norms. Because the MMPI-2 norms were collected approximately 20 years before the MMPI-2-RF was developed, Tellegen and Ben-Porath (2008) demonstrated the comparability of scores of a 1990 college student sample who completed the MMPI-2 and a college sample that completed the MMPI-2-RF approximately 20 years later, thus justifying the current use of the older norms. As discussed earlier in this chapter, only non-gendered norms are available for the MMPI-2-RF, whereas both gendered and nongendered norms are available for the MMPI-2. Although one could argue that using only nongendered norms can conceal differences between men and women, Ben-Porath and Forbey (2003) demonstrated that differences between MMPI-2 scores based on the two sets of norms did not differ meaningfully.

Both the MMPI-2 and MMPI-2-RF take advantage of computer technology for scoring and interpretation. In addition to hand-score materials, Pearson Assessments offers both computer scoring and computer interpretation services to users of both forms, with reports tailored to specific settings (e.g., outpatient, inpatient, preemployment screening).

With all these similarities between the MMPI-2 and MMPI-2-RF, what are the important differences between the two forms, and how are potential users to decide which form to use for specific assessment purposes? In this author's opinion the greatest advantage of the MMPI-2-RF over the MMPI-2 is that the hierarchical structure of the former allows for a more direct the linking of test results to contemporary models of personality and psychopathology. The MMPI-2-RF's emphasis on continuous as opposed to categorical descriptions of psycho-pathology is in line with changes being discussed for the DSM-V (e.g., Widiger, Livesley, & Clark, 2009).

The Emotional/Internalizing Dysfunction (EID) and Behavioral Dysfunction (BXD) scales of the MMPI-2-RF and their associated RC and Specific Problems scales map well onto the bifurcation of internalizing and externalizing disorders (Krueger, Caspi, Moffit, & Silva, 1998; Krueger & Markon, 2006). Sellbom,

Ben-Porath, and Stafford (2009) demonstrated that the externalizing scales of the MMPI-2-RF fit well with the conceptualization of Krueger et al. (2007) of a broad disinhibition factor (BXD) and subordinate factors of activation/aggression (RC9 and ACT) and substance abuse (RC4 and SUB). Additionally, Sellbom, Ben-Porath, and Bagby (2008) examined the MMPI-2-RF scales in relation to Watson's (2005) reconceptualization of internalizing distress and fear disorders. Demoralization (RCd) was a primary marker of distress disorders, and Dysfunctional Negative Emotions (RC7) was a primary marker of fear disorders. Low positive emotions (RC2) was a specific marker of depression and social phobia. The PSY-5 scales (Harkness, McNulty, & Ben-Porath, 1995) can be linked to a large body of literature concerning the Five-Factor Model of personality.

Some users see the brevity of the MMPI-2-RF as advantageous—338 items in the MMPI-2-RF compared with 567 in the MMPI-2. The importance of the different number of items in the two versions will depend, to a large extent, on the purposes of assessments and the settings in which assessments are conducted. For many test takers, completing the MMPI-2 will call for a bit more time than the MMPI-2-RF but will represent no significant hardship. Other test takers will find completing the larger number of items on the MMPI-2 to be burdensome. In neuropsychological evaluations, for example, test takers with significant cognitive deficits often are asked to complete a long battery of assessment instruments. In situations such as this, using the shorter MMPI-2-RF may be more appropriate than the longer MMPI-2. Similarly, some depressed patients or those with other significant psychological turmoil may find the shorter MMPI-2-RF more tolerable, and therefore they are more likely to produce valid protocols with this form.

Another practical advantage of the MMPI-2-RF is that interpretation of protocols is less complex than for MMPI-2 protocols. A simple and straightforward interpretive strategy is presented in Ben-Porath and Tellegen (2008b). A clear structure is provided for organizing information from the test's many scales. The time needed to interpret an MMPI-2-RF protocol is likely to be somewhat less than for the MMPI-2, especially for students and others not familiar with the MMPI instruments. However, it should be noted that the same level of professional training is required for using both versions of the test.

There also are some disadvantages of using the MMPI-2-RF instead of the MMPI-2. Perhaps the greatest disadvantage is that there is less research available to guide interpretation of the MMPI-2-RF scales, since the assessment instrument is relatively new. Tellegen and Ben-Porath (2008) presented correlations between substantive scales and external criterion measures for large samples in a variety of settings. These data are useful in starting to understand how to interpret MMPI-2-RF scores, but they pale in comparison to the massive research base that has accumulated for the MMPI and MMPI-2 since 1943, the year in which the MMPI was published. Some MMPI-2-RF studies have started to appear in professional journals, and it is likely that these data will continue to accumulate and further inform interpretation. It will be especially important to conduct additional MMPI-2-RF research in diverse settings and with more diverse populations.

The original Clinical scales of the MMPI, which were carried over virtually unchanged to the MMPI-2, are not available in the MMPI-2-RF. They have been replaced by the Restructured Clinical (RC) scales. Although the RC scales offer advantages over the Clinical scales (e.g., they are more homogeneous, less saturated with demoralization), there are some disadvantages to not having the Clinical scales available in the MMPI-2-RF. A large and useful research base has accumulated to guide the interpretation of the Clinical scales. Although the database concerning interpretation of the RC scales is increasing steadily, it will be quite some time before it is as large as that for the Clinical scales. The absence of the Clinical scales in the MMPI-2-RF also means that users cannot rely on code-type interpretations, a mainstay of MMPI interpretation since Hathaway and Meehl (1956) stressed their importance. Of course, one could argue that code types evolved largely as a way to deal with the heterogeneity of the Clinical scales and are not necessary because of the homogeneity of the RC and other MMPI-2-RF scales. Although that may indeed be the case, not having the code types renders useless the large body of research data that inform interpretation. Arbisi, Ben-Porath, and Forbey (2003) found that code types based on the original Clinical scales of the MMPI-2 did not add incrementally to individual RC scales in predicting external criterion measures in a psychiatric inpatient setting. It remains to be seen whether code types based on the RC scales will add incrementally to the individual RC scales in predicting conceptually relevant extratest characteristics.

The brevity of the MMPI-2-RF, which was discussed earlier as an advantage, can also be a disadvantage. Because many items in the MMPI-2 are not included in the MMPI-2-RF, some scales that could be scored for the MMPI-2 cannot be scored for the MMPI-2-RF. This author has found some of these scales that cannot be scored for the MMPI-2-RF to be quite interesting and informative. For example, a wealth of information is available to guide interpretation of the MacAndrew Alcoholism Scale–Revised (MAC-R) (MacAndrew, 1965). Similarly, the Hostility (Ho) scale (Cook & Medley, 1954) of the MMPI-2, which has come to have an important role in health psychology settings, is not available in the MMPI-2-RF. The MMPI instruments have always been and continue to be pathology oriented. Most of the inferences based on scales of the MMPI-2 and MMPI-2-RF deal with symptoms, problems, and shortcomings. However, there are some exceptions to this focus. For example, this author has found the Ego Strength (Es) scale (Barron, 1953) of the MMPI and MMPI-2 to be quite helpful because it can offer important information about psychological resources of test taker. The Es scale is not available on the MMPI-2-RF, nor does the test include a similar measure of psychological resources.

So, what is one to conclude about choosing the MMPI-2 or the MMPI-2-RF in conducting assessments? As with most things, it all depends. In some settings where brevity is important, the MMPI-2-RF would be preferable. In settings where only a screening instrument is needed (e.g., preemployment) the MMPI-2-RF has significant advantages. In settings where the goal of assessment is a comprehensive understanding of test takers, this author would choose the MMPI-2 because it is his opinion that interpretations based on the MMPI-2 can yield a more in-depth analysis of personality and psychopathology. In forensic settings, the acceptance of a relatively new assessment instrument is predicated on accumulated research supporting the use of the instrument and the extent to which the instrument is accepted by the professional community as a whole. Consequently, the professional who uses the MMPI-2-RF in forensic settings should be prepared to address challenges based on the instrument's novelty.

INTERPRETATION

Interpretive Guidelines

In the sections that follow interpretive guidelines are offered for the Validity and substantive scales of the MMPI-2-RF. The suggested interpretations for the Validity scales are based entirely on the guidelines offered by Ben-Porath and Tellegen (2008b). The suggested interpretations for the substantive scales are based on guidelines suggested in the interpretive manual, this author's examination of the empirical correlate data presented in the technical manual, and other research that has been reported since the MMPI-2-RF was published in 2008. Inferences were generated from the technical manual based on correlations between scales and criterion measures that were of at least a small effect size ($r \geq .20$; Cohen, Cohen, West, & Aiken, 2002).

As with the scales of the MMPI-2, inferences based on substantive scales should be treated as hypotheses that are to be compared with other information available about test takers (e.g., interview, other tests, behavioral observations). T scores much higher than 65 suggest greater likelihood that the listed descriptors will apply to a test taker and that listed symptoms will be more severe than those associated with less elevated scores. Although the interpretation of low scores on some MMPI-2-RF scales is recommended in the interpretive manual, little research is available to guide interpretation of low scores. The interpretive guidelines presented in this chapter for low scores are based on information in Ben-Porath and Tellegen (2008b) and on negative correlations between scales and external criterion measures presented in Tellegen and Ben-Porath (2008).

Interpretive Guidelines for Validity Scales

Cannot Say (CNS) Scale

When the test taker omits fewer than 15 items the protocol is interpretable. However, when 15 or more items are omitted, caution is indicated in the interpretation of the substantive scales because the omission of items tends to lead to lower scores on these scales. One should examine the percentage of items omitted from each scale. If more than 10% of items are omitted from a scale, the scale should not be interpreted. This information is readily available in MMPI-2-RF score reports and interpretive reports.

Variable Response Consistency–Revised (VRIN-r) Scale

High Scores (T ≥ 70)
Scores at this level indicate that the test taker responded in an inconsistent manner. T scores between 70 and 79 suggest that the protocol should be interpreted with caution. When T scores are ≥ 80, inconsistent responding is so pervasive that the protocol should not be interpreted.

Average Scores (T = 39–69)
The test taker responded in a consistent manner, and the protocol is interpretable.

Low Score (T = 30–38)
The test taker was remarkably consistent, and perhaps overly cautious, in responding, but the protocol is interpretable.

True Response Inconsistency–Revised (TRIN-r) Scale

High Scores (T ≥ 70)
High scores on this scale indicate that the test taker responded in an inconsistent manner with fixed responding. When a designation of T is associated with the score, the fixed responding is likely to be yea-saying, whereas a designation of F associated with the score indicates that the fixed responding is likely to be nay-saying. T scores between 70 and 79 indicate a tendency toward fixed responding, and the protocol should be interpreted with caution. When T scores are ≥80 the fixed responding is pervasive enough that the protocol should not be interpreted.

Average Scores (T = 50–69)
Scores in this range indicate that there is no evidence of fixed responding, and the protocol is interpretable.

Infrequent Responses (F-r) Scale

T = 120
Scores at this level indicate that the test taker has reported a large number of symptoms that are rarely endorsed by most individuals. The VRIN-r and TRIN-r scales should be consulted to determine whether F-r scale scores are the product of inconsistent responding. If evidence of inconsistency is not found, the scores likely represent an attempt on the part of the test taker to appear to have much more severe psychopathology or distress than is actually the case. Protocols with F-r scale scores at this level should be considered invalid and should not be interpreted.

T = 100–119
Scores at this level may indicate inconsistent responding, severe emotional distress, or overreporting. Check the VRIN-r and TRIN-r scales. If these scales are not at acceptable levels, the protocol should be considered invalid and should not

be interpreted. If these scores are at acceptable levels, it is important to determine whether the F-r scale scores are reflecting severe psychopathology or overreporting. For individuals for whom there is neither history nor any current indication of serious dysfunction, scores at this level likely indicate overreporting, and the protocol should not be interpreted. For individuals with a history or current indications of serious dysfunction, the scores at this level should be interpreted as reflecting genuine psychopathology, and the protocol can be interpreted. Protocols with F-r scale scores at this level are more likely to reflect genuine psychopathology if the F_p scale is at an acceptable level (see later).

$T = 90\text{--}99$
Scores at this level are to be interpreted similarly to T scores between 110 and 119, except the likelihood of overreporting is less than at the higher levels.

$T = 79\text{--}89$
Inconsistent responding or overreporting of symptoms is possible at this level, but scores are more likely to be reflective of serious psychopathology, especially if the F_p scale score is at an acceptable level (see later). The protocol can be interpreted, but with the caution that scores may to some extent overestimate the severity of symptoms and problems.

$T < 79$
When scores are at this level there is no evidence of significant overreporting, and the protocol can be interpreted.

Infrequent Psychopathology (F_p-r) Scale

$T \geq 100$
Scores at this level indicate an invalid protocol that should not be interpreted because the test taker has endorsed many very rare symptoms. Scores at this level can result from inconsistent responding (check VRIN-r and TRIN-r) or from overreporting of severe psychological symptoms and problems in order to appear more maladjusted than is really the case.

$T = 80\text{--}99$
Scores at this level can indicate inconsistent responding (check VRIN-r and TRIN-r). For individuals with histories or current corroborating evidence of severe dysfunction, scores at this level likely reflect genuine psychopathology. For those without histories or corroborating evidence of severe dysfunction, scores at this level likely reflect overreporting.

$T = 70\text{--}79$
Scores at this level may indicate inconsistent responding (check VRIN-r and TRIN-r), overreporting, or genuine psychopathology. Scores should be interpreted similarly to those at the 80–99 level, except at this level the likelihood of genuine psychopathology is greater than at the higher levels.

T < 70
There is no evidence of overreporting that would compromise protocol validity.

Infrequent Somatic Responses (F_s) Scale

T ≥ 100
Scores at this level indicate overreporting of somatic symptoms rarely described by persons with genuine medical problems. The scores may result from inconsistent responding (check VRIN-r and TRIN-r). If these scales are at acceptable levels, the F_s scores are likely to be reflecting overreporting of physical complaints, and scores on the somatic substantive scales (i.e., RC1 and SP Somatic scales) should be interpreted with considerable caution.

T = 80–99
Scores at this level indicate possible overreporting of somatic symptoms either as a product of inconsistent responding (check VRIN-r and TRIN-r) or as indicating an effort to appear to have more somatic problems than is actually the case. In individuals with no histories or corroborating evidence of physical health problems, scores at this level likely represent overreporting of somatic symptoms, and scores on the Specific Problems somatic scales should be interpreted with caution.

T < 80
There is no evidence of overreporting of somatic symptoms, and scores on the substantive scales can be interpreted.

Symptom Validity (FBS-r) Scale

T ≥ 100
Scores at this level suggest that test takers have reported a very unusual combination of symptoms that likely reflect noncredible reporting of somatic and/or cognitive symptoms. Because scores at this level can result from inconsistent responding, check the VRIN-r and TRIN-r scales. If inconsistent responding can be ruled out, scores on RC1 and the SP Cognitive and Somatic scales should be interpreted with great caution.

T = 80–99
Scores at this level indicate possible reporting of unusual combinations of somatic and/or cognitive symptoms. Because scores at this level can be the product of inconsistent responding, check the VRIN-r and TRIN-r scales. If inconsistent responding can be ruled out, scores may result from credible reporting of serious somatic problems and/or cognitive deficits or overreporting of these symptoms in order to appear to have medical or neurological problems that do not exist or to exaggerate genuine symptoms. Scores on the RC1 scale and the SP Somatic and Cognitive symptom scales should be interpreted with caution.

T < 80

When scores are at this level there is no evidence of significant overreporting of somatic and/or cognitive symptoms, and scales that assess such symptoms can be interpreted.

Uncommon Virtues (L-r) Scale

T ≥ 80

Scores at this level indicate that test takers have presented themselves in an overly positive and virtuous manner to such an extent that scores on substantive scales should not be interpreted. Since scores at this level can be a product of inconsistent responding, the VRIN-r and TRIN-r scales should be examined. Absence of elevation on substantive scales is uninterpretable, and elevated scores on the substantive scales may underestimate problems assessed by those scales.

T = 70–79

Scores at this level indicate that test takers likely presented themselves in a very positive way. Because the scores may be the product of inconsistent responding, check the VRIN-r and TRIN-r scales. Scores on substantive scales should be interpreted with caution. The absence of elevations on substantive scales is uninterpretable, and elevated scores on substantive scales may underestimate the problems assessed by the scales. Scores at this level may also indicate someone with an upbringing that strongly stressed traditional values.

T = 65–69

Scores at this level may be the product of inconsistent responding (check VRIN-r and TRIN-r) or an effort by test takers to present themselves in an unrealistically favorable light. Absence of elevations on substantive scales are uninterpretable, and elevated scores may underestimate problems assessed by those scales. Scores at this level may also indicate that the test takers were raised in a very traditional way.

T < 65

When scores are at this level there is no evidence of significant underreporting, and substantive scales can interpreted.

Adjustment Validity (K-r) Scale

T ≥ 70

Scores at this level indicate that test takers have presented themselves as remarkably well adjusted. Because scores at this level can be a product of inconsistent responding, check the VRIN-r and TRIN-r scales. If inconsistent responding can be ruled out, interpretation should proceed with considerable caution, as the scores likely represent an attempt on the part of test takers to present themselves as much better adjusted than they really are. Absence of elevations on substantive scales is uninterpretable, and elevated scores on substantive scales likely understate the problems assessed by those scales.

$T = 66–69$

Because scores at this level can be a product of inconsistent responding, check the VRIN-r and TRIN-r scales. If inconsistent responding can be ruled out, scores may reflect either underreporting of symptoms and problems or very good psychological adjustment. For persons for whom there is no corroborating evidence of good psychological adjustment, absence of elevation on substantive scales is uninterpretable. Elevations on substantive scales may underestimate the problems assessed by those scales.

$T = 60–65$

Scores at this level indicate possible underreporting of symptoms and problems. Inconsistent responding should be ruled out by checking the VRIN-r and TRIN-r scales. For persons for whom there is corroborating evidence of poor adjustment, absence of elevations on substantive scales should be interpreted with caution. Elevated scores on substantive scales may underestimate the problems assessed by those scales. Scores at this level are common among persons who complete the MMPI-2-RF in nonclinical settings (e.g., custody evaluations, preemployment screening).

$T < 60$

When scores are at this level, there is no evidence of significant underreporting, and scores on substantive scales may be interpreted.

Interpretive Guidelines for Higher-Order Scales

Emotional/Internalizing Dysfunction (EID)
High scores (T ≥ 65) indicate persons who

1. are experiencing a great deal of emotional turmoil (when T score ≥ 80, the distress is likely to be perceived as a crisis)
2. feel overwhelmed by their life situations
3. feel vulnerable, helpless, and unable to cope
4. have depression as a prominent presenting problem
5. are likely to feel sad and blue
6. lack energy and motivation to get things done
7. may have suicidal ideation and histories of suicide attempts
8. report anxiety
9. present somatic complaints
10. are likely to have obsessive thoughts and to have difficulty concentrating
11. may feel mistreated

12. feel angry
13. should be evaluated for depressive disorder, anxiety disorder, and somatoform disorder
14. are likely to be motivated for treatment because of emotional turmoil

Low scores (T < 39) indicate individuals who report a better than average level of emotional adjustment.

Thought Dysfunction (THD)

High scores (T ≥ 65) indicate individuals who

1. have reported symptoms of thought dysfunction
2. may experience auditory or visual hallucinations
3. may have delusions of grandeur or persecution
4. may engage in magical thinking
5. feel that life is a strain
6. report somatic complaints
7. feel depressed
8. are suspicious and untrusting
9. have low frustration tolerance
10. sometimes act aggressively toward others
11. do not communicate effectively
12. do not make good impressions on other people
13. do not seem motivated to work or achieve
14. may have problems with the law dating back to adolescence
15. should be evaluated for psychotic disorders (e.g., schizophrenia, delusional disorder)
16. should be evaluated for antipsychotic medications
17. may require treatment in a structured environment

Low scores (T < 39) on this scale are not interpreted.

Behavioral/Externalizing Dysfunction (BXD)

High scores (T ≥ 65) indicate persons who

1. report engaging in a wide variety of externalizing behaviors that have gotten them into difficulties
2. may have histories of arrests and convictions dating back to adolescence
3. may abuse alcohol and other substances
4. are aggressive in relationships
5. have low frustration tolerance
6. often show poor judgment
7. are cynical and untrusting
8. often feel that they have been mistreated
9. have histories of problems in school, at home, and at work
10. are narcissistic, selfish, and self-indulgent

11. typically do not report great emotional distress but may report some symptoms of anxiety and depression
12. often are given Cluster B personality disorder and/or substance abuse/dependence diagnoses
13. typically are not interested in changing but may agree to treatment to avoid negative consequences
14. need to develop better self-control
15. may terminate treatment prematurely

Low scores (T < 39) indicate persons who

1. report higher than average levels of behavioral constraint
2. are unlikely to engage in externalizing, acting-out behaviors

Interpretive Guidelines for Restructured Clinical (RC) Scales

As discussed earlier in this chapter, the RC scales of the MMPI-2-RF are identical to the RC scales of the MMPI-2. Thus, the interpretive guidelines reported in Chapter 7 of this book apply to the MMPI-2-RF RC scales.

Demoralization (RCd)

Very high scores (T ≥ 80) indicate persons who

1. are experiencing significant emotional turmoil
2. report feeling depressed
3. report feeling anxious and unable to concentrate
4. report somatic complaints that may increase in times of stress
5. feel overwhelmed by the demands of their life situations
6. feel incapable of coping with their current life circumstances
7. should be evaluated for suicide risk
8. may be motivated for treatment because of emotional distress
9. need intervention to relieve emotional distress

Moderately high scores (T = 65–79) indicate persons who

1. feel sad and unhappy
2. feel anxious much of the time
3. are dissatisfied with their life situations
4. have poor self-concepts and feel like failures
5. are pessimistic about their lives getting better

Low scores (T < 39) indicate persons who report a higher than average level of morale and life satisfaction.

Somatic Complaints (RC1)

High scores (T ≥ 65) indicate persons who

1. report multiple somatic complaints that may include gastrointestinal problems, head pain, and neurological symptoms

2. develop increased somatic symptoms at times of increased stress
3. are quite resistant to considering psychological factors that may be related to somatic symptoms
4. should be further evaluated for somatoform disorders if physical explanations for their somatic symptoms can be ruled out

Low scores (T < 39) indicate persons who report a sense of physical well-being.

Low Positive Emotions (RC2)
High scores (T ≥ 65) indicate persons who

1. lack positive emotional experiences in life
2. have deficits in ability to experience joy and happiness (anhedonia)
3. are unhappy and demoralized
4. are at increased risk for depression
5. may have thoughts about suicide
6. lack energy to handle demands of their life situations
7. find it difficult to take charge, make decisions, and get things done
8. tend to be introverted, passive, and withdrawn in social situations
9. often feel bored and isolated
10. are pessimistic
11. have low expectations of success and are not likely to place themselves in competitive situations
12. should be evaluated for antidepressant medication
13. if T ≥ 75, may need inpatient treatment for depression
14. may have difficulty engaging in treatment because of low positive emotionality

Low scores (T < 39) indicate persons who

1. report a high level of psychological well-being
2. report a wide range of emotionally positive experiences
3. report feeling confident and energetic
4. are extraverted and socially engaged
5. are optimistic about the future

Cynicism (RC3)
High scores (T ≥ 65) indicate persons who

1. have cynical beliefs
2. see other people as untrustworthy, uncaring, and concerned only about themselves
3. are hostile and feel alienated from others
4. may have difficulty forming therapeutic relationships
5. need help in developing interpersonal trust

Low scores (T < 39) indicate persons who

1. disavow cynical beliefs
2. see others as well-intentioned and trustworthy
3. may be naïve, gullible, and overly trusting of others

Antisocial Behavior (RC4)

High scores (T ≥ 65) indicate persons who

1. report histories of antisocial behaviors
2. find it difficult to conform to societal norms and expectations
3. have problems with authority figures
4. are likely to have been in trouble with the law
5. are at increased risk for substance abuse
6. behave aggressively toward other people
7. are critical, argumentative, and antagonistic
8. have conflictual relationships with other people
9. may have significant family problems
10. are not likely to be motivated for treatment
11. may not be very compliant in treatment
12. need help in developing better self-control

Low scores (T < 39) indicate persons who

1. have higher levels of behavioral constraint
2. are unlikely to report histories of antisocial conduct or substance abuse

Ideas of Persecution (RC6)

High scores (T ≥ 65) indicate persons who

1. feel targeted, controlled, or victimized by others
2. are suspicious of the motivations of others
3. have difficulty forming relationships
4. if T > 80, may indicate paranoid delusions and/or hallucinations
5. if T > 80, should be evaluated further for psychotic disorders
6. may have difficulty in forming therapeutic relationships

Low scores (T < 39) on this scale are not interpreted.

Dysfunctional Negative Emotions (RC7)

High scores (T ≥ 65) indicate persons who

1. report negative emotional experiences including anxiety, fear, and irritability
2. worry excessively
3. experience intrusive ideation
4. report feeling sad and unhappy
5. are insecure and excessively sensitive to perceived criticism
6. are self-critical and guilt prone
7. ruminate and brood about perceived failures

8. may be motivated for treatment because of emotional distress
9. should be evaluated for anxiolytic medications

Low scores (T < 39) indicate persons who report below-average levels of negative emotional experiences.

Aberrant Experiences (RC8)
High scores (T ≥ 65) indicate persons who

1. report unusual sensory, perceptual, cognitive, or motor experiences
2. may experience hallucinations and/or delusions
3. may experience bizarre sensory experiences
4. have impaired reality testing
5. may report feeling anxious and/or depressed
6. have impaired occupational and interpersonal functioning
7. in mental health settings, should be evaluated for psychotic disorders
8. may require treatment in structured settings
9. should be evaluated for antipsychotic medications
10. may find it difficult to participate appropriately in treatment because of disordered thinking

Low scores (T < 39) on this scale are not interpreted.

Hypomanic Activation (RC9)
High scores (T ≥ 65) indicate persons who

1. experience thought racing
2. experience high energy levels
3. have heightened mood
4. are irritable and aggressive
5. show poor impulse control
6. may engage in antisocial behaviors
7. may abuse substances
8. are sensation seekers and risk takers
9. if T > 75, may experience manic episodes
10. should be evaluated for bipolar disorders
11. may find appropriate participation in treatment difficult because of excessive behavioral activation
12. should be evaluated for mood-stabilizing medications

Low scores (T < 39) indicate persons who have below average levels of activation and engagement with their environments.

Interpretive Guidelines for Specific Problems (SP) Scales

Malaise (MLS)
High scores (T ≥ 65) indicate individuals who

1. report feelings of ill health and fatigue that may interfere with work and other activities
2. have vague somatic complaints
3. feel sad and depressed
4. feel unable to deal with stressors in their life situations
5. are pessimistic about the likelihood of their lives getting better
6. may feel angry much of the time
7. feel mistreated by others
8. should be evaluated for depressive disorders and/or somatoform disorders
9. may be unwilling and/or unable to participate in treatment because of malaise

Low scores (T < 39) indicate persons who report a general sense of physical well-being.

Gastrointestinal Complaints (GIC)
High scores (T ≥ 65) indicate individuals who

1. report gastrointestinal complaints (e.g., nausea, vomiting)
2. may report manifestations of depression (e.g., sad mood, decreased energy, suicidal ideation)
3. often are given depressive disorder diagnoses
4. should be evaluated for somatoform disorders if physical explanations of somatic symptoms can be ruled out
5. may benefit from learning stress reduction techniques

Low scores (T < 39) on this scale are not interpreted.

Head Pain Complaints (HPC)
High scores (T ≥ 65) indicate individuals who

1. report head and/or neck pain
2. experience increased pain during times of stress
3. may lack energy and feel overwhelmed by the demands of their life situations
4. tend to feel sad and depressed
5. in mental health settings, often are given depressive disorder diagnoses and treated with antidepressant medications
6. should be considered for somatoform diagnoses if physical explanations for the reported pain can be ruled out
7. may benefit from learning pain management techniques

Low scores (T < 39) on this scale are not interpreted.

Neurological Complaints (NUC)
High scores (T ≥ 65) indicate persons who

1. report problems with motor control (e.g., balance, dizziness, paralysis)
2. in mental health settings, may report feeling depressed and anxious
3. do not cope well with stress
4. lack energy to meet the demands of everyday life
5. should be considered for somatoform diagnoses if physical explanations for somatic symptoms can ruled out
6. may benefit from medical and/or behavioral management of symptoms if physical origin of neurological complaints has been established

Low scores (T < 39) on this scale are not interpreted.

Cognitive Complaints (COG)
High scores (T ≥ 65) indicate persons who

1. report problems with memory and concentration
2. do not cope well with stress
3. often feel inadequate and inferior
4. sometimes report perceptual aberrations or strange thoughts
5. in mental health settings, may report feeling anxious and depressed
6. should be referred for neurological evaluation
7. should be considered for somatoform diagnoses if physical explanations for the cognitive problems can be ruled out

Low scores (T < 39) on this scale are not interpreted.

Suicidal/Death Ideation (SUI)
High scores (T ≥ 65) indicate persons who

1. report suicidal ideation and/or histories of suicide attempts
2. should receive a detailed suicide assessment
3. feel quite depressed
4. feel overwhelmed and helpless
5. feel pessimistic about the likelihood of their lives getting better
6. may report anxiety, rumination, and specific fears
7. often receive diagnoses of depressive disorders and are treated with anti-depressant medications

Low scores (T < 39) on this scale are not interpreted.

Helplessness/Hopelessness (HLP)
High scores (T ≥ 65) indicate persons who

1. are expressing unhappiness with their lives
2. feel that they cannot make significant changes in their lives
3. are pessimistic about the likelihood of their lives getting better
4. experience a great deal of emotional turmoil
5. feel depressed
6. feel inadequate and inferior

7. feel angry because of perceived mistreatment by others
8. are suspicious of the motives of others
9. may see suicide as the only solution to their problems
10. often have histories of suicide attempts
11. often receive depressive disorder diagnoses and are treated with antidepressant medications
12. may benefit from treatment to increase feelings of hope

Low scores (T < 39) on this scale are not interpreted.

Self-Doubt (SFD)

High scores (T ≥ 65) indicate persons who

1. report lack of self-confidence
2. report feelings of uselessness
3. feel inferior to other people
4. feel sad and depressed
5. may have suicidal ideation and histories of suicide attempts
6. report anxiety, obsessiveness, and rumination
7. feel that they get a raw deal from life
8. feel angry and resentful about perceived mistreatment
9. in mental health settings, often receive depressive disorder diagnoses and are treated with antidepressant medications
10. may benefit from treatment to increase self-esteem

Low scores (T < 39) on this scale are not interpreted.

Inefficacy (NFC)

High scores (T ≥ 65) indicate persons who

1. report being very indecisive
2. try to avoid making difficult decisions in life
3. are not very self-reliant
4. may experience depression and anxiety
5. feel insecure and inadequate
6. give up easily
7. may benefit from treatment to decrease indecisiveness

Low scores (T < 39) on this scale indicate persons who are efficacious and decisive in stressful situations.

Stress/Worry (STW)

High scores (T ≥ 65) indicate person who

1. feel anxious and worried about many things
2. feel there is much to do and little time to do it
3. feel overwhelmed
4. do not cope well with stress

5. may develop somatic symptoms when stress levels increase
6. in mental health settings, may be depressed and anxious
7. may experience suicidal ideation
8. often feel like failures
9. are pessimistic about the future
10. may benefit from learning stress management techniques

Low scores (T < 39) indicate persons who report below-average levels of stress and worry.

Anxiety (AXY)

High scores (T ≥ 65) indicate persons who

1. report frequent and pervasive feelings of anxiety, dread, and fear
2. experience intrusive ideation
3. have difficulty in concentrating
4. experience nightmares and disturbed sleep
5. feel depressed
6. may have suicidal ideation
7. report somatic complaints
8. do not cope well with stress
9. feel overwhelmed by the demands of their lives
10. are pessimistic about the likelihood of things getting better
11. should be evaluated for anxiolytic medications

Low scores (T < 39) on this scale are not interpreted.

Anger Proneness (ANP)

High scores (T ≥ 65) indicate individuals who

1. report having a low frustration tolerance
2. are impatient and easily irritated
3. do not cope well with stress and feel that life is a strain
4. may report anxiety, depression, and somatic symptoms
5. may have histories of school problems and juvenile delinquency
6. may benefit from learning anger management techniques

Low scores (T < 39) on this scale are not interpreted.

Behavior-Restricting Fears (BRF)

High scores (T ≥ 65) indicate persons who

1. report multiple specific fears that restrict normal activities inside and outside the home
2. feel uneasy when away from home
3. may express fear of darkness, dirt, money, or pointed objects
4. report feeling generally anxious and depressed
5. may report somatic complaints

6. are seen by others as socially awkward and not very self-reliant
7. do not cope well with stress
8. are not achievement oriented
9. should be evaluated for anxiety disorders, particularly agoraphobia

Low scores (T < 39) on this scale are not interpreted.

Multiple Specific Fears (MSF)
High scores (T ≥ 65) indicate persons who

1. report having multiple fears
2. report fear of natural events (e.g., windstorms, earthquakes)
3. report fear of animals (e.g., snakes, spiders)
4. tend to feel anxious and depressed
5. may report somatic complaints
6. do not cope well with stress
7. do not engage in risky behaviors
8. are not achievement oriented
9. lack energy
10. are pessimistic about the future
11. in inpatient mental health settings, may report magical thinking, hallucinations, or other symptoms of psychosis
12. in substance abuse settings, tend to have more severe addictions
13. may benefit from behavioral approaches to fear reduction

Low scores (T < 39) indicate persons who report a lower than average number of specific fears.

Juvenile Conduct Problems (JCP)
High scores (T ≥ 65) indicate persons who

1. report school difficulties including behavior problems and truancy
2. may report having stolen things when young
3. have histories of acting out both as adolescents and adults
4. are likely to have histories of trouble with the law
5. are likely to have histories of abusing alcohol and other substances
6. show poor judgment
7. are emotionally labile
8. may act out in aggressive ways
9. tend to have problems with authority figures
10. have stormy relationships, especially with family members
11. tend to blame families for their difficulties
12. do not report many internalizing symptoms, but in mental health settings may report feeling anxious and depressed
13. often are given diagnoses of antisocial personality disorder and/or substance abuse/dependence
14. are not likely to be motivated for treatment

Low scores (T < 39) on this scale are not interpreted.

Substance Abuse (SUB)
High scores (T ≥ 65) on this scale indicate persons who

1. are openly acknowledging use and probably abuse of alcohol, marijuana, and/or other substances
2. report using substances in order to relax
3. tend to have problems with authority figures
4. may at times be physically aggressive
5. tend to be argumentative and provocative
6. have stormy interpersonal relationships
7. have difficulty trusting others
8. in mental health settings may feel depressed
9. often receive substance abuse/dependence diagnoses
10. should receive detailed substance abuse evaluation
11. may benefit from substance abuse treatment program

Scores below 65 are not interpreted because they could indicate either absence of substance abuse or denial of existing substance abuse.

Aggression (AGG)
High scores (T ≥ 65) indicate persons who

1. report feeling angry
2. report acting out in aggressive ways toward other people
3. acknowledge breaking things and hurting other people in fights
4. experience pleasure from making other people afraid of them
5. are cynical and suspicious of motives of others
6. may have histories of violent behavior
7. tend to have problems with authority figures
8. are seen by others as antisocial
9. tend to have histories of misbehavior in school
10. have had difficulties with the law
11. tend to abuse alcohol and other substances
12. may report physical problems
13. may feel sad and anxious
14. may have underlying feelings of inadequacy
15. may benefit from learning anger management techniques

Low scores (T < 39) indicate individuals who report below-average levels of aggressive behavior.

Activation (ACT)
High scores (T ≥ 65) indicate persons who

1. describe periods of excessive energy and excitement
2. report that at times they have difficulty controlling their thoughts, speech, or behavior

3. may have histories of mood swings and hypomanic behavior
4. have periods of accelerated speech and decreased need for sleep
5. may have histories of substance abuse and juvenile delinquency
6. in inpatient settings, may show evidence of magical thinking, perceptual aberrations, or hallucinations
7. if T > 80, should be evaluated for bipolar disorder
8. may benefit from mood-stabilizing medications

Low scores (T < 39) indicate persons who report below average levels of energy and activation.

Family Problems (FML)
High scores (T ≥ 65) indicate persons who

1. report having negative attitudes toward their families (because of item wording, it is not possible to tell whether they are describing current families, families of origin, or both)
2. describe conflicts with their families
3. do not feel supported by their families
4. report being mistreated, and even abused, by their families
5. in mental health settings, may feel depressed, anxious, helpless, and hopeless and may have suicidal ideation
6. tend to have histories of juvenile delinquency and substance abuse
7. may benefit from having family members involved in treatment program

Low scores (T < 39) indicate persons who report comparatively conflict-free family environments, past and present.

Interpersonal Passivity (IPP)
High scores (T ≥ 65) indicate persons who

1. describe themselves as passive and unassertive in interpersonal situations
2. report that they do not express opinions or feelings strongly
3. have difficulty making decisions
4. do not want to be in positions of leadership
5. are seen by others as passive and submissive
6. are not achievement or power oriented
7. are introverted
8. feel insecure
9. in mental health settings, tend to report feeling depressed and having suicidal ideation
10. may describe low sex drive and feelings of sexual inadequacy
11. should be evaluated for disorders involving passive, submissive behaviors (e.g., dependent personality disorder)
12. may benefit from treatment to reduce passive, submissive behaviors

Low scores (T < 39) indicate persons who describe themselves as

1. having strong opinions
2. standing up for themselves
3. being assertive and direct
4. being able to lead others

Social Avoidance (SAV)

High scores (T ≥ 65) indicate persons who

1. describe themselves as being socially awkward
2. do not like being in social situations involving many people
3. are seen by others as introverted and shy
4. lack self-confidence and feel like failures
5. feel hopeless and helpless
6. do not make good first impressions
7. tend to be passive in relationships
8. in mental health settings may report anxiety, depression, and somatic complaints
9. may benefit from treatment to reduce social avoidance

Low scores (T < 39) indicate persons who report enjoying social situations and events.

Shyness (SHY)

High scores (T ≥ 65) indicate persons who

1. report being shy, easily embarrassed, and uncomfortable around other people
2. tend to be socially anxious
3. find it difficult to interact with other people, especially those whom they do not know well
4. are seen by others as socially awkward and passive in relationships
5. are self-doubting and self-degrading
6. may be in considerable emotional turmoil
7. do not react well to stress
8. in mental health settings, may report anxiety, depression, and health concerns
9. should be evaluated for social phobia

Low scores (T < 39) indicate persons who report little or no social anxiety.

Disaffiliativeness (DSF)

High scores (T ≥ 65) indicate persons who

1. report that they prefer being alone rather than around other people
2. report that they do not want to hear other people's opinions
3. report that they do not want to talk with other people about their problems

4. are seen by others as introverted, uncomfortable in social situations, and not having close relationships
5. in mental health settings, are likely to be experiencing a great deal of emotional turmoil including anxiety, depression, and somatic symptoms
6. feel that life is a strain
7. are pessimistic about the likelihood of things getting better
8. may have difficulty developing therapeutic alliances

Low scores (T < 39) on this scale are not interpreted.

Interpretive Guidelines for Interest Scales

Aesthetic–Literary Interests (AES)
High scores (T ≥ 65) indicate persons who

1. report an above-average interest in activities or occupations that are aesthetic or literary in nature (e.g., writing, music, theater)
2. are seen by others as not having stereotypically masculine interests
3. in mental health settings, are more likely to have symptoms of internalizing disorders and less likely to have symptoms of externalizing disorders

Low scores (T < 39) indicate persons who report little interest in activities or occupations of an aesthetic or literary nature (e.g., writing, music, theater).

Mechanical–Physical Interests (MEC)
High scores (T ≥ 65) indicate persons who

1. report an above-average interest in activities or occupations of a mechanical or physical nature (e.g., sports, mechanics)
2. in clinical settings are more likely to report symptoms of externalizing disorders and less likely to report symptoms of internalizing disorders

Low scores (T < 39) indicate persons who report little interest in activities or occupations of a mechanical or physical nature (e.g., sports, mechanics).

Interpretive Guidelines for the Personality Psychopathology Five (PSY-5) Scales

Aggressiveness–Revised (AGGR-r)
High scores (T ≥ 65) indicate persons who

1. report that they are interpersonally dominant, assertive, and aggressive
2. report histories of physical fights
3. report that they try to control other people through threat and intimidation
4. tend to be aggressive in response to threat from others
5. are extroverted

6. indicate that they are self-confident and would be good leaders of other people
7. are seen by others as quite aggressive
8. may have histories of assaultiveness and physical abusiveness
9. are domineering and overbearing in relationships
10. are narcissistic
11. have unrealistic self-appraisals
12. may benefit from examining costs and benefits of aggressive behavior
13. may benefit from learning anger control techniques

Low scores (T < 39) indicate persons who

1. report being interpersonally passive and submissive
2. are likely to be less aggressive than the average person
3. are introverted
4. are conforming

Psychoticism–Revised (PSYC-r)
High scores (T ≥ 65) indicate persons who

1. are likely reporting unusual thought processes and/or perceptual experiences
2. in inpatient settings may report hallucinations, delusions of persecution or grandeur, and/or ideas of reference
3. in inpatient settings may receive psychotic diagnoses and may be treated with antipsychotic medications
4. display symptoms of demoralization (e.g., depression, hopelessness)
5. feel that life is a strain
6. do not cope well with the demands of their life situations
7. may develop somatic symptoms at times of increased stress
8. should be evaluated for psychotic disorders and/or Cluster A personality disorders (e.g., paranoid, schizoid)

Low scores (T < 39) indicate persons who do not report symptoms of thought disturbance.

Disconstraint–Revised (DISC-r)
High scores (T ≥ 65) indicate persons who

1. report various manifestations of disconstrained, undercontrolled behavior
2. may have had behavior problems in school
3. may have histories of problems with the law
4. use alcohol and/or other drugs excessively
5. may have histories of aggressive, and at times violent, behaviors
6. are nonconforming
7. are impulsive

    8. show poor judgment
    9. report family problems
  10. are narcissistic
  11. overvalue their own worth
  12. in forensic settings, may receive diagnoses of antisocial personality disorder
  13. are not likely to be motivated for treatment
  14. may be noncompliant in treatment
  15. may benefit from learning better impulse control

Low scores (T < 39) indicate persons who

    1. report overly constrained behavior
    2. are passive and submissive in relationships
    3. are seen by others as dependable, conscientious, and agreeable

Negative Emotionality/Neuroticism–Revised (NEGE-r)

High scores (T $\geq$ 65) on this scale indicate persons who

    1. report overwhelming negative emotions
    2. feel anxious much of the time
    3. feel depressed
    4. may experience suicidal ideation
    5. worry about many things
    6. seem to understand that many of their worries are not justified
    7. feel insecure, inadequate, and inferior
    8. are irritable and easily angered
    9. are pessimistic about the likelihood of things getting better for them
  10. may develop somatic complaints at times of increased stress
  11. should be evaluated for anxiety and depressive disorders
  12. should be evaluated for anxiolytic medications
  13. may be motivated for treatment because of emotional distress

Low scorers (T < 39) are persons who

    1. report below-average levels of negative emotional experiences
    2. are extroverted
    3. cope well with stress
    4. are seen by others as enthusiastic, agreeable, and optimistic

Introversion/Low Positive Emotionality–Revised (INTR-r)

High scores (T $\geq$ 65) on this scale indicate persons who

    1. report a lack of positive emotional experiences
    2. report avoiding social situations
    3. feel overwhelmed and that life is a strain
    4. feel hopeless and pessimistic about the likelihood of their lives getting better

5. do not cope well with stress
6. may develop somatic symptoms at times of increased stress
7. lack energy to get things done
8. feel anxious much of the time
9. feel sad and depressed
10. are quite socially awkward and introverted
11. are very sensitive to criticism
12. have a poor self-concepts and feel that they are failures
14. should be evaluated for Cluster C personality disorders (e.g., avoidant, dependent)
15. should be evaluated for antidepressant medications
16. may have difficulty engaging in therapy because of lack of positive emotions

Low scores (T < 39) indicate persons who

1. report feeling energetic and having many positive emotional experiences
2. cope well with stress
3. are extroverted
4. are achievement oriented

Interpretive Strategy

The MMPI-2-RF's authors have suggested a strategy for interpreting MMPI-2-RF protocols (Ben-Porath & Tellegen, 2008b; Y.S. Ben-Porath, personal communication, January 2009). The first step is to examine the Validity scales to determine whether interpretation of the substantive scales is warranted. If Validity scale scores suggest that the test taker approached the test in an invalid manner (e.g., omitted items, responded inconsistently, over-reported, under-reported), no further consideration is given to other MMPI-2-RF scores. However, sometimes Validity scale scores suggest some overreporting or underreporting but not to an extent that would invalidate the protocol. In these cases substantive scales are interpreted, but caution is advised. Guidelines for interpreting Validity scales are presented in Ben-Porath and Tellegen (2008b) and were summarized earlier in this chapter.

If a protocol is deemed valid and interpretable, the substantive scales are then interpreted. The interpretation of these scales is hierarchical in nature. Inferences are made first about general areas of dysfunction (i.e., somatic/cognitive, emotional, thought, and behavioral), and then about more specific aspects of dysfunction. Six areas are addressed: (1) somatic/cognitive dysfunction, (2) emotional dysfunction, (3) thought dysfunction, (4) behavioral dysfunction, (5) interpersonal functioning, and (6) interests. Two additional areas deal with diagnostic and treatment considerations.

The Higher-Order (H-O), Restructured Clinical (RC), Specific Problems (SP), and Personality Psychopathology Five (PSY-5) scales for each of the areas of dysfunction are listed in Table 14.2. The H-O scales allow inferences about general areas of dysfunction (i.e., emotional, thought, and behavioral). There are RC scales associated with each H-O scale that allow inferences about particular facets of dysfunction suggested by elevated scores on the H-O scales. Likewise, there are SP scales associated with the RC scales that permit inferences about even more specific facets of dysfunction suggested by elevations on RC scales. The first four areas are addressed in the order of their prominence in the MMPI-2-RF protocol. Determine prominence by using the RC1 scale for somatic/cognitive area and the three Higher-Order (H-O) scales for the general emotional (EID), thought (THD), and behavioral (BXD) areas. Start the interpretation with the area having the highest T score. If that T score is ≥ 65, generate inferences based on the score. This gives a general idea of the most salient problems that the test taker is likely to have. If the highest score is for an H-O scale, examine the RC scales associated with the H-O scale (RCd, RC2, and RC7 for EID; RC6 and RC8 for THD; and RC4 and RC9 for BXD). If the T score for an RC scale is ≥ 65, generate inferences about the RC scale and then examine and interpret SP scales that are facets of the RC scale, making inferences about scales with T scores ≥ 65. Inferences based on the RC scales typically will be more specific than those based on the H-O scale. If there are no elevated scores for the RC scales associated with the H-O scale, go directly to the Specific Problems scales associated with the RC scales and interpret any scales with T scores ≥ 65. Inferences based on the SP scales will be more focused than those based on the H-O and RC scales. Relevant PSY-5 scales should also be interpreted at this point (INTR-r for RC2, NEGE-r for RC7, PSYC-r for THD, and AGG-r and DISC-r for BXD). If the RC1 scale score is higher than the three H-O scale scores, interpret the RC1 scale first, followed by the Specific Problems scales associated with RC1.

After completing the interpretation of scales in the most prominent area, go to the H-O scale with the next highest T score and repeat the process that was used for the highest scale and its associated scales. Repeat the process for the areas with the third and fourth highest scores. There is one exception to this process. If the EID scale T score is ≥ 65, interpretation of the EID, RC, and SP scales associated with the EID scale should immediately follow the interpretation of any elevated scales in the somatic/cognitive area.

If there are no H-O scales with T scores ≥ 65, start interpreting the substantive scales by considering the highest RC scale score and its associated SP scales. If no RC scales have T scores ≥ 65, go directly to the Specific Problems scales, starting with the scale that has the highest T score.

Next examine the Interpersonal Functioning scales. Inferences based on these scales involve views of family life, cynicism, passivity, shyness, and disaffiliativeness. The two Interest scales (aesthetic/literary and mechanical/physical) are interpreted next.

Ben-Porath and Tellegen (2008b) do not address the issue of item-level interpretation. However, the MMPI-2 Score Report and Interpretive Report list "critical responses" given by test takers. Ben-Porath and Tellegen (2008c) discuss item-level interpretation. Seven MMPI-2-RF substantive scales––Suicidal/Death Ideation (SUI), Helplessness/Hopelessness (HLP), Anxiety (AXY), Ideas of Persecution

Table 14.2 Recommended Structure and Sources of Information for MMPI-2-RF Interpretation

TOPIC	MMPI-2-RF SOURCES
1. Protocol Validity	
a. Content Non-Responsiveness	CNS, VRIN-r, TRIN-r
b. Overreporting	F-r, F_P-r, F_S, FBS-r
c. Underreporting	L-r, K-r
2. Substantive Scale Interpretation	
a. Somatic/Cognitive Dysfunction	RC1, MLS, GIC, HPC, NUC, COG
b. Emotional Dysfunction	1. EID
	2. RCd, SUI, HLP, SFD, NFC
	3. RC2
	4. RC7, STW, AXY, ANP, BRF, MSF
	5. NEGE-r, INTR-r
c. Thought Dysfunction	1. THD
	2. RC6
	3. RC8
	4. PSYC-r
d. Behavioral Dysfunction	1. BXD
	2. RC4, JCP, SUB
	3. RC9, AGG, ACT
	4. AGG-r, DISC-r
e. Interpersonal Functioning	1. FML, RC3, IPP, SAV, SHY, DSF
f. Interests	AES, MEC
g. Diagnostic Considerations	Most substantive scales
h. Treatment Considerations	Most substantive scales

SOURCE: Excerpted (Table 5.1) from Ben-Porath, Y.S., & Tellegen, A. (2008). *MMPI-2-RF manual for administration, scoring, and interpretation*. Copyright © 2008 by the Regents of the University of Minnesota. Reproduced by permission of the University of Minnesota Press. All rights reserved. "Minnesota Multiphasic Personality Inventory-2-RF® " and "MMPI-2-RF® " are trademarks owned by the Regents of the University of Minnesota.

(RC6), Aberrant Experiences (RC8), Substance Abuse (SUB), and Aggression (AGG)––were identified as having critical item content that may require immediate attention and follow-up. Items answered in the scored direction are examined for scales for which T scores are ≥ 65. The test authors indicate that the critical responses can be used to guide follow-up interviews with test takers.

All the substantive scales (H-O, RC, SP, and PSY-5) are sources of information about diagnostic impressions and treatment implications. Ben-Porath and Tellegen (2008b) indicated that inferences about diagnostic considerations are based in part on empirical data and are in part inferential. They also stated that inferences about treatment are not based on empirical data.

Illustrative Case

It may be instructive to apply the preceding strategy to the scores for the illustrative case (Jeff) appended to this chapter. Readers should note that this is the same case discussed in Chapter 11 in relation to the MMPI-2 interpretive strategy.

Examination of Jeff's Validity scale scores indicates that he approached the test in an appropriate manner and that the substantive scales are interpretable. He omitted only one item and answered consistently (VRIN-r = T43; TRIN-r = T57 in true direction). He was not at all defensive (L-r = T42; K-r = T38). Among the over-reporting scales, only the F-r scale T score was significantly elevated (F-r = T70). However, at this level the F-r scale score likely indicates genuine emotional distress/psychopathology rather than overreporting.

Next, examine his Higher-Order (H-O) and RC1 scale scores. Because his highest score is on the Emotional/Internalizing Dysfunction (EID) scale and because that scale is ≥ T65, we would infer that he is reporting significant signs of emotional dysfunction. Then interpret the RC scales associated with EID—RCd, RC2, and RC7. Interpretation of these scales will give a more specific picture of Jeff's symptoms and problems. The RCd scale T score of 77 suggests that Jeff is reporting feeling sad, unhappy, and dissatisfied with his current life situation. The Specific Problems scales associated with RCd are interpreted next. T scores above 65 on the Inefficacy (NFC) and Self-Doubt (SFD) scales suggest that Jeff is reporting that he lacks self-confidence and feels useless. He also is reporting being indecisive, inefficacious, and incapable of coping with his current difficulties. Empirical correlates associated with elevated scores on the NFC and SFD scales indicate that Jeff feels insecure and inferior and that he engages in self-degrading and intropunitive behaviors. Further, he has difficulty dealing with small inconsequential matters. He is not very self-reliant and is passive in relationships. Because the RC2 and INTR-r scale T scores are not greater than 65, no inferences are made based on these scales.

The RC7 scale T score of 75 suggests that Jeff is reporting negative emotional experiences including anxiety, anger, and fear. This is consistent with the NEGE-r T score of 77, which indicates that Jeff likely has a disposition to experience emotions of these types. T scores greater than 65 on the STW, ANP, and NEGE-r scales indicate that Jeff is reporting multiple problems involving stress and worry, including preoccupation with disappointments, difficulties, and time pressure. He also may be reporting specific worries about misfortune and finances. The ANP scale T score of 80 indicates that Jeff is reporting that he gets upset easily, is impatient with others, becomes easily angered, and sometimes even is overcome with anger. Empirical correlates of the Specific Problems and PSY-5 scales are consistent with Jeff's self-report. He is likely to be stress reactive and worry prone, and he may engage in obsessive rumination. He tends to feel angry and irritable, has a temper, and is argumentative. He is likely to feel anxious and insecure, he worries excessively, and he may experience intrusive ideation. He is self-critical and guilt prone.

Because the EID scale T score was ≥ 65, we would next interpret scores for scales in the Somatic/Cognitive area. Although Jeff's RC1 scale is not significantly elevated, we would next interpret the MLS T score of 87. This very high score indicates that Jeff has reported that feelings of ill health interfere with work and other activities. He may feel weak and tired and lack energy for the activities of everyday life. Persons with elevated MLS scale scores may or may not report specific somatic or cognitive complaints. The absence of significant elevation on the GIC, HPC, and NUC scales suggests that Jeff is not presenting multiple somatic complaints.

The next highest H-O scale score is for Behavioral Dysfunction (BXD), which has a T score of 65. Because this is a borderline elevation, inferences can be made based on the scale, but one should have less confidence in the inferences than would be warranted if the score were higher. The BXD scale score suggests that Jeff reported externalizing, acting-out behavior, which may have gotten him into difficulties.

The RC scales associated with the BXD scale are RC4 and RC9. The RC4 T score of 71 suggests that Jeff reported a history of antisocial behavior. Next, examine the Specific Problems scales associated with RC4. The JCP T score of 63 is not high enough to warrant interpretation. The SUB T score of 69 indicates that Jeff reported past and current substance use/abuse. Because Jeff's RC9 scale T score is 48, no inferences are generated based on this scale. However, we would still examine scores on the Specific Problems and PSY-5 scales associated with RC9 (ACT, AGGR-r, and DISC-r). Because T scores on these scales are not greater than 65, no interpretations are made.

Because Jeff's remaining H-O scale T score (THD) is only 39, no interpretation is appropriate. Likewise, there are no significant elevations for either of the RC scales (RC6, RC8) associated with THD. The PSY-5 scale associated with the THD scale (PSYC-r) has a T score of 47, so this scale is not interpreted.

We next turn to the Interpersonal Functioning scales. The RC3, FML, SAV, and DSF scales are not interpreted because their T scores are below 65. The IPP T score of 74 indicates that Jeff reported being unassertive, passive, and submissive in interpersonal relationships, characteristics that are consistent with perceptions of others. In addition, Jeff is likely to be seen as emotionally overcontrolled. The T score of 75 on the SHY scale indicates that Jeff reported being shy, uncomfortable, and easily embarrassed around others. Empirical correlates of the SHY scale indicate that others see Jeff as introverted, inhibited, anxious, and nervous in social situations.

Jeff's T score of 39 on the Aesthetic–Literary Interests (AES) scale indicates that he reported below-average interest in activities or occupations of an aesthetic or literary nature. His T Score of 52 on the Mechanical–Physical Interests (MEC) scale indicates that he reported an average interest in activities or occupations of a mechanical or physical nature.

Of the seven scales for which critical responses should be examined if T scores are ≥ 65, Jeff had an elevated score on only one scale. His T score for the SUB scale was 69. His responses to items in this scale indicate that he acknowledged use of marijuana and excessive use of alcohol. He further indicated that he sometimes takes drugs or sleeping pills that were not ordered by doctors. He stated directly that he has an alcohol or drug problem. These responses would prompt follow-up questions and quite possibly a detailed evaluation for chemical dependency.

We next examine all of Jeff's scores to determine whether there is evidence to suggest that specific mental disorders should be considered. Jeff's scores on the EID, RC, Specific Problems, and PSY-5 scales suggest that several internalizing diagnoses should be considered. The MLS (T = 87) scale score indicates that Jeff reported that feelings of ill health interfere with work and other activities. If physical origins for his health concerns can be ruled out, further evaluation for somatoform disorder is indicated. His scores on the RC7 (T = 75), STW (T = 81), and SHY (T = 75) scales suggest that anxiety disorder diagnoses should be considered (e.g., obsessive compulsive, social phobia, and generalized anxiety disorder). Jeff's BXD scale T score of 65 is only marginally elevated, but it raises the possibility of externalizing disorders. His RC4 scale score of 71 reinforces this notion. However, the absence of elevations on the RC9, DISC-r, and AGGR-r scales and all but one of the Specific Problems scales associated with BXD tempers our interpretation. The significant elevation on the SUB scale (T = 69) suggests that Jeff should be further evaluated for a substance abuse or dependence disorder. It may well be that the primary factor leading to elevations on the BXD and RC4 scales is his acknowledged substance use/abuse.

Jeff's scores also indicate further evaluation for several personality disorder diagnoses. His scores on the NEGE-r (T = 77) scale and the IPP scale (T = 74) suggest that he should be evaluated further for Cluster C personality disorders (e.g., dependent, obsessive–compulsive).

Finally, we examine Jeff's scores again to determine whether inferences concerning treatment are warranted. We find that Ben-Porath and Tellegen (2008b) suggest a large number of treatment-related inferences.

T scores $\geq$ 65 on the EID, RC7, and NEGE-r scales suggest that Jeff is likely to be motivated for treatment because of his high level of emotional distress. However, a T score of 65 on the BXD scale indicates that he might not be internally motivated for treatment. Because his BXD scale score is considerably lower than the EID, RC7, and NEGE-r scale scores, the interpretation would emphasize the motivation because of emotional turmoil.

Several scores suggest characteristics that may interfere with effective treatment. An elevated score on the MLS scale (T = 87) indicates general fatigue and pessimism about the likelihood of things getting better that may make it difficult for Jeff to actively engage in the therapy process. An elevated score on the RC4 scale (T = 71) and a moderately elevated score on the BXD scale (T = 65) raise the possibility of noncompliance in treatment. Jeff's indecisiveness (NFC = 80) may interfere with establishing goals in therapy.

Scores on several scales suggest potential targets for treatment. Relief of psychological distress as a target is suggested by elevated T scores on the RCd (T = 77) and RC7 (T = 75) scales. The T score of 77 on the NEGE-r scale suggests that Jeff should be evaluated for anxiolytic medications. The SFD scale T score of 76 suggests that low self-esteem and self-doubt may be appropriate targets. Shyness in social situations is suggested as a treatment target by the SHY scale T score of 69. Stress management is suggested by the T score of 81 on the STW scale. Reduction of passive, submissive behaviors as a target is suggested by the T score of 74 on the

IPP scale. Helping Jeff develop better self-control is suggested by elevated scores on the RC4 (T = 71) and BXD (T = 65) scales. Anger management is suggested by Jeff's T score of 80 on the ANP scale. Jeff's T score of 69 on the SUB scale indicates that a detailed chemical dependency evaluation is indicated.

In summary, Jeff appears to have approached the MMPI-2-RF in a valid manner. He responded consistently, was not defensive, and did not over-report symptoms and problems. His problems are primarily internalizing in nature. He seems to be experiencing a great deal of emotional distress, feels overwhelmed by the demands of his life situation, and believes that he cannot do anything to make things better. His symptoms are likely to include feelings of ill health, anxiety, and, to a lesser extent, depression. He worries excessively about inconsequential things, and he may ruminate about perceived failures in his life. Jeff tends to be irritable and easily upset, and at times may not control his anger effectively. Jeff openly acknowledges that he uses alcohol and marijuana excessively, likely in an attempt to dampen his negative emotions. Jeff has a poor self-concept, lacks self-confidence, and expects to fail in life. He is likely to be passive and dependent in relationships and to feel shy and awkward in social situations.

Jeff is likely to be motivated for treatment because of the psychological distress that he is experiencing. However, there are factors that may interfere with effective treatment. He may lack the energy to actively participate in the therapy process, and he may not be compliant in treatment. His indecisiveness may make it difficult to establish treatment goals. He is pessimistic about being able to make changes that will lead to improvements in his life.

A primary focus of treatment should be to reduce his psychological distress. This may be accomplished by evaluating him for anxiolytic and antidepressant medications and helping him develop stress management techniques. Reduction of passive–dependent behaviors and increasing self-esteem are also important goals. Developing better self-control, especially in terms of expressing anger, will be helpful. Jeff's open acknowledgment of substance abuse indicates that a thorough chemical dependency evaluation and possibly treatment are indicated.

This interpretation of Jeff's MMPI-2-RF protocol was completed before the appended MMPI-2-RF Interpretive Report was examined. The interpretation of Jeff's scores presented here is very similar to the computer interpretive report. This is not at all surprising because the clinician-generated and computerized interpretations utilized the MMPI-2-RF authors' interpretive strategy and interpretive guidelines.

It can also be instructive to compare the MMPI-2-RF clinician-generated and computer interpretive reports to the corresponding MMPI-2 reports presented in Chapters 11 and 12. The MMPI-2 and MMPI-2-RF reports are in agreement that Jeff's protocols are valid and interpretable. The reports are in agreement that Jeff is experiencing considerable psychological turmoil and that depression and anxiety are salient features of his presentation.

All the interpretations mention somatic symptoms, but they are emphasized more in the MMPI-2-RF interpretations. Because Clinical scale 1, RC1, and the Health Concerns Content scale were not significantly elevated, somatic concerns were not salient in the MMPI-2 interpretations. Although RC1 and most of the Specific Problems scales associated with it were not elevated in the MMPI-2-RF protocol, the significant elevation (T = 87) on the MLS Specific Problems scale led to somatic issues being more salient in the MMPI-2-RF interpretations.

The MMPI-2 and MMPI-2-RF interpretations differ in terms of how much emphasis is placed on antisocial characteristics. The MMPI-2 interpretations recognize that Jeff may have problems with social conformity and acceptance of authority, but they conclude that he is not likely to act out in antisocial ways, except for excessive use of alcohol and marijuana. By contrast, the MMPI-2-RF interpretations include statements that Jeff reports a history of antisocial behavior and is likely to have been involved with the criminal justice system. It should be noted that Jeff's history, as corroborated by his sister, did not include any difficulties with the law. The extent to which anger problems are emphasized also differs in the MMPI-2 and MMPI-2-RF interpretations. The MMPI-2 interpretations acknowledge that Jeff does not express anger openly most of the time but may occasionally verbalize angry feelings. The MMPI-2-RF interpretation sees problems with anger control as a more important issue and one that should be a treatment target.

The MMPI-2-RF interpretations emphasize Jeff's negative characteristics to the neglect of positive ones. The MMPI-2 interpretations mention that Jeff is neat, meticulous, persistent, and reliable. Although there are problems in interpersonal functioning, he seems to have the capacity to form deep emotional ties. Others often see him as sensitive, kind, softhearted, and peaceable and react to him in nurturing and helping ways. These characteristics are absent in the MMPI-2-RF interpretation.

The MMPI-2 and MMPI-2-RF interpretations are in agreement that Jeff should be evaluated further for depression-related and anxiety disorders, including obsessive–compulsive disorder. They also agree that a detailed chemical dependency evaluation should be completed to determine if a substance abuse/dependence diagnosis is in order. The MMPI-2-RF interpretations also suggest that, if physical causes for his feeling of poor health can be ruled out, somatoform disorder should be considered. Although consideration of Axis II disorders is often difficult from MMPI data, the interpretations are in agreement that Jeff should be evaluated for dependent personality disorder.

There are similarities and differences in how treatment-related issues are addressed in the MMPI-2 and MMPI-2-RF interpretations. The interpretations are in agreement that, because of his considerable emotional distress, Jeff is likely to be motivated for treatment. However, the MMPI-2-RF interpretation expressed more concern that his acting-out tendencies and lack of energy can result in treatment noncompliance, and no inferences are made about treatment progress or outcome. The MMPI-2 interpretation indicates that Jeff is likely to remain in treatment longer than many mental health center outpatients and that slow but positive change can be expected.

Both sets of interpretations indicate that Jeff should be evaluated for anxiolytic and antidepressant medications to help reduce distress. The MMPI-2 interpretations do not suggest specific psychotherapeutic approaches for Jeff, but the MMPI-2-RF interpretations suggest stress management and anger management approaches.

In summary, there are far more similarities than differences in the MMPI-2 and MMPI-2-RF interpretations of Jeff's protocols. Perhaps because of the larger research basis that informs interpretation, the MMPI-2 interpretations seem to be richer and more detailed than the MMPI-2-RF interpretation. Perhaps in settings where the goal of the assessment is not a detailed understanding of the test taker, the briefer, less detailed MMPI-2-RF interpretations would be sufficient.

CLOSING COMMENTS

As mentioned at the beginning of this chapter, the MMPI-2-RF represents the most recent development in the long history of the MMPI. The rationale underlying this alternative form and initial data concerning its validity in a variety of settings are promising. However, more MMPI-2-RF research is needed before we will be able to adequately judge its utility in comparison to the more familiar and more researched MMPI-2.

CHAPTER APPENDIX

Minnesota Multiphasic
Personality Inventory-2
Restructured Form™

Interpretive Report: Clinical Settings

MMPI-2-RF®
Minnesota Multiphasic Personality Inventory-2-Restructured Form™
Yossef S. Ben-Porath, PhD, & Auke Tellegen, PhD

ID Number:	000182672
Age:	24
Gender:	Male
Marital Status:	Never Married
Years of Education:	12
Date Assessed:	09/02/1998

PEARSON   ✪ *PsychCorp*

Copyright © 2008 by the Regents of the University of Minnesota. All rights reserved.
Distributed exclusively under license from the University of Minnesota by NCS Pearson, Inc. Portions reproduced from the MMPI-2-RF test booklet. Copyright © 2008 by the Regents of the University of Minnesota. All rights reserved. Portions excerpted from the *MMPI-2-RF Manual for Administration, Scoring, and Interpretation*. Copyright © 2008 by the Regents of the University of Minnesota. All rights reserved.

MMPI-2-RF and the **MMPI-2-RF logo** are registered trademarks and **Minnesota Multiphasic Personality Inventory-2-Restructured Form** is a trademark of the University of Minnesota. **Pearson,** the **PSI logo,** and **PsychCorp** are trademarks in the U.S. and/or other countries of Pearson Education, Inc., or its affiliate(s).

TRADE SECRET INFORMATION
Not for release under HIPAA or other data disclosure laws that exempt trade secrets from disclosure.

[1.4 / 1 / 2.5.7]

Reproduced by permission of the University of Minnesota Press. All rights reserved. "Minnesota Multiphasic Personality Inventory-2-RF® " and "MMPI-2-RF® " are trademarks owned by the University of Minnesota.

MMPI-2-RF Validity Scales

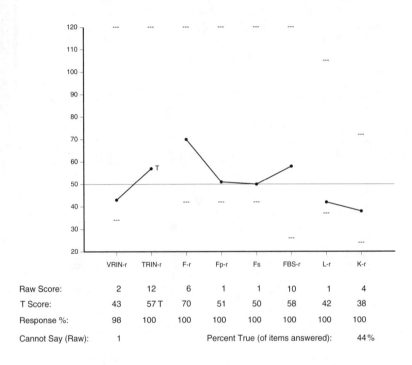

	VRIN-r	TRIN-r	F-r	Fp-r	Fs	FBS-r	L-r	K-r
Raw Score:	2	12	6	1	1	10	1	4
T Score:	43	57 T	70	51	50	58	42	38
Response %:	98	100	100	100	100	100	100	100

Cannot Say (Raw):   1   Percent True (of items answered):   44%

The highest and lowest T scores possible on each scale are indicated by a "---"; MMPI-2-RF T scores are non-gendered.

VRIN-r	Variable Response Inconsistency	Fs	Infrequent Somatic Responses
TRIN-r	True Response Inconsistency	FBS-r	Symptom Validity
F-r	Infrequent Responses	L-r	Uncommon Virtues
Fp-r	Infrequent Psychopathology Responses	K-r	Adjustment Validity

MMPI-2-RF Higher-Order (H-O) and Restructured Clinical (RC) Scales

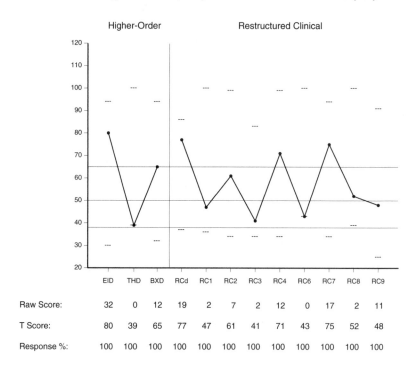

	EID	THD	BXD	RCd	RC1	RC2	RC3	RC4	RC6	RC7	RC8	RC9
Raw Score:	32	0	12	19	2	7	2	12	0	17	2	11
T Score:	80	39	65	77	47	61	41	71	43	75	52	48
Response %:	100	100	100	100	100	100	100	100	100	100	100	100

The highest and lowest T scores possible on each scale are indicated by a "---"; MMPI-2-RF T scores are non-gendered.

EID Emotional/Internalizing Dysfunction	RCd Demoralization	RC6 Ideas of Persecution
THD Thought Dysfunction	RC1 Somatic Complaints	RC7 Dysfunctional Negative Emotions
BXD Behavioral/Externalizing Dysfunction	RC2 Low Positive Emotions	RC8 Aberrant Experiences
	RC3 Cynicism	RC9 Hypomanic Activation
	RC4 Antisocial Behavior	

MMPI-2-RF Somatic/Cognitive and Internalizing Scales

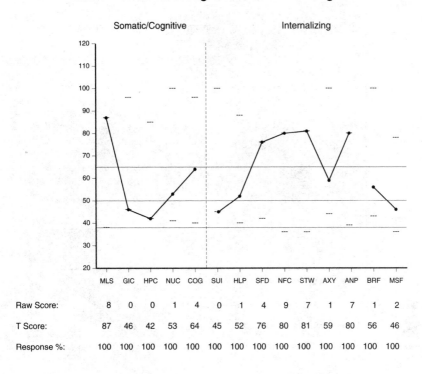

	MLS	GIC	HPC	NUC	COG	SUI	HLP	SFD	NFC	STW	AXY	ANP	BRF	MSF
Raw Score:	8	0	0	1	4	0	1	4	9	7	1	7	1	2
T Score:	87	46	42	53	64	45	52	76	80	81	59	80	56	46
Response %:	100	100	100	100	100	100	100	100	100	100	100	100	100	100

The highest and lowest T scores possible on each scale are indicated by a "---"; MMPI-2-RF T scores are non-gendered.

MLS	Malaise	SUI	Suicidal/Death Ideation	AXY	Anxiety
GIC	Gastrointestinal Complaints	HLP	Helplessness/Hopelessness	ANP	Anger Proneness
HPC	Head Pain Complaints	SFD	Self-Doubt	BRF	Behavior-Restricting Fears
NUC	Neurological Complaints	NFC	Inefficacy	MSF	Multiple Specific Fears
COG	Cognitive Complaints	STW	Stress/Worry		

MMPI-2-RF Externalizing, Interpersonal, and Interest Scales

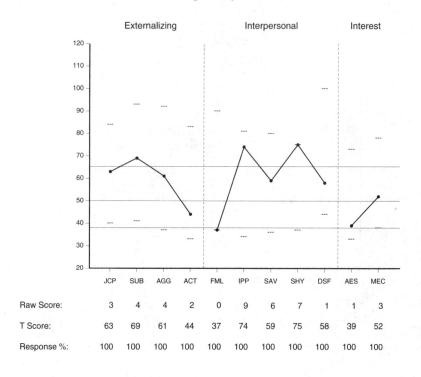

	JCP	SUB	AGG	ACT	FML	IPP	SAV	SHY	DSF	AES	MEC
Raw Score:	3	4	4	2	0	9	6	7	1	1	3
T Score:	63	69	61	44	37	74	59	75	58	39	52
Response %:	100	100	100	100	100	100	100	100	100	100	100

The highest and lowest T scores possible on each scale are indicated by a "---"; MMPI-2-RF T scores are non-gendered.

JCP	Juvenile Conduct Problems	FML	Family Problems	AES	Aesthetic-Literary Interests
SUB	Substance Abuse	IPP	Interpersonal Passivity	MEC	Mechanical-Physical Interests
AGG	Aggression	SAV	Social Avoidance		
ACT	Activation	SHY	Shyness		
		DSF	Disaffiliativeness		

MMPI-2-RF PSY-5 Scales

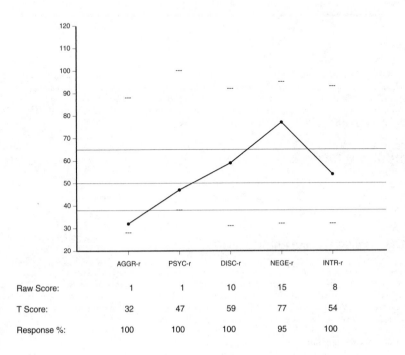

	AGGR-r	PSYC-r	DISC-r	NEGE-r	INTR-r
Raw Score:	1	1	10	15	8
T Score:	32	47	59	77	54
Response %:	100	100	100	95	100

The highest and lowest T scores possible on each scale are indicated by a "---"; MMPI-2-RF T scores are non-gendered.

AGGR-r   Aggressiveness-Revised
PSYC-r   Psychoticism-Revised
DISC-r   Disconstraint-Revised
NEGE-r   Negative Emotionality/Neuroticism-Revised
INTR-r   Introversion/Low Positive Emotionality-Revised

*This interpretive report is intended for use by a professional qualified to interpret the MMPI-2-RF.
The information it contains should be considered in the context of the test taker's background, the
circumstances of the assessment, and other available information.*

SYNOPSIS

This is a valid MMPI-2-RF protocol. Scores on the substantive scales indicate somatic complaints and
emotional, behavioral, and interpersonal dysfunction. Somatic complaints relate to malaise. Emotional-
internalizing findings include demoralization, self-doubt, stress and worry, and anger.
Behavioral-externalizing problems include antisocial behavior and substance abuse. Interpersonal
difficulties include passivity and social anxiety.

PROTOCOL VALIDITY

This is a valid MMPI-2-RF protocol. There are no problems with unscorable items. The test taker
responded to the items relevantly on the basis of their content, and there are no indications of over- or
under-reporting.

SUBSTANTIVE SCALE INTERPRETATION

*Clinical symptoms, personality characteristics, and behavioral tendencies of the test taker are
described in this section and organized according to an empirically guided framework. Statements
containing the word "reports" are based on the item content of MMPI-2-RF scales, whereas statements
that include the word "likely" are based on empirical correlates of scale scores. Specific sources for
each statement can be viewed with the annotation features of this report.*

Somatic/Cognitive Dysfunction

The test taker reports a general sense of malaise manifested in poor health, and feeling tired, weak, and
incapacitated[1]. He is indeed very likely to be preoccupied with poor health[2] and to complain of sleep
disturbance[2], fatigue[2], low energy[2], and sexual dysfunction[2].

Emotional Dysfunction

The test taker's responses indicate considerable emotional distress that is likely to be perceived as a
crisis[3]. More specifically, he reports feeling sad and unhappy and being dissatisfied with his current life
circumstances[4]. He is likely to complain of feeling depressed[5]. He also reports lacking confidence and
feeling useless[6], and is very likely to be prone to rumination, to experience self-doubt, to feel insecure
and inferior, and to be self-disparaging and intropunitive[7]. In addition, he reports being very indecisive
and inefficacious, believing he is incapable of making decisions and dealing effectively with crisis
situations, and even having difficulties dealing with small, inconsequential matters[8]. He is very unlikely

to be self-reliant[9]. He also reports multiple problems involving experiences of stress and worry, including preoccupation with disappointments, difficulties with time pressure, and specific worries over misfortune and finances[10]. He is very likely to be stress-reactive[11] and worry-prone[12] and to engage in obsessive rumination[13].

He reports various negative emotional experiences[14] and is likely to be self-critical and guilt-prone[15]. He also reports getting easily upset, being impatient with others, becoming easily angered, and sometimes even being overcome by anger[16]. He is indeed very likely to have problems with anger, irritability, and low tolerance for frustration[17]; to hold grudges[18]; to have temper tantrums[18]; and to be argumentative and abusive[18].

Thought Dysfunction

There are no indications of disordered thinking in this protocol.

Behavioral Dysfunction

The test taker's responses indicate significant externalizing, acting-out behavior, which is likely to have gotten him into difficulties[19]. More specifically, he reports a significant history of antisocial behavior[20] and is likely to have poor impulse control[21], to have been involved with the criminal justice system[22], and to have difficulties with individuals in positions of authority[23]. He is also likely to experience conflictual interpersonal relationships[23], to act out when bored[23], and to have antisocial characteristics[24]. He also reports significant past and current substance abuse[25], and is indeed likely to have a history of problematic use of alcohol or drugs[26], to be sensation-seeking[27], and to have had legal problems as a result of substance abuse[27].

Interpersonal Functioning Scales

The test taker reports being unassertive[28] and is indeed likely to be passive and submissive in interpersonal relationships[29]. He also reports being shy, easily embarrassed, and uncomfortable around others[30]. He is likely to be socially introverted[31] and inhibited[31] and to be anxious and nervous in social situations[31].

Interest Scales

The test taker reports an average number of interests in activities or occupations of an aesthetic or literary nature (e.g., writing, music, the theater)[32]. He also reports an average number of interests in activities or occupations of a mechanical or physical nature (e.g., fixing and building things, the outdoors, sports)[33].

DIAGNOSTIC CONSIDERATIONS

This section provides recommendations for psychodiagnostic assessment based on the test taker's MMPI-2-RF results. It is recommended that he be evaluated for the following:

Emotional-Internalizing Disorders

- Somatoform disorder, if physical origin for malaise has been ruled out[34]
- Depression-related disorder[35]
- Disorders involving excessive stress and worry such as obsessive-compulsive disorder[36]
- Anxiety-related disorders[37]
- Anger-related disorders[38]

Behavioral-Externalizing Disorders

- Antisocial personality disorder, substance use disorders, and other externalizing disorders[39]

Interpersonal Disorders

- Disorders characterized by passive-submissive behavior such as dependent personality disorder[40]
- Social phobia[41]

TREATMENT CONSIDERATIONS

This section provides inferential treatment-related recommendations based on the test taker's MMPI-2-RF scores.

Areas for Further Evaluation

- Origin of malaise complaints[42].

Psychotherapy Process Issues

- Malaise may impede his willingness or ability to engage in treatment[42].
- Serious emotional difficulties may motivate him for treatment[43].
- Indecisiveness may interfere with establishing treatment goals and progress in treatment[44].
- Acting-out tendencies can result in treatment non-compliance and interfere with the development of a therapeutic relationship[45].

Possible Targets for Treatment

- Psychological distress as an initial target[43]
- Low self-esteem and other manifestations of self-doubt[46]
- Stress management and excessive worry and rumination[36]
- Dysfunctional negative emotions[47]
- Anger management[38]
- Inadequate self-control[45]
- Reduction or cessation of substance abuse[48]
- Reducing passive, submissive behavior[40]
- Anxiety in social situations[49]

ITEM-LEVEL INFORMATION

Unscorable Responses

Following is a list of items to which the test taker did not provide scorable responses. Unanswered or double answered (both True and False) items are unscorable. The scales on which the items appear are in parentheses following the item content.

116.

Critical Responses

Seven MMPI-2-RF scales--Suicidal/Death Ideation (SUI), Helplessness/Hopelessness (HLP), Anxiety (AXY), Ideas of Persecution (RC6), Aberrant Experiences (RC8), Substance Abuse (SUB), and Aggression (AGG)--have been designated by the test authors as having critical item content that may require immediate attention and follow-up. Items answered by the individual in the keyed direction (True or False) on a critical scale are listed below if his T score on that scale is 65 or higher. The percentage of the MMPI-2-RF normative sample that answered each item in the keyed direction is provided in parentheses following the item content.

Substance Abuse (SUB, T Score = 69)

49.
141.
237.
266.

ENDNOTES

This section lists for each statement in the report the MMPI-2-RF score(s) that triggered it. In addition, each statement is identified as a <u>Test Response</u>, if based on item content, a <u>Correlate</u>, if based on empirical correlates, or an <u>Inference</u>, if based on the report authors' judgment. (This information can also be accessed on-screen by placing the cursor on a given statement.) For correlate-based statements, research references (Ref. No.) are provided, keyed to the consecutively numbered reference list following the endnotes.

[1] Test Response: MLS=87
[2] Correlate: MLS=87, Ref. 19
[3] Correlate: EID=80, Ref. 19
[4] Test Response: RCd=77
[5] Correlate: RCd=77, Ref. 1, 2, 4, 5, 6, 7, 9, 11, 14, 17, 18, 19, 20, 21, 22, 23
[6] Test Response: SFD=76
[7] Correlate: SFD=76, Ref. 19
[8] Test Response: NFC=80
[9] Correlate: NFC=80, Ref. 19
[10] Test Response: STW=81
[11] Correlate: RC7=75, Ref. 10, 15, 19; STW=81, Ref. 19
[12] Correlate: STW=81, Ref. 19
[13] Correlate: RC7=75, Ref. 3, 11, 14, 19, 20; STW=81, Ref. 19
[14] Test Response: RC7=75; NEGE-r=77
[15] Correlate: RC7=75, Ref. 19; NEGE-r=77, Ref. 19
[16] Test Response: ANP=80
[17] Correlate: RC7=75, Ref. 3, 12, 19, 20; ANP=80, Ref. 19
[18] Correlate: ANP=80, Ref. 19
[19] Correlate: BXD=65, Ref. 19
[20] Test Response: RC4=71
[21] Correlate: RC4=71, Ref. 3, 4, 5, 10, 12, 13, 15, 18, 19, 23
[22] Correlate: RC4=71, Ref. 1, 6, 13, 16, 19
[23] Correlate: RC4=71, Ref. 19
[24] Correlate: RC4=71, Ref. 6, 7, 14, 15, 16, 17, 18, 19, 22
[25] Test Response: SUB=69
[26] Correlate: RC4=71, Ref. 1, 2, 3, 5, 6, 7, 13, 14, 16, 18, 19, 22, 23; SUB=69, Ref. 19
[27] Correlate: SUB=69, Ref. 19
[28] Test Response: IPP=74
[29] Correlate: IPP=74, Ref. 19; AGGR-r=32, Ref. 19
[30] Test Response: SHY=75
[31] Correlate: SHY=75, Ref. 19
[32] Test Response: AES=39
[33] Test Response: MEC=52
[34] Correlate: MLS=87, Ref. 8
[35] Correlate: RCd=77, Ref. 18, 19
[36] Inference: STW=81

[37] Correlate: RC7=75, Ref. 11, 20
[38] Inference: ANP=80
[39] Correlate: BXD=65, Ref. 19; RC4=71, Ref. 7, 15, 18, 19, 22; SUB=69, Ref. 19
[40] Inference: IPP=74
[41] Correlate: RC7=75, Ref. 20; SHY=75, Ref. 19
[42] Inference: MLS=87
[43] Inference: RCd=77
[44] Inference: NFC=80
[45] Inference: BXD=65; RC4=71
[46] Inference: SFD=76
[47] Inference: RC7=75; NEGE-r=77
[48] Inference: SUB=69
[49] Inference: SHY=75

RESEARCH REFERENCE LIST

1. Arbisi, P. A., Sellbom, M., & Ben-Porath, Y. S. (2008). Empirical correlates of the MMPI-2 Restructured Clinical (RC) Scales in psychiatric inpatients. *Journal of Personality Assessment, 90,* 122-128.

2. Binford, A., & Liljequist, L. (2008). Behavioral correlates of selected MMPI-2 Clinical, Content, and Restructured Clinical Scales. *Journal of Personality Assessment, 60,* 608-614.

3. Forbey, J. D., & Ben-Porath, Y. S. (2007). A comparison of the MMPI-2 Restructured Clinical (RC) and Clinical Scales in a substance abuse treatment sample. *Psychological Services, 4,* 46-58.

4. Forbey, J. D., & Ben-Porath, Y. S. (2008). Empirical correlates of the MMPI-2 Restructured Clinical (RC) Scales in a non-clinical setting. *Journal of Personality Assessment, 90,* 136-141.

5. Forbey, J. D., Ben-Porath, Y. S., & Gartland, D. (2009). Validation of the MMPI-2 computerized adaptive version (MMPI-2-CA) in a correctional intake facility. *Psychological Services, 6,* 279-292.

6. Handel, R. W., & Archer, R. P. (2008). An investigation of the psychometric properties of the MMPI-2 Restructured Clinical (RC) Scales with mental health inpatients. *Journal of Personality Assessment, 90,* 239-249.

7. Kamphuis, J. H., Arbisi, P. A., Ben-Porath, Y. S., & McNulty, J. L. (2008). Detecting comorbid Axis-II status among inpatients using the MMPI-2 Restructured Clinical Scales. *European Journal of Psychological Assessment, 24,* 157-164.

8. Locke, D. E. C., Kirlin, K. A., Thomas, M. L., Osborne, D., Hurst, D. F., Drazkowsi, J. F., Sirven, J. I., & Noe, K. H. (2010). The Minnesota Multiphasic Personality Inventory-2-Restructured Form in the epilepsy monitoring unit. *Epilepsy & Behavior, 17*(2), 252-258.

9. McDevitt-Murphy, M. E., Weathers, F. W., Flood, A. M., Eakin, D. E., & Benson, T. A. (2007). The utility of the PAI and the MMPI-2 for discriminating PTSD, depression, and social phobia in trauma-exposed college students. *Assessment, 14,* 181-195.

10. Sellbom, M., & Ben-Porath, Y. S. (2005). Mapping the MMPI-2 Restructured Clinical (RC) Scales onto normal personality traits: Evidence of construct validity. *Journal of Personality Assessment, 85,* 179-187.

11. Sellbom, M., Ben-Porath, Y. S., & Bagby, R. M. (2008a). On the hierarchical structure of mood and anxiety disorders: Confirmatory evidence and elaboration of a model of temperament markers. *Journal of Abnormal Psychology, 117,* 576-590.

12. Sellbom, M., Ben-Porath, Y. S., & Bagby, R. M. (2008b). Personality and psychopathology: Mapping the MMPI-2 Restructured Clinical (RC) Scales onto the Five Factor Model of Personality. *Journal of Personality Disorders, 22,* 291-312.

13. Sellbom, M., Ben-Porath, Y. S., Baum, L. J., Erez, E., & Gregory, C. (2008). Predictive validity of the MMPI-2 Restructured Clinical (RC) Scales in a batterers' intervention program. *Journal of Personality Assessment, 90,* 129-135.

14. Sellbom, M., Ben-Porath, Y. S., & Graham, J. R. (2006). Correlates of the MMPI-2 Restructured Clinical (RC) Scales in a college counseling setting. *Journal of Personality Assessment, 86,* 89-99.

15. Sellbom, M., Ben-Porath, Y. S., Lilienfeld, S. O., Patrick, C. J., & Graham, J. R. (2005). Assessing psychopathic personality traits with the MMPI-2. *Journal of Personality Assessment, 85,* 334-343.

16. Sellbom, M., Ben-Porath, Y. S., & Stafford, K. P. (2007). A comparison of measures of psychopathic deviance in a forensic setting. *Psychological Assessment, 19,* 430-436.

17. Sellbom, M., Graham, J. R., & Schenk, P. (2006). Incremental validity of the MMPI-2 Restructured Clinical (RC) Scales in a private practice sample. *Journal of Personality Assessment, 86,* 196-205.

18. Simms, L. J., Casillas, A., Clark, L. A., Watson, D., & Doebbeling, B. I. (2005). Psychometric evaluation of the Restructured Clinical Scales of the MMPI-2. *Psychological Assessment, 17,* 345-358.

19. Tellegen, A., & Ben-Porath, Y. S. (2008). *The Minnesota Multiphasic Personality Inventory-2-Restructured Form (MMPI-2-RF): Technical manual.* Minneapolis: University of Minnesota Press.

20. Tellegen, A., Ben-Porath, Y. S., Sellbom, M., Arbisi, P. A., McNulty, J. L., & Graham, J. R. (2006). Further evidence on the validity of the MMPI-2 Restructured Clinical (RC) Scales: Addressing questions raised by Rogers et al. and Nichols. *Journal of Personality Assessment, 87,* 148-171.

21. Vachon, D. D., Sellbom, M., Ryder, A. G., Miller, J. D., & Bagby, R. M. (2009). A five-factor model description of depressive personality disorder. *Journal of Personality Disorders, 23,* 447-465.

22. Wolf, E. J., Miller, M. W., Orazem, R. J., Weierich, M. R., Castillo, D. T., Milford, J., Kaloupek, D. G., & Keane, T. M. (2008). The MMPI-2 Restructured Clinical Scales in the assessment of posttraumatic stress disorder and comorbid disorders. *Psychological Assessment, 20,* 327-340.

23. Wygant, D. B., Boutacoff, L. A., Arbisi, P. A., Ben-Porath, Y. S., Kelly, P. H., & Rupp, W. M. (2007). Examination of the MMPI-2 Restructured Clinical (RC) Scales in a sample of bariatric surgery candidates. *Journal of Clinical Psychology in Medical Settings, 14,* 197-205.

End of Report

This and previous pages of this report contain trade secrets and are not to be released in response to requests under HIPAA (or any other data disclosure law that exempts trade secret information from release). Further, release in response to litigation discovery demands should be made only in accordance with your profession's ethical guidelines and under an appropriate protective order.

ITEM RESPONSES

1: 2	2: 1	3: 2	4: 2	5: 1	6: 1	7: 1	8: 1	9: 2	10: 2
11: 2	12: 2	13: 1	14: 2	15: 2	16: 1	17: 2	18: 1	19: 1	20: 2
21: 1	22: 1	23: 1	24: 1	25: 2	26: 1	27: 1	28: 1	29: 1	30: 1
31: 2	32: 2	33: 2	34: 2	35: 1	36: 2	37: 2	38: 1	39: 2	40: 1
41: 2	42: 2	43: 2	44: 1	45: 1	46: 2	47: 1	48: 1	49: 1	50: 2
51: 2	52: 1	53: 1	54: 2	55: 2	56: 2	57: 2	58: 2	59: 1	60: 1
61: 2	62: 1	63: 1	64: 1	65: 1	66: 1	67: 1	68: 1	69: 1	70: 1
71: 2	72: 1	73: 2	74: 2	75: 1	76: 2	77: 2	78: 1	79: 2	80: 1
81: 2	82: 1	83: 1	84: 2	85: 1	86: 2	87: 2	88: 1	89: 1	90: 2
91: 1	92: 2	93: 2	94: 1	95: 1	96: 1	97: 2	98: 1	99: 2	100: 1
101: 2	102: 1	103: 2	104: 2	105: 2	106: 1	107: 2	108: 1	109: 2	110: 2
111: 2	112: 1	113: 1	114: 1	115: 2	116: /	117: 2	118: 1	119: 1	120: 2
121: 2	122: 2	123: 1	124: 2	125: 1	126: 2	127: 1	128: 2	129: 2	130: 2
131: 2	132: 1	133: 2	134: 2	135: 2	136: 1	137: 2	138: 2	139: 2	140: 1
141: 1	142: 2	143: 2	144: 1	145: 2	146: 2	147: 2	148: 2	149: 1	150: 2
151: 2	152: 1	153: 1	154: 1	155: 1	156: 1	157: 1	158: 1	159: 1	160: 1
161: 2	162: 1	163: 2	164: 2	165: 2	166: 1	167: 1	168: 2	169: 1	170: 2
171: 1	172: 1	173: 2	174: 2	175: 2	176: 2	177: 1	178: 2	179: 2	180: 2
181: 2	182: 2	183: 1	184: 2	185: 2	186: 1	187: 1	188: 2	189: 1	190: 2
191: 2	192: 2	193: 2	194: 2	195: 1	196: 2	197: 2	198: 1	199: 2	200: 1
201: 1	202: 2	203: 2	204: 2	205: 2	206: 1	207: 2	208: 2	209: 1	210: 2
211: 1	212: 1	213: 2	214: 2	215: 2	216: 2	217: 2	218: 2	219: 2	220: 1
221: 1	222: 2	223: 2	224: 1	225: 2	226: 1	227: 1	228: 2	229: 1	230: 2
231: 2	232: 1	233: 2	234: 2	235: 1	236: 2	237: 2	238: 1	239: 2	240: 2
241: 1	242: 2	243: 2	244: 2	245: 2	246: 1	247: 1	248: 1	249: 1	250: 1
251: 2	252: 2	253: 2	254: 1	255: 2	256: 2	257: 2	258: 2	259: 2	260: 2
261: 1	262: 2	263: 1	264: 2	265: 1	266: 1	267: 2	268: 2	269: 1	270: 2
271: 1	272: 1	273: 2	274: 1	275: 2	276: 2	277: 1	278: 1	279: 2	280: 1
281: 2	282: 1	283: 1	284: 2	285: 2	286: 1	287: 2	288: 1	289: 1	290: 1
291: 2	292: 2	293: 2	294: 2	295: 2	296: 2	297: 2	298: 2	299: 1	300: 1
301: 2	302: 2	303: 1	304: 2	305: 1	306: 2	307: 2	308: 2	309: 1	310: 2
311: 2	312: 1	313: 1	314: 2	315: 2	316: 2	317: 2	318: 1	319: 1	320: 2
321: 2	322: 1	323: 1	324: 1	325: 1	326: 2	327: 2	328: 2	329: 2	330: 2
331: 1	332: 2	333: 2	334: 2	335: 1	336: 2	337: 1	338: 1		

15

⁄⁄⁄ Assessing Adolescents:
The MMPI-A

Although the original MMPI was intended for use with adults, it quickly became popular as an instrument for assessing adolescents (e.g., Hathaway & Monachesi, 1963). Results of a survey by Archer, Maruish, Imhof, and Piotrowski (1991) indicated that the MMPI was the most widely used objective instrument for assessing adolescents. However, significant concerns were expressed about using the MMPI with adolescents because it had been developed with and normed on adults (e.g., Archer, 1987; Williams, 1986). Some of the items in the MMPI were awkward and inappropriate for many adolescents (e.g., satisfactory sex life, worry about money and business). Additionally, the MMPI had very few items dealing with experiences unique to adolescence (e.g., school, peer-group issues).

There were very few MMPI scales developed specifically for use with adolescents. Rather, scales developed using adult samples were adapted for adolescent use. For many of the scales that had been developed for use with adults, no adolescent normative data were available. Moreover, research studies demonstrated that the use of the adult MMPI norms overpathologized adolescent test takers (Archer, 1984, 1987; Klinge, Lachar, Grisell, & Berman, 1978). Unofficial norms were developed for use with younger persons (Marks, Seeman, & Haller, 1974). Some studies indicated that the use of these adolescent norms seemed to underpathologize disturbed adolescents assessed in clinical settings (Archer, Stolberg, Gordon, & Goldman, 1986; Klinge & Strauss, 1976), whereas other research supported the notion that scores based on these adolescent norms more accurately portrayed the clinical status of adolescents in a variety of clinical settings (e.g., Wimbish, 1984).

Another concern in using the MMPI with adolescents was the source of interpretive statements about scores and configurations of scores of adolescents. Should only descriptors developed specifically for adolescents be used, or can those developed on the basis of adult data also be used? Several studies suggested that the use of adult descriptors resulted in more accurate descriptions of adolescents (Ehrenworth & Archer, 1985; Lachar et al., 1976). Other studies (e.g., Wimbish, 1984) concluded that the most accurate inferences about adolescents came from the use of adolescent-based descriptors.

Based on these and other concerns, the committee responsible for developing the MMPI-2 decided to develop a separate instrument, the MMPI-A, specifically for use with adolescents between the ages of 14 and 18 (Butcher et al., 1992). Initial reviews of the MMPI-A were quite positive. Claiborn (1995) concluded that "the MMPI-A is an impressive inventory, sure to become a preeminent tool for assessing adolescent psychopathology. Its flaws are relatively minor, correctable, and enormously outweighed by the strength of the inventory" (p. 628). Lanyon (1995) observed that "in surveying the available test instruments for assessing psychopathology in adolescents, the MMPI-A would appear to have no serious competition" (p. 629).

Archer and Newsom (2000) surveyed 346 psychologists who worked with adolescent clients to determine their use of psychological tests. Results indicated that the MMPI-A was the fifth most frequently used test. Although the Wechsler Intelligence Scales, the Rorschach, the sentence completion tests, and the Thematic Apperception test were more frequently used, the MMPI-A was the most frequently used self-report instrument.

As stated previously and in Chapter 10 of this book, the MMPI-A is intended for use with adolescents between the ages of 14 and 18. Because both the MMPI-2 and the MMPI-A can be used with 18-year-olds, clinicians must decide which version is most appropriate for each 18-year-old. Generally, it is advisable to use the MMPI-2 for mature 18-year-olds who are in college or otherwise living independently of their parents and the MMPI-A for less mature persons who have not adopted independent lifestyles.

Shaevel and Archer (1996) conducted a study in which raw scores of 18-year-olds were plotted on both MMPI-A and MMPI-2 norms. The MMPI-A norms yielded higher T scores for the L and K scales and lower T scores for most of the Clinical scales. In some cases the differences were as large as 15 T-score points. The authors recommended that both the MMPI-A and MMPI-2 norms be used for 18-year-olds in which no clear indicators in their life situations suggest that one or the other form should be used. Because no extratest data were available for these adolescents, we cannot know which set of scores (MMPI-A or MMPI-2) more accurately reflected their actual characteristics. Osberg and Poland (2002) also compared scores of 18-year-old students derived from MMPI-2 norms and MMPI-A norms. Consistent with the Shaevel and Archer study, scores based on the MMPI-2 norms yielded higher scores on most scales. Using the SCL-90-R as a criterion measure, the authors concluded that the MMPI-A norms better represented the psychological status of participants.

The MMPI-A manual (Butcher et al., 1992) indicates that adolescents younger than 14 years of age are likely to have difficulty responding meaningfully to the test items. Thus, the official MMPI-A norms do not include adolescents younger than 14. However, Archer (1992b) published norms for 13-year-olds and opined that many adolescents of this age should be able to complete the MMPI-A validly. The MMPI-A manual (Butcher et al., 1992) indicates that a seventh-grade reading level is required to understand items in the test.

DEVELOPMENT OF THE MMPI-A[1]

Rationale

Because of concerns about using an adult instrument with adolescents, concurrently with the development of the MMPI-2, data were collected that later would be used to develop the MMPI-A, a version of the test designed specifically for use with adolescents (Butcher et al., 1992). Although there are marked similarities between the MMPI-A and MMPI-2, there also are some important differences.

Development of the MMPI-A Booklet

An experimental form (Form TX) was developed initially. It included the 550 items from the original MMPI with some items rewritten to eliminate awkward and archaic language. New items were added to assess treatment compliance, attitudes toward changing one's own behavior, treatment-related characteristics, and problems with alcohol and drugs. In addition, items were added dealing with adolescent-specific areas (e.g., school behavior, attitudes toward teachers, peer-group influences, eating problems, and relationships with parents and other adults).

Based on several criteria, items from the 704-item TX booklet were selected for inclusion in the MMPI-A. Most of the items scored on the standard MMPI scales were included (see Table 15.1). Several items from the standard scales were eliminated because they were judged to be inappropriate for this age group or had objectionable item content. To keep the length of the MMPI-A as brief as possible, some items that were scored only on Scales 5 and 0 were eliminated. Items were also included that were needed to score some of the more promising supplementary scales and newly developed adolescent Content scales.

Because of data indicating that the standard F scale did not work very well with adolescents, the scale underwent some significant modifications. The problem had been that even normal adolescents taking the test in a valid manner tended to produce high F-scale scores. Careful analysis indicated that many of the standard F-scale items were not endorsed as infrequently by adolescents as by adults. The F scale of the MMPI-A includes 66 items that were endorsed in the deviant direction by no more than 20% of the boys and girls in the normative sample. Only 37 of the 64 original F-scale items also are in the MMPI-A F scale. The F scale was divided into two parts: F1 consists of items in the first part of the test booklet, and F2 consists of items in the latter part of the test booklet.

After the 478 items were selected for the MMPI-A booklet, several items were rewritten to take into account wording carried over from the MMPI that was not appropriate for adolescents. Items were changed from past to present or present-perfect tense. Several studies have demonstrated that the rewritten items are essentially equivalent to the original ones (Archer & Gordon, 1994; Williams, Ben-Porath, & Hevern, 1994).

---

[1]Unless otherwise indicated, information concerning the development of the MMPI-A was abstracted from Williams, Butcher, Ben-Porath, and Graham (1992) and Butcher et al. (1992).

Table 15.1 Number of Items in the Basic Scales of the MMPI and MMPI-A

	NUMBER OF ITEMS	
SCALE	MMPI	MMPI-A
L	15	14
F	64	66
K	30	30
Hs	33	32
D	60	57
Hy	60	60
Pd	50	49
Mf	60	44
Pa	40	40
Pt	48	48
Sc	78	72
Ma	46	46
Si	70	62

SOURCE: Excerpted from Butcher, J.N., Williams, C.L., Graham, J.R., Archer, R.P., Tellegan, A., Ben-Porath, Y.S., & Kaemmer, B. (1992). Minnesota Multiphasic Personality Inventory® - Adolescent *(MMPI®-A) manual for administration, scoring and interpretation.* Copyright © 1992 by the Regents of the University of Minnesota. Reproduced by permission of the University of Minnesota Press. All rights reserved. "MMPI® -A" and "Minnesota Multiphasic Personality Inventory® -A," are trademarks owned by the Regents of the University of Minnesota.

MMPI-A Norms

There are 805 boys and 815 girls in the MMPI-A normative sample. They were solicited randomly from schools in seven states throughout the United States. They ranged in age from 14 to 18 years. Some preliminary data were collected for 13-year-olds, but because later analyses indicated that these younger persons had considerable difficulty completing the experimental booklet, they were eliminated from the sample (Butcher et al., 1992). Data presented in the MMPI-A manual (Butcher et al., 1992) indicate that the normative sample is approximately representative of the U.S. population in terms of ethnicity and socioeconomic status. Most of the adolescents in the normative sample were living in intact homes.

Although data concerning the effects of ethnic minority status on MMPI scores of adolescents were quite limited, Pancoast and Archer (1988) reviewed several studies and reported their own data suggesting that differences between African American and Caucasian adolescents were small and probably not clinically meaningful. They speculated that the somewhat higher scores for African Americans on some scales could reflect differences in socioeconomic status between African Americans and Caucasians.

The MMPI-A manual (Butcher et al., 1992) does not present data separately for the various ethnic groups represented in the normative sample. However, using large samples of nonclinical adolescents from the MMPI-A normative sample and adolescents from outpatient and inpatient treatment facilities, Schinka, Elkins, and Archer (1998) found that MMPI-A scores were not meaningfully influenced by age, sex, or ethnic identification.

Negy, Leal-Puente, Trainor, and Carlson (1997) reported data for 120 Mexican American adolescents in Texas. Their scores were remarkably similar to those of the MMPI-A normative sample. Negy et al. also reported that MMPI-A scores are related to socioeconomic status and level of acculturation, suggesting that Mexican Americans of lower socioeconomic status and lower acculturation could be disadvantaged on the test. However, they cautioned that it is also possible that adolescents of lower socioeconomic status and lower acculturation experience more psychopathology than those of higher socioeconomic status and higher acculturation. Clearly, additional research data are needed to address these issues.

Gumbiner (1998) reported MMPI-A data for very small groups of nonclinical Hispanic boys ($n = 30$) and girls ($n = 17$). The boys had higher mean scores than the MMPI-A normative boys, and the girls' scores were at or slightly below average on most scales. These results are difficult to interpret for several reasons. First, the samples are quite small. Second, the socioeconomic status of the Hispanic adolescents was much lower than that of the normative sample. Third, no extratest data were presented to determine if the differences between scores of the Hispanic boys and the normative boys represent test bias or accurately reflect real differences in conceptually relevant characteristics.

Gómez, Johnson, Davis, and Velásquez (2000) found that African American and Hispanic boys who were first-time offenders did not differ significantly on MMPI-A scales and that mean scores for both groups were not much different from those of the MMPI-A normative sample. Cashel, Rogers, Sewell, and Holliman (1998) found that Anglo-American delinquent boys scored significantly higher than African American and Hispanic boys on Scales 4 and 9. However, as has been the case with many studies of this kind, no extratest data were examined to determine if these MMPI-A differences were related to differences in conceptually relevant extratest characteristics.

Using the standard Mexican version of the MMPI-A, Lucio, Duran, Graham, and Ben-Porath (2002) determined the extent to which the F, F1, and F2 scales and the F-K index were able to discriminate between nonclinical Mexican adolescents who were instructed to appear to have serious emotional problems from Mexican adolescents in outpatient mental health treatment who completed the MMPI-A with standard instructions. They found that the three F scales and the F-K index all effectively differentiated the groups. Results, including optimal cut scores, were similar to previously reported data for U.S. adolescents.

Very little is known about the use of the MMPI-A with adolescents of other ethnic backgrounds. The study by Schinka, Elkins, et al. (1998) discussed earlier suggested that ethnic background (including being African American) did not have a meaningful effect on MMPI-A scores. This author could find no published research concerning the use of the MMPI-A with persons of Asian or American Indian backgrounds.

Unlike earlier MMPI adolescent norms that differed by age levels, only one set of norms is presented for boys and another for girls. This is because preliminary data analyses indicated that there were only minor differences between age groups within the MMPI-A normative sample. To maintain consistency with the MMPI-2, raw scores on the eight Clinical scales (1, 2, 3, 4, 6, 7, 8, 9), the Content and Content Component scales, and the Personality Psychopathology Five (PSY-5) scales are transformed to Uniform T scores using the same procedures developed for the MMPI-2. The rationale for the use of Uniform T scores and the procedures used to develop them are discussed in the MMPI-A manual (Butcher et al., 1992) and were described in Chapter 8 of this book. Scores on all other scales are transformed to linear T scores.

Compared with scores based on the adolescent norms of Marks et al. (1974) for the MMPI, the MMPI-A norms yield significantly lower T scores for most of the Clinical scales. Janus, Tolbert, Calestro, and Toepfer (1996) found that some of these differences in scores for adolescent psychiatric patients were greater than the five T-score point difference often used as a criterion for clinical meaningfulness. However, Janus et al. determined that interpretive descriptions based on code types resulting from the norms of Marks et al. and MMPI-A norms were not differentially accurate (as determined by members of the treatment staff).

That MMPI-A T scores are generally lower than those based on the MMPI adolescent norms led the developers of the MMPI-A (Butcher et al., 1992) to recommend that MMPI-A T scores of 65 or greater on the Clinical scales be considered clinically significant but that T scores between 60 and 64 also be interpreted as high scores. Greater confidence should be placed in inferences resulting from T scores that are greater than 65.

A major concern among users of the MMPI-A has been that adolescents with significant problems often do not have scores high enough to reflect those problems. For example, Hilts and Moore (2003) reported that 30% of male and 25% of female psychiatric inpatients produced valid MMPI-A protocols with no Clinical scales with T scores greater than 60. Several possible explanations for the significant number of adolescents in clinical settings having within-normal-limits (WNL) protocols have been offered. One possibility is that the absence of a K-correction, such as that used with the MMPI-2, could lead to lower scores on the Clinical scales for adolescents who approached the test defensively. However, Alperin, Archer, and Coates (1996) demonstrated that using a K-correction did not significantly reduce the number of WNL protocols among adolescent psychiatric patients. Another possibility is that adolescents in the MMPI-A normative sample answered items in the scored direction more often than adults in the MMPI-2 normative sample. Archer, Handel, and Lynch (2001) found that a substantial number of MMPI-A items did not differentiate between adolescents in the normative sample and adolescents in clinical settings. This would lead to raw scores on MMPI-A scales having lower T-score equivalents. Consistent with this possibility is the fact that approximately 12% of the adolescents in the MMPI-A normative sample indicated that they had been referred to a therapist or counselor within six months of the completion of the MMPI-A. Hand, Archer, Handel, and Forbey (2007) constructed revised MMPI-A norms by eliminating the adolescents in the normative sample who indicated that they had been referred to a counselor or therapist in the 6 months prior to completing the MMPI-A. Using the revised norms only slightly reduced the frequency of WNL protocols in several clinical settings. These findings suggest that perhaps some of the MMPI-A scales could be improved by eliminating the nondiscriminating items. In summary, the issue of lower scores among clinical adolescents is a complex one that will require more research to try to resolve. In the meantime, clinicians should be cautious about concluding that adolescents with WNL protocols in clinical settings are not experiencing significant psychopathology.

ADMINISTRATION AND SCORING

The MMPI-A can be administered using either a printed booklet or audio CD and a separate answer sheet. The test distributor, Pearson Assessments, also has software available for administering the test using a computer. In Chapter 2 of this book, information was provided concerning the equivalence of MMPI and MMPI-2 scores obtained from booklet, audio, or computer administration. Although no published data are available concerning the equivalence of scores resulting from booklet, audio, or computer administration of the MMPI-A, two doctoral dissertations (Carlson, 2001; Hays, 2003) reported research indicating that paper-and-pencil and computer-administered versions of the MMPI-A yielded equivalent scores.

Standard English and Spanish versions of the test are available for both the booklet and audio formats. The MMPI-A has been translated into other languages, including French, Italian, and Chinese. Users who require the test in a language other than English or Spanish should consult the test distributor, Pearson Assessments, for advice.

All of the considerations about administration of the MMPI-2, which were detailed in Chapter 2 of this book, also apply to the MMPI-A. In addition, it should be recognized that some adolescents may be too easily distracted, hyperactive, oppositional, or impulsive to complete the 478 items in a single session. When such problems are encountered, close supervision, frequent breaks, and praise and encouragement from the person administering the test may be helpful.

Once the MMPI-A has been administered, there are several scoring options available. Hand scoring can be accomplished using templates available from the test distributor. Completed answer sheets can be mailed to Pearson Assessments for scoring. Computerized scoring is available using software available from the test distributor. The software can produce an Extended Score Report that includes scores for all of the MMPI-A scales and subscales and profiles for some of them. A computerized narrative interpretive report (The Minnesota Report: Adolescent Interpretive System) also is available. Users should determine the scoring method to be used before administering the test because different answer sheets are needed for the various options.

MMPI-A VALIDITY SCALES

The L, F, and K scales from the original MMPI were maintained in the MMPI-A, although there were some significant changes made in the F scale. Two additional Validity scales, which have corresponding scales in the MMPI-2, were also developed. The Variable Response Inconsistency Scale (VRIN) assesses inconsistent responding and is useful in identifying random protocols. The True Response Inconsistency Scale (TRIN) assesses true and false response biases.

MMPI-A CLINICAL SCALES

The 10 standard Clinical scales of the MMPI were maintained in the MMPI-A. Although some of the scales have several fewer items than the original ones (see Table 15.1) and include some slightly rewritten items, the Clinical scales of MMPI-A are essentially the same as the corresponding scales of the MMPI and the MMPI-2. Consistent with traditional use of the MMPI with adolescents, none of the MMPI-A Clinical scales is K corrected.

MMPI-A HARRIS–LINGOES SUBSCALES

The Harris–Lingoes subscales were discussed in some detail in Chapter 6 of this book. These scales, in slightly modified form, are available in the MMPI-A. Two of the subscales have one less item in the MMPI-A than in the MMPI-2, and some of the items have been slightly rewritten. However, these changes are so minor that the scales are comparable in the two tests.

As discussed in Chapter 6 of this book, the Harris–Lingoes subscales can be useful in understanding why test takers obtain high scores on the Clinical scales. Analysis of subscale scores can help to determine which of a variety of descriptors for elevated Clinical scales should be emphasized for a particular test taker. High scores (T > 65) on the Harris–Lingoes subscales should be interpreted only when the T score on the parent scale is greater than 60.

Not much information is available concerning correlates of the Harris–Lingoes subscales for adolescents. Gallucci (1994) found that the Need for Affection (Hy2), Inhibition of Aggression (Hy5), and Naivete (Pa3) subscales functioned as inhibitory scales, whereas the Amorality (Ma1) and Psychomotor Acceleration (Ma2) subscales functioned as excitatory scales. The meaning of high scores on the Harris–Lingoes subscales can be inferred from the content of their items. Interpretive inferences for the Harris–Lingoes subscales were presented in Chapter 6 of this book. As with the MMPI-2, the Harris–Lingoes subscales of the MMPI-A probably are too short and unreliable to be used as independent scales on which to base interpretation. Likewise, because little is known about the meaning of below-average scores on the Harris–Lingoes subscales, low scores should not be interpreted.

MMPI-A SCALE 0 SUBSCALES

The subscales for Scale 0 that were described in Chapter 6 of this book also are available for the MMPI-A. These subscales have the same number of items as for the MMPI-2. As with the Harris–Lingoes subscales, analysis of elevated scores (T > 65) on these subscales can help clinicians understand why adolescent test takers obtained elevated scores on Scale 0. Like the Harris–Lingoes subscales, these subscales should not be used as independent scales for clinical interpretation, and low scores on the subscales should not be interpreted. High scores (T > 65) on these subscales should be interpreted only when the T score on Scale 0 is greater than 60.

MMPI-A SUPPLEMENTARY SCALES

Several scales that had been developed from the MMPI item pool were carried over to the MMPI-A, and several new scales were developed using the new MMPI-A item pool.

MacAndrew Alcoholism Scale–Revised (MAC-R)

The MacAndrew Alcoholism scale (MAC; MacAndrew, 1965) was developed using items from the original MMPI and became widely used as a way to screen for substance abuse problems. A revised version of the scale (MAC-R), with four items added to replace those deleted because of objectionable content, was included in the MMPI-2. The MMPI-A includes the revised version of the scale from the MMPI-2 minus one item, which has been replaced on the MMPI-A by another. Thus, the MAC-R scale of the MMPI-A has 49 items.

Previous research demonstrated that the MAC scale of the original MMPI was effective in identifying alcohol or other drug problems for adolescents as well as for adults (Graham, 1990). Weed, Butcher, and Williams (1994) found that the MAC-R scale of the MMPI-A discriminated quite well between adolescent substance abusers and adolescents in the MMPI-A normative sample but less well between the adolescent substance abusers and adolescent psychiatric patients who were not in substance abuse treatment programs. However, Archer, Bolinsky, Morton, and Farris (2003) found that the MAC-R scale was effective in differentiating between adolescents with comorbid substance abuse and other psychiatric disorders and adolescents with psychiatric disorders but not comorbid substance abuse disorders.

Gallucci (1997a) found that adolescent substance abusers who scored higher on the MAC-R scale of the MMPI-A received higher therapist ratings on a scale that assessed the frequency of substance abuse behaviors. Adolescents in Gallucci's study who scored higher on the MAC-R also were rated by therapists as less likely to anticipate the consequences of their behavior and more likely to be sensation seeking and aggressive. Gallucci (1997b) reported that adolescent substance abusers who scored higher on the MAC-R scale of the MMPI-A were more likely than lower scorers on this scale to be rated by treatment staff as showing behavioral undercontrol. Veltri et al. (2009) found that MAC-R scores were positively correlated with histories of substance abuse in both inpatient psychiatric and forensic samples.

Although research concerning optimal cut scores for the MAC-R for adolescents is limited, it is this author's recommendation that the same cut scores recommended for adults in Chapter 8 of this book be used for adolescents. Raw scores greater than 27 suggest a strong possibility of substance abuse problems, and additional information about substance use should be obtained. Raw scores of 23 or lower suggest that substance abuse problems are not likely. Raw scores between 24 and 27 are indeterminate concerning substance abuse.

Alcohol/Drug Problem Acknowledgment (ACK) Scale

The Alcohol/Drug Problem Acknowledgment (ACK) scale is a face-valid scale consisting primarily of items in which adolescents admit to using alcohol and/or other drugs and having some of the symptoms and problems associated with such use (Weed et al., 1994). Weed et al. reported that adolescents in treatment for substance abuse scored higher on the ACK scale than adolescents in the MMPI-A normative sample and adolescent psychiatric patients who were not in treatment for substance abuse. However, this study did not report classification accuracy using the ACK scale.

Gallucci (1997a) reported that adolescent substance abusers who scored higher on the ACK scale were rated by therapists as more frequently engaging in substance abuse behaviors and as not anticipating the consequences of their behavior. Gallucci (1997b) found that adolescent substance abusers who scored higher on the ACK scale were rated by treatment staff as more likely to show behavioral undercontrol. Veltri et al. (2009) found that ACK scores were positively correlated with histories of substance abuse in both inpatient psychiatric and forensic samples.

Because of the obvious nature of the items in the ACK scale, adolescents who are denying alcohol or drug problems can easily avoid detection. However, elevated scores on the ACK scale (T $\geq$ 60) indicate that adolescents are readily admitting to significant alcohol or other drug problems (Butcher et al., 1992).

Alcohol/Drug Problem Proneness (PRO) Scale

The Alcohol/Drug Problem Proneness (PRO) scale is an empirically derived scale developed to assess the likelihood of alcohol or other drug problems in adolescents (Weed et al., 1994). Items in the scale differentiated adolescent boys and girls in alcohol/drug treatment from adolescent boys and girls who were in treatment for psychological problems other than alcohol/ drug problems. The items in the scale deal with peer-group influence, sensation seeking, rule violation, negative attitudes toward achievement, problems with parents, and poor judgment (Butcher et al., 1992). Adolescents in treatment for substance abuse scored significantly higher on the PRO scale than adolescents in the MMPI-A normative sample and adolescent psychiatric patients who were not in substance abuse treatment programs.

Gallucci (1997a) reported that adolescent substance abusers who scored higher on the PRO scale were rated higher by therapists on a scale that assessed frequency of substance abuse behaviors. Higher scorers on the PRO scale also were rated as less likely to anticipate the consequences of their behavior and more likely to be impulsive and aggressive. Gallucci (1997b) also reported that adolescent substance abusers who scored higher on the PRO scale were rated by therapists as more likely to show behavioral undercontrol. Veltri et al. (2009) found that PRO scores were positively correlated with histories of substance abuse in both inpatient psychiatric and forensic samples.

The MMPI-A manual (Butcher et al., 1992) suggests that T scores equal to or greater than 60 indicate a potential for developing alcohol or drug problems. However, several issues limit the confidence that we can have in the PRO scale at this time. First, no data have yet been published concerning the classification accuracy that can be achieved with this scale. Second, the label of the scale may not be very appropriate. Using "proneness" in the label suggests that this scale may be assessing a vulnerability to substance abuse that may or may not yet have been realized. To date all of the data concerning this scale address current abuse, and no data have yet been published concerning potential for future abuse. Obviously, it should not be concluded from test data alone that an adolescent has problems with alcohol or other drugs. Elevated scores on this scale of the MMPI-A should be viewed as an indicator that more information should be obtained. Although preliminary data suggest that this may be a useful scale, more research is needed before we can determine whether it works as well as, or perhaps better than, the more familiar MAC-R in identifying alcohol or other drug problems in adolescents.

Immaturity (IMM) Scale

The Immaturity (IMM) scale was developed using items in the MMPI-A item pool (Archer, Pancoast, & Gordon, 1992). The scale is thought to assess the degree to which adolescents report behaviors, attitudes, and perceptions of self and others that reflect immaturity in terms of interpersonal style, cognitive complexity, self-awareness, judgment, and impulse control (Butcher et al., 1992). Tentative items for the scale were identified by correlating MMPI-A items with scores from a sentence completion test of ego maturation. The items were then rated by judges concerning their relevance to the construct of ego maturation. The scale was refined by deleting items that did not add to its internal consistency and by adding other items from the MMPI-A item pool that demonstrated both a conceptual and statistical relationship to the immaturity construct.

Preliminary data indicated that higher IMM scale scores were associated with a higher incidence of academic difficulties and with disobedient, defiant, and antisocial behaviors (Butcher et al., 1992). Also, scores were inversely related to chronological age. Imhof and Archer (1997) studied the IMM scale in a relatively small sample of adolescents in residential psychiatric treatment programs. Unlike results of earlier studies, IMM scale scores were not related to chronological age but were negatively correlated with reading ability. Comparing IMM scale scores to other self-report scales, the authors concluded that higher IMM scale scorers can be expected to have a more limited capacity to think in abstract terms, to be less likely to identify with the values and beliefs of their social group, to have less capacity to perceive the world from the viewpoint of others, and to exhibit lower levels of moral development.

Zinn, McCumber, and Dahlstrom (1999) found that IMM scale scores of college students were negatively related to level of ego development as measured by the Washington University Sentence Completion Test. Veltri et al. (2009) found very few external correlates of the IMM scale in their adolescent psychiatric and forensic samples. However, IMM scores were significantly correlated with histories of self-mutilation behaviors in their psychiatric sample and with histories of angry behavior in their forensic sample.

Anxiety (A) Scale

The Anxiety (A) scale was developed to assess the most important dimension that emerged when the Validity and Clinical scales of the MMPI were factor analyzed (Welsh, 1956). The MMPI-A version of this scale has 35 of its original 39 items. Archer, Gordon, Anderson, and Giannetti (1989) found correlate patterns that were consistent with those derived from studies of adults. Adolescents scoring high on the A scale were anxious, fearful, guilt-prone, and self-critical.

Repression (R) Scale

The Repression (R) scale was developed to assess a second dimension that emerged when the Validity and Clinical scales of the MMPI were factor analyzed (Welsh, 1956). The MMPI-A version of this scale has 33 of the original 40 items. In adults, higher scorers on the R scale were conventional, submissive people who tried to avoid unpleasant confrontations and disagreeable situations. Archer et al. (1989) reported that adolescents who scored high on the R scale were described as over-controlled, inhibited, and less spontaneous than other adolescents.

MMPI-A CONTENT SCALES

Using procedures similar to those applied in developing Content scales for the MMPI-2, Williams, Butcher, Ben-Porath, and Graham (1992) developed a set of 15 scales to assess the basic content dimensions represented in the MMPI-A item pool. The authors rationally identified tentative items for scales, and statistical procedures were used to refine the scales. Table 15.2 lists the MMPI-A Content scales and their internal-consistency and test–retest reliability coefficients. Some of the scales are slightly modified versions of scales in the MMPI-2 (e.g., Anxiety, Depression, and Health Concerns), whereas others were specifically developed to deal with adolescent problems and concerns (e.g., Conduct Problems, School Problems, and Low Aspirations).

Examination of the data in Table 15.2 indicates that the internal consistencies of the MMPI-A Content scales are adequate but somewhat lower than for the corresponding MMPI-2 Content scales. As would be expected, the temporal stability over a longer time period (1 year) is somewhat lower than for a shorter time period (1 week). The temporal stability of the MMPI-A Content scales is somewhat lower than for corresponding MMPI-2 scales but comparable to that usually reported for adolescent personality scales.

In an initial effort to demonstrate the validity of the MMPI-A Content scales, Williams et al. (1992) reported extratest correlates for the MMPI-A normative sample and for adolescents from several different clinical settings. Sources of

Table 15.2 Internal Consistency and Temporal Stability of the MMPI-A Content Scales

| | INTERNAL CONSISTENCY | | | | TEMPORAL STABILITY | |
| | CLINICAL SAMPLE | | NORMATIVE SAMPLE | | SHORT TERM[a] | LONG TERM[b] |
SCALES	BOYS ($n = 420$)	GIRLS ($n = 293$)	BOYS ($n = 805$)	GIRLS ($n = 815$)	BOYS AND GIRLS ($n = 154$)	BOYS AND GIRLS ($n = 81$)
Anxiety (A-anx)	.80	.86	.76	.80	.81	.65
Obsessiveness (A-obs)	.76	.80	.72	.72	.70	.50
Depression (A-dep)	.83	.89	.80	.83	.82	.66
Health Concerns (A-hea)	.78	.85	.81	.82	.76	.53
Bizarre Mentation (A-biz)	.73	.76	.75	.75	.68	.59
Anger (A-ang)	.75	.79	.69	.66	.72	.45
Cynicism (A-cyn)	.78	.83	.79	.81	.73	.51
Alienation (A-aln)	.72	.75	.69	.75	.62	.53
Conduct Problems (A-con)	.74	.79	.72	72	.62	.55
Low Self-Esteem (A-lse)	.73	.80	.71	.75	.78	.58
Low Aspirations (A-las)	.63	.63	.55	.59	.66	.61
Social Discomfort (A-sod)	.78	.85	.77	.78	.76	.68
Family Problems (A-fam)	.82	.82	.81	.82	.82	.51
School Problems (A-sch)	.70	.74	.69	.69	.64	.73
Negative Treatment Indicators (A-trt)	.77	.80	.72	.75	.68	.40

[a] 1-week test–retest of normative subset of normative sample, boys and girls combined.
[b] 1-year test–retest of nonclinical sample, boys and girls combined.

SOURCE FOR INTERNAL CONSISTENCY AND SHORT-TERM STABILITY DATA: Excerpted (Tables 21 & 22) from Butcher, J.N., Williams, C.L., Graham, J.R., Archer, R.P., Tellegan, A., Ben-Porath, Y.S., & Kaemmer, B. (1992). Minnesota Multiphasic Personality Inventory® –Adolescent (MMPI® -A): Manual for administration, scoring and interpretation. Copyright © 1992 by the Regents of the University of Minnesota. Reproduced by permission of the University of Minnesota Press. All rights reserved. "MMPI® -A" and "Minnesota Multiphasic Personality Inventory® -A" are trademarks owned by the Regents of the University of Minnesota.

SOURCE FOR LONG-TERM STABILITY DATA: Stein, L.A.R., McClinton, B.K., & Graham, J.R. (1998). Long-term stability of Maple-A scales. Journal of Personality Assessment, 70, 103–108. Copyright © 1998, Lawrence Erlbaum Associates, Inc. Reproduced by permission.

extratest data included adolescent self-report, parent ratings, clinician ratings, and information obtained from records of patients. The results suggested validity for the MMPI-A Content scales for which construct-relevant external measures were available. However, relevant external measures for some Content scales were not available in their research.

In a similar study, Veltri et al. (2009) correlated Content scale scores with information from adolescents' records in psychiatric inpatient and forensic settings. Their results supported the convergent and discriminant validity of most of the Content scales. In a study conducted in an adolescent residential treatment facility, Forbey and Ben-Porath (2003a) found that the Content scales added incrementally to the Clinical scales in predicting clinician ratings of psychological symptomatology. Incremental validity of the Content scales also was demonstrated for samples of psychiatric inpatients and adolescents from the community (Rinaldo & Baer, 2003). Kopper, Osman, Osman, and Hoffman

(1998) found that for inpatient boys the Alienation and Anxiety Content scales were related to scores on a self-report measure of suicide probability. For girls the Family Problems, Conduct Problems, and School Problems Content scales were related to self-reported suicide probability.

Arita and Baer (1998) reported extratest correlates for the Anxiety (A-anx), Depression (A-dep), Health Concerns (A-hea), Alienation (A-aln), Anger (A-ang), Conduct Problems (A-con), and Social Discomfort (A-sod) Content scales for adolescents being treated at a private psychiatric hospital. Archer and Krishnamurthy (1994) reported that Scale 2 and the Depression (A-dep) Content scales were about equally effective in identifying adolescents with diagnoses of depression. They also reported that the Conduct Problems (A-con) and Cynicism (A-cyn) Content scales and the Immaturity (IMM) scale were related to conduct disorder diagnoses. Pena, Megargee, and Brody (1996) reported that delinquent boys scored significantly and meaningfully higher than boys in the MMPI-A normative sample on the A-ang, A-cyn, A-con, and A-fam Content scales.

Although preliminary validity data concerning the MMPI-A Content scales are encouraging, more research is needed to determine to what extent these content-based scales add to the basic Validity and Clinical scales in understanding adolescents who complete the MMPI-A. The Content scales should be used in conjunction with the basic Validity and Clinical scales. High Content scale scores often clarify the reasons for elevated scores on these other scales and help clinicians determine which of the many descriptors typically associated with these other scales should be emphasized. Scores on the Content scales should be viewed as direct communications from adolescent test takers to examiners. Because the items of the Content scales are obvious and face-valid, adolescents who are trying to manage impressions of adjustment or maladjustment can do so on these scales. Therefore, the scales are most useful when the Validity scales do not indicate defensiveness or exaggeration.

Although the MMPI-A Content scales are more homogeneous than the Clinical scales (see Table 15.2), Sherwood, Ben-Porath, and Williams (1997) were able to identify meaningful clusters of items within most of the Content scales. Utilizing statistical and rational procedures similar to those used to develop the MMPI-2 Content Component scales (see Chapter 6 of this book), they developed Component scales for 13 of the 15 MMPI-A Content scales. Table 15.3 lists the MMPI-A Content Component scales.

Information concerning internal consistency and test–retest reliability for the Content Component Scales in the MMPI-A normative sample and in an adolescent clinical sample is reported in Ben-Porath, Graham, Archer, Tellegen, and Kaemmer (2006). The internal consistency values ranged from .31 to .81, with means of .56 for the normative boys and .62 for the normative girls. Corresponding values for the clinical sample were quite similar to those for the normative sample. One-week test–retest reliability of the Content Component scales ranged from .35 to .80, with a mean value of .65. Obviously, some of the Content Component scales are heterogeneous and unstable enough that they should not be treated as stand-alone scales. However, the Component scales can

T able 15.3 MMPI-A Content Component Scales

Depression (A-dep)
  A-dep1: Dysphoria (5 items)
  A-dep2: Self-Depreciation (5 items)
  A-dep3: Lack of Drive (7 items)
  A-dep4: Suicidal Ideation (4 items)

Health Concerns (A-hea)
  A-hea1: Gastrointestinal Complaints (4 items)
  A-hea2: Neurological Symptoms (18 items)
  A-hea3: General Health Concerns (8 items)

Alienation (A-aln)
  A-aln1: Misunderstood (5 items)
  A-aln2: Social Isolation (5 items)
  A-aln3: Interpersonal Skepticism (5 items)

Bizarre Mentation (A-biz)
  A-biz1: Psychotic Symptomatology (11 items)
  A-biz2: Paranoid Ideation (5 items)

Anger (A-ang)
  A-ang1: Explosive Behavior (8 items)
  A-ang2: Irritability (8 items)

Cynicism (A-cyn)
  A-cyn1: Misanthropic Beliefs (13 items)
  A-cyn2: Interpersonal Suspiciousness (9 items)

Conduct Problems (A-con)
  A-con1: Acting-Out Behaviors (10 items)
  A-con2: Antisocial Attitudes (8 items)
  A-con3: Negative Peer Group Influences (3 items)

Low Self-Esteem (A-lse)
  A-lse1: Self-Doubt (13 items)
  A-lse2: Interpersonal Submissiveness (5 items)

Low Aspirations (A-las)
  A-las1: Low Achievement Orientation (8 items)
  A-las2: Lack of Initiative (7 items)

Social Discomfort (A-sod)
  A-sod1: Introversion (14 items)
  A-sod2: Shyness (10 items)

Family Problems (A-fam)
  A-fam1: Familial Discord (21 items)
  A-fam2: Familial Alienation (11 items)

School Problems (A-sch)
  A-sch1: School Conduct Problems (4 items)
  A-sch2: Negative Attitudes (8 items)

Negative Treatment Indicators (A-trt)
  A-trt1: Low Motivation (11 items)
  A-trt2: Inability to Disclose (8 items)

SOURCE: Excerpted (Table 2) from Sherwood, N.E., Ben-Porath, Y.S., & Williams, C.L. (1997). MMPI-A Content Component scales: Development, psychometric characteristics, and clinical application. Copyright © 1997 by the Regents of the University of Minnesota. Reproduced by permission of the University of Minnesota Press. All rights reserved. "MMPI® -A" and "Minnesota Multiphasic Personality Inventory® -A" are trademarks owned by the Regents of the University of Minnesota.

be useful in determining what kinds of items adolescents endorsed that led to their elevated scores on the Content scales. When a test taker has a T score of 60 or greater for a Content scale, the Component scales for that Content scale can be examined. If there is a difference of at least 10 T-score points between the Content Component scales, the features associated with the more elevated Content Component scale should be emphasized in interpreting the Content scale. The MMPI-A manual supplement (Ben-Porath et al., 2006) offers interpretive guidelines for the Content Component scales. Special attention should be given to the Suicidal Ideation (A-dep4) Content Component scale, as even a single item in the scored direction can indicate that a suicide risk evaluation should be completed.

MMPI-A PERSONALITY PSYCHOPATHOLOGY FIVE (PSY-5) SCALES

The development of the MMPI-2 PSY-5 scales was discussed in Chapter 7 of this book. McNulty, Harkness, Ben-Porath, and Williams (1997) developed corresponding scales for the MMPI-A. MMPI-2 PSY-5 items that also are in the MMPI-A item pool were included in preliminary scales. Items unique to the MMPI-A were reviewed by undergraduates, and those judged to be measuring PSY-5 constructs were added to the preliminary scales. Using data from the MMPI-A normative sample and the clinical sample included in the MMPI-A manual (Butcher et al., 1992), statistical analyses were then used to refine the scales.

The labels of the MMPI-A PSY-5 scales, which are the same as the corresponding MMPI-2 scales, are reported in Table 15.4 along with internal consistency values for the MMPI-A normative and clinical samples. The values are generally similar to the values reported for the MMPI-2 PSY-5 scales (see Chapter 7 of this book). Stein, McClinton, and Graham (1998) reported one-year test–retest reliability coefficients for a sample of public school adolescents. The

Table 15.4 Internal Consistency Estimates for the MMPI-A PSY-5 Scales

PSY-5 SCALE	NORMATIVE SAMPLE		CLINICAL SAMPLE	
	BOYS	GIRLS	BOYS	GIRLS
Aggressiveness	.74	.73	.79	.82
Psychoticism	.76	.74	.74	.78
Disconstraint	.74	.72	.72	.75
Negative Emotionality/ Neuroticism	.75	.76	.79	.80
Introversion/Low Positive Emotionality	.78	.75	.71	.77

SOURCE: Excerpted (Table 4) from Ben-Porath, Y.S., Graham, J.R., Archer, R.P., Tellegen, A.J., & Kaemmer, B. (2006). *Supplement to the MMPI®-A Manual for administration, scoring, and interpretation.* Copyright © 2006 by the Regents of the University of Minnesota. Reproduced by permission of the University of Minnesota Press. All rights reserved. "MMPI® -A" and "Minnesota Multiphasic Personality Inventory® -A" are trademarks owned by the Regents of the University of Minnesota.

values ranged from .44 for Psychoticism to .68 for Disconstraint. Although the temporal stability of the scales is lower than for the corresponding adult scales, the values are comparable to those for other measures of adolescent personality characteristics.

Several studies have identified extratest correlates for the MMPI-A PSY-5 scales. McNulty, Harkness, et al. (1997) correlated PSY-5 scores with parent ratings, staff ratings, and information obtained from a review of the records of boys and girls from several treatment facilities. The results supported the construct validity of the PSY-5 scales. Scores on the Aggressiveness (AGGR) scale were most strongly related to externalizing behaviors of various kinds, including aggressive behavior toward others. Psychoticism scale scores were associated with psychotic symptoms of various kinds. Scores on the Disconstraint (DISC) scale were associated with externalizing behaviors, including drug use, delinquency, and sexual acting out. However, DISC scale scores were not strongly related to aggressive behaviors. As expected, scores on the Negative Emotionality/Neuroticism (NEGE) scale were related most strongly to internalizing behaviors. Finally, high scorers on the Introversion/Low Positive Emotionality (INTR) scale were characterized as internalizers.

Veltri et al. (2009) reported extratest correlates for the MMPI-A PSY-5 scales for clinical and forensic samples. Their results were very similar to those of McNulty, Harkness, et al. (1997). High scorers on the AGGR scale were more likely to appear angry and to get into fights. High scorers on the PSYC scale were described as experiencing hallucinations and flashbacks. Higher scores on the DISC scale were associated with a variety of externalizing behaviors, including drug use, school behavior problems, and difficulties with the law. The strongest correlates for the NEGE and INTR scales were internalizing in nature (e.g., anxiety and depression).

RELIABILITY AND VALIDITY OF THE MMPI-A

Table 15.5 reports internal-consistency and short-term temporal-stability coefficients for the basic Validity and Clinical scales of the MMPI-A for boys and girls in the normative sample (Butcher et al., 1992) and longer-term temporal stability for a small group of nonclinical adolescents (Stein, McClinton, & Graham, 1998). The internal-consistency coefficients are slightly lower than the corresponding values for the MMPI-2, but most of the scales have relatively good internal consistency, especially considering that no efforts were made to ensure internal consistency when the scales were originally developed. As would be expected, the longer-term temporal stability (1 year) of the scales was somewhat lower than the shorter-term temporal stability (1 week). The temporal stability of most scales is slightly lower than for the MMPI-2. This is in keeping with generally lower stability of personality test scores for adolescents than for adults. As is the case with the MMPI-2, Scale 6 has the lowest test–retest reliability coefficient of any of the Clinical scales.

Because the Validity scales of the MMPI-A are very similar to those of the MMPI-2, we would expect them to function similarly. The VRIN scale was

Table 15.5 Internal Consistency and Temporal Stability of MMPI-A Validity and Clinical Scales

| | INTERNAL CONSISTENCY | | TEMPORAL STABILITY | |
| | | | SHORT TERM[a] | LONG TERM[b] |
SCALE	BOYS (*n* = 805)	GIRLS (*n* = 815)	BOY & GIRLS (*n* = 154)	BOY & GIRLS (*n* = 81)
L	.64	.58	.61	.45
F	.90	.82	.55	.32
F1	.80	.73	.49	.43
F2	.85	.84	.55	.24
K	.72	.70	.75	.60
Hs	.78	.79	.79	.63
D	.65	.66	.78	.66
Hy	.63	.55	.70	.50
Pd	.63	.68	.80	.68
Mf	.43	.40	.82	.59
Pa	.57	.59	.65	.51
Pt	.84	.86	.83	.69
Sc	.88	.89	.83	.54
Ma	.61	.61	.70	.54
Si	.79	.80	.84	.75

[a] 1-week test–retest interval.

[b] 1-year test–retest interval.

SOURCE FOR INTERNAL CONSISTENCY AND SHORT-TERM STABILITY DATA: Excerpted (Tables 13 and 14) from Butcher, J.N., Williams, C.L., Graham, J.R., Archer, R.P., Tellegen, A., Ben-Porath, Y.S., & Kaemmer, B. (1992). *Minnesota Multiphasic Personality Inventory-Adolescent (MMPI-A): Manual for administration, scoring, and interpretation.* Copyright © 1992 by the Regents of the University of Minnesota. Reproduced by permission of the University of Minnesota Press. All rights reserved. "MMPIr-A" and "Minnesota Multiphasic Personality Inventory-A" are trademarks owned by the Regents of the University of Minnesota

SOURCE FOR LONG-TERM STABILITY DATA: Stein, L.A.R., McClinton, B.K., Graham, J.R. (1998). Long-term stability of MMPI-A Scales. *Journal of Personality Assessment, 70,* 103-108. Copyright © 1998, Lawrence Erlbaum Associates, Inc. Reproduced by permission.

designed to detect random responding. The MMPI-A manual (Butcher et al., 1992) recommended that T scores of 75 or higher should raise concerns about random responding. MMPI-A protocols with such high VRIN scores should not be interpreted. Several studies have demonstrated the utility of the VRIN scale in identifying random responding (e.g., Archer & Elkins, 1999; Baer, Ballenger, Berry, & Wetter, 1997; Baer, Kroll, Rinaldo, & Ballenger, 1999; Pinsoneault, 2005). However, optimal T-score cutoffs ranging from T > 65 to T > 90 have been reported. Obviously, higher cutoff scores will result in fewer false positive identifications, but at the cost of more false negative identifications.

As with the MMPI-2, the MMPI-A TRIN scale was developed to identify test takers who respond indiscriminately true or false to items without consideration of item content. The MMPI-A manual (Butcher et al., 1992) recommended that TRIN T scores equal to or higher than 75 suggest that test takers responded inconsistently to the items by answering true or false indiscriminately without consideration of item content. Archer (2005) recommended that TRIN scale T scores between 70 and 79 indicate marginal levels of response inconsistency, whereas TRIN T scores equal to or greater than 80 indicate unacceptable levels of response inconsistency. Handel, Arnau, Archer, and Dandy (2006) reported data leading them to conclude that a TRIN scale T-score cutoff of 65 was optimal in situations where the base rate of indiscriminate true or false responding is relative low. Obviously, protocols with such high TRIN scale scores should not be interpreted.

There are several ways in which the validity of the MMPI-A substantive scales can be assessed. To the extent that scores and configurations of scores on the MMPI-A are congruent with corresponding scores on the MMPI, interpretive information that has accumulated for the MMPI can be generalized to the MMPI-A. In addition, it is important to demonstrate that the MMPI-A scales have relevant external correlates.

The MMPI-A manual (Butcher et al., 1992) reported data concerning congruence between scores and code types based on the MMPI-A scores and code types based on the MMPI using the adolescent norms of Marks et al. (1974). When code types are well defined (at least five T-score points between the lowest scale in the code type and the next highest scale), code types from the two versions of the test are quite congruent. In the MMPI-A normative sample, 95.1% of the boys and 87.8% of the girls had the same one-point code type. Corresponding rates for the clinical sample were 95.4% and 94.4%. In the normative sample, 95.2% of the boys and 81.8% of the girls had the same two-point code type when the definition criterion of five T-score points was used. The corresponding rates for the clinical boys and girls were 95.0% and 91.0%, respectively. Clearly, profile configurations are quite similar for the MMPI and the MMPI-A.

The data concerning congruence do not address the important question of which code type more accurately reflects what a test taker is really like when different code types are found for the two versions of the test. To answer this question it would be necessary to compare the inferences based on the two code types with external information about each person and determine which inferences are more accurate. Graham, Timbrook, Ben-Porath, and Butcher (1991) demonstrated a methodology for assessing relative accuracy for adults and reported that MMPI-2 code types yielded inferences that were at least as accurate, and perhaps more so, than inferences based on the MMPI code types.

Although configurations are quite similar for the two versions of the test with adolescents, average T scores are somewhat different. For most scales, T scores on the MMPI-A are about five points lower than on the MMPI with adolescent norms. For boys, Scale 4 is about 10 T-score points lower on the MMPI-A, and for girls Scale 9 is about 10 T-score points lower on the MMPI-A. For both boys and girls, scores on Scale 0 are about the same for the two versions of the test. There are several possible reasons for these normative differences. It may be that contemporary adolescents endorse more items in the scored direction on most scales because they are more deviant. However, it may also be that they are endorsing more items in the scored direction because current test instructions encourage test takers to answer all the items if they possibly can. When the earlier MMPI normative data were collected, test takers were not given as much encouragement to answer all the items, and they typically omitted more items than contemporary adolescents do. When test takers answer more items, they are likely to endorse some of them in the scored direction.

Because of the considerable congruence between the MMPI and MMPI-A, when MMPI-A results are being interpreted, it is appropriate to use much of the information that has been reported for the MMPI with adolescents (e.g., Archer, 1992b; Archer, Gordon, Giannetti, & Singles, 1988; Belter, Foster, & Imm, 1996; Gallucci, 1994; Hathaway & Monachesi, 1963; Marks et al., 1974; Williams & Butcher, 1989a, 1989b; Wrobel & Lachar, 1992). This information has been summarized by Archer (2005) and Butcher and Williams (1992).

It also is important to demonstrate directly the validity of the MMPI-A scales. The MMPI-A manual (Butcher et al., 1992) reports some external correlates for scores for normal adolescents and adolescents in a variety of clinical settings. These data suggest that there are reliable correlates of the MMPI-A scales and that the correlates are remarkably similar to those previously published for the MMPI scales. Pena et al. (1996) found that delinquent boys scored higher than boys in the MMPI-A normative sample on relevant Clinical and Content scales. Cashel, Rogers, Sewell, and Holleman (1998) identified meaningful correlates for most of the MMPI-A Clinical, Content, and Supplementary scales in a correctional setting.

Arita and Baer (1998) reported that evidence for the convergent and discriminant validity of selected MMPI-A Content scales in a clinical setting was generally strong. Gallucci (1997a) reported correlates of MMPI-A substance abuse scales for a sample of substance-abusing adolescents. Veltri et al. (2009) reported correlates of MMPI-A scales for boys and girls in inpatient psychiatric and forensic settings. Correlates were similar for boys and girls and were similar to those previously identified for MMPI and MMPI-A scales. Convergent validity was strong, but discriminant validity was only modest.

Recognizing that the scales and subscales of the MMPI-A are not likely to be independent, in large part due to item overlap, Archer, Belevich, and Elkins (1994) factor analyzed scores of the adolescents in the MMPI-A normative ssample on 69 scales and subscales. They identified eight dimensions that accounted for 94% of the variance in these scores. The factor structure identified by Archer et al. was later replicated for a sample of juvenile delinquents (Archer, Bolinskey, Morton, & Farris, 2002). Relationships between the factor dimensions and extratest criterion measures were reported by Pogge, Stokes, McGrath, Bilginer, and Deluca (2002) for a sample of adolescent psychiatric inpatients. Archer and Krishnamurthy (1994) developed the MMPI-A Structural Summary as a way of organizing scores using the following general factor dimensions: (1) General Maladjustment, (2) Immaturity, (3) Disinhibition/Excitatory Potential, (4) Social Discomfort, (5) Health Concerns, (6) Naivete, (7) Familial Alienation, and (8) Psychoticism. For details concerning the utilization of the Structural Summary approach to MMPI-A interpretation, readers should consult Archer and Krishnamurthy's (2002) interpretive guide.

INTERPRETING THE MMPI-A VALIDITY SCALES

Cannot Say Scale

As with the MMPI-2, excessive item omissions lead to artificially lowered scores on the MMPI-A scales. Every effort should be made to encourage adolescents to answer as many of the items as possible. If more than 30 items are omitted, the protocol should be considered invalid and no scales should be interpreted (Butcher et al., 1992). If more than 10 items are omitted, the protocol should be interpreted with caution, and the omitted items should be examined to make sure that they are not concentrated on specific scales.

Variable Response Inconsistency (VRIN) Scale

The Variable Response Inconsistency (VRIN) scale assesses the extent to which test takers have responded consistently to the items in the inventory. The MMPI-A manual recommends that the possibility of random responding be considered when VRIN-scale T scores for adolescents are equal to or greater than 75. Baer et al. (1997) demonstrated empirically that the VRIN scale is quite effective in identifying random responding on the MMPI-A. These investigators found that a VRIN-scale T-score cutoff of 51 or greater correctly identified both totally and partially random responding. However, this author recommends using the T-score cutoff of 75 or greater as recommended in the MMPI-A manual. Baer et al. noted that when random responding occurs only in the latter quarter of the test, the VRIN scale may be less effective in detecting the random responding because relatively few VRIN-scale item pairs occur within the last quarter of the test.

True Response Inconsistency (TRIN) Scale

The True Response Inconsistency (TRIN) scale assesses the extent to which adolescent test takers have responded to MMPI-A items with indiscriminate true or false responding. This scale has not yet been validated with adolescents and should be used cautiously until more data are available. The MMPI-A manual (Butcher et al., 1992) recommends that T scores equal to or greater than 75 indicate the possibility of a true or false response bias. As with the TRIN scale of the MMPI-2, T scores on the TRIN scale are always 50 or higher, with T or F added to the T score to indicate either a true or false response bias.

Infrequency (F, F1, and F2) Scales

The MMPI-A F scale is divided into two parts (F1 and F2). The F1 scale gives information about the first part of the test (items 1–236), and the F2 scale gives information about the second part of the test (items 242–470). As long as T scores are used, scores on the F, F1, and F2 scales can be interpreted similarly. The F-scale raw score is the sum of the F1 and F2 scale scores.

T scores between 70 and 74 on one or more of the F scales suggest a possible problematic response pattern (Butcher et al., 1992). T scores equal to or greater than 75 indicate even greater likelihood of problematic responding. When an adolescent obtains a T score of 70 or greater on one of the F scales, the first thing that should be done is to rule out random or careless responding. The VRIN scale (see earlier) is very useful in this regard. Next, the possibility of true response bias should be ruled out. The TRIN scale (see earlier) is helpful in evaluating this possibility. If the F scale is elevated and the VRIN or TRIN scale suggests invalidity, none of the MMPI-A scales should be interpreted. However, if the F1 scale is within acceptable limits and the F2 scale suggests invalid responding, the basic Validity and Clinical scales can be interpreted, but none of the other scales can. If response bias is ruled out based on the VRIN- and TRIN-scale scores, a high score on one or more of the F scales is likely to be suggestive of either serious psychopathology or exaggeration of symptoms and problems.

L Scale

High scores on the L scale indicate that adolescents have approached the test in a defensive manner. They have tried to present themselves in an unrealistically favorable light, denying minor flaws and weaknesses and claiming excessive virtues (Butcher et al., 1992). T scores equal to or greater than 65 on the L scale suggest that adolescents have approached the test in such a defensive manner that the resulting scores may not reflect accurately what they really are like. If the high L-scale score is accompanied by high scores on Clinical, Content, or other substantive scales, these scales can be interpreted, but it should be acknowledged that the scores may under-represent symptoms and problems. If the L-scale score is high and there are no high scores on the problem-oriented scales, it is not possible to determine if the adolescent has serious problems and is covering them up or has average adjustment and is simply overstating virtues. T scores between 60 and 64 on the L scale indicate some defensiveness, which should be taken into account in interpreting the other scales.

Correction (K) Scale

Although scores on the MMPI-A Clinical scales are not K corrected, the K scale can be considered a measure of defensiveness in adolescents. T scores equal to or greater than 65 suggest the possibility that the adolescent has approached the test in an invalid manner. The TRIN scale (see earlier) should be consulted to rule out the possibility of a false response bias. The MMPI-A manual (Butcher et al., 1992) recommends that an adolescent MMPI-A protocol should not be invalidated solely on the basis of the K scale. However, it should be acknowledged that when the K-scale score is high (T ≥ 65), scores on the other scales may under-represent problems and symptoms.

IDENTIFYING OVERREPORTING AND UNDERREPORTING ON THE MMPI-A

Overreporting

Compared with adults, relatively little research was conducted concerning adolescents overreporting on the MMPI. Archer, Gordon, and Kirchner (1987) concluded that an extremely elevated raw score (≥ 26) on the F scale along with elevated scores on most Clinical scales easily detected adolescents who were instructed to overreport. However, this study did not include a comparison group of clinical adolescents. Herkov, Archer, and Gordon (1991) compared nonclinical adolescents who were instructed to overreport and adolescent psychiatric patients who took the MMPI with standard instructions and found that elevated F-scale scores (T $\geq$ 100) were effective in differentiating these two groups.

Stein, Graham, and Williams (1995) published the first overreporting study with the MMPI-A. These investigators compared nonclinical adolescents who took the MMPI-A with standard instructions, nonclinical adolescents who were instructed to overreport, and adolescent psychiatric patients who took the test with standard instructions. They found that, although most scales were somewhat lower than in adult overreporting studies, the pattern of scores for the adolescents who were overreporting was remarkably similar to what had previously been reported for adults who were overreporting. Although the F, F1, and F2 scales and the F-K index all discriminated well between adolescents who were overreporting and both nonclinical and clinical adolescents who took the test with standard instructions, the F scale was the best indicator of overreporting. An F-scale raw score of 23 (T = 77 for boys and T = 89 for girls) was most effective in discriminating boys and girls who were overreporting from both nonclinical and clinical boys and girls who completed the test with standard instructions.

In a study of overreporting among adolescent offenders, Rogers, Hinds, and Sewell (1996) found that F, F1, and F2 all were effective in identifying adolescents who were overreporting and that the F-K index (> 20) yielded the best positive and negative predictive powers. These investigators also found that a separate instrument, the Structured Interview of Reported Symptoms (SIRS; Rogers, 1992) also was quite effective in identifying the adolescents who were overreporting. The combined use of the MMPI-A validity indicators and SIRS scores was more effective in identifying overreporting than either of the individual measures.

In summary, it would appear that when adolescents approach the MMPI-A with the intention of feigning serious psychopathology, they have very high F, F1, and F2 scores and below average K scores. As with adults, these adolescents also have very high scores on most of the Clinical scales. The optimal score or index for identifying overreporting will likely differ from setting to setting and must be established according to the kinds of classification errors that one wants to minimize. However, whenever there are extremely high scores on the F scale and random and all-true or all-false responding have been ruled out by referring to the VRIN and TRIN scales, the possibility of overreporting should be considered seriously.

Underreporting

To date, only two studies have examined underreporting on the MMPI-A. Stein and Graham (1999) determined how well the MMPI-A Validity scales could detect underreporting among adolescents in a correctional/clinical inpatient setting. Adolescents who underreported tended to report fewer symptoms and problems, resulting in higher scores on scales L and K and lower scores on the Clinical scales. The underreporting pattern was similar to those reported in adult studies. The L scale seemed to work well for both boys and girls. Approximately 85% of correctional girls who were instructed to underreport and approximately 87% of noncorrectional girls who took the test with standard instructions were correctly identified by the L scale. Corresponding data for the correctional and noncorrectional boys were 77% and 72%, respectively. Because of the relatively small sample size in the Stein et al., study optimal cutoff scores for the various MMPI-A Validity scales could not be firmly established.

Baer, Ballenger, and Kroll (1998) utilized community and clinical samples and instructed adolescents to complete the MMPI-A with standard instructions or with instructions to try to demonstrate excellent psychological adjustment. They also found that the L scale was the most effective way to identify underreporting, but several less familiar scales also showed some promise.

INTERPRETING THE MMPI-A CLINICAL SCALES

The MMPI-A manual (Butcher et al., 1992) suggests that T scores of 65 or greater on the Clinical scales should be considered clinically significant. T scores between 60 and 64 on the Clinical scales also can be interpreted as high scores, although one should have less confidence in inferences based on scores at this lower level. Because very little is known about the meaning of low scores on the Clinical scales for adolescents, low scores should not be interpreted at this time. The interpretations of high scores on the Clinical scales are based on research with the original MMPI and with the MMPI-A. As with the MMPI-2, it should be acknowledged that not every interpretive statement will apply to every adolescent who has a high score on a particular scale. The inferences should be treated as hypotheses to be validated on the basis of other information available about each adolescent.

Scale 1 (Hypochondriasis)

High scores on Scale 1 generally indicate preoccupation with health, illness, and bodily functioning. Although adolescents with genuine physical disorders may obtain moderately elevated scores (T = 60–64), higher scores suggest somatic complaints that have a psychological component. High-scoring boys and girls may report fatigue and lack of energy, and high-scoring girls may report eating problems. Adolescents who score high on Scale 1 tend to have histories of poor academic performance. They are insecure, fear failure, and blame themselves for problems. They are self-centered, demanding, and attention-seeking. They tend to be somewhat isolated from other people.

Scale 2 (Depression)

In clinical settings, high scores on Scale 2 tend to be associated with depression, low energy, guilt, pessimism, and suicidal ideation. In clinical settings, adolescents with high scores on Scale 2 often receive diagnoses of depression or dysthymia. High scorers also frequently report somatic symptoms, anxiety, fear, worry, and eating problems. They lack self-confidence, are self-critical, and perform poorly in school. They tend to be overcontrolled, submissive, shy, timid, and socially withdrawn. Because of their emotional distress, high scorers are likely to be motivated to participate in psychotherapy.

Scale 3 (Hysteria)

High scores on Scale 3 are associated with somatic symptoms, poor concentration, and sleep disturbance. In clinical samples, high scorers may report depression and suicidal ideation. High scorers are immature, self-centered persons who are socially involved and demand attention and affection. They tend to deny difficulties and lack insight into their own motives.

Scale 4 (Psychopathic Deviate)

High scores on Scale 4 are associated with a variety of acting-out and delinquent behaviors. In clinical and correctional settings, high scorers on this scale often receive conduct disorder diagnoses. High scorers resent authority and have academic and behavior problems in school and conflicts with their families. They are quite sensitive to criticism and to restrictions on their behavior. High scorers tend to be seen by others as active, assertive, and independent. They often admit to alcohol or other drug problems. High scorers often are impulsive, oppositional, and aggressive. They may show poor judgment and do not seem to profit from their experiences. They are self-centered persons who do not accept responsibility for their own behavior. In clinical settings, high scorers may have histories of being physically abused (boys) or sexually abused (girls). High Scale 4 scorers typically are not motivated to participate in psychotherapy.

Scale 5 (Masculinity–Femininity)

For boys, high T scores on Scale 5 suggest stereotypically feminine interest patterns; for girls, high T scores suggest stereotypically masculine interest patterns. Boys with high T scores on Scale 5 are less likely than other boys to get into trouble with the law. Girls with high T scores on Scale 5 are more likely than other girls to have academic and behavior problems in school, to have histories of learning disability, and to act out in a variety of ways. Interestingly, Hathaway and Monachesi (1963) reported that both boys and girls with higher T scores on Scale 5 were less likely to act out in delinquent ways.

Scale 6 (Paranoia)

Adolescents who score high on Scale 6 often have academic and behavior problems in school. They are moody, changeable, and unpredictable. They are suspicious, guarded, evasive, and withdrawn interpersonally and are very sensitive to criticism and rejection. They tend to blame others for their own problems and difficulties. In clinical settings, self-mutilation and suicidal ideation are more common among high scorers than adolescent patients in general.

Scale 7 (Psychasthenia)

High scores on Scale 7 tend to be associated with anxiety, depression, and other emotional turmoil. High scorers often have difficulty concentrating and attending, and they are indecisive. They have poor self-concepts, are self-critical and perfectionistic, and feel guilty about perceived failures. Suicidal ideation is more common among high scorers on Scale 7 than adolescent patients in general. High scorers tend to be shy and socially introverted. Clinical records of high-scoring boys may indicate histories of being sexually abused.

Scale 8 (Schizophrenia)

In clinical settings, high scorers on Scale 8 may manifest psychotic symptoms (e.g., delusions, hallucinations, or ideas of reference). They may appear to be fearful, confused, and disorganized. They are likely to be emotionally unstable and to show large shifts in mood. Somatic symptoms and drug use also may be characteristic of high scorers on this scale. High scorers tend to have academic and behavior problems in school. They are quite vulnerable to stress and resort to excessive fantasy during times of increased stress. At times their reality testing may be impaired. They have low self-esteem and feel inferior to others. They are described as isolated, aloof, mistrustful, and uninvolved with others. High scorers may have histories of being sexually abused. The prognosis for successful psychotherapy is not very good for high scorers on Scale 8.

Scale 9 (Hypomania)

High scorers on Scale 9 often have histories of acting-out behaviors that may include school problems and drug use. They often seem to have difficulty focusing on problems. They are resentful of authority and often behave quite impulsively. They are optimistic and socially extroverted persons. They are self-centered and may be grandiose in their self-appraisal. High scorers on this scale often are seen by others as deceitful and self-indulgent. They often are not very motivated to engage in psychotherapy.

Scale 0 (Social Introversion)

High scorers on Scale 0 are introverted, shy, and timid, and they have difficulty making friends. They lack self-confidence, are emotionally overcontrolled, and blame themselves for problems. They have strong needs for attention, affection, and support. In clinical settings, they may report feeling depressed and suicidal. They tend not to use alcohol or drugs or to be involved in delinquent behaviors.

INTERPRETING THE MMPI-A SUPPLEMENTARY SCALES

MacAndrew Alcoholism Scale–Revised (MAC-R)

High scorers on the MAC-R scale are more likely than other adolescents to have problems with substance use/abuse. Raw scores greater than 27 suggest a strong possibility of such problems. Raw scores between 24 and 27 are indeterminate concerning substance abuse. Raw scores of 23 or lower suggest that substance abuse problems are not likely. High scorers on the MAC-R scale also are likely to display behavior undercontrol, and they are not likely to anticipate the consequences of their behavior.

Alcohol/Drug Problem Proneness (PRO) Scale

High scores on the PRO scale are associated with adolescent substance abuse problems. While not much information is available about PRO scale cutoff scores, the scale's authors recommended that T scores greater than 60 should raise concerns about substance abuse problems. It should be noted that all of the research to date deals with current substance abuse and not with potential for future abuse. High scorers on this scale also tend to be impulsive, aggressive, and behaviorally undercontrolled.

Alcohol/Drug Problem Acknowledgment (ACK) Scale

High scorers on the ACK scale are likely to be directly admitting problems with alcohol and other substances. The T-score cutoff recommended by the scale's authors is 60 or greater. High scorers on the scale also tend to be impulsive and behaviorally undercontrolled.

Immaturity (IMM) Scale

High scorers on the IMM scale are likely to have a lower level of ego development than others of their chronological age. They have limited capacity to think in abstract terms, are less likely to identify with values and beliefs of their social group, and have less capacity to see the world from the viewpoint of others. They also have lower levels of moral development. They are likely to have academic difficulties and to be somewhat rebellious and defiant toward authority figures.

Anxiety (A) Scale

High scorers on the A scale typically are not very well adjusted or effective. They are anxious, fearful, guilt-prone, and self-critical. They feel overwhelmed and unable to cope effectively with the demands of everyday life.

Repression (R) Scale

High scorers on the R scale tend to be overcontrolled and inhibited individuals. They are rather passive in relationships and try to avoid unpleasant confrontations and disagreeable situations.

INTERPRETING THE MMPI-A CONTENT SCALES

The MMPI-A Content scales can be very helpful in understanding patterns of scores on the basic Clinical scales. A rather wide variety of descriptors can be applied to an adolescent who has a high score on a Clinical scale. Examination of the Content scales can offer direction concerning which of these descriptors should be emphasized in interpreting the high Clinical scale score. For example, descriptors for high scores on Scale 4 for adolescents include family problems, school problems, and delinquency. If the Content scales indicate elevation on the Family Problems (A-fam) Content scale but not on the School Problems (A-sch) or Conduct Problems (A-con) scales, interpretation of the Scale 4 elevation would emphasize the adolescent's problems and conflicts with family, rather than school difficulties or problems with the law.

Scores on the MMPI-A Content scales give important information about what the adolescent wants the examiner to know about him or her. The content of the scales is very obvious, and adolescents may be aware of what information they convey as they respond to the items. Adolescents who are interested in creating particular impressions of themselves can do so by manipulating their responses to the items in these scales. Therefore, scores on the Content scales will be most informative when test takers approach the test in an honest, candid manner. The Content scales should not be interpreted when the Validity scales suggest that the adolescent has been quite defensive or has exaggerated symptoms and problems in responding to test items.

Scores on the MMPI-A Content scales are expressed as Uniform T scores, as are scores on the eight basic Clinical scales. Inferences can be made about T scores equal to or greater than 60, but greatest emphasis should be placed on T scores that are equal to or greater than 65. The descriptions of high scorers on the MMPI-A Content scales that follow are based on consideration of the items in each scale and on empirically derived descriptors that have been reported for the scales (Arita & Baer, 1998; Veltri et al., 2009; Williams et al., 1992). As with the Clinical scales, not every descriptor associated with a Content scale will apply to every adolescent who has a high score on the scale. Inferences should be treated as hypotheses that are to be validated based on other information available about the adolescent.

Anxiety (A-anx)

Adolescents who score high on the MMPI-A Anxiety (A-anx) scale are reporting many symptoms of anxiety, including tension, frequent worrying, and sleep disturbances. They report problems with concentration, confusion, and inability to stay on a task. They may believe that life is a strain and that their difficulties are insurmountable. They may worry about losing their minds or feel that something dreadful is about to happen to them. They seem to be aware of their problems and how they differ from others. Correlate data indicate that scores on the A-anx scale are related to general maladjustment as well as to specific symptoms such as anxiety, depression, withdrawal, and somatic complaints.

Obsessiveness (A-obs)

Adolescents who score high on the MMPI-A Obsessiveness (A-obs) scale report worrying beyond reason, often over trivial matters. They may have ruminative thoughts about bad words or counting unimportant things. They have times when they are unable to sleep because of their worries. They report difficulty making decisions and dread making changes in their lives. They report that others sometimes lose patience with them, and they often are regretful about things they have said or done. Correlate data suggest that the A-obs scale is related to general maladjustment and also to dependent, anxious behaviors in clinical boys and suicidal ideation and/or gestures in clinical girls. Further research with persons known to be exhibiting obsessive symptoms is needed to clarify the interpretation of the scale.

Depression (A-dep)

Adolescents who score high on the MMPI-A Depression (A-dep) scale report many symptoms of depression, including fatigue and crying spells. They are dissatisfied with their lives and feel that others are happier than they are. They may be expressing many self-depreciative thoughts and feel that life is neither interesting nor worthwhile. They may report feeling blue and wishing they were dead, and suicidal ideation is possible. They experience social problems, report feeling lonely even when with other people, and tend to be socially withdrawn. The future seems too uncertain for them to make serious plans, and they may have periods when they are unable to "get going." They may be characterized by a sense of hopelessness and not caring. Correlate data indicate that for normal girls and for clinical boys and girls, high scores on the A-dep scale are indicative of depression and dysphoria. For clinical cases suicidal ideation and/or gestures may be present.

Health Concerns (A-hea)

Adolescents who score high on the MMPI-A Health Concerns (A-hea) scale report numerous physical complaints and indicate that physical problems interfere with enjoyment of school activities and contribute to school absence. They worry about their health and may feel that their problems would disappear if only their health would improve. Correlate data offer considerable support for the A-hea scale as a measure of somatic complaints in clinical cases. For normal boys and girls, higher scores on this scale seem to be related to misbehavior, poor academic performance, and other school problems.

Bizarre Mentation (A-biz)

Adolescents scoring high on the MMPI-A Bizarre Mentation (A-biz) scale report very strange thoughts and experiences, which may include auditory, visual, or olfactory hallucinations. They may feel that something is wrong with their minds. They may feel that they are being plotted against or that someone is trying to poison them. They may believe that others are trying to steal their thoughts, possibly through hypnosis. They may believe that evil spirits or ghosts possess or influence them. Correlate data indicate that the A-biz scale is a measure of general maladjustment in nonclinical settings, with higher scorers having problems in school and receiving low grades. For boys and girls in clinical settings, high scores on the

A-biz scale are suggestive of bizarre sensory experiences and other symptoms and behaviors that may be indicative of psychosis.

Anger (A-ang)

Adolescents who score high on the MMPI-A Anger (A-ang) scale report anger control problems. They often feel like swearing or smashing things. They may get into fights, especially when drinking. They may get into trouble for breaking or destroying things. They report feeling irritable and impatient with others, and they may throw temper tantrums to get their way. They do not like being hurried or having people get ahead of them in line. Correlate data for clinical cases indicate that higher scorers on the A-ang scale may have histories of assault and other acting-out behaviors. They tend to externalize blame for their problems and difficulties. In clinical settings boys may have histories of having been sexually abused.

Cynicism (A-cyn)

Adolescents scoring high on the MMPI-A Cynicism (A-cyn) scale report misanthropic attitudes. They may feel that others are out to get them and will use unfair means to gain an advantage. They look for hidden motives whenever someone does something nice for them. They believe that it is safer to trust nobody because people make friends in order to use them. Others are seen as inwardly disliking to help another person. They feel misunderstood by others and see others as jealous of them. Correlate data indicate that the A-cyn scale is not necessarily related to acting-out behavior. It may be more of an attitudinal than a behavioral measure.

Alienation (A-aln)

High scorers on the MMPI-A Alienation (A-aln) scale report considerable emotional distance from others. They believe that they are getting a raw deal from life and that no one, including parents, cares about or understands them. They do not believe that they are liked by others, nor do they get along well with peers. They have difficulty self-disclosing and report feeling awkward when having to talk in a group. They do not appreciate hearing others give their opinions. They do not believe that others are sympathetic and feel that other people often block their attempts at success. Correlate data indicate that for both normative and clinical cases, the A-aln scale is related to social problems and feelings of emotional distance from others. High scorers on this scale often report symptoms of depression and anxiety.

Conduct Problems (A-con)

Adolescents scoring high on the MMPI-A Conduct Problems (A-con) scale report behavioral problems, which may include stealing, shoplifting, lying, breaking or destroying things, being disrespectful, swearing, and being oppositional. They say that their peers are often in trouble and frequently talk them into doing things they know they should not do. At times they may try to make others afraid of them, just for the fun of it. They are entertained by criminal behavior and do not blame people for taking advantage of others. They admit doing bad things in the past that they cannot tell anybody about. Correlate data, which were similar across normative and clinical samples, genders, and criterion measures, indicate that high scorers on the A-con scale tended to have various kinds of behavior problems, including delinquency, anger, aggressiveness, and substance abuse. High scorers tend to externalize blame for their problems and difficulties.

Low Self-Esteem (A-lse)

Adolescents scoring high on the MMPI-A Low Self-Esteem (A-lse) scale report very negative opinions of themselves, including being unattractive, lacking self-confidence, feeling useless, having little ability, having several faults, and not being able to do anything well. They say that they are likely to yield to others' pressure, changing their minds or giving up in arguments. They let other people take charge when problems have to be solved, and they do not feel that they are capable of planning their own future. They become uncomfortable when others say nice things about them, and at times they may become confused and forgetful. Correlate data indicate that higher scores on the A-lse scale are related to negative views of self and poor school performance. Depression and suicidal ideation may be present among high scorers.

Low Aspirations (A-las)

High scorers on the MMPI-A Low Aspirations (A-las) scale report low need to achieve, and they do not expect to be successful. They do not like to study and read about things, dislike science and lectures on serious topics, and prefer work that allows them to be careless. They avoid newspaper editorials and believe that the comic strips are the only interesting part of the newspaper. They report difficulty starting things and give up quickly when things go wrong. They let other people solve their problems, and they avoid facing difficulties. They believe that others block their success. They report that others tell them they are lazy. Correlate data support the A-las scale as a measure of poor achievement and limited participation in school activities. In addition, the scale is related to antisocial tendencies, such as running away, truancy, and sexual acting out in girls.

Social Discomfort (A-sod)

Adolescents with high scores on the MMPI-A Social Discomfort (A-sod) scale report that they find it very difficult to be around others. They report being shy and prefer to be alone. They dislike having people around them and frequently avoid others. They do not like parties, crowds, dances, or other social gatherings. They tend not to speak unless spoken to, and others have told them they are hard to get to know. They have difficulty making friends and do not like to meet strangers. Correlate data suggest that the A-sod scale is a measure of social discomfort and social withdrawal. High scorers also tend to have low energy levels. Both boys and girls who score higher on this scale are likely to feel anxious and depressed. In addition, for girls higher scores are related to eating problems and are contrain-dicative of aggressive and irresponsible acting-out behaviors.

Family Problems (A-fam)

Adolescents with high scores on the MMPI-A Family Problems (A-fam) scale report serious problems with their parents and other family members. Family dis-cord, jealousy, fault-finding, anger, serious disagreements, lack of love and under-standing, and limited communication characterize the families. These adolescents do not seem to feel that they can count on their families in times of trouble. They wish for the day when they are able to leave home. They feel their parents fre-quently punish them without cause and treat them more like children than adults. They report that their parents dislike their peer group. Correlate data indicate that high scores on the A-fam scale are related to disagreements with and between par-ents and to a variety of delinquent and neurotic symptoms and behaviors.

School Problems (A-sch)

High scorers on the MMPI-A School Problems (A-sch) scale report numerous dif-ficulties in school. High scorers report poor grades, suspension, truancy, negative attitudes toward teachers, and dislike of school. The only pleasant aspect of school is being with friends. High scorers say that they do not participate in school activi-ties, and they feel that school is a waste of time. They report frequent boredom and sleepiness at school, and they have been told that they are lazy. Some high scorers may report being afraid to go to school. Correlate data indicate that high scores on the A-sch scale are indicative of both academic and behavioral problems at school. The scale may also be a measure of general maladjustment.

Negative Treatment Indicators (A-trt)

High scorers on the MMPI-A Negative Treatment Indicators (A-trt) scale may report negative attitudes toward doctors and health professionals. They do not believe that others are capable of understanding their problems and difficulties and do not care what happens to them. They are unwilling to take charge and face their problems and difficulties and do not assume responsibility for the negative events in their lives. They do not feel that they can plan their own futures. They report having some faults and bad habits that they feel are insurmountable. They report great unwillingness to discuss their problems with others and indicate that there are some issues that they would never be able to share with anyone. They report feeling nervous when others ask them personal questions and have secrets best kept to themselves. Treatment outcome studies with adolescents are needed to establish the external validity of the A-trt scale. Correlate data do not indicate that the scale is simply a measure of general maladjustment.

INTERPRETING CONTENT COMPONENT SCALES

Sherwood et al. (1997) developed Component scales for some of the MMPI-A Content scales. They offered some evidence that the Component scales can be helpful in understanding which Content scale correlates should be emphasized in particular cases. They suggested that the Component scales be interpreted only when the parent Content scale T score is between 60 and 75 and a component scale T score is greater than 65. The assumption is that for Content scale T scores greater than 75 a wide array of symptoms and problems is likely to apply. Although Sherwood et al. did not specify that there should be at least a 10 T-score point difference between component scales before interpreting them, this recommendation, which was made for the MMPI-2 Content Component scales, would seem to be appropriate for the MMPI-A scales as well.

McCarthy and Archer (1998) reported that for nine of the MMPI-A Content scales, factor analyses yielded only a single factor. For the remaining Content scales, two or three factors were identified. These results are only partially consistent with those of Sherwood et al. (1997). Obviously, more research is needed to better understand the dimensionality of these Content scales.

INTERPRETING PERSONALITY PSYCHOPATHOLOGY FIVE (PSY-5) SCALES

Raw scores for each of the PSY-5 scales are converted to Uniform T scores. T scores equal to or greater than 65 are considered to be high scores. As with other MMPI-A scale scores, interpretations can be made for T scores between 60 and 65. However, greater confidence should be placed on T scores of 65 or higher.

Aggressiveness (AGGR)

Adolescents with high scores on the AGGR scale typically engage in a variety of externalizing behaviors. They may have histories of difficulties with the law. Drug use and sexual acting out are common among high scorers. High scorers also are seen by others as angry and aggressive.

Psychoticism (PSYC)

High scores on the PSYC scale are associated with bizarre and possibly psychotic behaviors, including hallucinations. High scorers may also experience anxiety, obsessive thinking, and somatic symptoms.

Disconstraint (DISC)

High scorers on the DISC scale are characterized by a variety of externalizing behaviors. They may abuse alcohol and other drugs, get into trouble at school and with the law, and act out in sexual ways.

Negative Emotionality/Neuroticism (NEGE)

High scores on the NEGE scale are associated with a variety of internalizing symptoms and behaviors. High scorers report feeling anxious and tense. They are self-critical and feel guilty about perceived shortcoming and failures. They also report feeling sad or blue and seem to lack energy for activities of daily life.

Introversion/Low Positive Emotionality (INTR)

High scores on the INTR scale are associated with internalizing disorders. High scorers report feeling anxious and depressed. They tend to be socially introverted and deficient in the ability to experience joy and other positive emotions.

INTERPRETING MMPI-A CRITICAL ITEMS

The use of critical items in interpreting the MMPI-2 was discussed in Chapter 6 of this book. Although previous critical item sets were developed for adults, there has been some speculation that they could also be used with adolescents. Archer and Jacobson (1993) examined endorsement frequencies of the Koss-Butcher and Lachar-Wrobel critical items for the MMPI-2 normative sample, for the MMPI-A normative sample, and for a sample of adolescents receiving mental health services. As expected, they found that nonclinical adolescents endorsed critical items much more frequently than nonclinical adults and that there were not many differences in endorsement frequencies between normal and clinical adolescents. They interpreted these data as indicating that the Koss-Butcher and Lachar-Wrobel critical item lists would probably have little utility with adolescents and that it would be very difficult to develop a critical items list specifically for the MMPI-A.

Forbey and Ben-Porath (1998) used a combined empirical-rational strategy to develop a critical item set for the MMPI-A. They compared endorsement frequencies for the MMPI-A normative sample and several adolescent clinical samples and identified a set of items infrequently endorsed in the scored direction by the normative adolescents and frequently endorsed by the clinical adolescents. They then examined each item in the list and retained only those whose content was judged to be of critical significance. The resulting critical item list includes 82 items that were rationally grouped into 15 categories: Aggression, Anxiety, Cognitive Problems, Conduct Problems, Depression/Suicidal Ideation, Eating Problems, Family Problems, Hallucinatory Experiences, Paranoid Ideation, School Problems, Self-Denigration, Sexual Concerns, Somatic Complaints, Substance Use/Abuse, and Unusual Thinking.

Forbey and Ben-Porath (1998) concluded that their critical items "represent those developmentally appropriate adolescent concerns that, due to their critical nature, should be brought to a clinician's immediate attention." They indicated that examination of the critical items can provide important information about the nature and severity of problems that an adolescent has reported. However, they cautioned that an adolescent's responses to single test items should not be taken at face value as psychometrically sound indicators of psychopathology or maladjustment. The critical items endorsed by a test taker are listed in the MMPI-A computerized reports available from Pearson Assessments.

MMPI-A INTERPRETIVE STRATEGY

The MMPI-2 interpretive strategy, which was presented in Chapter 10 of this book, can also be applied to the MMPI-A, although modifications must be made to take into account the special life circumstances of adolescents. Archer, Krishnamurthy, and Jacobson (1994) and Ben-Porath and Davis (1996) have published books of case studies illustrating MMPI-A interpretation.

Butcher and Williams (1992) suggested that the following questions should be addressed in interpreting MMPI-A results:

1. Are there extratest factors that can explain the MMPI-A results?
2. What are the individual's response attitudes?
3. What are the individual's reported symptoms and behaviors? What is the likelihood of acting-out behaviors? If present, are the acting-out problems likely to be seen across settings or in specific settings? How severe is the acting out likely to be?
4. Do problems in school play a significant role in the adolescent's clinical picture? What, if any, are they likely to be?
5. Does the adolescent admit to having a problem with alcohol or other drugs? Does he or she have the potential for developing such a problem?
6. What are the individual's interpersonal relationships like? Are there negative peer group influences? Are family problems significant? How does he or she respond to authority? Are alienation, cynicism, and isolation important factors?
7. Does the MMPI-A suggest a need for evaluation of possible physical and/or sexual abuse?
8. What strengths or assets are apparent in the individual?
9. What are the diagnostic implications of the MMPI-A results?
10. What treatment implications or recommendations are suggested on the basis of the MMPI-A results?

Information concerning these questions comes from examination of the individual Validity, Clinical, Supplementary, Content, Content Component, and PSY-5 scales. As suggested earlier in this chapter, T scores of 60 or greater on these scales should be considered interpretable. Greater confidence should be placed in inferences based on scales with T scores equal to or greater than 65. Because of limited information concerning the meaning of low scores on the MMPI-A, below-average scores should not be interpreted except as indicating that test takers did not admit to the problems and symptoms associated with higher scores on those scales. We cannot know if the low scorers do not have the problems and symptoms associated with high scores, are consciously denying them, or simply are not aware of them.

Sometimes the inferences based on high scores on individual scales will appear to be inconsistent, and it will be necessary to reconcile these apparent inconsistencies. The same approach recommended in Chapter 10 of this book for the MMPI-2 is appropriate for the MMPI-A. First, consider the possibility that the apparently inconsistent inferences accurately reflect different facets of the adolescent's personality and behavior. If it seems that some of the inferences are indeed inconsistent, a decision must be made concerning which inferences should be emphasized in the interpretation. In general, greater emphasis should be placed on inferences based on higher scores. Also, because the standard Validity and Clinical scales have been more thoroughly researched, greater emphasis should be placed on inferences based on these scales than on inferences based on other substantive scales. As with the MMPI-2, sometimes inferences are not based directly on scores from the MMPI-A scales. Rather, it is necessary to make higher-order inferences about adolescents based on an overall understanding of that person. Such higher-order inferences are quite acceptable, but the test interpreter should acknowledge that they do not come directly from the MMPI-A scales.

The use of code type interpretation with the MMPI-A has been quite controversial. Although the early work of Marks et al. (1974) suggested that MMPI code types of adolescents could be used to make inferences about them, later research offered only limited support for the use of code types with adolescents (Ehrenworth & Archer, 1985; Williams & Butcher, 1989a). Using a methodology similar to that of Ehrenworth and Archer, Janus et al. (1996) found that code-type descriptions based on MMPI-A norms were slightly more accurate than code type descriptions in the study of Ehrenworth and Archer.

Although research to address the extratest correlates of code types based on MMPI-A scales and norms is lacking, Archer (2005) made a convincing argument that the congruence of Clinical scales of the MMPI and MMPI-A justifies using code-type descriptors based on MMPI research with adults and adolescents to generate inferences based on MMPI-A code types. Drawing on such descriptors, he provided inferences for 29 of the most frequently occurring code types among adolescents. Consideration of all of these code types is beyond the scope of this chapter. Clinicians who want to use MMPI-A code types as sources of inferences should consult Archer's (2005) book. As discussed in Chapter 5 of this book, one should have more confidence on inferences based on code types that are defined and elevated.

Extratest Factors

Several factors external to the MMPI-A may affect test performance and need to be taken into account in interpreting test results. Gender is an important variable; research has indicated that somewhat different descriptors are appropriate for boys and girls who have high scores on some MMPI-A scales (Butcher et al., 1992; Williams & Butcher, 1989a; Wrobel & Lachar, 1992). Reading ability is also an important factor to be considered. The MMPI-A requires approximately a seventh-grade reading ability. Limited education, English as a second language, or other factors that affect reading ability should be taken into account. When such factors are present, special attention should be given to the Validity scales. Circumstances of the testing may also be important. An adolescent who is forced into the testing situation by parents or teachers may respond differently from one who takes the test because she or he is acknowledging problems and seeking help. Finally, extraordinary life circumstances that could affect test results should be considered. For example, having recently experienced a catastrophic event, such as sexual assault or the death of a parent, could lead to extreme responding on the MMPI-A, which would not reflect typical functioning of the adolescent.

Response Attitudes

Before generating inferences concerning the adolescent's symptoms, personality, and behavior, it is necessary to consider response attitudes. Are there indications that the adolescent approached the test in a manner that invalidates the results? Are there response attitudes that are not extreme enough to invalidate the results but that should be taken into account in interpreting the results? The standard Validity scales of the MMPI-A should be consulted in trying to answer these questions.

MMPI-A results should be considered invalid and uninterruptible if more than 30 items are omitted, if the VRIN T score is 75 or higher, or if the TRIN T score is 75 or higher (in either the true or false direction). T scores equal to or greater than 75 on the L or K scales suggest that the test taker approached the test in a defensive, denying manner and that the scores on the other scales probably underrepresent problems and symptoms. Scores equal to or greater than 65 on the F, Fl, or F2 scales suggest the possibility of problematic responding. In such cases the VRIN and TRIN scores should be consulted to rule out the possibility of random responding or a true or false response bias. If these possibilities are ruled out, the elevated F scores may be indicating either serious maladjustment or exaggeration of symptoms and problems. Other information, especially the circumstances of the testing, should be considered in determining the most likely reasons for the high F-scale scores. If it seems likely that the adolescent is exaggerating, it should be understood that the scores on the other scales probably overestimate problems and symptoms.

Symptoms and Behaviors

Assuming that it has been concluded that the MMPI-A results are valid and interpretable, the individual Clinical, Supplementary, Content, Content Component, and PSY-5 scale scores can be consulted to generate inferences concerning symptoms and behaviors. Although inferences can be generated from all high scores, several scales and subscales are especially important in relation to particular symptoms and problem behaviors. Inferences also can be made if a two- or three-point code type is present and has been described previously in the literature (see Archer, 2005).

Anxiety

Anxiety and excessive worry are suggested by high scores on Scale 7, on the Anxiety (A-anx) and Obsessiveness (A-obs) Content scales, and on the Anxiety (A) Supplementary scale. High scorers on Scale 2, on the Depression (A-dep) Content scale, and on the PSY-5 NEGE scale often report symptoms of anxiety.

Depression

High scores on Scale 2 and the Depression (A-dep) Content scale are the major indicators of depression and possibly suicidal ideation, particularly in clinical settings. However, high scores on scales 3, 7, and 0; on the Low Self-Esteem (A-lse), Obsessiveness (A-obs), Social Discomfort (A-sod), and Anxiety (A-anx) Content scales; and on the Sc2 (Emotional Alienation) and Sc4 (Lack of Ego Mastery, Conative) Harris–Lingoes subscales also can be suggestive of depression and/or suicidal ideation. Finally, high scorers on the INTR PSY-5 scale often report symptoms of depression. Because the Suicidal Ideation Content Component Scale is made up of items dealing directly with suicidal ideas and intention, any raw score greater than zero should taken very seriously.

Somatic Concerns

High scores on Scale 1 and on the Health Concerns (A-hea) Content scale are the clearest indicators of somatic symptoms. However, high scores on Scales 2, 3, and 8 and on the Anxiety (A-anx) Content scale also can be indicative of somatic symptoms. Eating problems in girls have been associated with high scores on Scales 1 and 2 and on the Social Discomfort (A-sod) Content scale. Sleep difficulties are suggested by high scores on Scale 3, on the Obsessiveness (A-obs) and Anxiety (A-anx) Content scales, and on the D1 (Subjective Depression) Harris–Lingoes subscale.

Psychotic Symptoms

High scores on Scale 8, on the Bizarre Mentation (A-biz) Content scale, and on the PSY-5 Psychoticism (PSYC) scale indicate the possibility of psychotic behaviors, including delusions, hallucinations, ideas of reference, or disorganized thinking. High scores on the Pa1 (Persecutory Ideas), Sc3 (Lack of Ego Mastery, Cognitive), and Sc6 (Bizarre Sensory Experiences) Harris–Lingoes subscales are additional indicators of psychosis.

Poor Self-Esteem

High scores on the Low Self-Esteem (A-lse) Content scale suggest problems with self-confidence. High scores on several Clinical scales (1, 2, 7, 8, 0) also tend to be associated with lack of self-confidence. High scores on Scale 9 are indicative of positive self-perceptions that may at times be somewhat grandiose.

Anger

High scores on Scales 4 and 9 and on the Aggressiveness (AGGR) PSY-5 scale are suggestive of anger and resentment. High scores on the Anger (A-ang) and Conduct Problems (A-con) Content scales indicate problems with anger control.

Acting-Out Behaviors

Delinquent and acting-out behaviors are suggested by high scores on several scales and subscales. The best indicators of such behavior are high scores on Scales 4 and 9, on the Conduct Problems (A-con) Content scale, and on the PSY-5 Disconstraint (DISC) scale. High scores on Scale 2 tend to contraindicate acting-out behavior. Some data indicate that girls who have higher T scores on Scale 5 tend to act out in various ways, whereas boys with higher T scores on Scale 5 tend not to act out.

Girls with high scores on the Social Discomfort (A-sod) Content scale tend not to act out. Acting out also is characteristic of adolescents who have high scores on the Anger (A-ang) and Low Aspirations (A-las) Content scales and on the Pd2 (Authority Problems) and Ma1 (Amorality) Harris–Lingoes subscales.

School Problems

The School Problems (A-sch) Content scale was developed specifically to assess academic and behavioral problems in school. In addition, academic problems are suggested by high scores on Scales 1, 2, 4, 5 (girls), 6, and 8 and on the Health Concerns (A-hea), Bizarre Mentation (A-biz), Low Self-Esteem (A-lse), and Low Aspirations (A-las) Content scales. Behavioral problems in school are suggested by high scores on Scales 4, 5 (girls), 6, 8, and 9; on the Health Concerns (A-hea) and Bizarre Mentation (A-biz) Content scales; and on the PSY-5 DISC scale. The relationship between school problems and so many MMPI-A scales seems to indicate that adolescents develop school problems for a variety of reasons and that school problems can contribute to a variety of symptoms.

Alcohol/Drug Problems

Adolescents who have moderate (T = 60–64) or high (T ≥ 65) scores on the Alcohol/Drug Problem Acknowledgment (ACK) scale are openly admitting to the use of alcohol and/or drugs and the problems associated with such use. However, the absence of high scores on ACK is difficult to interpret. Because of the obvious content of most items in this scale, the absence of high scores could indicate either that substance abuse problems are not present or that they are present and are being deliberately denied. Moderate (T = 60–64) or high (T ≥ 65) scores on the MacAndrew Alcoholism Scale–Revised (MAC-R) and the Alcohol/Drug Problem Proneness (PRO) scale suggest problems with alcohol and/or drugs whether or not the adolescents are acknowledging such problems. The likelihood of abuse is greatest if an adolescent has high scores on all three of these scales. Other indicators of possible alcohol or other drug problems include high scores on Scales 4, 8, and 9 and on the Disconstraint (DISC) PSY-5 scale. High scores on Scale 2 tend not to be associated with substance abuse. As with the MMPI-2, one should not conclude from MMPI-A data that an adolescent is a substance abuser. However, high scores on the scales mentioned here should alert the clinician to the possibility of substance abuse problems that should be evaluated more completely.

Interpersonal Relationships

Adolescents who have high scores on Scale 0, on the Social Discomfort (A-sod) Content scale, and on the PSY-5 Introversion/Low Positive Emotionality (INTR) scale are likely to be shy, introverted, and uncomfortable in social situations. High scores on Scales 2 and 7 and on the Si1 (Shyness/Self-Consciousness) subscale further support the impression of shyness and introversion. On the other hand, high scores on the Hy1 (Denial of Social Anxiety) and Pd3 (Social Imperturbability) Harris–Lingoes subscales and on Scale 9 suggest extroversion and gregariousness.

Social withdrawal and isolation are suggested by high scores on Scales 1, 6, and 8; on the Alienation (A-aln) and Social Discomfort (A-sod) Content scales; on the Pd4 (Social Alienation) and Sc1 (Social Alienation) Harris–Lingoes subscales; and on the Si2 (Social Avoidance) subscale. Adolescents who have high scores on Scale 6, on the Cynicism (A-cyn) Content scale, or on the Pa1 (Persecutory Ideas) Harris–Lingoes subscale are likely to be cynical, guarded, and untrusting in relationships. High scores on the Anger (A-ang) Content scale are associated with irritability and lack of anger control.

High scores on Scale 4, the Family Problems (A-fam) Content scale, and the Pd1 (Familial Discord) Harris–Lingoes subscale indicate that adolescents are describing their family circumstances very negatively. They do not see their families as loving or supportive, and they tend to be angry, resentful, and rebellious toward family members. Adolescents who have high scores on the Conduct Problems (A-con) or Low Self-Esteem (A-lse) Content scales or on the Alcohol/Drug Problem Proneness (PRO) scale tend to be influenced easily by peers to become involved in antisocial or delinquent acts.

Physical or Sexual Abuse

It is not possible to determine from test data whether or not an adolescent has been physically or sexually abused. However, some MMPI-A data suggest that adolescents with high scores on certain scales are more likely than other adolescents to have histories of having been abused. High scores on Scale 4 or on the Family Problems (A-fam) Content scale for boys suggest that the possibility of physical abuse be considered carefully. High scores on Scales 8 (boys and girls), 4 (girls), and 7 (boys) suggest that the possibility of sexual abuse should be considered carefully. Histories of sexual abuse may be associated with high scores on the Family Problems (A-fam) Content scale for girls and with high scores on the Depression (A-dep), Anger (A-ang), Low Self-Esteem (A-lse), or School Problems (A-sch) Content scales for boys. It should be emphasized again that high scores on these various scales should not be used to determine if abuse has occurred. Rather, high scores on these scales should alert clinicians to assess the possibility of abuse carefully if this is not already a goal of the assessment.

Strengths and Assets

Although the scales of the MMPI-A were designed to measure problems and symptoms, it is important to try to address strengths and assets when giving feedback to the adolescents, their parents, or school staff. As stated earlier in this chapter, we cannot know if low scores on the MMPI-A scales are indicative of a lack of problems and symptoms or simply denial of them. However, it is appropriate to emphasize in an interpretation that low scores indicate that the adolescents are not reporting the problems and symptoms relevant to the scales; for example, low scorers on Scale 2 are not reporting depression and sadness, low scorers on Scale 4 are not espousing antisocial attitudes, and low scorers on Scale 0 are not describing themselves as shy and introverted. Similarly, low scorers on the Low Aspirations

(A-las) Content scale are indicating that they have interest in achieving, low scorers on the Conduct Problems (A-con) Content scale are claiming that they do not engage in acting-out behaviors, and low scorers on the Family Problems (A-fam) Content scale are denying negative attitudes about their families.

Although the limited empirical data available for MMPI-A scales do not suggest many positive characteristics associated with high scores, research conducted on the original MMPI scales suggests some characteristics of high scorers that could be viewed as positive (Archer, 1987). High scorers on Scale 3 are described as achievement-oriented, socially involved, and friendly. High scorers on Scale 4 tend to be sociable, gregarious persons who create favorable first impressions on other people. High-scoring boys on Scale 5 are seen by others as intelligent and attaining higher levels of academic achievement. High scorers on Scale 7 can be described as conscientious. High scale 8 scorers tend to approach problems in creative ways. High Scale 9 scorers are likely to be energetic, extroverted, and self-confident. High scorers on Scale 0 are less likely to be involved in delinquent activities.

High scores on some of the Harris–Lingoes subscales also suggest some positive characteristics. For example, high scores on Hy1 (Denial of Social Anxiety) or Pd3 (Social Imperturbability) subscales indicate adolescents who say they are comfortable and confident in social situations. High Ma4 (Ego Inflation) scorers tend to have very favorable self-concepts (perhaps unrealistically so at times).

Diagnostic Considerations

Although there is not much research available that directly addresses the most likely diagnoses for adolescents who produce particular scores or patterns of scores on the MMPI or MMPI-A, some inferences can be made on the basis of high scores on certain scales. High scores on Scale 1 and/or the Health Concerns (A-hea) Content scale are consistent with somatoform disorder diagnoses; high scores on Scale 2, on the Depression (A-dep) Content scale, and on the Introversion/Low Positive Emotionality (INTR) PSY-5 scale are consistent with depression or anxiety disorder diagnoses; high scores on Scales 4 and/or 9, on the Conduct Disorders (A-con) Content scale, and on the PSY-5 Disconstraint (DISC) scale often are consistent with conduct disorder diagnoses; high scores on Scale 7, on the Anxiety (A-anx) Content scale, and on the Negative Emotionality/Neuroticism (NEGE) PSY-5 scale are consistent with anxiety disorder diagnoses; high scores on Scale 8, on the Bizarre Mentation (A-biz) Content scale, and on the PSY-5 Psychoticism (PSYC) scale are consistent with the possibility of psychotic disorders; and high scores on one or more of the alcohol/drug problem scales (MAC-R, PRO, ACK) suggest that the possibility of a substance use disorder should be explored carefully.

It should be emphasized that diagnoses cannot and should not be assigned to adolescents solely on the basis of MMPI-A data. The criteria for most diagnostic categories include information that must be obtained from sources other than test data (e.g., observation, interview, history). Often the best approach is to generate a comprehensive description of the adolescent's symptoms, personality, and behavior and compare this description with the various categories described in the most current version of the diagnostic manual.

Treatment Implications

There are very limited empirical data for adolescents concerning relationships between MMPI or MMPI-A scores and treatment-related characteristics. The MMPI-A Negative Treatment Indicators (A-trt) scale was designed to assess characteristics of adolescents that would interfere with effective psychological treatment. High scorers on this scale typically express negative attitudes toward doctors and health professionals, believe that others do not care what happens to them, accept little responsibility for their own behavior, and feel unable and/or unwilling to change. Obviously, characteristics such as these have very negative implications for treatment. However, it must be emphasized that there have not yet been any outcome studies conducted to evaluate the validity of the A-trt scale. In addition, evidence concerning the saturation of the adult version of the A-trt scale with demoralization suggests caution in interpreting high scores on the scale when adolescents are in considerable psychological turmoil.

High scorers on Scales 2 and 7 often are experiencing enough emotional distress that they are motivated to participate in psychotherapy. By contrast, high scorers on Scales 4 and 9 often blame others for their problems, so they are not very motivated to engage in psychotherapy. The prognosis for successful psychological treatment is not very positive for high scorers on Scale 8.

It is often necessary and appropriate to make higher-order inferences concerning treatment-related issues. For example, it is reasonable to infer that an adolescent who admits to a great deal of psychological turmoil (as indicated by high scores on many scales) will be more willing to cooperate in treatment than someone who does not admit to such turmoil, and that an adolescent who produces a very defensive pattern on the Validity scales of the MMPI-A would not be very open and cooperative in a therapeutic relationship. Adolescents whose MMPI-A scores (e.g., Scales 4, 9, A-ang, A-cyn, AGGR, DISC) suggest considerable anger and resentment will be likely to be rather uncooperative in therapy and will often test limits in relationships with therapists.

ILLUSTRATIVE CASE

To illustrate the interpretive strategy just described, the MMPI-A scores of an adolescent girl will be interpreted. The computerized Extended Score Report that is appended to this chapter includes her scores, profiles, and critical item endorsements. It should be understood that the interpretive inferences derived from her MMPI-A scores should be treated as hypotheses to be evaluated on the basis of other information available about her. The MMPI-A results should be only part of a more comprehensive evaluation.

Background and Referral Concerns

Megan was a 15-year-old girl who was referred for psychological evaluation primarily because of problems with concentration and attention. She was an honor roll student in elementary school, but her grades had continued to decline since she was in middle school. In addition to her academic problems, Megan had been displaying increased irritability and anger with adult authority figures. She reported experiencing severe headaches on an almost daily basis.

Megan was a young girl of mixed ethnicity. Her biological father was Caucasian and her biological mother was American Indian. Her parents were divorced when she was two years old. Her mother remarried, and the family lived abroad during her early years because of her stepfather's government employment. She had a younger half-brother. Megan's developmental history was essentially normal and uneventful, although shortly after birth she was placed in a neonatal intensive care unit for a brief time for initial oxygen support.

Because of her report of frequent headaches, Megan was evaluated by a neuropsychologist who included the MMPI-A in the test battery. Her WISC-IV Full Scale IQ score was within an average range, but her processing speed was quite slow. No problems with memory were detected. There were indications of severe impairment in attention and concentration. Preliminary diagnoses were dysthymic disorder and math learning disability. Major depression and ADHD were to be ruled out.

Megan completed the MMPI-A in a cooperative manner. She worked a bit more slowly than the average adolescent of her age, and she asked no questions during the testing.

Extratest Factors

Megan was cooperative throughout the psychological evaluation. She completed the MMPI-A in approximately 90 minutes, asking no questions and making no comments during the testing.

Response Attitudes

Megan completed the MMPI-A in a valid manner. She omitted no items, and her VRIN scale T score of 43 and her TRIN scale T score of 54 indicate that she responded consistently to the items. Her T scores of 43 on the L scale and 37 on the K scale suggest that she was not at all defensive. In fact, these scores indicate that she was less defensive than the average adolescent. Her scores on the F1 (T = 63), F2 (T = 60), and F (T = 61) were somewhat above average but were not high enough to indicate that she was overreporting problems and symptoms. Rather, the scores are likely to reflect problems and symptoms that she was really experiencing. In summary, there is no reason that we cannot interpret the substantive scales with confidence that they will give an accurate picture of her psychological status.

Symptoms

Megan has a defined and elevated three-point code (782), but no descriptive information is available for this code type. She does not have a defined two-point code because the difference between her second most elevated Clinical scale score (Scale 8) is only one T-score point greater than her third highest Clinical scale score (Scale 2). Thus, no code type interpretation is made, and the focus of the interpretation will be on single scales.

Anxiety

Megan appears to be experiencing significant psychological distress. She has T scores greater than 65 on three Clinical scales and six Content scales. Her T score of 78 on Scale 7 suggests anxiety, worry, and problems with concentration and attention. Sometimes elevated Scale 7 scores also indicate obsessiveness, but because her Obsessiveness (A-obs) Content scale is not significantly elevated this is not likely for Megan.

Depression

Elevated scores on Scale 2 (T = 67) and on the Depression Content (A-dep) scale (T = 71) suggest that she is likely to be feeling sad and depressed. She endorsed two items on the Suicidal Ideation (A-dep4) Content Component scale. The content of these items indicates that Megan feels that the future seems hopeless and that she has thought about killing herself. Obviously, this self-report should be taken seriously, and a suicide-risk evaluation should be undertaken.

Somatic Concerns

Megan is not likely to be presenting health-related concerns (T score for Scale 1 = 48; T score for A-hea = 45).

Psychotic Symptoms

Megan's T score of 68 on Scale 8 raises some initial concerns about psychotic symptoms. However, T scores of 48 on the Bizarre Mentation (A-biz) Content scale and 58 on the Psychoticism (PSYC) PSY-5 scale are not consistent with psychotic symptoms. Examination of the Harris–Lingoes subscales suggests that Scale 8 is elevated primarily because of feelings of alienation (Sc1, Sc2) and hopelessness (Sc4). She did not endorse any of the clearly psychotic critical items.

Poor Self-Esteem

Megan's T score of 73 on the Low Self-Esteem (A-lse) Content scale indicates that she is likely to have a very negative self-concept, often feeling like a failure and comparing herself unfavorably with other people. Additional evidence of low self-esteem comes from elevated scores on Scales 2, 7, and 8.

Anger

Megan does not have elevated scores on several primary indicators of anger [Scales 4 and 9; Aggressiveness (AGGR) PSY-5 scale]. However, her T score of 67 on the Anger (A-ang) Content scale suggests that she may harbor feelings of anger toward others. Given the elevated score on the Family Problems (A-fam) Content scale (T = 73), her parents may be a primary target of her anger. The absence of elevations on Scales 4 and 9, the Conduct Problems (A-con) Content scale, and the Aggressiveness (AGGR) PSY-5 scale suggest that her anger is not likely to be expressed in direct, uncontrolled ways.

Acting-Out Behaviors

There are no strong indicators of acting-out behaviors in Megan's MMPI-A scores. Scores on the primary indicators of acting out [Scales 4 and 9, Conduct Problems (A-con) Content scale, Disconstraint (DISC) scale] are all within normal limits.

School Problems

Megan's moderately elevated score (T = 63) on the School Problems (A-sch) Content scales suggests that she may have difficulties in school. She endorsed several critical items suggesting that she has misbehaved in class and has been sent to the principal's office because of misbehavior. Her T score of 61 on the Low Aspirations (A-las) Content scale indicates that she probably is not very interested in learning and achievement.

Alcohol/Drug Problems

Data concerning substance abuse problems are mixed. Megan's T score of 56 on the Alcohol/Drug Problem Acknowledgment (ACK) scale indicates that she is not admitting use or misuse of substances. Examination of critical item responses indicates no admission of substance use or abuse. The T score of 51 on the MacAndrew Alcoholism Scale–Revised (MAC-R) is not consistent with substance abuse problems. However, the T score of 67 on the Alcohol/Drug Problem Proneness (PRO) scale raises some concern about substance abuse problems. It should be recognized that this scale does not include items dealing directly with substance use or abuse and its items cover a wide array of content, including family and school problems, antisocial behaviors and beliefs, and peer group influence.

Interpersonal Relationships

Megan does not seem to be a particularly outgoing, gregarious young woman (Scale 4, T = 59; Scale 9, T = 52). Her above average scores on Scale 0 (T = 59) and on the Social Discomfort (A-sod) Content scale (T = 55) suggest that she is likely to be somewhat shy and uncomfortable in social situations. Elevated scores on Scales 2 (T = 67) and 7 (T = 78) also suggest some social discomfort and raise the possibility that she tends to be rather passive and dependent in most relationships. The exception may be with family members (A-fam, T = 73), who are seen as not being very understanding or supportive.

Physical or Sexual Abuse

There is no indication in Megan's scores or item endorsements to suggest that she has been sexually or physically abused. It was noted that she endorsed a critical item suggesting that she has been in trouble because of her sexual behavior.

Strengths

The MMPI-A is a problem and psychopathology oriented instrument, and not much information is available about positive characteristics associated with its scales. However, several inferences are possible based on Megan's scores. Her high scores on Scales 2 (T = 67) and 7 (T = 78) suggest that in many ways she may be a responsible and reliable person and that she is likely to have the capacity for developing intimate relationships. One could also discuss the things that her scores suggest that she is not. She is not likely to have psychotic symptoms and probably does not have a serious substance abuse problem.

Diagnostic Considerations

Megan's MMPI-A scores are consistent with several diagnoses. Her high scores on Scale 7 (T = 78), on the Anxiety Content (A-anx) scale (T = 69), and on the Negative Emotionality/Neuroticism (NEGE) scale (T = 74) are consistent with an anxiety disorder diagnosis. Her high scores on Scales 2 (T = 67) and the Depression (A-dep) Content scale (T = 71) are consistent with diagnoses of depression or dysthymia. Although she is not acknowledging problems with alcohol or other substances and probably does not have a diagnosable substance disorder, her rather high score on the Alcohol/Drug Problem Proneness (PRO) scale (T = 67) suggests that such diagnoses be ruled out.

Treatment Implications

Megan's deteriorating academic performance and the considerable emotional turmoil that she is experiencing (Scale 2, T = 67; Scale 7, T = 78; A-dep, T = 71; A-anx, T = 69; NEGE, T = 74) indicate that she could benefit from psychological treatment and that she would be willing to engage in such treatment. Her willingness to admit to problems and symptoms while completing the MMPI-A (F1, T = 63; F2, T = 60; F, T = 61) and her lack of defensiveness (L, T = 43; K, T = 37) suggest that she will be willing to discuss problems during therapy. In therapy she is likely to be somewhat passive (Scale 2, T = 67; Scale 7, T = 78). She may feel incapable of dealing with her problems and of making positive changes (A-trt, T = 78).

A primary goal for therapy should be reduction of her psychological distress. Because she admitted to feeling hopeless and to having considered killing herself (A-dep4, T = 60; Critical Items #177 and #399), a detailed suicide risk assessment is in order. Additional issues to be addressed in therapy are her low self-esteem (A-lse, T = 73) and her anger (A-ang, T = 67). Because it seems that her anger probably involves her parents (A-fam, T = 73), consideration should be given to involving them in a treatment plan. Megan is not expressing much interest in learning and achievement (A-las, T = 61), so it would be important to find something that interests her and to encourage her increased involvement in that area. Because she seems to view others, particularly authority figures, as not being very supportive and understanding (A-fam, T = 73; A-trt, T = 78), it would be important for a therapist to communicate to Megan that she is understood.

Summary

Megan approached the MMPI-A in a valid manner, acknowledging problems and symptoms. She is in a great deal of emotional turmoil, feeling depressed, anxious, and overwhelmed. She feels quite hopeless about the future and has considered killing herself. She has very low self-esteem and often compares herself unfavorably with other people. She sees other people, especially parents and other authority figures, as not understanding and supportive. These perceptions lead to feelings of anger, resentment, and at times rebellion.

The diagnoses that are most consistent with her MMPI-A scores are anxiety disorder and depressive disorder or dysthymia. It is not likely that she has a serious substance abuse problem, but her responses to some items also endorsed by adolescent substance abusers suggest that a substance disorder be ruled out.

Megan's deteriorating school performance and her emotional distress indicate that she needs psychological intervention. She is likely to be somewhat ambivalent about treatment, feeling the need for help with her distress but believing that she will not be able to make significant positive changes. A primary goal for therapy is reduction of her psychological turmoil. Because of her admitted thoughts about killing herself, suicide risk and monitoring should be part of treatment. She can also use help in developing a more positive self-concept.

Information from assessment data other than the MMPI-A also have implications for treatment. Because of her complaints of almost daily headaches, a referral for a neurological examination should be considered. The problems with concentration and attention and other learning-related problems suggest that a treatment program should also involve development of strategies to help her cope with deficits in skills and abilities associated with effective learning.

CHAPTER APPENDIX

Minnesota Multiphasic Personality Inventory— ADOLESCENT™

MMPI-A™

Minnesota Multiphasic Personality Inventory-Adolescent™

Extended Score Report

ID Number: 123456789
Age: 15
Gender: Female
Date Assessed: 10/11/2010

PEARSON

🟡 PsychCorp

Copyright © 1992, 2006 by the Regents of the University of Minnesota. All rights reserved.
Portions reproduced from the MMPI-A test booklet. Copyright © 1942, 1943 (renewed 1970), 1992 by the Regents of the University of Minnesota. All rights reserved. Portions excerpted from the *MMPI-A Manual for Administration, Scoring, and Interpretation.* Copyright © 1992 by the Regents of the University of Minnesota. All rights reserved. Portions excerpted from the *Supplement to the MMPI-A Manual for Administration, Scoring, and Interpretation: The Content Component Scales, The Personality Psychopathology Five (PSY-5) Scales, The Critical Items.* Copyright © 2006 by the Regents of the University of Minnesota. All rights reserved. Distributed exclusively under license from the University of Minnesota by NCS Pearson, Inc.

Minnesota Multiphasic Personality Inventory-Adolescent and **MMPI-A** are trademarks of the University of Minnesota. **Pearson, the PSI logo,** and **PsychCorp** are trademarks in the U.S. and/or other countries of Pearson Education, Inc., or its affiliate(s).

TRADE SECRET INFORMATION
Not for release under HIPAA or other data disclosure laws that exempt trade secrets from disclosure.

[3.8 / 1 / 2.5.7]

Reproduced by permission of the University of Minnesota Press. All rights reserved. "Minnesota Multiphasic Personality Inventory® -Adolescent" and MMPI® -A" are trademarks owned by the University of Minnesota.

MMPI-A VALIDITY AND CLINICAL SCALES PROFILE

	VR	TR	F₁	F₂	F	L	K	Hs	D	Hy	Pd	Mf	Pa	Pt	Sc	Ma	Si
Raw Score:	2	10	7	9	16	1	6	8	30	23	26	27	16	39	40	24	34
T Score:	43	54	63	60	61	43	37	48	67	49	59	53	56	78	68	52	59
Response %:	100	100	100	100	100	100	100	100	100	100	100	100	100	100	100	100	100

Cannot Say (Raw): 0

Percent True: 55

Percent False: 45

Welsh Code: 7'82+-40659/31: F-/L:K#

509

MMPI-A CONTENT SCALES PROFILE

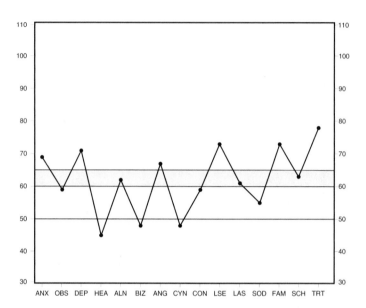

	ANX	OBS	DEP	HEA	ALN	BIZ	ANG	CYN	CON	LSE	LAS	SOD	FAM	SCH	TRT
Raw Score:	16	11	19	6	10	3	13	13	12	13	9	10	23	10	19
T Score:	69	59	71	45	62	48	67	48	59	73	61	55	73	63	78
Response %:	100	100	100	100	100	100	100	100	100	100	100	100	100	100	100

MMPI-A SUPPLEMENTARY SCALES PROFILE

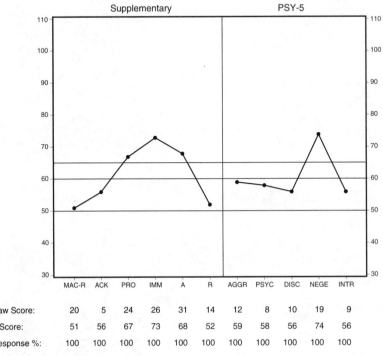

	MAC-R	ACK	PRO	IMM	A	R	AGGR	PSYC	DISC	NEGE	INTR
Raw Score:	20	5	24	26	31	14	12	8	10	19	9
T Score:	51	56	67	73	68	52	59	58	56	74	56
Response %:	100	100	100	100	100	100	100	100	100	100	100

ADDITIONAL SCALES

	Raw Score	T Score	Resp %
Harris-Lingoes Subscales			
Depression Subscales			
Subjective Depression (D_1)	17	65	100
Psychomotor Retardation (D_2)	7	62	100
Physical Malfunctioning (D_3)	5	58	100
Mental Dullness (D_4)	9	70	100
Brooding (D_5)	6	60	100
Hysteria Subscales			
Denial of Social Anxiety (Hy_1)	1	37	100
Need for Affection (Hy_2)	3	42	100
Lassitude-Malaise (Hy_3)	10	69	100
Somatic Complaints (Hy_4)	4	47	100
Inhibition of Aggression (Hy_5)	4	58	100
Psychopathic Deviate Subscales			
Familial Discord (Pd_1)	4	51	100
Authority Problems (Pd_2)	4	59	100
Social Imperturbability (Pd_3)	2	43	100
Social Alienation (Pd_4)	9	66	100
Self-Alienation (Pd_5)	8	63	100
Paranoia Subscales			
Persecutory Ideas (Pa_1)	8	64	100
Poignancy (Pa_2)	5	57	100
Naivete (Pa_3)	3	46	100
Schizophrenia Subscales			
Social Alienation (Sc_1)	13	70	100
Emotional Alienation (Sc_2)	6	70	100
Lack of Ego Mastery, Cognitive (Sc_3)	7	67	100
Lack of Ego Mastery, Conative (Sc_4)	10	71	100
Lack of Ego Mastery, Defective Inhibition (Sc_5)	8	68	100
Bizarre Sensory Experiences (Sc_6)	4	46	100
Hypomania Subscales			
Amorality (Ma_1)	3	55	100
Psychomotor Acceleration (Ma_2)	6	44	100
Imperturbability (Ma_3)	2	44	100
Ego Inflation (Ma_4)	5	52	100

	Raw Score	T Score	Resp %
Social Introversion Subscales (Ben-Porath, Hostetler, Butcher, & Graham)			
Shyness/Self-Consciousness (Si_1)	8	55	100
Social Avoidance (Si_2)	1	45	100
Alienation--Self and Others (Si_3)	13	63	100
Content Component Scales (Sherwood, Ben-Porath, & Williams)			
Adolescent Depression			
Dysphoria (A-dep$_1$)	4	64	100
Self-Depreciation (A-dep$_2$)	5	68	100
Lack of Drive (A-dep$_3$)	5	65	100
Suicidal Ideation (A-dep$_4$)	2	60	100
Adolescent Health Concerns			
Gastrointestinal Complaints (A-hea$_1$)	0	44	100
Neurological Symptoms (A-hea$_2$)	2	42	100
General Health Concerns (A-hea$_3$)	2	50	100
Adolescent Alienation			
Misunderstood (A-aln$_1$)	5	69	100
Social Isolation (A-aln$_2$)	2	54	100
Interpersonal Skepticism (A-aln$_3$)	3	65	100
Adolescent Bizarre Mentation			
Psychotic Symptomatology (A-biz$_1$)	3	51	100
Paranoid Ideation (A-biz$_2$)	0	43	100
Adolescent Anger			
Explosive Behavior (A-ang$_1$)	5	62	100
Irritability (A-ang$_2$)	7	60	100
Adolescent Cynicism			
Misanthropic Beliefs (A-cyn$_1$)	10	58	100
Interpersonal Suspiciousness (A-cyn$_2$)	3	43	100
Adolescent Conduct Problems			
Acting-Out Behaviors (A-con$_1$)	7	69	100
Antisocial Attitudes (A-con$_2$)	5	61	100
Negative Peer Group Influences (A-con$_3$)	0	42	100
Adolescent Low Self-Esteem			
Self-Doubt (A-lse$_1$)	10	73	100
Interpersonal Submissiveness (A-lse$_2$)	3	59	100

	Raw Score	T Score	Resp %
Adolescent Low Aspirations			
Low Achievement Orientation (A-las$_1$)	4	52	100
Lack of Initiative (A-las$_2$)	4	60	100
Adolescent Social Discomfort			
Introversion (A-sod$_1$)	2	46	100
Shyness (A-sod$_2$)	8	67	100
Adolescent Family Problems			
Familial Discord (A-fam$_1$)	15	66	100
Familial Alienation (A-fam$_2$)	5	63	100
Adolescent School Problems			
School Conduct Problems (A-sch$_1$)	2	65	100
Negative Attitudes (A-sch$_2$)	4	59	100
Adolescent Negative Treatment Indicators			
Low Motivation (A-trt$_1$)	6	62	100
Inability to Disclose (A-trt$_2$)	8	77	100

Uniform T scores are used for Hs, D, Hy, Pd, Pa, Pt, Sc, Ma, the content scales, the content component scales, and the PSY-5 scales. The remaining scales and subscales use linear T scores.

CRITICAL ITEMS (Forbey & Ben-Porath)

The MMPI-A contains a number of items whose content may indicate the presence of psychological problems when endorsed in the deviant direction. These "critical items," developed for use in clinical settings, may provide an additional source of hypotheses about the respondent. However, caution should be used in interpreting critical items since responses to single items are very unreliable and should not be treated as scores on full-length scales -- for example, an individual could easily mismark or misunderstand a single item and not intend the answer given. The content of the items and the possibility of misinterpretation make it important to keep the test results strictly confidential. Special caution should be exercised when interpreting these items in nonclinical settings.

Aggression
303.
453.

Anxiety
173.
297.
309.
353.

Cognitive Problems
158.
288.

Conduct Problems
354.

Depression/Suicidal Ideation
  62.
177.
399.

Family Problems
365.
366.

Paranoid Ideation
  95.

School Problems
101.
389.

Self-Denigration
219.

Sexual Concerns
31.
59.

Somatic Complaints
138.
175.

Substance Use/Abuse
161.

431.

End of Report

NOTE: This and previous pages of this report contain trade secrets and are not to be released in response to requests under HIPAA (or any other data disclosure law that exempts trade secret information from release). Further, release in response to litigation discovery demands should be made only in accordance with your profession's ethical guidelines and under an appropriate protective order.

ITEM RESPONSES

```
  1: 2    2: 1    3: 2    4: 2    5: 2    6: 2    7: 2    8: 2    9: 2   10: 2
 11: 2   12: 1   13: 1   14: 2   15: 1   16: 2   17: 2   18: 1   19: 1   20: 1
 21: 1   22: 2   23: 1   24: 1   25: 2   26: 1   27: 2   28: 1   29: 1   30: 2
 31: 2   32: 1   33: 2   34: 1   35: 1   36: 2   37: 2   38: 1   39: 1   40: 2
 41: 2   42: 2   43: 1   44: 1   45: 1   46: 1   47: 2   48: 1   49: 1   50: 2
 51: 2   52: 1   53: 1   54: 1   55: 1   56: 2   57: 2   58: 2   59: 2   60: 2
 61: 1   62: 1   63: 2   64: 2   65: 2   66: 2   67: 2   68: 2   69: 2   70: 1
 71: 1   72: 1   73: 1   74: 1   75: 2   76: 2   77: 1   78: 2   79: 2   80: 2
 81: 1   82: 1   83: 2   84: 2   85: 1   86: 2   87: 1   88: 2   89: 1   90: 2
 91: 1   92: 2   93: 2   94: 1   95: 1   96: 1   97: 2   98: 1   99: 2  100: 1
101: 1  102: 1  103: 1  104: 1  105: 2  106: 2  107: 1  108: 2  109: 1  110: 2
111: 1  112: 1  113: 1  114: 2  115: 2  116: 1  117: 1  118: 2  119: 2  120: 1
121: 1  122: 1  123: 1  124: 1  125: 1  126: 2  127: 2  128: 2  129: 2  130: 1
131: 2  132: 2  133: 1  134: 2  135: 1  136: 2  137: 1  138: 2  139: 1  140: 1
141: 2  142: 2  143: 2  144: 2  145: 1  146: 2  147: 2  148: 1  149: 2  150: 2
151: 1  152: 1  153: 1  154: 1  155: 1  156: 1  157: 1  158: 2  159: 2  160: 1
161: 1  162: 1  163: 2  164: 1  165: 2  166: 1  167: 2  168: 2  169: 1  170: 2
171: 2  172: 1  173: 1  174: 1  175: 1  176: 1  177: 1  178: 1  179: 1  180: 2
181: 1  182: 1  183: 1  184: 2  185: 1  186: 2  187: 2  188: 1  189: 1  190: 2
191: 2  192: 1  193: 2  194: 1  195: 2  196: 2  197: 2  198: 1  199: 2  200: 2
201: 2  202: 1  203: 2  204: 1  205: 1  206: 2  207: 2  208: 1  209: 1  210: 1
211: 1  212: 1  213: 1  214: 2  215: 2  216: 2  217: 1  218: 1  219: 1  220: 1
221: 2  222: 2  223: 2  224: 2  225: 1  226: 1  227: 2  228: 1  229: 2  230: 2
231: 2  232: 2  233: 2  234: 1  235: 1  236: 2  237: 2  238: 2  239: 1  240: 1
241: 2  242: 2  243: 1  244: 2  245: 1  246: 1  247: 2  248: 1  249: 1  250: 2
251: 2  252: 2  253: 1  254: 2  255: 1  256: 1  257: 2  258: 1  259: 1  260: 2
261: 2  262: 1  263: 1  264: 2  265: 1  266: 1  267: 2  268: 2  269: 1  270: 1
271: 1  272: 1  273: 2  274: 2  275: 1  276: 2  277: 1  278: 2  279: 1  280: 1
281: 1  282: 2  283: 2  284: 1  285: 1  286: 1  287: 2  288: 1  289: 1  290: 1
291: 2  292: 1  293: 2  294: 1  295: 2  296: 1  297: 1  298: 1  299: 2  300: 2
301: 2  302: 1  303: 1  304: 2  305: 1  306: 1  307: 1  308: 1  309: 1  310: 2
311: 1  312: 2  313: 1  314: 2  315: 2  316: 1  317: 1  318: 1  319: 1  320: 1
321: 2  322: 1  323: 2  324: 1  325: 2  326: 1  327: 1  328: 2  329: 2  330: 1
331: 1  332: 2  333: 2  334: 2  335: 1  336: 1  337: 2  338: 1  339: 1  340: 1
341: 1  342: 2  343: 2  344: 1  345: 2  346: 1  347: 1  348: 1  349: 2  350: 2
351: 2  352: 2  353: 1  354: 1  355: 2  356: 1  357: 1  358: 1  359: 1  360: 2
361: 1  362: 1  363: 1  364: 1  365: 2  366: 1  367: 1  368: 1  369: 1  370: 1
371: 1  372: 1  373: 1  374: 1  375: 2  376: 2  377: 1  378: 1  379: 1  380: 2
381: 1  382: 1  383: 1  384: 1  385: 1  386: 1  387: 1  388: 1  389: 1  390: 1
391: 1  392: 2  393: 2  394: 1  395: 2  396: 1  397: 1  398: 1  399: 1  400: 1
401: 1  402: 2  403: 2  404: 1  405: 2  406: 2  407: 1  408: 1  409: 2  410: 1
411: 2  412: 1  413: 2  414: 2  415: 2  416: 1  417: 2  418: 2  419: 2  420: 1
421: 1  422: 1  423: 1  424: 2  425: 2  426: 2  427: 2  428: 2  429: 2  430: 1
```

431: 2 432: 1 433: 2 434: 1 435: 1 436: 1 437: 2 438: 1 439: 2 440: 2
441: 2 442: 1 443: 2 444: 1 445: 2 446: 2 447: 2 448: 1 449: 1 450: 1
451: 2 452: 1 453: 1 454: 2 455: 1 456: 1 457: 2 458: 2 459: 2 460: 1
461: 1 462: 1 463: 2 464: 2 465: 1 466: 1 467: 2 468: 1 469: 1 470: 2
471: 1 472: 1 473: 1 474: 2 475: 1 476: 2 477: 2 478: 2

REFERENCES

Aaronson, A.L., Dent, O.B., Webb, J.T., & Kline, C.D. (1996). Graying of the critical items: Effects of aging on responding to MMPI-2 critical items. *Journal of Personality Assessment, 66,* 169–176.

Adams, K.M., & Shore, D.L. (1976). The accuracy of an automated MMPI interpretation system in a psychiatric setting. *Journal of Clinical Psychology, 32,* 80–82.

Adkins, J.W., Weathers, F.W., McDevitt-Murphy, M., & Daniels, J.B. (2008). Psychometric properties of seven self-report measures of posttraumatic stress disorder in college students with mixed civilian trauma exposure. *Journal of Anxiety Disorders, 22,* 1393–1402.

Adler, T. (1990, April). Does the "new" MMPI beat the "classic"? *APA Monitor,* pp. 18–19.

Akerlind, I., Hornquist, J.O., & Bjurulf, P. (1992). Psychological factors in the long-term prognosis of chronic low back pain patients. *Journal of Clinical Psychology, 48,* 596–606.

Alfano, D.P., Paniak, C.E., Christopher, E., & Finlayson, M.A. (1993). The MMPI and closed head injury: A neurocorrective approach. *Neuropsychiatry, Neuropsychology, and Behavioral Neurology, 6,* 111–116.

Alker, H.A. (1978). Minnesota Multiphasic Personality Inventory. In O.K. Buros (Ed.), *Eighth mental measurements yearbook* (pp. 931–935). Highland Park, NJ: Gryphon.

Allard, G., & Faust, D. (2000). Errors in scoring objective personality tests. *Assessment, 7,* 119–129.

Allen, J. (1998). Personality assessment with American Indians and Alaska natives: Instrument considerations and service delivery style. *Journal of Personality Assessment, 70,* 17–42.

Almagor, M., & Koren, D. (2001). The adequacy of the MMPI-2 Harris–Lingoes sub-scales: A cross-cultural factor analytic study of scales D, Hy, Pd, Pa, Sc, and Ma. *Psychological Assessment, 13,* 199–215.

Alperin, J.J., Archer, R.P., & Coates, G.D. (1996) Development and effects of an MMPI-A K-correction procedure. *Journal of Personality Assessment, 67,* 155–168.

American Psychiatric Association. (1987). *Diagnostic and statistical manual of mental disorders* (3rd ed., revised). Washington, DC: Author.

American Psychological Association. (2002). Ethical principles of psychologists and code of conduct. *American Psychologist, 57,* 1060–1073.

American Psychological Association. (1994). Guidelines for child custody evaluations in divorce proceedings. *American Psychologist, 49,* 677–680.

American Psychological Association. (1986). *Guidelines for computer-based tests and interpretations.* Washington, DC: Author.

Anderson, B.N. (1969). *The utility of the Minnesota Multiphasic Personality Inventory in a private psychiatric hospital setting.* Unpublished master's thesis, Ohio State University, Columbus, OH.

Anderson, W., & Bauer, B. (1985). Clients with MMPI high D-Pd: Therapy implications. *Journal of Clinical Psychology, 41,* 181–189.

Anthony, N. (1971). Comparison of clients' standard, exaggerated, and matching MMPI profiles. *Journal of Consulting and Clinical Psychology, 36,* 100–103.

Apfeldorf, M., & Hunley, P.J. (1975). Application of MMPI alcoholism scales to older alcoholics and problem drinkers. *Journal of Studies on Alcohol, 37,* 645–653.

Applegate, K.L., Keefe, F.J., Siegler, I.C., Bradley, L.A., McKee, D.C., Cooper, K.S., & Riordan, P. (2005). Does personality at college entry predict number of reported pain conditions at mid-life? A longitudinal study. *The Journal of Pain, 6,* 92–97.

Arbisi, P.A., & Ben-Porath, Y.S. (1995). An MMPI-2 infrequent response scale for use with psychopathological populations: The Infrequency Psychopathology scale, F(p). *Psychological Assessment, 7,* 424–431.

Arbisi, P.A., & Ben-Porath, Y.S. (1997). Characteristics of the MMPI-2 F(p) scale as a function of diagnosis in an inpatient sample of veterans. *Psychological Assessment, 9,* 102–105.

Arbisi, P.A., & Ben-Porath, Y.S. (1998). The ability of Minnesota Multiphasic Personality Inventory-2 validity scales to detect fake-bad responses in psychiatric inpatients. *Psychological Assessment, 10,* 221–228.

Arbisi, P.A., & Ben-Porath, Y.S. (1999). The use of the Minnesota Multiphasic Personality Inventory-2 in the psychological assessment of persons with TBI: Correction factors and other clinical caveats and conundrums. *NeuroRehabilitation, 13,* 117–125.

Arbisi, P.A., Ben-Porath, Y.S., & Forbey, J.D. (2003, March). *Can the MMPI-2 Restructured Clinical (RC) Scales predict criteria measured by the Clinical Scale code types?* Paper presented at the Midwinter Meeting of the Society for Personality Assessment. San Francisco, CA.

Arbisi, P.A., Ben-Porath, Y.S., & McNulty, J. (2002). A comparison of MMPI-2 validity in African American and Caucasian psychiatric inpatients. *Psychological Assessment, 14,* 3–15.

Arbisi, P.A., Ben-Porath, Y.S., & McNulty, J. (2003a). Empirical correlates of common MMPI-2 two-point codes in male psychiatric inpatients. *Assessment, 10,* 237–247.

Arbisi, P.A., Ben-Porath, Y.S., & McNulty, J. (2003b). Refinement of the MMPI-2 F(p) scale is not necessary: A response to Gass and Luis. *Assessment, 10,* 123–128.

Arbisi, P.A., & Butcher, J.N. (2004). Relationship between personality and health symptoms: Use of the MMPI-2 in medical assessments. *International Journal of Clinical and Health Psychology, 4,* 571–595.

Arbisi, P.A., Sellbom, M., & Ben-Porath, Y.S. (2008). Empirical correlates of the MMPI-2 Restructured Clinical (RC) scales in psychiatric inpatients. *Journal of Personality Assessment, 90,* 122–128.

Archer, R.P. (1984). Use of the MMPI with adolescents: A review of salient issues. *Clinical Psychology Review, 41,* 241–251.

Archer, R.P. (1987). *Using the MMPI with adolescents.* Hillsdale, NJ: Lawrence Erlbaum Associates.

Archer, R.P. (1992a). Minnesota Multiphasic Personality Inventory-2. In J.J. Kramer & J.C. Conoley (Eds.), *Eleventh mental measurements yearbook* (pp. 558–562). Lincoln, NE: Buros Institute of Mental Measurements.

Archer, R.P. (1992b). *MMPI-A: Assessing adolescent psychopathology.* Hillsdale, NJ: Lawrence Erlbaum Associates.

Archer, R.P. (2005). *MMPI-A: Assessing adolescent psychopathology* (3rd ed.). Mahwah, NJ. Lawrence Erlbaum Associates.

Archer, R.P., Aiduk, R., Griffin, R., & Elkins, D.E. (1996). Incremental validity of the MMPI-2 content scales in a psychiatric sample. *Assessment, 3,* 79–90.

Archer, R.P., Belevich, J.K., & Elkins, D.E. (1994). Item-level and scale level factor structures on the MMPI-A. *Journal of Personality Assessment, 62,* 332–345.

Archer, R.P., Bolinskey, P.K., Morton, T.L., & Farris, K.L. (2002). A factor structure for the MMPI-A: Replication with male delinquents. *Assessment, 9,* 319–326.

Archer, R.P., Bolinskey, P.K., Morton, T.L., & Farris, K.L. (2003). MMPI-A characteristics of male adolescents in juvenile justice and clinical treatment settings. *Assessment, 10,* 400–410.

Archer, R.P., & Elkins, D.E. (1999). Identification of random responding on the MMPI-A. *Journal of Personality Assessment, 73,* 407–421.

Archer, R.P., Elkins, D.E., Aiduk, R., & Griffin, R. (1997). The incremental validity of MMPI-2 supplementary scales. *Assessment, 4,* 193–205.

Archer, R.P., Fontaine, J., & McCrae, R.R. (1998). Effects of two MMPI-2 validity scales on basic scale relations to external criteria. *Journal of Personality Assessment, 70,* 87–102.

Archer, R.P., & Gordon, R.A. (1994). Psychometric stability of MMPI-A modifications. *Journal of Personality Assessment, 62,* 416–426.

Archer, R.P., Gordon, R.A., Anderson, G.L., & Giannetti, R. (1989). MMPI special scale clinical correlates for adolescent inpatients. *Journal of Personality Assessment, 53,* 654–664.

Archer, R.P., Gordon, R.A., Giannetti, R., & Singles, J.M. (1988). MMPI scale clinical correlates for adolescent inpatients. *Journal of Personality Assessment, 52,* 707–721.

Archer, R. P., Gordon, R. A., & Kirchner, F. H. (1987). Response-set characteristics among adolescents. *Journal of Personality Assessment, 51,* 506–516.

Archer, R.P., Griffin, R., & Aiduk, R. (1995). MMPI-2 clinical correlates for the common codes. *Journal of Personality Assessment, 65,* 391–407.

Archer, R.P., Handel, R.W., & Lynch, K.D. (2001). The effectiveness of the MMPI-A items in discriminating between normative and clinical samples. *Journal of Personality Assessment, 77,* 420–435.

Archer, R.P., & Jacobson, J.M. (1993). Are critical items "critical" for the MMPI-A? *Journal of Personality Assessment, 61,* 547–556.

Archer, R.P., & Krishnamurthy, R. (1994). A structural summary approach for the MMPI-A: Development and empirical correlates. *Journal of Personality Assessment, 63,* 554–573.

Archer, R.P., & Krishnamurthy, R. (2002). *Essentials of MMPI-A assessment.* New York: Wiley.

Archer, R.P., Krishnamurthy, R., & Jacobson, J.M. (1994). *MMPI-A casebook.* Tampa, FL: Psychological Assessment Resources.

Archer, R.P., Maruish, M., Imhof, E.A., & Piotrowski, C. (1991). Psychological test usage with adolescent clients: 1990 survey findings. *Professional Psychology: Research and Practice, 22,* 247–252.

Archer, R.P., & Newsom, C.R. (2000). Psychological test usage with adolescent clients: Survey update. *Assessment, 7,* 227–235.

Archer, R.P., Pancoast, D.L., & Gordon, R.A. (1992). The development of the MMPI-A Immaturity Scale: Findings for normal and clinical samples. Unpublished manuscript.

Archer, R.P., Stolberg, A.L., Gordon, R.A., & Goldman, W.R. (1986). Parent and child MMPI responses: Characteristics among families with adolescents in inpatient and outpatient settings. *Journal of Abnormal Child Psychology, 14,* 181–190.

Arita, A.A., & Baer, R.A. (1998). Validity of selected MMPI-A content scales. *Psychological Assessment, 10,* 59–63.

Arnau, R.C., Handel, R.W., & Archer, R.P. (2005). Principal components analyses of the MMPI-2 PSY-5 scales: Identification of facet subscales. *Assessment, 12,* 186–198.

Arnau, R.C., Handel, R.W., Archer, R.P., Bisconer, S., & Gross, D. (2004, May). *External correlates of the MMPI-2 Personality Psychopathology Five (PSY-5) facet subscales in an adult inpatient psychiatric sample.* Paper presented at the 39th Annual Symposium on Recent Developments in the Use of the MMPI-2 and MMPI-A. Minneapolis, MN.

Arthur, G. (1944). An experience in examining an Indian twelfth-grade group with the Multiphasic Personality Inventory. *Mental Hygiene, 25,* 243–250.

Atkinson, L. (1986). The comparative validities of the Rorschach and MMPI: A meta-analysis. *Canadian Psychology, 27,* 238–247.

Avery, R.D., Mussio, S.J., & Payne, G. (1972). Relationships between MMPI scores and job performance measures of fire fighters. *Psychological Reports, 31,* 199–202.

Bacchiochi, J.R., & Bagby, R.M. (2003, June). *Development of the Malingering Discriminant Function Index (M-DFI).* Paper presented at the 38th Annual Symposium on Recent Developments on the MMPI-2/MMPI-A, Minneapolis, MN.

Baer, R.A., Ballenger, J., Berry, D.T.R., & Wetter, M.W. (1997). Detection of random responding on the MMPI-A. *Journal of Personality Assessment, 68,* 139–151.

Baer, R.A., Ballenger, J., & Kroll, L.S. (1998). Detection of underreporting on the MMPI-A in clinical and community samples. *Journal of Personality Assessment, 71,* 98–113.

Baer, R.A., Kroll, L.S., Rinaldo, J., & Ballenger, J. (1999). Detecting and discriminating between random responding and overreporting on the MMPI-A. *Journal of Personality Assessment, 72,* 308–320.

Baer, R.A., & Miller, J. (2002). Underreporting of psychopathology on the MMPI-2: A meta-analytic review. *Psychological Assessment, 14,* 16–26.

Baer, R.A., & Sekirnjak, G. (1997). Detection of underreporting on the MMPI-2 in a clinical population: Effects of information about validity scales. *Journal of Personality Assessment, 69,* 555–567.

Baer, R.A., Wetter, M.W., & Berry, D.T.R. (1992). Detection of underreporting of psychopathology on the MMPI: A meta-analysis. *Clinical Psychology Review, 12,* 509–525.

Baer, R.A., Wetter, M.W., & Berry, D.T.R. (1995). Effects of information about validity scales on underreporting of symptoms on the MMPI-2: An analogue investigation. *Assessment, 2,* 189–200.

Baer, R.A., Wetter, M.W., Nichols, D.S., Greene, R., & Berry, D.T.R. (1995). Sensitivity of MMPI-2 validity scales to underreporting of symptoms. *Psychological Assessment, 7,* 419–423.

Bagby, R.M. (2005, April). *Detecting overreporting on the MMPI-2.* Workshop presented at the 40th Annual MMPI-2/MMPI-A Workshops. Fort Lauderdale, FL.

Bagby, R.M., Buis, T., & Nicholson, R.A. (1995). Relative effectiveness of the standard validity scales in detecting fake-bad and fake-good responding: Replication and extension. *Psychological Assessment, 7,* 84–92.

Bagby, R.M., Marshall, M.B., Basso, M.R., Nicholson, R.A., Bacchiochi, J., & Miller, L.S. (2005). Distinguishing bipolar depression, major depression, and schizophrenia with the MMPI-2 clinical and content scales. *Journal of Personality Assessment, 84,* 89–95.

Bagby, R.M., Nicholson, R.A., Bacchiochi, J.R., Ryder, A.G., & Bury, A.S. (2002). The predictive capacity of the MMPI-2 and PAI validity scales and indexes to detect coached and uncoached feigning. *Journal of Personality Assessment, 78,* 69–86.

Bagby, R.M., Nicholson, R.A., Buis, T., Radovanovic, H., & Fidler, B.J. (1999). Defensive responding on the MMPI-2 in family custody and access evaluations. *Psychological Assessment, 11,* 24–28.

Bagby, R.M., Rogers, R., & Buis, T. (1994). Detecting malingered and defensive responding on the MMPI-2 in a forensic inpatient sample. *Journal of Personality Assessment, 62,* 191–203.

Bagby, R.M., Rogers, R., Buis, T., Nicholson, R.A., Cameron, S.L., Rector, N.A., ... Seeman, M.V. (1997). Detecting feigned depression and schizophrenia on the MMPI-2. *Journal of Personality Assessment, 68,* 650–664.

Bagby, R.M., Rogers, R., Nicholson, R.A., Buis, T., Seeman, M.V., & Rector, N.A. (1997). Effectiveness of the MMPI-2 validity indicators in the detection of defensive responding in clinical and non-clinical samples. *Journal of Personality Assessment, 68,* 650–664.

Bagby, R.M., Ryder, A.G., Ben-Dat, D., Bacchiochi, J., & Parker, J.D.A. (2002). Validation of the dimensional factor structure of the Personality Psychopathology Five in clinical and nonclinical samples. *Journal of Personality Disorders, 16,* 304–316.

Bagby, R.M., Sellbom, M., Costa, P.T., Jr., & Widiger, T.A. (2008). Predicting *Diagnostic and Statistical Manual of Mental Disorders-IV* personality disorders with the five-factor model of personality and the personality psychopathology five. *Personality and Mental Health, 2,* 55–69.

Ball, J.C. (1960). Comparison of MMPI profile differences among Negro–White adolescents. *Journal of Clinical Psychology, 16,* 304–307.

Ball, J.D., Archer, R.P., & Imhof, E.A. (1994). Time requirements of psychological testing: A survey of practitioners. *Journal of Personality Assessment, 63,* 239–249.

Barefoot, J.C., Dahlstrom, W.G., & Williams, R.B. (1983). Hostility, CHD incidence, and total mortality: A 25-year follow-up study of 255 physicians. *Psychosomatic Medicine, 45,* 59–63.

Barefoot, J.C., Dodge, K.A., Peterson, B.L., Dahlstrom, W.G., & Williams, R.B. (1989). The Cook–Medley Hostility scale: Item content and ability to predict survival. *Psychosomatic Medicine, 51,* 46–57.

Barker, H.R., Fowler, R.D., & Peterson, L.P. (1971). Factor analytic structure of the short form MMPI in a VA hospital population. *Journal of Clinical Psychology, 27,* 228–233.

Barrash, J., Rodriguez, E.M., Scott, D.H., Mason, E.E., & Sines, J.O. (1987). The utility of MMPI subtypes for the prediction of weight loss after bariatric surgery. *International Journal of Obesity, 11,* 115–128.

Barron, F. (1953). An ego strength scale which predicts response to psychotherapy. *Journal of Consulting Psychology, 17,* 327–333.

Barron, F., & Leary, T. (1955). Changes in psychoneurotic patients with and without psychotherapy. *Journal of Consulting Psychology, 19,* 239–245.

Barthlow, D.L., Graham, J.R., Ben-Porath, Y.S., & McNulty, J.L. (1999). Incremental validity of the MMPI-2 content scales in an outpatient mental health setting. *Psychological Assessment, 11,* 39–47.

Barthlow, D.L., Graham, J.R., Ben-Porath, Y.S., & McNulty, J.L. (2004). Construct validity of the MMPI-2 College Maladjustment (Mt) scale. *Assessment, 11,* 251–262.

Barthlow, D.L., Graham, J.R., Ben-Porath, Y.S., Tellegen, A., & McNulty, J.L. (2002). The appropriateness of the MMPI-2 K correction. *Assessment, 9,* 219–229.

Bartol, C.R. (1991). Predictive validation of the MMPI for small-town police officers who fail. *Professional Psychology: Research and Practice, 22,* 127–132.

Bathurst, K., Gottfried, A.W., & Gottfried, A.E. (1997). Normative data for the MMPI-2 in child custody litigation. *Psychological Assessment, 9,* 205–211.

Belter, R.W., Foster, K.Y., & Imm, P.S. (1996). Convergent validity of selected scales of the MMPI and the Achenbach Child Behavior Checklist–Youth Self-Report. *Psychological Reports, 79,* 1901–1100.

Belter, R., & Piotrowski, C. (2001). Current status of doctoral-level training in psychological testing. *Journal of Clinical Psychology, 57,* 717–726.

Ben-Porath, Y.S. (2003). Assessing personality and psychopathology with self-report inventories. In J. Graham & J. Naglieri (Eds.), *Handbook of psychology, Volume 10: Assessment psychology* (pp. 553–577). Hoboken, NJ: John Wiley & Sons, Inc.

Ben-Porath, Y.S., & Butcher, J.N. (1986). Computers in personality assessment: A brief past, an ebullient present, and an expanding future. *Computers in Human Behavior, 2,* 167–182.

Ben-Porath, Y.S., & Butcher, J.N. (1989a). Psychometric stability of rewritten MMPI items. *Journal of Personality Assessment, 53,* 645–653.

Ben-Porath, Y.S., & Butcher, J.N. (1989b). The comparability of MMPI and MMPI-2 scales and profiles. *Psychological Assessment: A Journal of Consulting and Clinical Psychology, 1,* 345–347.

Ben-Porath, Y.S., Butcher, J.N., & Graham, J.R. (1991). Contribution of the MMPI-2 content scales to the differential diagnosis of schizophrenia and major depression. *Psychological Assessment: A Journal of Consulting and Clinical Psychology, 3,* 634–640.

Ben-Porath, Y.S., & Davis, D.L. (1996). *Case studies for interpreting the MMPI-A.* Minneapolis: University of Minnesota Press.

Ben-Porath, Y.S., & Forbey, J.D. (2003). *Non-gendered norms for the MMPI-2.* Minneapolis: University of Minnesota Press.

Ben-Porath, Y.S., & Forbey, J.D. (2004, May). *Detrimental effects of the K correction on clinical scale validity.* Paper presented at the 39th Annual Symposium on Recent Developments of the MMPI-2/MMPI-A. Minneapolis, MN.

Ben-Porath, Y.S., & Graham, J.R. (1991). Resolutions to interpretive dilemmas created by the Minnesota Multiphasic Personality Inventory-2 (MMPI-2): A reply to Strassberg. *Journal of Psychopathology and Behavioral Assessment, 13,* 173–179.

Ben-Porath, Y.S., Graham, J.R., Archer, R.P., Tellegen, A., & Kaemmer, B. (2006). *Supplement to the MMPI-A Manual for Administration, Scoring, and Interpretation: The Content Component Scales; the Personality Psychopathology Five (PSY-5) Scales, and the Critical Items.* Minneapolis: University of Minnesota Press.

Ben-Porath, Y.S., Graham, J.R., & Tellegen, A. (2009). *MMPI-2 Symptom Validity (FBS) Scale: Development, research findings, and interpretive recommendations.* Minneapolis: University of Minnesota Press.

Ben-Porath, Y.S., Hostetler, K., Butcher, J.N., & Graham, J.R. (1989). New subscales for the MMPI-2 social introversion (Si) scale. *Psychological Assessment: A Journal of Consulting and Clinical Psychology, 1,* 169–174.

Ben-Porath, Y.S., McCully, E., & Almagor, M. (1993). Incremental validity of the MMPI-2 content scales in the assessment of personality and psychopathology by self-report. *Journal of Personality Assessment, 61,* 557–575.

Ben-Porath, Y.S., & Sherwood, N.E. (1993). *The MMPI-2 content component scales.* Minneapolis: University of Minnesota Press.

Ben-Porath, Y.S., Shondrick, D.D., & Stafford, K.P. (1995). MMPI-2 and race in a forensic diagnostic sample. *Criminal Justice and Behavior, 22,* 19–32.

Ben-Porath, Y.S., Slutske, W.S., & Butcher, J.N. (1989). A real-data simulation of computerized adaptive administration of the MMPI. *Psychological Assessment: A Journal of Consulting and Clinical Psychology, 1,* 18–22.

Ben-Porath, Y.S., & Stafford, K.P. (1993, August). *Empirical correlates of MMPI-2 scales in a forensic diagnostic sample: An interim report.* Paper presented at the 101st Annual Meeting of the American Psychological Association, Toronto, Ontario.

Ben-Porath, Y.S., & Tellegen, A. (1996). How (not) to evaluate the comparability of the MMPI and MMPI-2 profile configurations: A reply to Humphrey and Dahlstrom. *Journal of Personality Assessment, 65,* 52–58.

Ben-Porath, Y.S., & Tellegen, A. (2008a). Empirical correlates of the MMPI-2 Restructured Clinical (RC) scales in mental health, forensic, and non-clinical settings: An introduction. *Journal of Personality Assessment, 90,* 119–121.

Ben-Porath, Y.S., & Tellegen, A. (2008b). *MMPI-2-RF: Manual for administration, scoring, and interpretation.* Minneapolis: University of Minnesota Press.

Ben-Porath, Y.S., Tellegen, A., & Graham, J.R. (2009). *The MMPI-2 Symptom Validity Scale (FBS).* Minneapolis, MN: University of Minnesota Press.

Benton, A.L. (1949). The MMPI: A review. In O.K. Buros (Ed.), *The third mental measurements yearbook* (pp. 104–107). Rutgers, NJ: Rutgers University Press.

Berk, E., Black, J., Locastrok, J., Wickis, J., Simpson, T., Keane, T.M., & Penk, W. (1989). Traumatogenicity: Effects of self-reported noncombat trauma on MMPIs of male Vietnam combat and noncombat veterans treated for substance abuse. *Journal of Clinical Psychology, 45,* 704–717.

Bernstein, I.H. (1980). Security guards' MMPI profiles: Some normative data. *Journal of Personality Assessment, 44,* 377–380.

Berry, D.T., Wetter, M.W., Baer, R.A., Larsen, L., Clark, C., & Monroe, K. (1992). MMPI-2 random responding indices: Validation using a self-report methodology. *Psychological Assessment, 4,* 340–345.

Berry, D.T.R., Adams, J.J., Clark, C.D., Thacker, S.R., Burger, T.L., Wetter, M.W., Baer, R.A., & Borden, J.W. (1996). Detection of a cry for help on the MMPI-2: An analog investigation. *Journal of Personality Assessment, 67,* 26–36.

Berry, D.T.R., Adams, J.J., Smith, T., Greene, R.L., Sekirnjak, G.C., Wieland, G., & Tharp, B. (1997). MMPI-2 clinical scales and 2-point code types: Impact of varying levels of omitted items. *Psychological Assessment, 9,* 158–160.

Berry, D.T.R., Baer, R.A., & Harris, M.J. (1991). Detection of malingering on the MMPI: A meta-analysis. *Clinical Psychology Review, 11,* 585–598.

Berry, D.T.R., Wetter, M.W., Baer, R.A., Widiger, T.A., Sumpter, J.C., Reynolds, S.K., & Hallam, R.A. (1991). Detection of random responding on the MMPI-2: Utility of F, Back F, and VRIN scales. *Psychological Assessment, 3,* 418–423.

Berry, D.T.R., Wetter, M.W., Baer, R.A., Youngjohn, J.R., Gass, C.S., Lamb, D.G., & Bucholz, W.D. (1995). Overreporting of closed-head injury symptoms on the MMPI-2. *Psychological Assessment, 7,* 517–523.

Beutler, L.E., Storm, A., Kirkish, P., Scogin, F., & Gaines, J.A. (1985). Parameters in the prediction of police officer performance. *Professional Psychology: Research and Practice, 16,* 324–335.

Bianchini, K.J., Etherton, J.L., Greve, K.W., Heinly, M.T., &Meyers, J.E. (2008). Classification accuracy of MMPI-2 validity scales in the detection of pain-related malingering: A known-groups study. *Assessment, 15*, 435–449.

Binder, L.M., & Rohling, L.M. (1996). Money matters: Meta-analytic review of the effects of financial incentives on recovery after closed-head injury. *American Journal of Psychiatry, 153*, 7–10.

Binford, A., & Liljequist, L. (2008). Behavioral correlates of selected MMPI-2 Clinical, Content, and Restructured Clinical Scales. *Journal of Personality Assessment, 90*, 608–614.

Black, J.D. (1953). *The interpretation of MMPI profiles of college women.* Unpublished doctoral dissertation, University of Minnesota, Minneapolis.

Block, J. (1965). *The challenge of response sets: Unconfounding meaning, acquiescence, and social desirability in the MMPI.* New York: Appleton-Century-Crofts.

Block, J., & Bailey, D.Q. (1955). *Q-sort item analyses of a number of MMPI scales.* Officer Education Research Laboratory (Technical Memorandum No. OERL-TM-55-7).

Blumenthal, J.A., Barefoot, J., Burg, M.M., & Williams, R.B., Jr. (1987). Psychological correlates of hostility among patients undergoing coronary angiography. *British Journal of Medical Psychology, 60*, 349–355.

Boerger, A.R., Graham, J.R., & Lilly, R.S. (1974). Behavioral correlates of single-scale MMPI code types. *Journal of Consulting and Clinical Psychology, 42*, 398–402.

Bohn, M.J., Carbonell, J.L., & Megargee, E.I. (1995). The applicability and utility of the MMPI-based offender classification system in a correctional mental health unit. *Criminal Behavior & Mental Health, 5*, 14–33.

Bombardier, C.H., Divine, G.W., Jordan, J.S., Brooks, B.W., & Neelon, F.A. (1993). Minnesota Multiphasic Personality Inventory (MMPI) cluster groups among chronically ill patients: Relationship to illness adjustment and treatment outcome. *Journal of Behavioral Medicine, 16*, 467–484.

Boone, D.E. (1994). Validity of the MMPI-2 Depression content scale with psychiatric inpatients. *Psychological Reports, 74*, 159–162.

Booth-Kewley, S., & Friedman, H.S. (1987). Psychological predictors of heart disease: A quantitative review. *Psychological Bulletin, 101*, 343–362.

Borum, R., & Grisso, T. (1995). Psychological test use in criminal forensic evaluations. *Professional Psychology: Research & Practice, 26*, 465–473.

Borzecki, M., Wormith, J.S., & Black, W.H. (1988). An examination of differences between native and non-native psychiatric offenders on the MMPI. *Canadian Journal of Behavioral Science, 20*, 287–301.

Bosquet, M., & Egeland, B. (2000). Predicting parenting behaviors from Antisocial Practices content scale scores on the MMPI-2 administered during pregnancy. *Journal of Personality Assessment, 74*, 147–162.

Bow, J.N., Flens, J.R., Gould, J.W., & Greenhut, D. (2005). An analysis of administration, scoring, and interpretation of the MMPI-2 and MCMI-II/III in child custody evaluations. *Journal of Child Custody, 2*, 1–22.

Bow, J.N., Gould, J.W., Flens, J.R., & Greenhut, D. (2006). Testing in child custody evaluations: Selection, usage, and Daubert admissibility. *Journal of Forensic Psychology Practice, 6*(2), 17–38.

Bow, J., & Quinnell, F.A. (2001). Psychologists' current practices and procedures in child custody evaluations: Five years after American Psychological Association guidelines. *Professional Psychology: Research and Practice, 32*, 261–268.

Bowler, R.M., Hartney, C., & Ngo, L.H. (1998). Amnestic disturbance and posttraumatic stress disorder in the aftermath of a chemical release. *Archives of Clinical Neuropsychology, 13*, 455–471.

Brems, C., & Lloyd, P. (1995). Validation of the MMPI-2 Low Self-Esteem content scale. *Journal of Personality Assessment, 65,* 550–556.

Bringmann, W.G., Balance, W.D., & Giesbrecht, C.A. (1972). The computer vs. the technologist: Comparison of psychological reports on normal and elevated MMPI profiles. *Psychological Reports, 31,* 211–217.

Brodsky, S.L. (1991). *Testifying in court.* Washington, DC: American Psychological Association.

Brophy, A.L. (1995). Educational level, occupation, and the MMPI-2 F–K index. *Psychological Reports, 77,* 175–178.

Brophy, A.L. (1997). MMPI and MMPI-2 scores on the Cook–Medley Hostility scale. *Psychological Reports, 80,* 1087–1090.

Brown, A., & Zeichner, A. (1989). Concurrent incidence of depression and physical symptoms among hostile young women. *Psychological Reports, 65,* 739–744.

Brown, T.G., & Fayek, A. (1993). Comparison of demographic characteristics and MMPI scores from alcohol and poly-drug alcohol and cocaine abusers. *Alcoholism Treatment Quarterly, 10,* 123–135.

Brozek, J. (1955). Personality changes with age: An item analysis of the MMPI. *Journal of Gerontology, 10,* 194–206.

Bubenzer, D.L., Zimpfer, D.G., & Mahrle, C.L. (1990). Standardized individual appraisal in agency and private practice. *Journal of Mental Health Counseling, 12,* 51–66.

Bunde, J., & Suls, J. (2006). A quantitative analysis of the relationship between the Cook-Medley Hostility scale and traditional coronary artery disease risk factors. *Health Psychology, 25,* 493–500.

Burkhart, B.R., Christian, W.L., & Gynther, M.D. (1978). Item subtlety and faking on the MMPI: A paradoxical relationship. *Journal of Personality Assessment, 42,* 76–80.

Burkhart, B.R., Gynther, M.D., & Fromuth, M.E. (1980). The relative validity of subtle versus obvious items on the MMPI Depression scale. *Journal of Clinical Psychology, 36,* 748–751.

Bury, A.S., & Bagby, R. (2002). The detection of feigned uncoached and coached posttraumatic stress disorder with the MMPI-2 in a sample of workplace accident victims. *Psychological Assessment, 14,* 472–484.

Buss, A.H., & Perry, M. (1992). The Aggression Questionnaire. *Journal of Personality and Social Psychology, 63,* 452–459.

Butcher, J.N. (1972). *Objective personality assessment: Changing perspectives.* New York: Academic Press.

Butcher, J.N. (1978). Computerized scoring and interpreting services. In O.K. Buros (Ed.), *Eighth mental measurements yearbook* (pp. 942–945). Highland Park, NJ: Gryphon.

Butcher, J.N. (1979). Use of the MMPI in personnel selection. In J.N. Butcher (Ed.), *New developments in the use of the MMPI* (pp. 165–201). Minneapolis: University of Minnesota Press.

Butcher, J.N. (1985). Personality assessment in industry: Theoretical issues and illustrations. In H.J. Bernardin (Ed.), *Personality assessment in organizations* (pp. 277–310). New York: Praeger.

Butcher, J.N. (1987). The use of computers in psychological assessment: An overview of practices and issues. In J.N. Butcher (Ed.), *Computerized psychological assessment* (pp. 3–14). New York: Basic Books.

Butcher, J.N. (1988, March). *Use of the MMPI in personnel screening.* Paper presented at the 23rd Annual Symposium on Recent Developments in the Use of the MMPI, St. Petersburg Beach, FL.

Butcher, J.N. (1989a). *The Minnesota Report: Adult Clinical System*. Minneapolis: National Computer Systems.

Butcher, J.N. (1989b). *User's guide for the Minnesota Personnel Report*. Minneapolis: National Computer Systems.

Butcher, J.N. (1990a). Education level and MMPI-2 measured pathology: A case of negligible influence. *MMPI-2 News and Profiles: A Newsletter of the MMPI-2 Workshops and Symposia, 1,* 3.

Butcher, J.N. (1990b). *MMPI-2 in psychological treatment*. New York: Oxford University Press.

Butcher, J.N. (1991). Screening for psychopathology: Industrial applications of the Minnesota Multiphasic Personality Inventory (MMPI-2). In J. Jones, B.D. Steffey, & D. Bray (Eds.), *Applying psychology in business: The manager's handbook* (pp. 835–850). Boston: Lexington Books.

Butcher, J.N. (1993). *Minnesota Multiphasic Personality Inventory-2 (MMPI-2): Users guide for the Minnesota Report: Adult clinical system—Revised*. Minneapolis: National Computer Systems.

Butcher, J.N. (1994). Psychological assessment of airline pilot applicants with the MMPI-2. *Journal of Personality Assessment, 62,* 31–44.

Butcher, J.N. (1995). Personality patterns of personal injury litigants: The role of computer-based MMPI-2 evaluations. In Y.S. Ben-Porath, J.R. Graham, G.C.N. Hall, R.D. Hirshman, & M.S. Zaragoza (Eds.), *Forensic applications of the MMPI-2* (pp. 179–201). Thousand Oaks, CA: Sage.

Butcher, J.N. (1996). Translation and adaptation of the MMPI-2 for international use. In J.N. Butcher (Ed.), *International adaptations of the MMPI-2: Research and clinical applications* (pp. 26–43). Minneapolis: University of Minnesota Press.

Butcher, J.N. (2001). *The Minnesota Report: Revised Personnel System*. Minneapolis, MN: Pearson Assessments.

Butcher, J.N. (2005). *The Minnesota Report: Adult Clinical System—Revised (4th Edition)*. Minneapolis: Pearson Assessments.

Butcher, J.N., Aldwin, C.M., Levenson, M.R., Ben-Porath, Y.S., Spiro, A., & Bosse, R. (1991). Personality and aging: A study of the MMPI-2 among older men. *Psychology and Aging, 6,* 361–370.

Butcher, J.N., Arbisi, P.A., Atlis, M.M., & McNulty, J.L. (2003). The construct validity of the Lees–Haley Fake Bad Scale: Does this measure somatic malingering and feigned emotional distress? *Archives of Clinical Neuropsychology, 18,* 473–485.

Butcher, J.N., Atlis, M., & Fang, L. (2000). The effects of altered instructions on the MMPI-2 responses of persons who are not motivated to deceive. *Journal of Personality Assessment, 75,* 492–501.

Butcher, J.N., Ball, B., & Ray, E. (1964). Effects of socio-economic level on MMPI differences in Negro–White college students. *Journal of Counseling Psychology, 11,* 183–187.

Butcher, J.N., Braswell, L., & Raney, D. (1983). A cross-cultural comparison of American Indian, Black, and White inpatients on the MMPI and presenting symptoms. *Journal of Consulting and Clinical Psychology, 51,* 587–594.

Butcher, J.N., Cabiya, J., Lucio, E., & Garrido, M. (2007). *Assessing Hispanic clients using the MMPI-2 and MMPI-A*. Washington, DC: American Psychological Association.

Butcher, J.N., Dahlstrom, W.G., Graham, J.R., Tellegen, A., & Kaemmer, B. (1989). *Minnesota Multiphasic Personality Inventory-2 (MMPI-2): Manual for administration and scoring*. Minneapolis: University of Minnesota Press.

Butcher, J.N., Graham, J.R., & Ben-Porath, Y.S. (1995). Methodological problems and issues in MMPI, MMPI-2, and MMPI-A research. *Psychological Assessment, 7,* 320–329.

Butcher, J.N., Graham, J.R., Ben-Porath, Y.S., Tellegen, A., Dahlstrom, W.G., & Kaemmer, B. (2001). *MMPI-2 (Minnesota Multiphasic Personality Inventory-2): Manual for administration, scoring, and interpretation, revised edition.* Minneapolis: University of Minnesota Press.

Butcher, J.N., Graham, J.R., Williams, C.L., & Ben-Porath, Y.S. (1990). *Development and use of the MMPI-2 content scales.* Minneapolis: University of Minnesota Press.

Butcher, J.N., Hamilton, C.K., Rouse, S.V., & Cumella, E.J. (2006). The deconstruction of the Hy scale of MMPI-2: Failure of RC3 in measuring somatic symptom expression. *Journal of Personality Assessment, 87,* 186–192.

Butcher, J.N., & Han, K. (1995). Development of an MMPI-2 scale to assess the presentation of self in a superlative manner: The S scale. In J.N. Butcher & C.D. Spielberger (Eds.), *Advances in personality assessment* (Vol. 10, pp. 25–50). Hillsdale, NJ: Lawrence Erlbaum Associates.

Butcher, J.N., Keller, L.S., & Bacon, S.F. (1985). Current developments and future directions in computerized personality assessment. *Journal of Consulting and Clinical Psychology, 53,* 803–815.

Butcher, J.N., Kendall, P.C., & Hoffman, N. (1980). MMPI short forms: CAUTION. *Journal of Consulting Psychology, 48,* 275–278.

Butcher, J.N., Morfitt, R.C., Rouse, S.V., & Holden, R.R. (1997). Reducing MMPI-2 defensiveness: The effect of specialized instructions on retest validity in a job applicant sample. *Journal of Personality Assessment, 68,* 385–401.

Butcher, J.N., & Tellegen, A. (1966). Objections to MMPI items. *Journal of Consulting and Clinical Psychology, 30,* 527–534.

Butcher, J.N., & Williams, C.L. (1992). *Essentials of MMPI-2 and MMPI-A interpretation.* Minneapolis: University of Minnesota Press.

Butcher, J.N., & Williams, C.L. (2000). *Essentials of MMPI-2 and MMPI-A interpretation* (2nd ed.). Minneapolis: University of Minnesota Press.

Butcher, J.N., Williams, C.L., Graham, J.R., Archer, R.P., Tellegen, A., Ben-Porath, Y.S., & Kaemmer, B. (1992). *Minnesota Multiphasic Personality Inventory—Adolescent (MMPI-A): Manual for administration, scoring, and interpretation.* Minneapolis: University of Minnesota Press.

Butler, R.W., Foy, D.W., Snodgrass, L., Hurwicz, M., & Goldfarb, J. (1988). Combat-related posttraumatic stress disorder in a nonpsychiatric population. *Journal of Anxiety Disorders, 2,* 111–120.

Caillouet, B.A., Boccaccini, M.T., Varela, J.G., Davis, R.D., & Rostow, C.D. (2010). Predictive validity of the MMPI-2 PSY-5 and facets for law enforcement officer employment outcomes. *Criminal justice and Behavior, 37,* 217–238.

Caldwell, A.B. (1969). *MMPI critical items.* Unpublished manuscript. (Available from Caldwell Report, 1545 Sawtelle Bl., No. 14, Los Angeles, CA 90025.)

Caldwell, A.B. (1988). *MMPI supplemental scale manual.* Los Angeles: Caldwell Report.

Caldwell, A.B. (1991). Commentary on "The Minnesota Multiphasic Personality Inventory-2: A review." *Journal of Counseling & Development, 69,* 568–569.

Caldwell, A.B. (2006). Maximal measurement or meaningful measurement: The interpretive challenges of the MMPI-2 Restructured Clinical (RC) scales. *Journal of Personality Assessment, 87,* 193–201.

Caldwell, A.B., Jr. (2005). The use of the MMPI-2 and the Rorschach in the child custody context: How can the MMPI-2 help child custody examiners. *Journal of Child Custody, 2,* 83–117.

Calvin, J. (1974). *Two dimensions or fifty: Factor analytic studies with the MMPI.* Unpublished materials, Kent State University, Kent, OH.

Calvin, J. (1975). *A replicated study of the concurrent validity of the Harris subscales for the MMPI.* Unpublished doctoral dissertation, Kent State University, Kent, OH.

Camara, W.J., Nathan, J.S., & Puente, A.E. (2000). Psychological test usage: Implications in professional psychology. *Professional Psychology: Research and Practice, 31,* 141–154.

Campos, L.P. (1989). Adverse impact, unfairness, and bias in the psychological screening of Hispanic peace officers. *Hispanic Journal of Behavioral Sciences, 11,* 122–135.

Cannon, D.S., Bell, W.E., Andrews, R.H., & Finkelstein, A.S. (1987). Correspondence between MMPI PTSD measures and clinical diagnosis. *Journal of Personality Assessment, 51,* 517–521.

Canul, G.D., & Cross, J.J. (1994). The influence of acculturation and racial identity attitudes on Mexican-Americans' MMPI-2 performance. *Journal of Clinical Psychology, 50,* 736–745.

Capwell, D.F. (1945). Personality patterns of adolescent girls: II. Delinquents and nondelinquents. *Journal of Applied Psychology, 29,* 289–297.

Carbone, E.G., Cigrang, J.A., Todd, S.L., & Fiedler, E.R. (1999). Predicting outcome of military basic training for individuals referred for psychological evaluation. *Journal of Personality Assessment, 72,* 256–265.

Carlson, D.A. (2001). Computerized vs. written administration of the MMPI-A in clinical and non-clinical settings. *Dissertations Abstracts International: Section B: The Sciences and Engineering, 62,* 2-B.

Carmody, T.P., Crossen, J.R., & Wiens, A.N. (1989). Hostility as a health risk factor: Relationships with neuroticism, Type A behavior, attentional focus, and interpersonal style. *Journal of Clinical Psychology, 45,* 754–762.

Carr, A.C., Ghosh, A., & Ancill, R.J. (1983). Can a computer take a psychiatric history? *Psychological Medicine, 13,* 151–158.

Carr, J.L., & Graham, J.R. (1996). Assessing anger with the Minnesota Multiphasic Personality Inventory. In C.D. Spielberger & I.G. Sarason (Eds.), *Stress and emotion: Anxiety, anger, and curiosity* (Vol. 16, pp. 67–82). Washington, DC: Taylor and Francis.

Carson, R.C. (1969). Interpretive manual to the MMPI. In J.N. Butcher (Ed.), *Research developments and clinical applications* (pp. 279–296). New York: McGraw-Hill.

Cashel, L., Rogers, R., Sewell, K.W., & Holliman, N.B. (1998). Preliminary validation of the MMPI-A for a male delinquent sample: An investigation of clinical correlates and discriminative validity. *Journal of Personality Assessment, 71,* 49–69.

Castlebury, F.K., & Durham, T.W. (1997). The MMPI-2 GM and GF scales as measures of psychological well-being. *Journal of Clinical Psychology, 53,* 879–893.

Castro, Y., Gordon, K.H., Brown, J.S., Anestis, J.C., & Joiner, T.E. (2008). Examination of racial differences on the MMPI-2 clinical and restructured clinical scales in an outpatient sample. *Assessment, 15,* 277–286.

Cavaiola, A.A., Strohmetz, D.B., Wolf, J.M., & Lavender, N.J. (2002). Comparison of DWI offenders with non-DWI individuals on the MMPI-2 and the Michigan Alcoholism Screening Test. *Addictive Behaviors, 28,* 971–977.

Chang, A.F., Caldwell, A.B., & Moss, T. (1973). Stability of personality traits in alcoholics during and after treatment as measured by the MMPI: A one-year follow-up study. Proceedings of the 81st Annual Convention of the American Psychological Association, 8, 387–388.

Chang, P.N., Nesbit, M.E., Youngren, N., & Robison, L.L. (1988). Personality characteristics and psychosocial adjustment of long-term survivors of childhood cancer. *Journal of Psychosocial Oncology, 5*, 43–58.

Chase, L.L. (1974). An evaluation of MMPI interpretation systems (doctoral dissertation, University of Minnesota, Minneapolis). *Dissertation Abstracts International, 35*, 3009.

Cheung, F.M., & Song, W. (1989). A review on the clinical applications of the Chinese MMPI. *Psychological Assessment, 1*, 230–237.

Chojnacki, J.T., & Walsh, W.B. (1992). The consistency of scores and configural patterns between the MMPI and MMPI-2. *Journal of Personality Assessment, 59*, 276–289.

Chojnacki, J.T., & Walsh, W.B. (1994). The consistency between scores on the Harris–Lingoes subscales of the MMPI and MMPI-2. *Journal of Personality Assessment, 62*, 57–165.

Chu, C. (1966). *Object cluster analysis of the MMPI.* Unpublished doctoral dissertation, University of California, Berkeley, CA.

Cigrang, J.A., & Staal, M.A. (2001). Readministration of the MMPI-2 following defensive invalidity in a military job applicant sample. *Journal of Personality Assessment, 76*, 472–481.

Claiborn, D.D. (1995). Review of the Minnesota Multiphasic Personality Inventory–Adolescent. In J.C. Conoley & J.C. Impara (Eds.), *The twelfth mental measurements yearbook* (pp. 626–628). Lincoln, University of Nebraska Press.

Clark, C., & Klonoff, H. (1988). Empirically derived MMPI profiles: Coronary bypass surgery. *The Journal of Nervous and Mental Disease, 176*, 101–106.

Clark, C.G., & Miller, H.L. (1971). Validation of Gilberstadt and Duker's 8–6 profile type on a Black sample. *Psychological Reports, 29*, 259–264.

Clark, M.E. (1994). Interpretive limitations of the MMPI-2 Anger and Cynicism content scales. *Journal of Personality Assessment, 63*, 89–96.

Clark, M.E. (1996). MMPI-2 Negative Treatment Indicators content and content component scales: Clinical correlates and outcome prediction for men with chronic pain. *Psychological Assessment, 8*, 32–38.

Clark, S.A., Velasquez, R.J., & Callahan, W.J. (1992). MMPI-ER two point code of industrially injured Hispanic workers by DSM-III-R diagnosis. *Psychological Reports, 71*, 107–112.

Clavelle, P.R. (1992). Clinicians' perceptions of the comparability of the MMPI and MMPI-2. *Psychological Assessment, 4*, 466–472.

Clayton, M.R., & Graham, J.R. (1979). Predictive validity of Barron's Es scale: The role of symptom acknowledgment. *Journal of Consulting and Clinical Psychology, 47*, 424–425.

Cleckley, H. (1982). *The mask of sanity* (5th ed.). St. Louis, MO: Mosby.

Clements, R., & Heintz, J.M. (2002). Diagnostic accuracy and factor structure of the AAS and APS scales of the MMPI-2. *Journal of Personality Assessment, 79*, 564–582.

Clopton, J.R., Shanks, D.A., & Preng, K.W. (1987). Classification accuracy of the MacAndrew scale with and without K corrections. *The International Journal of the Addictions, 22*, 1049–1051.

Cofer, C.N., Chance, J., & Judson, A.J. (1949). A study of malingering on the MMPI. *Journal of Psychology, 27*, 491–499.

Cohen, J., Cohen, P., West, S.G., & Aiken, L.S. (2002). *Applied multiple regression/correlation analysis for the behavioral sciences.* Mahwah, NJ: Lawrence Erlbaum Associates.

Colligan, R.C., & Offord, K.P. (1988). The risky use of the MMPI hostility scale in assessing risk for coronary heart disease. *Psychosomatics, 29,* 188–196.

Colligan, R.C., & Offord, K.P. (1990). MacAndrew versus MacAndrew: The relative efficacy of the MAC and the SAP scales for the MMPI in screening male adolescents for substance misuse. *Journal of Personality Assessment, 55,* 708–716.

Colligan, R.C., & Offord, K.P. (1992). Age, stage, and the MMPI: Changes in response patterns over an 85-year age span. *Journal of Clinical Psychology, 48,* 476–493.

Colligan, R.C., Osborne, D., & Offord, K.P. (1980). Linear transformation and the interpretation of MMPI T scores. *Journal of Clinical Psychology, 36,* 162–165.

Colligan, R.C., Osborne, D., Swenson, W.M., & Offord, K.P. (1983). *The MMPI: A contemporary normative study.* New York: Praeger.

Colligan, R.C., Rasmussen, N.H., Agerter, D.C., Offord, K.P., Malinchoc, M., O'Byrne, M.M., & Benson, J.T. (2008). The MMPI-2: A contemporary normative study of midwestern family medicine outpatients. *Journal of Clinical Psychology in Medical Settings, 15,* 98–119.

Comrey, A.L. (1957a). A factor analysis of items on the MMPI depression scale. *Educational and Psychological Measurement, 17,* 578–585.

Comrey, A.L. (1957b). A factor analysis of items on the MMPI hypochondriasis scale. *Educational and Psychological Measurement, 17,* 566–577.

Comrey, A.L. (1957c). A factor analysis of items on the MMPI hysteria scale. *Educational and Psychological Measurement, 17,* 586–592.

Comrey, A.L. (1958a). A factor analysis of items on the F scale of the MMPI. *Educational and Psychological Measurement, 18,* 621–632.

Comrey, A.L. (1958b). A factor analysis of items on the MMPI hypomania scale. *Educational and Psychological Measurement, 18,* 313–323.

Comrey, A.L. (1958c). A factor analysis of items on the MMPI paranoia scale. *Educational and Psychological Measurement, 18,* 99–107.

Comrey, A.L. (1958d). A factor analysis of items on the MMPI psychasthenia scale. *Educational and Psychological Measurement, 18,* 293–300.

Comrey, A.L. (1958e). A factor analysis of items on the MMPI psychopathic deviate scale. *Educational and Psychological Measurement, 18,* 91–98.

Comrey, A.L., & Marggraff, W. (1958). A factor analysis of items on the MMPI schizophrenia scale. *Educational and Psychological Measurement, 18,* 301–311.

Cook, G. (1969). The court unit: Patient characteristics and differences between patients judged competent and incompetent. *Journal of Clinical Psychology, 25,* 140–143.

Cook, G., Pogany, E., & Johnston, N.G. (1974). A comparison of Blacks and Whites committed for evaluation of competency to stand trial on criminal charges. *Journal of Psychiatry and Law, 2,* 319–337.

Cook, W.N., & Medley, D.M. (1954). Proposed hostility and pharisaic-virtue scales for the MMPI. *Journal of Applied Psychology, 38,* 414–418.

Cooper-Hakim, A., & Viswesvaran, C. (2002). A meta-analytic review of the MacAndrew Alcoholism scale. *Educational and Psychological Measurement, 62,* 818–829.

Costa, P.T., & McCrae, R.R. (1992). *NEO PI-R professional manual.* Odessa, FL: Psychological Assessment Resources.

Costa, P.T., Zonderman, A.B., McCrae, R.R., & Williams, R.R. (1986). Cynicism and paranoid alienation in the Cook and Medley Ho scale. *Psychosomatic Medicine, 48,* 283–285.

Costello, R.M. (1977). Construction and cross-validation of an MMPI Black–White scale. *Journal of Personality Assessment, 41,* 514–519.

Costello, R.M., Hulsey, T.L., Schoenfeld, L.S., & Ramamurthy, S. (1987). P-A-I-N: A four cluster MMPI typology for chronic pain. *Pain, 30,* 199–209.

Costello, R.M., Schneider, S.L., & Schoenfeld, L.S. (1996). Validation of a preemployment MMPI index correlated with interdisciplinary suspension days of police officers. *Psychology: Crime and Law, 2,* 299–306.

Costello, R.M., Schoenfeld, L.S., & Kobos, J. (1982). Police applicant screening: An analogue study. *Journal of Clinical Psychology, 38,* 216–221.

Costello, R.M., Schoenfeld, L.S., Ramamurthy, S., & Hobbs-Hardee, B. (1989). Sociodemographic and clinical correlates of P-A-I-N. *Journal of Psychosomatic Research, 33,* 315–321.

Costello, R.M., Tiffany, D.W., & Gier, R.H. (1972). Methodological issues and racial (Black–White) comparisons on the MMPI. *Journal of Consulting and Clinical Psychology, 38,* 161–168.

Cottle, W.C. (1950). Card versus booklet forms of the MMPI. *Journal of Applied Psychology, 34,* 255–259.

Cowan, M.A., Watkins, B.A., & Davis, W.E. (1975). Level of education, diagnosis and race-related differences in MMPI performance. *Journal of Clinical Psychology, 31,* 442–444.

Craig, R.J. (2005). Assessing contemporary substance abusers with the MMPI MacAndrews Alcoholism scale: A review. *Substance Use & Misuse, 40,* 427–450.

Craig, R.J., & Olson, R.E. (2004). Predicting methadone maintenance treatment outcomes using the addiction severity index and the MMPI-2 content scales (negative treatment indicators and cynicism scales). *The American Journal of Drug and Alcohol Abuse, 30,* 823–839.

Crovitz, E., Huse, M.N., & Lewis, D.E. (1973). Selection of physicians' assistants. *Journal of Medical Education, 48,* 551–555.

Crumpton, C.A. (1975). An evaluation and comparison of three automated MMPI interpretive reports (doctoral dissertation, University of Texas, Austin). *Dissertation Abstracts International, 35,* 6090.

Cumella, E.J., Wall, A.D., & Kerr-Almeida, N. (2000). MMPI-2 in the inpatient assessment of women with eating disorders. *Journal of Personality Assessment, 75,* 387–403.

Dahlstrom, W.G. (1972). Whither the MMPI? In J.N. Butcher (Ed.), *Objective personality assessment: Changing perspectives* (pp. 85–115). New York: Academic Press.

Dahlstrom, W.G. (1980). Altered versions of the MMPI. In W.G. Dahlstrom & L. Dahlstrom (Eds.), *Basic readings on the MMPI: A new selection on personality measurement* (pp. 386–393). Minneapolis: University of Minnesota Press.

Dahlstrom, W.G. (1992). Comparability of two-point high-point code types with MMPI norms to MMPI-2 norms for the restandardization sample. *Journal of Personality Assessment, 59,* 153–164.

Dahlstrom, W.G., & Archer, R.P. (2000). A shortened version of the MMPI-2. *Assessment, 7,* 131–137.

Dahlstrom, W.G., & Dahlstrom, L. (Eds.). (1980). *Basic readings on the MMPI: A new selection on personality measurement.* Minneapolis: University of Minnesota Press.

Dahlstrom, W.G., & Humphrey, D.H. (1996). Comparability of MMPI and MMPI-2 profile patterns: Ben-Porath and Tellegen's inappropriate invocation of Mahalanobis's D^2 function. *Journal of Personality Assessment, 66,* 350–354.

Dahlstrom, W.G., Lachar, D., & Dahlstrom, L.E. (1986). *MMPI patterns of American minorities.* Minneapolis: University of Minnesota Press.

Dahlstrom, W.G., & Tellegen, A.K. (1993). *Socioeconomic status and the MMPI-2: The relation of MMPI-2 patterns to levels of education and occupation.* Minneapolis: University of Minnesota Press.

Dahlstrom, W.G., & Welsh, G.S. (1960). *An MMPI handbook: A guide to use in clinical practice and research.* Minneapolis: University of Minnesota Press.

Dahlstrom, W.G., Welsh, G.S., & Dahlstrom, L.E. (1972). *An MMPI handbook: Vol. I. Clinical interpretation.* Minneapolis: University of Minnesota Press.

Dahlstrom, W.G., Welsh, G.S., & Dahlstrom, L.E. (1975). *An MMPI handbook: Vol. II. Research applications.* Minneapolis: University of Minnesota Press.

Dancyger, I.F., Sunday, S.R., Eckert, E.D., & Halmi, K.A. (1997). A comparative analysis of Minnesota Multiphasic Personality Inventory profiles of anorexia nervosa at hospital admission, discharge, and 10-year follow up. *Comprehensive Psychiatry, 38,* 185–191.

Daniel, A.E., Beck, N.C., Herath, A., Schmitz, M., & Menninger, K. (1985). Factors correlated with psychiatric recommendations of incompetency and insanity. *Journal of Psychiatry & Law, 12,* 527–544.

Daubert v. Merrell Dow Pharmaceuticals, 727 F. Supp. 570 (S.D.Cal. 1989), aff'd, 951F.2d 1128 (9th Cir. 1990), vacated, 1123 S.Ct. 2786 (1993).

Davis, K.R., & Sines, J.O. (1971). An antisocial behavior pattern associated with a specific MMPI profile. *Journal of Consulting and Clinical Psychology, 36,* 229–234.

Davis, R.D., Wagner, E.E., & Patty, C.C. (1994). Maximized split-half reliabilities for Harris–Lingoes subscales: A follow-up with larger Ns. *Perceptual & Motor Skills, 78,* 881–882.

Davis, W.E. (1975). Race and the differential "power" of the MMPI. *Journal of Personality Assessment, 39,* 138–140.

Dean, A.C., Boone, K.B., Kim, M.S., Curiel, A.R., Martin, D.J., Victor, T.L., Zeller, M.A., & Lang, Y.K. (2008). Examination of the impact of ethnicity on the Minnesota Multiphasic Personality Inventory-2 (MMPI-2) Fake Bad Scale. *Clinical Neuropsychologist, 22,* 1054–1060.

Dearth, C.S., Berry, D.T.R., Vickery, C.D., Vagnini, V.L., Baser, R.E., Orey, S.A., & Cragar, D.E. (2005). Detection of feigned head injury symptoms on the MMPI-2 in head injured patients and community controls. *Archives of Clinical Neuropsychology, 20,* 95–110.

Deiker, T.E. (1974). A cross-validation of MMPI scales of aggression on male criminal criterion groups. *Journal of Consulting and Clinical Psychology, 42,* 196–202.

Detrick, P., Chibnall, J.T., & Rosso, M. (2001). Minnesota Multiphasic Personality Inventory-2 in police officer selection: Normative data and relation to the Inwald Personality Inventory. *Professional Psychology: Research and Practice, 32,* 484–490.

Diamond, R., Barth, J.T., & Zillmer, E.A. (1988). Emotional correlates of mild closed head trauma: The role of the MMPI. *The International Journal of Clinical Neuropsychology, 10,* 35–40.

Dikmen, S., Hermann, B.P., Wilensky, A.J., & Rainwater, G. (1983). Validity of the Minnesota Multiphasic Personality Inventory (MMPI) to psychopathology in patients with epilepsy. *Journal of Nervous and Mental Disease, 171,* 114–122.

Distler, L.S., May, P.R., & Tuma, A.H. (1964). Anxiety and ego strength as predictors of response to treatment in schizophrenic patients. *Journal of Consulting Psychology, 28,* 170–177.

Dodrill, C.B. (1986). Psychosocial consequences of epilepsy. In S. Filskov & T. Boll (Eds.), *Handbook of clinical neuropsychology, Vol. 2* (pp. 338–363). New York: Wiley.

Dolan, M.P., Roberts, W.R., Penk, W.E., Robinowitz, R., & Atkins, H.G. (1983). Personality differences among Black, White and Hispanic-American male heroin addicts on MMPI content scales. *Journal of Clinical Psychology, 39,* 807–813.

Dong, Y.T., & Church, A.T. (2003). Cross-cultural equivalence and validity of the Vietnamese MMPI-2: Assessing psychological adjustment of Vietnamese refugees. *Psychological Assessment, 15,* 370–377.

Dragon, W.R., & Ben-Porath, Y.S., (2007, April). *Examining the impact of unscorable item responses on the validity and interpretability of MMPI-2 substantive scale scores.* Paper presented at the 42nd Annual Meeting on Recent Developments in MMPI-2 and MMPI-A Research, Fort Lauderdale, FL.

Drake, L.E. (1946). A social I.E. scale for the MMPI. *Journal of Applied Psychology, 30,* 51–54.

Drake, L.E., & Oetting, E.R. (1959). *An MMPI codebook for counselors.* Minneapolis: University of Minnesota Press.

DuAlba, L., & Scott, R.L. (1993). Somatization and malingering for worker's compensation applicants: A cross-cultural MMPI study. *Journal of Clinical Psychology, 49,* 913–917.

Dubinsky, S., Gamble, D.J., & Rogers, M.L. (1985). A literature review of subtle–obvious items on the MMPI. *Journal of Personality Assessment, 49,* 62–68.

Duckworth, J., & Anderson, W. (1986). *MMPI interpretation manual for counselors and clinicians.* Muncie, IN: Accelerated Development, Inc.

Duckworth, J.C. (1991a). Response to Caldwell and Graham. *Journal of Counseling & Development, 69,* 572–573.

Duckworth, J.C. (1991b). The Minnesota Multiphasic Personality Inventory-2: A review. *Journal of Counseling & Development, 69,* 564–567.

Duckworth, J.C., & Duckworth, E. (1975). *MMPI interpretation manual for counselors and clinicians.* Muncie, IN: Accelerated Development, Inc.

Duckworth, M.P., & Iezzi, T. (2005). Chronic pain and posttraumatic stress symptoms in litigating motor vehicle accident victims. *The Clinical Journal of Pain, 21,* 251–261.

Duff, F.L. (1965). Item subtlety in the personality inventory scales. *Journal of Consulting Psychology, 29,* 565–570.

Dunnette, M.D., Bownas, D.A., & Bosshardt, M.J. (1981). *Electric power plant study: Prediction of inappropriate, unreliable or aberrant job behavior in nuclear power plant settings.* Minneapolis: Personnel Decisions Research Institute.

Duris, M., Bjorck, J.P., & Gorsuch, R.L. (2007). Christian subcultural differences in item perceptions of the MMPI-2 lie scale. *Journal of Psychology and Christianity, 26,* 356–366.

Dush, D.M., Simons, L.E., Platt, M., Nation, P.C., & Ayres, S.Y. (1994). Psychological profiles distinguishing litigating and nonlitigating pain patients: Subtle, and not so subtle. *Journal of Personality Assessment, 62,* 299–313.

Dusky v. United States, 362 U.S. 402 (1960).

Dwyer, S.A., Graham, J.R., & Ott, E.K. (1992). *Psychiatric symptoms associated with the MMPI-2 content scales.* Unpublished manuscript, Kent State University, Kent, OH.

Edwards, A.L. (1957). *The social desirability variable in personality assessment and research.* New York: Dryden.

Edwards, A.L. (1964). Social desirability and performance on the MMPI. *Psychometrika, 29,* 295–308.

Edwards, A.L., & Edwards, L.K. (1992). Social desirability and Wiggins's MMPI content scales. *Journal of Personality and Social Psychology, 62,* 147–153.

Edwards, D.W., Morrison, T.L., & Weissman, H.N. (1993). The MMPI and MMPI-2 in an outpatient sample: Comparisons of code types, validity scales, and clinical scales. *Journal of Personality Assessment, 61,* 1–18.

Edwards, E.L., Holmes, C.B., & Carvajal, H.H. (1998). Oral and booklet presentation of MMPI-2. *Journal of Clinical Psychology, 54,* 593–596.

Edwards, L.K., & Clark, C.L. (1987). A comparison of the first factor of the MMPI and the first factor of the EMPI: The PSD factor. *Journal of Educational and Psychological Measurement, 47,* 1165–1173.

Edwin, E., Andersen, A.E., & Rosell, F. (1988). Outcome prediction by MMPI subtypes of anorexia nervosa. *Psychosomatics: Journal of Consultation Liaison, 29,* 273–282.

Egeland, B., Erickson, M.F., Butcher, J.N., & Ben-Porath, Y.S. (1991). The MMPI-2 profiles of women at risk for child abuse. *Journal of Personality Assessment, 57,* 254–263.

Egger, J.I.M., de Mey, H.R.A., Derksen, J.J.L., & van der Staak, C.P.F. (2003). Cross-cultural replication of the five-factor model and comparison of the NEO-PI-R and MMPI-2 PSY-5 scales in a Dutch psychiatric sample. *Psychological Assessment, 15,* 81–88.

Ehrenworth, N.V., & Archer, R.P. (1985). A comparison of clinical accuracy ratings of interpretive approaches for adolescent MMPI responses. *Journal of Personality Assessment, 49,* 413–421.

Eichman, W.J. (1961). Replicated factors on the MMPI with female NP patients. *Journal of Consulting Psychology, 25,* 55–60.

Eichman, W.J. (1962). Factored scales for the MMPI: A clinical and statistical manual. *Journal of Clinical Psychology, 18,* 363–395.

Elhai, J.D., Gold, P.B., Frueh, B.C., & Gold, S.N. (2000). Cross-validation of the MMPI-2 in detecting malingered posttraumatic stress disorder. *Journal of Personality Assessment, 75,* 449–463.

Elhai, J.D., Naifeh, J.A., Zucker, I.S., Gold, S.N., Deitsch, S.E., & Frueh, B.C. (2004). Discriminating malingered from genuine civilian posttraumatic stress disorder. *Assessment, 11,* 139–144.

Elhai, J.D., Ruggiero, K.J., Frueh, B.C., Beckham, J.C., & Gold, P.B. (2002). The Infrequency-Posttraumatic Stress Disorder Scale (Fptsd) for the MMPI-2: Development and initial validation with veterans presenting with combat-related PTSD. *Journal of Personality Assessment, 79,* 531–549.

Elion, V.H., & Megargee, E.I. (1975). Validity of the MMPI Pd scale among Black males. *Journal of Consulting and Clinical Psychology, 43,* 166–172.

Endicott, J., & Spitzer, R.L. (1978). A diagnostic interview: The schedule for affective disorders and schizophrenia. *Archives of General Psychiatry, 35,* 837–844.

Ends, E.J., & Page, C.W. (1957). Functional relationships among measures of anxiety, ego strength, and adjustment. *Journal of Clinical Psychology, 13,* 148–150.

Englert, D.R., Weed, N.C., & Watson, G.S. (2000). Convergent, discriminant, and internal properties of the Minnesota Multiphasic Personality Inventory (2nd ed.): Low Self-Esteem content scale. *Measurement and Evaluation in Counseling and Development, 33,* 42–49.

Epstein, J., & Rotunda, R.J. (2000). The utility of computer versus clinician-authored assessments in aiding the prediction of patient symptomatology. *Computers in Human Behavior, 16,* 519–536.

Eschenback, A.E., & Dupree, L. (1959). The influence of stress on MMPI scale scores. *Journal of Clinical Psychology, 15,* 42–45.

Evan, W.M., & Miller, J.R. (1969). Differential effects on response bias of computer vs. conventional administration of a social science questionnaire. *Behavior Science, 14,* 216–227.

Evans, D.R. (1977). Use of the MMPI to predict effective hotline workers. *Journal of Clinical Psychology, 33,* 1113–1114.

Eyde, L.D., Kowal, D.M., & Fishburne, F.J. (1991). The validity of computer-based test interpretations of the MMPI. In T.B. Gutkin & S.L. Wise (Eds.), *The computer and the decision-making process* (pp. 75–123). Hillsdale, NJ: Lawrence Erlbaum Associates.

Ezzo, F.R., Pinsoneault, T.B., & Evans, T.M. (2007). A comparison of MMPI-2 profiles between child maltreatment cases and two types of custody cases. *Journal of Forensic Psychology Practice, 7,* 29–43.

Fairbank, J., McCaffrey, R., & Keane, T. (1985). Psychometric detection of fabricated symptoms of post-traumatic stress disorder. *American Journal of Psychiatry, 142,* 501–503.

Fantoni-Salvador, P., & Rogers, R. (1997). Spanish versions of the MMPI-2 and PAI: An investigation of concurrent validity with Hispanic patients. *Assessment, 4,* 29–39.

Finger, M.S., & Ones, D.A. (1999). Psychometric equivalence of the computer and booklet forms of the MMPI: A meta-analysis. *Psychological Assessment, 11,* 58–66.

Finn, S.E. (1996). Assessment feedback integrating MMPI-2 and Rorschach findings. *Journal of Personality Assessment, 67,* 543–557.

Finn, S.E. (2007). *In our clients' shoes: Theory and techniques of therapeutic assessment.* Mahwah, NJ: Erlbaum.

Finn, S.E., & Tonsager, M.E. (1992). Therapeutic effects of providing MMPI-2 test feedback to college students awaiting therapy. *Psychological Assessment, 4,* 278–287.

Fisher, G. (1970). Discriminating violence emanating from over-controlled vs. under-controlled aggressivity. *British Journal of Social and Clinical Psychology, 9,* 54–59.

Flynn, C.F., Sipes, W.E., Grosenbach, M.J., & Ellsworth, J. (1994). Top performer survey: Computerized psychological assessment in aircrew. *Aviation, Space, and Environmental Medicine, 65,* 39–44.

Forbey, J. D., & Ben-Porath, Y. S. (1998). *A critical item set for the MMPI-A.* Minneapolis: University of Minnesota Press.

Forbey, J.D., & Ben-Porath, Y.S. (2003a). Incremental validity of the MMPI-A Content scales in a residential treatment facility. *Assessment, 10,* 191–202.

Forbey, J.D., & Ben-Porath, Y.S. (2003b, June). *The MMPI-2 computer adaptive version (MMPI-2-CA): A preliminary investigation.* Paper presented at the 38th Annual Symposium on Recent Developments on the MMPI2/MMPI-A, Minneapolis, MN.

Forbey, J.D., & Ben-Porath, Y.S. (2004, May). *Further validation of the computerized-adaptive MMPI-2.* Poster presented at the annual MMPI/MMPI-2 symposium, Minneapolis, MN.

Forbey, J.D., & Ben-Porath, Y.S. (2007). Computerized adaptive personality testing: A review and illustration with the MMPI-2 computerized adaptive version. *Psychological Assessment, 19,* 14–24.

Forbey, J.D., & Ben-Porath, Y.S. (2008). Empirical correlates of the MMPI-2 Restructured Clinical (RC) scales in a nonclinical setting. *Journal of Personality Assessment, 90,* 136–141.

Forbey, J.D., Ben-Porath, Y.S., Graham, J.R., & Black, M.S. (2004). The potential of computerized adaptive testing with the MMPI-2 in a correctional facility. *Ohio Corrections Research Compendium, 2,* 201–207.

Forbey, J.D., Ben-Porath, Y.S., & Tellegen, A. (2004, March). *Associations between and the relative contributions of the MMPI-2 Restructured Clinical (RC) and content scales.* Paper presented at the Society for Personality Assessment, Miami, FL.

Fordyce, W.E. (1979). *Use of the MMPI in the assessment of chronic pain* (Clinical Notes on the MMPI No. 3). Minneapolis, MN: National Computer Systems.

Fordyce, W.E., Bigos, S.J., Batti'e, M.C., & Fisher, L.D. (1992). MMPI Scale 3 as a predictor of back injury report: What does it tell us? *Clinical Journal of Pain, 8,* 222–226.

Fow, N., Sittig, M., Dorris, D., Breisinger, G., & Anthony, K. (1994). An analysis of the relationship of gender and age to MMPI scores of patients with chronic pain. *Journal of Clinical Psychology, 50,* 538–554.

Fowler, R.D. (1969). Automated interpretation of personality test data. In J.N. Butcher (Ed.), *MMPI: Research developments and clinical applications* (pp. 105–126). New York: McGraw-Hill.

Fowler, R.D. (1975). *A method for the evaluation of the abuse prone patient.* Paper presented at the meeting of the American Academy of Family Physicians, Chicago, IL.

Fowler, R.D., & Butcher, J.N. (1986). Critique of Matarazzo's views on computerized testing: All sigma and no meaning. *American Psychologist, 41,* 94–96.

Fowler, R.D., & Coyle, F.A. (1968). Overlap as a problem in atlas classification of MMPI profiles. *Journal of Clinical Psychology, 24,* 435.

Fowler, R.D., Teel, S.K., & Coyle, F.A. (1967). The measurement of alcoholic response to treatment by Barron's Ego Strength scale. *Journal of Psychology, 67,* 65–68.

Fraboni, M., Cooper, D., Reed, T., & Saltstone, R. (1990). Offense type and two-point MMPI code profiles: Discriminating between violent and nonviolent offenders. *Journal of Clinical Psychology, 46,* 774–777.

Fredericksen, S.J. (1976, March). *A comparison of selected personality and history variables in highly violent, mildly violent, and nonviolent female offenders.* Paper presented at the 11th Annual MMPI Symposium, Minneapolis, MN.

Frueh, B.C., Gold, P.B., de Arellano, M.A., & Brady, K.L. (1997). A racial comparison of combat veterans evaluated for PTSD. *Journal of Personality Assessment, 68,* 692–702.

Frueh, B.C., Smith, D.W., & Libet, J.M. (1996). Racial differences on psychological measures in combat veterans seeking treatment for PTSD. *Journal of Personality Assessment, 66,* 41–53.

Frye v. United States, 293 F.1012 (D.C.Cir. 1923).

Gallagher, R.W. (1997). *Detection of malingering at the time of intake in a correctional setting with the MMPI-2 validity scales.* Unpublished doctoral dissertation, Kent State University, Kent, OH.

Gallagher, R.W., Ben-Porath, Y.S., & Briggs, S. (1997). Inmate views about the purpose and use of the MMPI-2 at the time of correctional intake. *Criminal Justice and Behavior, 24,* 360–369.

Gallen, R.T., & Berry, D.T.R. (1996). Detection of random responding in MMPI-2 protocols. *Assessment, 3,* 171–178.

Gallucci, N.T. (1994). Criteria associated with clinical scales of Harris–Lingoes subscales of the Minnesota Multiphasic Personality Inventory with adolescent inpatients. *Psychological Assessment, 6,* 179–187.

Gallucci, N.T. (1997a). Correlates of MMPI-A Substance abuse scales. *Assessment, 4,* 87–94.

Gallucci, N. T. (1997b). On the identification of patterns of substance abuse with the MMPI-A. *Psychological Assessment, 9,* 224–232.

Gallucci, N.T., Kay, D.C., & Thornby, J.I. (1989). The sensitivity of 11 substance abuse scales from the MMPI to change in clinical status. *Psychology of Addictive Behaviors, 3,* 29–33.

Gantner, A.B., Graham, J.R., & Archer, R.P. (1992). The usefulness of the MAC scale in normal, psychiatric, and substance abuse settings. *Psychological Assessment, 4,* 133–137.

Garb, H.N. (1984). The incremental validity of information used in personality assessment. *Clinical Psychology Review, 4,* 641–655.

Garb, H.N. (1989). Clinical judgment, clinical training, and professional experience. *Psychological Bulletin, 105,* 387–396.

Garetz, F.K., & Anderson, R.W. (1973). Patterns of professional activities of psychiatrists: A follow-up of 100 psychiatric residents. *American Journal of Psychiatry, 130,* 981–984.

Gass, C.S. (1991). MMPI-2 interpretation and closed head injury: A correction factor. *Psychological Assessment, 3,* 27–31.

Gass, C.S. (1992). MMPI-2 interpretation of patients with cerebrovascular disease: A correction factor. *Archives of Clinical Neuropsychology, 7,* 17–27.

Gass, C.S., & Lawhorn, L. (1991). Psychological adjustment following stroke: An MMPI study. *Psychological Assessment: A Journal of Consulting and Clinical Psychology, 3,* 628–633.

Gass, C.S., & Luis, C.A. (2001a). MMPI-2 short form: Psychometric characteristics in a neuropsychological setting. *Assessment, 8,* 213–219.

Gass, C.S., & Luis, C.A. (2001b). MMPI-2 scale F(p) and symptom feigning: Scale refinement. *Assessment, 8,* 425–429.

Gassen, M.D., Pietz, C.A., Spray, B.J., & Denney, R.L. (2007). Accuracy of Megargee's Criminal Offender Infrequency (FC) scale in detecting malingering among forensic examinees. *Criminal Justice and Behavior, 34,* 493–504.

Gatchel, R.J., Mayer, T.G., & Eddington, A. (2006). MMPI disability profile: The least known, most useful screen for psychopathology in chronic occupational spinal disorders. *Spine, 31,* 2973–2978.

Gatchel, R.J., Polatin, P.B., & Kinney, R.K. (1995). Predicting outcome of chronic back pain using clinical predictors of psychopathology: A prospective analysis. *Health Psychology, 14,* 415–420.

Gayton, W.F., Burchstead, G.N., & Matthews, G.R. (1986). An investigation of the utility of an MMPI post-traumatic stress disorder subscale. *Journal of Clinical Psychology, 42,* 916–917.

Gerson, A., & Fox, D. (2003). Fibromyalgia revisited: Axis II factors in MMPI and historical data in compensation claimants. *American Journal of Forensic Psychology, 21,* 21–25.

Gervais, R.O., Ben-Porath, Y.S., & Wygant, D.B. (2009). Empirical correlates and interpretation of the MMPI-2-RF Cognitive Complaints (COG) Scale. *The Clinical Neuropsychologist, 23,* 996–1015.

Gervais, R.O., Ben-Porath, Y.S., Wygant, D.B., & Green, P. (2007). Development and validation of a response bias scale (RBS) for the MMPI-2. *Assessment, 14,* 196–208.

Gervais, R.O., Ben-Porath, Y.S., Wygant, D.B., & Green, P. (2008). Differential sensitivity of the Response Bias Scale (RBS) and MMPI-2 validity scales to memory complaints. *Clinical Neuropsychologist, 22,* 1061–1079.

Getter, H., & Sundland, D.M. (1962). The Barron Ego Strength scale and psychotherapy outcome. *Journal of Consulting Psychology, 26,* 195.

Gilberstadt, H., & Duker, J. (1965). *A handbook for clinical and actuarial MMPI interpretation*. Philadelphia: Saunders.

Gilmore, J.D., Lash, S.J., Foster, M.A., & Blosser, S.L. (2001). Adherence to substance abuse treatment: Clinical utility of two MMPI-2 scales. *Journal of Personality Assessment, 77,* 524–540.

Gironda, R.J. (1999). *Comparative validity of MMPI-2 scores of African-Americans and Caucasians in a forensic diagnostic sample*. Unpublished doctoral dissertation, Kent State University, Kent, OH.

Gironda, R., & Clark, M. (2009). Psychometric properties of the MMPI-2 Restructured Form. *The Journal of Pain, 10,* 11.

Gocka, E. (1965). *American Lake norms for 200 MMPI scales*. Unpublished materials, Veterans Administration Hospital, American Lake, WA.

Gocka, E., & Holloway, H. (1963). *Normative and predictive data on the Harris and Lingoes subscales for a neuropsychiatric population* (Report No. 7). American Lake, WA: Veterans Administration Hospital.

Gold, P.B., & Frueh, B.C. (1998). Compensation-seeking and extreme exaggeration of psychopathology among combat veterans evaluated for posttraumatic stress disorder. *The Journal of Nervous and Mental Disease, 187,* 680–684.

Goldberg, L.R. (1965). Diagnosticians vs. diagnostic signs: The diagnosis of psychosis vs. neurosis for the MMPI. *Psychological Monographs, 79* (9, Whole No. 602).

Goldberg, L.R. (1968). Simple models or simple processes. *American Psychologist, 23,* 483–496.

Gómez, F.C., Jr., Johnson, R., Davis, Q., & Velásquez, R.J. (2000). MMPI-A performance of African and Mexican American adolescent first-time offenders. *Psychological Reports, 87,* 309–314.

Good, P.K., & Brantner, J.P. (1961). *The physician's guide to the MMPI*. Minneapolis: University of Minnesota Press.

Gottesman, I.I. (1959). More construct validation of the Ego Strength scale. *Journal of Consulting Psychology, 23,* 342–346.

Gottesman, I.I., & Prescott, C.A. (1989). Abuses of the MacAndrew MMPI alcoholism scale: A critical review. *Clinical Psychology Review, 9,* 223–242.

Gough, H.G. (1950). The F minus K dissimulation index for the MMPI. *Journal of Consulting Psychology, 14,* 408–413.

Gough, H.G. (1954). Some common misconceptions about neuroticism. *Journal of Consulting Psychology, 18,* 287–292.

Gough, H.G., McClosky, H., & Meehl, P.E. (1951). A personality scale for dominance. *Journal of Abnormal and Social Psychology, 46,* 360–366.

Gough, H.G., McClosky, H., & Meehl, P.E. (1952). A personality scale for social responsibility. *Journal of Abnormal and Social Psychology, 47,* 73–80.

Gough, H.G., McKee, M.G., & Yandell, R.J. (1955). *Adjective check list analyses of a number of selected psychometric and assessment variables*. Officer Education Research Laboratory (Technical Memorandum No. OERL-TM-5S-10).

Graham, J.R. (1967). A Q-sort study of the accuracy of clinical descriptions based on the MMPI. *Journal of Psychiatric Research, 5,* 297–305.

Graham, J.R. (1971a). Feedback and accuracy of clinical judgments from the MMPI. *Journal of Consulting and Clinical Psychology, 36,* 286–291.

Graham, J.R. (1971b). Feedback and accuracy of predictions of hospitalization from the MMPI. *Journal of Clinical Psychology, 27,* 243–245.

Graham, J.R. (1978). A review of some important MMPI special scales. In P. McReynolds (Ed.), *Advances in psychological assessment* (Vol. IV, pp. 311–331). San Francisco: Jossey-Bass.

Graham, J.R. (1987). *The MMPI: A practical guide* (2nd ed.). New York: Oxford University Press.

Graham, J.R. (1988, August). *Establishing validity of the revised form of the MMPI.* Symposium presentation at the 96th Annual Convention of the American Psychological Association, Atlanta, GA.

Graham, J.R. (1990). *MMPI 2: Assessing personality and psychopathology.* New York: Oxford.

Graham, J.R., Barthlow, D.L., Stein, L.A.R., Ben-Porath, Y.S., & McNulty, J.L. (2002). Assessing general maladjustment with the MMPI-2. *Journal of Personality Assessment, 78,* 334–347.

Graham, J.R., Ben-Porath, Y.S., Forbey, J.D., & Sellbom, M. (2003, June). *Relationship between T-score levels on MMPI-2 scales and symptom severity.* Paper presented at the 38th Annual Symposium on Recent Developments on the MMPI-2/MMPI-A, Minneapolis, MN.

Graham, J.R., Ben-Porath, Y.S., & McNulty, J.L. (1997). Empirical correlates of low scores on MMPI-2 scales in an outpatient mental health setting. *Psychological Assessment, 9,* 386–391.

Graham, J.R., Ben-Porath, Y.S., & McNulty, J.L. (1999). *MMPI-2 correlates for outpatient mental health settings.* Minneapolis: University of Minnesota Press.

Graham, J.R., & Lilly, R.S. (1984). *Psychological testing.* Englewood Cliffs, NJ: Prentice-Hall.

Graham, J.R., & Lilly, R.S. (1986, March). *Linear T scores versus normalized T scores: An empirical study.* Paper presented at the 21st Annual Symposium on Recent Developments in the Use of the MMPI, Clearwater Beach, FL.

Graham, J.R., & Mayo, M.A. (1985, March). *A comparison of MMPI strategies for identifying Black and White male alcoholics.* Paper presented at the 20th Annual Symposium on Recent Developments in the Use of the MMPI, Honolulu, HI.

Graham, J.R., & McCord, G. (1985). Interpretation of moderately elevated MMPI scores for normal subjects. *Journal of Personality Assessment, 49,* 477–484.

Graham, J.R., Schroeder, H.E., & Lilly, R.S. (1971). Factor analysis of items on the Social Introversion and Masculinity–Femininity scales of the MMPI. *Journal of Clinical Psychology, 27,* 367–370.

Graham, J.R., Smith, R.L., & Schwartz, G.F. (1986). Stability of MMPI configurations for psychiatric inpatients. *Journal of Consulting and Clinical Psychology, 54,* 375–380.

Graham, J.R., & Strenger, V.E. (1988). MMPI characteristics of alcoholics: A review. *Journal of Consulting and Clinical Psychology, 56,* 197–205.

Graham, J.R., Timbrook, R.E., Ben-Porath, Y.S., & Butcher, J.N. (1991). Code-type congruence between MMPI and MMPI-2: Separating fact from artifact. *Journal of Personality Assessment, 57,* 205–215.

Graham, J.R., Watts, D., & Timbrook, R.E. (1991). Detecting fake-good and fake-bad MMPI-2 profiles. *Journal of Personality Assessment, 57,* 264–277.

Grayson, H.M. (1951). *A psychological admissions testing program and manual.* Los Angeles: Veterans Administration Center, Neuropsychiatric Hospital.

Green, C.J. (1982). The diagnostic accuracy and utility of MMPI and MCMI computer interpretive reports. *Journal of Personality Assessment, 46,* 359–365.

Greene, R.L. (1980). *The MMPI: An interpretive manual.* New York: Grune & Stratton.

Greene, R.L. (1987). Ethnicity and MMPI performance: A review. *Journal of Consulting and Clinical Psychology, 55,* 497–512.

Greene, R.L. (1991). *The MMPI-2/MMPI: An interpretive manual.* Boston: Allyn and Bacon.

Greene, R.L., Robin, R.W., Albaugh, B., Caldwell, A., & Goldman, D. (2003). Use of the MMPI-2 in American Indians: II. Empirical Correlates. *Psychological Assessment, 15,* 360–369.

Greene, R.L., Weed, N.C., Butcher, J.N., Arredondo, R., & Davis, H.G. (1992). A cross-validation of MMPI-2 substance abuse scales. *Journal of Personality Assessment, 58,* 405–410.

Greenglass, E.R., & Julkunen, J. (1991). Cook–Medley Hostility, Anger, and Type A behavior pattern in Finland. *Psychological Reports, 68,* 1059–1066.

Greiffenstein, M.F., Baker, W.J., Gola, T., Donders, J., & Miller, L. (2002). The Fake Bad Scale in atypical and severe closed head injury litigants. *Journal of Clinical Psychology, 58,* 1591–1600.

Greist, J.H., & Klein, M.H. (1980). Computer programs for patients, clinicians, and researchers in psychiatry. In J.B. Sidowski, J.H. Johnson, & T.A. Williams (Eds.), *Technology in mental health care delivery systems* (pp. 161–182). Norwood, NJ: Ablex.

Grossman, L.S., Haywood, T.W., Ostrov, E., Wasyliw, O., & Cavanaugh, J.L., Jr. (1990). Sensitivity of MMPI validity scales to motivational factors in psychological evaluations of police officers. *Journal of Personality Assessment, 55,* 549–561.

Grossman, L.S., & Wasyliw, O.E. (1988). A psychometric study of stereotypes: Assessment of malingering in a criminal forensic group. *Journal of Personality Assessment, 52,* 549–563.

Grove, W.M., Zald, D.H., Lebow, B.S., Snitz, B.E., & Nelson, C. (2000). Clinical versus mechanical prediction: A meta-analysis. *Psychological Assessment, 12,* 19–30.

Guck, T.P., Meilman, P.W., & Skultety, F.M. (1987). Pain assessment index: Following multidisciplinary pain treatment. *Journal of Pain and Symptom Management, 2,* 23–27.

Gucker, D., & McNulty, J.L. (2004, May). *The MMPI-2, defensiveness and an analytic strategy.* Paper presented at the 39th Annual Symposium on Recent Developments in the Use of the MMPI-2 and MMPI-A, Minneapolis, MN.

Gumbiner, J. (1998). MMPI-A profiles of Hispanic adolescents. *Psychological Reports, 82,* 659–672.

Guthrie, G.M. (1949). *A study of the personality characteristics associated with the disorders encountered by an internist.* Unpublished doctoral dissertation, University of Minnesota, Minneapolis.

Guthrie, G.M. (1952). Common characteristics associated with frequent MMPI profile types. *Journal of Clinical Psychology, 8,* 141–145.

Gynther, M.D. (1979). Aging in personality. In J.N. Butcher (Ed.), *New developments in the use of the MMPI* (pp. 39–68). Minneapolis: University of Minnesota Press.

Gynther, M.D., Altman, H., & Sletten, I.W. (1973). Replicated correlates of MMPI two-point types: The Missouri Actuarial System. *Journal of Clinical Psychology* (Suppl. 39).

Gynther, M.D., Burkhart, B.R., & Hovanitz, C. (1979). Do face-valid items have more predictive validity than subtle items? The case of the MMPI Pd scale. *Journal of Consulting and Clinical Psychology, 47,* 295–300.

Hagen, M.A., & Castagna, N. (2001). The real numbers: Psychological testing in custody evaluations. *Professional Psychology: Research and Practice, 32,* 269–271.

Haggard, R.A., Stowell, A.W., Bernstein, D., & Gatchel, R.J. (2008). Relationship between the MMPI-2 and psychosocial measures in a heterogeneous pain population. *Rehabilitation Psychology, 53,* 471–478.

Haisch, D.C., & Meyers, L.S. (2004). MMPI-2 assessed post-traumatic stress disorder related to job stress, coping, and personality in police agencies. *Stress and Health, 20,* 223–229.

Hall, G.C.N., Bansal, A. & Lopez, I.R. (1999). Ethnicity and psychopathology: A meta-analytic review of 31 years of comparative MMPI/MMPI-2 research. *Psychological Assessment, 11,* 186–197.

Hall, G.C.N., Graham, J.R., & Shepherd, J.B. (1991). Three methods of developing MMPI taxonomies of sexual offenders. *Journal of Personality Assessment, 56,* 2–13.

Han, K., Weed, N.C., Calhoun, R.F., & Butcher, J.N. (1995). Psychometric characteristics of the MMPI-2 Cook–Medley Hostility scale. *Journal of Personality Assessment, 65,* 567–585.

Hand, C.G., Archer, R.P., Handel, R.W., & Forbey, J.D. (2007). The classification accuracy of the Minnesota Multiphasic Personality Inventory–Adolescent: Effects of modifying the normative sample. *Assessment, 14,* 80–85.

Handel, R.W., & Archer, R.P. (2008). An investigation of the psychometric properties of the MMPI-2 Restructured Clinical (RC) Scales with mental health inpatients. *Journal of Personality Assessment, 90,* 239–249.

Handel, R.W., Arnau, R.C., Archer, R.P., & Dandy, K.L. (2006). An evaluation of the MMPI-2 and MMPI-A True Response Inconsistency (TRIN) scales. *Assessment, 13,* 98–106.

Handel, R.W., Ben-Porath, Y.S., Tellegen, A., & Archer, R.P. (2010). Psychometric functioning of the MMPI-2-RF VRIN-r and TRIN-r Scales with varying degrees of randomness, acquiescence, and counter-acquiescence. *Psychological Assessment, 22,* 87–95.

Handel, R.W., Ben-Porath, Y.S., & Watt, M. (1999). Computerized adaptive assessment with the MMPI in a clinical setting. *Psychological Assessment, 11,* 369–380.

Hanvik, L.J. (1949). *Some psychological dimensions of low back pain.* Unpublished doctoral dissertation, University of Minnesota, Minneapolis, MN.

Hanvik, L.J. (1951). MMPI profiles in patients with low back pain. *Journal of Consulting Psychology, 15,* 250–253.

Hardy, J.D., & Smith, T.W. (1988). Cynical hostility and vulnerability to disease: Social support, life stress, and physiological response to conflict. *Health Psychology, 7,* 447–459.

Hare, R.D. (1991). *The Hare Psychopathy Checklist—Revised.* Toronto: Multihealth Systems.

Hargrave, G.E., & Hiatt, D. (1987, May). *Use of the MMPI to predict aggression in law enforcement officer applicants.* Paper presented at the 22nd Annual Symposium on Recent Developments in the Use of the MMPI, Seattle, WA.

Hargrave, G.E., Hiatt, D., Ogard, E.M., & Karr, C. (1994). Comparison of the MMPI and the MMPI-2 for a sample of peace officers. *Psychological Assessment, 6,* 27–32.

Harkness, A.R., & Lilienfeld, S.O. (1997). Individual differences science for treatment planning: Personality traits. *Psychological Assessment, 9,* 349–360.

Harkness, A.R., & McNulty, J.L. (2006). An overview of personality: The MMPI-2 Personality Psychopathology-Five scales (PSY-5). In J.N. Butcher (Ed.), *MMPI-2: A practitioner's guide* (pp. 73–97). Washington, DC: American Psychological Association.

Harkness, A.R., & McNulty, J.L. (2007, August). *Restructured versions of the MMPI-2 Personality Psychopathology Five (PSY-5) Scales.* Paper presented at the 115th Annual Convention of the American Psychological Association, San Francisco, CA.

Harkness, A.R., McNulty, J.L., & Ben-Porath, Y.S. (1995). The Personality Psychopathology Five (PSY-5): Constructs and MMPI-2 scales. *Psychological Assessment, 7,* 104–114.

Harkness, A.R., McNulty, J.L., Ben-Porath, Y.S., & Graham, J.R. (2002). *MMPI-2 Personality Psychopathology Five (PSY-5) scales: Gaining an overview for case conceptualization and treatment planning.* Minneapolis: University of Minnesota Press.

Harkness, A.R., Spiro, A., Butcher, J.N., & Ben-Porath, Y.S. (1995, August). *Personality Psychopathology Five (PSY-5) in the Boston VA Normative Aging Study.* Paper presented at the 103rd Annual Convention of the American Psychological Association, New York, NY.

Harrell, T.H., Honaker, L.M., & Parnell, T. (1992). Equivalence of the MMPI-2 with the MMPI in psychiatric patients. *Psychological Assessment, 4,* 460–465.

Harrell, T.W., & Harrell, M.S. (1973). The personality of MBAs who reach general management early. *Personnel Psychology, 26,* 127–134.

Harris, R., & Christiansen, C. (1946). Prediction of response to brief psychotherapy. *Journal of Psychology, 21,* 269–284.

Harris, R., & Lingoes, J. (1955). *Subscales for the Minnesota Multiphasic Personality Inventory.* Mimeographed materials, The Langley Porter Clinic.

Harris, R., & Lingoes, J. (1968). *Subscales for the Minnesota Multiphasic Personality Inventory.* Mimeographed materials, The Langley Porter Clinic.

Harrison, P.L., Kaufman, A.S., Hickman, J.A., & Kaufman, N.L. (1988). A survey of tests used for adult assessment. *Journal of Psychoeducational Assessment, 6,* 188–198.

Harrison, R.H., & Kass, E.H. (1968). MMPI correlates of Negro acculturation in a northern city. *Journal of Personality and Social Psychology, 10,* 262–270.

Hart, K.E. (1966). Perceived availability of different types of social support among cynically hostile women. *Journal of Clinical Psychology, 52,* 383–387.

Hartman, B.J. (1987). Psychological screening of law enforcement candidates. *American Journal of Forensic Psychology, 1,* 5–10.

Hathaway, S.R. (1947). A coding system for MMPI profiles. *Journal of Consulting Psychology, 11,* 334–337.

Hathaway, S.R. (1956). Scales 5 (Masculinity-Femininity), 6 (Paranoia), and 8 (Schizophrenia). In G.S. Welsh & W.G. Dahlstrom (Eds.), *Basic readings on the MMPI in psychology and medicine* (pp. 104–111). Minneapolis: University of Minnesota Press.

Hathaway, S.R. (1965). Personality inventories. In B.B. Wolman (Ed.), *Handbook of clinical psychology* (pp. 451–476). New York: McGraw-Hill.

Hathaway, S.R., & Briggs, P.F. (1957). Some normative data on new MMPI scales. *Journal of Clinical Psychology, 13,* 364–368.

Hathaway, S.R., & McKinley, J.C. (1940). A multiphasic personality schedule (Minnesota): I. Construction of the schedule. *Journal of Psychology, 10,* 249–254.

Hathaway, S.R., & Meehl, P.E. (1952). *Adjective check list correlates of MMPI scores.* Unpublished materials, University of Minnesota.

Hathaway, S.R., & Meehl, P.E. (1956). Psychiatric implications of code types. In G.S. Welsh & W.G. Dahlstrom (Eds.), *Basic readings on the MMPI in psychology and medicine* (pp. 136–150). Minneapolis: University of Minnesota Press.

Hathaway, S.R., & Monachesi, E.D. (1953). *Analyzing and predicting juvenile delinquency with the MMPI.* Minneapolis: University of Minnesota Press.

Hathaway, S.R., & Monachesi, E.D. (1957). The personalities of predelinquent boys. *Journal of Criminal Law, Criminology, and Political Science, 48,* 149–163.

Hathaway, S.R., & Monachesi, E.D. (1963). *Adolescent personality and behavior: MMPI patterns of normal, delinquent, dropout, and other outcomes.* Minneapolis: University of Minnesota Press.

Hawk, G.L., & Cornell, D.G. (1989). MMPI profiles of malingerers diagnosed in pretrial forensic evaluations. *Journal of Clinical Psychology, 45,* 673–678.

Hawkinson, J.R. (1961). *A study of the construct validity of Barron's Ego Strength scale with a state mental hospital population.* Unpublished doctoral dissertation, University of Minnesota, Minneapolis, MN.

Hays, S.K. (2003). A computer-administered version versus paper-and-pencil-administered version of the MMPI-A. *Dissertations Abstracts International: Section B: The Sciences and Engineering, 63,* 12-B.

Hearn, M.D., Murray, D.M., & Luepker, R.V. (1989). Hostility, coronary heart disease, and total mortality: A 33-year follow-up of university students. *Journal of Behavioral Medicine, 12,* 105–121.

Hedayat, M.M., & Kelly, D.B. (1991). Relationship of MMPI dependency and dominance scale scores to staff's ratings, diagnoses, and demographic data for day-treatment clients. *Psychological Reports, 68,* 259–266.

Hedlund, J.L. (1977). MMPI clinical scale correlates. *Journal of Consulting and Clinical Psychology, 45,* 739–750.

Hedlund, J.L., Morgan, D.W., & Master, F.D. (1972). The Mayo Clinic automated MMPI program: Cross-validation with psychiatric patients in an army hospital. *Journal of Clinical Psychology, 28,* 505–510.

Heilbrun, A.B. (1979). Psychopathy and violent crime. *Journal of Consulting and Clinical Psychology, 47,* 509–516.

Heilbrun, K., & Heilbrun, A.B. (1995). Risk assessment with the MMPI-2 in forensic evaluations. In Y.S. Ben-Porath, J.R. Graham, G.C.N. Hall, R.D. Hirshman, & M.S. Zaragoza (Eds.), *Forensic applications of the MMPI-2* (pp. 160–178). Thousand Oaks, CA: Sage.

Heinicke, C.M., Diskin, S.D., Ramsey-Klee, D.M., & Oates, D.S. (1986). Pre- and post-antecedents of 2-year-old attention, capacity for relationships, and verbal expressiveness. *Developmental Psychology, 22,* 777–787.

Helmes, E., & Reddon, J.R. (1993). A perspective on developments in assessing psychopathology: A critical review of the MMPI and MMPI-2. *Psychological Bulletin, 113,* 453–471.

Henning, J.J., Levy, R.H., & Aderman, M. (1972). Reliability of MMPI tape recorded and booklet administrations. *Journal of Clinical Psychology, 28,* 372–373.

Henrichs, T.F. (1964). Objective configural rules for discriminating MMPI profiles in a psychiatric population. *Journal of Clinical Psychology, 20,* 157–159.

Henrichs, T.F. (1981). *Using the MMPI in medical consultation* (Clinical Notes on the MMPI, No. 6). Minneapolis, MN: National Computer Systems.

Henrichs, T.F. (1990). The effect of methods of accurate feedback on clinical judgments based upon the MMPI. *Journal of Clinical Psychology, 46,* 778–781.

Henrichs, T.F., & Waters, W.F. (1972). Psychological adjustment and responses to open-heart surgery: Some methodological considerations. *British Journal of Psychiatry, 120,* 491–496.

Herkov, M.J., Archer, R.P., & Gordon, R.A. (1991). An MMPI response-set among adolescents: An evaluation of the limitations of the subtle/obvious subscales. *Psychological Assessment, 3,* 424–426.

Herreid, C.F., & Herreid, J.R. (1966). Differences in MMPI scores in native and non-native Alaskans. *The Journal of Social Psychology, 70,* 191–198.

Hiatt, D., & Hargrave, G.E. (1988). MMPI profiles of problem peace officers. *Journal of Personality Assessment, 52,* 722–731.

Hilts, D., & Moore, J.M., Jr. (2003). Normal range MMPI-A profiles among psychiatric inpatients. *Assessment, 10,* 266–272.

Himelstein, P. (1964). Further evidence of the Ego Strength scale as a measure of psychological health. *Journal of Consulting Psychology, 28,* 90–91.

Hiscock, M., & Hiscock, C.K. (1989). Refining the forced-choice method for detection of malingering. *Journal of Clinical and Experimental Neuropsychology, 11,* 967–974.

Hjemboe, S., Almagor, M., & Butcher, J.N. (1992). Empirical assessment of marital distress: The Marital Distress Scale (MDS) for the MMPI-2. In J.N. Butcher & C.D. Spielberger (Eds.), *Advances in personality assessment: Vol. 9* (pp. 141–152). Hillsdale, NJ: Lawrence Erlbaum Associates.

Hjemboe, S., & Butcher, J.N. (1991). Couples in marital distress: A study of personality factors as measured by the MMPI-2. *Journal of Personality Assessment, 57,* 216–237.

Hoelzle, J.B., & Meyer, J. (2008). The factor structure of the MMPI-2 Restructured Clinical (RC) Scales. *Journal of Personality Assessment, 90,* 443–455.

Hoffman, H., Loper, R.G., & Kammeier, M.L. (1974). Identifying future alcoholics with the MMPI alcoholism scales. *Quarterly Journal of Studies on Alcohol, 35,* 490–498.

Holcomb, W.R., & Adams, N. (1982). Racial influences on intelligence and personality measures of people who commit murder. *Journal of Clinical Psychology, 38,* 793–796.

Holmes, D.S. (1967). Male-female differences in MMPI Ego Strength: An artifact. *Journal of Consulting Psychology, 31,* 408–410.

Honaker, L.M. (1988). The equivalency of computerized and conventional MMPI administration: A critical review. *Clinical Psychology Review, 8,* 561–577.

Honaker, L.M., Harrell, T.H., & Buffaloe, J.D. (1988). Equivalency of microtest computer MMPI administration for standard and special scales. *Computers in Human Behavior, 4,* 323–337.

Houston, K.B., & Kelly, K.E. (1989). Hostility in unemployed women: Relation to work and marital experiences, social support, stress, and anger expression. *Personality and Social Psychology Bulletin, 15,* 175–182.

Houston, K.B., Smith, M.A., & Cates, D.S. (1989). Hostility patterns and cardiovascular reactivity to stress. *Psychophysiology, 26,* 337–342.

Houston, K.B., & Vavak, C.R. (1991). Cynical hostility: Developmental factors, psychosocial correlates, and health behaviors. *Health Psychology, 10,* 9–17.

Hovey, H.B. (1953). MMPI profiles and personality characteristics. *Journal of Consulting Psychology, 17,* 142–146.

Hovey, H.B., & Lewis, E.G. (1967). *Semiautomatic interpretation of the MMPI.* Brandon, VT: Clinical Psychology Publishing Company.

Hsu, L.M. (1984). MMPI T scores: Linear versus normalized. *Journal of Consulting and Clinical Psychology, 52,* 821–823.

Huber, N.A., & Danahy, S. (1975). Use of the MMPI in predicting completion and evaluating changes in a long-term alcoholism treatment program. *Journal of Studies on Alcohol, 36,* 1230–1237.

Huff, F.W. (1965). Use of actuarial description of abnormal personality in a mental hospital. *Psychological Reports, 17,* 224.

Humphrey, D.H., & Dahlstrom, W.G. (1995). The impact of changing from the MMPI to the MMPI-2 on profile configurations. *Journal of Personality Assessment, 64,* 428–439.

Hutton, H.E., & Miner, M.H. (1995). The validation of the Megargee–Bohn Typology in African American and Caucasian forensic psychiatric patients. *Criminal Justice and Behavior, 22,* 233–245.

Hutton, H.E., Miner, M.H., Blades, J.R., & Langfeldt, V.C. (1992). Ethnic differences on the MMPI Overcontrolled–Hostility scale. *Journal of Personality Assessment, 58,* 260–268.

Hutton, H.E., Miner, M.H., & Langfeldt, V.C. (1993). The utility of the Megargee-Bohn typology in a forensic psychiatric hospital. *Journal of Personality Assessment, 60,* 572–587.

Hyer, L., Fallon, J.H., Jr., Harrison, W.R., & Boudewyns, P.A. (1987). MMPI over-reporting by Vietnam combat veterans. *Journal of Clinical Psychology, 43,* 79–83.

Hyer, L., Woods, M.G., Summers, M.N., Boudewyns, P., & Harrison, W.R. (1990). Alexithymia among Vietnam veterans with post-traumatic stress disorder. *Journal of Clinical Psychiatry, 51,* 243–247.

Imhof, E.A. & Archer, R.P. (1997). Correlates of the MMPI-A Immaturity (IMM) Scale in an adolescent psychiatric sample. *Assessment, 4,* 169–179.

Inman, T.H., Vickery, C.D., Berry, D.T.R., Lamb, D.G., Edwards, C.L., & Smith, G.T. (1998). Development and initial validation of a new procedure for evaluating adequacy of effort given during neuropsychological testing: The Letter Memory Test. *Psychological Assessment, 10,* 128–139.

Inwald, R.E. (1988). Five-year follow-up study of departmental terminations as predicted by 16 preemployment psychological indicators. *Journal of Applied Psychology, 4,* 703–710.

Iverson, G.L., & Barton, E. (1999). Interscorer reliability of the MMPI-2: Should TRIN and VRIN be computer scored? *Journal of Clinical Psychology, 55,* 65–69.

Iverson, G.L., Franzen, M.D., & Hammond, J.A. (1995). Examination of inmates' ability to malinger on the MMPI-2. *Psychological Assessment, 7,* 118–121.

Jackson, D.N., Fraboni, M., & Helmes, E. (1997). MMPI-2 content scales: How much content do they measure? *Assessment, 4,* 111–117.

Jackson, D.N., & Messick, S. (1961). Acquiescence and desirability as response determinants on the MMPI. *Educational and Psychological Measurement, 21,* 771–790.

Jansen, D.G., & Garvey, F.J. (1973). High-, average-, and low-rated clergymen in a state hospital clinical program. *Journal of Clinical Psychology, 29,* 89–92.

Janus, M.D., Tolbert, H., Calestro, K., & Toepfer, S. (1996). Clinical accuracy ratings of MMPI approaches for adolescents: Adding ten years and the MMPI-A. *Journal of Personality Assessment, 67,* 364–383.

Johnson, J.R., Null, C., Butcher, J.N., & Johnson, K.N. (1984). Replicated item level factor analysis of the full MMPI. *Journal of Personality and Social Psychology, 47,* 105–114.

Johnson, M.E., & Brems, C. (1990). Psychiatric inpatient MMPI profiles: An exploration for potential racial bias. *Journal of Counseling Psychology, 37,* 213–215.

Johnson, M.E., Jones, G., & Brems, C. (1996). Concurrent validity of the MMPI-2 feminine gender role (GF) and masculine gender role (GM) scales. *Journal of Personality Assessment, 66,* 153–168.

Kamphuis, J.H., Arbisi, P.A., Ben-Porath, Y.S., & McNulty, J.L. (2008). Detecting comorbid axis-II status among inpatients using the MMPI-2 Restructured Clinical Scales. *European Journal of Psychological Assessment, 24,* 157–164.

Katz, M.M., & Lyerly, S.B. (1963). Methods for measuring adjustment and social behavior in the community: I. Rationale, description, discriminative validity and scale development. *Psychological Reports, 13*, 503–535.

Kawachi, I., Sparrow, D., Kubazansky, L.D., Spiro, A., Vokonas, P.S., & Weiss, S.T. (1998). Prospective study of a self-report Type A scale and risk of coronary heart disease: Test of the MMPI-2 Type A scale. *Circulation, 98*, 405–412.

Keane, T.M., Malloy, P.F., & Fairbank, J.A. (1984). Empirical development of an MMPI subscale for the assessment of combat-related post-traumatic stress disorder. *Journal of Consulting and Clinical Psychology, 52*, 888–891.

Keiller, S.W., & Graham, J.R. (1993). Interpreting low scores on the MMPI-2 clinical scales. *Journal of Personality Assessment, 61*, 211–223.

Kelch, L.W., & Wagner, E.E. (1992). Maximized split-half reliabilities and distributional characteristics for Harris–Lingoes subscales with few items: A reevaluation for the MMPI-2. *Perceptual & Motor Skills, 75*, 847–850.

Keller, J.W., & Piotrowski, C. (1989, March). *Psychological testing patterns in outpatient mental health facilities: A national study.* Paper presented at the meeting of the Southeastern Psychological Association, Washington, DC.

Keller, L.S., & Butcher, J.N. (1991). *Assessment of chronic pain with the MMPI-2.* Minneapolis: University of Minnesota Press.

Kelley, C.K., & King, G.D. (1979a). Cross validation of the 2–8/8–2 MMPI code type for young adult psychiatric outpatients. *Journal of Personality Assessment, 43*, 143–149.

Kelley, C.K., & King, G.D. (1979b). Behavioral correlates of the 2–7–8 MMPI profile type in students at a university mental health center. *Journal of Consulting and Clinical Psychology, 47*, 679–685.

Kelley, C.K., & King, G.D. (1979c). Behavioral correlates of infrequent two-point MMPI code types at a university mental health center. *Journal of Clinical Psychology, 35*, 576–585.

Kelly, W.L. (1974). Psychological prediction of leadership in nursing. *Nursing Research, 23*, 38–42.

Kenderdine, S.K., Phillips, E.J., & Scurfield, R.M. (1992). Comparison of the MMPI-PTSD subscale with PTSD and substance abuse patient populations. *Journal of Clinical Psychology, 48*, 136–139.

Kendrick, S., & Hatzenbeuhler, L. (1982). The effect of oral administration by a live examiner on the MMPI: A split-half design. *Journal of Clinical Psychology, 38*, 788–792.

Kinder, B.N., Curtiss, G., & Kalichman, S. (1992). Affective differences among empirically derived subgroups of headache patients. *Journal of Personality Assessment, 52*, 516–524.

King, G.D. (1978). Minnesota Multiphasic Personality Inventory. In O.K. Buros (Ed.), *Eighth mental measurements yearbook* (pp. 935–938). Highland Park, NJ: Gryphon.

Kirkcaldy, B.D., & Kobylinska, E. (1988). Psychological characteristics of breast cancer patients. *Psychotherapy & Psychosomatics, 48*, 32–43.

Kleinmuntz, B. (1960). An extension of the construct validity of the Ego Strength scale. *Journal of Consulting Psychology, 24*, 463–464.

Kleinmuntz, B. (1961). The college maladjustment scale (Mt): Norms and predictive validity. *Educational and Psychological Measurement, 21*, 1029–1033.

Kleinmuntz, B. (1963). MMPI decision rules for the identification of college maladjustment: A digital computer approach. *Psychological Monographs, 77* (14, Whole No. 577).

Kline, J.A., Rozynko, V.V., Flint, G., & Roberts, A.C. (1973). Personality characteristics of male Native-American alcoholic patients. *International Journal of the Addictions, 8,* 729–732.

Klinge, V., Lachar, D., Grisell, J., & Berman, W. (1978). Effects of scoring norms on adolescent psychiatric drug users' and nonusers' MMPI profiles. *Adolescence, 13,* 1–11.

Klinge, V., & Strauss, M.E. (1976). Effects of scoring norms on adolescent psychiatric patients' MMPI profiles. *Journal of Personality Assessment, 40,* 13–17.

Knapp, R.R. (1960). A reevaluation of the validity of MMPI scales of dominance and responsibility. *Educational and Psychological Measurement, 20,* 381–386.

Koeppl, P.M., Bolla-Wilson, K., & Bleecker, M.L. (1989). The MMPI: Regional difference or normal aging? *Journal of Gerontology: Psychological Sciences, 44,* 95–99.

Kopper, B.A., Osman, A., & Barrios, F.X. (2001). Assessment of suicidal ideation in young men and women: The incremental validity of the MMPI-2 content scales. *Death Studies, 25,* 593–607.

Kopper, B.A., Osman, A., Osman, J.R., & Hoffman, J. (1998). Clinical utility of the MMPI-A content scales and Harris–Lingoes subscales in the Assessment of suicidal risk factors in psychiatric adults. *Journal of Clinical Psychology, 54,* 191–200.

Koretzky, M.B., & Peck, A.H. (1990). Validation and cross-validation of the PTSD subscale of the MMPI with civilian trauma victims. *Journal of Clinical Psychology, 46,* 296–300.

Kornfeld, A.D. (1995). Police officer candidate MMPI-2 performance: Gender, ethnic, and normative factors. *Journal of Clinical Psychology, 51,* 536–540.

Koss, M.P. (1979). MMPI item content: Recurring issues. In J.N. Butcher (Ed.), *New developments in the use of the MMPI* (pp. 3–38). Minneapolis: University of Minnesota Press.

Koss, M.P. (1980). Assessing psychological emergencies with the MMPI. In J. Butcher, W. Dahlstrom, M. Gynther, & W. Schofield (Eds.), *Clinical notes on the MMPI* (No. 4). Minneapolis, MN: National Computer Systems.

Koss, M.P., Butcher, J.N., & Hoffman, N. (1976). The MMPI critical items: How well do they work? *Journal of Consulting and Clinical Psychology, 44,* 921–928.

Kostlan, A. (1954). A method for the empirical study of psychodiagnosis. *Journal of Consulting Psychology, 18,* 83–88.

Kramer, J.J., & Conoley, J.C. (Eds.). (1992). *The eleventh mental measurements yearbook.* Lincoln, NE: Buros Institute of Mental Measurements.

Kranitz, L. (1972). Alcoholics, heroin addicts and non-addicts: Comparisons on the MacAndrew Alcoholism scale on the MMPI. *Quarterly Journal of Studies on Alcohol, 33,* 807–809.

Krishnamurthy, R., Archer, R.P., & Huddleston, E.N. (1995). Clinical research note on psychometric limitations of two Harris–Lingoes subscales for the MMPI-2. *Assessment, 2,* 301–304.

Krueger, R.F., Caspi, A., Moffitt, T.E., & Silva, P.A. (1998). The structure and stability of common mental disorders (DSM-III-R): A longitudinal-epidemiological study. *Journal of Abnormal Psychology, 107,* 216–227.

Krueger, R.F., & Markon, K.E. (2006). Reinterpreting comorbidity: A model-based approach to understanding and classifying psychopathology. *Annual Review of Clinical Psychology, 2,* 111–133.

Kwan, K.K. (1999). MMPI and MMPI-2 performance of the Chinese: Cross-cultural applicability. *Professional Psychology: Research and Practice, 30,* 260–268.

Kwon, P. (2002). Comment on "Effects of acculturation on the MMPI-2 scores of Asian American students." *Journal of Personality Assessment, 78,* 187–189.

Lachar, D. (1974a). *The MMPI: Clinical assessment and automated interpretation*. Los Angeles: Western Psychological Services.

Lachar, D. (1974b). Prediction of early U.S. Air Force cadet adaptation with the MMPI. *Journal of Counseling Psychology, 21*, 404–408.

Lachar, D., Hays, J.R., & Buckle, K.E. (1991, August). *An exploratory study of MMPI-2 single-scale correlates*. Symposium presentation at the 99th Annual Convention of the American Psychological Association, San Francisco, CA.

Lachar, D., Klinge, V., & Grisell, J.L. (1976). Relative accuracy of automated MMPI narratives generated from adult norm and adolescent norm profiles. *Journal of Consulting and Clinical Psychology, 44*, 20–24.

Lachar, D., & Wrobel, T.A. (1979). Validation of clinicians' hunches: Construction of a new MMPI critical item set. *Journal of Consulting and Clinical Psychology, 47*, 277–284.

Ladd, J.S. (1998). The F(p) Infrequency–Psychopathology scale with chemically dependent inpatients. *Journal of Clinical Psychology 54*, 665–671.

Lally, S.J. (2003). What tests are acceptable for use in forensic evaluations? A survey of experts. *Professional Psychology: Research and Practice, 34*, 491–498.

Lane, P.J. (1976). *Annotated bibliography of the Megargee et al.'s Overcontrolled–Hostility (O–H) scale and the overcontrolled personality literature*. Unpublished materials. Florida State University, Tallahassee, FL.

Lanyon, R.I. (1968). *A handbook of MMPI group profiles*. Minneapolis: University of Minnesota Press.

Lanyon, R. I. (1995). Review of the Minnesota Multiphasic Personality Inventory–Adolescent. In J.C. Conoley & J.C. Impara (Eds.), *The twelfth mental measurements year book* (pp. 238–239). Lincoln, University of Nebraska Press.

Lapham, S.C., Skipper, B.J., Owen, J.P., Kleyboecker, K., Teaf, D., Thompson, B., & Simpson, G. (1995). Alcohol abuse screening instruments: Normative data collected from a first DWI offender screening program. *Journal of Studies on Alcohol, 56*, 51–59.

Larrabee, G.J. (2003). Detection of symptom exaggeration with the MMPI-2 in litigants with malingered neurocognitive deficit. *The Clinical Neuropsychologist, 17*, 54–68.

Lauterbach, D., Garcia, M., & Gloster, A. (2002). Psychometric properties and predictive validity of the Mt scale of the MMPI-2. *Assessment, 9*, 390–400.

Lawrence, S.B. (1985). Clinical evaluation of competence to stand trial. In C.P. Ewing (Ed.), *Psychology, psychiatry, and the law: A clinical and forensic handbook* (pp. 41–66). Sarasota, FL: Professional Resource Exchange, Inc.

Leath, J.R., & Pricer, R. (1968). *Reliability of the MMPI tape form with institutionalized epileptics of average intelligence*. Unpublished manuscript. Abilene State School, Abilene, TX.

Lee, H.B., Cheung, F.M., Man, H., & Hsu, S.Y. (1992). Psychological characteristics of Chinese low back pain patients: An exploratory study. *Psychology and Health, 6*, 119–128.

Lee, T.T.C., Graham, J.R., Sellbom, M., & Gervais, R.O. (2010, March). *Is the Symptom Validity Scale (FBS) biased against women?* Paper presented at the Society for Personality Assessment annual meeting, San Jose, CA.

Lees-Haley, P.R. (1992). Psychodiagnostic test usage by forensic psychologists. *American Journal of Forensic Psychology, 10*, 25–30.

Lees-Haley, P.R., English, L.T., & Glenn, W.J. (1991). A fake-bad scale on the MMPI-2 for personal injury claimants. *Psychological Reports, 68*, 203–210.

Lees-Haley, P.R., Smith, H.H., Williams, C.W., & Dunn, J.T. (1996). Forensic neuropsychological test usage: An empirical survey. *Archives of Clinical Neuropsychology, 11,* 45–51.

Legan, L., & Craig, R.J. (1996). Correspondence of MMPI and MMPI-2 with chemically dependent patients. *Journal of Clinical Psychology, 52,* 589–597.

Leon, G.R., Finn, S.E., Murray, D., & Bailey, J.M. (1988). Inability to predict cardiovascular disease from hostility scores or MMPI items related to Type A behavior. *Journal of Consulting and Clinical Psychology, 56,* 597–600.

Leon, G.R., Gillum, B., Gillum, R., & Gouze, M. (1979). Personality stability and change over a 30-year period—middle age to old age. *Journal of Consulting and Clinical Psychology, 47,* 517–524.

Leonelli, B.T., Chang, C., Bock, D.R., & Schilling, S.G. (2000). Interpretation of a full-information item-level factor analysis of the MMPI-2: Normative sampling and non-pathognomonic descriptors. *Journal of Personality Assessment, 74,* 400–422.

Lessenger, L.H. (1997). Acculturation and MMPI-2 scale scores of Mexican American substance abuse patients. *Psychological Reports, 80,* 1181–1182.

Levenson, M.R., Aldwin, C.M., Butcher, J.N., DeLabry, L., Workman-Daniels, K., & Bosse, R. (1990). The MAC scale in a normal population: The meaning of "false positives." *Journal of Studies on Alcohol, 51,* 457–462.

Levitt, E.E. (1990). A structural analysis of the impact of MMPI-2 on MMPI-1. *Journal of Personality Assessment, 55,* 562–577.

Levitt, E.E., Browning, J.M., & Freeland, L.J. (1992). The effect of MMPI-2 on the scoring of special scales derived from MMPI-1. *Journal of Personality Assessment, 59,* 22–31.

Lewandowski, D., & Graham, J.R. (1972). Empirical correlates of frequently occurring two-point code types: A replicated study. *Journal of Consulting and Clinical Psychology, 39,* 467–472.

Lewinsohn, P.M. (1965). Dimensions of MMPI change. *Journal of Clinical Psychology, 21,* 37–43.

Lezak, M.D. (1987). Norms for growing older. *Developmental Neuropsychology, 3,* 1–12.

Liao, H., Arvey, R.D., Butler, R.J., & Nutting, S.M. (2000). Correlates of work injury frequency and duration among firefighters. *Journal of Occupational Health Psychology, 6,* 229–242.

Lilienfeld, S.O. (1996). The MMPI-2 Antisocial Practices content scale: Construct validity and comparison with the Psychopathic Deviate scale. *Psychological Assessment, 8,* 281–293.

Lilienfeld, S.O. (1999). The relation of the MMPI-2 Pd Harris–Lingoes subscales to psychopathy, psychopathy facets, and antisocial behavior: Implications for clinical practice. *Journal of Clinical Psychology, 55,* 241–255.

Lilienfeld, S.O., & Andrews, B.P. (1996). Development and preliminary validation of a self-report measure of psychopathic personality traits in noncriminal populations. *Journal of Personality Assessment, 66,* 488–524.

Lim, J., & Butcher, J.N. (1996). Detection of faking on the MMPI-2: Differentiation among faking-bad, denial, and claiming extreme virtue. *Journal of Personality Assessment, 67,* 1–25.

Lingoes, J. (1960). MMPI factors of the Harris and Wiener subscales. *Journal of Consulting Psychology, 24,* 74–83.

Little, K.B., & Shneidman, E.S. (1959). Congruencies among interpretations of psychological test and anamnestic data. *Psychological Monographs, 73* (6, Whole No. 476).

Litz, B.T., Penk, W.E., Walsh, S., Hyer, L., Blake, D.D., Marx, B., & Bitman, D. (1991). Similarities and differences between MMPI and MMPI-2 applications to the assessment of post-traumatic stress disorder. *Journal of Personality Assessment, 57,* 238–253.

Livingston, R.B., Jennings, E., Colotla, V.A., Reynolds, C.R., & Shercliffe, R.J. (2006). MMPI-2 code-type congruence of injured workers. *Psychological Assessment, 18,* 126–130.

Long, K.A., & Graham, J.R. (1991). The Masculinity–Femininity scale of MMPI-2: Is it useful with normal men? *Journal of Personality Assessment, 57,* 46–51.

Long, K.A., Graham, J.R., & Timbrook, R.E. (1994). Socioeconomic status and MMPI-2 interpretation. *Measurement and Evaluation in Counseling and Development, 27,* 158–177.

Lubin, B., Larsen, R.M., & Matarazzo, J.D. (1984). Patterns of psychological test usage in the United States: 1935–1982. *American Psychologist, 39,* 451–454.

Lubin, B., Larsen, R.M., Matarazzo, J.D., & Seever, M. (1985). Psychological test usage patterns in five professional settings. *American Psychologist, 40,* 857–861.

Lucas, R.W., Mullin, P.J., Luna, C.B., & McInroy, D.C. (1977). Psychiatrists and a computer as interrogators of patients with alcohol-related illnesses: A comparison. *British Journal of Psychiatry, 131,* 160–167.

Lucio, E., Duran, C., Graham, J.R., & Ben-Porath, Y. S. (2002). Identifying faking bad on the MMPI-A with Mexican adolescents. *Assessment, 9,* 62–69.

Lushene, R.E. (1967). *Factor structure of the MMPI item pool.* Unpublished master's thesis, Florida State University, Tallahassee, FL.

Lyons, J.A., & Keane, T.M. (1992). Keane PTSD scale: MMPI and MMPI-2. *Journal of Traumatic Stress, 5,* 111–117.

Lyons, J.A., & Scotti, J.R. (1994). Comparability of two administration formulas of the Keane Posttraumatic Stress Disorder scale. *Psychological Assessment, 6,* 209–211.

Lyons, J.A., & Wheeler-Cox, T. (1999). MMPI, MMPI-2, and PTSD: Overview of scores, scales, and profiles. *Journal of Traumatic Stress, 12,* 175–183.

MacAndrew, C. (1965). The differentiation of male alcoholic out-patients from nonalcoholic psychiatric patients by means of the MMPI. *Quarterly Journal of the Studies on Alcohol, 26,* 238–246.

MacDonald, G.L. (1952). A study of the shortened group and individual forms of the MMPI. *Journal of Clinical Psychology, 8,* 309–311.

Marks, P.A., & Seeman, W. (1963). *Actuarial description of abnormal personality.* Baltimore, MD: Williams & Wilkins.

Marks, P.A., Seeman, W., & Haller, D.L. (1974). *The actuarial use of the MMPI with adolescents and adults.* Baltimore, MD: Williams & Wilkins.

Marsella, A.J., Sanborn, K.O., Kameoka, V., Shizuru, L., & Brennan, J. (1975). Cross-validation of self-report measures of depression among normal populations of Japanese, Chinese, and Caucasian ancestry. *Journal of Clinical Psychology, 31,* 281–287.

Marshall, W.L., & Hall, G.C.N. (1995). The value of the MMPI in deciding forensic issues in accused sexual offenders. *Sexual Abuse: Journal of Research and Treatment, 7,* 205–219.

Martin, M.A., Allan, A., & Allan, M.M. (2001). The use of psychological tests by Australian psychologists who do assessments for the courts. *Australian Journal of Psychology, 53,* 77–82.

Maruta, T., Hamburgen, M.E., Jennings, C.A., Offord, K.P., Colligan, R.P., Frye, R., & Malinchoc, M. (1993). Keeping hostility in perspective: Coronary heart disease and the hostility scale on the Minnesota Multiphasic Personality Inventory. *Mayo Clinic Proceedings, 68,* 109–114.

Matarazzo, J.D. (1986). Computerized clinical psychological test interpretations: Unvalidated plus all mean and no sigma. *American Psychologist, 41,* 14–24.

Maxon, L.S., & Neuringer, C. (1970). Evaluating legal competency. *Journal of Genetic Psychology, 117,* 267–273.

McCaffrey, R.J., Hickling, E.J., & Marrazo, M.J. (1989). Civilian-related post-traumatic stress disorder: Assessment-related issues. *Journal of Clinical Psychology, 45,* 72–76.

McCarthy, L., & Archer, R.P. (1998). Factor structure of the MMPI-A content scales: Item-level and scale-level findings. *Journal of Personality Assessment, 70,* 84–97.

McClinton, B.K., Graham, J.R., & Ben-Porath, Y.S. (1995, March). *Ethnicity and MMPI-2 substance abuse scales.* Paper presented at the 30th Annual Symposium on Recent Developments in the Use of the MMPI-2 and MMPI-A, St. Petersburg Beach, FL.

McCrae, R.R., Costa, P.T., Dahlstrom, W.G., Barefoot, J.C., Siegler, I.C., & Williams, R.B. (1989). A caution on the use of the MMPI K-correction in research on psychosomatic medicine. *Psychosomatic Medicine, 51,* 58–65.

McCranie, E.W., Watkins, L.O., Brandsma, J.M., & Sisson, B.D. (1986). Hostility, coronary heart disease (CHD) incidence, and total mortality: Lack of association in a 25-year follow-up study of 478 physicians. *Journal of Behavioral Medicine, 9,* 119–125.

McCreary, C., & Padilla, E. (1977). MMPI differences among Black, Mexican-American, and White male offenders. *Journal of Clinical Psychology, 33,* 171–177.

McCurdy, B.A., & Kelly, D.B. (1997). Correlations of the MMPI-2 low self-esteem scale with two self-esteem measures. *Psychological Reports, 81,* 826.

McFall, M.E., Moore, J.E., Kivlahan, D.R., & Capestany, F. (1988). Differences between psychotic and nonpsychotic patients on content dimensions of the MMPI Sc scale. *The Journal of Nervous and Mental Disease, 176,* 732–736.

McFall, M.E., Smith, D.E., Roszell, D.K., Tarver, D.J., & Malas, K.L. (1990). Convergent validity of measures of PTSD in Vietnam combat veterans. *American Journal of Psychiatry, 147,* 645–648.

McGrath, R.E., Pogge, D.L., & Kravic, C. (2003). Development of a short form for the MMPI-2 based on scale elevation congruence. *Assessment, 10,* 13–28.

McGrath, R.E., Sweeney, M., O'Malley, W.B., & Carlton, T.K. (1998). Identifying psychological contributions to chronic pain complaints with the MMPI-2: The role of the K scale. *Journal of Personality Assessment, 70,* 448–459.

McKee, G.R., Shea, S.J., Mogy, R.B., & Holden, C.E. (2001). MMPI-2 profiles of filicidal, mariticidal, and homicidal women. *Journal of Clinical Psychology, 57,* 367–374.

McKinley, J.C., & Hathaway, S.R. (1940). A multiphasic personality schedule (Minnesota): II. A differential study of hypochondriasis. *Journal of Psychology, 10,* 255–268.

McKinley, J.C., & Hathaway, S.R. (1944). The MMPI: V. Hysteria, hypomania, and psychopathic deviate. *Journal of Applied Psychology, 28,* 153–174.

McKinley, J.C., Hathaway, S.R., & Meehl, P.E. (1948). The MMPI: VI. The K scale. *Journal of Consulting Psychology, 12,* 20–31.

McNeal, T.P. (1997). *Examining the validity of computer based test interpretation with interpretive Q-sorts.* Unpublished master's thesis, University of Mississippi, Oxford.

McNulty, J.L., Ben-Porath, Y.S., & Graham, J.R. (1998). An empirical examination of the correlates of well-defined and not defined MMPI-2 code types. *Journal of Personality Assessment, 71,* 393–410.

McNulty, J.L., Ben-Porath, Y.S., Graham, J.R., & Stein, L.A.R. (1997, June). *Using the content component scales to facilitate content scale interpretation.* Paper presented at the 32nd Annual Symposium on Recent Developments in the Use of the MMPI (MMPI-2 and MMPI-A), Minneapolis, MN.

McNulty, J.L., Forbey, J.D., Graham, J.R., Ben-Porath, Y.S., Black, M.S., Anderson, S.V., & Burlew, A.K. (2003). MMPI-2 validity scale characteristics in a correctional sample. *Assessment, 10,* 288–298.

McNulty, J.L., Graham, J.R., Ben-Porath, Y.S., & Stein, L.A.R. (1997). Comparative validity of MMPI-2 scores of African American and Caucasian mental health center clients. *Psychological Assessment, 9,* 464–470.

McNulty, J.L., Harkness, A.R., Ben-Porath, Y.S., & Williams, C.L. (1997). Assessing the personality psychopathology five (PSY-5) in adolescents: New MMPI-A scales. *Psychological Assessment, 9,* 250–259.

Meehl, P.E. (1951). *Research results for counselors.* St. Paul, MN: State Department of Education.

Meehl, P.E. (1956). Wanted—a good cookbook. *American Psychologist, 11,* 263–272.

Meehl, P.E., & Dahlstrom, W.G. (1960). Objective configural rules for discriminating psychotic from neurotic MMPI profiles. *Journal of Consulting Psychology, 24,* 375–387.

Meehl, P.E., & Hathaway, S.R. (1946). The K factor as a suppressor variable in the MMPI. *Journal of Applied Psychology, 30,* 525–564.

Megargee, E.I. (1979). Development and validation of an MMPI-based system for classifying criminal offenders. In J.N. Butcher (Ed.), *New developments in the use of the MMPI* (pp. 303–324). Minneapolis: University of Minnesota Press.

Megargee, E.I. (1994). Using the Megargee MMPI-based classification system with MMPI-2s of male prison inmates. *Psychological Assessment, 6,* 337–344.

Megargee, E.I. (1997). Using the Megargee MMPI-based classification system with the MMPI-2's of female prison inmates. *Psychological Assessment, 9,* 75–82.

Megargee, E.I. (2000). *User's guide for the MMPI-2 Criminal Justice and Correctional Report.* Minneapolis: Pearson Assessments.

Megargee, E.I. (2004, May). *Development and initial validation of an MMPI-2 infrequency scale (Fc) for use with criminal offenders.* Paper presented at the 39th Annual Symposium on Recent Developments on the MMPI-2/MMPI-A, Minneapolis, MN.

Megargee, E. I. (2006). *Using the MMPI-2 in criminal justice and correctional settings.* Minneapolis, MN: University of Minnesota Press.

Megargee, E.I., Bohn, M.J., Meyer, J.E., Jr., & Sink, F. (1979). *Classifying criminal offenders: A new system based on the MMPI.* Beverly Hills, CA: Sage.

Megargee, E.I., & Carbonell, J.L. (1995). Use of the MMPI-2 in correctional settings. In Y.S. Ben-Porath, J.R. Graham, G.C.N. Hall, R.D. Hirshman, & M.S. Zaragoza (Eds.), *Forensic applications of the MMPI-2* (pp. 127–159). Thousand Oaks, CA: Sage.

Megargee, E.I., Carbonell, J.L., Bohn, M.J., Jr., & Sliger, G.L. (2001). *Classifying criminal offenders with the MMPI-2: The Megargee system.* Minneapolis: University of Minnesota Press.

Megargee, E.I., Cook, P.E., & Mendelsohn, G.A. (1967). The development and validation of an MMPI scale of assaultiveness in overcontrolled individuals. *Journal of Abnormal Psychology, 72,* 519–528.

Meikle, S., & Gerritse, R. (1970). MMPI cookbook pattern frequencies in a psychiatric unit. *Journal of Clinical Psychology, 26,* 82–84.

Meloy, J.R., & Gacono, C. (1995). Assessing the psychopathic personality. In J. Butcher (Ed.), *Clinical personality assessment: Practical approaches* (pp. 410–422). New York: Oxford University Press.

Melton, G.B., Petrila, J., Poythress, N., & Slobogin, C. (1987). *Psychological evaluations for the courts: A handbook for mental health professionals and lawyers.* New York: Guilford.

Melton, G.B., Weithorn, L.A., & Slobogin, C. (1985). *Community mental health centers and the courts: An evaluation of community-based forensic services.* Lincoln: University of Nebraska Press.

Merritt, R.D., Balogh, D.W., & Kok, C.J. (1998). DSM-IV Cluster A personality disorder diagnosis among young adults with a 2-7-8 MMPI profile. *Assessment, 5,* 273–285.

Messick, S., & Jackson, D.N. (1961). Acquiescence and the factorial interpretation of the MMPI. *Psychological Bulletin, 58,* 299–304.

Michael, K.D., Furr, R.M., Masters, K.S., Collett, B.R., Spielmans, G.I., Ritter, K., et al. (2009). Using the MMPI-2 to predict symptom reduction during psychotherapy in a sample of community outpatients. *Journal of Contemporary Psychotherapy, 39,* 157–163.

Mihura, J.L., Schlottmann, S., & Scott, A.B. (2000). Are the MMPI subtle subscales subtle measures of their scales? *Journal of Clinical Psychology, 56,* 139–148.

Miller, C.S., Shields, A.L., Campfield, D., Wallace, K.A., & Weiss, R.D. (2007). Substance use scales of the Minnesota Multiphasic Personality Inventory: An exploration of score reliability via meta-analysis. *Educational and Psychological Measurement, 67,* 1052–1065.

Miller, H.A. (2004). Examining the use of the M-FAST with criminal defendants incompetent to stand trial. *International Journal of Offender Therapy and Comparative Criminology, 48,* 268–280.

Miller, H.B., & Paniak, C.E. (1995). MMPI and MMPI-2 profile and code type congruence in a brain-injured sample. *Journal of Clinical & Experimental Neuropsychology, 17,* 58–64.

Miller, H.R., & Streiner, D.L. (1990). Using the Millon Clinical Multiaxial Inventory's Scale B and the MacAndrew Alcoholism scale to identify alcoholics with concurrent psychiatric diagnoses. *Journal of Personality Assessment, 54,* 736–746.

Miller, M.W., Kaloupek, D.G., Dillon, A.L., & Keane, T.M. (2004). Externalizing and internalizing subtypes of combat-related PTSD: A replication and extension using the PSY-5 Scales. *Journal of Abnormal Psychology, 113,* 635–645.

Monahan, J. (1981). *Predicting violent behavior: An assessment of clinical techniques.* Beverly Hills, CA: Sage.

Monnot, M.J., Quirk, S.W., Hoerger, M., & Brewer, L. (2009). Racial bias in personality assessment: Using the MMPI-2 to predict psychiatric diagnoses of African American and Caucasian chemical dependency inpatients. *Psychological Assessment, 21,* 137–151.

Montgomery, G.T., Arnold, B.R., & Orozco, S. (1990). MMPI supplemental scale performance of Mexican Americans and level of acculturation. *Journal of Personality Assessment, 54,* 328–342.

Moore, J.E., McFall, M.E., Kivlahan, D.R., & Capestany, F. (1988). Risk of misinterpretation of MMPI Schizophrenia scale elevations in chronic pain patients. *Pain, 32,* 207–213.

Moreland, K.L. (1985a). Computer-assisted psychological assessment in 1986: A practical guide. *Computers in Human Behavior, 1,* 221–233.

Moreland, K.L. (1985b). *Test–retest reliability of 80 MMPI scales.* Unpublished materials. (Available from National Computer Systems, Minneapolis, MN.)

Moreland, K.L., & Walsh, S. (1991, August). *Comparative concurrent validity of the MMPI-2 using MMPI and MMPI-2 based descriptors*. Symposium presentation at the 99th Annual Convention of the American Psychological Association, San Francisco, CA.

Morrison, T.L., Edwards, D.W., & Weissman, H.N. (1994). The MMPI and MMPI-2 as predictors of psychiatric diagnosis in an outpatient sample. *Journal of Personality Assessment, 62*, 17–30.

Mrazek, D.A., Klinnert, M.D., Mrazek, P., & Macey, T. (1991). Early asthma onset: Consideration of parenting issues. *Journal of the American Academy of Child Adolescent Psychiatry, 30*, 277–282.

Muller, B.P., & Bruno, L.N. (1988, March). *The MMPI and the Inwald Personality Inventory in the psychological screening of police candidates*. Paper presented at the 23rd Annual Symposium on Recent Developments in the Use of the MMPI, St. Petersburg, FL.

Munley, P.H., Bains, D.S., Bloem, W.D., & Busby, R.M. (1995). Post-traumatic stress disorder and the MMPI-2. *Journal of Traumatic Stress, 8*, 171–178.

Munley, P.H., Germain, J.M., Tovar-Murray, D., & Borgman, A.L. (2004). MMPI-2 code types and measurement error. *Journal of Personality Assessment, 82*, 179–188.

Neal, B. (1986). The K scale (MMPI) and job performance. In J. Reese & H. Goldstein (Eds.), *Psychological services for law enforcement* (pp. 83–90). Washington, DC: United States Government Printing Office.

Neal, L.A., Busuttil, W., Rollins, J., Herepath, R., Strike, P., & Turnbull, G. (1994). Convergent validity of measures of post-traumatic stress disorder in a mixed military and civilian population. *Journal of Traumatic Stress, 7*, 447–455.

Neal, L.A., Hill, N., Hughes, J., Middleton, A., & Busuttil, W. (1995). Convergent validity of measures of PTSD in an elderly population of former prisoners of war. *International Journal of Geriatric Psychiatry, 10*, 617–622.

Negy, C., Leal-Puente, L., Trainor, D.J., & Carlson, R. (1997). Mexican American adolescents' performance on the MMPI-A. *Journal of Personality Assessment, 69*, 205–214.

Nelson, D.V., Novy, D.M., Averill, P.M., & Berry, L.A. (1996). Ethnic comparability of the MMPI in pain patients. *Journal of Clinical Psychology, 52*, 485–497.

Nelson, L.D., Elder, J.T., Groot, J., Tehrani, P., & Grant, A.C. (2004). Personality testing and epilepsy: Comparison of two MMPI-2 correction procedures. *Epilepsy & Behavior, 5*, 911–918.

Nelson, L.D., & Marks, P.A. (1985). Empirical correlates of infrequently occurring MMPI code types. *Journal of Clinical Psychology, 41*, 477–482.

Nelson, N.W., Sweet, J.J., & Demakis, G.J. (2006). Meta-analysis of the MMPI-2 fake bad scale: Utility in forensic practice. *The Clinical Neuropsychologist, 20*, 39–58.

Nelson, N.W., Sweet, J.J., & Heilbronner, R.L. (2007). Examination of the new MMPI-2 Response Bias Scale (Gervais): Relationship with MMPI-2 validity scales. *Journal of Clinical and Experimental Neuropsychology, 29*, 67–72.

Newman, M.L., & Greenway, P. (1997). Therapeutic effects of providing MMPI-2 test feedback to clients at a university counseling service: A collaborative approach. *Psychological Assessment, 9*, 122–131.

Newmark, C.S. (1971). MMPI: Comparison of the oral form pressented by a live examiner and the booklet form. *Psychological Reports, 29*, 797–798.

Nichols, D.S. (1992). Minnesota Multiphasic Personality Inventory-2. In J.J. Kramer & J.C. Conoley (Eds.), *Eleventh mental measurements yearbook* (pp. 562–565). Lincoln, NE: Buros Institute of Mental Measurements.

Nichols, D.S. (2006). The trials of separating bath water from baby: A review and critique of the MMPI-2 Restructured Clinical scales. *Journal of Personality Assessment, 87,* 121–138.

Nichols, D.S., & Greene, R.L. (1991, March). *New measures for dissimulation on the MMPI/MMPI-2.* Paper presented at the 26th Annual Symposium on Recent Developments in the Use of the MMPI, St. Petersburg, FL.

Nichols, D.S., Greene, R.L., & Schmolck, P. (1989). Criteria for assessing inconsistent patterns of item endorsement on the MMPI: Rationale, development, and empirical trials. *Journal of Clinical Psychology, 45,* 239–250.

Nichols, D.S., Greene, R.L., Williams, C.L. (2009). *Gender bias in the MMPI-2 Fake Bad Scale (FBS) and FBS-r in MMPI-2-RF.* Paper presented at Society of Personality Assessment Chicago.

Nichols, W. (1980). The classification of law offenders with the MMPI: A methodological study. (Doctoral Dissertation, University of Alabama, 1979.) *Dissertation Abstracts International, 41,* No. 1, 333B.

Nicholson, R.A., Mouton, G.J., Bagby, R.M., Buis, T., Peterson, S.A., & Buigas, R.A. (1997). Utility of MMPI-2 indicators of response distortion: Receiver operating characteristic analysis. *Psychological Assessment, 9,* 471–479.

Noblitt, J.R. (1995). Psychometric measures of trauma among psychiatric patients reporting ritual abuse. *Psychological Reports, 77,* 743–747.

Nockleby, D.M., & Deaton, A.V. (1987). Denial versus distress: Coping patterns in post head trauma patients. *The International Journal of Clinical Neuropsychology, 10,* 145–148.

Nussbaum, D., Choudhry, R., & Martin-Doto, C. (1996). Cognitive impulsivity, verbal intelligence and locus of control in violent and nonviolent mentally disordered offenders. *American Journal of Forensic Psychology, 14,* 5–30.

Ogloff, J.R.P. (1995). The legal basis of forensic applications of the MMPI-2. In Y.S. Ben-Porath, J.R. Graham, G.C.N. Hall, R.D. Hirschman, & M.S. Zaragoza (Eds.), *Forensic applications of the MMPI-2* (pp. 18–47). Thousand Oaks, CA: Sage.

Ogloff, J.R.P., & Douglas, K.S. (2003). Psychological assessment in forensic settings. In J. Graham & J. Naglieri (Eds.), *Handbook of psychology: Assessment psychology, Vol. 10* (pp. 345–363). New York: John Wiley.

Okazaki, S., & Sue, S. (1995). Cultural considerations in psychological assessment of Asian-Americans. In J.N. Butcher (Ed.), *Clinical personality assessment: Practical approaches* (pp. 107–119). New York: Oxford University Press.

O'Laughlin, S., & Schill, T. (1994). The relationship between self-monitored aggression and the MMPI-2 F, 4, 9 composite and anger content scale scores. *Psychological Reports, 74,* 733–734.

Olmstead, D.W., & Monachesi, E.D. (1956). A validity check on MMPI scales of responsibility and dominance. *Journal of Abnormal and Social Psychology, 53,* 140–141.

O'Reilly, B.P., Graham, J.R., Hjemboe, S.M., & Butcher, J.N. (2003, June). *The construct validity of the MMPI-2 Marital Distress Scale.* Paper presented at the 38th Annual Symposium on Recent Developments on the MMPI-2/MMPI-A. Minneapolis, MN.

Orr, S.P., Claiborn, B.A., Forgue, D.F., DeJong, J.B., Pitman, R.K., & Herz, L.R. (1990). Psychometric profile of post-traumatic stress disorder, anxious, and healthy Vietnam veterans and correlations with psychophysiologic responses. *Journal of Consulting and Clinical Psychology, 58,* 329–335.

Osberg, T.M., & Harrigan, P. (1999). Comparative validity of the MMPI-2 Wiener–Harmon Subtle–Obvious scales in male prison inmates. *Journal of Personality Assessment, 72,* 36–48.

Osberg, T.M., Haseley, E.N., & Kamas, M.M. (2008). The MMPI-2 clinical scales and Restructured Clinical (RC) scales: Comparative psychometric properties and relative diagnostic efficiency in young adults. *Journal of Personality Assessment, 90,* 81–92.

Osberg, T.M., & Poland, D.L. (2001). Validity of the MMPI-2 basic and Harris-Lingoes subscales in a forensic sample. *Journal of Clinical Psychology, 57,* 1269–1380.

Osberg, T.M., & Poland, D.L. (2002). Comparative accuracy of the MMPI-2 and the MMPI-A in the diagnosis of psychopathology in 18-year-olds. *Psychological Assessment, 14,* 164–169.

Osborne, D. (1979). Use of the MMPI with medical patients. In J.N. Butcher (Ed.), *New developments in the use of the MMPI* (pp. 141–163). Minneapolis: University of Minnesota Press.

Otto, R.K., Buffington-Vollum, J.K., & Edens, J.R. (2003). Child custody evaluation. In A.M. Goldstein (Ed.), *Forensic psychology* (pp. 179–207). New York: Wiley.

Otto, R.K., & Collins, R.P. (1995). Use of the MMPI-2/MMPI-A in child custody evaluations. In Y.S. Ben-Porath, J.R. Graham, G.C.N. Hall, R.D. Hirshman, & M.S. Zaragoza (Eds.), *Forensic applications of the MMPI-2* (pp. 222–252). Thousand Oaks, CA: Sage.

Otto, R.K., Lang, A.R., Megargee, E.I., & Rosenblatt, A.I. (1988). Ability of alcoholics to escape detection by the MMPI. *Journal of Consulting and Clinical Psychology, 56,* 452–457.

Pace, T.M., Robbins, R.R., Choney, S.K., Hill, J.S., Lacey, K., & Blair, G. (2006). A cultural-contextual perspective on the validity of the MMPI-2 with American Indians. *Cultural Diversity and Ethnic Minority Psychology, 12,* 320–333.

Page, R.D., & Bozlee, S. (1982). A cross-cultural MMPI comparison of alcoholics. *Psychological Reports, 50,* 639–646.

Palav, A., Ortega, A., & McCaffrey, R.J. (2001). Incremental validity of the MMPI-2 content scales: A preliminary study with brain-injured patients. *Journal of Head Trauma Rehabilitation, 16,* 275–283.

Pallone, N.J. (1992). The MMPI in police officer selection: Legal constraints, case law, empirical data. *Journal of Offender Rehabilitation, 17,* 171–188.

Pancoast, D. L., & Archer, A. P. (1988). MMPI adolescent norms: Patterns and trends across 4 decades. *Journal of Personality Assessment, 52,* 691–706.

Panton, J.H. (1958). MMPI profile configurations among crime classification groups. *Journal of Clinical Psychology, 14,* 305–308.

Panton, J.H. (1959). The response of prison inmates to MMPI subscales. *Journal of Social Therapy, 5,* 233–237.

Paolo, A.M., & Ryan, J.J. (1992). Detection of random response sets on the MMPI-2. *Psychotherapy in Private Practice, 11,* 1–8.

Parker, C.A. (1961). The predictive use of the MMPI in a college counseling center. *Journal of Counseling Psychology, 8,* 154–158.

Parker, K.C., Hanson, R.K., & Hunsley, J. (1988). MMPI, Rorschach, and WAIS: A meta-analytic comparison of reliability, stability, and validity. *Psychological Bulletin, 103,* 367–373.

Pena, L.M., Megargee, E.I., & Brody, E. (1996). MMPI-A patterns of male juvenile delinquents. *Psychological Assessment, 8,* 388–397.

Penk, W.E., Robinowitz, R., Roberts, W.R., Dolan, M.P., & Atkins, H.G. (1981). MMPI differences of male Hispanic-American, Black and White heroin addicts. *Journal of Consulting and Clinical Psychology, 49,* 488–490.

Pepper, L.J., & Strong, P.N. (1958). *Judgmental subscales for the Mf scale of the MMPI.* Unpublished materials, Hawaii Department of Health, Honolulu, HI.

Persky, V.W., Kempthorne-Rawson, J., & Shekelle, R.B. (1987). Personality and risk of cancer: 20-year follow-up of the Western Electric Study. *Psychosomatic Medicine, 49,* 435–449.

Persons, R.W., & Marks, P.A. (1971). The violent 4–3 MMPI personality type. *Journal of Consulting and Clinical Psychology, 36,* 189–196.

Peterson, C.D., & Dahlstrom, W.G. (1992). The derivation of gender-role scales GM and GF for MMPI-2 and their relationship to scale 5 (Mf). *Journal of Personality Assessment, 59,* 486–499.

Peterson, D.R. (1954). Predicting hospitalization of psychiatric outpatients. *Journal of Abnormal and Social Psychology, 49,* 260–265.

Petroskey, L.J., Ben-Porath, Y.S., & Stafford, K.P. (2003). Correlates of the Minnesota Multiphasic Personality Inventory-2 (MMPI-2) Personality Psychopathology-Five (PSY-5) scales in a forensic assessment setting. *Assessment, 10,* 393–399.

Pinsoneault, T.B. (1996). Equivalency of computer-assisted and paper and pencil administered versions of the Minnesota Multiphasic Personality Inventory-2. *Computers in Human Behavior, 12,* 291–300.

Pinsoneault, T.B. (2005). Detecting random, partially random, and nonrandom Minnesota Multiphasic Personality Inventory–Adolescent protocols. *Psychological Assessment, 17,* 476–480.

Pinsoneault, T.B. (2007). Detecting random, partially random, and nonrandom Minnesota Multiphasic Personality Inventory-2 protocols. *Psychological Assessment, 19,* 159–164.

Piotrowski, C., & Belter, R.W. (1999). Internship training in psychological assessment: Has managed care had an impact? *Assessment, 6,* 381–389.

Piotrowski, C., & Keller, J.W. (1984). Attitudes toward clinical assessment by members of AABT. *Psychological Reports, 55,* 831–838.

Piotrowski, C., & Keller, J.W. (1989). Psychological testing in outpatient mental health facilities: A national survey. *Professional Psychology: Research and Practice, 20,* 423–425.

Piotrowski, C., & Lubin, B. (1990). Assessment practices of health psychologists: Survey of APA Division 38 practitioners. *Professional Psychology: Research and Practice, 21,* 99–106.

Piotrowski, C., Shery, D., & Keller, J.W. (1985). Psychodiagnostic test usage: A survey of the Society for Personality Assessment. *Journal of Personality Assessment, 49,* 115–119.

Platt, J.R., & Husband, S.D. (1987). Posttraumatic stress disorder and motor vehicle accident victims. *American Journal of Forensic Psychology, 5,* 35–42.

Pogge, D.L., Stokes, J.M., McGrath, R.E., Bilginer, L., & DeLuca, V.A. (2002). MMPI-A Structural Summary variables: Prevalence and correlates in an adolescent outpatient psychiatric sample. *Assessment, 9,* 334–342.

Pollack, D., & Shore, J.H. (1980). Validity of the MMPI with Native Americans. *American Journal of Psychiatry, 137,* 946–950.

Pope, K.S. (1992). Responsibilities in providing psychological test feedback to clients. *Psychological Assessment, 4,* 268–271.

Pope, K.S., Butcher, J.N., & Seelen, J. (2000). *The MMPI, MMPI-2, & MMPI-A in court: A practical guide for expert witnesses and attorneys, second edition.* Washington, DC: American Psychological Association.

Pope, M.K., Smith, T.W., & Rhodewalt, F. (1990). Cognitive, behavioral, and affective correlates of the Cook and Medley Hostility scale. *Journal of Personality Assessment, 54*, 501–514.

Poston, J.M., & Hanson, W.E. (2010). Meta-analysis of psychological assessment as a therapeutic intervention. *Psychological Assessment, 22*, 203–212.

Priest, W., & Meunier, G.F. (1993). MMPI-2 performance of elderly women. *Clinical Gerontologist, 14*, 3–11.

Pritchard, D.A., & Rosenblatt, A. (1980). Racial bias in the MMPI: A methodological review. *Journal of Consulting and Clinical Psychology, 48*, 263–267.

Prokop, C.K. (1986). Hysteria scale elevations in low back pain patients: A risk factor for misdiagnosis. *Journal of Consulting and Clinical Psychology, 54*, 558–562.

Quay, H. (1955). The performance of hospitalized psychiatric patients on the Ego Strength scale of the MMPI. *Journal of Clinical Psychology, 11*, 403–405.

Quereshi, M.Y., & Kleman, R.L. (1996). Factor analysis of MMPI-2 basic scales among college students. *Current Psychology, 15*, 167–178.

Query, W.T., Megran, J., & McDonald, G. (1986). Applying post-traumatic stress disorder MMPI subscale to World War II POW veterans. *Journal of Clinical Psychology, 42*, 315–317.

Quilty, L.C., & Bagby, R.M. (2007). Psychometric and structural analysis of the MMPI-2 Personality Psychopathology Five (PSY-5) facet subscales. *Assessment, 14*, 375–384.

Reed, M.K., Walker, B., Williams, G., McLeod, S., & Jones, S. (1996). MMPI-2 patterns in African-American females. *Journal of Clinical Psychology, 52*, 437–441.

Reese, P.M., Webb, J.T., & Foulks, J.D. (1968). A comparison of oral and booklet forms of the MMPI for psychiatric inpatients. *Journal of Clinical Psychology, 21*, 436–437.

Rhodes, R.J. (1969). The MacAndrew Alcoholism scale: A replication. *Journal of Clinical Psychology, 25*, 189–191.

Rich, C.C., & Davis, H.G. (1969). Concurrent validity of MMPI alcoholism scales. *Journal of Clinical Psychology, 25*, 425–426.

Richard, L.S., Wakefield, J.A., & Lewak, R. (1990). Similarity of personality variables as predictors of marital satisfaction: A Minnesota Multiphasic Personality Inventory (MMPI) item analysis. *Personality and Individual Differences, 11*, 39–43.

Ricketts, A.J. (2003). *Validity of MMPI-2 content scales and content component scales in a forensic diagnostic sample.* Unpublished doctoral dissertation, Kent State University, Kent, OH.

Ridenour, T.A., Miller, A.R., Joy, K.L., & Dean, R.S. (1997). "Profile" analysis of the personality characteristics of child molesters using the MMPI-2. *Journal of Clinical Psychology, 53*, 575–586.

Riley, J.L., III, & Robinson, M.E. (1998). Validity of MMPI-2 profiles in chronic back pain patients: Differences in path models of coping and somatization. *The Clinical Journal of Pain, 14*, 324–335.

Rinaldo, J.C.B., & Baer, R.A. (2003). Incremental validity of the MMPI-A Content scales in the prediction of self-reported symptoms. *Journal of Personality Assessment, 80*, 309–318.

Robers, H.P.H. (1992). Ethnicity and the MMPI-2: Cultural implications and limitations for Chinese Americans. *Dissertation Abstracts International, 52*, 2311B.

Robin, R.W., Greene, R.L., Albaugh, B., Caldwell, A., & Goldman, D. (2003). Use of the MMPI-2 in American Indians: I. Comparability of the MMPI-2 between two tribes and with the MMPI-2 normative group. *Psychological Assessment, 15*, 351–359.

Robinson, M.E., Greene, A.F., & Geisser, M.E. (1993). Specificity of MMPI cluster types to chronic illness. *Psychology and Health, 8,* 285–294.

Rogers, R. (1992). *Structured interview of reported symptoms.* Odessa, FL: Psychological Assessment Resources.

Rogers, R., Bagby, R.M., & Chakraborty, D. (1993). Feigning schizophrenic disorders on the MMPI-2: Detection of coached simulators. *Journal of Personality Assessment, 60,* 215–226.

Rogers, R., Bagby, R.M., & Dickens, S.E. (1992). *Structured Interview of Reported Symptoms (SIRS).* Odessa, FL: Psychological Assessment Resources.

Rogers, R., Gillis, J.R., McMain, S., & Dickens, S.E. (1988). Fitness evaluations: A retrospective study of clinical, criminal, and sociodemographic characteristics. *Canadian Journal of Behavioral Science, 20,* 192–200.

Rogers, R., Hinds, J.D., & Sewell, K.W. (1996). Feigning psychopathology among adolescent offenders: Validation of the SIRS, MMPI-A, and SIMS. *Journal of Personality Assessment, 67,* 244–257.

Rogers, R., & McKee, G.R. (1995). Use of the MMPI-2 in the assessment of criminal responsibility. In Y.S. Ben-Porath, J.R. Graham, G.C.N. Hall, R.D. Hirshman, & M.S. Zaragoza (Eds.), *Forensic applications of the MMPI-2* (pp. 103–126). Thousand Oaks, CA: Sage.

Rogers, R., Sewell, K.W., Harrison, K.S., & Jordan, M.J. (2006). The MMPI-2 Restructured Clinical scales: A paradigmatic shift in scale development. *Journal of Personality Assessment, 87,* 139–147.

Rogers, R., Sewell, K.W., Martin, M.A., & Vitacco, M.J. (2003). Detection of feigned mental disorders: A meta-analysis of the MMPI-2 and malingering. *Assessment, 10,* 160–177.

Rogers, R., Sewell, K.W., & Salekin, R.T. (1994). A meta-analysis of malingering on the MMPI. *Psychological Assessment, 1,* 227–237.

Rogers, R., Sewell, K.W., & Ustad, K.L. (1995). Feigning among chronic outpatients on the MMPI-2: A systematic examination of fake-bad indicators. *Assessment, 2,* 81–89.

Rohan, W.P. (1972). MMPI changes in hospitalized alcoholics: A second study. *Quarterly Journal of Studies on Alcohol, 33,* 65–76.

Rohan, W.P., Tatro, R.L., & Rotman, S.R. (1969). MMPI changes in alcoholics during hospitalization. *Quarterly Journal of Studies on Alcohol, 30,* 389–400.

Roman, D.D., Tuley, M.R., Villanueva, M.R., & Mitchell, W.E. (1990). Evaluating MMPI validity in a forensic psychiatric population: Distinguishing between malingering and genuine psychopathology. *Criminal Justice and Behavior, 17,* 186–198.

Roper, B.L., Ben-Porath, Y.S., & Butcher, J.N. (1991). Comparability of computerized adaptive and conventional testing with the MMPI-2. *Journal of Personality Assessment, 57,* 278–290.

Roper, B.L., Ben-Porath, Y.S., & Butcher, J.N. (1995). Comparability and validity of computerized adaptive testing with the MMPI-2. *Journal of Personality Assessment 65,* 358–371.

Rosch, D.S., Crowther, J.H., & Graham, J.R. (1991). MMPI derived personality description and personality subtypes in an undergraduate bulimic population. *Psychology of Addictive Behaviors, 5,* 15–22.

Rosen, A. (1963). Diagnostic differentiation as a construct validity indication for the MMPI Ego Strength scale. *Journal of General Psychology, 69,* 65–68.

Rosenberg, N. (1972). MMPI alcoholism scales. *Journal of Clinical Psychology, 28,* 515–522.

Rouhbakhsh, P., Lewis, V., & Allen-Byrd, L. (2004). Recovering alcoholic families: When is normal not normal and when is not normal healthy? *Alcoholism Treatment Quarterly, 22,* 35–53.

Rouse, S.V., Butcher, J.N., & Miller, K.B. (1999). Assessment of substance abuse in psychotherapy clients: The effectiveness of the MMPI-2 substance abuse scales. *Psychological Assessment, 11,* 101–107.

Rozensky, R.H., Honor, L.F., Rasinski, K., Tovian, S.M., & Herz, G.I. (1986). Paper-and-pencil versus computer-administered MMPI's: A comparison of patients' attitudes. *Computers in Human Behavior, 2,* 111–116.

Ryan, J.J., Dunn, G.E., & Paolo, A.M. (1995). Temporal stability of the MMPI-2 in a substance abuse sample. *Psychotherapy in Private Practice, 14,* 33–41.

Salekin, K.L., Ogloff, J.R.P., Ley, R.G., & Salekin, R.T. (2002). The Overcontrolled Hostility scale: An evaluation of its applicability with an adolescent population. *Criminal Justice and Behavior, 29,* 718–733.

Sawrie, S.M., Kabat, M.H., Dietz, C.B., Greene, R.L., Arredondo, R., & Mann, A.W. (1996). Internal structure of the MMPI-2 Addiction Potential Scale in alcoholic and psychiatric inpatients. *Journal of Personality Assessment, 66,* 177–193.

Schaffer, C.E., Pettigrew, C.G., Blouin, D., & Edwards, D.W. (1983). Multivariate classification of female offender MMPI profiles. *Journal of Crime and Justice, 6,* 57–66.

Schill, T., & Wang, S. (1990). Correlates of the MMPI-2 Anger content scale. *Psychological Reports, 67,* 800–802.

Schinka, J.A., Elkins, D.E., & Archer, R.P. (1998). Effects of psychopathology and demographic characteristics on MMPI-A scale scores. *Journal of Personality Assessment, 71,* 295–305.

Schinka, J.A., & LaLone, L. (1997). MMPI-2: Comparisons with a census-matched subsample. *Psychological Assessment, 9,* 307–311.

Schinka, J.A., LaLone, L., & Greene, G.L. (1998). Effects of psychopathology and demographic characteristics on MMPI-2 scale scores. *Journal of Personality Assessment, 70,* 197–211.

Schlenger, W.E., & Kulka, R.A. (1989). *PTSD scale development for the MMPI-2.* Research Triangle Park, NC: Research Triangle Institute.

Schretlen, D.J. (1988). The use of psychological tests to identify malingered symptoms of mental disorder. *Clinical Psychology Review, 8,* 451–476.

Schuldberg, D. (1992). Ego Strength revised: A comparison of the MMPI-2 and MMPI-1 versions of the Barron Ego Strength scale. *Journal of Clinical Psychology, 48,* 500–505.

Schwartz, G.F. (1977). *An investigation of the stability of single scale and two-point MMPI code types for psychiatric patients.* Unpublished doctoral dissertation, Kent State University, Kent, OH.

Schwartz, M.F., & Graham, J.R. (1979). Construct validity of the MacAndrew Alcoholism scale. *Journal of Consulting and Clinical Psychology, 47,* 1090–1095.

Segal, D.L., Hersen, M., VanHasselt, V.B., Silberman, C., & Roth, L. (1996). Diagnosis and assessment of personality disorders in older adults: A critical review. *Journal of Personality Disorders, 10,* 384–399.

Sellbom, M., & Bagby, R.M. (2008). Validity of the MMPI-2-RF (Restructured Form) L-r and K-r Scales in detecting underreporting in clinical and nonclinical samples. *Psychological Assessment, 20,* 370–376.

Sellbom, M., & Bagby, R.M. (2010). The detection of over-reported psychopathology with the MMPI-2-RF (Restructured Form) Validity Scales. *Psychological Assessment, 22,* 757–767.

Sellbom, M., & Ben-Porath, Y.S. (2005). Mapping the MMPI-2 Restructured Clinical (RC) Scales onto normal personality traits: Evidence of construct validity. *Journal of Personality Assessment, 85,* 179–187.

Sellbom, M., & Ben-Porath, Y.S. (2006). Forensic applications of the MMPI. In R. P. Archer (Ed.), *Forensic uses of clinical assessment instruments* (pp. 19–55). Mahwah, NJ: Lawrence Erlbaum Associates.

Sellbom, M., Ben-Porath, Y.S., & Bagby, R.M. (2008). On the hierarchical structure of mood and anxiety disorders: Confirmatory evidence and elaboration of a model of temperament markers. *Journal of Abnormal Psychology, 117,* 576–590.

Sellbom, M., Ben-Porath, Y.S., & Graham, J.R. (2004). *Correlates of the MMPI-2 Restructured Clinical (RC) scales in a college counseling setting.* Unpublished manuscript, Kent State University, Kent, OH.

Sellbom, M., Ben-Porath, Y. S., & Graham, J. R. (2006). Correlates of the MMPI-2 Restructured Clinical (RC) Scales in a college counseling setting. *Journal of Personality Assessment, 86,* 89–99.

Sellbom, M., Ben-Porath, Y.S., Graham, J.R., Arbisi, P.A., & Bagby, R.M. (2005). Susceptibility of the MMPI-2 clinical, Restructured Clinical (RC), and content scales to over- and under-reporting. *Assessment, 12,* 79–85.

Sellbom, M., Ben-Porath, Y.S., Lilienfeld, S.O., Patrick, C.J., & Graham, J.R. (2005). Assessing psychopathic personality traits with the MMPI-2. *Journal of Personality Assessment, 85,* 334–343.

Sellbom, M., Ben-Porath, Y.S., & Stafford, K.P. (2009, March). *Examining the hierarchical structure of the MMPI-2-RF externalizing scales: Evidence of construct validity.* Paper presented at the Society for Personality Assessment Annual Meeting, Chicago, IL.

Sellbom, M., Fischler, G.L., & Ben-Porath, Y.S. (2007). Identifying MMPI-2 predictors of police officer integrity and misconduct. *Criminal Justice and Behavior, 34,* 985–1004.

Sellbom, M., Graham, J.R., & Schenk, P.W. (2005). Symptom correlates of MMPI-2 scales and code types in a private practice setting. *Journal of Personality Assessment, 84,* 163–171.

Sellbom, M., Graham, J.R., & Schenk, P.W. (2006). Incremental validity of the MMPI-2 Restructured Clinical (RC) scales in a private practice sample. *Journal of Personality Assessment, 86,* 196–205.

Sellbom, M., Toomey, J.A., Wygant, D.B., Kucharski, L.T., & Duncan, S. (2010). Utility of the MMPI-2-RF (Restructured Form) validity scales in detecting malingering in a criminal forensic setting: A known-groups design. *Psychological Assessment, 22,* 22–31.

Serkownek, K. (1975). *Subscales for scales 5 and 0 of the Minnesota Multiphasic Personality Inventory.* Unpublished materials.

Shaevel, B., & Archer, R.P. (1996). Effects of MMPI-2 and MMPI-A norms on T-score elevations for 18-year-olds. *Journal of Personality Assessment, 67,* 72–78.

Sharpe, J.P., & Desai, S. (2001). The revised NEO Personality Inventory and the MMPI-2 Psychopathology Five in the prediction of aggression. *Personality and Individual Differences, 31,* 505–518.

Shekelle, R.B., Gale, M., Ostfeld, A.M., & Paul, O. (1983). Hostility, risk of coronary heart disease, and mortality. *Psychosomatic Medicine, 45,* 109–114.

Shepherd, K.L. (1997). *Prediction of treatment outcome using the MMPI-2.* Unpublished doctoral dissertation, Kent State University, Kent, OH.

Sherriffs, A.C., & Boomer, D.S. (1954). Who is penalized by the penalty for guessing? *Journal of Educational Psychology, 45,* 81–90.

Sherwood, N.E., Ben-Porath, Y.S., & Williams, C.L. (1997). *The MMPI-A content component scales.* Minneapolis: University of Minnesota Press.

Shondrick, D.D., Ben-Porath, Y.S., & Stafford, K.P. (1992, May). *Forensic applications of the MMPI-2.* Paper presented at the 27th Annual Symposium on Recent Developments in the Use of the MMPI (MMPI-2 and MMPI-A), Minneapolis, MN.

Sieber, K.O., & Meyers, L.S. (1992). Validation of the MMPI-2 Social Introversion subscales. *Psychological Assessment, 4,* 185–189.

Siegel, J.C. (1996). Traditional MMPI-2 validity indicators and initial presentation in custody evaluations. *American Journal of Forensic Psychology, 14,* 55–63.

Silver, R.J., & Sines, L.K. (1962). Diagnostic efficiency of the MMPI with and without the K correction. *Journal of Clinical Psychology, 18,* 312–314.

Simia, G.H., & di Loreto, A.O. (1970). *Comparability of oral and booklet forms of the MMPI.* Unpublished manuscript. Riverwood Community Mental Health Center, St. Joseph, MI.

Simms, L.J., Casillas, A., Clark, L.A., Watson, D., & Doebbeling, B.N. (2005). Psychometric evaluation of the restructured clinical scales of the MMPI-2. *Psychological Assessment, 17,* 345–358.

Simonds, E.C., Handel, R.W., & Archer, R.P. (2008). Incremental validity of the Minnesota Multiphasic Personality Inventory—2 and Symptom Checklist-90-Revised with mental health inpatients. *Assessment, 15,* 78–86.

Sines, L.K. (1959). The relative contribution of four kinds of data to accuracy in personality assessment. *Journal of Consulting Psychology, 23,* 483–492.

Sinnett, E.R. (1962). The relationship between the Ego Strength scale and rated in-hospital improvement. *Journal of Clinical Psychology, 18,* 46–47.

Sinnett, E.R., Holen, M.C., & Albott, W.L. (1995). MMPI scores of female victims. *Psychological Reports, 76,* 139–144.

Sivec, H.J., Hilsenroth, M.J., & Lynn, S.J. (1995). Impact of simulating borderline personality disorder on the MMPI-2: A costs-benefits model employing base rates. *Journal of Personality Assessment, 64,* 295–311.

Sivec, H.J., Lynn, S.J., & Garske, J.P. (1994). The effect of somatoform disorder and paranoid psychotic role-related dissimulations as a response set on the MMPI-2. *Assessment, 1,* 69–81.

Slesinger, D., Archer, R.P., & Duane, W. (2002). MMPI-2 characteristics in a chronic pain population. *Assessment, 9,* 406–414.

Sliger, G.L. (1997). *The applicability of the Megargee MMPI-based offender classification system to the MMPI-2s of women inmates.* Unpublished doctoral dissertation, Florida State University, Tallahassee, FL.

Sloan, P. (1988). Post-traumatic stress in survivors of an airplane crash-landing: A clinical and exploratory research intervention. *Journal of Traumatic Stress, 1,* 211–229.

Sloan, P., Arsenault, L., Hilsenroth, M., & Harvill, L. (1996). Assessment of noncombat, war-related posttraumatic stress symptomatology: Validity of the PK, PS, and Es scales. *Psychological Assessment, 3,* 37–41.

Smart, C.M., Nelson, N.W., Sweet, J.J., Bryant, F.B., Berry, D.T.R., Granacher, R.P., & Heilbronner, R.L. (2008). Use of MMPI-2 to predict cognitive effort: A hierarchically optimal classification tree analysis. *Journal of the International Neuropsychological Society, 14,* 842–852.

Smith, C.P., & Graham, J.R. (1981). Behavioral correlates for the MMPI standard F scale and for a modified F scale for Black and White psychiatric patients. *Journal of Consulting and Clinical Psychology, 49,* 455–459.

Smith, S.R., Hilsenroth, M.J., Castlebury, F.D., & Durham, T.W. (1999). The clinical utility of the MMPI-2 Antisocial Practices content scale. *Journal of Personality Disorders, 13,* 385–393.

Smith, T.W. (1992). Hostility and health: Current status of a psychosomatic hypothesis. *Health Psychology, 11,* 139–150.

Smith, T.W., & Frohm, K.D. (1985). What's so unhealthy about hostility? Construct validity and psychosocial correlates of the Cook–Medley Ho scale. *Health Psychology, 4,* 503–520.

Smith, T.W., Saunders, J.D., & Alexander, J.F. (1990). What does the Cook and Medley Hostility scale measure? Affect, behavior, and attributions in the marital context. *Journal of Personality and Social Psychology, 58,* 699–708.

Snyder, D.K., Kline, R.B., & Podany, E.C. (1985). Comparison of external correlates of MMPI substance abuse scales across sex and race. *Journal of Consulting and Clinical Psychology, 53,* 520–525.

Snyter, C.M., & Graham, J.R. (1984). The utility of Subtle and Obvious MMPI subscales. *Journal of Clinical Psychology, 40,* 981–985.

Sobel, H.J., & Worden, W. (1979). The MMPI as a predictor of psychosocial adaptation to cancer. *Journal of Consulting and Clinical Psychology, 47,* 716–724.

Solway, K.S., Hays, J.R., & Zieben, M. (1976). Personality characteristics of juvenile probation officers. *Journal of Community Psychology, 4,* 152–156.

Spanier, G.B. (1976). Measuring dyadic adjustment: New scales for assessing the quality of marriage and similar dyads. *Journal of Marriage and the Family, 38,* 15–28.

Spiegel, D.E. (1969). SPI and MMPI predictors of psychopathology. *Journal of Projective Techniques and Personality Assessment, 33,* 265–273.

Spiro, A., Butcher, J.N., Levenson, M.R., Aldwin, C.M., & Bose, R. (2000). Change and stability in personality: A five-year study of the MMPI-2 in older men. In J.N. Butcher (Ed.), *Basic sources on the MMPI-2* (pp. 443–462). Minneapolis: University of Minnesota Press.

Steffan, J.S., Clopton, J.R., & Morgan, R.D. (2003). An MMPI-2 scale to detect malingered depression (Md scale). *Assessment, 10,* 382–392.

Stein, K.B. (1968). The TSC scales: The outcome of a cluster analysis of the 550 MMPI items. In P. McReynolds (Ed.), *Advances in psychological assessment, Vol. I* (pp. 80–104). Palo Alto, CA: Science and Behavior Books.

Stein, L.A.R., & Graham, J.R. (1999). Detecting fake-good MMPI-A profiles in a correctional facility. *Psychological Assessment, 11,* 386–395.

Stein, L.A.R., Graham, J.R., Ben-Porath, Y.S., & McNulty, J.L. (1999). Using the MMPI-2 to detect substance abuse in an outpatient mental health setting. *Psychological Assessment, 11,* 94–100.

Stein, L.A.R., Graham, J.R., & Williams, C.L. (1995). Detecting fake-bad MMPI-A profiles. *Journal of Personality Assessment, 65,* 415–327.

Stein, L.A.R., McClinton, B.K., & Graham, J.R. (1998). Long term stability of MMPI-A scales. *Journal of Personality Assessment, 70,* 103–108.

Stevens, M.J., Kwan, K.-L., & Graybill, D.F. (1993). Comparison of MMPI-2 scores of foreign Chinese and Caucasian-American students. *Journal of Clinical Psychology, 49,* 23–27.

Stone, L.A., Bassett, G.R., Brousseau, J.D., Demers, J., & Stiening, J.A. (1972). Psychological test scores for a group of MEDEX trainees. *Psychological Reports, 31,* 827–831.

Storm, J., & Graham, J.R. (2000). Detection of coached general malingering on the MMPI-2. *Psychological Assessment, 12,* 158–165.

Strassberg, D.S. (1991). Interpretive dilemmas created by the Minnesota Multiphasic Personality Inventory-2 (MMPI-2). *Journal of Psychopathology and Behavioral Assessment, 13,* 53–59.

Strassberg, D.S., Clutton, S., & Karboot, P. (1991). A descriptive and validity study of the Minnesota Multiphasic Personality Inventory-2 (MMPI-2) in elderly Australian sample. *Journal of Psychopathology and Behavioral Assessment, 13,* 301–311.

Strassberg, D.S., & Russell, S.W. (2000). MMPI-2 content scale validity within a sample of chronic pain patients. *Journal for Psychopathology and Behavioral Assessment, 22,* 47–60.

Strassberg, D.S., Tilley, D., Bristone, S., & Oei, T.P.S. (1992). The MMPI and chronic pain: A cross-cultural view. *Psychological Assessment, 4,* 493–497.

Strauss, M.E., Gynther, M.D., & Wallhermfechtel, J. (1974). Differential misdiagnosis of Blacks and Whites by the MMPI. *Journal of Personality Assessment, 38,* 55–60.

Strenger, V.E. (1989). *Content homogeneous subscales for scale 7 of the MMPI.* Unpublished master's thesis, Kent State University, Kent, OH.

Strong, D.R., Greene, R.L., Hoppe, C., Johnston, T., & Olesen, N. (1999). Taxometric analysis of impression management and self-deception on the MMPI-2 in child-custody litigants. *Journal of Personality Assessment, 73,* 1–18.

Strupp, H.H., & Bloxom, A.L. (1975). An approach to defining a patient population in psychotherapy research. *Journal of Counseling Psychology, 22,* 231–237.

Sullivan, D.L., Miller, C., & Smelser, W. (1958). Factors in the length of stay and progress in psychotherapy. *Journal of Consulting Psychology, 22,* 1–9.

Svanum, S., & Ehrmann, L.C. (1993). Screening for maladjustment in college students: An application of receiver operating characteristic curve to MMPI scales. *Journal of Personality Assessment, 60,* 397–410.

Svanum, S., McGrew, J., & Ehrmann, L. (1994). Validity of the substance abuse scales of the MMPI-2 in a college student sample. *Journal of Personality Assessment, 62,* 427–439.

Swan, G.E., Carmelli, D., & Rosenman, R.H. (1991). Cook and Medley Hostility and the Type A behavior pattern: Psychological correlates of two coronary-prone behaviors. In M.H. Strube (Ed.), *Type A behavior* (pp. 89–106). Newbury Park, CA: Sage.

Swanson, J., Holzer, C., Ganju, V., & Jono, R. (1990). Violence and psychiatric disorder in the community: Evidence from the Epidemiologic Catchment Area Surveys. *Hospital and Community Psychiatry, 41,* 761–770.

Swenson, W.M. (1961). Structured personality testing in the aged: An MMPI study of the gerontic population. *Journal of Clinical Psychology, 17,* 302–304.

Swenson, W.M., Pearson, J.S., & Osborne, D. (1973). *An MMPI source book: Basic item, scale, and pattern data for 50,000 medical patients.* Minneapolis: University of Minnesota Press.

Swenson, W.M., Rome, H.P., Pearson, J.S., & Brannick, T.L. (1965). A totally automated psychological test: Experience in a medical center. *Journal of the American Medical Association, 191,* 925–927.

Taft, R. (1957). The validity of the Barron Ego Strength scale and the Welsh Anxiety Index. *Journal of Consulting Psychology, 21,* 247–249.

Tamkin, A.S. (1957). An evaluation of the construct validity of Barron's Ego Strength scale. *Journal of Consulting Psychology, 13,* 156–158.

Tamkin, A.S., & Klett, C.J. (1957). Barron's Ego Strength scale: A replication of an evaluation of its construct validity. *Journal of Consulting Psychology, 21,* 412.

Tanner, B.A. (1990). Composite descriptions associated with rare MMPI two-point code types: Codes that involve scale 5. *Journal of Clinical Psychology, 46,* 425–431.

Tanner, B.A. (2007). A Windows program to aid in MMPI-2 interpretation. *Computers in Human Behavior, 23,* 52–57.

Taulbee, E.S., & Sisson, B.D. (1957). Configural analysis of MMPI profiles of psychiatric groups. *Journal of Consulting Psychology, 21,* 413–417.

Taylor, J.R., Strassberg, D.S., & Turner, C.W. (1989). Utility of the MMPI in a geriatric population. *Journal of Personality Assessment, 53,* 665–676.

Tellegen, A. (1982). *Brief manual for the Differential Personality Questionnaire.* Unpublished manuscript, University of Minnesota, Minneapolis.

Tellegen, A., & Ben-Porath, Y.S. (1992). The new uniform T scores for the MMPI-2: Rationale, derivation, and appraisal. *Psychological Assessment, 4,* 145–155.

Tellegen, A., & Ben-Porath, Y.S. (1996). Evaluating the similarity of MMPI-2 and MMPI profiles: Reply to Dahlstrom and Humphrey. *Journal of Personality Assessment, 66,* 640–644.

Tellegen, A., & Ben-Porath, Y.S. (2008). *MMPI-2-RF: Technical manual.* Minneapolis: University of Minnesota Press.

Tellegen, A., Ben-Porath, Y.S., McNulty, J.L., Arbisi, P.A., Graham, J.R., & Kaemmer, B. (2003). *MMPI-2 Restructured Clinical (RC) scales: Development, validation, and interpretation.* Minneapolis: University of Minnesota Press.

Tellegen, A., Ben-Porath, Y.S., & Sellbom, M. (2009). Construct validity of the MMPI-2 Restructured Clinical (RC) scales: Reply to Rouse, Greene, Butcher, Nichols, & Williams. *Journal of Personality Assessment, 91,* 211–221.

Tellegen, A., Ben-Porath, Y.S., Sellbom, M., Arbisi, P.A., McNulty, J.L., & Graham, J.R. (2006). Further evidence on the validity of the MMPI-2 Restructured Clinical (RC) scales: Addressing questions raised by Rogers, Sewell, Harrison, and Jordan and Nichols. *Journal of Personality Assessment, 87,* 148–171.

Terman, L.M., & Miles, C.C. (1936). *Sex and personality: Studies in masculinity and femininity.* New York: McGraw-Hill.

Timbrook, R.E. (1998). *Comparison of clinician's interpretations of MMPI and MMPI-2 profiles with congruent and incongruent code types in a psychiatric sample.* Unpublished doctoral dissertation, Kent State University, Kent, OH.

Timbrook, R.E., & Graham, J.R. (1992). *The meaning of low scores on the MMPI-2 clinical and content scales in a psychiatric setting.* Unpublished manuscript, Kent State University, Kent, OH.

Timbrook, R.E., & Graham, J.R. (1994). Ethnic differences on the MMPI-2? *Psychological Assessment, 6,* 212–217.

Timbrook, R.E., Graham, J.R., Keiller, S.W., & Watts, D. (1993). Comparison of the Wiener–Harmon Subtle–Obvious scales and the standard validity scales in detecting valid and invalid MMPI-2 profiles. *Psychological Assessment, 5,* 53–61.

Tolin, D.F., Maltby, N., Weathers, F.W., Litz, B.T., Knight, J., & Keane, T.M. (2004). The use of the MMPI-2 Infrequency-Psychopathology scale in the assessment of posttraumatic stress disorder in male veterans. *Journal of Psychopathology and Behavioral Assessment, 26,* 23–29.

Tombaugh, T.N. (1997). The Test of Memory Malingering (TOMM): Normative data from cognitively intact and cognitively impaired individuals. *Psychological Assessment, 9,* 260–268.

Tran, B.N. (1996). Vietnamese translation and adaptation of the MMPI-2. In J.N. Butcher (Ed.), *International adaptations of the MMPI-2: Research and clinical applications* (pp. 175–193). Minneapolis: University of Minnesota Press.

Trent, C.R., Rushlau, M.G., Munley, P.H., Bloem, W., & Driesenga, S. (2000). An ethnocultural study of posttraumatic stress disorder in African-American and White American Vietnam War veterans. *Psychological Reports, 87,* 585–592.

Trull, T.J., Useda, J.D., Costa, P.T., & McCrae, R.R. (1995). Comparison of the MMPI-2 Personality Psychopathology Five (PSY-5), the NEO-PI, and the NEO-PI-R. *Psychological Assessment, 7,* 508–516.

Tryon, R.C. (1966). Unrestricted cluster and factor analysis, with application to the MMPI and Holzinger-Harman problems. *Multivariate Behavioral Research, 1,* 229–244.

Tryon, R.C., & Bailey, D. (Eds.). (1965). *Users' manual of the BC TRY system of cluster and factor analysis* (taped version). Berkeley, CA: University of California Computer Center.

Tsai, D.C., & Pike, P.L. (2000). Effects of acculturation on the MMPI-2 scores of Asian American students. *Journal of Personality Assessment, 74,* 216–230.

Tsushima, W.T., Bridenstine, M.P., & Balfour, J.F. (2004). MMPI-2 scores in the outcome prediction of gastric bypass surgery. *Obesity Surgery, 14,* 528–532.

Tsushima, W.T., & Onorato, V.A. (1982). Comparison of MMPI scores of White and Japanese-American medical patients. *Journal of Consulting and Clinical Psychology, 50,* 150–151.

Tsushima, W.T., & Stoddard, V.M. (1990). Ethnic group similarities in the biofeedback treatment of pain. *Medical Psychotherapy: An International Journal, 3,* 69–75.

Uecker, A.E. (1970). Differentiating male alcoholics from other psychiatric inpatients: Validity of the MacAndrew scale. *Quarterly Journal of Studies on Alcohol, 31,* 379–383.

Uecker, A.E., Boutilier, L.R., & Richardson, E.H. (1980). "Indianism" and MMPI scores of men alcoholics. *Journal of Studies on Alcohol, 41,* 357–362.

Urmer, A.H., Black, H.O., & Wendland, L.V. (1960). A comparison of taped and booklet forms of the Minnesota Multiphasic Personality Inventory. *Journal of Clinical Psychology, 16,* 33–34.

Vanderploeg, R.D., Sisson, G.F.P., & Hickling, E.J. (1987). A reevaluation of the use of the MMPI in the assessment of combat-related post-traumatic stress disorder. *Journal of Personality Assessment, 51,* 140–150.

Velasquez, R.J. (1995). Personality assessment of Hispanic clients. In J.N. Butcher (Ed.), *Clinical personality assessment: Practical approaches* (pp. 120–139). New York: Oxford University Press.

Velasquez, R.J., Ayala, G.X., & Mendoza, S.A. (1998). *Psychodiagnostic assessment of U.S. Latinos: MMPI, MMPI-2, and MMPI-A results.* East Lansing, MI: Julian Samora Institute.

Velasquez, R.J., & Callahan, W.J. (1990a). MMPI comparisons of Hispanic- and White-American veterans seeking treatment for alcoholism. *Psychological Reports, 67,* 95–98.

Velasquez, R.J., & Callahan, W.J. (1990b). MMPIs of Hispanic, Black, and White DSM-III schizophrenics. *Psychological Reports, 66,* 819–822.

Velasquez, R.J., Callahan, W.J., & Carrillo, R. (1989). MMPI profiles of Hispanic-American inpatient and outpatient sex offenders. *Psychological Reports, 65,* 1055–1058.

Velasquez, R.J., Callahan, W.J., & Carrillo, R. (1991). MMPI differences among Mexican-American male and female psychiatric inpatients. *Psychological Reports 68,* 123–127.

Velasquez, R.J., Callahan, W.J., & Young, R. (1993). Hispanic and White MMPI comparisons: Does psychiatric diagnosis make a difference? *Journal of Clinical Psychology, 49,* 528–534.

Velasquez, R.J., Gonzales, R.J., Butcher, J.N., Castillo-Canez, I., Apodaca, J.X., & Chavira, D. (1997). Use of MMPI-2 with Chicanos: Strategies for counselors. *Journal of Multicultural Counseling and Development, 25,* 107–120.

Veltri, C.O., Graham, J.R., Sellbom, M., Ben-Porath, Y.S., Forbey, J.D., O'Connell, C., et al. (2009). Correlates of MMPI-A scales in acute psychiatric and forensic samples. *Journal of Personality Assessment, 91,* 288–300.

Vendrig, A.A. (1999). Prognostic factors and treatment-related changes associated with return to work in the multimodal treatment of chronic back pain. *Journal of Behavioral Medicine, 22,* 217–232.

Vendrig, A.A., Derksen, J.J.L., & de Mey, H.R. (1999). Utility of selected MMPI-2 scales in the outcome prediction for patients with chronic back pain. *Psychological Assessment, 11,* 381–385.

Vendrig, A.A., Derksen, J.J.L., & de Mey, H.R. (2000). MMPI-2 Personality Psychopathology Five (PSY-5) and prediction of treatment outcome for patients with chronic back pain. *Journal of Personality Assessment, 74,* 423–438.

Venn, J. (1988). MMPI profiles of Native, Mexican and Caucasian-American male alcoholics. *Psychological Reports, 62,* 427–432.

Verona, E., & Carbonell, J.L. (2000). Female violence and personality: Evidence of a pattern of overcontrolled hostility among one-time violent female offenders. *Criminal Justice and Behavior, 27,* 176–195.

Viglione, D.J., Wright, D.M., Dizon, N.T., Moynihan, J.E., DuPuis, S., & Pizitz, T.D. (2001). Evading detection on the MMPI-2: Does caution produce more realistic patterns of responding? *Assessment, 8,* 237–250.

Vincent, K.R. (1990). The fragile nature of MMPI code types. *Journal of Clinical Psychology, 46,* 800–802.

Wallace, A., & Liljequist, L. (2005). A comparison of the correlational structures and elevation patterns of the MMPI-2 Restructured Clinical (RC) and clinical scales. *Assessment, 12,* 290–294.

Waller, N.G. (1999). Searching for structure in the MMPI. In S.T. Embretson & S.L. Hershberger (Eds.), *The new rules of measurement: What every psychologist and educator should know* (pp. 185–217). Mahwah, NJ: Lawrence Erlbaum Associates.

Walters, G.D. (1987). Child sex offenders and rapists in a military setting. *International Journal of Offender Therapy and Comparative Criminology, 31,* 261–269.

Walters, G.D., Greene, R.L., & Jeffrey, T.B. (1984). Discriminating between alcoholic and nonalcoholic Blacks and Whites on the MMPI. *Journal of Personality Assessment, 48,* 486–488.

Walters, G.D., Greene, R.L., Jeffrey, T.B., Kruzich, D.J., & Haskin, J.J. (1983). Racial variations on the MacAndrew Alcoholism scale of the MMPI. *Journal of Consulting and Clinical Psychology, 51,* 947–948.

Wang, L., Zhang, J., Shi, Z., Zhou, M., & Li, Z. (2010). Internal consistencies and structural analysis of the MMPI-2 PSY-5 Facet subscales in Chinese population. *Journal of Psychopathology and Behavioral Assessment, 32,* 150–155.

Ward, L.C. (1991). A comparison of T scores from the MMPI and the MMPI-2. *Psychological Assessment: A Journal of Consulting and Clinical Psychology, 3,* 688–690.

Ward, L.C. (1997). Confirmatory factor analyses of the Anxiety and Depression content scales of the MMPI-2. *Journal of Personality Assessment, 68,* 678–691.

Ward, L.C., & Jackson, D.B. (1990). A comparison of primary alcoholics, secondary alcoholics, and nonalcoholic psychiatric patients on the MacAndrew Alcoholism scale. *Journal of Personality Assessment, 54,* 729–735.

Ward, L.C., & Perry, M.S. (1998). Measures of social introversion by the MMPI-2. *Journal of Personality Assessment, 70,* 171–182.

Wasyliw, O.E., Haywood, T.W., Grossman, L.S., & Cavanaugh, J.L. (1993). The psychometric assessment of alcoholism in forensic groups: The MacAndrew scale and response bias. *Journal of Personality Assessment, 60,* 252–266.

Watkins, C.E., Jr., Campbell, V.L., & McGregor, P. (1988). Counseling psychologists' uses of and opinions about psychological tests: A contemporary perspective. *Counseling Psychologist, 16,* 476–486.

Watson, C.G., Juba, M., Anderson, E.D., & Manifold, V. (1990). What does the Keane et al. PTSD scale for the MMPI measure? *Journal of Clinical Psychology, 46,* 600–606.

Watson, C.G., Kucala, T., & Manifold, V. (1986). A cross-validation of the Keane and Penk MMPI scales as measures of post-traumatic stress disorder. *Journal of Clinical Psychology, 42,* 727–732.

Watson, C.G., Kucala, T., Manifold, V., Vassar, P., & Juba, M. (1988). Differences between posttraumatic stress disorder patients with delayed and undelayed onsets. *Journal of Nervous and Mental Disease, 176,* 568–572.

Watson, C.G., Plemel, D., DeMotts, J., Howard, M.T., Tuorila, J., Moog, R., Thomas, D., & Anderson, D. (1994). A comparison of four PTSD measures' convergent validities in Vietnam veterans. *Journal of Stress and Coping, 7,* 75–82.

Watson, C.G., Thomas, D., & Anderson, P.E. (1992). Do computer administered Minnesota Multiphasic Personality Inventories underestimate booklet-based scores? *Journal of Clinical Psychology, 48,* 744–748.

Watson, D. (2005). Rethinking the mood and anxiety disorders: A quantitative hierarchical model for DSM-V. *Journal of Abnormal Psychology, 114,* 522–536.

Watson, D., & Tellegen, A. (1985). Toward a consensual structure of mood. *Psychological Bulletin, 98,* 219–235.

Weaver, G.M., & Wootton, R.R. (1992). The use of the MMPI special scales in the assessment of delinquent personality. *Adolescence, 27,* 545–554.

Webb, J.T., Miller, M.L., & Fowler, R.D. (1969). Validation of a computerized MMPI interpretation system. *Proceedings of the 77th Annual Convention of the American Psychological Association, 4,* 523–524.

Webb, J.T., Miller, M.L., & Fowler, R.D. (1970). Extending professional time: A computerized MMPI interpretation service. *Journal of Clinical Psychology, 26,* 210–214.

Weed, N.C., Ben-Porath, Y.S., & Butcher, J.N. (1990). Failure of Wiener and Harmon Minnesota Multiphasic Personality Inventory (MMPI) subtle scales as personality descriptors and as validity indicators. *Psychological Assessment: A Journal of Consulting and Clinical Psychology, 2,* 281–285.

Weed, N.C., Butcher, J.N., & Ben-Porath, Y.S. (1995). MMPI-2 measures of substance abuse. In J.N. Butcher & C.D. Spielberger (Eds.), *Advances in personality assessment* (Vol. 10, pp. 121–145). Hillsdale, NJ: Lawrence Erlbaum Associates.

Weed, N.C., Butcher, J.N., McKenna, T., & Ben-Porath, Y.S. (1992). New measures for assessing alcohol and drug abuse with the MMPI-2: The APS and AAS. *Journal of Personality Assessment, 58,* 389–404.

Weed, N.C., Butcher, J.N., & Williams, C. (1994). Development of the MMPI-A alcohol/drug problems scales. *Journal of Studies on Alcohol, 55,* 296–302.

Weed, N.C., & Han, K. (1992, May). *Is K correct?* Paper presented at the 27th Annual Symposium on Recent Developments in the Use of the MMPI (MMPI-2 and MMPI-A), Minneapolis, MN.

Weiner, I.B. (1987). Writing forensic reports. In I.B. Weiner & A.K. Hess (Eds.), *Handbook of forensic psychology* (pp. 511–528). New York: Wiley.

Weiner, I.B. (1995). How to anticipate ethical and legal challenges in personality assessments. In J.N. Butcher (Ed.), *Clinical personality assessment: Practical approaches* (pp. 95–103). New York: Oxford University Press.

Weisenburger, S.M., Harkness, A.R., McNulty, J.L., Graham, J.R., & Ben-Porath, Y.S. (2008). Interpreting low Personality Psychopathology-Five Aggressiveness scores on the MMPI-2: Graphical, robust, and resistant data analysis. *Psychological Assessment, 20*, 403–408.

Weiss, J.M. (2000). Idiographic use of the MMPI-2 in the assessment of dangerousness among incarcerated felons. *International Journal of Offender Therapy and Comparative Criminology, 44*, 70–83.

Welsh, G.S. (1948). An extension of Hathaway's MMPI profile coding system. *Journal of Consulting Psychology, 12*, 343–344.

Welsh, G.S. (1956). Factor dimensions A and R. In G.S. Welsh & W.G. Dahlstrom (Eds.), *Basic readings on the MMPI in psychology and medicine* (pp. 264–281). Minneapolis: University of Minnesota Press.

Welsh, G.S. (1965). MMPI profiles and factors A and R. *Journal of Clinical Psychology, 21*, 43–47.

Wetter, M.W., Baer, R.A., Berry, D.T.R., & Reynolds, S.K. (1994). The effect of symptom information on faking on the MMPI-2. *Assessment, 1*, 199–207.

Wetter, M.W., Baer, R.A., Berry, D.T.R., Robison, L.H., & Sumpter, J. (1993). MMPI-2 profiles of motivated fakers given specific symptom information: A comparison to matched patients. *Psychological Assessment, 5*, 317–323.

Wetter, M.W., Baer, R.A., Berry, D.T.R., Smith, G.T., & Larsen, L.H. (1992). Sensitivity of MMPI-2 validity scales to random responding and malingering. *Psychological Assessment, 4*, 369–374.

Wetter, M.W., & Corrigan, S.K. (1995). Providing information to clients about psychological tests: A survey of attorneys' and law students' attitudes. *Professional Psychology: Research and Practice, 26*, 1–4.

Wetter, M.W., & Deitsch, S.E. (1996). Faking specific disorders and temporal response consistency on the MMPI-2. *Psychological Assessment, 8*, 39–47.

Wetter, M.W., & Tharpe, B. (1995, March). *Sensitivity of the TRIN scale on the MMPI-2.* Paper presented at the 30th Annual Symposium on Recent Developments in the Use of the MMPI-2 and MMPI-A, St. Petersburg Beach, FL.

Wetzel, R.D., & Yutzy, S. (1994). Effect of reducing cut-off scores on Keane's Posttraumatic Stress Disorder scale. *Psychological Reports, 75*, 1296–1298.

Wetzler, S., Khadivi, A., & Moser, R.K. (1998). The use of the MMPI-2 for the assessment of depressive and psychotic disorders. *Assessment, 5*, 249–261.

Whitney, K.A., Davis, J.J., Shepard, P.H., & Herman, S.M. (2008). Utility of the Response Bias Scale (RBS) and other MMPI-2 validity scales in predicting TOMM performance. *Archives of Clinical Neuropsychology, 23*(7–8), 777–786.

Whitworth, R.H., & McBlaine, D.D. (1993). Comparison of the MMPI and MMPI-2 administered to Anglo- and Hispanic-American university students. *Journal of Personality Assessment, 61*, 19–27.

Whitworth, R.H., & Unterbrink, C. (1994). Comparison of MMPI-2 clinical and content scales administered to Hispanic and Anglo-Americans. *Hispanic Journal of Behavioral Sciences, 16,* 255–264.

Widiger, T.A. (1997). Mental disorders as discrete clinical conditions: Dimensional versus categorical classification. In S. Turner and M. Hersen (Eds.), *Adult psychopathology and diagnosis, 3rd edition* (pp. 3–23). New York: Wiley.

Widiger, T.A., Livesley, W.J. & Clark, L.A. (2009). An integrative dimensional classification of personality disorder. *Psychological Assessment, 21,* 243–255.

Wiener, D.N. (1947). Differences between the individual and group forms of the MMPI. *Journal of Consulting Psychology, 11,* 104–106.

Wiener, D.N. (1948). Subtle and obvious keys for the MMPI. *Journal of Consulting Psychology, 12,* 164–170.

Wiggins, J.S. (1959). Interrelations among MMPI measures of dissimulation under standard and social desirability instructions. *Journal of Consulting and Clinical Psychology, 23,* 419–427.

Wiggins, J.S. (1969). Content dimensions in the MMPI. In J.N. Butcher (Ed.), *MMPI: Research developments and clinical applications* (pp. 127–180). New York: McGraw-Hill.

Wiggins, J.S. (1973). *Personality and prediction: Principles of personality assessment.* Reading, MA: Addison-Wesley.

Wilderman, J.E. (1984). *An investigation of the clinical utility of the College Maladjustment scale.* Unpublished master's thesis, Kent State University, Kent, OH.

Williams, A.F., McCourt, W.F., & Schneider, L. (1971). Personality self-descriptions of alcoholics and heavy drinkers. *Quarterly Journal of Studies on Alcohol, 32,* 310–317.

Williams, C.L. (1986). MMPI profiles from adolescents: Interpretive strategies and treatment considerations. *Journal of Child and Adolescent Psychotherapy, 3,* 179–193.

Williams, C.L., Ben Porath, Y.S., & Hevern, V. (1994). Item level improvements for use of the MMPI with adolescents. *Journal of Personality Assessment, 63,* 284–294.

Williams, C.L., & Butcher, J.N. (1989a). An MMPI study of adolescents: I. Empirical validity of the standard scales. *Psychological Assessment: A Journal of Consulting and Clinical Psychology, 1,* 251–259.

Williams, C.L., & Butcher, J.N. (1989b). An MMPI study of adolescents: II. Verification and limitations of code type classifications. *Psychological Assessment: A Journal of Consulting and Clinical Psychology, 1,* 260–265.

Williams, C.L., Butcher, J.N., Ben Porath, Y.S., & Graham, J.R. (1992). *MMPI A content scales: Assessing psychopathology in adolescents.* Minneapolis: University of Minnesota Press.

Williams, H.L. (1952). The development of a caudality scale for the MMPI. *Journal of Clinical Psychology, 8,* 293–297.

Williams, J.E., & Weed, N.C. (2004a). Relative user ratings of MMPI-2 computer-based test interpretations. *Assessment, 11,* 316–329.

Williams, J.E., & Weed, N.C. (2004b). Review of computer-based test interpretation software for the MMPI-2. *Journal of Personality Assessment, 83,* 78–83.

Williams, R.B., Haney, T.L., Lee, K.L., Kong, Y.H., Blumenthal, J.A., & Whalen, R.E. (1980). Type A behavior, hostility, and coronary atherosclerosis. *Psychosomatic Medicine, 42,* 539–549.

Wimbish, L.G. (1984). *The importance of appropriate norms for the computerized inter-pretation of adolescent MMPI profiles.* Unpublished doctoral dissertation, Ohio State University, Columbus, OH.

Windle, M. (1994). Characteristics of alcoholics who attempted suicide: Co-occurring disorders and personality differences with a sample of male Vietnam era veterans. *Journal of Studies on Alcohol, 55,* 571–577.

Wirt, R.D. (1955). Further validation of the Ego Strength scale. *Journal of Consulting Psychology, 19,* 444.

Wirt, R.D. (1956). Actuarial prediction. *Journal of Consulting Psychology, 20,* 123–124.

Wisniewski, N.M., Glenwick, D.S., & Graham, J.R. (1985). MacAndrew scale and socio-demographic correlates of adolescent alcohol and drug use. *Addictive Behaviors, 10,* 55–67.

Wolf, A.W., Schubert, D.S.P., Patterson, M., Grande, T., & Pendleton, L. (1990). The use of the MacAndrew Alcoholism scale in detecting substance abuse and antisocial per-sonality. *Journal of Personality Assessment, 54,* 747–755.

Wolf, E.J., Miller, M.W., Orazem, R.J., Weierich, M.R., Castillo, D.T., Milford, J.,…Keane, T.M. (2008). The MMPI-2 Restructured Clinical Scales in the assessment of posttrau-matic stress disorder and comorbid disorders. *Psychological Assessment, 20,* 327–340.

Wolf, S., Freinek, W.R., & Shaffer, J.W. (1964). Comparability of complete oral and book-let forms of the MMPI. *Journal of Clinical Psychology, 20,* 375–378.

Wolfson, K.P., & Erbaugh, S.E. (1984). Adolescent responses to the MacAndrew Alcoholism scale. *Journal of Consulting and Clinical Psychology, 52,* 625–630.

Wong, J.L., & Besett, T.M. (1999). Sex differences on the MMPI-2 substance abuse scales in psychiatric inpatients. *Psychological Reports, 84,* 582–584.

Woo, M., & Oei, T.P.S. (2006). The MMPI-2 Gender-Masculine and Gender-Feminine scales: Gender roles as predictors of psychological health in clinical patients. *International Journal of Psychology, 41,* 413–422.

Woo, M., & Oei, T.P.S. (2008). Empirical investigations of the MMPI-2 Gender-Masculine and Gender-Feminine scales. *Journal of Individual Differences, 29,* 1–10.

Wooten, A.J. (1984). Effectiveness of the K correction in the detection of psychopathology and its impact on profile height and configuration among young adult men. *Journal of Consulting and Clinical Psychology, 52,* 468–473.

Wrobel, N.H., & Lachar, D. (1992). Refining adolescent MMPI interpretations: Moderating effects of gender in prediction of descriptions from parents. *Psychological Assessment, 4,* 375–381.

Wrobel, N.H., Wrobel, T.A., & McIntosh, J.W. (1988). Application of the Megargee MMPI typology to a forensic psychiatric population. *Criminal Justice and Behavior, 15,* 247–254.

Wygant, D.B., Ben-Porath, Y.S., Arbisi, P.A., Berry, D.T.R., Freeman, D.B., & Heilbronner, R.L. (2009). Examination of the MMPI-2 Restructured Form (MMPI-2-RF) validity scales in civil forensic settings: Findings from simulation and known group samples. *Archives of Clinical Neuropsychology, 24,* 671–680.

Wygant, D.B., Boutacoff, L.I., Arbisi, P.A., Ben-Porath, Y.S., Kelly, P.H., & Rupp, W.M. (2007). Examination of the MMPI-2 Restructured Clinical (RC) scales in a sample of bariatric surgery candidates. *Journal of Clinical Psychology in Medical Settings, 14,* 197–205.

Wygant, D.B., Sellbom, M., Graham, J.R., & Schenk, P.W. (2004, March). *Incremental validity of the MMPI-2 Personality Psychopathology Five (PSY-5) scales in assessing self-reported personality disorder criteria.* Paper presented at the annual meeting of the Society for Personality Assessment, Miami, FL.

Wygant, D.B., Sellbom, M., Graham, J.R., & Schenk, P.W. (2006). Incremental Validity of the MMPI-2 PSY-5 scales in assessing self-reported personality disorder criteria. *Assessment, 13,* 178–186.

Wygant, Y.S., Ben-Porath, Y.S., & Arbisi, P.A. (May, 2004). *Development and initial validation of a scale to detect somatic over-reporting.* Paper presented at the 39th Annual Symposium on Recent Developments in the Use of the MMPI-2 and MMPI-A. Minneapolis, MN.

Youngjohn, J.R., Davis, D., & Wolf, I. (1997). Head injury and the MMPI-2: Paradoxical severity effects and the influence of litigation. *Psychological Assessment, 9,* 177–184.

Zager, L.D., & Megargee, E.I. (1981). Seven MMPI drug abuse scales: An empirical investigation of their interrelationships, convergent, and discriminant validity, and degree of racial bias. *Journal of Personality and Social Psychology, 40,* 532–544.

Zalewski, C.E., & Gottesman, I.I. (1991). (Hu)Man versus mean revisited: MMPI group data and psychiatric diagnosis. *Journal of Abnormal Psychology, 100,* 562–568.

Zinn, S., McCumber, S., & Dahlstrom, W.G. (1999). Cross-validation and extension of the MMPI-A IMM scale. *Assessment, 6,* 1–6.

Ziskin, J. (1981). *Use of the MMPI in forensic settings* (Clinical Notes on the MMPI, No. 9). Minneapolis, MN: National Computer Systems.

▨ Appendix A

Koss–Butcher Critical Item Numbers

Acute Anxiety State: 2F, 3F, 5T, 10F, 15T, 28T, 39T, 59T, 140F, 172T, 208F, 218T, 223F, 301T, 444T, 463T, 469T

Depressed Suicidal Ideation: 9F, 38T, 65T, 71T, 75F, 92T, 95F, 130T, 146T, 215T, 233T, 273T, 303T, 306T, 388F, 411T, 454T, 485T, 506T, 518T, 520T, 524T

Threatened Assault: 37T, 85T, 134T, 213T, 389T

Situational Stress Due to Alcoholism: 125F, 264T, 487T, 489T, 502T, 511T, 518T

Mental Confusion: 24T, 31T, 32T, 72T, 96T, 180T, 198T, 299T, 311T, 316T, 325T

Persecutory Ideas: 17T, 42T, 99T, 124T, 138T, 144T, 145T, 162T, 216T, 228T, 241T, 251T, 259T, 314F, 333T, 361T

SOURCE: Excerpted (Appendix D) from Butcher, J.N., Graham, J.R., Ben-Porath, Y.S., Tellegen, A., Dahlstrom, W.G., & Kaemmer, B. (2001). *MMPI®-2 (Minnesota Multiphasic Personality Inventory®-2) Manual for Administration, Scoring, and Interpretation, Revised Edition.* Minneapolis: University of Minnesota Press. Copyright © 2001 by the Regents of the University of Minnesota. Used by permission of the University of Minnesota Press. All rights reserved. "MMPI®" and "Minnesota Multiphasic Personality Inventory®" are trademarks owned by the Regents of the University of Minnesota.

◈ Appendix B

Intercorrelations of MMPI–2 Scales for Normative Sample[a]

SCALE	VRIN	TRIN	F	F_B	F_p	L	K	S	Hs	D	Hy	Pd	Mf	Pa	Pt	Sc	Ma	Si
VRIN	—	05	40	41	25	-11	-40	-39	38	28	-04	26	01	10	44	44	13	37
TRIN	02	—	09	23	08	-12	-29	-25	00	-08	-30	00	-03	-01	22	20	20	08
F	35	18	—	65	61	-04	-36	-43	46	36	07	52	13	29	55	69	32	37
F_B	37	23	57	—	51	-06	-44	-49	48	34	01	48	04	31	63	70	32	40
F_p	26	14	54	55	—	26	-17	-19	27	22	01	24	-02	17	27	39	22	20
L	-03	-03	-09	-06	15	—	37	46	-05	09	15	-19	-18	-04	-31	-28	-19	-10
K	-40	-26	-40	-48	-25	28	—	81	-33	-10	44	-21	-02	-01	-68	-60	-35	-49
S	-35	-25	-45	-50	-26	34	82	—	-41	-18	29	-41	-12	-06	-72	-67	-46	-45
Hs	30	10	41	48	25	-06	-45	-48	—	53	41	33	04	23	53	56	15	37
D	29	-03	-34	39	17	00	-29	-33	56	—	35	34	18	26	47	39	-21	50
Hy	01	-16	10	08	-02	10	24	14	01	35	—	25	22	32	-05	01	09	-22
Pd	29	03	56	46	28	-19	-28	-45	53	37	26	—	23	41	46	55	36	13
Mf	-06	-08	-11	-12	-19	-11	-03	-05	36	12	10	01	—	29	22	24	07	10
Pa	13	-02	36	35	17	-07	-15	-15	01	31	22	41	13	—	34	39	15	06
Pt	40	20	55	62	30	-28	-71	-73	24	61	09	51	09	43	—	84	33	59
Sc	42	22	71	71	45	-25	-62	-67	59	48	15	64	-02	47	84	—	46	48
Ma	13	24	38	33	25	-17	-36	-50	60	-07	01	42	-06	21	37	51	—	-17
Si	38	05	35	42	21	-04	-56	-47	25	60	-14	16	08	17	63	49	-11	—

[a]Correlations for men are above the diagonal. Correlations for women are below diagonal. Decimal points are omitted.

SOURCE: Excerpted (Appendix F–1) from Butcher, J.N., Graham, J.R., Ben-Porath, Y.S., Tellegen, A., Dahlstrom, W.G., & Kaemmer, B. (2001). MMPI®-2(Minnesota Multiphasic Personality Inventory®-2) Manual for Administration, Scoring, and Interpretation, Revised Edition. Minneapolis: University of Minnesota Press. Used by permission of the University of Minnesota. Copyright © 2001 by the Regents of the University of Minnesota Press. All rights reserved. "MMPI®" and "Minnesota Multiphasic Personality Inventory®" are trademarks owned by the Regents of the University of Minnesota.

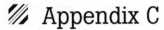 Appendix C

Percentile Equivalents for Uniform T Scores

UNIFORM T SCORE	PERCENTILE EQUIVALENT
30	≤1
35	4
40	15
45	34
50	55
55	73
60	85
65	92
70	96
75	98
80	≥99

SOURCE: Excerpted (Table 4) from Butcher, J.N., Graham, J.R., Ben-Porath, Y.S., Tellegen, A., Dahlstrom, W.G., & Kaemmer, B. (2001). *MMPI® -2(Minnesota Multiphasic Personality Inventory® -2) Manual for Administration, Scoring, and Interpretation, Revised Edition.* Minneapolis, MN: University of Minnesota Press. Copyright © 2001 by the Regents of the University of Minnesota. Used by permission of the University of Minnesota Press. All rights reserved. "MMPI® " and "Minnesota Multiphasic Personality Inventory® " are trademarks owned by the Regents of the University of Minnesota.

Appendix D

Data for Four Practice Cases

PRACTICE CASE 1: GEORGE

George was referred by his family physician to a psychologist in private practice. He had been involved in a minor automobile accident approximately 6 months prior to the referral. Although numerous medical evaluations had been negative, George continued to complain of pain in his neck and back. The referring physician asked for recommendations concerning the most appropriate treatment strategies for George.

George is a 22-year-old African American man. He graduated from college with a political science major and is a full-time first-year law student. George has never been married and currently lives alone in an apartment near the college campus where he is a student. He dates occasionally, but he has never been involved in a serious, lasting relationship. George's father owns an automobile dealership, and his mother is employed as a receptionist in a dentist's office.

George reports that he has never had psychological problems and has never received mental health services. He admits to occasional use of alcohol but denies abuse of alcohol or other substances. He states that he has taken various medications that have been prescribed for pain, but he takes them only as directed by his physician.

Although he is in almost constant pain, George has been attending his law classes regularly and is receiving above average grades. In interview he denies depression or dysphoria but admits that at times he feels tense and worried, especially about his law classes.

George was administered the MMPI-2 in the psychologist's office. He seemed to take the test seriously, and he completed it in just over 1 hour. He asked no questions during the testing.

**Minnesota Multiphasic
Personality Inventory®-2**

MMPI®-2

Minnesota Multiphasic Personality Inventory®-2

Extended Score Report

ID Number:	000173541
Age:	22
Gender:	Male
Date Assessed:	10/19/1998

PEARSON

⑫*PsychCorp*

Copyright © 1989, 1994, 2000, 2003, 2006 by the Regents of the University of Minnesota. All rights reserved.
Portions reproduced from the MMPI-2 test booklet. Copyright © 1942, 1943 (renewed 1970), 1989 by the Regents of the
University of Minnesota. All rights reserved. Portions excerpted from the *MMPI-2 Manual for Administration, Scoring, and
Interpretation, Revised Edition.* Copyright © 2001 by the Regents of the University of Minnesota. All rights reserved.
Distributed exclusively under license from the University of Minnesota by NCS Pearson, Inc.

Minnesota Multiphasic Personality Inventory and **MMPI** are registered trademarks of the University of Minnesota.
Pearson, the **PSI logo,** and **PsychCorp** are trademarks in the U.S. and/or other countries of Pearson Education, Inc., or its
affiliate(s).

TRADE SECRET INFORMATION
Not for release under HIPAA or other data disclosure laws that exempt trade secrets from disclosure.

[5.1 / 153 / 2.3.17]

Reproduced by permission of the University of Minnesota Press. All rights reserved. "MMPI® " and
"Minnesota Multiphasic Personality Inventory® " are trademarks owned by the University of Minnesota.

MMPI-2 VALIDITY AND CLINICAL SCALES PROFILE

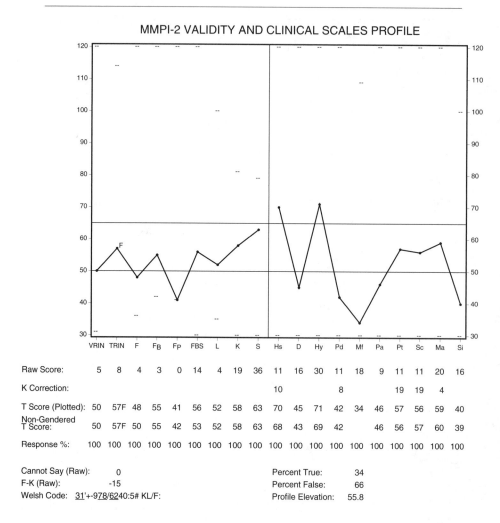

	VRIN	TRIN	F	F_B	Fp	FBS	L	K	S	Hs	D	Hy	Pd	Mf	Pa	Pt	Sc	Ma	Si
Raw Score:	5	8	4	3	0	14	4	19	36	11	16	30	11	18	9	11	11	20	16
K Correction:										10		8			19	19	4		
T Score (Plotted):	50	57F	48	55	41	56	52	58	63	70	45	71	42	34	46	57	56	59	40
Non-Gendered T Score:	50	57F	50	55	42	53	52	58	63	68	43	69	42		46	56	57	60	39
Response %:	100	100	100	100	100	100	100	100	100	100	100	100	100	100	100	100	100	100	100

Cannot Say (Raw):   0
F-K (Raw):   -15
Welsh Code: 31'+-978/6240:5# KL/F:

Percent True: 34
Percent False: 66
Profile Elevation: 55.8

The highest and lowest T scores possible on each scale are indicated by a "--".

For information on FBS, see Ben-Porath, Y. S., & Tellegen, A. (2006). The FBS: Current Status, a report on the Pearson web site (www.pearsonassessments.com/tests/mmpi_2.htm).

MMPI-2 **NON-K-CORRECTED** VALIDITY/CLINICAL SCALES PROFILE

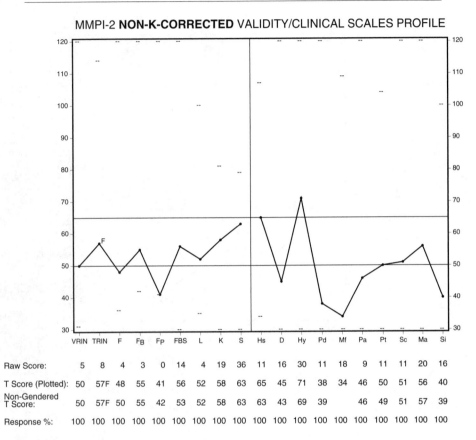

	VRIN	TRIN	F	F_B	Fp	FBS	L	K	S	Hs	D	Hy	Pd	Mf	Pa	Pt	Sc	Ma	Si
Raw Score:	5	8	4	3	0	14	4	19	36	11	16	30	11	18	9	11	11	20	16
T Score (Plotted):	50	57F	48	55	41	56	52	58	63	65	45	71	38	34	46	50	51	56	40
Non-Gendered T Score:	50	57F	50	55	42	53	52	58	63	63	43	69	39		46	49	51	57	39
Response %:	100	100	100	100	100	100	100	100	100	100	100	100	100	100	100	100	100	100	100

Cannot Say (Raw):	0	Percent True:	34
Profile Elevation:	52.8	Percent False:	66

The highest and lowest T scores possible on each scale are indicated by a "--".

Non-K-corrected T scores allow interpreters to examine the relative contributions of the Clinical Scale raw score and the K correction to K-corrected Clinical Scale T scores. Because all other MMPI-2 scores that aid in the interpretation of the Clinical Scales (the Harris-Lingoes subscales, Restructured Clinical Scales, Content and Content Component Scales, PSY-5 Scales, and Supplementary Scales) are not K-corrected, they can be compared most directly with non-K-corrected T scores.

For information on FBS, see Ben-Porath, Y. S., & Tellegen, A. (2006). The FBS: Current Status, a report on the Pearson web site (www.pearsonassessments.com/tests/mmpi_2.htm).

581

MMPI-2 RESTRUCTURED CLINICAL SCALES PROFILE

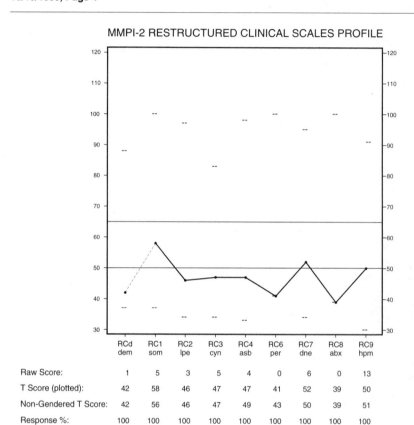

	RCd dem	RC1 som	RC2 lpe	RC3 cyn	RC4 asb	RC6 per	RC7 dne	RC8 abx	RC9 hpm
Raw Score:	1	5	3	5	4	0	6	0	13
T Score (plotted):	42	58	46	47	47	41	52	39	50
Non-Gendered T Score:	42	56	46	47	49	43	50	39	51
Response %:	100	100	100	100	100	100	100	100	100

The highest and lowest T scores possible on each scale are indicated by a "--".

LEGEND

dem= Demoralization	**cyn** = Cynicism	**dne** = Dysfunctional Negative Emotions
som= Somatic Complaints	**asb** = Antisocial Behavior	**abx** = Aberrant Experiences
lpe = Low Positive Emotions	**per** = Ideas of Persecution	**hpm**= Hypomanic Activation

For information on the RC scales, see Tellegen, A., Ben-Porath, Y.S., McNulty, J.L., Arbisi, P.A., Graham, J.R., & Kaemmer, B. 2003. The MMPI-2 Restructured Clinical (RC) Scales: Development, Validation, and Interpretation. Minneapolis: University of Minnesota Press.

MMPI-2 CONTENT SCALES PROFILE

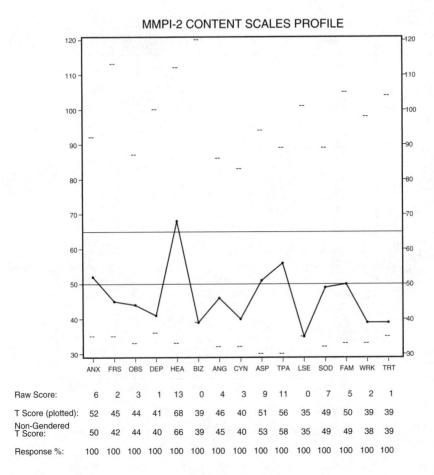

	ANX	FRS	OBS	DEP	HEA	BIZ	ANG	CYN	ASP	TPA	LSE	SOD	FAM	WRK	TRT
Raw Score:	6	2	3	1	13	0	4	3	9	11	0	7	5	2	1
T Score (plotted):	52	45	44	41	68	39	46	40	51	56	35	49	50	39	39
Non-Gendered T Score:	50	42	44	40	66	39	45	40	53	58	35	49	49	38	39
Response %:	100	100	100	100	100	100	100	100	100	100	100	100	100	100	100

The highest and lowest T scores possible on each scale are indicated by a "--".

583

MMPI-2 SUPPLEMENTARY SCALES PROFILE

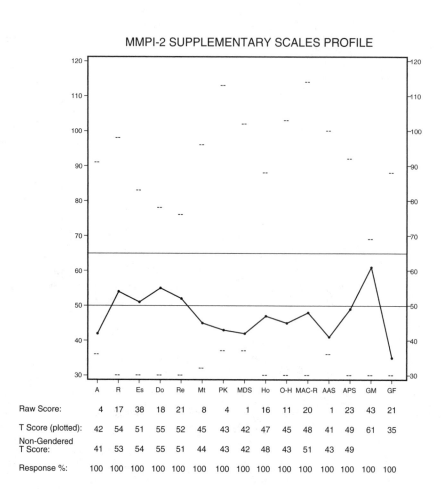

	A	R	Es	Do	Re	Mt	PK	MDS	Ho	O-H	MAC-R	AAS	APS	GM	GF
Raw Score:	4	17	38	18	21	8	4	1	16	11	20	1	23	43	21
T Score (plotted):	42	54	51	55	52	45	43	42	47	45	48	41	49	61	35
Non-Gendered T Score:	41	53	54	55	51	44	43	42	48	43	51	43	49		
Response %:	100	100	100	100	100	100	100	100	100	100	100	100	100	100	100

The highest and lowest T scores possible on each scale are indicated by a "--".

584

MMPI-2 PSY-5 SCALES PROFILE

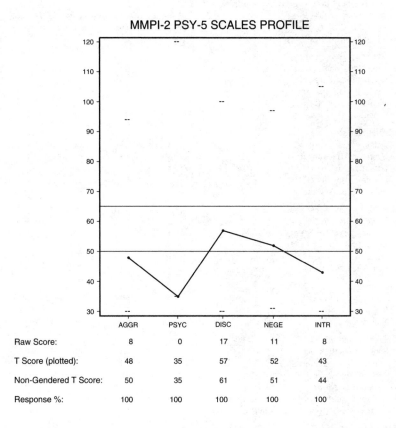

	AGGR	PSYC	DISC	NEGE	INTR
Raw Score:	8	0	17	11	8
T Score (plotted):	48	35	57	52	43
Non-Gendered T Score:	50	35	61	51	44
Response %:	100	100	100	100	100

The highest and lowest T scores possible on each scale are indicated by a "--".

585

ADDITIONAL SCALES
(to be used as an aid in interpreting the parent scales)

	Raw Score	T Score	Non-Gendered T Score	Resp %
Harris-Lingoes Subscales				
Depression Subscales				
Subjective Depression (D_1)	5	45	44	100
Psychomotor Retardation (D_2)	7	59	58	100
Physical Malfunctioning (D_3)	5	67	65	100
Mental Dullness (D_4)	2	48	48	100
Brooding (D_5)	1	45	44	100
Hysteria Subscales				
Denial of Social Anxiety (Hy_1)	5	56	56	100
Need for Affection (Hy_2)	10	63	63	100
Lassitude-Malaise (Hy_3)	5	61	60	100
Somatic Complaints (Hy_4)	5	62	59	100
Inhibition of Aggression (Hy_5)	3	48	47	100
Psychopathic Deviate Subscales				
Familial Discord (Pd_1)	2	51	51	100
Authority Problems (Pd_2)	4	53	57	100
Social Imperturbability (Pd_3)	5	57	58	100
Social Alienation (Pd_4)	1	35	34	100
Self-Alienation (Pd_5)	0	34	34	100
Paranoia Subscales				
Persecutory Ideas (Pa_1)	0	40	39	100
Poignancy (Pa_2)	1	41	40	100
Naivete (Pa_3)	7	60	60	100
Schizophrenia Subscales				
Social Alienation (Sc_1)	2	47	46	100
Emotional Alienation (Sc_2)	3	69	68	100
Lack of Ego Mastery, Cognitive (Sc_3)	1	48	49	100
Lack of Ego Mastery, Conative (Sc_4)	3	55	55	100
Lack of Ego Mastery, Defective Inhibition (Sc_5)	3	61	60	100
Bizarre Sensory Experiences (Sc_6)	2	51	50	100
Hypomania Subscales				
Amorality (Ma_1)	4	66	68	100
Psychomotor Acceleration (Ma_2)	6	53	54	100
Imperturbability (Ma_3)	4	53	54	100
Ego Inflation (Ma_4)	2	43	43	100
Social Introversion Subscales				
Shyness/Self-Consciousness (Si_1)	1	39	39	100
Social Avoidance (Si_2)	6	62	64	100
Alienation--Self and Others (Si_3)	2	41	41	100

		Non-Gendered		
	Raw Score	T Score	T Score	Resp %
Content Component Scales				
Fears Subscales				
Generalized Fearfulness (FRS$_1$)	2	62	58	100
Multiple Fears (FRS$_2$)	0	37	34	100
Depression Subscales				
Lack of Drive (DEP$_1$)	1	46	46	100
Dysphoria (DEP$_2$)	0	42	41	100
Self-Depreciation (DEP$_3$)	0	41	41	100
Suicidal Ideation (DEP$_4$)	0	45	46	100
Health Concerns Subscales				
Gastrointestinal Symptoms (HEA$_1$)	3	83	79	100
Neurological Symptoms (HEA$_2$)	3	60	58	100
General Health Concerns (HEA$_3$)	3	64	64	100
Bizarre Mentation Subscales				
Psychotic Symptomatology (BIZ$_1$)	0	44	44	100
Schizotypal Characteristics (BIZ$_2$)	0	41	41	100
Anger Subscales				
Explosive Behavior (ANG$_1$)	1	45	46	100
Irritability (ANG$_2$)	3	51	51	100
Cynicism Subscales				
Misanthropic Beliefs (CYN$_1$)	3	41	42	100
Interpersonal Suspiciousness (CYN$_2$)	0	34	35	100
Antisocial Practices Subscales				
Antisocial Attitudes (ASP$_1$)	7	52	54	100
Antisocial Behavior (ASP$_2$)	2	52	56	100
Type A Subscales				
Impatience (TPA$_1$)	4	57	58	100
Competitive Drive (TPA$_2$)	3	50	51	100
Low Self-Esteem Subscales				
Self-Doubt (LSE$_1$)	0	39	40	100
Submissiveness (LSE$_2$)	0	41	40	100
Social Discomfort Subscales				
Introversion (SOD$_1$)	6	53	55	100
Shyness (SOD$_2$)	1	41	41	100
Family Problems Subscales				
Family Discord (FAM$_1$)	1	40	39	100
Familial Alienation (FAM$_2$)	2	58	59	100

	Raw Score	T Score	Non-Gendered T Score	Resp %
Negative Treatment Indicators Subscales				
Low Motivation (TRT$_1$)	0	42	42	100
Inability to Disclose (TRT$_2$)	1	45	46	100

Uniform T scores are used for Hs, D, Hy, Pd, Pa, Pt, Sc, Ma, the content scales, the content component scales, and the PSY-5 scales. The remaining scales and subscales use linear T scores.

OMITTED ITEMS

Those items for which there is no response or for which both true and false responses have been entered are considered "omitted." The potential for lowering the elevation of individual scales or the overall profile and rendering the administration invalid increases with the number of omitted items. Defensiveness, confusion, carelessness, and indecision are among the common reasons for omitting items. Examination of the content of the items that were omitted by the respondent may reveal specific problem areas or suggest reasons for their not responding appropriately to all items. Following are the items that were omitted:

None omitted.

CRITICAL ITEMS

The MMPI-2 contains a number of items whose content may indicate the presence of psychological problems when endorsed in the deviant direction. These "critical items," developed for use in clinical settings, may provide an additional source of hypotheses about the respondent. However, caution should be used in interpreting critical items since responses to single items are very unreliable and should not be treated as scores on full-length scales -- for example, an individual could easily mismark or misunderstand a single item and not intend the answer given. The content of the items and the possibility of misinterpretation make it important to keep the test results strictly confidential. Special caution should be exercised when interpreting these items in nonclinical settings.

Acute Anxiety State (Koss-Butcher Critical Items)
28.
59.
218.
223.
301.
444.
463.

Depressed Suicidal Ideation (Koss-Butcher Critical Items)
38.

Mental Confusion (Koss-Butcher Critical Items)
180.

Antisocial Attitude (Lachar-Wrobel Critical Items)
27.

35.
105.
227.

254.

Family Conflict (Lachar-Wrobel Critical Items)
21.

Somatic Symptoms (Lachar-Wrobel Critical Items)
18.
28.
33.
44.
53.

59.
111.

Anxiety and Tension (Lachar-Wrobel Critical Items)
218.
223.
301.
320.
405.
463.

Deviant Thinking and Experience (Lachar-Wrobel Critical Items)
122.

Depression and Worry (Lachar-Wrobel Critical Items)
180.

End of Report

NOTE: This and previous pages of this report contain trade secrets and are not to be released in response to requests under HIPAA (or any other data disclosure law that exempts trade secret information from release). Further, release in response to litigation discovery demands should be made only in accordance with your profession's ethical guidelines and under an appropriate protective order.

ITEM RESPONSES

1: 1	2: 1	3: 1	4: 2	5: 2	6: 1	7: 1	8: 1	9: 1	10: 1
11: 2	12: 1	13: 2	14: 1	15: 2	16: 2	17: 2	18: 1	19: 1	20: 1
21: 1	22: 2	23: 2	24: 2	25: 2	26: 2	27: 1	28: 1	29: 2	30: 2
31: 2	32: 2	33: 2	34: 1	35: 1	36: 2	37: 2	38: 1	39: 2	40: 2
41: 1	42: 2	43: 1	44: 1	45: 2	46: 2	47: 1	48: 2	49: 1	50: 2
51: 1	52: 2	53: 1	54: 2	55: 1	56: 2	57: 1	58: 1	59: 1	60: 2
61: 1	62: 2	63: 1	64: 2	65: 2	66: 2	67: 2	68: 1	69: 2	70: 2
71: 2	72: 2	73: 2	74: 2	75: 1	76: 2	77: 1	78: 1	79: 1	80: 2
81: 2	82: 2	83: 1	84: 2	85: 2	86: 2	87: 2	88: 2	89: 2	90: 1
91: 1	92: 2	93: 1	94: 2	95: 1	96: 2	97: 2	98: 2	99: 2	100: 2
101: 2	102: 1	103: 2	104: 2	105: 1	106: 1	107: 1	108: 1	109: 1	110: 2
111: 1	112: 2	113: 2	114: 2	115: 1	116: 1	117: 2	118: 1	119: 2	120: 1
121: 1	122: 1	123: 1	124: 2	125: 1	126: 1	127: 2	128: 2	129: 1	130: 2
131: 1	132: 2	133: 1	134: 2	135: 2	136: 1	137: 2	138: 2	139: 1	140: 1
141: 2	142: 1	143: 1	144: 2	145: 2	146: 2	147: 2	148: 2	149: 2	150: 2
151: 2	152: 2	153: 2	154: 2	155: 2	156: 2	157: 2	158: 2	159: 1	160: 1
161: 2	162: 2	163: 1	164: 1	165: 1	166: 2	167: 2	168: 2	169: 1	170: 2
171: 1	172: 2	173: 2	174: 1	175: 2	176: 1	177: 1	178: 2	179: 2	180: 1
181: 2	182: 2	183: 1	184: 2	185: 2	186: 2	187: 2	188: 2	189: 1	190: 2
191: 2	192: 1	193: 2	194: 1	195: 2	196: 1	197: 2	198: 2	199: 1	200: 1
201: 1	202: 2	203: 1	204: 1	205: 2	206: 1	207: 2	208: 1	209: 1	210: 2
211: 2	212: 2	213: 2	214: 1	215: 2	216: 2	217: 2	218: 1	219: 2	220: 2
221: 2	222: 1	223: 2	224: 1	225: 2	226: 2	227: 1	228: 2	229: 2	230: 2
231: 1	232: 2	233: 2	234: 2	235: 2	236: 2	237: 1	238: 1	239: 1	240: 2
241: 2	242: 2	243: 2	244: 2	245: 1	246: 2	247: 2	248: 1	249: 2	250: 2
251: 2	252: 2	253: 2	254: 1	255: 1	256: 2	257: 2	258: 2	259: 2	260: 1
261: 1	262: 1	263: 2	264: 2	265: 2	266: 1	267: 1	268: 2	269: 2	270: 2
271: 2	272: 2	273: 2	274: 2	275: 2	276: 1	277: 2	278: 1	279: 2	280: 1
281: 2	282: 2	283: 2	284: 1	285: 2	286: 2	287: 2	288: 2	289: 2	290: 2
291: 2	292: 2	293: 2	294: 2	295: 1	296: 2	297: 2	298: 2	299: 2	300: 2
301: 1	302: 1	303: 2	304: 1	305: 2	306: 2	307: 2	308: 2	309: 2	310: 2
311: 2	312: 2	313: 2	314: 2	315: 2	316: 2	317: 2	318: 1	319: 2	320: 1
321: 2	322: 2	323: 2	324: 2	325: 2	326: 2	327: 2	328: 2	329: 1	330: 1
331: 2	332: 2	333: 2	334: 2	335: 1	336: 2	337: 2	338: 2	339: 2	340: 2
341: 2	342: 1	343: 1	344: 2	345: 1	346: 2	347: 2	348: 2	349: 2	350: 1
351: 2	352: 2	353: 1	354: 1	355: 2	356: 1	357: 2	358: 2	359: 2	360: 1
361: 2	362: 1	363: 2	364: 2	365: 2	366: 2	367: 1	368: 1	369: 2	370: 2
371: 2	372: 2	373: 2	374: 2	375: 2	376: 2	377: 2	378: 2	379: 2	380: 2
381: 2	382: 2	383: 1	384: 2	385: 1	386: 2	387: 2	388: 1	389: 2	390: 2
391: 2	392: 2	393: 1	394: 2	395: 2	396: 2	397: 2	398: 2	399: 2	400: 2
401: 1	402: 2	403: 2	404: 2	405: 2	406: 2	407: 2	408: 2	409: 2	410: 2
411: 2	412: 2	413: 1	414: 1	415: 2	416: 2	417: 2	418: 1	419: 1	420: 1
421: 2	422: 1	423: 2	424: 2	425: 2	426: 2	427: 1	428: 1	429: 1	430: 2
431: 2	432: 2	433: 1	434: 2	435: 2	436: 1	437: 1	438: 2	439: 2	440: 1

441: 1 442: 1 443: 1 444: 1 445: 2 446: 2 447: 2 448: 2 449: 2 450: 2
451: 2 452: 2 453: 1 454: 2 455: 1 456: 1 457: 2 458: 2 459: 1 460: 1
461: 2 462: 1 463: 1 464: 2 465: 1 466: 2 467: 1 468: 2 469: 2 470: 2
471: 2 472: 2 473: 2 474: 1 475: 2 476: 2 477: 1 478: 2 479: 2 480: 2
481: 1 482: 2 483: 2 484: 2 485: 2 486: 1 487: 2 488: 2 489: 2 490: 2
491: 2 492: 1 493: 1 494: 1 495: 1 496: 2 497: 2 498: 2 499: 2 500: 2
501: 1 502: 2 503: 2 504: 2 505: 2 506: 2 507: 2 508: 2 509: 2 510: 1
511: 2 512: 2 513: 2 514: 2 515: 2 516: 2 517: 2 518: 2 519: 2 520: 2
521: 1 522: 1 523: 1 524: 2 525: 2 526: 2 527: 2 528: 2 529: 2 530: 2
531: 2 532: 2 533: 2 534: 1 535: 1 536: 2 537: 2 538: 2 539: 2 540: 2
541: 1 542: 2 543: 2 544: 2 545: 2 546: 2 547: 2 548: 2 549: 2 550: 1
551: 2 552: 2 553: 2 554: 2 555: 2 556: 2 557: 1 558: 2 559: 2 560: 2
561: 1 562: 2 563: 2 564: 1 565: 2 566: 2 567: 1

PRACTICE CASE 2: ALICE

Alice completed the MMPI-2 as part of the admission process at an inpatient chemical dependency treatment program. She had been referred to the program by the court following her second conviction within 1 year for driving under the influence of alcohol. Completion of the treatment program is part of her probation.

Alice is a 43-year-old Caucasian woman. She graduated from a vocational high school and has been employed at several different clerical jobs. At the time of the evaluation she was not employed and was receiving unemployment benefits. She has been divorced for approximately 5 years. Her 10-year-old daughter and her 8-year-old son live with her in an apartment. Her ex-husband is supposed to pay child support but has been very irregular in doing so. Alice has dated occasionally since her divorce, but she is not seriously involved with anyone.

Alice is the second of three children in her family. She has an older brother and a younger sister. Her parents have been married for 40 years. Her father is a retired high school English teacher, and her mother has never been employed outside of the home.

Alice admits that she has a problem with alcohol and seems motivated to complete the treatment program. She says that she started using alcohol when she was in high school and feels that her use increased dramatically during the divorce process. Alice denies having serious psychological or emotional problems and has not been involved in mental health treatment. However, she admits that at times she feels overwhelmed by the responsibilities of raising her two children without much help from their father.

Alice seemed motivated to complete the MMPI-2, although it took her more than 2 hours to do so. Several times during the testing she asked for clarification concerning the meaning of some of the items.

**Minnesota Multiphasic
Personality Inventory®-2**

MMPI®-2

Minnesota Multiphasic Personality Inventory®-2

Extended Score Report

ID Number:	001091873
Age:	43
Gender:	Female
Date Assessed:	10/19/1998

PEARSON

PsychCorp

Copyright © 1989, 1994, 2000, 2003, 2006 by the Regents of the University of Minnesota. All rights reserved.
Portions reproduced from the MMPI-2 test booklet. Copyright © 1942, 1943 (renewed 1970), 1989 by the Regents of the
University of Minnesota. All rights reserved. Portions excerpted from the *MMPI-2 Manual for Administration, Scoring, and
Interpretation, Revised Edition.* Copyright © 2001 by the Regents of the University of Minnesota. All rights reserved.
Distributed exclusively under license from the University of Minnesota by NCS Pearson, Inc.

Minnesota Multiphasic Personality Inventory and **MMPI** are registered trademarks of the University of Minnesota.
Pearson, the **PSI logo,** and **PsychCorp** are trademarks in the U.S. and/or other countries of Pearson Education, Inc., or its
affiliate(s).

TRADE SECRET INFORMATION
Not for release under HIPAA or other data disclosure laws that exempt trade secrets from disclosure.

[5.1 / 153 / 2.3.17]

Reproduced by permission of the University of Minnesota Press. All rights reserved. "MMPI® " and
"Minnesota Multiphasic Personality Inventory® " are trademarks owned by the University of Minnesota.

MMPI-2 VALIDITY AND CLINICAL SCALES PROFILE

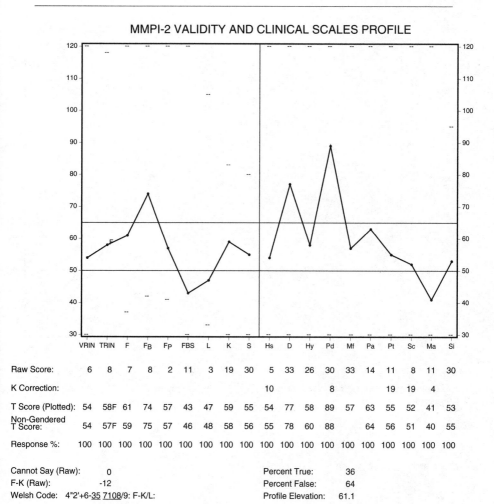

	VRIN	TRIN	F	F_B	Fp	FBS	L	K	S	Hs	D	Hy	Pd	Mf	Pa	Pt	Sc	Ma	Si
Raw Score:	6	8	7	8	2	11	3	19	30	5	33	26	30	33	14	11	8	11	30
K Correction:										10			8			19	19	4	
T Score (Plotted):	54	58F	61	74	57	43	47	59	55	54	77	58	89	57	63	55	52	41	53
Non-Gendered T Score:	54	57F	59	75	57	46	48	58	56	55	78	60	88		64	56	51	40	55
Response %:	100	100	100	100	100	100	100	100	100	100	100	100	100	100	100	100	100	100	100

Cannot Say (Raw): 0
F-K (Raw): -12
Welsh Code: 4"2'+6-35 7108/9: F-K/L:

Percent True: 36
Percent False: 64
Profile Elevation: 61.1

The highest and lowest T scores possible on each scale are indicated by a "--".

For information on FBS, see Ben-Porath, Y. S., & Tellegen, A. (2006). The FBS: Current Status, a report on the Pearson web site (www.pearsonassessments.com/tests/mmpi_2.htm).

MMPI-2 **NON-K-CORRECTED** VALIDITY/CLINICAL SCALES PROFILE

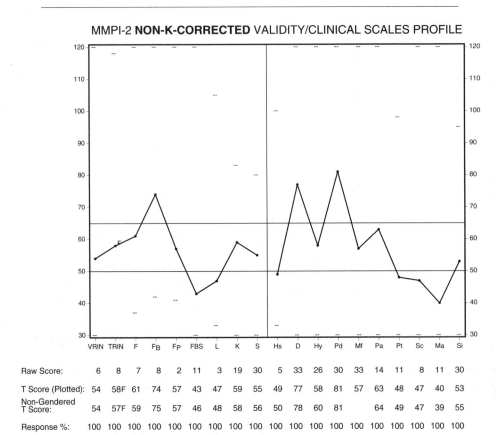

	VRIN	TRIN	F	F_B	Fp	FBS	L	K	S	Hs	D	Hy	Pd	Mf	Pa	Pt	Sc	Ma	Si
Raw Score:	6	8	7	8	2	11	3	19	30	5	33	26	30	33	14	11	8	11	30
T Score (Plotted):	54	58F	61	74	57	43	47	59	55	49	77	58	81	57	63	48	47	40	53
Non-Gendered T Score:	54	57F	59	75	57	46	48	58	56	50	78	60	81		64	49	47	39	55
Response %:	100	100	100	100	100	100	100	100	100	100	100	100	100	100	100	100	100	100	100

Cannot Say (Raw):	0	Percent True:	36
Profile Elevation:	57.9	Percent False:	64

The highest and lowest T scores possible on each scale are indicated by a "--".

Non-K-corrected T scores allow interpreters to examine the relative contributions of the Clinical Scale raw score and the K correction to K-corrected Clinical Scale T scores. Because all other MMPI-2 scores that aid in the interpretation of the Clinical Scales (the Harris-Lingoes subscales, Restructured Clinical Scales, Content and Content Component Scales, PSY-5 Scales, and Supplementary Scales) are not K-corrected, they can be compared most directly with non-K-corrected T scores.

For information on FBS, see Ben-Porath, Y. S., & Tellegen, A. (2006). The FBS: Current Status, a report on the Pearson web site (www.pearsonassessments.com/tests/mmpi_2.htm).

MMPI-2 RESTRUCTURED CLINICAL SCALES PROFILE

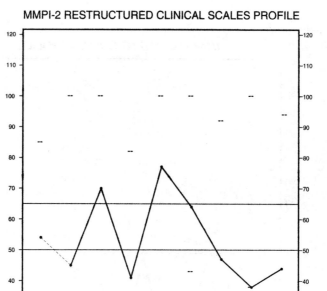

	RCd dem	RC1 som	RC2 lpe	RC3 cyn	RC4 asb	RC6 per	RC7 dne	RC8 abx	RC9 hpm
Raw Score:	7	2	9	2	13	2	5	0	8
T Score (plotted):	54	45	70	41	77	64	47	38	44
Non-Gendered T Score:	55	47	69	41	73	61	48	39	43
Response %:	100	100	100	100	100	100	100	100	100

The highest and lowest T scores possible on each scale are indicated by a "--".

LEGEND

dem= Demoralization	**cyn** = Cynicism	**dne** = Dysfunctional Negative Emotions
som= Somatic Complaints	**asb** = Antisocial Behavior	**abx** = Aberrant Experiences
lpe = Low Positive Emotions	**per** = Ideas of Persecution	**hpm**= Hypomanic Activation

For information on the RC scales, see Tellegen, A., Ben-Porath, Y.S., McNulty, J.L., Arbisi, P.A., Graham, J.R., & Kaemmer, B. 2003. The MMPI-2 Restructured Clinical (RC) Scales: Development, Validation, and Interpretation. Minneapolis: University of Minnesota Press.

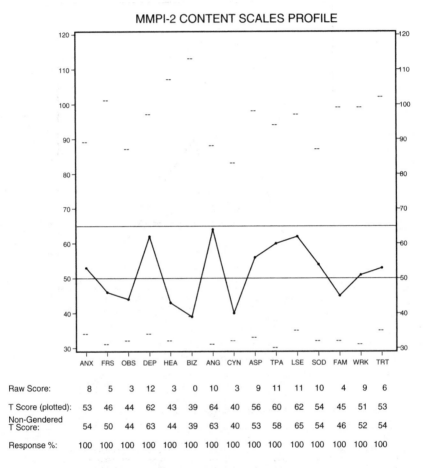

MMPI-2 CONTENT SCALES PROFILE

	ANX	FRS	OBS	DEP	HEA	BIZ	ANG	CYN	ASP	TPA	LSE	SOD	FAM	WRK	TRT
Raw Score:	8	5	3	12	3	0	10	3	9	11	11	10	4	9	6
T Score (plotted):	53	46	44	62	43	39	64	40	56	60	62	54	45	51	53
Non-Gendered T Score:	54	50	44	63	44	39	63	40	53	58	65	54	46	52	54
Response %:	100	100	100	100	100	100	100	100	100	100	100	100	100	100	100

The highest and lowest T scores possible on each scale are indicated by a "--".

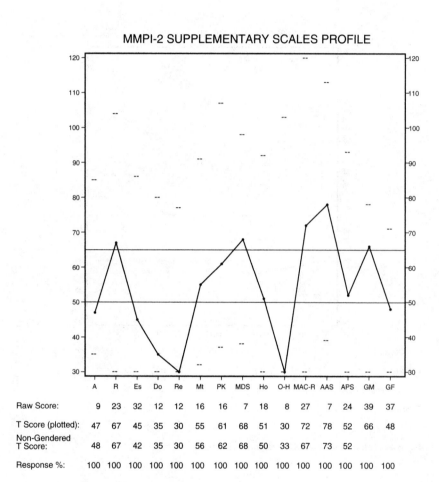

MMPI-2 SUPPLEMENTARY SCALES PROFILE

	A	R	Es	Do	Re	Mt	PK	MDS	Ho	O-H	MAC-R	AAS	APS	GM	GF
Raw Score:	9	23	32	12	12	16	16	7	18	8	27	7	24	39	37
T Score (plotted):	47	67	45	35	30	55	61	68	51	30	72	78	52	66	48
Non-Gendered T Score:	48	67	42	35	30	56	62	68	50	33	67	73	52		
Response %:	100	100	100	100	100	100	100	100	100	100	100	100	100	100	100

The highest and lowest T scores possible on each scale are indicated by a "--".

MMPI-2 PSY-5 SCALES PROFILE

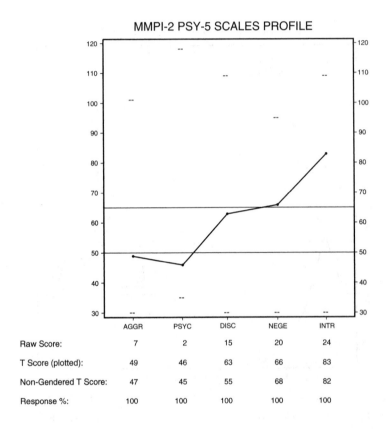

	AGGR	PSYC	DISC	NEGE	INTR
Raw Score:	7	2	15	20	24
T Score (plotted):	49	46	63	66	83
Non-Gendered T Score:	47	45	55	68	82
Response %:	100	100	100	100	100

The highest and lowest T scores possible on each scale are indicated by a "--".

ADDITIONAL SCALES
(to be used as an aid in interpreting the parent scales)

	Raw Score	T Score	Non-Gendered T Score	Resp %
Harris-Lingoes Subscales				
Depression Subscales				
Subjective Depression (D_1)	16	70	72	100
Psychomotor Retardation (D_2)	7	57	58	100
Physical Malfunctioning (D_3)	6	70	73	100
Mental Dullness (D_4)	7	70	71	100
Brooding (D_5)	5	63	65	100
Hysteria Subscales				
Denial of Social Anxiety (Hy_1)	6	61	62	100
Need for Affection (Hy_2)	7	50	51	100
Lassitude-Malaise (Hy_3)	10	79	81	100
Somatic Complaints (Hy_4)	0	37	38	100
Inhibition of Aggression (Hy_5)	1	31	32	100
Psychopathic Deviate Subscales				
Familial Discord (Pd_1)	3	56	57	100
Authority Problems (Pd_2)	6	77	70	100
Social Imperturbability (Pd_3)	6	64	63	100
Social Alienation (Pd_4)	6	60	60	100
Self-Alienation (Pd_5)	8	72	72	100
Paranoia Subscales				
Persecutory Ideas (Pa_1)	2	51	52	100
Poignancy (Pa_2)	2	46	47	100
Naivete (Pa_3)	7	60	60	100
Schizophrenia Subscales				
Social Alienation (Sc_1)	3	50	50	100
Emotional Alienation (Sc_2)	1	49	49	100
Lack of Ego Mastery, Cognitive (Sc_3)	1	49	49	100
Lack of Ego Mastery, Conative (Sc_4)	2	49	49	100
Lack of Ego Mastery, Defective Inhibition (Sc_5)	0	40	40	100
Bizarre Sensory Experiences (Sc_6)	1	45	45	100
Hypomania Subscales				
Amorality (Ma_1)	2	54	52	100
Psychomotor Acceleration (Ma_2)	2	35	34	100
Imperturbability (Ma_3)	4	56	54	100
Ego Inflation (Ma_4)	1	37	37	100
Social Introversion Subscales				
Shyness/Self-Consciousness (Si_1)	3	44	44	100
Social Avoidance (Si_2)	6	65	64	100
Alienation--Self and Others (Si_3)	6	52	53	100

601

	Raw Score	T Score	Non-Gendered T Score	Resp %
Content Component Scales				
Fears Subscales				
Generalized Fearfulness (FRS$_1$)	0	42	43	100
Multiple Fears (FRS$_2$)	4	45	50	100
Depression Subscales				
Lack of Drive (DEP$_1$)	5	65	67	100
Dysphoria (DEP$_2$)	2	53	55	100
Self-Depreciation (DEP$_3$)	4	68	70	100
Suicidal Ideation (DEP$_4$)	1	61	62	100
Health Concerns Subscales				
Gastrointestinal Symptoms (HEA$_1$)	0	43	44	100
Neurological Symptoms (HEA$_2$)	1	45	46	100
General Health Concerns (HEA$_3$)	2	56	57	100
Bizarre Mentation Subscales				
Psychotic Symptomatology (BIZ$_1$)	0	44	44	100
Schizotypal Characteristics (BIZ$_2$)	0	41	41	100
Anger Subscales				
Explosive Behavior (ANG$_1$)	3	61	60	100
Irritability (ANG$_2$)	5	59	61	100
Cynicism Subscales				
Misanthropic Beliefs (CYN$_1$)	2	40	39	100
Interpersonal Suspiciousness (CYN$_2$)	1	40	40	100
Antisocial Practices Subscales				
Antisocial Attitudes (ASP$_1$)	4	45	45	100
Antisocial Behavior (ASP$_2$)	4	81	72	100
Type A Subscales				
Impatience (TPA$_1$)	5	64	64	100
Competitive Drive (TPA$_2$)	3	52	51	100
Low Self-Esteem Subscales				
Self-Doubt (LSE$_1$)	7	71	73	100
Submissiveness (LSE$_2$)	2	51	53	100
Social Discomfort Subscales				
Introversion (SOD$_1$)	8	61	61	100
Shyness (SOD$_2$)	1	40	41	100
Family Problems Subscales				
Family Discord (FAM$_1$)	2	42	44	100
Familial Alienation (FAM$_2$)	0	41	41	100

	Raw Score	T Score	Non-Gendered T Score	Resp %
Negative Treatment Indicators Subscales				
Low Motivation (TRT$_1$)	2	51	53	100
Inability to Disclose (TRT$_2$)	2	53	53	100

Uniform T scores are used for Hs, D, Hy, Pd, Pa, Pt, Sc, Ma, the content scales, the content component scales, and the PSY-5 scales. The remaining scales and subscales use linear T scores.

OMITTED ITEMS

Those items for which there is no response or for which both true and false responses have been entered are considered "omitted." The potential for lowering the elevation of individual scales or the overall profile and rendering the administration invalid increases with the number of omitted items. Defensiveness, confusion, carelessness, and indecision are among the common reasons for omitting items. Examination of the content of the items that were omitted by the respondent may reveal specific problem areas or suggest reasons for their not responding appropriately to all items. Following are the items that were omitted:

None omitted.

CRITICAL ITEMS

The MMPI-2 contains a number of items whose content may indicate the presence of psychological problems when endorsed in the deviant direction. These "critical items," developed for use in clinical settings, may provide an additional source of hypotheses about the respondent. However, caution should be used in interpreting critical items since responses to single items are very unreliable and should not be treated as scores on full-length scales -- for example, an individual could easily mismark or misunderstand a single item and not intend the answer given. The content of the items and the possibility of misinterpretation make it important to keep the test results strictly confidential. Special caution should be exercised when interpreting these items in nonclinical settings.

Acute Anxiety State (Koss-Butcher Critical Items)
3.
5.
10.
39.
444.

Depressed Suicidal Ideation (Koss-Butcher Critical Items)
9.
71.
75.
95.
130.
454.
485.
518.

Threatened Assault (Koss-Butcher Critical Items)
213.
389.

Situational Stress Due to Alcoholism (Koss-Butcher Critical Items)
125.
487.
489.
518.

Mental Confusion (Koss-Butcher Critical Items)
 31.

Persecutory Ideas (Koss-Butcher Critical Items)
145.

Antisocial Attitude (Lachar-Wrobel Critical Items)
 35.
105.
227.
240.
266.

Family Conflict (Lachar-Wrobel Critical Items)
 21.
125.

Somatic Symptoms (Lachar-Wrobel Critical Items)
142.

Sexual Concern and Deviation (Lachar-Wrobel Critical Items)
 12.

Anxiety and Tension (Lachar-Wrobel Critical Items)
261.
405.

Sleep Disturbance (Lachar-Wrobel Critical Items)
 5.
 39.

Depression and Worry (Lachar-Wrobel Critical Items)
 3.
 10.
 73.
 75.
130.
415.
454.

Substance Abuse (Lachar-Wrobel Critical Items)
429.

Problematic Anger (Lachar-Wrobel Critical Items)
213.
389.

End of Report

NOTE: This and previous pages of this report contain trade secrets and are not to be released in response to requests under HIPAA (or any other data disclosure law that exempts trade secret information from release). Further, release in response to litigation discovery demands should be made only in accordance with your profession's ethical guidelines and under an appropriate protective order.

ITEM RESPONSES

1: 2	2: 1	3: 2	4: 2	5: 1	6: 1	7: 1	8: 1	9: 2	10: 2
11: 2	12: 2	13: 2	14: 1	15: 2	16: 2	17: 2	18: 2	19: 1	20: 1
21: 1	22: 2	23: 2	24: 2	25: 2	26: 2	27: 2	28: 2	29: 1	30: 2
31: 1	32: 2	33: 1	34: 1	35: 1	36: 2	37: 2	38: 2	39: 1	40: 2
41: 1	42: 2	43: 2	44: 2	45: 2	46: 2	47: 1	48: 2	49: 2	50: 2
51: 1	52: 1	53: 2	54: 2	55: 2	56: 1	57: 1	58: 1	59: 2	60: 2
61: 2	62: 1	63: 2	64: 2	65: 2	66: 2	67: 2	68: 2	69: 1	70: 2
71: 1	72: 2	73: 1	74: 1	75: 2	76: 1	77: 1	78: 2	79: 2	80: 2
81: 2	82: 1	83: 1	84: 2	85: 2	86: 2	87: 2	88: 1	89: 1	90: 1
91: 1	92: 2	93: 1	94: 2	95: 2	96: 2	97: 2	98: 2	99: 2	100: 2
101: 2	102: 1	103: 1	104: 2	105: 1	106: 1	107: 2	108: 1	109: 2	110: 2
111: 2	112: 2	113: 2	114: 1	115: 1	116: 1	117: 1	118: 1	119: 1	120: 2
121: 1	122: 2	123: 2	124: 2	125: 2	126: 1	127: 1	128: 1	129: 2	130: 1
131: 2	132: 2	133: 2	134: 2	135: 1	136: 2	137: 2	138: 2	139: 1	140: 1
141: 2	142: 2	143: 1	144: 2	145: 1	146: 2	147: 2	148: 2	149: 2	150: 2
151: 2	152: 1	153: 1	154: 1	155: 2	156: 2	157: 2	158: 2	159: 1	160: 2
161: 2	162: 2	163: 1	164: 1	165: 1	166: 2	167: 2	168: 2	169: 2	170: 2
171: 1	172: 2	173: 1	174: 1	175: 2	176: 1	177: 2	178: 2	179: 1	180: 2
181: 1	182: 2	183: 1	184: 1	185: 2	186: 1	187: 2	188: 1	189: 2	190: 2
191: 2	192: 1	193: 2	194: 2	195: 2	196: 2	197: 2	198: 2	199: 2	200: 2
201: 2	202: 1	203: 1	204: 2	205: 2	206: 1	207: 2	208: 1	209: 2	210: 1
211: 2	212: 2	213: 1	214: 1	215: 2	216: 2	217: 1	218: 2	219: 1	220: 2
221: 2	222: 1	223: 1	224: 1	225: 2	226: 2	227: 1	228: 2	229: 2	230: 2
231: 2	232: 1	233: 2	234: 2	235: 2	236: 1	237: 2	238: 2	239: 2	240: 1
241: 2	242: 2	243: 2	244: 2	245: 2	246: 2	247: 2	248: 2	249: 1	250: 1
251: 2	252: 2	253: 2	254: 2	255: 1	256: 2	257: 2	258: 2	259: 2	260: 1
261: 2	262: 1	263: 2	264: 2	265: 2	266: 2	267: 2	268: 2	269: 2	270: 2
271: 2	272: 2	273: 2	274: 2	275: 1	276: 1	277: 2	278: 1	279: 2	280: 1
281: 2	282: 2	283: 2	284: 2	285: 2	286: 2	287: 2	288: 2	289: 2	290: 1
291: 2	292: 2	293: 1	294: 2	295: 1	296: 2	297: 2	298: 2	299: 2	300: 2
301: 2	302: 1	303: 2	304: 2	305: 1	306: 2	307: 2	308: 2	309: 2	310: 2
311: 2	312: 2	313: 2	314: 1	315: 1	316: 2	317: 2	318: 1	319: 2	320: 2
321: 1	322: 2	323: 2	324: 2	325: 2	326: 2	327: 2	328: 2	329: 2	330: 1
331: 2	332: 2	333: 2	334: 2	335: 1	336: 2	337: 2	338: 2	339: 2	340: 1
341: 2	342: 2	343: 2	344: 1	345: 2	346: 2	347: 1	348: 2	349: 2	350: 1
351: 2	352: 2	353: 2	354: 1	355: 2	356: 2	357: 1	358: 2	359: 2	360: 1
361: 2	362: 1	363: 2	364: 2	365: 1	366: 2	367: 1	368: 2	369: 1	370: 2
371: 2	372: 2	373: 2	374: 2	375: 1	376: 2	377: 1	378: 1	379: 2	380: 2
381: 1	382: 2	383: 1	384: 1	385: 2	386: 2	387: 2	388: 1	389: 1	390: 1
391: 2	392: 2	393: 2	394: 2	395: 2	396: 2	397: 1	398: 1	399: 2	400: 2
401: 1	402: 1	403: 2	404: 1	405: 2	406: 1	407: 2	408: 2	409: 1	410: 1
411: 2	412: 1	413: 2	414: 1	415: 1	416: 2	417: 2	418: 1	419: 1	420: 1
421: 2	422: 1	423: 1	424: 2	425: 2	426: 1	427: 1	428: 1	429: 2	430: 1
431: 1	432: 2	433: 1	434: 2	435: 2	436: 2	437: 1	438: 2	439: 2	440: 1

```
441: 2  442: 2  443: 2  444: 1  445: 2  446: 1  447: 2  448: 2  449: 2  450: 2
451: 2  452: 1  453: 2  454: 1  455: 1  456: 1  457: 1  458: 2  459: 1  460: 1
461: 1  462: 2  463: 2  464: 2  465: 2  466: 2  467: 2  468: 2  469: 2  470: 2
471: 2  472: 1  473: 2  474: 1  475: 2  476: 1  477: 2  478: 2  479: 1  480: 1
481: 1  482: 2  483: 1  484: 1  485: 1  486: 1  487: 1  488: 2  489: 1  490: 2
491: 2  492: 1  493: 1  494: 1  495: 1  496: 2  497: 1  498: 1  499: 2  500: 1
501: 2  502: 2  503: 2  504: 2  505: 2  506: 2  507: 1  508: 2  509: 2  510: 2
511: 2  512: 1  513: 2  514: 2  515: 2  516: 2  517: 1  518: 1  519: 2  520: 2
521: 1  522: 1  523: 1  524: 2  525: 2  526: 2  527: 2  528: 2  529: 2  530: 2
531: 2  532: 2  533: 1  534: 1  535: 2  536: 2  537: 2  538: 2  539: 2  540: 2
541: 1  542: 2  543: 2  544: 1  545: 1  546: 2  547: 1  548: 2  549: 1  550: 2
551: 2  552: 1  553: 2  554: 2  555: 2  556: 1  557: 2  558: 2  559: 2  560: 2
561: 1  562: 2  563: 2  564: 2  565: 2  566: 2  567: 2
```

PRACTICE CASE 3: ALBERT

Albert was referred for psychological assessment by the criminal court as part of a presentence evaluation. He recently pled guilty to a disorderly conduct charge following his arrest for fighting at a local bar.

Albert is a 21-year-old Caucasian man. He dropped out of school in the ninth grade. His grades in school were very poor, and he was suspended several times for fighting. He was not a popular person in school, and he tended to associate with other students who also had behavior problems in school. Albert has dated regularly since he was in junior high school. He has never been married, but he has a steady girlfriend.

Albert is an only child. His parents have been married for 25 years. His father is a supervisor for a local manufacturing company, and his mother is an elementary school teacher.

Albert has a lengthy history of difficulties with the law. He has several juvenile offenses and spent some time in a juvenile detention center. As an adult he has had two previous misdemeanor convictions and spent 5 months in jail after being found guilty of assaulting a girlfriend.

Albert also has a history of mental health treatment. He has been hospitalized three times. He received a diagnosis of bipolar disorder and was treated with lithium. Albert denies significant psychological or emotional problems at the present time, but he acknowledges some anxiety about the outcome of the presentence evaluation. Albert has a long history of substance use and abuse. He started using alcohol when he was 13 years old and has also used LSD, cocaine, and many other drugs. He denies ever having had chemical dependency treatment.

Albert was somewhat reluctant to complete the MMPI-2, stating that he was not sure that it was in his best interest to do so. However, after some assurance that it could be helpful, he completed the test in approximately 90 minutes. He did not ask any questions or make any comments during the testing.

MMPI®-2
Minnesota Multiphasic Personality Inventory®-2
Extended Score Report

ID Number: 000091010
Age: 21
Gender: Male
Date Assessed: 10/19/1998

PEARSON

®PsychCorp

Copyright © 1989, 1994, 2000, 2003, 2006 by the Regents of the University of Minnesota. All rights reserved.
Portions reproduced from the MMPI-2 test booklet. Copyright © 1942, 1943 (renewed 1970), 1989 by the Regents of the
University of Minnesota. All rights reserved. Portions excerpted from the *MMPI-2 Manual for Administration, Scoring, and
Interpretation, Revised Edition.* Copyright © 2001 by the Regents of the University of Minnesota. All rights reserved.
Distributed exclusively under license from the University of Minnesota by NCS Pearson, Inc.

Minnesota Multiphasic Personality Inventory and **MMPI** are registered trademarks of the University of Minnesota.
Pearson, the **PSI logo,** and **PsychCorp** are trademarks in the U.S. and/or other countries of Pearson Education, Inc., or its
affiliate(s).

TRADE SECRET INFORMATION
Not for release under HIPAA or other data disclosure laws that exempt trade secrets from disclosure.

[5.1 / 153 / 2.3.17]

Reproduced by permission of the University of Minnesota Press. All rights reserved. "MMPI® " and
"Minnesota Multiphasic Personality Inventory® " are trademarks owned by the University of Minnesota.

MMPI-2 VALIDITY AND CLINICAL SCALES PROFILE

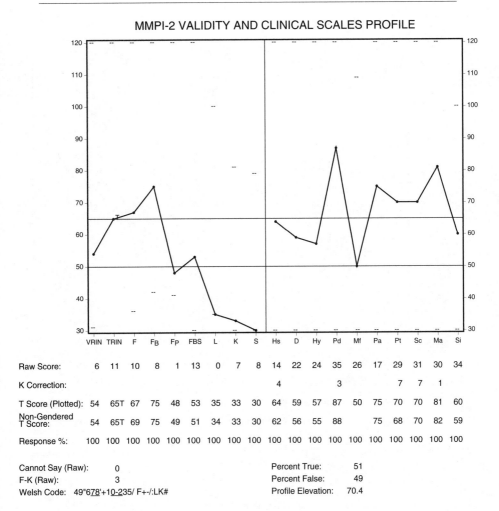

	VRIN	TRIN	F	FB	Fp	FBS	L	K	S	Hs	D	Hy	Pd	Mf	Pa	Pt	Sc	Ma	Si
Raw Score:	6	11	10	8	1	13	0	7	8	14	22	24	35	26	17	29	31	30	34
K Correction:										4		3			7	7	1		
T Score (Plotted):	54	65T	67	75	48	53	35	33	30	64	59	57	87	50	75	70	70	81	60
Non-Gendered T Score:	54	65T	69	75	49	51	34	33	30	62	56	55	88		75	68	70	82	59
Response %:	100	100	100	100	100	100	100	100	100	100	100	100	100	100	100	100	100	100	100

Cannot Say (Raw): 0
F-K (Raw): 3
Welsh Code: 49"678'+10-235/ F+-/:LK#

Percent True: 51
Percent False: 49
Profile Elevation: 70.4

The highest and lowest T scores possible on each scale are indicated by a "--".

For information on FBS, see Ben-Porath, Y. S., & Tellegen, A. (2006). The FBS: Current Status, a report on the Pearson web site (www.pearsonassessments.com/tests/mmpi_2.htm).

MMPI-2 **NON-K-CORRECTED** VALIDITY/CLINICAL SCALES PROFILE

	VRIN	TRIN	F	F_B	Fp	FBS	L	K	S	Hs	D	Hy	Pd	Mf	Pa	Pt	Sc	Ma	Si
Raw Score:	6	11	10	8	1	13	0	7	8	14	22	24	35	26	17	29	31	30	34
T Score (Plotted):	54	65T	67	75	48	53	35	33	30	71	59	57	91	50	75	76	75	85	60
Non-Gendered T Score:	54	65T	69	75	49	51	34	33	30	68	56	55	92		75	74	74	85	59
Response %:	100	100	100	100	100	100	100	100	100	100	100	100	100	100	100	100	100	100	100

Cannot Say (Raw):	0	Percent True:	51
Profile Elevation:	73.6	Percent False:	49

The highest and lowest T scores possible on each scale are indicated by a "--".

Non-K-corrected T scores allow interpreters to examine the relative contributions of the Clinical Scale raw score and the K correction to K-corrected Clinical Scale T scores. Because all other MMPI-2 scores that aid in the interpretation of the Clinical Scales (the Harris-Lingoes subscales, Restructured Clinical Scales, Content and Content Component Scales, PSY-5 Scales, and Supplementary Scales) are not K-corrected, they can be compared most directly with non-K-corrected T scores.

For information on FBS, see Ben-Porath, Y. S., & Tellegen, A. (2006). The FBS: Current Status, a report on the Pearson web site (www.pearsonassessments.com/tests/mmpi_2.htm).

MMPI-2 RESTRUCTURED CLINICAL SCALES PROFILE

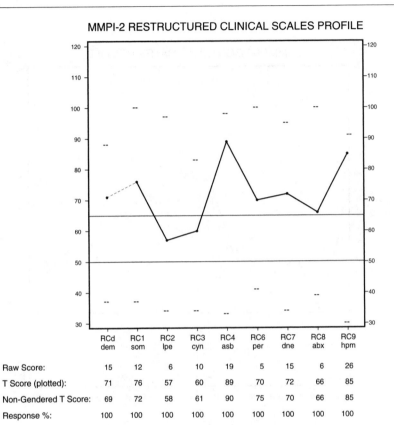

	RCd dem	RC1 som	RC2 lpe	RC3 cyn	RC4 asb	RC6 per	RC7 dne	RC8 abx	RC9 hpm
Raw Score:	15	12	6	10	19	5	15	6	26
T Score (plotted):	71	76	57	60	89	70	72	66	85
Non-Gendered T Score:	69	72	58	61	90	75	70	66	85
Response %:	100	100	100	100	100	100	100	100	100

The highest and lowest T scores possible on each scale are indicated by a "--".

LEGEND
dem= Demoralization	**cyn** = Cynicism	**dne** = Dysfunctional Negative Emotions
som= Somatic Complaints	**asb** = Antisocial Behavior	**abx** = Aberrant Experiences
lpe = Low Positive Emotions	**per** = Ideas of Persecution	**hpm**= Hypomanic Activation

For information on the RC scales, see Tellegen, A., Ben-Porath, Y.S., McNulty, J.L., Arbisi, P.A., Graham, J.R., & Kaemmer, B. 2003. The MMPI-2 Restructured Clinical (RC) Scales: Development, Validation, and Interpretation. Minneapolis: University of Minnesota Press.

613

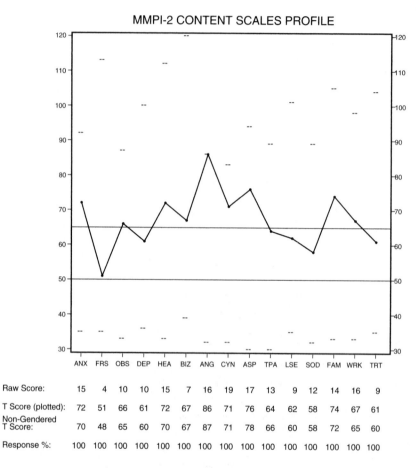

MMPI-2 CONTENT SCALES PROFILE

	ANX	FRS	OBS	DEP	HEA	BIZ	ANG	CYN	ASP	TPA	LSE	SOD	FAM	WRK	TRT
Raw Score:	15	4	10	10	15	7	16	19	17	13	9	12	14	16	9
T Score (plotted):	72	51	66	61	72	67	86	71	76	64	62	58	74	67	61
Non-Gendered T Score:	70	48	65	60	70	67	87	71	78	66	60	58	72	65	60
Response %:	100	100	100	100	100	100	100	100	100	100	100	100	100	100	100

The highest and lowest T scores possible on each scale are indicated by a "--".

614

MMPI-2 SUPPLEMENTARY SCALES PROFILE

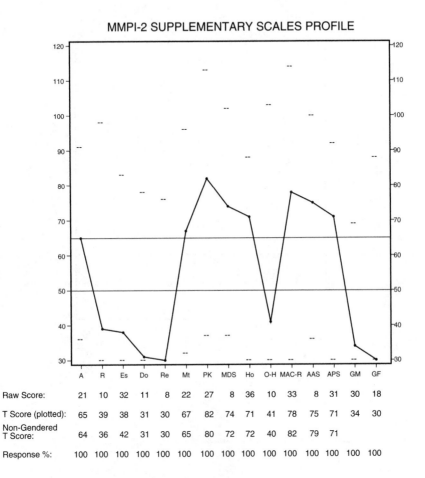

	A	R	Es	Do	Re	Mt	PK	MDS	Ho	O-H	MAC-R	AAS	APS	GM	GF
Raw Score:	21	10	32	11	8	22	27	8	36	10	33	8	31	30	18
T Score (plotted):	65	39	38	31	30	67	82	74	71	41	78	75	71	34	30
Non-Gendered T Score:	64	36	42	31	30	65	80	72	72	40	82	79	71		
Response %:	100	100	100	100	100	100	100	100	100	100	100	100	100	100	100

The highest and lowest T scores possible on each scale are indicated by a "--".

615

MMPI-2 PSY-5 SCALES PROFILE

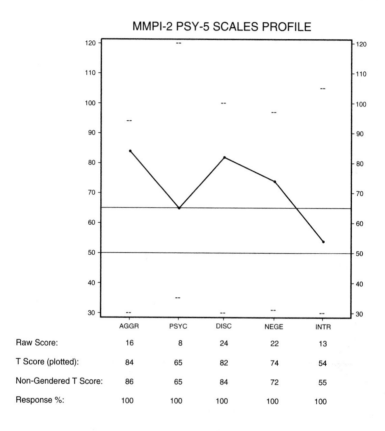

	AGGR	PSYC	DISC	NEGE	INTR
Raw Score:	16	8	24	22	13
T Score (plotted):	84	65	82	74	54
Non-Gendered T Score:	86	65	84	72	55
Response %:	100	100	100	100	100

The highest and lowest T scores possible on each scale are indicated by a "--".

ADDITIONAL SCALES
(to be used as an aid in interpreting the parent scales)

	Raw Score	T Score	Non-Gendered T Score	Resp %
Harris-Lingoes Subscales				
Depression Subscales				
Subjective Depression (D_1)	15	71	69	100
Psychomotor Retardation (D_2)	5	48	47	100
Physical Malfunctioning (D_3)	5	67	65	100
Mental Dullness (D_4)	6	67	66	100
Brooding (D_5)	6	74	70	100
Hysteria Subscales				
Denial of Social Anxiety (Hy_1)	4	51	51	100
Need for Affection (Hy_2)	3	36	35	100
Lassitude-Malaise (Hy_3)	6	66	64	100
Somatic Complaints (Hy_4)	9	82	76	100
Inhibition of Aggression (Hy_5)	1	33	32	100
Psychopathic Deviate Subscales				
Familial Discord (Pd_1)	7	84	82	100
Authority Problems (Pd_2)	7	73	77	100
Social Imperturbability (Pd_3)	5	57	58	100
Social Alienation (Pd_4)	10	82	81	100
Self-Alienation (Pd_5)	8	72	72	100
Paranoia Subscales				
Persecutory Ideas (Pa_1)	8	88	88	100
Poignancy (Pa_2)	5	68	67	100
Naivete (Pa_3)	3	41	41	100
Schizophrenia Subscales				
Social Alienation (Sc_1)	10	80	78	100
Emotional Alienation (Sc_2)	1	50	49	100
Lack of Ego Mastery, Cognitive (Sc_3)	3	60	61	100
Lack of Ego Mastery, Conative (Sc_4)	3	55	55	100
Lack of Ego Mastery, Defective Inhibition (Sc_5)	6	82	80	100
Bizarre Sensory Experiences (Sc_6)	8	80	78	100
Hypomania Subscales				
Amorality (Ma_1)	3	58	60	100
Psychomotor Acceleration (Ma_2)	10	73	74	100
Imperturbability (Ma_3)	3	47	48	100
Ego Inflation (Ma_4)	6	69	68	100
Social Introversion Subscales				
Shyness/Self-Consciousness (Si_1)	8	59	58	100
Social Avoidance (Si_2)	4	54	55	100
Alienation--Self and Others (Si_3)	10	65	64	100

617

	Raw Score	T Score	Non-Gendered T Score	Resp %
Content Component Scales				
Fears Subscales				
Generalized Fearfulness (FRS$_1$)	0	44	43	100
Multiple Fears (FRS$_2$)	4	54	50	100
Depression Subscales				
Lack of Drive (DEP$_1$)	3	57	56	100
Dysphoria (DEP$_2$)	2	58	55	100
Self-Depreciation (DEP$_3$)	3	62	62	100
Suicidal Ideation (DEP$_4$)	1	62	62	100
Health Concerns Subscales				
Gastrointestinal Symptoms (HEA$_1$)	2	70	67	100
Neurological Symptoms (HEA$_2$)	5	74	70	100
General Health Concerns (HEA$_3$)	4	72	72	100
Bizarre Mentation Subscales				
Psychotic Symptomatology (BIZ$_1$)	2	64	64	100
Schizotypal Characteristics (BIZ$_2$)	5	73	73	100
Anger Subscales				
Explosive Behavior (ANG$_1$)	7	83	88	100
Irritability (ANG$_2$)	7	72	71	100
Cynicism Subscales				
Misanthropic Beliefs (CYN$_1$)	11	63	64	100
Interpersonal Suspiciousness (CYN$_2$)	8	71	73	100
Antisocial Practices Subscales				
Antisocial Attitudes (ASP$_1$)	12	66	68	100
Antisocial Behavior (ASP$_2$)	5	74	79	100
Type A Subscales				
Impatience (TPA$_1$)	4	57	58	100
Competitive Drive (TPA$_2$)	5	60	62	100
Low Self-Esteem Subscales				
Self-Doubt (LSE$_1$)	4	59	59	100
Submissiveness (LSE$_2$)	2	55	53	100
Social Discomfort Subscales				
Introversion (SOD$_1$)	7	56	58	100
Shyness (SOD$_2$)	4	58	57	100
Family Problems Subscales				
Family Discord (FAM$_1$)	7	70	69	100
Familial Alienation (FAM$_2$)	4	76	77	100

			Non-Gendered	
	Raw Score	**T Score**	**T Score**	**Resp %**
Negative Treatment Indicators Subscales				
Low Motivation (TRT$_1$)	4	66	64	100
Inability to Disclose (TRT$_2$)	2	52	53	100

Uniform T scores are used for Hs, D, Hy, Pd, Pa, Pt, Sc, Ma, the content scales, the content component scales, and the PSY-5 scales. The remaining scales and subscales use linear T scores.

OMITTED ITEMS

Those items for which there is no response or for which both true and false responses have been entered are considered "omitted." The potential for lowering the elevation of individual scales or the overall profile and rendering the administration invalid increases with the number of omitted items. Defensiveness, confusion, carelessness, and indecision are among the common reasons for omitting items. Examination of the content of the items that were omitted by the respondent may reveal specific problem areas or suggest reasons for their not responding appropriately to all items. Following are the items that were omitted:

None omitted.

CRITICAL ITEMS

The MMPI-2 contains a number of items whose content may indicate the presence of psychological problems when endorsed in the deviant direction. These "critical items," developed for use in clinical settings, may provide an additional source of hypotheses about the respondent. However, caution should be used in interpreting critical items since responses to single items are very unreliable and should not be treated as scores on full-length scales -- for example, an individual could easily mismark or misunderstand a single item and not intend the answer given. The content of the items and the possibility of misinterpretation make it important to keep the test results strictly confidential. Special caution should be exercised when interpreting these items in nonclinical settings.

Acute Anxiety State (Koss-Butcher Critical Items)
10.
39.
140.
208.
218.
301.
444.
469.

Depressed Suicidal Ideation (Koss-Butcher Critical Items)
38.

75.
130.
233.
273.
388.
485.
506.
518.

Threatened Assault (Koss-Butcher Critical Items)
 37.
 85.
134.
213.
389.

Situational Stress Due to Alcoholism (Koss-Butcher Critical Items)
125.
264.
487.
489.
502.
511.
518.

Mental Confusion (Koss-Butcher Critical Items)
 32.
316.

Persecutory Ideas (Koss-Butcher Critical Items)
 99.
124.

251.
259.
314.
333.
361.

Antisocial Attitude (Lachar-Wrobel Critical Items)
 27.

 35.
 84.
105.
227.
254.
266.
324.

Family Conflict (Lachar-Wrobel Critical Items)
 21.
 83.
125.
288.

Somatic Symptoms (Lachar-Wrobel Critical Items)
33.
40.
47.
159.
164.
176.
224.
229.

247.
295.

Sexual Concern and Deviation (Lachar-Wrobel Critical Items)
34.
121.

Anxiety and Tension (Lachar-Wrobel Critical Items)
218.
261.
301.
320.
405.

Sleep Disturbance (Lachar-Wrobel Critical Items)
39.
140.

Deviant Thinking and Experience (Lachar-Wrobel Critical Items)
32.
122.
298.
316.

Depression and Worry (Lachar-Wrobel Critical Items)
10.
73.
75.
130.
150.
273.
339.

Deviant Beliefs (Lachar-Wrobel Critical Items)
99.
106.

259.
314.
333.
361.

Substance Abuse (Lachar-Wrobel Critical Items)
168.

264.
429.

Problematic Anger (Lachar-Wrobel Critical Items)
85.
134.
213.
389.

End of Report

NOTE: This and previous pages of this report contain trade secrets and are not to be released in response to requests under HIPAA (or any other data disclosure law that exempts trade secret information from release). Further, release in response to litigation discovery demands should be made only in accordance with your profession's ethical guidelines and under an appropriate protective order.

ITEM RESPONSES

1: 1	2: 1	3: 1	4: 2	5: 2	6: 2	7: 1	8: 1	9: 1	10: 2
11: 2	12: 1	13: 2	14: 1	15: 2	16: 1	17: 2	18: 2	19: 1	20: 2
21: 1	22: 1	23: 2	24: 2	25: 1	26: 1	27: 1	28: 2	29: 1	30: 2
31: 2	32: 1	33: 2	34: 2	35: 1	36: 2	37: 1	38: 1	39: 1	40: 1
41: 1	42: 2	43: 1	44: 2	45: 1	46: 1	47: 2	48: 2	49: 2	50: 1
51: 1	52: 1	53: 2	54: 2	55: 1	56: 1	57: 1	58: 1	59: 2	60: 2
61: 1	62: 2	63: 2	64: 2	65: 2	66: 2	67: 1	68: 1	69: 1	70: 2
71: 2	72: 2	73: 1	74: 2	75: 2	76: 1	77: 1	78: 1	79: 2	80: 2
81: 1	82: 1	83: 2	84: 1	85: 1	86: 1	87: 1	88: 1	89: 1	90: 2
91: 2	92: 2	93: 1	94: 1	95: 1	96: 2	97: 2	98: 1	99: 1	100: 2
101: 2	102: 1	103: 2	104: 2	105: 1	106: 2	107: 1	108: 1	109: 1	110: 1
111: 2	112: 1	113: 1	114: 2	115: 1	116: 1	117: 2	118: 2	119: 2	120: 1
121: 2	122: 1	123: 1	124: 1	125: 2	126: 1	127: 1	128: 1	129: 2	130: 1
131: 2	132: 1	133: 1	134: 1	135: 1	136: 1	137: 1	138: 2	139: 1	140: 2
141: 2	142: 1	143: 2	144: 2	145: 2	146: 2	147: 2	148: 2	149: 2	150: 1
151: 2	152: 1	153: 1	154: 2	155: 1	156: 2	157: 2	158: 2	159: 2	160: 2
161: 2	162: 2	163: 1	164: 2	165: 1	166: 2	167: 1	168: 1	169: 1	170: 1
171: 2	172: 2	173: 1	174: 1	175: 2	176: 2	177: 1	178: 2	179: 1	180: 2
181: 1	182: 2	183: 1	184: 2	185: 2	186: 1	187: 2	188: 1	189: 1	190: 1
191: 2	192: 1	193: 2	194: 2	195: 1	196: 1	197: 1	198: 2	199: 1	200: 2
201: 1	202: 1	203: 1	204: 1	205: 1	206: 1	207: 2	208: 2	209: 1	210: 1
211: 2	212: 1	213: 1	214: 1	215: 2	216: 2	217: 2	218: 1	219: 1	220: 2
221: 1	222: 1	223: 1	224: 2	225: 1	226: 1	227: 1	228: 2	229: 1	230: 1
231: 1	232: 1	233: 1	234: 2	235: 2	236: 2	237: 2	238: 1	239: 2	240: 2
241: 2	242: 1	243: 2	244: 1	245: 1	246: 2	247: 1	248: 1	249: 1	250: 1
251: 1	252: 2	253: 1	254: 1	255: 1	256: 2	257: 2	258: 2	259: 1	260: 1
261: 2	262: 1	263: 1	264: 1	265: 1	266: 2	267: 1	268: 2	269: 1	270: 2
271: 1	272: 2	273: 1	274: 1	275: 1	276: 1	277: 1	278: 1	279: 2	280: 1
281: 2	282: 2	283: 2	284: 1	285: 1	286: 1	287: 2	288: 1	289: 1	290: 1
291: 2	292: 1	293: 2	294: 2	295: 2	296: 2	297: 2	298: 1	299: 2	300: 1
301: 1	302: 1	303: 2	304: 1	305: 1	306: 2	307: 2	308: 2	309: 1	310: 1
311: 2	312: 2	313: 2	314: 2	315: 2	316: 1	317: 2	318: 1	319: 2	320: 1
321: 2	322: 2	323: 2	324: 1	325: 2	326: 1	327: 2	328: 2	329: 2	330: 1
331: 2	332: 2	333: 1	334: 2	335: 2	336: 2	337: 2	338: 2	339: 1	340: 2
341: 1	342: 2	343: 1	344: 1	345: 2	346: 1	347: 2	348: 1	349: 2	350: 1
351: 2	352: 1	353: 2	354: 1	355: 2	356: 2	357: 1	358: 2	359: 1	360: 2
361: 1	362: 1	363: 2	364: 1	365: 1	366: 2	367: 1	368: 2	369: 1	370: 1
371: 2	372: 2	373: 1	374: 1	375: 2	376: 1	377: 2	378: 1	379: 2	380: 2
381: 2	382: 1	383: 2	384: 1	385: 1	386: 1	387: 2	388: 2	389: 1	390: 1
391: 2	392: 2	393: 1	394: 1	395: 2	396: 1	397: 2	398: 2	399: 2	400: 2
401: 2	402: 2	403: 1	404: 1	405: 2	406: 1	407: 2	408: 2	409: 2	410: 1
411: 2	412: 1	413: 2	414: 1	415: 2	416: 2	417: 1	418: 1	419: 1	420: 1
421: 2	422: 1	423: 1	424: 1	425: 2	426: 1	427: 1	428: 1	429: 2	430: 1
431: 1	432: 2	433: 1	434: 1	435: 2	436: 2	437: 1	438: 1	439: 2	440: 2

```
441: 2   442: 1   443: 2   444: 1   445: 1   446: 2   447: 2   448: 2   449: 1   450: 2
451: 2   452: 1   453: 2   454: 2   455: 1   456: 1   457: 1   458: 1   459: 1   460: 1
461: 1   462: 1   463: 2   464: 2   465: 2   466: 2   467: 1   468: 2   469: 1   470: 1
471: 2   472: 2   473: 1   474: 1   475: 1   476: 2   477: 1   478: 2   479: 1   480: 2
481: 1   482: 1   483: 2   484: 2   485: 1   486: 1   487: 1   488: 2   489: 1   490: 2
491: 2   492: 1   493: 1   494: 1   495: 2   496: 2   497: 1   498: 2   499: 1   500: 2
501: 1   502: 1   503: 2   504: 2   505: 1   506: 1   507: 1   508: 2   509: 1   510: 2
511: 1   512: 2   513: 1   514: 2   515: 2   516: 2   517: 2   518: 1   519: 2   520: 2
521: 1   522: 1   523: 2   524: 2   525: 1   526: 1   527: 2   528: 2   529: 1   530: 2
531: 2   532: 1   533: 2   534: 2   535: 2   536: 2   537: 1   538: 1   539: 2   540: 1
541: 1   542: 1   543: 2   544: 2   545: 2   546: 2   547: 2   548: 1   549: 1   550: 1
551: 1   552: 2   553: 2   554: 1   555: 2   556: 1   557: 2   558: 2   559: 1   560: 2
561: 1   562: 2   563: 2   564: 2   565: 2   566: 2   567: 2
```

PRACTICE CASE 4: LARRY

Larry completed the MMPI-2 as part of the admission process at a psychiatric inpatient unit. He recently had been discharged from the Army because of psychiatric problems and was transferred to the hospital for treatment.

Larry is a 20-year-old Caucasian man who graduated from high school. In school his grades were above average. He was not very popular and did not date. His only school activity was the computer club. He did not get into any trouble in school and has never been in trouble with the law.

Larry is the younger of two children in his family. His brother is a senior college student majoring in business. His parents were divorced when he was 10 years old, and he and his brother were raised by their mother, although they have stayed involved with their father. His mother works as a nursing assistant at a community hospital, and his father is a police officer.

Larry has had no prior mental health treatment. While still in the Army he experienced hallucinations and persecutory delusions. He had frequent suicidal ideation and on one occasion took a large number of aspirins in an apparent suicide attempt. Larry has no history of substance abuse.

Larry was somewhat agitated and had difficulty attending to the MMPI-2. However, breaking the test administration into several shorter sessions over a 2-day period resulted in successful completion of the test.

MMPI®-2
Minnesota Multiphasic
Personality Inventory®-2

MMPI®-2
Minnesota Multiphasic Personality Inventory®-2
Extended Score Report

ID Number:	000056860
Age:	20
Gender:	Male
Date Assessed:	10/19/1998

PEARSON

⑭PsychCorp

Copyright © 1989, 1994, 2000, 2003, 2006 by the Regents of the University of Minnesota. All rights reserved.
Portions reproduced from the MMPI-2 test booklet. Copyright © 1942, 1943 (renewed 1970), 1989 by the Regents of the
University of Minnesota. All rights reserved. Portions excerpted from the *MMPI-2 Manual for Administration, Scoring, and
Interpretation, Revised Edition*. Copyright © 2001 by the Regents of the University of Minnesota. All rights reserved.
Distributed exclusively under license from the University of Minnesota by NCS Pearson, Inc.

Minnesota Multiphasic Personality Inventory and **MMPI** are registered trademarks of the University of Minnesota.
Pearson, the **PSI logo,** and **PsychCorp** are trademarks in the U.S. and/or other countries of Pearson Education, Inc., or its
affiliate(s).

TRADE SECRET INFORMATION
Not for release under HIPAA or other data disclosure laws that exempt trade secrets from disclosure.

[5.1 / 153 / 2.3.17]

Reproduced by permission of the University of Minnesota Press. All rights reserved. "MMPI® " and
"Minnesota Multiphasic Personality Inventory® " are trademarks owned by the University of Minnesota.

MMPI-2 VALIDITY AND CLINICAL SCALES PROFILE

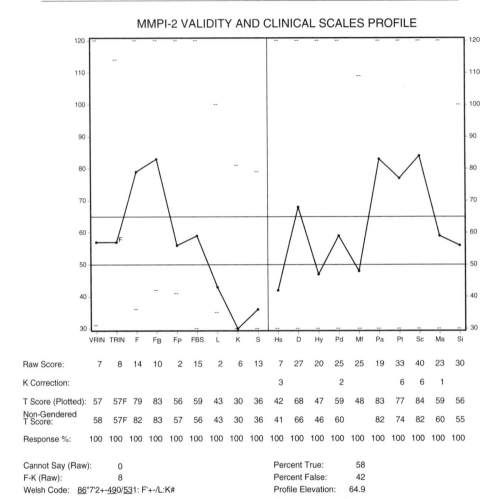

	VRIN	TRIN	F	F_B	F_P	FBS	L	K	S	Hs	D	Hy	Pd	Mf	Pa	Pt	Sc	Ma	Si
Raw Score:	7	8	14	10	2	15	2	6	13	7	27	20	25	25	19	33	40	23	30
K Correction:										3			2			6	6	1	
T Score (Plotted):	57	57F	79	83	56	59	43	30	36	42	68	47	59	48	83	77	84	59	56
Non-Gendered T Score:	58	57F	82	83	57	56	43	30	36	41	66	46	60		82	74	82	60	55
Response %:	100	100	100	100	100	100	100	100	100	100	100	100	100	100	100	100	100	100	100

Cannot Say (Raw):	0	Percent True:	58
F-K (Raw):	8	Percent False:	42
Welsh Code: 86"7'2+-490/531: F'+-/L:K#		Profile Elevation:	64.9

The highest and lowest T scores possible on each scale are indicated by a "--".

For information on FBS, see Ben-Porath, Y. S., & Tellegen, A. (2006). The FBS: Current Status, a report on the Pearson web site (www.pearsonassessments.com/tests/mmpi_2.htm).

628

MMPI-2 **NON-K-CORRECTED** VALIDITY/CLINICAL SCALES PROFILE

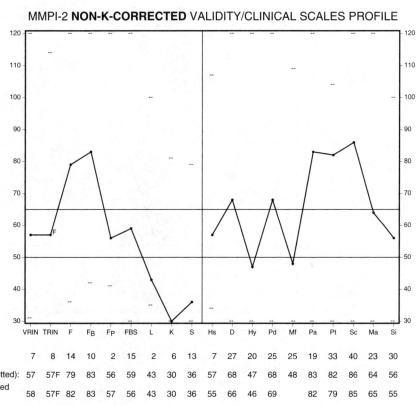

	VRIN	TRIN	F	F$_B$	Fp	FBS	L	K	S	Hs	D	Hy	Pd	Mf	Pa	Pt	Sc	Ma	Si
Raw Score:	7	8	14	10	2	15	2	6	13	7	27	20	25	25	19	33	40	23	30
T Score (Plotted):	57	57F	79	83	56	59	43	30	36	57	68	47	68	48	83	82	86	64	56
Non-Gendered T Score:	58	57F	82	83	57	56	43	30	36	55	66	46	69		82	79	85	65	55
Response %:	100	100	100	100	100	100	100	100	100	100	100	100	100	100	100	100	100	100	100

Cannot Say (Raw):	0	Percent True:	58
Profile Elevation:	69.4	Percent False:	42

The highest and lowest T scores possible on each scale are indicated by a "--".

Non-K-corrected T scores allow interpreters to examine the relative contributions of the Clinical Scale raw score and the K correction to K-corrected Clinical Scale T scores. Because all other MMPI-2 scores that aid in the interpretation of the Clinical Scales (the Harris-Lingoes subscales, Restructured Clinical Scales, Content and Content Component Scales, PSY-5 Scales, and Supplementary Scales) are not K-corrected, they can be compared most directly with non-K-corrected T scores.

For information on FBS, see Ben-Porath, Y. S., & Tellegen, A. (2006). The FBS: Current Status, a report on the Pearson web site (www.pearsonassessments.com/tests/mmpi_2.htm).

MMPI-2 RESTRUCTURED CLINICAL SCALES PROFILE

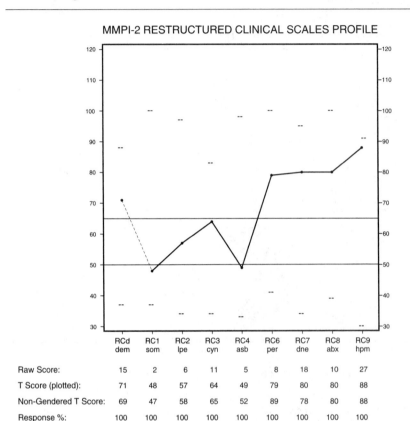

	RCd dem	RC1 som	RC2 lpe	RC3 cyn	RC4 asb	RC6 per	RC7 dne	RC8 abx	RC9 hpm
Raw Score:	15	2	6	11	5	8	18	10	27
T Score (plotted):	71	48	57	64	49	79	80	80	88
Non-Gendered T Score:	69	47	58	65	52	89	78	80	88
Response %:	100	100	100	100	100	100	100	100	100

The highest and lowest T scores possible on each scale are indicated by a "--".

LEGEND

dem = Demoralization **cyn** = Cynicism **dne** = Dysfunctional Negative Emotions
som = Somatic Complaints **asb** = Antisocial Behavior **abx** = Aberrant Experiences
lpe = Low Positive Emotions **per** = Ideas of Persecution **hpm** = Hypomanic Activation

For information on the RC scales, see Tellegen, A., Ben-Porath, Y.S., McNulty, J.L., Arbisi, P.A., Graham, J.R., & Kaemmer, B. 2003. The MMPI-2 Restructured Clinical (RC) Scales: Development, Validation, and Interpretation. Minneapolis: University of Minnesota Press.

MMPI-2 CONTENT SCALES PROFILE

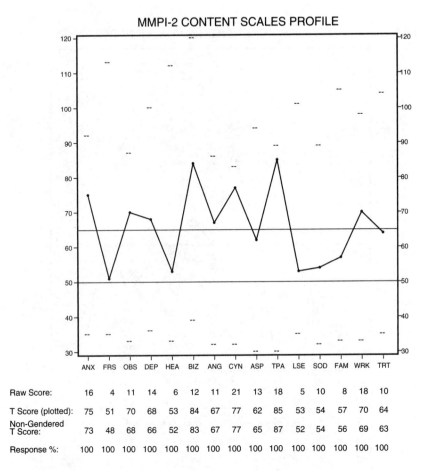

	ANX	FRS	OBS	DEP	HEA	BIZ	ANG	CYN	ASP	TPA	LSE	SOD	FAM	WRK	TRT
Raw Score:	16	4	11	14	6	12	11	21	13	18	5	10	8	18	10
T Score (plotted):	75	51	70	68	53	84	67	77	62	85	53	54	57	70	64
Non-Gendered T Score:	73	48	68	66	52	83	67	77	65	87	52	54	56	69	63
Response %:	100	100	100	100	100	100	100	100	100	100	100	100	100	100	100

The highest and lowest T scores possible on each scale are indicated by a "--".

MMPI-2 SUPPLEMENTARY SCALES PROFILE

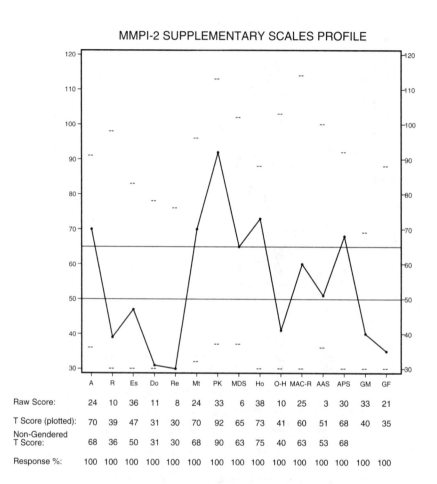

	A	R	Es	Do	Re	Mt	PK	MDS	Ho	O-H	MAC-R	AAS	APS	GM	GF
Raw Score:	24	10	36	11	8	24	33	6	38	10	25	3	30	33	21
T Score (plotted):	70	39	47	31	30	70	92	65	73	41	60	51	68	40	35
Non-Gendered T Score:	68	36	50	31	30	68	90	63	75	40	63	53	68		
Response %:	100	100	100	100	100	100	100	100	100	100	100	100	100	100	100

The highest and lowest T scores possible on each scale are indicated by a "--".

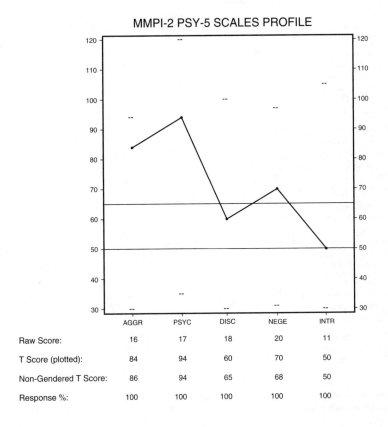

MMPI-2 PSY-5 SCALES PROFILE

	AGGR	PSYC	DISC	NEGE	INTR
Raw Score:	16	17	18	20	11
T Score (plotted):	84	94	60	70	50
Non-Gendered T Score:	86	94	65	68	50
Response %:	100	100	100	100	100

The highest and lowest T scores possible on each scale are indicated by a "--".

ADDITIONAL SCALES
(to be used as an aid in interpreting the parent scales)

	Raw Score	T Score	Non-Gendered T Score	Resp %
Harris-Lingoes Subscales				
Depression Subscales				
Subjective Depression (D₁)	18	79	77	100
Psychomotor Retardation (D₂)	5	48	47	100
Physical Malfunctioning (D₃)	3	51	50	100
Mental Dullness (D₄)	11	91	90	100
Brooding (D₅)	7	79	76	100
Hysteria Subscales				
Denial of Social Anxiety (Hy₁)	1	34	35	100
Need for Affection (Hy₂)	2	32	31	100
Lassitude-Malaise (Hy₃)	9	79	77	100
Somatic Complaints (Hy₄)	5	62	59	100
Inhibition of Aggression (Hy₅)	0	30	30	100
Psychopathic Deviate Subscales				
Familial Discord (Pd₁)	2	51	51	100
Authority Problems (Pd₂)	5	60	64	100
Social Imperturbability (Pd₃)	2	39	40	100
Social Alienation (Pd₄)	11	87	87	100
Self-Alienation (Pd₅)	9	77	77	100
Paranoia Subscales				
Persecutory Ideas (Pa₁)	11	106	106	100
Poignancy (Pa₂)	5	68	67	100
Naivete (Pa₃)	1	32	31	100
Schizophrenia Subscales				
Social Alienation (Sc₁)	10	80	78	100
Emotional Alienation (Sc₂)	8	117	116	100
Lack of Ego Mastery, Cognitive (Sc₃)	8	90	91	100
Lack of Ego Mastery, Conative (Sc₄)	9	87	86	100
Lack of Ego Mastery, Defective Inhibition (Sc₅)	6	82	80	100
Bizarre Sensory Experiences (Sc₆)	6	70	69	100
Hypomania Subscales				
Amorality (Ma₁)	2	50	52	100
Psychomotor Acceleration (Ma₂)	8	63	64	100
Imperturbability (Ma₃)	1	35	36	100
Ego Inflation (Ma₄)	8	82	81	100
Social Introversion Subscales				
Shyness/Self-Consciousness (Si₁)	8	59	58	100
Social Avoidance (Si₂)	2	45	46	100
Alienation--Self and Others (Si₃)	12	71	70	100

	Raw Score	T Score	Non-Gendered T Score	Resp %
Content Component Scales				
Fears Subscales				
Generalized Fearfulness (FRS_1)	2	62	58	100
Multiple Fears (FRS_2)	2	45	42	100
Depression Subscales				
Lack of Drive (DEP_1)	4	62	61	100
Dysphoria (DEP_2)	4	74	69	100
Self-Depreciation (DEP_3)	4	69	70	100
Suicidal Ideation (DEP_4)	1	62	62	100
Health Concerns Subscales				
Gastrointestinal Symptoms (HEA_1)	0	44	44	100
Neurological Symptoms (HEA_2)	1	47	46	100
General Health Concerns (HEA_3)	1	48	49	100
Bizarre Mentation Subscales				
Psychotic Symptomatology (BIZ_1)	4	84	85	100
Schizotypal Characteristics (BIZ_2)	7	86	86	100
Anger Subscales				
Explosive Behavior (ANG_1)	4	64	67	100
Irritability (ANG_2)	6	67	66	100
Cynicism Subscales				
Misanthropic Beliefs (CYN_1)	13	69	70	100
Interpersonal Suspiciousness (CYN_2)	8	71	73	100
Antisocial Practices Subscales				
Antisocial Attitudes (ASP_1)	10	60	62	100
Antisocial Behavior (ASP_2)	3	59	64	100
Type A Subscales				
Impatience (TPA_1)	6	68	70	100
Competitive Drive (TPA_2)	8	77	79	100
Low Self-Esteem Subscales				
Self-Doubt (LSE_1)	3	54	54	100
Submissiveness (LSE_2)	1	48	47	100
Social Discomfort Subscales				
Introversion (SOD_1)	5	50	52	100
Shyness (SOD_2)	4	58	57	100
Family Problems Subscales				
Family Discord (FAM_1)	6	65	64	100
Familial Alienation (FAM_2)	0	40	41	100

	Raw Score	T Score	Non-Gendered T Score	Resp %
Negative Treatment Indicators Subscales				
Low Motivation (TRT$_1$)	3	60	58	100
Inability to Disclose (TRT$_2$)	3	60	61	100

Uniform T scores are used for Hs, D, Hy, Pd, Pa, Pt, Sc, Ma, the content scales, the content component scales, and the PSY-5 scales. The remaining scales and subscales use linear T scores.

OMITTED ITEMS

Those items for which there is no response or for which both true and false responses have been entered are considered "omitted." The potential for lowering the elevation of individual scales or the overall profile and rendering the administration invalid increases with the number of omitted items. Defensiveness, confusion, carelessness, and indecision are among the common reasons for omitting items. Examination of the content of the items that were omitted by the respondent may reveal specific problem areas or suggest reasons for their not responding appropriately to all items. Following are the items that were omitted:

None omitted.

CRITICAL ITEMS

The MMPI-2 contains a number of items whose content may indicate the presence of psychological problems when endorsed in the deviant direction. These "critical items," developed for use in clinical settings, may provide an additional source of hypotheses about the respondent. However, caution should be used in interpreting critical items since responses to single items are very unreliable and should not be treated as scores on full-length scales -- for example, an individual could easily mismark or misunderstand a single item and not intend the answer given. The content of the items and the possibility of misinterpretation make it important to keep the test results strictly confidential. Special caution should be exercised when interpreting these items in nonclinical settings.

Acute Anxiety State (Koss-Butcher Critical Items)
   3.
   5.
  10.
  15.
  39.
 140.
 172.
 223.
 444.
 463.
 469.

Depressed Suicidal Ideation (Koss-Butcher Critical Items)
   9.
  38.

  65.
  92.
  95.
 130.
 233.

273.
388.
411.
518.

Threatened Assault (Koss-Butcher Critical Items)
  37.
  85.
134.
213.
389.

Situational Stress Due to Alcoholism (Koss-Butcher Critical Items)
502.
518.

Mental Confusion (Koss-Butcher Critical Items)
  31.
  32.
180.
198.
311.
316.

Persecutory Ideas (Koss-Butcher Critical Items)
  17.
  42.
  99.
124.

138.
144.
145.
241.
251.
259.
314.

Antisocial Attitude (Lachar-Wrobel Critical Items)
  27.

  35.
105.
254.
266.
324.

Somatic Symptoms (Lachar-Wrobel Critical Items)
  44.
176.

Sexual Concern and Deviation (Lachar-Wrobel Critical Items)
  12.
166.

Anxiety and Tension (Lachar-Wrobel Critical Items)
  15.
  17.
172.
223.
320.
463.

Sleep Disturbance (Lachar-Wrobel Critical Items)
   5.
  30.
  39.
140.
328.

Deviant Thinking and Experience (Lachar-Wrobel Critical Items)
  32.
  60.
122.
198.
307.
316.
319.

Depression and Worry (Lachar-Wrobel Critical Items)
   3.
  10.
  65.
  73.
130.
150.
165.
180.
273.
339.

411.
415.

Deviant Beliefs (Lachar-Wrobel Critical Items)
 42.
 99.
138.
144.
259.
314.
466.

Problematic Anger (Lachar-Wrobel Critical Items)
 85.
134.
213.
389.

End of Report

NOTE: This and previous pages of this report contain trade secrets and are not to be released in response to requests under HIPAA (or any other data disclosure law that exempts trade secret information from release). Further, release in response to litigation discovery demands should be made only in accordance with your profession's ethical guidelines and under an appropriate protective order.

ITEM RESPONSES

1: 1	2: 1	3: 2	4: 2	5: 1	6: 1	7: 1	8: 1	9: 2	10: 2
11: 2	12: 2	13: 1	14: 1	15: 1	16: 1	17: 1	18: 2	19: 2	20: 1
21: 2	22: 1	23: 1	24: 2	25: 2	26: 2	27: 1	28: 2	29: 1	30: 1
31: 1	32: 1	33: 1	34: 1	35: 1	36: 2	37: 1	38: 1	39: 1	40: 2
41: 1	42: 1	43: 1	44: 1	45: 2	46: 1	47: 1	48: 1	49: 1	50: 1
51: 1	52: 1	53: 2	54: 1	55: 1	56: 1	57: 1	58: 1	59: 2	60: 1
61: 1	62: 2	63: 2	64: 2	65: 1	66: 1	67: 2	68: 1	69: 2	70: 2
71: 2	72: 2	73: 1	74: 2	75: 1	76: 1	77: 1	78: 1	79: 1	80: 2
81: 1	82: 2	83: 1	84: 2	85: 1	86: 1	87: 1	88: 1	89: 1	90: 1
91: 1	92: 1	93: 1	94: 1	95: 2	96: 2	97: 2	98: 1	99: 1	100: 2
101: 2	102: 1	103: 1	104: 1	105: 1	106: 1	107: 1	108: 1	109: 1	110: 1
111: 2	112: 2	113: 1	114: 2	115: 1	116: 1	117: 1	118: 1	119: 2	120: 1
121: 1	122: 1	123: 2	124: 1	125: 1	126: 1	127: 1	128: 2	129: 2	130: 1
131: 1	132: 1	133: 1	134: 1	135: 1	136: 1	137: 1	138: 1	139: 1	140: 2
141: 1	142: 1	143: 1	144: 1	145: 1	146: 2	147: 1	148: 2	149: 2	150: 1
151: 1	152: 1	153: 1	154: 2	155: 2	156: 2	157: 1	158: 1	159: 1	160: 1
161: 1	162: 2	163: 2	164: 1	165: 2	166: 1	167: 1	168: 2	169: 1	170: 1
171: 2	172: 1	173: 2	174: 1	175: 2	176: 2	177: 1	178: 1	179: 1	180: 1
181: 2	182: 2	183: 1	184: 2	185: 1	186: 1	187: 2	188: 1	189: 1	190: 1
191: 1	192: 1	193: 2	194: 2	195: 2	196: 1	197: 2	198: 1	199: 1	200: 1
201: 1	202: 1	203: 1	204: 1	205: 1	206: 2	207: 2	208: 1	209: 1	210: 1
211: 2	212: 1	213: 1	214: 1	215: 2	216: 2	217: 1	218: 2	219: 1	220: 2
221: 1	222: 1	223: 2	224: 1	225: 1	226: 1	227: 2	228: 2	229: 2	230: 1
231: 1	232: 2	233: 1	234: 2	235: 2	236: 2	237: 1	238: 2	239: 2	240: 2
241: 1	242: 1	243: 1	244: 1	245: 2	246: 2	247: 2	248: 2	249: 2	250: 1
251: 1	252: 2	253: 2	254: 1	255: 1	256: 1	257: 2	258: 2	259: 1	260: 1
261: 1	262: 1	263: 1	264: 2	265: 1	266: 2	267: 1	268: 2	269: 2	270: 2
271: 1	272: 1	273: 1	274: 1	275: 1	276: 1	277: 2	278: 1	279: 2	280: 1
281: 2	282: 2	283: 1	284: 1	285: 1	286: 1	287: 2	288: 2	289: 1	290: 2
291: 2	292: 2	293: 2	294: 2	295: 1	296: 2	297: 2	298: 2	299: 2	300: 2
301: 2	302: 1	303: 2	304: 1	305: 1	306: 2	307: 1	308: 2	309: 1	310: 2
311: 1	312: 2	313: 1	314: 2	315: 1	316: 1	317: 2	318: 1	319: 1	320: 1
321: 1	322: 2	323: 1	324: 1	325: 2	326: 2	327: 1	328: 1	329: 1	330: 2
331: 1	332: 1	333: 2	334: 2	335: 2	336: 2	337: 1	338: 1	339: 1	340: 2
341: 2	342: 1	343: 1	344: 1	345: 1	346: 1	347: 2	348: 1	349: 2	350: 1
351: 1	352: 1	353: 2	354: 1	355: 2	356: 1	357: 2	358: 1	359: 1	360: 1
361: 2	362: 1	363: 1	364: 1	365: 1	366: 1	367: 2	368: 2	369: 2	370: 1
371: 2	372: 2	373: 1	374: 1	375: 1	376: 2	377: 1	378: 1	379: 2	380: 2
381: 2	382: 2	383: 1	384: 2	385: 1	386: 1	387: 2	388: 2	389: 1	390: 1
391: 2	392: 2	393: 1	394: 2	395: 2	396: 1	397: 2	398: 1	399: 2	400: 2
401: 1	402: 2	403: 1	404: 1	405: 1	406: 1	407: 2	408: 1	409: 1	410: 2
411: 1	412: 2	413: 2	414: 1	415: 1	416: 1	417: 1	418: 2	419: 1	420: 1
421: 2	422: 1	423: 1	424: 1	425: 1	426: 2	427: 1	428: 1	429: 1	430: 1
431: 2	432: 1	433: 2	434: 1	435: 2	436: 2	437: 1	438: 2	439: 2	440: 1

441: 2 442: 2 443: 2 444: 1 445: 1 446: 2 447: 2 448: 1 449: 2 450: 2
451: 2 452: 1 453: 2 454: 2 455: 1 456: 1 457: 2 458: 2 459: 1 460: 1
461: 1 462: 1 463: 1 464: 2 465: 1 466: 1 467: 2 468: 1 469: 1 470: 1
471: 2 472: 1 473: 2 474: 1 475: 1 476: 2 477: 1 478: 2 479: 1 480: 1
481: 1 482: 1 483: 2 484: 1 485: 2 486: 1 487: 2 488: 2 489: 2 490: 2
491: 2 492: 1 493: 1 494: 1 495: 2 496: 2 497: 1 498: 2 499: 1 500: 2
501: 1 502: 1 503: 2 504: 2 505: 2 506: 2 507: 1 508: 1 509: 2 510: 1
511: 2 512: 2 513: 1 514: 1 515: 2 516: 2 517: 1 518: 1 519: 1 520: 2
521: 1 522: 1 523: 1 524: 2 525: 2 526: 2 527: 2 528: 2 529: 2 530: 1
531: 2 532: 1 533: 1 534: 2 535: 1 536: 2 537: 1 538: 2 539: 2 540: 2
541: 1 542: 2 543: 1 544: 2 545: 1 546: 1 547: 1 548: 2 549: 1 550: 2
551: 1 552: 1 553: 2 554: 2 555: 2 556: 2 557: 2 558: 2 559: 2 560: 2
561: 1 562: 2 563: 2 564: 1 565: 2 566: 2 567: 2

AUTHOR INDEX

SUBJECT INDEX